CW01300953

A SCHOLAR AND A GENTLEMAN: EDWARD HASTED, THE HISTORIAN OF KENT

Shirley Burgoyne Black

Darenth Valley Publications
Otford, Kent

First published in the United Kingdom in 2001 by
Darenth Valley Publications
33 Tudor Drive, Otford, Sevenoaks, Kent TN14 5QP

Copyright © Shirley Burgoyne Black 2001

All rights reserved. No part of this publication may be reproduced, stored in or introduced into a retrieval system, or transmitted, in any form or by any means, electronic, mechanical, photocopying, recording or otherwise, without the prior written permission of the copyright owner of this book.

British Library Cataloguing in Publication Data
A catalogue record for this book is available from the British Library

ISBN 0 9507334 8 2

Cover illustration: The North View of the Ruins of St Augustine's Abbey at Canterbury, from Volume IV of *The History and Topographical Survey of the County of Kent*
(By permission of the British Library)

For Tony

Shirley Burgoyne Black has been a resident of Kent since 1962, although born and brought up in Middlesex. After a first degree in languages at King's College London she worked in several fields, including technical translating, teaching, and librarianship. In 1991 she obtained a Ph.D. in Economic and Social History at the University of Kent at Canterbury, and since then has been an independent scholar. Her books include *An Eighteenth Century Mad-Doctor: William Perfect of West Malling*, and *A Farningham Childhood: Chapters from the Life of Marianne Farningham*. She is married and has two children.

Contents

List of Illustrations   ix

Preface   xi

Edward Hasted 1732-1812. Known ancestors and descendants   xiv

Prolegomena   1

1   Moses, Mary, Joseph and Katherine   3
2   The Hasteds of Hawley   29
3   Hasted at Sutton-at-Hone   53
4   The Lethieullier Chapter   81
5   Hasted and the History of Sequestrations   97
6   Throwley: The Preparation of the *History*, I   113
7   Hasted in London   137
8   A Tradition of Service   155
9   'The more the antiquarian toils, the more he sees beyond him to encounter': The Preparation of the *History*, II   177
10   Hasted in Canterbury   203
11   The Route to Calais   233
12   'Monsieur Ested'   267
13   In the King's Bench   289
14   The Scholar in the Garret   323
15   Corsham   339
16   The Kentish Legacy   369
17   Epilogue   393

Appendices   409

Notes   413

List of Subscribers   447

Index   451

List of Illustrations

Frontispiece   Edward Hasted, the Kentish historian
1   Katherine Walker, mother of Katherine Yardley
2   Joseph Hasted, the historian's grandfather
3   Katherine Yardley, Joseph Hasted's wife and grandmother of the historian
4   Edward Hasted, only son of Joseph and Katherine, father of the historian
5   Estate map of Joseph Hasted
6   Hatchment of Joseph Hasted
7   Ann Dorman, the historian's wife
8   Mary Dorman
9   St John's Jerusalem at Sutton-at-Hone, Hasted's home from 1757 to 1768
10   Pedigree of Hasted and Dingley, in Hasted's hand
11   Franks, Horton Kirby, a drawing by Hasted
12/13   Part of the Plan of Canterbury in 1800, engraved by John Barlow
14   Dr Andrew Coltee Ducarel
15   John Thorpe, of Bexley
16   Thomas Astle
17   Part of the pedigree of Smith or Smythe of Westenhanger, drawn up by Hasted
18   'Edward Hasted at sixty-nine'
19   Title-page of Volume 3 of the octavo edition
20   Vignette by John Barlow for the dedication in Volume 10 of the octavo edition
21   'The North View of the Ruins of St Augustine's Abbey at Canterbury', engraved by John Barlow
22   Lady Margaret Hungerford, from the painting by Cornelius Johnson, 1631
23   Lady Hungerford's Almshouses at Corsham in Wiltshire
24   Undated pencil drawing of the historian

Acknowledgments

The frontispiece and illustrations 1-4, 6-8 are reproduced by permission of Maidstone Museum. Illustrations 10 (Add.5486), 11 (Add.5486), 15 (206.g.11), 17 (Add.5520), 20 (578.f.7), 21 (G.165-8, Vol.4) and 24 (Add.32,353) are reproduced by permission of the British Library. The copyright of illustration 9 belongs to the National Trust. I am grateful to the British Museum for permission to reproduce illustration no.16, to the Centre for Kentish Studies for permission to reproduce illustration no.5, to Rochester Guildhall Museum and Medway Council for permission to reproduce no.18, and to the London Borough of Lambeth, Archives Department, for permission to reproduce no.14.

Preface

The long eighteenth century was the great era of the county history, and Kent's Edward Hasted sits squarely in the middle of it. Today, however, the names of the country's Hanoverian topographers are barely remembered and few, if any, have had their lives studied in detail. The explosion of research, particularly in the twentieth century, has extended our knowledge of the areas they wrote about far beyond anything they could attain to, and left them offering what can seem very limited views of place and people. But there is still much that can be gleaned from these old histories, a Hutchins's *Dorset*, a Blomefield's *Norfolk*, a Hasted's *Kent*. They provide a starting-point for anyone interested in the history of their locality and were ground-breakers for the massive *Victoria County Histories* of our own day. And they are, for their own period, a kind of latter-day Domesday Book.

Today's researchers are so accustomed to the support of catalogues, calendars and indexes that these are seldom acknowledged as the framework on which they build. By contrast, those earlier researchers had no such basic tools, and we should not forget or underestimate the labour involved in ferreting out information without them, the journeys on horseback that were required to look at a set of deeds, or the conditions of temperature or lighting under which this had to be done.

It was during the course of research for a doctorate, among the rich archival holdings of Kent, that I came across enough mentions of the name of Edward Hasted to make me feel that a life of the historian would be an interesting one to piece together. Ten years in his company have fully confirmed that impression. The work has snowballed, as one piece of information has led on to another, and in spite of the lack of Hasted's own private papers and the remoteness of the subject in time, the life which it is now possible to present to the reader is a surprisingly intimate one.

There is a large correspondence relating to the *History*, covering around four decades, and this, discursive in the manner of the day, provides a good substitute for a more private correspondence and has been drawn on extensively. In quoting from these letters I have on the whole retained their spelling, although punctuation has usually been modernised. The text of those letters taken from the Hasted-Astle correspondence, printed in *Archaeologia Cantiana* in 1905, is based on that transcript, although with the occasional error corrected. This applies also to quotations taken from Hasted's own Anecdotes, a short account of the family and of his life, which goes no further than 1770, printed in

Preface

Archaeologia Cantiana in 1904. The MSS of both these items are now in the Centre for Kentish Studies at Maidstone.

I am indebted to the facilities of all those libraries and archive offices in which I worked, including the British Library, the Public Record Office, Canterbury Cathedral Archives, Rochester Guildhall Museum, Rochester Bridge Trust, the Centre for Kentish Studies at Maidstone, Medway Archives and Local Studies Centre, Wiltshire County Record Office at Trowbridge, the Isle of Wight Record Office at Newport, Surrey County Record Office at Kingston, Lambeth Palace Library, Colindale Newspaper Library, the Guildhall Library, London, the City of London Record Office and the Archives Municipales de la Ville de Calais. What may seem a confusing reference to Hasted manuscripts as being both in the British Museum and in the British Library is caused by the fact that they were originally acquired by the British Museum but now form part of the holdings of the British Library, created as a separate entity in 1973.

I should like to thank the Royal Society and the Society of Antiquaries for permission to quote from, respectively, their Journal Books and their Minute Books. The Kent Archaeological Society kindly made a small grant towards the cost of the illustrations.

I am particularly indebted to Mr Guy Hitchings, of Speldhurst, and to Mrs Janet Adamson, of Folkestone Library, for directing my attention to new Hasted material, and to Dr Peter Draper, of Stansted, Sevenoaks, Mr Bryan Gipps, of Egerton, and Mr Anthony Whittaker, of Brenchley, for allowing me to examine and use Hasted archival material in their possession. I should also like to thank my son for considerable help in formatting the text, and my daughter for time spent in printing it out. A kind friend, who preferred not to be named, helped with the translations of the Latin. And thanks are also due to the many subscribers, who showed their confidence in this work and helped to make publication possible. It is pleasant to record that there are among them several whose ancestors were subscribers to Hasted's original *History*.

Four Edward Hasteds make an appearance in the story: father, son (the historian himself), grandson and great-grandson. I distinguish between the first three by referring to the father as Edward Hasted, to the historian simply as Hasted — as he is known throughout the county — and to his son as Edward, or, as he became, the Revd Edward Hasted. The fourth, short-lived and far away, is unlikely to cause confusion.

Finally, how should the name Hasted be pronounced? Evidence in the records, such as finding Mrs Hasted's name written in a rates book as Hastings, or Edward Hasted's as Haister, seems to show that, whatever the name had been before, by the eighteenth century it was being pronounced with a long 'a' as in 'fate'. This pronunciation is confirmed by

Preface

a brief note inserted in *Archaeologia Cantiana* 66 (1953) by the late curator of Maidstone Museum, Allen Grove, in which he quotes from an MS by one Edward Hughes:

> I, long intimate with the parish of Hollingbourne, and in frequent communication with people who knew the Revd Edwd Hasted, always heard the name as *Haste-ed* — only from Mr Russell, a stranger, had it come to me as *Hassted*: but now, May 1903, Mr Louis King has appealed to me on the point: he too had ever pronounced it as I have done, but he says that everyone he meets with in London who may have to refer to the historian sounds it the other way as seemingly justified by the spelling. I shall of course continue to [use] the local and doubtless family pronunciation.

My hope is that there will continue to be many, in Kent, in London, and indeed in the British Isles generally, who find that they 'have to refer to the historian' Edward Hasted — however they may choose to pronounce his name!

Shirley Burgoyne Black
April 2001.

EDWARD HASTED 1732-1812
KNOWN ANCESTORS AND DESCENDANTS

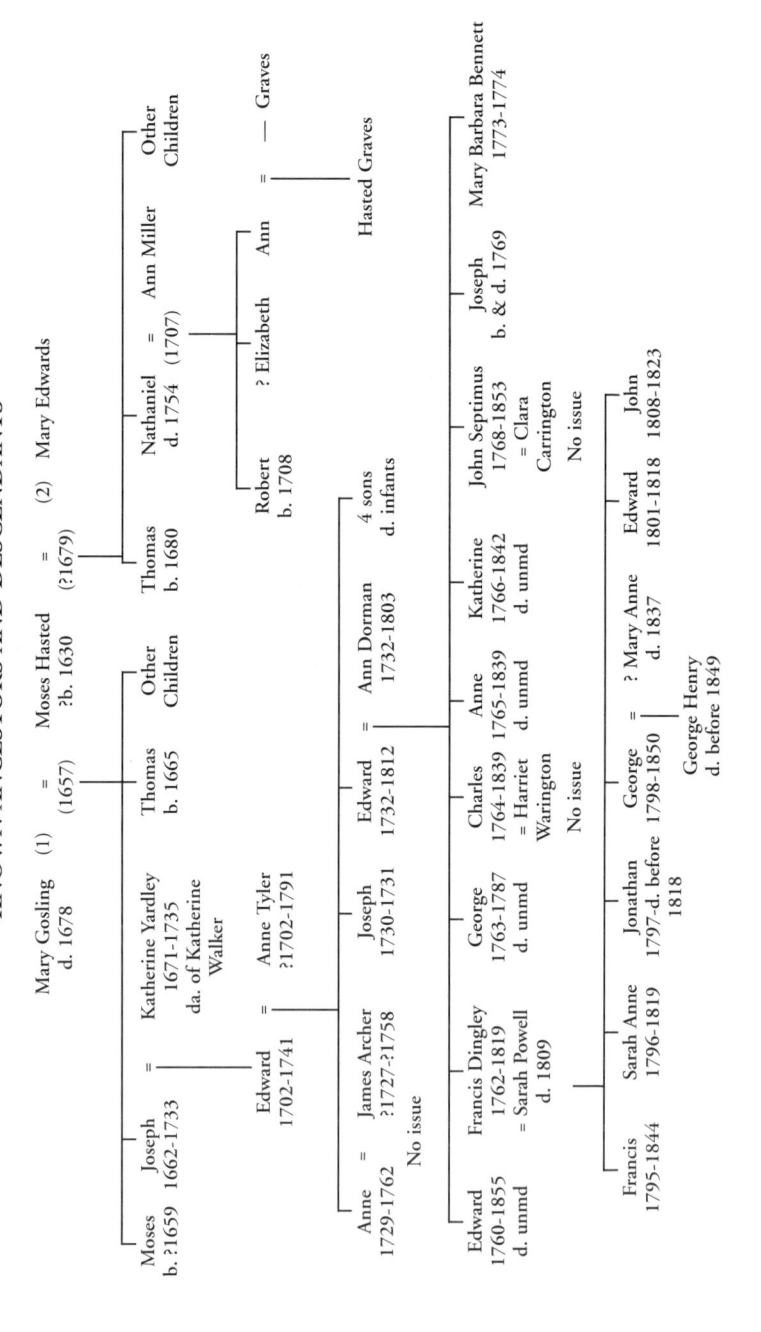

Mary Gosling (1) = Moses Hasted (2) = Mary Edwards
d. 1678   (1657)   ?b. 1630   (?1679)

Children of Moses Hasted:
- Joseph 1662-1733
- Katherine Yardley 1671-1735, da. of Katherine Walker = Thomas b. 1665
- Other Children
- Thomas b. 1680 = Ann Miller
- Other Children

Thomas b. 1680 = Ann Miller:
- Nathaniel d. 1754 (1707) = ? Elizabeth
  - Robert b. 1708
  - Ann = — Graves
    - Hasted Graves

Katherine Yardley = Thomas b. 1665:
- Edward 1702-1741 = Anne Tyler ?1702-1791
- Joseph 1730-1731
- Edward 1732-1812 = Ann Dorman 1732-1803
- 4 sons d. infants

Anne 1729-1762 = James Archer ?1727-?1758
No issue

Children of Edward 1732-1812 and Ann Dorman:
- Edward 1760-1855 d. unmd
- Francis Dingley 1762-1819 = Sarah Powell d. 1809
- George 1763-1787 d. unmd
- Charles 1764-1839 d. unmd
- Anne 1765-1839 d. unmd
- Katherine 1766-1842 d. unmd
- John Septimus 1768-1853 = Clara Carrington No issue
- Joseph b. & d. 1769 = Mary Barbara Bennett 1773-1774

Children of Francis Dingley and Sarah Powell:
- Francis 1795-1844
- Sarah Anne 1796-1819
- Jonathan 1797-d. before 1818
- George 1798-1850 = ? Mary Anne d. 1837
- Edward 1801-1818
- John 1808-1823

George Henry d. before 1849

xiv

Prolegomena

The eighteenth century into which Edward Hasted was born was the period when the classical renaissance came to its full flowering in England. After two politically turbulent centuries, the relative calm brought by the accession of the Hanoverian dynasty allowed the arts to flourish publicly as never before. The result was what is now termed the neoclassical period, which drew inspiration not only from the ancient civilisations of Greece and Rome, but also from those fourteenth and fifteenth century Italian works which had fed from the same source.

The spirit of enquiry which had marked the Italian renaissance was not wanting in English neoclassicism. Two aspects of it were the Grand Tour, the travels abroad undertaken by those who could afford it to complete their education, and the experiments carried out in the field of science which would, at the end of the century, explode into the industrial revolution.

Quieter branches of knowledge were extended at the same time. English topography, the discovery of England itself, and indeed, of Scotland and Wales too, became a subject of absorbing interest: both Samuel Johnson and James Boswell were to find an eager market for accounts of their tour in the Hebrides. Questionnaires were drawn up which might be circulated to those inhabitants willing to cooperate, for the purpose of writing up parish, town or city; and numerous Fellows of learned societies enthusiastically announced an intention of publishing a detailed history of a particular county.

It was in the nature of things that many such proposals should remain proposals only, or should get no further than a collection of notes and heterogeneous manuscripts, bequeathed, eventually, to a friend, and consigned, finally, to the dust and mice of an attic.

Edward Hasted proved to be one of the very few to project such a history and to have the ability and the stamina to see it through to completion. For this he deserves a place among the names of those who are remembered. But his personal life, a chequered one, is also interesting, as typical in many ways of the life of a gentleman of his time. The century was a severe one, and did not by any means always smile on those who made her illustrious. The historian of Kent was born in the same year and in the same month as Warren Hastings, destined to become Governor General of India. It is unlikely that the two men ever met. Hasted's career lay in the field of scholarship and in the voluntary, unspectacular one of local government administration within his own county of Kent;

he travelled, but he never went to India. Yet, like Hastings, Edward Hasted was to be forced to live through a fall from grace, and India was to be as fateful for the Hasted family as it was for Warren Hastings.

Chapter 1

Moses, Mary, Joseph and Katherine

Edward Hasted himself provides a few sparse facts relating to his birth and ancestry in a manuscript which he headed 'Anecdotes of the Hasted family, drawn up to the best of my recollection and to the best of my remembrance in the year 1800 by me Edward Hasted'. The Anecdotes were written in two small leather-covered notebooks, their intended contents summed up in the two Latin quotations with which they open, and which translate as: 'We also flourished, but that flowering decayed; it perished lamentably through base trickery'; and: 'I have sinned, I have repented; the past is expunged'.

Perhaps the Anecdotes were originally planned as a kind of confessional, but they cover no more than the first half of the historian's life, and the whole story was never told. A few years later Hasted again seems to have experienced a compulsion to summarise the main events of his life, and he made a series of brief entries on a sheet of paper, taking the story down to 1807. It is quite possible that both these attempts at a short account of his life were written for no one but himself. He certainly did not intend to leave material around which could be used to fill in the known outline of the bohemian existence of his later years: his will contained instructions to his executor to destroy all letters 'improper to be made public'. The two small memorandum books which held the unfinished Anecdotes were explicitly exempted from the pyre and bequeathed to the historian's eldest son, the Revd Edward Hasted, because they contained 'the account of the family of Hasted'.

The first page of the Anecdotes sets out the Hasted genealogy:

> I was born at Dove Court in Lombard Street on Decr 31st, 1732, Xtned at the adjoining church next the post office. My father Edward Hasted was the son of Joseph H. of Chatham, gentn., by Katherine Yardley his wife, and was born in 1702. Joseph Hasted was the son of Moses H. of Canterbury by his 1st wife Mary Goslin, md in 1657 in St Peter's church in that city. She died in 1678 and was buried in St George's church there. She had besides 2 other sons who dyed young. His 2d wife was Mary dar. of Mr Edwards of Faversham, gentn, by whom he left a son Nathaniel, who was a citizen of London and painter-stainer there, who md Anne Miller of the town of Nottingham. ... Joseph Hasted the eldest son by the 1st wife was born in the year 1662, was a freeman of the City of Canterbury, and became chief painter to the Royal

Navy at Chatham, where he resided at a house which he had purchased of Commissioner Lee at the corner of King Street on Smithfield Bank over the Brook there.[1]

As the writer of a topographical history of his county and the owner of lands which had by then been in his family for three generations, Hasted could hardly avoid giving some account of himself in his book, which is largely concerned with the descent of land. Although the Hasteds owned land in some dozen parishes, Hasted chose, not unnaturally, to give this information under the entry for the parish of Eastling, where they had, if not their largest, their most prestigious holding. Here, he ventured much further back than seventeenth-century Moses. In the second edition the entry is as follows:

> The family of Hasted, or as they were antiently written, both Halsted and Hausted, was of eminent note in very early times, as well from the offices they bore, as their several possessions in different counties, and bore for their arms, Gules, a chief chequy, or and azure. William Hausted was keeper of the king's exchange in London, in the 5th year of Edward II, from whom these of Kent hold themselves to be descended, one of whom, John Hausted, clerk, or as his descendants wrote themselves, Hasted, born in Hampshire, is recorded to have been chaplain to Queen Elizabeth, and a person much in favor with her, whom he so far displeased by entering into the state of marriage, which he did with a daughter of George Clifford, esq. of Bobbing, and sister of Sir Coniers Clifford, governor of Connaught, in Ireland, that he retired to the Isle of Wight, where he was beneficed, and dying there about the year 1596, was buried in the church of Newport. His great-grandson Joseph Hasted, gent. was of Chatham, and dying in 1732, was buried in Newington church, as was his only son Edward, who was of Hawley, esq. the purchaser of Huntingfield Court as before-mentioned.[2]

The first edition of the *History* had contained a much longer pedigree for the family, beginning with Richard de Hausted, possessor of Halstead in Essex in the reign of King Stephen, and citing also Agnes Hausted, a benefactress of Davington priory in the reign of Henry III, and Rowland de Aysted, mentioned in a Swanscombe record of around the same time. The family's orginal arms, Gules, a chief chequy or and azure, were traced back by Hasted to Robert de Halsted, who held land in the county of Leicester in the reign of Edward I, while the addition of an eagle, 'displayed ermine, beaked and legged or', was dated to 1628, with a confirmation of these arms to Laurence Halsted (or Hasted) by Sir William Segar, Garter King of Arms.[3]

Unfortunately, however, the historian was able to show no definite link either between these individuals, or between any of them and his own immediate family. Writing in 1763 to his friend Thomas Astle he seems to have thought that Laurence Hasted was his great-great-grandfather, but by the time the folio volume containing the account of his family came out in 1783 he had changed his mind and opted for descent from the Isle of Wight Hasteds, giving his grandfather Joseph a great-grandfather in the person of the Revd John Hausted, and a grandfather in the son of this divine, also called John, who is stated to have been the father of Moses, the historian's own great-grandfather.

It is only fair to Hasted to say that he gives his sources for the mentions of all the earlier Hasteds, that he clearly spent much time in endeavouring to establish a valid pedigree, and that he could not know, as we know today, thanks to the far greater number of genealogical works of reference which are available to us, how common the name Hasted or Halsted was in some counties, which must reduce the chance of direct links between any two individuals of the same name at different periods. For the later part of the account his authorities were, he tells us, parish registers, family papers and letters, and 'pictures, which by tradition are original portraits of the persons above-mentioned'.

Towards the end of his life, while at Corsham, Hasted was to copy out, very possibly at the request of his son Edward, a pedigree of the family which he had drawn up, based on his research and in line with the account of the family given in his *History*, although going no further back than the Revd John Hausted of Newport in the Isle of Wight, whose son John is said to have married Jane Hacket and to have been the father of Moses Hasted.[4]

It is possible that the Isle of Wight Hasteds, or Hausteds, were the more readily accepted into the story because of the family's connection, through Edward Hasted senior's marriage, with the Dingleys. There is no doubt at all that the historian's mother was related to the Dingleys of Wolverton, a manor in the parish of Shorwell, who were said by Sir John Oglander, the island's late sixteenth- early seventeenth-century antiquarian, to have come to the Isle of Wight from Kent in the reign of Richard II.[5] Half a century later, around 1445, Lewis Dingley had married a Margaret Hackett of Chedham in Sussex. In the Hasted pedigree John Hasted, the son of the Revd John Hausted, is shown as marrying Jane Hacket (although no date is given for this), something which would have provided evidence of an even earlier link between the

Hasteds and the Dingleys than the one created by the marriage of the historian's father to Anne Tyler, whose mother had been a Dingley. However, there is no evidence for the descent of Hasted's own line from the Isle of Wight family of that name, which seems, in any case, to have been of little standing: Oglander (whose manuscript memoirs would have been unknown to Hasted) made several lists and also wrote accounts of the most important families in the island in his time (when the Dingleys ranked third), but the name Hasted appears in none of them. It must, finally, be significant that in the Anecdotes, which contain the historian's more private account of his family, there is no mention whatever of the Revd John Hausted. Instead, we are taken no further back than Joseph's parents, Moses Hasted, of Canterbury, and his wife, the former Mary Goslin.

Moses, Hasted's great-grandfather, is the first of the family for whom we have any parish register entry in Kent. He was probably born around 1630, for the register of St Peter's, Canterbury, tells us that

> Moses Harsted and Mary Goslinge bothe of the parishe of St Peters in Canterbury weare maryed the 21 of June 1657.[6]

In the still medieval city of Canterbury, with its fifteen tiny interlocking parishes, there was inevitably some overlapping of jurisdictions. Moses and Mary were married by banns, but the record relating to the calling of these is to be found in the register of St Alphage's, the parish containing the market, just outside the cathedral precincts, where it was customary to have them announced — no doubt to suitable and unsuitable comments from bystanders. Accordingly, among the entries for 1657 in the St Alphage's register, we find the following:

> Moses Hastted and Mary Goslin both of the parish of St Petters haue bin published 3 seuerall market dayes May the 30 June the 3 and 10th.[7]

The lists of Canterbury freemen show that in 1641 one John Gosling took out his freedom of the city, by redemption, as a shoemaker.[8] The fact that his freedom had to be purchased, and that it was not obtained by virtue of his being the son of a freeman, or having served an apprenticeship in the city, almost certainly shows Gosling to have been a relative newcomer: judging by his name, he may well have been of Huguenot descent. Canterbury, in the sixteenth and seventeenth centuries, was host to vast numbers of Huguenot refugees, who came over in waves as persecution drove them from their homes in France and the Low Countries. The name Goslin or Gosling can be a form of the French 'Gosselin', a name which appears in the registers of the Walloon church in the city in the 1680s and 1690s. There is a strong possibility, therefore, that Hasted's great-grandmother, Mary Goslin or Gosling, was descended from a Walloon family which had come to England in the late sixteenth or early seventeenth century, and had settled in or around Canterbury with thousands of other 'strangers' as they were known: Strangers Lane, some way outside the city walls, beyond Wincheap, still bears witness to their former presence. By 1641 the Goslings were obviously well enough established for John, perhaps a son or a grandson of immigrants, to purchase his freedom and set up his own business.

The likelihood of Mary Gosling being the daughter of John Gosling the shoemaker is increased by the fact that Moses, as later records tell us, was a tailor. The alliance of a tailor and of a shoemaker's daughter would have been a very suitable one, and it would almost certainly have been in such circles that Moses the tailor would have sought a wife.

This is the point at which the history of Hasted's own family has so far been taken to begin with any reliability, speculation having usually provided him with forebears among the yeomen of Kent. There is however nothing to suggest that the family was an old Kentish one, and proof has been wanting of any earlier appearance of them there than the date of Moses' marriage in 1657 which, given the context in which it took place, may be assumed to be his first. There is, nevertheless, one piece of evidence with an earlier date which must be brought in here.

Among the family papers preserved by Hasted's son, the Revd Edward Hasted, is the will of a certain Robert Halsted, haberdasher, alderman of the city of Rochester, who died in 1649.[9] There is nothing else to connect Robert with the Canterbury Hasteds, but one must ask why, otherwise, does this will turn up among the family papers? Robert, who named his wife Joane as executrix, clearly came from Burnley, in Lancashire: he left bequests not only to his kinsmen Henry, William and Richard Halsted, of Worsthorne in Burnley, but also to the poor of Worsthorne and Burnley. Robert had been comfortably off: he owned the Swan in Rochester High Street, and had a lease of part of the Castle ditch. The City of Rochester archives show that he was invited to join what was known as the Common Counsell in September 1636, and that some six years later, in April 1643, he became an alderman of the city.[10] In his will Robert requested that two friends, Mr Edwarde Hawthorn, another Rochester alderman, and Mr John Bagnell, a silkman of London, would assist his wife in settling his affairs, and to each of them he left a handsome present.

There appear to have been no direct descendants of Robert's marriage. The Swan, and the lease of the Castle ditch, were both left to Robert's wife, Joane, for life; after her decease they were to go to Robert Halsted, the son of William Halsted of Worsthorne.

There is a certain ostentation in Robert's manner of leaving legacies to his Burnley 'kinsmen', whom he was unlikely to have seen for many years. It is quite possible that when he came down from Lancashire he had not come alone, and that there were closer relatives, geographically speaking, whom he preferred not to remember in his will. He had certainly stayed in London, on the way down into Kent, long enough to acquire a friend for life in John Bagnell, the silkman, with whom he had perhaps later maintained trading relations. A branch of Hasteds, or Halsteds, appears to have settled in Stepney round about the same time, and it does not seem fanciful to suggest that Robert may have come down to London with a brother, who remained there, marrying, and begetting progeny with more success than Robert in Rochester, and yet with whom Robert broke off all contact. Moses Hasted, the tailor of Canterbury, could have been a nephew of Robert the haberdasher.

What, in this case, might have caused the split between the brothers? A possible clue lies in Moses' very name. Although a sound Biblical one, it is not common in Church of England registers in the seventeenth century, and taken with the other Old Testament names which occur subsequently in the family — Joseph, Nathaniel, Isaac — could indicate allegiance to, and possibly marriage within, some other sect on the part of Moses' father. The large riverside parish of Stepney, east of the City of London, had at this time a growing shipbuilding industry. In the early seventeenth century the expansion of London's shipyards and the development of supporting trades was attracting not only Englishmen migrating from other parts of the country in search of work, but refugees from the wars of religion on the continent, particularly French and Flemish Huguenots, followers of the Protestant reformed church of Jean Calvin. There would be nothing unusual in the marriage of an exile from the north of England with the daughter of an exile from France. Moses' father, in fact, seems to have married into the London Huguenot community — tolerated, on account of the persecution it was undergoing in France and the Low Countries, but by no means wholly approved by the Church of England — and members of a Hasted family are traceable within various London Huguenot churches during the next hundred years.[11] It could thus have been due to his Huguenot inheritance that Moses received his slightly unusual first name — Old Testament names were overwhelmingly favoured by the Huguenots — and due to this also that we have the otherwise baffling emergence of Moses, alone, in Canterbury in 1657.

There is unfortunately no record of Moses' father's marriage. A considerable number of Huguenot congregations, of varying size, were established in London from 1550, but survival of their earliest records is understandably patchy. Nevertheless, we know, apart from finding Hasteds in the registers of the Huguenot churches of Crispin Street, Leicester Fields and St Jean Spitalfields between 1711 and 1759 (see Appendix 1), that Moses had London connections. Around 1700 we find one of his sons by his second marriage, Nathaniel, spending several years in the London parish of Stepney, where there is considerable evidence of other Hasteds being established.[12] The custom of the times suggests that as a young man venturing to seek a living in or near the City of London Nathaniel would almost certainly have gone to stay with relatives. A supposed portrait of Moses describes him as 'of Canterbury and London', and we have Hasted's own statement that Moses died in London, which again would suggest relatives there.

It certainly seems justifiable to suggest a connection with the Huguenots in London, and the argument is reinforced by the fact that Moses, as a young man, went to Canterbury, one of the principal Huguenot settlements in England outside London, where he may well have had relatives on his mother's side, and that he in his turn was to marry someone who was almost certainly the descendant of a Huguenot immigrant.

All in all, therefore, there are definite pointers to the southern branch of the family having moved down into Kent from London. And if the will of Robert Halsted is in any way connected with the family — as it almost certainly must be for the Revd Edward Hasted to have preserved it among what are otherwise purely family papers — the further clue to descent from a Lancashire family has to be accepted. There are numerous occasions on which Joseph Hasted's name was spelt Halsted, and it seems to have been only in his time that the form Hasted was finally adopted. Robert Halsted, although so written in his will, actually signed his name 'Hallsted' on the one occasion, in 1647, when he was called upon to append a signature to the minutes in the Meeting Day book of the Mayor and Aldermen of the City of Rochester.[13] Finally, it should be said that among all the counties of England Lancashire and Yorkshire are unequalled for the proliferation of the surname Hasted, Halsted or Hallstead.

The Medway towns, therefore, would seem to have become home to at least one other member of the Hasted family, and may also have provided a temporary shelter for Moses on his way to Canterbury from

London. There is no official record of the birth of a child to Moses and Mary until 1665, but an entry in one of Hasted's great commonplace books seems to show that the birth of their son Joseph, grandfather of the future historian, took place in Chatham in 1662. It reads as follows:

> Joseph Hausted painter by contract to the yard there was born Decr 19th at 1/2 past 7 o'clock P.M. 1662. Old Mr Austen of Chatham cest his nativity.[14]

By 1665, however, the couple were back in Canterbury, for an entry in the register of St Peter's notes that,

> Thomas the Sonne of Moyses Hasted and Mary his wife was baptised maye 14th 1665.[15]

If Moses and Mary had indeed been living in Chatham, they had done well to move back to Canterbury: in 1666 the plague was to rage in the Medway towns almost as ferociously as it had done in London, with the mortality among children particularly high. Later evidence shows that these were not the only children born to them, and that at least two, Moses and Joseph, survived these worrying years.

From now on the family was probably settled in Canterbury. Moses would appear to have worked for some time as a journeyman tailor, but by 1670 he had clearly saved enough to set up in business by himself. There was a necessary and expensive formality to be completed beforehand, however, and in July 1670 Moses Hasted was reported in Canterbury's Court of Burghmote minutes as guilty of exercising his trade as a tailor without having first become free of the city. The result was an order made by the Court:

> That Mr Chamberlaine shall take course in Law against Moses Halstead of the said Citty Taylor hee having not taken out his freedome and using and exercising his said trade in the said Citty not being a freeman.[16]

There was no delay in bringing the defaulting tailor to book, for the accounts show that only a month later Moses Hasted paid to the city's account the sume of ffive pounds, parcell of the sume of ten pounds agreed by order of Burghmote to be paied for his ffine to be admitted to the Libties of this City but he is not yet admitted nor sworne.[17]

By the following April Moses had put together the remaining five pounds of his admission money: the city's accounts note:

Item. The xxith day of Aprill Ano Dni 1671 Moses Hasted of this Citty Tailer was admitted and sworne to the Libties and ffreedome of this Citty for the ffine of ten pounds: whereof the sume of five pounds parcell was paied unto Mr Alderman Hills Late Chamberlaine of this Citty, as by his last yeares accompt appeares. And the other ffive pounds is now paied unto this Accomptant. Which said ffreedome is with proviso that the same do not extend to make the Sons or daughters of the said Moses ffree, but himself and his Apprentices only.[18]

The proviso that no sons or daughters should benefit by his freedom was a not uncommon one, and was stipulated because Moses already had children. Only children whose father was a freeman at the time of their birth were able to inherit the freedom of the city, and Moses had only acquired his freedom fourteen years after his marriage to Mary Gosling. In such a case, the obvious way of ensuring that sons would become freemen was by the simple expedient of apprenticing them to their father. Accordingly, among the Inrolments of Apprentices for 1676 we find the following entry:

Item. the xxiiijth of July, Ano dni 1676 receaved of Moses Hasted of this City Taylor for inrolling the Indenture of apprenticepp of Moses Hasted his Son bound to him by Indenture dated the 6th of January 1673 for vii years …… 6s.3d.[19].

Joseph, who was clearly younger than his brother, was similarly apprenticed in his turn. An entry in the Inrolments of Apprentices shows that in May 1675 he too was apprenticed to Moses Hasted the tailor for seven years: it was the simplest way to train him up to a trade, and put him in a position to obtain his own freedom of the city. But in Joseph's case we are faced with a confusion of entries, which could, perhaps, have been due to forgetfulness as much as anything. By 1676 the fourteen-year-old boy apparently had a much clearer idea of what he wanted to do — perhaps he was already showing signs of the artistic skill which was later to enable him to obtain the position of gilder in the naval dockyard at Chatham, and he was, instead, apprenticed to a painter-stainer, Robert Parkinson, who enrolled the apprenticeship the following year:

> Item. xxx Julij 1677 Received of Robert Parkinson Painter Stainer for inrolling the Indenture of Apprenticepp of Joseph Hasted bound to him by Indenture dated the fourth of September anno dni 1676 for the term of seven yeares to be accompted from the date the sum of 2s.1d.[20]

It would not have been difficult to break an indenture made between father and son. The difficulty arises because Moses enrolled the indenture of apprenticeship binding Joseph to him to learn the tailoring trade in May 1680, four years after he appears to have started on his apprenticeship with Robert Parkinson. It is possible that the apprenticing of one's own children was seen as something of a formality, which could be useful — as, indeed it was to prove in later years to Joseph — merely to enable them to gain the city's freedom. Moses may have realised that he had meant to enrol Joseph's indenture of apprenticeship to himself at the time it was made, early in May 1675, and decided that he would do so anyway, five years later, although by then Joseph's career had taken another turn.

Much had been happening in the Hasted family over the last few years to distract the busy and apparently successful tailor. In December 1677 he had buried a son, unnamed in the register, and less than six months later this death — whether of a baby or of an older child we cannot know — was followed by the death of his wife, who was buried on the 1st May 1678.[21] Mary Gosling must have been around 40 at the time of her death, and it is quite possible that a late and perhaps difficult birth, of a child who also died, had left her an ailing woman.

A year or so later Moses had married for a second time. Hasted tells us that his second wife, Mary Edwards, was the daughter of Mr Edwards, of Faversham, gentleman, and it is the fact that Moses, the second time round, was able to choose a wife from a higher level of society, which proves that he must have been successful at his trade. It is at this point that Moses would appear to have moved away from his Huguenot background. There is a single record of the birth of a son to Moses and his new wife. In the register of St George's, Canterbury, it is noted that:

> Thomas sonne of Moses Hasted and Mary his wife baptized 12th August 1680,[22]

but Hasted mentions another, Nathaniel, who later became a painter-stainer and a citizen of London. This is fully borne out by the records of the Company of Painter-Stainers: Nathaniel Hasted became a freeman of the City of London by redemption in this company in February 1715.[23] Hasted also tells us that Nathaniel married a certain Ann Miller, of Nottingham. This, too, is confirmed by the records: Ann, who must have been one of the many thousands who were drawn from their home towns at this time by the magnet of London, was married to Nathaniel in September 1707 at St Dunstan's church, Stepney, where the couple had a son, Robert, christened in July of the following year.[24]

Only three months after Nathaniel and Ann were married at St Dunstan's we find another Hasted marriage: in December 1707 a certain Moses Heasted of Spitalfields, whose occupation was given as a brazier, was to marry Sarah List at the same church.[25] Despite the variant spelling, the appearance of a Moses, marrying around the same time and in the same church as Nathaniel, almost certainly indicates that they were kinsmen, if not brothers. And there may have been more of them. Who, for example, was Benjamin Hasted who married Catherine Halley at St Nicholas, Rochester, in 1700?[26]

But before we accuse Hasted of simplifying the record for the sake of enhancing it, and purposely leaving out any mention of the family's humbler members, it has to be borne in mind that he may simply not have known very much about his own family: he was only a small boy when his father died, and at that stage, like most people, would have known very little if anything of relatives whom he never saw. By his father's early death he was deprived of his main source of family history. He himself was to be responsible for instituting in his family the tradition of a family Bible (using for the purpose a folio edition printed in the reign of Henry VIII) in which were to be recorded its births, marriages and deaths, and there would have been few, if any, other family records available to him. Naturally, his own immediate predecessors had the greatest importance for him — and he had a particular reason for remembering Nathaniel, whom he probably knew, for his great-uncle died only in 1754, when he himself was twenty-one.[27]

The founder of the family fortunes was undoubtedly Joseph, who was apparently Moses Hasted's eldest surviving son. The historian, in his Anecdotes, gives us a lively and appealing picture of him, in descriptions which he himself must have heard from his father — perhaps as a small boy sitting on his knee — for he never knew his grandfather. The story of the family's coat of arms, assumed by old Joseph, was probably also one which he heard at the same time, gazing meanwhile both fascinated and frightened at the charge on the red shield: 'an eagle displayed ermine, beaked and legged or' — these were the days when it was quite possible to see a great eagle sweeping over your fields. The little boy would probably no more have questioned the family's right to bear arms than he would have questioned their right to wear clothes.

Joseph's career is sketched briefly in the Anecdotes: freeman of the city of Canterbury, chief painter to the Royal Navy at Chatham, in which employment he 'acquired a very handsome fortune with a fair reputation', marriage to Katherine Yardley, purchase of a number of estates in the Medway area, investments in one or more of the large joint-stock companies set up around the end of the seventeenth century, together with considerable losses in the South Sea Bubble.[28] The records, however, reveal a considerably faster route to the acquisition of wealth and the title of 'gentleman' than Hasted suggests.

While it is impossible to know for certain which, of the two apprenticeships we find him bound to, was the one he completed, the evidence of his later career suggests that the young Joseph became a painter-stainer, and not a tailor. It is true that in 1705 he claimed and obtained his freedom of the city of Canterbury by virtue of an apprenticeship served with his father, the tailor, but this apprenticeship may have been something of a fiction.[29] Hasted may not have had access to the Canterbury Burghmote minutes which show that he was also apprenticed to Robert Parkinson, for he suggests that he served his apprenticeship as a painter to a Mr Walker in London, an uncle of his future wife, Katherine Yardley. It seems more likely, however, that Joseph had already completed his apprenticeship to Robert Parkinson by the time he went to work for Mr Walker. There was indeed a John Walker, noted in 1684 in the Register of Apprentice Bindings belonging to the Painter-Stainers Company, among the names of masters taking apprentices, but Joseph does not figure as one of them.[30] Interestingly, however, we find one of the Stepney Hasteds, this time with his name spelt Hastead, entering the same trade around the same time, when in 1688 Thomas Hastead, 'Son of Thomas Hastead of Stepney in the County of Middlesex, Marriner', was bound apprentice for seven years to Richard Lateward. Joseph may just possibly have been the first of the family to become a painter-stainer, but if so he clearly inaugurated a family tradition which continued for several generations, for a grandson of his half-brother Nathaniel, Hasted Graves, was to follow the same calling.

There are no parish accounts for Chatham between 1696 and 1702, so it is not possible to establish precisely when Joseph Hasted went to live there, although it was some time between those years. It may well have been in 1700, when he married his master's niece, Katherine Yardley. Until then, as Hasted suggests in the Anecdotes, he may have been living and working in London. He was nearly thirty-eight, and it seems unlikely that he had not been married before. Katherine appears to have been a spinster, and was about twenty-nine at the time of her marriage, which took place at Limpsfield in Surrey on 29 August 1700.[31]

Neither Joseph nor Katherine appears to have had any connection with Limpsfield, and the fact that they chose to get married there, outside London and Kent where both had relatives, and that the wedding was by licence and not by banns, strongly suggests an elopement and marriage in some haste, without the knowledge of their Kentish or London relatives. It seems very possible that Katherine was a small heiress, bringing with her to the marriage enough money to launch Joseph on his career as a purchaser of land. If this was the case both chose their partner well, for Katherine's money, if such it was, was on the whole prudently invested.

By 1702, if not before, the couple were settled in Chatham, among Katherine's Yardley and Walker relatives. Judging from their position in earlier church rate books these appear to have been people of some substance.[32] In 1687, for example, Yardleys were paying a rate of 6s. and Walkers one of 8s., extremely high church rates which were only exceeded by those paid by Sir Phineas Pett, which amounted to 10s. The church rate of 2s. paid by Joseph Hasted in 1702 placed him, too, among the principal inhabitants of that part of Chatham in which he lived, known variously as the West or Middle Borough, and where he seems to have remained until 1711. The assessment of that year finds him in the East Borough, paying a church rate which has increased to 5s.

There is another gap of ten years in the Chatham rates books between 1713 and 1723, so we cannot know precisely when Joseph purchased the house described by Hasted as having belonged to Commissioner Lee of Deptford Dockyard, 'at the corner of King Street on Smithfield Bank over the Brook there'. By 1724, however, we find him paying a church rate of 10s. for a house assessed on a rental value of £20, and can probably assume that he had already been there for some years. He was to remain there until his death, early in 1733.[33]

The house of a former Commissioner must have been a stately and even an elegant one, requiring appropriate furnishing and fittings. Houses were frequently sold with their furniture in those days — not surprisingly, since much of it was far too massive to be moved — and the Hasteds probably continued living with the tables, presses and four-poster beds which had served Commissioner Lee. But they undoubtedly added various items of their own. Among these were some family portraits, including one each of Joseph and Katherine, done when he was around fifty and his wife some ten years younger. These form part of a series of four, all painted in oils, oval in shape, and enclosed in rectangular black frames with gilt ornamentation in the corners. The remaining two show Katherine's mother, as Katherine Walker, and a young boy brandishing a bow, with a small dog on a table — the only portrait we have of their son Edward, the father of the historian.[34]

Joseph, handsome in red velvet coat and full-bottomed wig, gazes shrewdly out at the world. His wife, Katherine, with a somewhat compliant air, is considerably less good-looking than her husband. But the artist has done excellent work on the rich brown of her dress, and the dark shawl falling from one shoulder, and hers is perhaps the finest portrait of them all. Her mother, Katherine Walker, looks if anything younger than her daughter, and it is possible that this was repainted from an older portrait, quite possibly from a miniature, so that it could hang with the others. Certainly her hairstyle, and the dress with its slashed sleeves, which allows a somewhat uncomfortable display of bust, seem to indicate that this portrait was originally painted some years earlier. The wealth and standing of the Walkers, already noted, is underlined by Katherine's necklace of large pearls, and by the pearls which decorate her sleeves. The fourth portrait shows a richly dressed boy of perhaps eight or nine years old, with the eyes and nose of his mother, and the determined mouth of his father. All in all, it is an honest and appealing group of portraits, and must have looked very well on the panelled walls of Joseph Hasted's big house.

The Hasteds were certainly highly respected in the area. In 1778 one of the historian's correspondents, the Revd Thomas Austen, reminiscing about his childhood in Chatham, was to recall that the Hasteds had lived next door but one to the house in which he had been born, on Chatham Brook, and that Mrs Hasted had become godmother to one of his brothers: 'and such connections then were valuable events'. The produce of Mrs Hasted's garden, too, had been such as only lavish expenditure could bring forth: 'Oh, the fine grapes, pears, etc. we boys enjoy'd from her garden near the market place!'.[35]

The Anecdotes mention a number of Rochester and Chatham families, including those of Hawes, Chicheley, Taylor, Ayres, Bryant, Austen and Page, to whom Joseph and Katherine were related — wholly, it seems, through Katherine, which is hardly surprising given the number of Yardleys to be found in the area. Although Hasted does not mention the Petts in this connection, both Phineas Pett, Keeper of the Plank Yard at Chatham under Charles I and designer and builder, in 1637, of the famous ship the *Sovereign of the Seas*, as well as his son John, had married Yardleys: Phineas, the widow of Robert Yardley, Susan, in 1627, and John, Susan's daughter, Katherine.

Hasted attributes his grandfather's fortune solely to his work as a painter-stainer in the government's service at Chatham, telling us that he was employed on the gilding of the sterns and other carved work of the great ships known as men-of-war, until the vast expense of such gilding caused it to be abandoned. Just how elaborate this work was, and how much delicate gilding was required, can be seen from the *Kentish Post*'s description of the figurehead of a man-of-war launched at Chatham in April, 1761:

> The Ocean man of war launched on Tuesday at Chatham is looked upon as one of the best built ships in the Navy; she has a figurehead representing Old Ocean, the God of the Seas and Rivers, with an urn in his hands, out of which he is pouring the rivers into the sea, attended by young Neptune, nereids, Triton, etc., most beautifully carved, painted, and finished in a masterly manner.

It is obvious that the person responsible for supervising the painting of such intricate work, as well as for handling the quantities of expensive gold leaf which the gilding required, would have been very well paid.

However, the name of Joseph Hasted is not to be found in either the ordinary or the extraordinary lists of Chatham dockyard, although his grandson describes him as having been 'chief painter to the Royal Navy at Chatham'. This seeming mystery is resolved by the entry in the historian's commonplace book relating to his grandfather's birth where he states more specifically that Joseph was 'painter by contract to the yard' at Chatham.[36] This explains why Joseph's name never appears on the Chatham yard books: as a painter by contract he did not count as a government employee.

Hasted tells us that as the size of the navy increased under Queen Anne the cost of gilding became so enormous 'that it was wholly left off at the end of that or very beginning of the next reign of K. Geo. 1st, and common paint was instituted in the room of it', whereupon his grandfather 'resigned his place as not worth his keeping'.[37] It is possible to see a certain amount of family myth in this. Firstly, as we have seen, there was no 'place' or government position to resign. Secondly, it seems rather unlikely that Joseph would have been able to amass a fortune in land solely on the basis of his trade as a painter or gilder. It also seems unlikely that, if he had given up business twenty years before, we should still find him labelled as a painter until his death in 1733. This, however, is how one occasionally finds him described in the Freeholders' Lists — lists of those liable for jury service, which were kept by the Clerk of the Peace for the county, and which also served as check-lists of those entitled to vote at county elections.[38]

Although Joseph was in Chatham from at least 1702 he does not appear to have become a freeholder there until 1707, when the name Richard Walker, yeoman, disappears from the lists, and the name of Jos. Hasted, yeoman, appears in its stead. Richard Walker was almost certainly an uncle of Joseph's wife, Katherine, with whom he had been working, and whose house and business he would now appear to have taken over. From then on Joseph Hasted's name appears regularly in the Chatham Freeholders' List. He is usually given the courtesy title of 'yeoman', and, very occasionally, that of 'Gent'. Nevertheless, his trade remained with him all his life, and in the list of 1731, which was the last one in which his name appeared and which also shows occupations, he is marked simply 'painter' — denoted by his trade along with a number of other men who were similarly in the process of carrying their families on to a higher plane, like William Duddy, already a member of the commonalty, as it was known, and as such an elector of the Rochester bridge wardens, who is here simply noted as a glazier.

In becoming a freeholder, and a well-to-do freeholder, Joseph entered the ranks of those of whom voluntary duties in the service of local government, either at parish or county level, could be expected. From 1707, as we have seen, he figured among those who were liable to be called for jury service when the quarter sessions jury was chosen from Chatham. The person responsible for compiling the Freeholders' List in each Hundred or Half Hundred was the high constable, and Joseph himself filled this prestigious position from 1710 to 1711, with his signature to be found at the foot of the list for 1710. As high constable he was also responsible for collecting the county rate and the gaol rate for the Half Hundred of Chatham, and another quarter sessions record, the List of County Stock, shows that Joseph Hasted was present at Maidstone at both the Easter and Michaelmas general quarter sessions for that year, handing over, on the first occasion, a county rate of 8s., and on the second, a gaol rate of 6s.6d.[39]

Joseph does not seem to have served as churchwarden or overseer for his parish, probably avoiding office in the accepted manner by payment of a fine, but he occasionally attended a church vestry meeting. He witnessed the auditing and passing of the churchwardens' accounts on 10 April 1710, for example, when we find his signature among those of the men present on that date.[40] But he seems to have been a rather infrequent attender: we do not find his signature again until 6 March

Moses, Mary, Joseph and Katherine

1725, when the vestry was considering an increase in the number of poor chargeable to the rates, as well as the completion of a charity house which had recently been erected in Chatham, both of these being matters guaranteed to bring about a well attended vestry. On this occasion the two Chatham churchwardens, Mr John Cazeneuve, a distiller, and Mr John Proby, of the dockyard, were authorized to borrow a sum not exceeding £100 to finish the house, and the vestry agreed to 'save them harmless', and indemnify them in the event of the sum not being covered by a future rate.[41]

There seems every likelihood that Joseph, as a wealthy master, although still remaining in business, ceased doing any painting himself well before his death. His farms and land, as well as the tenements and houses he owned, would have required regular oversight at the very least, if not constant supervision and attention to repairs, if he was to get his due rents and income from his tenants.

For whether or not the title of 'gentleman' was a disputed one for Joseph Hasted, there is no doubt about his steady acquisition of land. His grandson in his Anecdotes was to call them 'estates', but this is rather too splendid a title for what were sometimes parcels of land of less than two acres: in the common fields at Cliffe, for example, Joseph owned or leased strips of no more than three and seven yards, although in the same parish he also owned Court Sole, a farm of nearly sixty acres. Taken all together, however, and subsequently added to here and there by his son Edward, they could certainly be termed an estate, amounting to around eight hundred acres of land, plus some fifty houses, spread among the parishes of Lower Halstow, Upchurch, Newington, Lynsted, Teynham, Eastling, Linton, Cliffe, Gillingham, Shorne, Hartlip, St James in the Isle of Grain, St Margaret's Rochester, and Chatham.

Hasted says of his grandfather that he began purchasing estates in 1718, but the records show that he already owned a number of properties by this time. One of his earliest purchases was a farm of around sixty acres, Burntflower Farm, in Linton, which he acquired in 1711 from two sets of owners, Thomas Hope and John Earle, and their wives Elizabeth and Barbara, who had been the daughters of John Fisher, yeoman, the previous owner. Joseph Hasted appears to have paid a total of £748 for the farm: £375 to the Hopes, £153 to the Earles, and £220 with which he bought back a mortgage lease which a certain John Smith, a blacksmith of Offham, had acquired on the property.[42] Clearly, Joseph already disposed of considerable sums of money, and was looking for ways in which to invest it. It may be, therefore, that he had begun investing in land even earlier than this. The small strips in the common fields at Cliffe, for example, could represent his earliest purchases; indeed, lying as they do in a parish considerably nearer Chatham than the manor of Teynham (which covered the parishes of both Teynham and Lynsted) further to the east, they seem more likely as first purchases than a sixty-acre farm.

Most of the property Joseph acquired must have been manorial, owing annual quitrents (paid in lieu of services) and the usual court duties to the lord of the manor in question, but many manorial records have now disappeared. However, the Court Book for the manor of Teynham, dating from 1704, is still in existence, and shows us Joseph Hasted acquiring several freehold properties there prior to 1718. In 1714 he bought a farm and land in Teynham from Sir John Bunce, on which was payable a quitrent of twenty-three shillings and elevenpence-halfpenny, and in 1715 he made two purchases in the manor, acquiring a farm in Lynsted called Cambridge, with a quitrent of ten shillings and fourpence-halfpenny, from Thomas Greenstreete, as well as a house and land near Cellar Hill, in the same parish, with a quitrent of five shillings and eightpence-halfpenny. Another property in Lynsted was acquired in 1717, when he bought land known as Bishop's Garden from Lewis Theobald, with a quitrent of seven shillings and sixpence. No other actual purchase by Joseph Hasted is recorded in the Court Book, but in 1732 the court found that he was then holding a barn and lands at or near Barrow Green in Teynham which owed a quitrent of eight shillings yearly, and that, as the incoming tenant, he had not yet paid the relief levied on it, nor the annual quitrent — an oversight which was probably due to the steward's book-keeping, since it was he who had failed to note that the property had changed hands.[43]

Not all of Joseph's property was freehold. The manor of Horsham, for example, which he held from 1721, and which extended over a number of parishes, including Upchurch, Halstow, Newington, Hartlip and Rainham, was leased from the Warden and Fellows of All Souls' College, Oxford.[44] This consisted of more than one thousand acres of meadow, pasture, arable, wood and other lands, the rents for which were payable not only in money, but also in quarters of wheat, bushels of malt, and firkins or bushels of 'good well fed oysters'![45]

And an entry in the insurance records of the Sun Fire Office shows that he was mortgagee of at least one very substantial property: the dwelling house of Thomas Vacher, a Milton-next-Gravesend vintner, which was insured in 1730 and 1731 for a total of £800.[46]

Those holding manorial lands were liable to be elected to perform manorial office, and the manor of Teynham Court Book shows that Joseph Hasted was required to fill two such offices in 1716 and 1717.[47] In October 1716 he was chosen to serve as beadle for the year, with the duty of collecting the reliefs, fines, alienations and amerciaments due to the lord of the manor, while the following October, this time with the word 'Gent' after his name, he was elected into the higher office of reeve, responsible for the collection of the tenants' quitrents. In practice this seems to have meant paying in advance the total sum due to the lord of the manor, and then reimbursing oneself by a subsequent collection of quitrents from those concerned.

When Joseph could make an advantageous sale he appears to have done so, for at the time of his death in 1733 he was not the owner of all the lands noted in the Court Book as purchased by him. But he still retained five holdings in the manor, on which a total of £2.11s.1d. in quitrents was payable: Dane Gardens, Lewson, Cambridge, Well Farm and Hays.

By then Joseph's largest number of holdings, as also his greatest acreage, apart from the manor of Horsham, lay in the parish of Cliffe, which was notoriously unhealthy. More than fifty years later its vicar, the Revd John Simpkinson, in one of his answers to the 1788 Visitation Return required by Archbishop Moore, had no hesitation in admitting that he spent as little time as possible there:

> I reside a part of the year at Westbourne in Sussex, distant from Cliffe about seventy miles, and a part of the year in London, distant about thirty miles. I visit my parish three or four times in the year. The reason of my absence is the unhealthiness of my parish which I have learnt from almost fatal experience.[48]

It was very probably the unhealthiness of the area, where malaria, then known as the ague, seems to have been endemic, which kept down the price of land and made it attractive to men such as Joseph Hasted, intent on acquiring and expanding a landholding. He was by no means the only Chatham-based tradesman who was busily buying up land in the surrounding parishes: the name of Mawdistly Best, of the brewing family, was to appear in both Lynsted and Teynham only a short while later.

Joseph never lived at Cliffe, where he owned the 58-acre farm, Court Sole, as well as sixty-five acres of the Cock farm, some scattered acres, and several strips in the common fields. His grandson gives his principal farms as being at Newington and Lower Halstow. Lower Halstow, with the churchyard of its small Saxon church surrounded on two sides by the mouth of a creek where a small river joins the Medway, must also have been very damp — the names of two of Joseph's holdings there, the Spray Farm and Boatfield, are both redolent of the water — and in fact he appears to have chosen for his residence the hillier ground of

Newington, and the village of Upchurch, slightly further inland than Lower Halstow, although still alongside the Medway.

His grandson gives us a very attractive vignette of this ship's painter turned landowner. After Joseph came into possession of his lands, says Hasted,

> he retained a parlour in each of his principal farms, both at Newington and Halstow, to which he used frequently to ride and pass a day (for he kept a riding horse both for himself and servant) to see after his workmen and repairs, and see after the management of his estates. It is remarkable that he generally chewed rhubarb whilst he was on these excursions, which he found an excellent preventive medicine against agues and bad air and fogs.[49]

The air of Cliffe marshes may well have been liable to aggravate the asthma from which Joseph suffered, and perhaps his faith in the rhubarb — a popular remedy of the time — was not misplaced.

It was common for owners of large estates to have their landholdings mapped in an estate book, and Joseph Hasted was no exception in beginning such a book, or having one begun for him. It is a modest enough attempt, and in fact was never finished: of the four maps which it contains only one is fully drawn and coloured, and has the measurements entered on it. This is a map which shows 'Lands in Upchurch and Halstow belonging to Joseph Hasted Esqr', words that appear in a lozenge which could perhaps have been added by a child, that only child to whom Joseph's myriad of holdings would in due course descend. The map itself contains some delightful details: houses with their smoking chimneys, two big Kentish barns, the church at Upchurch with its strange conical cap over the spire, and the Three Tuns, complete with sign. The second and third maps in the book show Newington and the New — and in the second map we perhaps have a tiny drawing of the Hasted farm where Joseph and Katherine sometimes lived — while the fourth map, which was never completed, shows Cellar Hill Farm in Lynsted, just south of the London-Dover road.[50]

In spite of Joseph's numerous land-holdings and farms the main Hasted residence continued to be Chatham. Hasted the historian gives a charming picture in the Anecdotes of his grandparents' life there:

> Being looked on at Chatham as very rich, they were looked on accordingly with much respect. Their housekeeping was

exceedingly plentiful, but their visitors who partook of it were in general their relations, according to the fashion of the times; their hours were early, they rose in the morn at 5 o'clock and played together at backgammon till breakfast at 8 o'clock. They had at morn some thick cake and mead, they dined at 12, drank tea at 4, and supped at 8. He brewed his own beer, which he prided himself much in, especially his strong beer, which he kept to the age of several years. Their beverage after dinner was elder wine, which, as well as several other sorts, she made herself being an excellent housewife.[51]

Nevertheless, there must have been friends as well as relatives who were welcomed to the Hasted table. Friendships were formed in those times which would continue down to their grandson's day. Among families whom Hasted was to know particularly well those of Fullagar, Thorneycroft and Henniker were probably also known to his grandfather: Fullagars and Thorneycrofts were tenants, like old Joseph, of land in the manor of Teynham; John Henniker was living in Chatham over the same period as Joseph, although in a more modestly rated property, and one of the signatories to the will of Robert Halsted in Rochester, many years earlier, had been a certain Luce Henniker.

It was probably fairly late in his life, supported by his evident wealth, and perhaps also encouraged to it by his son, now resident in London, and by his son's well (although distantly) connected wife, that old Joseph was persuaded to set in motion a search for the family's armorial bearings. They were an essential part of gentility, 'everybody' had them, including, according to Hasted, the Walkers and the Yardleys, and the provision of a pedigree may well have been a line of business offered by rather less than scrupulous attorneys, whose day-to-day work frequently involved them in genealogical research. Overlooking the seemingly humble origins of a tailor in Canterbury and a host of riverine relatives, it appears to have been suggested to the Hasteds that they might claim descent from one Laurence Hasted of Sonning in Berkshire, who had received a grant of arms in 1628. Assuming the validity of this pedigree, it was these arms which Joseph Hasted was to adopt, and which the family henceforth bore so proudly:

> Gules, an eagle displayed ermine beaked and legged or, a chief chequy or and azure. Crest: A demi-eagle displayed ermine issuing out of a mural crown on a wreath of its colours.

There was certainly no grant of arms to Joseph Hasted himself,[52] and we shall see that his grandson worried from time to time about the lack of proof of the family's right to bear the Hasted arms. However, in the climate of the early eighteenth century, Joseph and Katherine were quite satisfied with the ancestry proposed for them, and proceeded to have the crest engraved on their plate and, no doubt, emblazoned on their carriage. It was not, after all, crucial to their status: that was assured by the solidity of both plate and carriage, and by the soundness of Joseph's investments.

*   *   *

The Hasted 'family portraits'

Hasted was scrupulous in always requiring evidence for his statements. This applied no less to his own genealogy than to those of other Kentish families. By his own admission, however, the authorities on which he was obliged to rely, in the case of his own descent, were surprisingly slight: parish registers, family papers and letters, and 'pictures, which by tradition are original portraits of the persons above-mentioned'. It was due to the existence of the portraits alone that he felt able to trace his descent from a great-great-grandfather in the person of the son of the Revd John Hausted, of Hampshire and the Isle of Wight, but it is clear that he was not always in possession of them, since for many years he considered Laurence Hasted of Sonning to have stood in this relation to him. In 1763 he was writing to his friend Thomas Astle, who was then working at the British Museum, to ask whether Astle could find anything relating to 'a coat of arms granted by Segar, Garter, to Laurence Hasted, my gt gt grandfather, of Sunning in Berks, in the year 1628'.[53] Twenty years later, however, by the time of the appearance of Volume II of his *History*, the volume which contains an account of his family, he had changed his mind, and now felt able to trace the Kentish Hasteds back to a Tudor divine, the Revd John Hausted. This gentleman, according to the label on his portrait, had been a chaplain to Queen Elizabeth I until, marrying a daughter of George Clifford, he had retired to the Isle of Wight where he was beneficed; dying around 1596 he had been buried in the church at Newport. The pedigree of the family, which Hasted wrote out some years later, probably for his son Edward, contains the same descent, although in rather more detail. How and when had a belief in the family's descent from Laurence Hasted of Sonning been replaced by one in its descent from the Revd John Hausted?

There were in fact nine portraits relating to his ancestry which Hasted listed on the copy of the pedigree and which he noted as now in his son's house at Hollingbourne. The four which are latest in date are those which had undoubtedly belonged to Joseph Hasted: the portraits, already described, of himself, his wife, his son and his wife's mother. The other five, earlier in date, consist of the small oil portrait of the Revd John Hausted, a small and very amateur chalk painting of Catherine Clifford, said to be his wife, and oils of Sir Conyers Clifford, brother of Catherine Clifford and governor of Connaught, Ireland, done in 1595, as well as two of gentlemen who seem originally to have been unidentified: the first of these a three-quarter-length portrait of someone thought to be a son of the Revd John Hausted and his wife, and the second a three-quarter-length of a gentleman of the time of Charles II, of aristocratic appearance. How had these five portraits come into Hasted's possession?

A few other portraits are also listed on the pedigree, and against two of these — small half-length portraits of King Charles I and his sister the Electress Palatine — Hasted has noted that they were 'bought at Lord Teynham's sale at Linsted Lodge'. No date is given for this, but the tenth Baron Teynham had died in 1781 — after holding the title for more than fifty years — and it is possible that his death had been the occasion for selling some of the accumulated contents of the family seat, as could not infrequently happen — often for the purpose of clearing debts. It seems not unlikely that the five portraits in question were purchased at the same time. Sir Conyers Clifford and Catherine Clifford are stated by Hasted to have been the children of George Clifford of Bobbing, a parish not far removed from Teynham, and it is therefore quite possible that they were related to the Teynhams. This would explain the presence of this group of portraits in Lord Teynham's house, which could well be where Hasted came across them. The name Hausted, however, when Hasted saw it attached to a portrait, would have been sufficient to excite in him the thought that here, at last, was the evidence of his own descent for which he had been searching for so long: that the Revd John Hausted could — indeed, must — be an ancestor, and hence that the other portraits associated with him formed in fact a set of lost family portraits. He was of course perfectly aware that his family had held Teynham manorial land since the time of Joseph, and it was but a short step from there to arguing that what had once been the Hasted family portraits had somehow passed into the keeping of Lord Teynham.

Thus Hasted may have reasoned. The price asked at the sale was probably trifling — paintings fetched very little in those days — and Hasted was at last provided with what he could consider as hard evidence of the family's descent. The fifth portrait was perhaps pointed to by those engaged in the sale as belonging to the same group: who then was this gentleman of the time of Charles II likely to be but the son of the son of the Revd John Hausted, and could he not then be Moses Hasted, the very link which Hasted needed to confirm the two previous generations? It was only, as Hasted honestly admitted, 'by tradition' that the sitters in the portraits were thought to be the persons whose names they now bear. The Revd John Hausted would seem to have been named; Sir Conyers Clifford certainly was. But the gentleman taken to be the son of the Revd John Hausted was probably not then definitely identified, as he is not now, and the same was undoubtedly true of the profusely curled, aristocratic-looking gentleman who gazes languidly out of the fifth portrait, clasping the edge of his cloak or gown with a delicate hand. The label attached to this portrait is almost certainly not original, and its legend — 'Moses Hasted, of Canterbury and London' — seems vague and unsatisfactory, were there nothing else to make it seem a highly unlikely one. For Moses Hasted had been a hard-working tailor, who married the daughter of a shoemaker, had some difficulty in putting together the money needed to buy his freedom of the city of Canterbury, and sought apprenticeships for his sons. Such was certainly not the life of the gentleman shown in this portrait, whose bland features are far removed from what must have been the characterful ones of an industrious artisan.

Nevertheless, Hasted, who was not in possession of all the facts we now have with regard to Moses, allowed himself to be persuaded to the contrary. The five portraits would seem to have been purchased, and became part of the evidence on which the Hasted descent was to be based in both first and second editions of the *History*. The date 1781, although a relatively late one, certainly seems possible as the year in which Hasted acquired the portraits, since there is evidence that in the early part of 1782 he was anxiously consulting J.C.Brooke, Somerset Herald, on the subject of his pedigree, to receive the somewhat doubting reply:

> I received the favour of your letter dated 5th of last month, and am very glad if the anecdotes I sent you concerning the family of Halsted were of any use to you: I wish it may be in your power to connect your family to theirs, as those only who descend from the person to whom the coat was granted by Segar, have legally a right to bear it.[54]

There was, in addition, to be an unexplained delay in the appearance of Volume II of the *History*. Advertised for the end of 1782, review copies appear to have been distributed in November, but there was then a six-month delay — covered by an apology in the newspapers — before the general distribution took place in May 1783. It is just possible that this could have been caused by a need to reprint the page dealing with the Hasted family, in order to take account of what the historian saw as new evidence relating to his ancestry.

As has been shown, this was an erroneous descent. Hasted's progenitors probably came down to the south of England from the north, Huguenot elements came into the family on the distaff side, and it remains to this day virtually impossible to find named ancestors beyond the worthy Moses, who did indeed have links, in families as humble as his own, in London as well as Canterbury.

It was perhaps with memories of how he had himself come by the portraits that the historian was to stipulate in his will that if, after his eldest son's decease, Edward's brothers did not want them, they were to be destroyed, 'to prevent their coming into the hands of brokers and exposed to a sale for a few shillings'.[55] Fortunately, by the time of the death of the last remaining of his sons, who was ironically to be Edward himself, these instructions had been totally forgotten. Passing to the Olivers, the family of Edward's executors, all nine portraits were to be given, in 1880, by Mrs Henry Wright and Miss Oliver to Maidstone Museum, in whose keeping they now remain.

THE OGLANDER MEMOIRS.

WOOLVERTON.

Dinglye came olso into owre Island in Rychard ye Seconde's reygne, beinge of an awntient famely in Kent. John Dinglye, ye grandfathor of Sir John nowe livinge, wase long Liftennant of this Island under Sir George Carye, whose sistor, a handsome woman, Sir William Moore, of Losely, maryed, but dyed without issue. Mr. Rychard Woorseley and he weare both in love with her at one time, but Mr. Woorseley sourrendered to his good frynd Mr. William More, afterwardes knyghted. The fyrst of this famely that came into owre Island wase ————ton, by whome they now enjoye ———— daughter and heyre of that awntient famely ———————— sonn and

Chapter 2

The Hasteds of Hawley

Joseph's landholdings, dispersed as they were, could have provided the basis for a fine estate. Many important estates at this time consisted, or had earlier consisted, of dispersed holdings, and the Hasted lands required only careful management to take their place among the smaller landed estates in Kent. It was a tragedy for the family that Joseph's son, who should have been a key figure in such a consolidation, was to die too early to make more than a slight impact on the property, outliving his father as he did by no more than eight years. And although Joseph was to have the pleasure of seeing his son begin to take the family on to a higher social plane, Edward, as frequently happens, particularly with the children of wealthy older parents, seems to have taken some time to settle down.

According to his own son the historian, Edward Hasted was born in 1702, when his father would have been forty, apparently Joseph and Katherine's only child.[56] He was obviously an intelligent boy, and was given a good education by his parents, who sent him to the grammar school at Luddesdown, near Cobham, kept at that time by the Revd Stephen Thornton, rector of the parish. Hasted says of Thornton that he

> brought his school to such repute that the gentry from all this part of the country put their sons under his tuition; among them were those of Selby, Fortrye, Faunce, Hornsby, Market, James, Saxby, and others whose names I don't now recollect.[57]

It could be said that the day when little Edward Hasted first entered Mr Thornton's academy was the day on which he made his entrance among the minor gentry of the county.

It is Edward, aged perhaps eight years old, who looks out at us from the fourth painting in Joseph's set of family portraits now hanging in the Archbishop's Palace at Maidstone. With a bow in his hand, he seems to be accoutred like a young huntsman, his eager spaniel only awaiting the word of command to go and retrieve the bird he has shot, perhaps over the marshes near his Chatham home. Edward, as an only child, could have been rather a lonely little boy, but he was probably allowed plenty of pets, and the dog who shares his portrait was perhaps a favourite. The Hasteds seem always to have been fond of animals, and Edward may well have been indulged with as many as he wanted, dogs, and possibly ponies too. That he was over-indulged is probable: turning into self-indulgence, this was to lead in due course to his corpulence and to an early death.

Edward's marriage, which Hasted describes as 'not much to his father's inclination, as his wife had no fortune', was clearly another area in which a self-willed boy got his own way. Joseph had made a prudent marriage when he chose Katherine Yardley for his wife, and he would no doubt have liked to see his son do likewise. But Edward copied his father only in so far as he ran off to Surrey to get married. In the register of the parish of Headley, near Dorking, we find among the marriages the following entry for 28 September 1722:

> Edward Hasted of Putny Gentleman and Ann Tyler of Richmond.[58]

What Edward Hasted was doing in Putney it is impossible to know. What we can be fairly sure of, however, is that Anne and Edward were married by licence, and that both were minors, that is, under twenty-one. Later in the century Hardwicke's Marriage Act of 1753 was to be designed to put an end to just such marriages, making the parents' consent essential for the marriage of minors, but in the meantime the vicar of a place such as Headley — whose tiny population would otherwise have rarely required him to perform the rites of matrimony more than once in two years — was kept in almost permanent work by the flow of couples arriving at his church door from far and wide.

Headley, on the Surrey downs, seems to have been a romantic spot, much favoured by lovers like Edward and Anne, and ideal for runaway marriages. John Aubrey, Surrey's first historian, recounts of its shepherds at the end of the seventeenth century that they were skilled in hurling small stones at their sheep to round them up or keep them from straying into the corn, using for the purpose a split horn nailed to the end of a long staff. 'Such,' says Aubrey, 'I have seen in old hangings ... and before the first edition of Sir Philip Sidney's Arcadia, but never saw the thing, before I pass'd over these pleasant downs'.[59] The village itself he describes as very small and 'much encompass'd with wood'; the tiny church, which stood at some distance from the village, must have been even more secluded. The parish register shows couples flocking to it throughout the early decades of the eighteenth century from all over Surrey — Epsom and Dorking, Cheam and Abinger — as well as from other counties, Sussex, Middlesex, and Kent.

Anne Tyler, describing herself as 'of Richmond' when she married, certainly seems to have come of a family with Surrey connections, although Hasted describes her father George Tyler as a watchmaker and goldsmith of Change Alley, Lombard Street, in London. He mentions, however, that the Tylers had relations in Sutton and Ewell;

and a rent-charge for land in the manor of Chipstead in Reigate Hundred, in Surrey, which the historian sold jointly with his mother in 1763, had descended to Anne from Henry Tyler of Cheam, who in 1629 had granted it to his son Richard, the father of George Tyler.[60] Anne's mother, Elizabeth Dingley, was very possibly the Elizabeth who was married to George Tyler at Croydon in 1685.[61] George was a first cousin once removed, and Anne was therefore descended from Dingleys on both sides. Hasted subsequently traced this side of his family back to a knight (in the pedigree he is termed a baronet) of the time of James I, Sir John Dingley, of Wolverton in the Isle of Wight. In right of her descent from Sir John Dingley his mother was able to quarter in her coat of arms thirteen different coats which were quartered by him: Hasted provides the list of these in both his Anecdotes and the pedigree — and it is doubtless here that one can find the basis for what he calls in the Anecdotes his mother's 'excessive pride'. But he was clearly making no idle boast when he claimed cousinship with Robert Dingley of Lamorbey near Bexley, merchant, architect and philanthropist, and founder of the Magdalen Hospital for Penitent Prostitutes.

Did Edward and his young bride enjoy an extended honeymoon, or was Edward perhaps already working in an attorney's office in London? For two years we lose track of him, as, curiously, we do to a certain extent of his son the historian after his marriage, some thirty years later, to Ann Dorman. But we come across Edward again in 1724, finally settling to a career when on the 23 April he is admitted student at Lincoln's Inn as Edward Hasted of Chatham, Kent.[62]

The 8 December of that same year, 1724, was an important day for Edward Hasted, when he took part in two private ceremonies in the City of London. In the first of these, which was shared with three other gentlemen, Edward Hasted, having first been presented to the Court of the City of London by Miles Man, clerk to the Town Clerk, was admitted into the freedom of the City by redemption in the Company of Wax Chandlers, that is to say, by purchasing his livery, as it was known, for the sum of forty-six shillings and eightpence.[63] The second ceremony, in which he was again presented to the Court, concerned Edward Hasted alone. The Repertory or Minute Book of the Court contains the following entry:

> This day Edward Hasted Citizen and Waxchandler of London being presented unto this Court by Mr Sheriffes and having produced Mr Chamberlains Receipt for Twenty one Pounds for this Citties third part of the Sum of Sixty Three Pounds agreed by him to be given to the Right Honourable the Lord Mayor and the

said Mr Sheriffes for his admission to the place or office of one of the Clerksitters of the Poultry Compter pursuant to the Act of Common Council in that Case Made and Provided Is by this Court admitted into the said Place and Office of one of the Clerksitters of the Poultry Compter in the room and stead of Denham Hamond (who this Day Surrendered the Same) to Have Hold Exercise and Enjoy the said Place with all Fees Proffitts and other Comodities thereunto due and of Right belonging so long as He shall well and honestly Use and behave himself therein.[64]

Accordingly Edward Hasted was sworn into office, taking and subscribing the necessary oaths as a clerksitter for the Poultry Compter, one of the five debtors' gaols of the City of London. It is of interest to note that he followed Denham Hammond into this office. There must have been a close link between the two men, since Hasted tells us that his father had served his clerkship to Denham Hammond, and that he became one of his partners 'in the law business'. Hammond was to become Comptroller of the City of London in 1736, but when he died in May 1740 Edward Hasted was not, this time round, to be again his successor. This is hardly surprising, since the sum paid for the appointment by the incoming Comptroller, Dutton Seaman, a total of £3600, was undoubtedly well above what Edward Hasted could afford. The cost and value of such posts seems to have been rising considerably over this period. Another appointment as clerksitter at the same Compter went for £330 in 1736, although Edward Hasted had given only £63 for his in 1724, and on his demise in 1741 his position as clerksitter was to go to William Stewart for £315.[65]

As was not infrequently the case with such posts, the position of a clerksitter seems to have had accommodation attached to it: an entry in the Waxchandlers' Clerks' Book for the 8 December 1724 gives Edward Hasted's address as the Poultry Compter.[66] In 1726, however, we find the name of Edward Hastead (sic) among those of the ratepayers of St Mary Woolnoth, and indeed, he appears to have owed rates on his house at this time to the tune of 14s.7½d.[67] This is the parish in which lay Dove Court, off Lombard Street, where the future historian was to be born in 1732, so Edward and his wife clearly lived here for some years. It was perhaps not mere chance which led the young couple to take a house off Lombard Street: Change Alley, where lived Anne's father, the watchmaker and goldsmith, was another turning off the same street, and only a stone's throw from Dove Court.

Hasted states, both in the Anecdotes and on his pedigree (and he obviously had this from his mother's own lips) that he was one of seven children born to her, six sons and one daughter, of whom five older brothers died in infancy; but we do not find an entry in the baptismal register of St Mary Woolnoth until 1729, when Hasted's only sister, Anne, who had been born on the 6 February, was christened there on the 20th of that month. The only other Hasted entry in this register is for Joseph, born on his grandfather's birthday, 19 December, in 1730, and christened there the following January. Unfortunately Joseph lived only a few weeks. There is a record of his burial in the vault and the ringing of the great bell for him on 4 March 1731.[68] However, in default of further Hasted entries in the registers we find burial records for members of three families which were or were to be closely connected with the Hasted story: Yardley, Dingley and Lethieullier.

There is no entry relating to the historian's own birth or christening in the registers of St Mary Woolnoth, but Hasted in his Anecdotes states clearly that he was christened there, having been born in December 1732 in Dove Court, off Lombard Street, 'the corner house on the right hand as you enter the court from Sherborne Lane'. Dove Court no longer exists, but Sherborne Lane is still to be found, running between Lombard Street and St Swithins Lane.

The actual date of the historian's birth presents a small problem. It was certainly around Christmas, as letters from friends sending seasonal greetings often added good wishes for his birthday as well. In the Anecdotes, Hasted himself gives the date as the 31 December 1732, but in the pedigree he states it as 20 December. A copy of a legal document, drawn up in connection with the sale of Burntflower Farm in 1759, shows that there was some uncertainty over the precise day, noting that 'the said Edward Hasted the son attained his age of 21 years on the ... day of December 1753'.

This uncertainty was caused by the reform of the English calendar in 1752 to bring it into line with the more exact Gregorian calendar, already in common use over much of Europe. For this purpose it was necessary to shorten 1752 by eleven days. The law which effected this stipulated that in spite of this shortening the full number of years and days had to be worked to complete any contract undertaken before this, and the same ruling applied to birthdays and the attaining, in particular, of the age of twenty-one.[69] Hasted's birthday, therefore, was probably first moved in December 1752. The fact that it became 31 December must lead us to suppose that he had been born on the 20 December, and this is confirmed by his own statement in the family pedigree.

For the second time, Edward and Anne had had a son born very close to the date of Edward's father's birthday, and old Joseph hastened up to London from Chatham to be one of the christening party, which no doubt included the Tylers from Change Alley as well. Joseph was one of the godfathers, with one of Edward Hasted's friends, a Mr Bignel of the Six Clerks' office in Chancery, as the other. Mrs Katherine Hasted, the baby's grandmother, who was to be godmother, was represented by a proxy: she had broken her arm in a fall one Sunday morning when on the way to church, and now seldom ventured out.[70]

St Mary Woolnoth, the church to which the christening party now made its way, was only a short distance from the Hasted house. Hasted describes it as 'the adjoining church next the Post Office'. Even today, there is still a post office behind it. When Edward and Anne Hasted took their small son to be christened there in the January of 1733, the General Post Office had been occupying the site for more than sixty years, but the church itself was a totally new structure, although on an ancient site. Damaged in the Great Fire, it had been, first, repaired by Wren, and then totally rebuilt to a beautiful baroque design by Wren's gifted pupil, Nicholas Hawksmoor. The building entered by the christening party had gracious fluted Corinthian columns grouped in threes at each corner of a square nave, which itself soared up into airy space, part clerestory part lantern, its lightness hardly arrested by the plaster ceiling. It must have provided a most fitting background for the small gathering of gentlemen in high full wigs and delicately buckled shoes, with their ladies in full gowns under loose coats and lace mantillas, and the clergyman in his flowing black robes.

Little Edward, on what was undoubtedly his first excursion outside the house, would have been well wrapped up — his parents had lost too many sons already not to be nervous about him. The January air was damp and foggy, and full of noxious substances from the city's many workshops. The baby took no harm from them, but it was otherwise with his seventy-year-old grandfather. The damp, dirty air aggravated Joseph's asthma, and to this were now added a very bad cough and cold. In alarm, the family quickly arranged for him to be taken to the better air of Hackney, then well outside the metropolis and considered particularly healthy, but there was to be no improvement: Joseph Hasted's busy and fruitful existence came to an end on 22 January 1733.[71] He had lived to see his son an undisputed gentleman and to set eyes on the only grandson who would live, and who would carry the family name, if not to glory, at least to renown. From all the evidence, Joseph can be said to have had a long and happy life, a combination which was to be denied to both his son and his grandson.

Joseph had made his will nearly two years before, on the 25 August 1731, so that it contained no provision for little Edward. But it was a generous will to those closest to him at the time, leaving bequests for mourning to his wife, son and daughter-in-law of £50, £25 and £20 respectively. To a Chatham friend, John Thurstone, a fellow tenant of the manor of Teynham, and his wife Martha, was left £10 each that they might buy mourning; his half-brother Nathaniel Hasted received £50, and little Anne, his granddaughter, £100. To Edward, his son, were bequeathed all the lands and tenements held of the Warden and Fellows of All Soul's College, Oxford, which Joseph had acquired in 1721, with most of the remainder of the property going to his wife Katherine until her decease, when it would pass to their son. The holdings in Lynsted and Teynham were excepted conditionally from this, however, and were only left to Katherine so long as she remained unmarried: on her remarriage, as on her decease, they were to pass immediately to Edward. In the event of Edward dying before his mother, and leaving no heirs, the Hasted estate was entailed on Joseph's half-brother, Nathaniel.[72]

Hasted tells us that the proviso relating to the property in Lynsted and Teynham offended his grandmother greatly — although whether at the suggestion that she might ever want to marry again, or at the mere imposition of a condition, he does not say. Her annoyance could perhaps also be construed as a sign that the Hasted estate had indeed been founded on money which Katherine had brought with her to the marriage.

On Joseph's only son, Edward, fell the responsibility of arranging for his father's funeral. In his will Joseph had expressed a desire to be buried at Rainham, but the historian tells us in the Anecdotes that before he died it was pointed out to him that he had no land there, and that Newington, where he held a considerable amount, would be more fitting. Indeed, most of the local farmers who formed the vestry there appear to have been tenants of Hasted land, and Edward seems to have had no difficulty in obtaining for his father burial in the parish church of St Mary the Virgin at Newington. The spot selected was in the north-east corner of the thirteenth-century south chancel. This housed the arcaded tomb known as the shrine of Robert, or St Robert, of Newington, thought to have been a murdered pilgrim of the thirteenth or fourteenth century. A late sixteenth-century brass also commemorated Francis Holbrook, his two wives and thirteen children. Since that date, however, the chancel seems to have had no other occupants of note, and the churchwardens were probably very pleased that the up and coming Hasted family should now choose to be buried there, with the likelihood that a profusion of Hasted memorials would come in time to decorate its bare walls. Joseph's body was accordingly carried down to Newington, and the funeral took place on the 29 January, with tenants of Hasted land in Newington and Upchurch acting as the bearers.

In Newington vestry minutes is the following memorandum, dated 10 June 1733:

> Mr Hasted paid by Henry Mercer into the Churchwardens hands Mr Richard Chrisfield the sum of three guineas for depositing his father in the chancel and for leave to erect such monument and inscription in ye said chancel as to the said Mr Hasted shall be agreeable.
> Mem: at the same time it was agreed at the vestry that for the future no more shall be demanded by the Parish of Mr Hasted than one Guinea for any corpse of his Family to be deposited in ye said Chancel. [73]

A duplicate of this statement was given to Edward, and he proceeded to commission a London mason, Thomas Ayling, to supply a black marble gravestone, suitably inscribed, as well as a monumental tablet for the wall. The tablet, for which several types of marble were used — black, white, white streaked with grey, and a pinkish-grey — was at once severe and elaborate. It combined the Hasted coat of arms, carved and painted, above a sarcophagus in bas-relief, with a rectangular panel for the inscription ample enough to commemorate others of the family in due course, and it terminated below in a wreath. The family papers, preserved for posterity by Edward's grandson, contain the accounts for the work. Carving and painting the arms and letters came to £23.13s.4d., and the total cost, including packing cases, 'carteg' and 'wharfeg', cramps, lead, mortar and blacking, as well as fixing in place at Newington and the cost of the black marble ledger stone over the grave, amounted to a grand total of £51.16s.2½d.[74]

However, the unfortunate Thomas Ayling seems to have been unable ever to touch his money, as he became the subject of an attachment in the Lord Mayor's court, brought by one Philip Fruchard, obviously one of Ayling's creditors. Edward Hasted received a receipt dated 16 July 1734 for £47.17s.0d. from Fruchard 'being the monys of the Deft Condemned in his hands in the above cause for my use'.[75]

Joseph had received a fitting commemoration. Perhaps Katherine saw to it that her son gave his attention to the matter. She may have guessed that he would be slower to attend to such things after her own death, which occurred only two years later, in March 1735. Her funeral, which may have taken place at Chatham, was, one would hope, carried out as she had wanted it, with six pall-bearers, all but one of them, Martha Thurstone, related to her: Mrs Ayerst, Mrs Taylour, Mrs Chicheley, Mrs Page and Mr Yardley. Her body was taken down to Newington and buried with that of her husband, in the north-east corner of the south chancel. Edward wrote out on a piece of paper the inscription which he intended should be put 'on the Flat Stone' — there is no mention of the tablet:

> Here also lyeth interred the Body of Katherine his wife who departed this Life the 10th day of March 1734 in the 65th year of her Age.[76]

But the instructions were never passed on. Thomas Ayling, the stonemason who had been employed earlier, was under an attachment, and in any case a local man would probably have been sought for a simple inscription. Had Edward Hasted lived longer he may, like Samuel Johnson, have turned his attention in old age to providing his mother with some commemoration before it was too late. But such an opportunity was to be denied him, and fate was to repay him with a similar neglect.

One should not be too hard on Edward on this account, however. He had been left with a complicated estate to administer; he was a busy lawyer with official employment in the City; and he was in the process of moving his family out of the smoke and grime of London to a small estate at Hawley, near Dartford, where he would accept with great goodwill the onerous unpaid duties which frequently fell to the lot of gentlemen resident in the countryside.

Katherine's will, made a few months before she died, consisted of no more than small monetary bequests: the distribution of the property had already been attended to by her husband. She left small legacies to the poor of the parishes of Chatham and Newington, and £20 each to her son and daughter-in-law with which to buy mourning apparel, while her brother and sister, Robert Yardley and Sarah Ward, were left 20s. apiece for a mourning ring. £30 was left to a niece, Mary, of whom she was clearly fond, a daughter of her brother Robert; £100 went to her granddaughter Anne, and, rectifying the omission of her grandson from Joseph's will, little Edward was to receive £200.[77] The residue of her estate would seem to have gone to her son Edward: indeed, Joseph had been careful to stipulate that his plate — engraved with the Hasted crest — should go to his son after Katherine's death.

The thirty-three-year-old Edward now came into his own as the senior member of the family, with a respectable house at Chatham, embellished with family portraits, as well as a house in London. Voting in the general election of 1734 for two 'Knights of the Shire' for Kent in right of a freehold in Eastling, he was listed among the county's freeholders whose abode was in London.[78] In addition to his professional interests he had an extremely complex estate to administer: Hasted himself mentions land in the parishes of Chatham, Rochester, Gillingham, Cliffe, Shorne, Linton, Eastling, Lynsted, Teynham, Newington, Upchurch and Halstow; the manor of Horsham, with lands and appurtenances in Upchurch and adjoining parishes, which was held on a lease from the Warden and Fellows of All Souls' College, Oxford; mortgages on property in Kent and Essex; and money in the public funds, including the Million Bank, founded in 1694 in connection with William III's Million Lottery.[79] A catalogue of the Hasted lands drawn up in the 1750s shows that they consisted of around sixty parcels of land, ranging in extent from half an acre to sixty, as well as an interest in numerous houses, cottages, a mill, a malt house, a lime kiln and a smith's forge — the tenements being mainly in Chatham, Gillingham and St Margaret's Rochester.[80]

To assist him in the administration of all this Edward had the services of the Rochester attorney, Henry Sheafe, who had worked for his father before him. Sheafe, who was for many years clerk to the wardens of Rochester Bridge, seems to have had a finger in most Rochester pies. These pies, and the good living which they represented, rendered him latterly, according to Hasted in his Anecdotes, 'too unwieldy from his size to ride any distance on horseback', but he seems, nevertheless, unlike Hasted's father, to have been able to survive with his corpulency into a relatively ripe old age. While the Hasted affairs remained in the hands of Henry Sheafe, and, subsequently, his assistant Robert Taylor, they were safe.

A single business letter of 1734, written by Henry Dalyson from Redbourne in Lincolnshire to Edward Hasted, and probably preserved by the historian because it referred to his father, shows Sheafe acting as the steward of some Dalyson land which Edward Hasted senior must have leased:

> Sir, In answer to your letter rec'd this day, that if it is your intention to have the Trees fell'd this Winter I leave it to You and Mr Sheafe's good management, and the sooner they are fell'd the better they will sell, before the sap rises ... Be pleased to desire Mr Sheafe to send me an Account when fell'd of the number and contents ... My humb. Servce to Madm Hasted and Mr Sheafe.[81]

Like his father before him, Edward Hasted seems to have had a head for business, and to have understood, initially at any rate, that it would be for him to consolidate his scattered patrimony. Immediately on the death of his father he made a purchase in Eastling, adding to the demesne lands bought in the same manor by his father a third part of the manor of Huntingfield, which contained the mansion of Huntingfield Court. From a lease which was drawn up some years later by the historian it would appear that Edward let out both the house, known also as Great Huntingfield, and its farm, Little Huntingfield, although keeping some 20 acres of woodland for his own use.[82] If he had any thoughts of settling at Huntingfield Court when he bought it, they must have been only fleeting. He was still a busy professional man in London whose presence was frequently required there, and his wife, always a Londoner at heart, would have bitterly opposed the idea of isolation in what, even today, is a remote and sparsely populated parish in east Kent. They therefore compromised by looking for a suitable country house whose proximity to London would make it more convenient for Edward, and more acceptable to Anne. Thus it was that in 1735 Edward Hasted moved his family out of London, taking a lease on a house at Hawley near Dartford, about sixteen miles from London, apparently the one mentioned in the *History* as owned by Samuel Percival and later known as The Rookery.[83]

A number of city merchants and professional men owned estates in the north-west Kent countryside, among them John Borrett, of Shoreham, Protonotary of the Court of Common Pleas, and John Lethieullier, of Sutton-at-Hone. The Lethieulliers were a family of Huguenot stock, several of whom had become wealthy merchants in the city of London. John Lethieullier, of Sutton Place, was the son of William Lethieullier, a Turkey merchant, and grandson of Sir John Lethieullier, sheriff and alderman of London, knighted in 1674. Since 1727 John Lethieullier had been Remembrancer of the City of London, and he was probably well acquainted with most of the other officials of the City of London, including Denham Hammond, shortly to become its Comptroller and Edward's former superior, as well as with Edward Hasted himself, who continued to hold his post of clerksitter at the Poultry Compter. It may well have been Lethieullier who recommended the Hawley property to Edward Hasted, knowing that the younger man wanted to establish himself within reasonable reach of London, and the Hasteds were probably delighted to settle in a neighbourhood where they already had an acquaintance.

It it quite possible that there was another factor in the increasingly close friendship between the Hasted and Lethieullier families, namely, the Huguenot ancestry that both could claim. That Edward laid some emphasis on this seems to be underlined by the fact that the Hasteds took as their housekeeper a Mrs Baptiste, a person whose name almost certainly indicates French, and very possibly Huguenot, connections. Hasted says of her that she was someone 'they had long known in friendship in a better state of life, but who by misfortunes had come to decay'. The Lethieulliers were related to the Desbouveries, from whom was to descend the family of Pleydell-Bouverie, Earls of Radnor: Catherine Lethieullier, in 1630, had married in London a son of Laurens Desbouverie, a wealthy Huguenot refugee at that time resident in Canterbury. Many years later this, too, was to prove a valuable acquaintance for Hasted the historian.

From now on, professional work in London and relaxation in the country seem to have gone hand in hand for Edward Hasted. He was called to the bar on 23 November 1736, and in 1737 became clerk of his livery company, the Wax Chandlers, perhaps exchanging his rooms at the Poultry Compter for a superior suite at Wax Chandlers' Hall in Gutter Lane, Cheapside, although he still retained his post as a clerksitter at the Compter.[84] At home, in nearby Dartford, an old posting town on the Dover road, all aspects of local society seem to have benefited from the educated participation of the Hasteds. The artistic talents of Joseph were not without an outlet in his son, who set on foot there a series of monthly concerts, for which he acted as both steward and treasurer. These must have provided a pleasant social occasion of the kind which particularly distinguished eighteenth century country towns. Anne, for her part, also had a lively social circle, and became well known for the public breakfasts which she organised for the ladies of the town and neighbourhood each Saturday, Dartford's market day, and which were probably held at the Bull. Public breakfasts seem to have remained popular over a long period: John Byng, the diarist, has left us a thumb-nail sketch of one he came across in Cheltenham in 1781:

> There is a gaiety in a public breakfast in a summer's morning, with music, that is to me very pleasing; every one then looks fresh and happy; the women are more in their natural looks, not disfigured by over-dress and paint, and the men are civil, and sober.[85]

There seems in addition to have been a considerable amount of entertaining at Hawley itself. Hasted in his Anecdotes gives a long list of his father's neighbours — not only the Lethieulliers of Sutton Place but also the Revd Mr Barrell, vicar of Sutton-at-Hone and his family, Mrs Hill of St John's, Mr and Mrs Leigh of Hawley and Mr and Mrs Lee of Darenth, the Revd Mr Taylor, vicar of Darenth, Sir Thomas and Lady Dyke of Lullingstone, the Blenchyndons of Swanscombe, the Melchiors (or Malchers) of Dartford, the Wheatleys of Erith, the Bedfords of Greensted Green, Mr Fullerton of Farningham, Mr Chiffinch of Northfleet, Mr Walter and Mrs Harris of Wilmington — all these were among those 'who had professed their attachment to (Edward) and had constantly partaken of his hospitality', but who were to fail so signally, after his death, to come forward and support his widow.

Other visitors came to stay: Hasted was to recollect Mr Stewart of the Poultry Compter and Henry Saxby of the Custom House, who were, he says, old cronies and schoolfellows of his father, as well as Mr Marye, his father's law clerk. These would no doubt be conducted round the small estate to see the latest improvements: a new stable for Edward's five horses — two kept for riding and three coach horses; a larger byre for the three cows, with sometimes a young calf also, curled up in the straw. But it was the garden which was Edward's great delight — his son tells us that he spent £100 a year on it — and here he was perhaps always his own first visitor: coming down to it early on a spring morning, to see how the new brick walk was shaping, how the Dutch bulbs did, and whether the apple blossom would open that day, having a word with the gardener Mr Aldridge and the under-gardener when he came across them, a happy man, planting Elysium.

Within the house, the civilised existence of an eighteenth-century gentleman's family was maintained by a housekeeper and three maids, and probably a cook also, although Hasted does not mention one, as well as two livery servants, the coachman and the footman. Perhaps the footman was also the servant who accompanied Edward on horseback when he rode out on local business: the coach and chariot would be used for more formal, and family, occasions. The chariot was probably the larger of the two, with an outside seat for servants, but both, according to Hasted's recollection of them, were decorated with carved woodwork. Sixty years later he was still able to describe in great detail the family's olive-painted coach, which was doubtless emblazoned with the Hasted crest, for although his mother sold the chariot on her husband's death she kept the coach, and Hasted must often have ridden in it as a boy:

> The coach I remember was in shape almost a triangle, V, and as well as the chariot had a deal of carve[d] work on the mouldings. There were 4 or 5 rows of brass nails on the leather parts of it, and on the braces before and behind very large brass buckles, and other ornaments on the straps. The carriage and wheels had near as much wood in them for strength as a modern waggon, for even the turnpike roads then required no small strength both for carriage and harness. The coach was painted a dark olive colour, and the inside was lined with scarlet cloth, of which colour was the hammercloth.[86]

Both the coachman sitting on the box and the footman, who rode behind, wore what would have been recognised locally as the Hasted livery, showing up well against the red of the hammercloth: 'a light blue suit with small gilt buttons down to the bottom of the skirt, a pair of scarlet stockings, a blue and gold shoulder knot with gilt tassells and a very broad gold lace on a square cocked hat'.

Seated inside the coach might frequently be seen a gentleman of middle height — his son states him to have been just under five and a half feet tall — rather portly, and fair in colouring, with an oval face, hazel eyes, a rather long aquiline or Roman nose and a somewhat prominent chin, wearing a large white frizzed wig under a square cocked hat. When dressed in his best attire he would appear in a snuff-coloured coat lined with scarlet silk, its large cuffs decorated with four or five buttons of the same colour. Beneath the coat was a black velvet waistcoat with long flaps, as long as the coat itself, which sat close to each other. A pair of light grey worsted stockings, ending in a pair of broad high-heeled shoes, rounded at the toes and decorated with thin-rimmed silver buckles, about the size of a shilling, completed the outfit. The whole countenance of this personage, says Hasted, 'bespoke affability and good nature. Such I believe my father's person was'.[87]

Indeed, on account of his 'good nature, affability and constant readiness to oblige and render himself serviceable to all his neighbours, from the highest to the meanest and most indigent among them,' Edward Hasted seems to have been popular in all quarters. 'By his knowledge of the law', continues Hasted,

> he became exceedingly usefull at all meetings of the gentry of the county on the business of the county, such as the assizes, petty and quarter sessions, commission of the land tax, and parochial meetings, which he, by their desire, constantly attended, when by his advice and moderation he was truly serviceable.'[88]

This is a very modest summary of the work carried out by Edward Hasted on local government affairs. Throughout the eighteenth century there were a great many public duties which country gentlemen were expected to perform voluntarily and without any remuneration, and Edward, enthusiastic and energetic, threw himself into a number of them and was not merely, as Hasted's comments imply, called in as an outside adviser when occasion required.

He was, for example, an active member of the important New Cross turnpike trust which had been set up in 1718. We find him present from 1 July 1738 at both general and committee meetings, the committee on which he sat being referred to as the 'Committee for surveying the road leading from the Limekilns in East Greenwich to the Town of Dartford'. There was usually a good representation of gentlemen from the Sutton-at-Hone and Dartford area: the names of those attending meetings at this time include several of Edward Hasted's near neighbours and acquaintances, among them Thomas Chiffinch, Francis Leigh, Thomas Faunce, and John Lethieullier. It is not without significance that Edward Hasted's name was usually written third or fourth in the list of attenders, showing that he was both known and respected; and there are a number of occasions when it is possible to deduce that he was called on to act as chairman.[89]

Attendance at trust meetings involved him in a not inconsiderable amount of travelling. General meetings were usually held at the Green Man at Blackheath, although the several committee meetings which resulted in the decision, in July 1739, to make a new road, thirty feet wide, up the middle of the east side of Shooters Hill, had been held at the Catherine Wheel and Starr on Shooters Hill itself. More frequently, however, the committee met at the George at Dartford, as it did on 29 September 1739 when Edward Hasted chaired a meeting composed of a number of his friends, Nathaniel Elwick, William Wheatley, John Fullerton, Samuel Malcher, Thomas Bedford, John Lidgbird, William James and Thomas Tryon, esqs, Captain Markett and Mr John Woodin[g]. At another meeting of the committee, also held at the George, on 10 May 1740,

> Capt. Wooding and Mr Hasted reported that they had according to the Order of the Committee attended the Justices of the Peace at their last monthly meeting for the Hundred of Dartford & Wilmington held at the Cock Inn at Dartford on Monday the 28th day of April last in order to settle the Satisfaction to be made to the Owners and Occupiers of Lands laid into the Road between Crayford and Dartford.[90]

One can see the widened, straighter roads of the nineteenth and twentieth centuries being brought into being under the care and attention of such committees. The same minute also shows that the committee had to act as the employer of the men working on its stretch of road, since it was resolved,

> That the Laborers now Employed on the road be Continued during their good behaviour, and that no Labourers be employed

on the Road within the Limits of this Committee for the future Except they are approved of by the Committee.[91]

There is no doubt that Edward Hasted took his duties as a trustee of the New Cross road very seriously: we find him present at nine meetings in 1738, at some twenty-five in 1739, and at thirty-seven in 1740. Contrary to what is sometimes alleged about turnpike trusts, attendances generally can be said to have been very good around this time: there were usually from five to eight people present at a committee and frequently in excess of twenty at a general meeting.

The services of Hasted's father to the county were not limited to turnpike trust work. On 3 November 1737 the Commissioners of Sewers for the Limitts extending from Gravesend Bridge to Sheerness and thence to Penshurst ordered that,

> There be a new Commission sued out with all convenient speed by Mr Henry Sheafe Clerk of the present Commission and that the Commissioners in the said present Commission of Sewers now living are desired to be Commissioners in such New Commission and to be added to them the several persons following.[92]

Among the twenty-nine new names which were added to the Commission, and which included the Earls of Westmorland, Jersey and Darnley, Lord Romney, Sir Edward Dering, Bt. and Dr John Thorpe, was that of Edward Hasted, esq. He was soon making regular appearances at the meetings of the commissioners, attending three in 1738, one in 1739, and two in 1740 — the Commissions of Sewers, bodies dating back to the sixteenth century, set up for the purpose of attending to the drainage of low-lying areas, made noticeably fewer demands on the time of those involved than the newly established turnpike trusts.

Kent's principal river, the Medway, was to become increasingly important in the economy of the county, and here, too, we find Edward Hasted eager to play a part. In 1739 he was named as one of the commissioners of the newly re-established Medway Navigation Company which was to flourish for more than one hundred and fifty years.[93] He was also beginning to make an appearance on another semi-official body, that of the commonalty of Rochester Bridge, the body of freeholders who voted for the wardens. We find his name written in, in pencil, in the election register (and misspelt Edw. Haister, esq.) for the single year 1740, when he would seem to have been summoned for the first time as one of the two Chatham electors, together with William Duddy. At the end of that meeting he was to sign the large leather-bound volume, in which the names of the new wardens and their twelve assistants were recorded, as a freeholder of contributory land in the manor and parish of Chatham, with his 'Habitation' also given as Chatham.[94]

We can thus see Edward Hasted entering with enthusiasm into the life of a country gentleman. He had not yet fully retired from his London affairs, but Kentish business seems to have begun to outweigh City matters in his mind. At the beginning of March 1741, for example, his diary must have shown the following dates and appointments, together, no doubt, with a few social engagements:

> 21 March: New Cross Turnpike — Committee meeting, George, Dartford
>
> 24 March: Election of Lord Mayor, Guildhall, London
>
> 4 April: New Cross Turnpike — Committee meeting, George, Dartford
>
> 17 April: Court of Sewers, Rochester

On the 21 March the New Cross committee, eager to see work on its section of road completed, decided that the six gentlemen present, of whom Edward Hasted was one, or any two of them, should be

> Impowered to Employ Teams of Labourers in laying the Land of Mr John Lampard into the Road removing and Levelling the Banks making a New Fence to the same and Carrying and Spreading Materials for amending the Road,[95]

— work very similar to that which is carried out today when a road is widened.

In order to attend this meeting Edward Hasted probably rode the mile or two into Dartford on horseback, accompanied by his servant. The meeting at London's Guildhall, three days later, presented an occasion of an entirely different nature. At the election, and the banquet which was to follow, it would have been quite improper to appear in dusty, travel-stained clothes, and a fresh outfit — perhaps that very one that his son remembered, consisting of snuff-coloured coat, black waistcoat and silver-buckled shoes — was carefully packed in a chest and taken up to London, to be donned on arrival in the City. Mrs Hasted, always eager to visit London, and little Edward, who was now about the age his father had been when he had his portrait painted, were to share in the excitement of the day; thirteen-year-old Anne would be passing a more prosaic day at Blacklands, her boarding-school in Chelsea. Accordingly, the coach was made ready to carry father, mother and son up to town in style. There was no need to take the more cumbersome chariot and additional servants, for a maid was kept permanently at Edward Hasted's City apartment at Wax Chandlers' Hall, and she would be able to attend on Mrs Hasted while they remained there. Quite possibly a stay of two or three days was envisaged, which might include a visit to the theatre, a return dinner with Mr Stewart of the Poultry Compter, and a tea-drinking with old uncle Nathaniel, whom Edward was likely to meet at the election, where he would be voting in his capacity as a freeman of the Painter-Stainers' Company.

No such engagements were ever fulfilled. The turnpike committee of the 4 April and the Court of Sewers of the 17 met without Edward Hasted. The election of the new Lord Mayor, Daniel Lambert, was the last function which Edward ever attended, for it was there, on the 24 March 1741, in a heated Guildhall and very possibly at the dinner following the election, that he suffered a stroke, and in the words of his son some sixty years later,

> The weather being exceedingly sultry and the Guildhall very much crowded, he was there, being rather corpulent, seized with an apoplectic fit ... and being carried to his apartments at Wax Chandlers' Hall in Gutter Lane, Cheapside, where his wife and son were waiting his return, he was there put to bed in that state from which he never recovered, but dyed within a few hours after, aet. 38. [96]

It must have been a sad and traumatic event for both wife and son, but particularly for the little boy of only eight years old. Hasted's father was to be carried down to Newington and buried in the south chancel beside his parents, where, only eight years before, he had 'paid by Henry Mercer into the Churchwardens' hands ... the sum of three guineas for depositing his father in the chancel', with an agreement for the payment of no more than one guinea for the subsequent interment there of 'any corpse of his family'.

Six Hasted tenants, provided with mourning hatbands and gloves, were called on to to meet the funeral procession which came down from London and to act as bearers at the funeral itself, which was conducted by the Revd Mr Franks, curate of Newington. As was customary, the bearers' labours were acknowledged, both before and after the event, by liquid refreshment prepared for them at the Bull — the bill for this and the other funeral expenses being the first of many which were to land on Madame Hasted's totally unprepared shoulders.

It was one of little Edward's earliest duties, as the son and heir to whom his deceased father's manorial holdings now descended, to pay the fees or 'relief' which were demanded on this occasion. The Court Book of the manor of Teynham recites those same properties, which in 1733 had descended to his father from Joseph, as now passing from Edward Hasted the father to Edward Hasted the son: Dane Gardens, at Cellar Hill in Lynsted; a messuage, farm and lands at Lewsham Street; another messuage, farm and lands, known as Cambridge or Cambridges, in Lynsted; Well Farm, or the Burnthouse land, also in Lynsted; and land known as Hays, near Barrow Green in Teynham. The relief, amounting to £1.5s.6^1/$_2$d., which represented one-half of the total quitrent payable annually on the Hasted holdings, was paid in 1742, exactly the same sum which had been due on the death of old Joseph some eight years before.[97]

But it was of course on the young widow, with the assistance, as she supposed, of her late husband's clerk Mr Marye, that the responsibility of running a large but much dispersed estate, and the upbringing of an only son and daughter, now fell. It is possible that her own father was also dead by this time. She was desperately in need of assistance and advice, but the calamity of her husband's death seems to have occasioned total neglect of the Hasted establishment on the part of the whole neighbourhood. Much later, and perhaps in the light of similar neglect to which he himself was subjected by some of those whom he had felt entitled to consider as his friends, Hasted was to judge this episode severely, writing:

> Of the numerous friends who had professed their attachment to her husband and had constantly partaken of his hospitality not one of them appeared to advise her or offer the least assistance, but all as it were with one accord agreed to stay away.[98]

However, the neglect on this occasion may have been due to Anne's own excessive pride, which no doubt showed itself in a certain haughtiness of manner: the friends of the husband, in more fortunate days, had not been encouraged to become friends of the wife.

Things went badly for the Hasteds from now on. No will could be found, and the family was forced to conclude that Edward had relied on the Kentish custom of gavelkind to dispose of his estate between its members. According to this, the freehold property was divided between his wife and his son, the leasehold between wife, son and daughter. With hindsight, one can say that it seems highly improbable that a barrister should have been content with this rough and ready distribution of his estate, particularly given the fact that it was so dispersed. It was also less than kind to his widow, whose dower of half the freehold property would be forfeit on her remarriage.

It seems clear from the historian's subsequent account of the disorder which ensued in Mrs Hasted's affairs that her dead husband was indeed served badly by all those on whom he might have expected to be able to rely. Not only did his Kentish friends turn a cold shoulder to the plight of his widow, but his clerk, Marye, very probably a Londoner, who had also been looked on as a friend of the family and frequently entertained as a visitor, increased her confusion by insisting on the immediate disposal of much that was of value: the family plate, Edward Hasted's collection of gold medals, his cellar of wine. Marye, if anyone, must have known of the existence of a will, had there been one, and it seems quite possible that such a person would have had few scruples in suppressing it. There can be little doubt that he encouraged Mrs Hasted to believe herself to be worse off than she was, perhaps intending to help himself to the Hasted money as time went by. It was due to the picture he painted of her situation that poor Anne made stringent and, it would appear, unnecessary economies, cutting down on the number of servants and on the expense of the garden, selling the chariot and keeping only the coach, and fetching her daughter home from her Chelsea boarding-school. It was just as well that Marye soon overreached himself, in losing at the gaming tables a large sum of money with which he had been entrusted to pay the rent of the Hasted lands leased from All Souls' College. His villainy stood revealed, and Mrs Hasted finally turned for help in her affairs to the old Strood firm of attorneys which had served her husband and his father before him.[99]

This was a wise move, and for a few years things went better for the Hasteds. Mr Henry Sheafe and Mr Robert Taylor, his assistant, managed to recover some of the money Marye had made free with, and were able to assure Mrs Hasted that she could in fact continue to live in considerable style and comfort. They gave her the excellent advice to live nearer her estates, where she could more easily consult with her attorneys about them, and where, too, she would have the credit and standing which naturally accrued to the owner of so much property. Anne Hasted took their advice, and accordingly, about 1742, moved to Chatham, where she took Rome House, an old mansion built around the beginning of the seventeenth century. A lease of the early nineteenth century — it was not demolished until 1882 — describes it as having had stables, coach-houses, outhouses, yard and gardens, and it was obviously both spacious and prestigious.

Poor Anne, who had clearly had eighteen very distressing months since the death of her husband, felt able to relax once more in Chatham. Hasted describes the contrast for her between living 'retired' in a country village such as Hawley, and 'the gay round of company which these towns of Chatham and Rochester afforded her'. She herself was, as Hasted later described her, 'a young widow, cheerful and sprightly', and she now had a companion in the person of her daughter Anne, a pretty, vivacious girl, of medium height, perhaps not unlike her brother in looks — he describes her as having an oval face, aquiline nose, and light brown hair. Anne's formal schooling had been terminated abruptly when she was taken away from Blacklands. We are not told whether her education was continued at Chatham, although Hasted mentions that she still took music lessons.

His own education continued without interruption. In 1740, after three years at the school kept by the vicar of Darenth, the Revd Mr Taylor, he had been sent to the King's School at Rochester, and he was to remain there for four years. The proximity of Rome House meant that he was now able to go home for the holidays, however short, an escape dear to his heart and something which had not always been possible when the Hasteds lived in Hawley.

Life in Chatham, in fact, seems to have been to the taste of all the family. The town contained, for a start, all the many relatives of the children's Chatham grandmother: the Yardleys and Walkers, the Hawes, the Chicheleys, the Taylors, the Ayres and the Bryants, with some of whom, no doubt, acquaintance was made afresh by Mrs Hasted, and whose presence in Chatham perhaps rendered the place even more welcoming and homely for the children than it was for their mother.

It must have been during this period of his life that Hasted laid the foundations for many of the friendships which were to enrich his life in later years. The family of Samuel Fullagar the attorney, later to be treasurer of West Kent Quarter Sessions, was an old Chatham one, as was that of the Austens of St Margarets, Rochester, to whom Hasted was also connected through his grandmother. The dedicatee of volume 7 of the second edition of the *History of Kent* was to be Joseph Musgrave, acknowledged as a former schoolfellow:

> Be pleased to accept this tribute of grateful respect for the friendship you have honored me with, a friendship begun in our early days, when we first imbibed the rudiments of our education at the same seminary of learning in the county of Kent, whilst we

were under our respective paternal roofs in the same neighbourhood.

Musgrave, in a letter of 1781, mentions 'the cheerful scenes of our early youth which I well remember were greatly heighten'd by the friendly aid of your sprightly Poney', and one can imagine the shouts as the two boys galloped up and down the paddock at Rome House, or played in its outhouses.[100] Sir John Henniker, another dedicatee of a volume of the second edition, by that time an MP and immensely rich, had also been a friend of the Chatham days. Henniker's family seems to have part-owned a substantial quay at Rochester: there is mention in the *Kentish Gazette* in November 1774 of Messrs Henneker and Nicholson's Quay Yard at Rochester being able to take a ship of over a thousand tons.

Hasted's sister, too, soon had her own circle of friends in Chatham and Rochester. Among them were Fanny Johnson, the daughter of Dr Pelham Johnson, MD, a friend of her mother, and Martha (Tatty) Soan, whose father, the Revd Jonathan Soan, was headmaster of the King's School which Hasted himself was attending at the time. It seems likely that Anne's brother also knew and loved Tatty Soan, although from afar, as an ink-stained schoolboy, for he recounts with considerable sadness the subsequent events in her life. She was to marry the Revd Roger Mostyn, rector of Eastling, a man much older than she was, who took her to live at the Parsonage House in this very isolated part of Kent. The great disparity in their ages made him, quite without cause, an extremely jealous husband, and that, combined with the loneliness of the place, broke her heart, says Hasted, so that she died, childless, at an early age. Hasted's bitterness at this recollection, fifty years later, seems only partly assuaged by the knowledge that Roger Mostyn's second wife, whom he married for her money, made him unhappy in his turn, 'and served him right for his usage of his former wife'.[101]

The young widow and her daughter were clearly much in demand. Visits and outings became the order of the day, particularly with the officers of Colonel Cockran's Marines, who were at that time stationed in Chatham, and to four of whom, Lieutenant Colonel Whiteford, Captain Sir Robert Abercrombye, Lieutenant John Campbell and Ensign Adam Fergusson, Joseph Hasted's old house on Smithfield Bank was now let. Lieutenant John Campbell, indeed, seems to have been much attracted by Miss Hasted, and to have proposed to her on more than one occasion. These (it would appear) Scottish gentlemen were, says Hasted, 'constant visitors at my mother's house, and on every party of pleasure with her and my sister'. But all was conducted, he assures us, with much decorum.

Nevertheless, as one of the principal naval bases in the country, with a constantly changing population of sailors and marines, the town was alive with dangers for a young girl, and Anne was not proof against them. Some time in 1746 she became acquainted with a young man called James Archer, and a few months later the whole of Chatham was to learn that the daughter of Mrs Hasted of Rome House had eloped with a marine. Their subsequent marriage in Exeter hardly mended matters: Archer's family, who lived in Kettering in Northamptonshire, were, says Hasted, 'poor people, little above common labourers'. Anne could not have made a worse choice, in terms of either the man or the manner of her marriage. It, was, says Hasted simply, 'a love match on her side, to accomplish which she totally disgraced and ruined herself'.[102]

The scandal of Anne's elopement brought to an end the few happy years in Chatham. Mrs Hasted could not bear to remain there. Hearing of a house in Margaret Street, Cavendish Square, which was to let next door to one already taken by some former Chatham friends, Captain Killegrew and his family, she fled to London. The St Marylebone Poor Rates for 1747 show her name written in against an empty space in Margaret Street — Hasted tells us that the house she moved to was a new one — and in 1748 she appears to have been paying rates there on an annual rental of £20. On one side of her were the Killegrews, with a £30 rental, and on the other, rated like Mrs Hasted on a £20 rental, was Lady Montagu, while beyond Lady Montagu lived the Earl of Warwick, whose larger property paid rates on an annual rental of £40.[103]

Bn in Dovecast Lombard S.t 1732
1734 went with my Father to Hadley
1737 went to school to the Rev.d M.r Taylor Darent
1740 went to school at the King's school Rochr.
       the Rev.d M.r Soan's
1742 Lived at Stone House in Holydays with my Mother
       at Chatham
1744 went to school at Eton recommended there
       be Mr Gilpin
1746 .. went to Eaton in surry under the
              M.r [   ] Staid till 1750
                Mother Mary [   ]

FIDEM   SERVABO

Chapter 3

Hasted at Sutton-at-Hone

For the next six years most of Mrs Hasted's attention was to be centred on Anne, always her favourite child, as Hasted was to remark without rancour many years later, but whose story had now taken such a disastrous turn. For much of that time her son was away from home, pursuing his education. In 1744 or 1745, on the recommendation of Mr Gilpin, he had gone from the King's School at Rochester to Eton: his name appears in the *Eton College Register* from 1745 to 1748.[104] It is worth commenting that two members of the Lethieullier family had also attended Eton, and it had perhaps been a wish of Hasted's father that his son should go to the school which was also the choice of the family to which he had, in some measure, attached himself. But at the age of fifteen the young Hasted was removed from Eton and sent to board at the house of a clergyman at Esher in Surrey — described by the historian of Rome Edward Gibbon, who became a student in the same establishment four years later, as 'a pleasant spot, which promised to unite the various benefits of air, exercise and study'. It is quite possible that Hasted's stay with the Revd Philip Francis, a noted translator of Horace, originated, like that of Gibbon, in ill-health, especially as he speaks of having been 'under the care' of Mr Francis. Gibbon's time at Esher lasted only a few months, but Hasted was to spend two years there. When he left in 1750 it was to follow in his father's footsteps by entering Lincoln's Inn as a law student, where he was put to study under an attorney, Mr Edmund Browne.[105]

The choice of Edmund Browne was not fortuitous. Mrs Hasted — still, on her move to London in 1747, an attractive and well-to-do widow — was as much in need of help and advice with her affairs as she had ever been. On quitting Chatham she had left behind the protection of the family attorney Henry Sheafe, and was now once more at the mercy of gentlemen who were on the lookout for such as she.

The first of these appears to have been a Mr Trehearne, who had, said Hasted, 'very handsome lodgings under the little piazza in Covent Garden', and who appeared to be a man of some substance, although what there was to support this appearance seems to have been a mystery. The young Hasted was clearly rather suspicious of him from the start, and was relieved when something happened to rupture the new friendship. At all events, he instinctively avoided the man thereafter, even though, in the smaller London of those days, this not infrequently meant cutting him dead.[106]

Trehearne's place, as an acquaintance, if not as a suitor, was soon taken by Edmund Browne, who was to prove an even more unsuitable ally. Where Trehearne may have relied on his personal address to charm Mrs Hasted's money in his direction, Browne, as an attorney, had the skills to channel it as he wanted. It was perhaps only due to his early death that the Hasted story did not end sooner, with a would-be historian forced to earn his living in the world, and an abrupt termination to the leisure which was to be the loom for a massive *History of Kent*.

It seems quite likely that Edmund Browne, by way of introduction to Mrs Hasted, claimed a former acquaintance with her late husband through membership of the same Inn of Court, Lincoln's Inn, where Browne had been admitted in 1731.[107] Whatever the basis of the friendship, however, Browne was soon the widow's closest confidant, and able to persuade her to place all her affairs in his hands.

The house taken by Mrs Hasted in London, on her flight from Chatham, was towards one end of Margaret Street, near the corner of Great Portland Street. Empty spaces still separated the houses, but the area was in the process of being developed very fast: in 1748 Captain Killegrew had only one neighbour between him and the corner of Great Portland Street, a certain Ryves esq., but by 1750 he had two, Lord Oliphant (who appears variously in the local rates as Elaphant and Olaphant) and William Gwynn.[108]

Margaret Street was evidently a very pleasant location. Although, as Hasted says, the house his mother took was smaller than Rome House, it seems to have been very convenient for a town house, with a small garden and its own coachhouse with a stable for two horses, as well as sufficient room for three servants. Here Anne Hasted was able to live with both dignity and style, keeping her coach and horses, and with an establishment of two maids and a footman. Hasted describes the quiet but elegant livery — a distinguishing mark of the many equipages trotting about the London streets — which his mother designed for her footman: 'A brown cloth frock and light blue waistcoat, both trimmed with blue and white livery lace, a plain hat with a silver button and loop, and leather breeches'.[109] He also mentions that the neighbouring houses were inhabited by 'persons of good fashion', and in the St Marylebone rates books we do indeed find those persons listed by Hasted: the Earl of Warwick, Lord Oliphant, Lady Betty Montagu, Colonel Watson, and the two Mr Gwynns among them.[110]

Mrs Hasted was not to remain long in Margaret Street, however. By the time of the Poor Rate made in June 1751 her house is marked 'Emty', which confirms the date given by Hasted in his *Anecdotes* for her move to another house, this time in Richmond in Surrey, and by 1752 her former house had a new tenant, Captain Ormond Thompson.[111]

What is not borne out by Hasted's account, however, is the annual rental paid by Mrs Hasted, which seems to indicate both that at this time Hasted himself knew little of his mother's financial affairs (hardly surprising, as he was still a student), and that she was not handling them herself. In the Anecdotes, Hasted says that the reason his mother gave up the Margaret Street house was the threat by her landlord to raise her rent from £42 to £50 a year. On the contrary, the St Marylebone rates show that, in common with several of her neighbours, Lady Montagu, Lord Oliphant and William Gwynn among them, Mrs Hasted should have been paying no more than £20 a year. Nor is this the only discrepancy. When Mrs Hasted left Margaret Street the incoming tenant, Captain Ormond Thompson, similarly paid no more than £20 for his annual rent. The threat of an increase to £50 was clearly a fabricated one. We cannot suppose that the landlord used it to get rid of an unsatisfactory tenant, for Mrs Hasted, with all her faults, was a cultivated and intelligent woman. The blame lies very clearly with the person who was now handling all her financial affairs — and mulcting her, most likely, on every transaction — and who in 1750 was successful in persuading her to move out of town into a house at Richmond of which he had the letting.

Hasted seldom has harsh words for anyone: Edmund Browne, on the contrary, is described in the Anecdotes in what, for Hasted, is strong language indeed:

> He was an attorney of Lincoln's Inn, a man of shrewd parts, cunning and ensnaring, of a smooth persuasive tongue, and one who had the look of roguery in his countenance.

He had, said Hasted, with a bitter wit, 'been bred up a Quaker, from which he warped to no religion at all'. [112]

This was the man who was responsible for Mrs Hasted's move to Richmond, and it was ironic that here she was prevailed on to pay that very same rental of £50 p.a. in order to avoid which she was leaving her comfortable and convenient house in Margaret Street.[113] But Browne undoubtedly represented the Richmond house as being far better value for £50 — although from Hasted's description it appears to have been little more than an exalted cottage, a small house with small rooms, with one very large room built on as an extra wing. And the attorney, playing on Mrs Hasted's tendency to an inordinate pride in her own lineage, probably argued that this bijou residence, in a select locality, would be eminently suitable for someone whose neighbours in Margaret Street had included among their number members of the aristocracy.

Richmond was to remain Mrs Hasted's home for three years, the home to which her son, in the intervals of his studies at Lincoln's Inn, returned from time to time. Possessing a beautiful view over the Thames, the house seems to have been charming in the summer, but appallingly damp and dreary in the winter. Mrs Hasted visited with very few families in the neighbourhood, and whole days, and even weeks, must have been spent in the sole company of the daughter whose marriage to a more suitable partner could have continued for both of them the ease and affluence of the earlier years, as well as providing a natural entrée into the society which Mrs Hasted craved and which, given the circumstances of her own married life, she had had some right to expect.

Anne and James, who were both minors when they married, had stayed in Exeter for some time, until Mrs Hasted purchased a commission for James and he went abroad with the army. On his return from duty the couple lived for a few months in lodgings only a short walk from Margaret Street. But Archer had proved totally incapable of supporting a wife, the marriage was not a success, and Anne had returned to live with her mother. Now, in the dank, uncomfortable and lonely surroundings of Richmond there must have been many bitter recriminations about the past between mother and daughter, and Hasted's visits no doubt frequently coincided with such scenes. It is not surprising that in 1752 he suddenly put London and all it contained behind him, and returned to the Kent of his childhood.

There was no family property in the Dartford area of Kent to which he could go, and the house at Hawley had a new tenant. But the Hasteds' former housekeeper, Mrs Baptiste, was still in the area. She was obviously a person of some breeding, originally a personal friend of the Hasteds, who had fallen on hard times to the extent of being grateful for the position of housekeeper in the Hawley establishment. Hasted must have known her well, and it is quite possible that in the Hawley days she had been something of a nanny to the little boy who was perhaps already conscious that his sister was his mother's 'favourite child'. When Mrs Hasted left Hawley in the aftermath of her husband's death, Mrs Baptiste, no longer required, had remained behind to marry Thomas Aldridge, who had been the head gardener at Hawley.[114]

It was, accordingly, to Mrs Aldridge, now widowed for the second time and living alone in her cottage at Sutton-at-Hone, that Hasted went on leaving London. Mrs Aldridge must have been quite elderly, however, for she appears to have died two years later, and Hasted tells us that on her death he 'hired the cottage myself and kept house in it'. In 1754 the name of Edward Hasted enters the churchwardens' accounts for the first time, when we find him rated for a cottage at Sutton-at-Hone with a rental of £4.10s. per annum.[115]

Although he must have been glad to leave the Richmond establishment behind him, Hasted did not break off relations with his mother and sister altogether, for in December 1753 he agreed to go to Bedford with an attorney, Henry Waterman, for a meeting with James Archer, when a deed of separation was drawn up between Archer and his sister. The deed contained a penalty bond which would be forfeit should Archer molest his wife in any way in the future. Under the terms of the gavelkind settlement which had been made on the death of their father Anne had been entitled to a third of the leasehold property, which on her marriage became the property of her husband. Archer had been given money on a number of occasions, in addition to the commission which Anne's mother had bought for him, and he must have been made to realise that Anne's share of the property, amounting, if sold, to some £950, had been bled dry. He appears to have been willing, on the present occasion, to take himself off for the sum of £20, and the Hasteds saw him no more. A record in the India Office Library, which agrees with Hasted's description of him as coming originally from Northamptonshire, shows that in 1754, as a 27-year-old ensign under Richard Gaillard, Captain of Artillery, he set sail for Bombay aboard the East India Company's ship *Pelham* with a company of 39 officers and men and 70 'Swiss soldiers'. The Hasteds were to learn later, quite by chance, that he had died in the East Indies around 1758.[116]

Hasted himself had come of age in December 1753, and it seems to have been at Edmund Browne's suggestion that the gavelkind settlement was set aside, so that instead of the freehold estates remaining divided between mother and son Mrs Hasted made over her interest in them to Edward, and he then undertook to pay his mother a regular annuity of £250 for life. A land transaction of this kind was a complicated process, and before it could be completed Edmund Browne was himself dead, succumbing at his chambers in Lincoln's Inn in 1754 to a short and violent fever which lasted just a few days, during which he never recovered his senses and which was due, said Hasted grimly, to 'the derangement of his affairs'. This meant in effect that Browne's sole heir, his only sister Mary, who was unmarried and lived in Gloucestershire, remained the tenant of the Hasted lands and was subsequently a party to the sale of some of them in 1759.[117]

Disgust with the man he had been given as a tutor may perhaps also have contributed to Hasted's determination to give up his law studies and leave London. His epitaph on Browne's death was that it freed his mother, 'and, I may say, luckily, from his control and self-interested designs'.[118] Nevertheless, the attorney did not die before persuading Mrs Hasted to take another house which was also unsuitable for her, although for a different reason.

Mrs Hasted had sense enough not to be duped where her health was concerned, and the damp, dreary house at Richmond was probably having a lowering effect on both her and her daughter. At the beginning of 1754, therefore, she determined to move back to London — but again, Browne knew of just the place for her of which, also again, and as if by chance, he was the letting agent. This was an almost equally expensive property in Princes Court in Westminster, the most fashionable part of London. It was set back a little from the street and had the luxury of a small garden behind it, where Hasted, on his visits to his mother, was to take pleasure in tending her rose-trees. The rental was £48 a year, and the house was considerably bigger than Mrs Hasted needed — large enough, when she finally left it in 1770, for the incoming tenant, who was none other than the radical John Wilkes, to arrange that it should have two print rooms, one for himself and one for his daughter Polly.[119] The house in Margaret Street, with two rooms to a floor, had been much more in line with Mrs Hasted's requirements: at Princes Court, which also had charming but expensive views, looking out over St James's Park and on to Birdcage Walk, there were three rooms to a floor. Taking such an expensive house in the heart of London would mean making further economies. But Mrs Hasted was not to be deterred, and selling her coach, dismissing the liveried footman and reducing her servants to two maids only, she moved in at midsummer 1754. It is quite likely that the well-to-do neighbourhood looked with some surprise on the meagreness of the new establishment: Hasted, in his Anecdotes, was to recall the discomforts which his mother was forced to bear here in order to keep up appearances. That she did so with some success, however, is shown by the fact that she was soon on visiting terms with some of her neighbours: Mrs Smith, who lived next door and with whom she was perhaps particularly friendly, as both women moved into Princes Court in the same year; Dr Pettingall, the minister at the Duke Street chapel which Mrs Hasted and her daughter attended, and his wife and daughters; a certain Mr Foote and his sister, of Manchester Buildings; and a Mrs Drew of Parliament Street. Despite the inconvenience of a limited income paid, as her son later admitted, very irregularly, and with a sizeable deduction every quarter for rent, Mrs Hasted, a Londoner who had returned to London, was to remain there for another sixteen years.

Her son, meanwhile, enjoying his new-found independence at Sutton-at-Hone, had no difficulty in re-establishing links with old friends of the family: the Lethieulliers of Sutton Place, the Leighs of Hawley and the Lees of Darenth, the Blenchyndons of Swanscombe, the Melchiors of Dartford, the Wheatleys of Erith, Sir Thomas and Lady Dyke of Lullingstone, the Revd Edmund Barrell, vicar of Sutton, and his old headmaster, the Revd Mr Taylor, vicar of Darenth. There were former friends of his father in most of the parishes around, with all of whom visits were exchanged and who were happy to renew relations with the son. And, of course, there were soon new friends also, such as the Faunces of Sutton-at-Hone, Edward Fowke of Hawley, and the Dormans.

Politically, Hasted's views conformed to those held generally in the neighbourhood. In the general election of 1754, the first in which he was qualified, by age and ownership of freehold property, to take part, we find him voting with the local majority and continuing his father's Tory support. Edward Hasted, in 1734, had been among the eleven of Sutton-at-Hone's thirteen-man electorate to vote for the successful Tory candidates, Sir Edward Dering and Viscount Vane, and his son, one of the sixteen freeholders entitled to vote in 1754, was one of thirteen who plumped their choice by casting a single vote in favour of Sir Edward Dering, who had remained one of the county's two MPs since 1734, having been returned with Sir Roger Twisden in 1741. Now, however, Twisden declined to stand on grounds of ill-health, and Dering, unable to find a suitable partner, lost his seat, leaving the Whig candidates Robert Fairfax and Lewis Monson Watson the comfortable winners — and the voters of Sutton, one may suppose, disconsolate.[120]

The Dormans, who had been yeomen farmers in Sutton-at-Hone for several generations, were among these freeholders. John Dorman, at this time one of the parish's largest ratepayers, assessed on a rental of £79, third only to two higher ones of £104 and £125, had signed his name to the church rate in 1748 alongside that of Thomas Aldridge. He had served as churchwarden, an office of some standing, in 1747, but died at the early age of 53 in the summer of 1750.[121] His carved headstone, still standing in Sutton-at-Hone churchyard, commemorates him as 'Many years a farmer in this parish; A constant attender on the worship of God in this church; Industrious, skilful and honest in his calling; Kind and attentive to his family; Courteous and friendly to all with whom he had to do'.

By the time Hasted moved down to Sutton-at-Hone John Dorman's widow Dorothy, who was to survive her husband by twenty years, appears to have been running the farm on her own, although probably with help from her son Thomas. Since Dorman and Aldridge had clearly known each other and had acted together on the church vestry, there is every likelihood that their wives were also friendly, especially as both women had been widowed around the same time. It seems most probable, therefore, that it was Mrs Aldridge who introduced Hasted to the Dorman household. It was not now a very large family: the Sutton-at-Hone registers show five children born to Dorothy Dorman, although these do not include the three eldest, Thomas, Mary and Elizabeth. Twin sons, John and Nicholas, born in 1730, had died shortly after their birth. Then had come Ann, born in September 1732, John, born in 1734, and Margaret, born at the beginning of 1738. [122] It was Ann, the third daughter and probably the eldest one now at home, who soon engaged the whole of Hasted's attention.

In the brief Chronology of his life which was bequeathed to his son with the Anecdotes, Hasted seems to indicate that he had been paying his addresses to Miss Ann Dorman for several years before they were married in July 1755. It was certainly not a question of the yeoman's daughter running after the young squire. The Revd Joseph Price of Monks Horton, an inveterate gossip, who clearly knew well the society in Canterbury of which the Hasteds, after 1768, became a part, commented in his diary that the historian had married 'a miller's daughter who did not want to have him'.[123] It is indeed likely that John Dorman, as well as farming land at Sutton-at-Hone, also owned one of the several mills at Dartford where there was an important corn market — he was assessed to rates there on a property worth £96 and an entry in John Lethieullier's diary points to this also.[124] What is of greater interest, however, is the emphatic statement that Ann had not wanted to marry Hasted, particularly in view of the fact that the first five years of the marriage were childless.

Nevertheless, by the summer of 1755 Hasted's addresses had been successful in winning the day, and an entry in the parish register of the church of St John the Baptist at Sutton-at-Hone reads:

> Edward Hasted Esqr of this parish and Ann Dorman of this parish were married in this church by licence this twenty first day of July in the year one thousand seven hundred and fifty five by me Richd Bathurst (Curate).[125]

The witnesses were Robert Northall, parish clerk and local farmer and victualler, and Thomas Faunce.

It was the curate, Richard Bathurst, rather than the vicar, the Revd Edmund Barrell, who was chosen to perform the ceremony, because he was related to Ann. In his letters to the historian Richard Bathurst regularly calls Edward and Ann his uncle and aunt, which must imply that his mother had been a Dorman — there are no Hasted candidates. There is a certain mystery surrounding his birth, however, as he is noted in

Hasted at Sutton-at-Hone

Hasted's pedigree of the Bathursts as 'born before marriage' — a marriage which never took place — but he was obviously recognised by his father, Edward Bathurst, a senior bencher of the Middle Temple, since he bore his name and would inherit the Bathurst property of Finchcocks at Goudhurst in 1767 before his father's death at the age of 92 in 1772. Edward Bathurst's will refers to his first wife, Elizabeth, who had died in 1715, and also to 'my beloved wife Mary Bathurst', but here the word 'wife' has been crossed out.[126] It is permissible to speculate, therefore, that Richard Bathurst's mother was also related to the Mary Dorman whom we shall later find living in considerable comfort although again in a slightly equivocal position, and who was to become the wealthiest member of the family.

The 21 July was no doubt a happy day in Sutton-at-Hone, with a copious wedding breakfast laid out at the Dorman farm, consumed amid the hearty good wishes of a large number of Dorman relatives. Hasted, on the other hand, was the sole representative of his own family. His mother had chosen to go down to Canterbury, where the young couple had decided to live initially, to oversee the preparations being made there for their reception, and had taken her daughter with her.

The supposed necessity for her presence in Canterbury had in fact provided Mrs Hasted with an excellent excuse for not attending the wedding. Hasted clearly already knew — as no doubt did Ann — that his mother strongly disapproved of his choice, but he must have thought that her views would mellow with time and that she would become reconciled to someone who had so much charm for him, as had happened in the case of his sister's husband. Nothing could have prepared him for the lifetime of unremitting disdain with which his wife was to be treated by his mother. His sister's life had been damaged irreparably by their mother's thoughtlessness in leading a young girl into the 'gay round of company' which she herself craved, in a dockyard town where the charms of a marine had proved irresistible. In the case of her son, too, she has similarly to be accused of extreme selfishness, as someone whose own feelings took primacy over those of everyone else.

The wedding-breakfast cannot have lasted long. As soon as the last toasts had been drunk, Hasted and Ann set off for Canterbury, arriving in the evening of the same day in the area known as Without Riding Gate where Hasted had taken a house, complete with two maid-servants. Ann, worn out with the events of the day and the very long drive, deserved a warm welcome. But that was something she was never to receive from the dowager Mrs Hasted. Their reception was icy: Hasted never forgot it, and it may well have cast a shadow over their marriage which it was difficult to throw off. In Mrs Hasted's eyes, her son had done an unpardonable thing in marrying beneath him. 'My mother,' said Hasted,

> tho' she acquiesced in my marriage, yet she never inwardly approved of it, and tho' she outwardly behaved civil to my wife yet her pride was so great that she could never stomach her, nor carry herself towards her with that cordiality that could produce that harmony which her relationships in the family, as my wife and her daughter-in-law, surely ought to have done ... My mother and sister staid with us, if I remember right, about 2 months and then returned home, keeping the whole time and at her parting, as she continued afterwards, a behaviour the same as an acquaintance, but not as a daughter, by which name she never called her, speaking of her to me by the words, your wife, and to her by the name of Mrs Hasted.[127]

Even the bitter irony of the loss of her own daughter at the age of thirty-three was to do nothing to soften the implacable resentment of Hasted's mother at what she considered her son's misalliance. It is not surprising that in the end the strain of presenting an urbane exterior on any number of fronts should have proved unendurable for him.

After this over-long and painful stay of two months, and the damage done to his feelings and those of his bride, as well, perhaps, as inflicted on his marriage, Hasted could not bring himself to see his mother again for another two years. But the fact that he was responsible for paying her annuity and that they still held some property in common, made it impossible for him not to remain in communication with her. The transfer of the freehold Hasted estates from shared gavelkind ownership to the vesting of them all in the son and heir, which had been begun by Edmund Browne, and which had remained incomplete at the latter's death in 1754, was not to be concluded for some years, when Hasted wished to sell some land. By 1755, a mere twenty-two-year-old, he had probably become too preoccupied with other matters to continue the legal intricacies involved in what was known as perfecting the recovery of his estates. For that was also the year in which, as well as marrying, he took a long lease of the old Commandery of the Knights Hospitallers of St John at Sutton-at-Hone with a view to settling there permanently.

The lease of the thirteenth-century Commandery had perhaps been available for some time. This was a manor which had been created in the time of Charles I by the division of a larger one, the manor of Sutton-at-Hone alias St John's, into two smaller ones, subsequently known as the manors of Sutton and of St John's alias Sutton manor. St

John's, which Hasted now held, contained close on 500 acres of land, a house, a mill and a cottage. As a manor it had a right to hold a court baron, and it had retained the right to hold the judicial court, the court leet, which had belonged to the original manor. Of what must have been fairly extensive buildings, only the chapel and tower of the Commandery now remained. These had been converted after the dissolution into a dwelling, which in 1660 had come into the possession of the Hill family, who still owned it.

Abraham Hill, one of the founders of the Royal Society, had purchased the manor in that year, perhaps in order to move his family out of London. A black marble gravestone in the south chancel of Sutton-at-Hone church commemorates his second wife Elizabeth, who died in 1672, but Abraham Hill himself does not seem to have spent much time there until after 1700. On his death in 1721, which was followed in a matter of weeks by that of his only son Richard, his unmarried daughter Frances had continued to live at St John's, clearly a woman of strong character and considerable education. She caused a large tablet, bearing a long Latin inscription, to be erected to her father's memory in the church of Sutton-at-Hone, as well as a smaller one to her brother Richard, who was also buried there. When she herself died in 1736 she was to be commemorated in the same church, both by a tablet ornamented with a three-quarter-length portrait in relief and by a ledger stone which, defying the feet of nearly three centuries of worshippers passing over her grave, still proclaims that she had 'served God in pure virginity and abstinence from wine and strong drink without a vow', and that 'The number of her years had taken very little from the comeliness of her person, less from the vivacity of her parts'. It was perhaps William Hill, her first cousin once removed, who thus eulogised his relative, since it was to William Hill, a Cornishman, that St John's now descended.[128]

William Hill, however, preferred to remain on the family's estates in Cornwall. By 1755 St John's would seem to have been uninhabited for twenty years and was probably in a very dilapidated state. Nevertheless, it obviously had a great deal of appeal for the young Hasted. One can imagine him taking Ann to look at it, running excitedly up creaking, worm-eaten stairs, opening doors which swept ponderous swathes through two decades of dust, while she stood forlornly below, seeing the whole ancient building, with which she had been vaguely familiar from childhood, as little more than a ruin. To Hasted, there was something irresistible about this relic of the old Hospitallers, whose walls incorporated here and there pieces of a past even more remote: the former Roman villa at Darenth had obviously served as a quarry for some of the building materials. If Hasted had done nothing else in his life, he would deserve some credit as the man whose imagination recreated a country house in an idyllic Kentish setting, which the Romans, nearly two thousand years ago, had found to be not unlike their own Emilia or Tuscany.

Once Hasted had decided to take the lease there was probably no dissuading him. However, even he saw that the house required some modernisation. The roof could be lowered to obtain a more pleasing aspect externally, and at the same time attics could be installed for the servants. A new staircase would be necessary, too. Hasted might have been happy to remain on the spot to supervise the rebuilding, but Ann was far from being convinced that the old Commandery would ever make an acceptable home, and in the end they reached a compromise. While rebuilding was in process they would live as far away as possible from the dust and dirt of the renovations.

Thus it was that the day of their marriage found Hasted and Ann undertaking the long drive from Sutton-at-Hone to Canterbury, where they were to spend the next two years. It would have been too dark for Ann, on arrival, to take in much of her surroundings, but the following morning must have seen her investigating her new domain with pleasure. The house Hasted had taken was a small brick-built one, with four rooms to a floor, which probably meant that it had a pleasing Georgian regularity, the front door flanked by the windows of the two main reception rooms. It stood in a good sized garden, and had besides a wash-house, a drying-yard, and a stable with stalls for two horses. And just down the road, through the still standing Riding Gate overshadowed by its round tower, lay the city of Canterbury, with its great cathedral, its shops and markets, its assemblies and occasional concerts, and seasons of plays given by the Canterbury Company of Comedians.

Still very much the medieval city, Canterbury itself must have been a place of great charm, and it is probable that both Hasted and Ann, when whey could forget the frost with which Mrs Hasted had blighted the first few months of their marriage, found plenty to occupy them: apart from anything else, they were keeping house together for the first time, and Ann, with two maids to supervise, was having her first taste of being mistress in her own establishment.

It also seems likely that it was in Canterbury that Hasted began to discover his true vocation as a historian — there had already been some finds at St John's to whet his appetite. It was probably during these months that he became friendly with the the noted Kentish antiquary and archaeologist, the Revd Bryan Faussett, who lived only a few miles away at Heppington, and whom he seems to have accompanied on a number of excavations. And, of course, there were were fairly frequent trips back to

Sutton-at-Hone, for Hasted at least, to supervise the rebuilding of St John's.

Quite apart from St John's, however, Hasted, although still only twenty-two, was already burdened with the cares of a considerable landowner. This meant making periodic visits to all his properties, giving orders for repairs, seeing that his rents were collected, and, when necessary, finding new tenants. It is perhaps significant that in the same year that he took St John's, we find him entering into a new lease for 25 years for his Eastling farms of Great and Little Huntingfield at a rent of £55 per annum with Mr Henry Chapman, a local butcher of some importance.[129] Little Huntingfield Farm, consisting of 20 acres of woodland, was described as having been until then in the possession or occupation of Edward Hasted, and he may originally have toyed with the idea of settling in Eastling, where the purchase made by his father in 1733 had extended the Hasted property. The lease of 1755, which reserved to Hasted all the timber-farming at both Little and Great Huntingfield, also had an industrial side to it. Chapman was to be allowed to dig chalk from half an acre of land called Hogg Hill, where there was apparently already a chalk pit, and to burn lime there, either for his own use or for sale. In addition, he was to supply Hasted with up to forty-thousand 'good well burnt bricks', for the purpose of making which he was allowed to dig loam and clay from a quarter of an acre of ground forming part of a hop-garden. Hasted was to pay ten shillings per thousand for them, delivered at Great Huntingfield. It seems possible that, in planning the rebuilding of St John's, Hasted had the availability of this cheap supply of bricks in mind.

By the spring of 1757 work on St John's was far enough advanced — indeed, one must hope for his wife's sake that it was now virtually finished — for Hasted to plan to move into it at midsummer. It was perhaps not the best of times in which to dispose of a house in East Kent — war had been declared on France in May 1756, due to what were termed France's 'unwarrantable proceedings in the West Indies and North America', there was much marauding in the Channel by both sides, and a frequent fear of a French landing on the exposed Kentish coast. Hasted had the foresight to begin advertising his house in the *Kentish Post* in the middle of May — 'To be Lett on Lease, and Enter'd on at Midsummer next' — but even so, it seems to have remained on the market for four months.[130] It continued to be advertised at roughly weekly intervals until 10 September, when it seems at last to have found a taker. By then Hasted had been at St John's for two months: he must have moved between the 9 and 16 July, when the advertisement, from having first described the house as 'Now in the Occupation of Edward Hasted, Esq.', was altered to 'Late in the Occupation of Edward Hasted, Esq.'. And interested parties, who had been originally directed, 'For further Particulars, inquire at the House; or, of William Morrice, Esq., at the next House', were instructed to address themselves only to William Morrice, mention of Hasted's tenancy, now very much in the past, being dropped.

The move back to Sutton-at-Hone no doubt gave rise to what Hasted was in the habit of calling 'a bustle', but when that was over one cannot imagine that the new 'young squire' — Sutton, as a manor divided into two smaller manors, already had an 'old' squire in the person of John Lethieullier of Sutton Place — failed to celebrate his installation at St John's with a lavish house-warming. It was to be the first of the numerous occasions on which 'my heart has been open to all my friends, and my hospitality equal to my heart', as he was to recall many years later.

The house into which its new owner now welcomed the Lethieulliers and the Leighs, the Dykes, the Barrells, the Blenchyndons, the Fowkes and the Faunces, as their carriages clattered over the little bridge that crossed an arm of the Darent — whose waters had been divided, probably centuries earlier, to form a moat round the building and its grounds — was relatively long and low, and displayed a variety of materials — flint, stone, brick and wood — with a short stuccoed west wing that rose a little higher than the rest of the house. The plainness of the wall which met the approaching visitor's eye could have appeared somewhat severe, but to overcome this two false windows had been inserted between the four which served the upper and lower rooms, and these, six windows in all, together with two dormer windows to the attics and the rusticated quoins at the angles of the wall, must have succeeded, then as now, in preventing the west face from appearing too forbidding.

The drive curved sharply round to the south-facing front of the house, where the aspect was at one and the same time both mellow and domestic, with a mingling of styles which Hasted's visitors were to find partly echoed by the interior. To the right lay the small area which had remained as a chapel when the Hospitallers' church had been first converted into a dwelling, and which still retained its three tall lancet windows in the east wall, with signs of former doors and windows to the south. Alongside this, behind one of these blocked-up doorways, was the large kitchen, unsuspected by the visitor, who would have been invited to enter the house through what was now its main entrance, slightly off-centre, cut through the thickness of the wall. The doorway, simple and unimposing, with wood standing in for rusticated stonework, and surmounted by a somewhat severe triangular pediment, had an air of combining the solidity of the seventeenth century with the grace of the eighteenth.

One passed through this straight into the first of the three reception rooms in the house, a pleasant, low-ceilinged rectangular room, with two sash windows which looked out on to the drive and the garden beyond. Such a room, with immediate access from outside, was to be ideal for Hasted the young magistrate on those occasions when he acted at home as a single justice in petty judicial and administrative matters. The second room was entered from the first through an impressively deep arch on the left of the room beyond the further window. Here the proportions were quite different, since this room occupied what had formerly been the base of the Commandery tower. At an earlier date the tower had been given a gallery, equivalent to a first floor, and this seems to have been used to determine the height of the ceiling here, markedly higher than that of the first room. Nevertheless, this room, roughly square in shape, was large enough to carry the extra height, and the effect was by no means unpleasing. A second arch, of a similar depth to the first, led from here into what was probably the dining-room, a room of handsome proportions, rectangular rather than square, panelled throughout, and well lit by two windows, one facing west, and a wider, more generous one, facing north.

This room, with the one above it, built on to the north wall of the original tower, constituted a totally new addition to the house. It seems quite likely that in planning his extension Hasted was influenced by the memory of the 'large handsome room' which had been added as a wing to the cottage his mother had lived in at Richmond, for this room occupies a similar position at St John's. Its ceiling was at the same level as that in the tower room, it was panelled, and and each of the two rooms had an identical fireplace, with a decorative overmantel, perhaps intended to hold one of the family portraits. There is no doubt that Hasted was successful in creating a room which was handsome without being austere — and which was made additionally welcoming on that summer evening in 1757 by the eager hospitality of the young host and hostess.

Before they sat down to dinner Hasted may well have conducted his friends all over his refurbished house — for the eighteenth century was as interested as the present one in visiting other people's homes. Both the first and the third reception rooms had doors which communicated with a hall at the back of the house, which was also part of Hasted's remodelling, and from here a wide, handsome staircase with a turned wooden balustrade and flat handrail led past a large circular-headed window up to a spacious landing.

What was probably Mrs Hasted's bedroom lay on the left. This, perhaps the most attractive room in the house, stretched across the whole width of the former chapel and had two windows on each side, north and south. It had been given a cornice, and on either side of the two south-facing windows there had just been room for two charming swags of flowers and fruit, done in plaster-work, with similar plaster-work over the fireplace. Another door from this room led off to the east of the house, to rooms perhaps intended for the children — who were to be a long time in coming — and to the back stairs, going down to the offices, and up to the servants' quarters in the attic.

To the right of the landing lay a small suite of three rooms, which were almost certainly occupied by Hasted himself. They were approached up a short flight of eight stairs — necessitated by the difference in height of the rooms below — leading up under an attractively curved ceiling to a door flanked by a pair of Tuscan pilasters. The first of these rooms was probably a dressing-room, from which one passed into the main bedroom, which constituted the upper floor of the new wing. Like the room below, this too had windows facing west and north. The third room was also entered from the dressing-room, but lay at the front of the house. There seems little doubt that this tiny room was intended by Hasted as his study, where books and manuscripts were to accumulate as the years passed, and the shelves climbed ever higher up the walls. Like Ann's room, it overlooked the drive and the garden beyond, which would have allowed Hasted to know who his visitors were before they were announced — although he seems seldom to have taken advantage of this to declare himself 'not at home', a procedure which in his eyes would have been tantamount to lying. In 1763 he was to confide to his friend Astle that he was 'pestered at Sutton' by 'the interruption of too many visitors' — the inevitable result of so friendly and hospitable a nature as his.

We can only guess at the number of servants needed at St John's, but it is unlikely to have been fewer than had been kept at Hawley. There, Hasted tells us, his father had two livery servants, coachman and footman, three maid-servants, and a housekeeper, as well as two gardeners; and Edward Hasted's own man-servant may have been additional to these. Hasted has a pleasant way of talking about his mother's small establishment as her 'family', and he seems, like his father, to have been a caring master and landlord. But the only servant of whom we know is William Child, who came from an old Wilmington family: there are gravestones to earlier members of it still standing in Sutton-at-Hone churchyard. William seems to have been Hasted's personal servant in the sixties, and may often have accompanied his master on rides and excursions. Edward Hasted, at Hawley, had kept three coach horses, and two riding horses, one for himself, and one for his servant, and it is difficult to imagine that his son, who was an excellent horseman, could have managed with any fewer. There was always a dog in the Hasted household, and cats as well. These can be deduced from various mentions, but sadly nothing tells us whether the domestic arrangements at St John's also included cows and chickens, although this is very likely: Hasted's father, we know, kept three cows.[131]

The Preface to a small book which Hasted brought out around 1767 contains a detailed and loving description of the house and its setting at Sutton:

> The mansion house of the knights of St John's of Sutton was pulled down soon after the Dissolution; but the chapel adjoining it, a stone building of great strength and beauty, had been made the dwelling-house. It stands on the banks of the river Darent, which here dividing itself, washes the east and west sides of the garden. The fruitful hills form an amphitheatre around it to the distance of some miles, and make the most beautiful prospect to be imagined, especially when the eye hath glanced over a large intermediate plain of rich and fertile meadows, which join the garden, whose verdure, opposed to the golden harvest of the hills, makes a most beautiful and pleasing variety.[132]

We can almost see Hasted and his wife, walking about their garden or seated under a tree, like Mr and Mrs Robert Andrews in the painting by Gainsborough, with a similar background of well-watered garden and cultivated hills, an idyll to the eighteenth-century mind, and perhaps not surpassed since.

In his Anecdotes Hasted confesses that as the squire of St John's he was guilty of a certain ostentation — 'wishing to live in the style of a gentleman with my carriage and servants' — but he was still very young, and the rental from the Hasted lands, amounting to nearly £1000 a year, must have seemed like Fortunatus' purse to someone who had perhaps been kept on a tight rein as a schoolboy and a student. It is clear, however, that the cost of turning St John's into a suitable eighteenth-century residence — Hasted nowhere admits how much this was, although he calls it an 'enormous expense' — gave the first, and very serious, blow to his finances, and is probably the reason why we find him, in 1759, selling a sizeable farm to the trustees of the Galfridus Mann estate, who were acting in the absence of the heir, the connoisseur and dilettante Sir Horace Mann, who was to spend most of his life in Florence.

The transaction is very well documented in the Mann/Cornwallis archives, which show that after the death of Edmund Browne in 1754 Hasted had neglected to complete the recovery of his estates, so that Browne's sister Mary, as his devisee, remained what was known as the 'tenant to the praecipe'. However, the matter had been completed insofar as Mrs Hasted's rent-charge of £250 was now payable yearly, and partly chargeable to the rents of Burntflower Farm, which Hasted now proposed to sell. It was therefore necessary to transfer the rent-charge to other Hasted property, and at the same time, the recovery of his estates, which had remained in suspension, was concluded.[133] There is a brief correspondence from the attorney Robert Taylor, who acted for the Hasted estates, to Samuel Eastchurch, who was also Deputy Clerk of the Peace for the county at this time, and who was acting for the Mann estates, although Hasted also employed in the matter the Henry Waterman who in 1753 had assisted in drawing up the deed of separation between his sister and her husband James Archer. And Robert Taylor seems to have deferred to the opinion of a certain 'Mr Bankes' in London, so the legal expenses for the whole transaction cannot have been inconsiderable.

On the 24 April Taylor was writing to Eastchurch from Strood:

> Sir, I did not receive the drafts by the Maidstone coach yesterday, and can't conveniently come to the Sessions today, so beg the favour of you to send the drafts by Mr Hasted who is at the Sessions and I believe will return tomorrow, And you will oblige Sir, etc.[134]

The drafts were obviously returned as suggested, for on the 5 May Taylor was to write again:

> I received yours of the 25th ult. with the drafts by Mr Hasted, and am clearly of an opinion with you, that if Miss Brown conveys in the manner Mr Banks has drawn the draft, Mr Hasted must levy a fine to secure his mother's annuity, which I think may be prevented by altering the drafts, and let Miss Brown join with Mr Hasted in the conveyance of the Linton Estate, and also in the deed to regrant the annuity to Mrs Hasted. I shall go to town next Monday, and will then settle this affair with Mr Banks, and let you know how we settle them and am, Sir, etc.[135]

Matters were now moving along briskly. On the 10 May Taylor was to write that he had seen Mr Bankes, and that he had approved of the method he had proposed, 'so that now I hope it will not be long before we get this affair finished'. The somewhat complicated transaction was finally completed, and Hasted received for his farm a purchase price of £1300 — very nearly twice what it had cost in 1711, when his grandfather had paid a total of £748 to its two sets of owners, Thomas and Elizabeth Hope, and John and Barbara Earle, and to the Offham blacksmith who held a mortgage on it.

Hasted's need for a sum of this size perhaps gives us some clue to the cost of rebuilding St John's. This had obviously created a debt, which the £1300 went some way to wipe out, although the Hasted finances must have remained weakened by it.

Small economies probably made little difference: Hasted had begun to live in some style, his generous hospitality was becoming famed, and he probably saw no way in which he could spend less. On his own admission, the first sufferer was his mother, now dependent on him for the payment of her annuity. This, according to the terms of the original indenture, was payable four times a year on quarter day, 'at or in the Common Dining Hall in Lincoln's Inn'.[136] Such details were probably mere formalities between the parties concerned: the essential was that the annuity should have been paid, and Hasted at the end of his life admitted that his mother seldom saw the full sum: 'she seldom received more than one half of it in a year, and that by mere driblets'. Nevertheless, one way and another, Mrs Hasted was to contrive to remain in London for another eleven years.

One of the ways resorted to, in 1763, was the sale of a small annual rent-charge payable out of a farm in Chipstead, Surrey, which had descended to her from her great-grandfather, Henry Tyler of Cheam. All other claimants to it — Mrs Hasted's half-brother and -sister, George and Lovis, or Louisa — were now dead, and an indenture of 10 May 1763 records the sale of it by Mrs Hasted and her son to Thomas Nuthall for £240.[137] This small windfall probably freed Hasted from immediate worries about his mother's annuity, and gave him more financial freedom for the next twelve months.

It was during the course of this year that he was to learn that Oakleys, or Homefield House, an old sixteenth-century house at Hawley, which stood almost opposite the entrance to the Commandery along the Dartford to Farningham road, was to be offered for sale in the autumn, together with its 75 acres of land, plus two acres of marshland in the salt marsh at Dartford and another two acres of enclosed arable land at Sutton-at-Hone known as Sutton Croft. This had come on the market as the result of the bankruptcy of two London stationers, William James and Nathaniel Poyntell, the wife of one of whom seems to have been a local woman with an interest in it. In September 1764 the premises were advertised for sale by auction in the *London Gazette* and elsewhere, and the indenture was subsequently to recite that at the auction at the Guildhall on 3 October, 'after several biddings for the said lands, tenements and estate the said Edward Hasted party to these presents was at the said meeting declared the best bidder for the same'. The successful bid had been for £980, and Hasted, having got £1300 for the 60 acres of Burntflower Farm in 1759, probably felt that he had done very well.[138]

The purchase was almost certainly made at the instigation of Hasted's attorney and financial adviser, Thomas Williams, who himself took over a small mortgage already existing on Oakleys of £119.17s.8d., 'in trust for him the said Edward Hasted, his heirs and assignees to attend and wait upon the freehold and inheritance of the premises'. Hasted was left to find the bulk of the purchase money, £860.2s.4d. He certainly could not raise such a sum easily, however, and a short-term mortgage of £400 on the security of the property was therefore arranged in November 1764, most probably by Williams, with a Mr James Whiffen of Beckenham. By the time the two-year loan period had expired, not only was Hasted unable to repay it, but he was again in need of money. Accordingly, a fresh loan was arranged for a further £400, again on the security of Oakleys, and again with Mr Whiffen, who now had a mortgage on most of the property. And this time Hasted was obliged to enter into a bond for £1600, binding himself to repay the loan of £836, as it had now become with interest, by the 20 December 1767.[139] One can see the traps being sprung, one by one. It is not surprising that Oakleys did not figure among the Hasted holdings when these were sold after the historian's death, and it is possible that this deal was a contributory cause of the abandonment of St John's the following year.

Yet Williams was to remain Hasted's financial adviser, who could always suggest some new way in which the Hasted property could be made to yield money when the historian was hard pressed. For many years the Hasted-Williams relationship seems to have been amicable enough, but in the end there was to be a bitter tussle between the two men over the Hasted estates, or rather, between Hasted and Thomas Williams's ghost, for by then the attorney was dead. Hasted knew from experience the duplicity which could be shown by an attorney, having seen his mother rescued from the clutches of Edmund Browne only by his death, and it is ironic that he, too, should have fallen a victim to an unscrupulous member of the same profession.

Strange as it may be, Hasted seems to have discovered that Thomas Williams was a distant relative, who thus required little introduction to be entrusted with his most intimate affairs. That Hasted was interested in establishing, if he could, a pedigree for Williams appears from one of his early commonplace books in which he was collecting coats of arms, and into which he copied the arms of 'Sir Thomas Williams of Eleham Court in Kent Knt and Baronet Principal Physitian to K. Chas.

2d'.[140] More convincingly, a pedigree of the Tylers, his own maternal grandfather's family, shows a Hester Tyler as the first wife of Rice Williams, by whom Rice had a son, Thomas Williams, who later became a stationer in London. Hester's father, William, appears to have been the eldest brother of the father of Henry Tyler of Cheam, who had left the useful Chipstead rent-charge in the family. If this pedigree is correct, Hasted and Thomas Williams of Dartford had a great-great-great-grandfather in common, and what is more, Thomas Williams is seen to descend from the senior line, William Tyler of Pembridge, County Hereford, while it was his youngest brother, Richard, who became the founder of the Surrey branch of the family, from which Hasted himself was descended through his mother.[141]

There was a great deal of land to be farmed at St John's, and at times Hasted's life may not have been unlike that of the neighbouring squire at Sutton Place, John Lethieullier, the former Remembrancer of the City of London, in its closeness to toil on the land. Ann, it should be remembered, had been a farmer's daughter, and although she was now a gentleman's wife that gentleman was a somewhat idiosyncratic one, who may have been as happy seeing his wife busy with farm chores or, like his grandmother, making excellent elder wine, as sitting idly in the parlour. Hasted was very friendly with Lethieullier, and many of his particular interests seem to have been given direction by acquaintances which he made via Sutton Place. There is the curious fact that Lethieullier had also got into the grip of Edmund Browne, whose machinations with regard to the Hasted estates were cut short by his early death. John Lethieullier was not so fortunate.

Other clues to life at St John's can be found in the recipes and notes which Hasted jotted down from time to time, often at the back of the commonplace book or notebook which he happened to be using at the time.[142] Two recipes, 'To Destroy Rats', indicate the prevalence of these vermin. Both concoct seemingly inviting but in fact lethal potions, and end with a reference to the risk or otherwise which they could present to domestic animals. The first one, which consisted of pieces of sponge cut to the size of guinea pieces and fried gently in dripping, without letting them become crisp, may well have been taken by Hasted from the *Kentish Post*, since a similar recipe appeared in the issue of 3 March 1759. These appetising morsels were to be placed where rats would find them, 'but out of the reach of your domestic animals'. The second recipe offered the rats a supposed sweetmeat of powdered nux vomica mixed with fresh butter or lard, wrapped up in paper, and it ended: 'But the chief excellency of this receipt is the safety of it to mankind and that it will hurt no other animals: a little oil, if either dog or cat may eat it, will soon cure them'.

Frances Hill is known to have removed the stained glass from the lancet windows in the chapel on the death of her father in 1721, but Hasted may have found some to replace this, as his notes contain a London address where the narrow lead could be bought in which stained glass was embedded, as well as two sets of instructions for gluing panes of such glass together. For one of these Hasted was indebted to John Latham, the distinguished naturalist and doctor of Dartford, with whom he must have been on friendly terms.

Two more recipes came from another doctor, Thomas Scrimsour, a former ship's surgeon and John Lethieullier's brother-in-law, who now lived with his wife Mary at Darenth. One was headed 'To give pictures or wood a varnish'. The other contained instructions 'For Black Leather Chairs' — which we may suppose Hasted had, and which were to be treated as follows:

> 2 oz. of ivory black and one pint of well boiled linseed oil well mixed together and rubbed over them pretty thin, and then dried before a moderate fire or in the sun. When dry the chairs to be rubbed with a brush and then with a flannel.

Other pests to be dealt with were maggots and caterpillars in the orchards which Abraham Hill had planted in the grounds, and another recipe contained instructions 'To destroy caterpillars':

> Take a chaffing dish with lighted charcoal and throwing some pinches of brimstone in powder on the coals, hold it under the branches. The vapour of the sulphur is mortal to these and other insects.

One can imagine St John's on a sunny summer's day, with the Darent sparkling on both sides of the house, and Hasted happily at work with his gardener among the fruit trees, master and man each bearing a smoking chaffing dish and moving slowly between the trees, while the maids at the back of the house together carry out into the sun several heavy black leather chairs, which have just been oiled in accordance with Dr Scrimsour's instructions.

For all his friends, whether they came with or without a recipe, or a piece of information which could be incorporated in the historical work which had begun to engage him, there was always a cordial welcome, and no doubt a glass of wine. Ann must have had many unexpected visitors to cope with, but she, too, seems to have proved a smiling hostess, and was always remembered in their letters by Hasted's correspondents.

Uninterrupted leisure, however, was soon to become a prized commodity. Hasted had no profession, having abandoned his law studies after two years, but he had inherited a fair-sized estate, and a considerable amount of a gentleman's time and energy had to be consumed in visits to his farms and other properties, which in Hasted's case were of course much dispersed. The historian has given us an appealing picture of his grandfather, accompanied by his manservant, riding out to his farms to see after his workmen and repairs, and the same picture, with a slight nod in the direction of changing fashions, probably holds true both for Hasted's father and for Hasted himself. In addition to this, however, the son seems to have been as ready as had been the father to oblige the county and accept numerous administrative positions all, in those days, performed without any remuneration. Already before his marriage he had agreed to become a trustee of the New Cross turnpike road, and he was later to allow his name to go forward as a trustee of several other roads, the Chalk road among them. The two years in Canterbury seem to have been free of such demands, but on his return he was soon put in the Commission of the Peace, and made a commissioner of sewers. He was a commissioner of the land tax, a Deputy Lieutenant for the county, and a warden of Rochester Bridge. There is no doubt that he was interested in all these aspects of administration, and that his legal expertise enabled him to participate fully in the local decision-making which they entailed, but as time passed duties were being heaped on him and he was becoming a very busy man.

There were also family obligations which could not be ignored. These included the occasional visit to his mother in London, and, in the summer, making arrangements for her to come down and visit him. But the coldness with which Mrs Hasted had first greeted her daughter-in-law persisted, and seems now to have been extended to all Hasted's friends — most strangely, since many of them had formerly been friends of her husband and as such must frequently have been welcomed into her own home. Instead of receiving his mother at St John's, therefore, Hasted found it was better to take a cottage or house for her in a neighbouring parish, where she would reside with her daughter in somewhat solitary state, enjoying a few weeks of country air.

Anne, after the separation from her husband and her subsequent widowhood, had become her mother's constant companion, refusing several offers of marriage, one of them from the Lieutenant, now Colonel, John Campbell, who had admired her in earlier days. Her death was as sudden and as unexpected as had been her elopement. One day in March

1762 she had walked into the City, and on her return had to hurry to take shelter from a storm. The great arch over the Horse Guards proved a draughty protection, however, and Anne caught a chill from which she died only a few days later. She was just thirty-three.[143]

Hasted went straight up to London to be with his mother in her grief. Arrangements had to be made for a hearse to transport his sister's remains down into Kent — she was to be buried at Newington, where her grandparents and her father already lay — while preparations for the funeral had to be taken in hand at the same time. Hasted's manservant was entrusted with overseeing the part the tenants would play in this. A long, detailed letter dated 26 March 1762 was sent by Hasted 'To Willm Child, at Mr Hasted's, at Sutton, near Dartford', containing the necessary instructions. William was ordered to make his way to Newington via Rochester:

> Then go on to Newington to Mr Mercer's and if he is not at home stay till you see him, if it is a day or two, give him the letter directed to him, and then go down to the church with him and there proceed according to the letter I have wrote him which he will shew you. Then go to the tenants undermentioned and tell [them], I shall take their attendance kind at my sister's funeral and that six of them will carry her to the church. I would beg them to meet at the Bull in Newington by one o'clock next Thursday and the funeral will be there by two. I would have you call on this occasion on those following: Luke Miles at Horsham, Stephen Richardson, Luke Colley at Upchurch, Jacob Skilder, Halstow, John Beanland, Richard Sears [and] Thos. Gibbon, Newington, Hen. Mercer, Wm Tress, Jas Hubbard of Hartlip, and Mr Elvy of Rainham.
>
> The first six I would have you desire to be bearers, excepting Stephen Richardson, who is too infirm, and if any of the other six are incapable, take the next in the list and so on. But I would have you desire them all to meet at the time and place aforesaid to be assisting, where they will have gloves and hatbands prepared for them, and some little matters for refreshment; and remember if you can to see them all and to give me a full account. And desire Mr Mercer to order at the Bull the same as at my father's funeral, for the tenants' refreshment.
>
> This is all I can think of, which I hope you will be particularly careful in, that nothing may be left undone.[144]

Hasted at Sutton-at-Hone

With its several omissions and mistakes, the letter to William Child shows signs of having been written in a great hurry. William carried also letters for Mercer and for Miss Peggy Dorman, Hasted's wife's sister Margaret, and was instructed to enquire of her whether one of the tenants, Beanland, had paid her any money for his master.

The funeral took place on 1 April. A small note of the expenses incurred on the occasion still exists among the family papers. The officiating clergyman, probably the Revd John Saunders, vicar of Newington, whom Hasted would also have known as the vicar of Farningham, which Saunders held in plurality, received a guinea, and the clerk £1.14s.0d. The six servants, or bearers, each received a pair of gloves at 1s. each, and three other friends were each given a pair of kid gloves, at 2s. each. Refreshments at the Bull for the bearers after the funeral came to 13s. The highest expenditure, amounting to £5.2s.0d., was on mourning rings, probably for Anne's mother and for her brother, Hasted himself.[145]

It seems likely that it was Mrs Hasted who was the person responsible for the idea of having a Hasted family vault constructed in Newington church since she contributed £30 towards it, for which Hasted promised to be accountable. There was not time to have a vault made before the day of the funeral, but the following month John Boyse and six men spent a day digging one out in the south chancel on the site of previous Hasted burials. The historian was to describe it as 'a goodly spacious vault ... arched with brick work and paved with large tiles, opening by a door with a handsome iron gratework into the churchyard eastward'. Boyse's bill for £27.5s.6d., which included labour and also '100 of playn Tiles', was paid on the 1 January 1763, but the vault does not seem to have been finally completed for another year or so, when Thomas Gibbons was paid for carpenter's work and materials, which included a gothic door case and door, protected by a palisado fence and gate. The total cost was £49.8s.5d. Anne's coffin was deposited here, next to the inner leaden one of her father, whose outer wooden coffin had completely rotted away. The coffins of Joseph and Katherine, too, had virtually disintegrated, with little remaining of their bodies but the bones. These were accordingly gathered up, and consigned to a single coffin, 'full trimmed with brass nails, plate [and] handles', which was deposited alongside the others in the Hasted vault. By an agreement dated the 23 May 1762 made with the vicar and the church vestry, the former contract between Hasted's father and the parish of Newington relating to burials in the chancel was renewed, and permission granted for the vault in the north-east corner of the south chancel; three guineas was to be paid for the first coffin deposited there, except for those which had already been buried in the chancel, and one guinea thereafter. And Hasted made a memo for himself that he paid the clerk half a guinea a year to keep the vault swept and clean.[146]

On a day heavy with mourning Mrs Hasted must have been taken to see the new vault, where the body of her only daughter now lay. The summer of 1762 was spent with her son at St John's, recovering from the sad event of Anne's death, and after this it became the custom for her to spend two or three months during the summer with her son and daughter-in-law. From 1763 to early 1765 we find Hasted renting a house in Farningham, a new one, entered as 'Mrs Pratt's house' in the parish rates books, for which he paid an annual rental of £11.15s., and it is likely that this was taken with his mother in mind.[147] Mrs Pratt, the landlady of Farningham's Bull inn, is the subject of a lively vignette in John Byng's 'Tour into Kent' of 1790,[148] and her house, judging by its rental, would seem to have been quite a genteel one, which would have suited the fastidious Mrs Hasted — who, in spite of her bereavement, still could not bring herself to stomach her son's wife.

The house at Farningham may also, on occasion, have provided Hasted himself with the peace and quiet which were becoming dear to him, just as happier events were starting to fill his house with noise and disturbance. In 1760, after nearly five childless years, Ann Hasted had become pregnant, and on 11 November was born a Hasted son and heir, baptised the following month in the local parish church and named Edward, after his father and grandfather. As sponsors, or godfathers, Hasted chose two local friends, Thomas Faunce, and Richard Leigh, while old Mrs Hasted became the child's godmother as well as grandmother. Three more sons were to follow in quick succession. Francis Dingley arrived thirteen months later, on 8 January 1762. His godparents were Robert Dingley of Lamienby, a relative of Hasted's mother, and Francis Leigh of Hawley, another member of the Leigh family, while the baby's Dorman grandmother, Mrs Dorothy Dorman, became his godmother. A third son, George, was born on 21 August 1763, and this time the godparents came from somewhat further afield: they were Edward Wilks of Faversham, a friend of Hasted, and an uncle and aunt on the Dorman side, Gabriel Thorne, husband of Ann's sister Elizabeth, together with her sister Mary Dorman. A fourth son, Charles, born less than a year later, on 25 July 1764, was given similar godparents: Edward Wilks, Gabriel Thorne, and Gabriel's wife Elizabeth.[149]

The choice of sponsors for his sons reflects to some extent Hasted's various activities and interests over this period. Thomas Faunce and Richard and Francis Leigh, at Sutton-at-Hone and Hawley, as well as being near neighbours, were colleagues on several of the administrative bodies which Hasted had been invited to join, and they frequently attended meetings together. Robert Dingley, who lived at Lamienby (now Lamorbey Park) in Bexley, was a prosperous London merchant, a member of the Russia Company, and an active philanthropist: a governor and inspector of Thomas Coram's London Foundling Hospital, and now generally recognised to have been largely responsible for the founding of the Magdalen Hospital for Penitent Prostitutes in 1758.[150] He was a cousin of Hasted's mother, and Hasted, who himself had very few close relatives, had been happy to renew acquaintance with him on his return to Sutton as a young man. The cordial relations seem to have been maintained: some years later we find Hasted's friend John Thorpe, another Bexley resident, checking on the writer's behalf a few facts about local families with the now elderly Dingley.

The unexpected choice of a friend from Faversham, who does not appear hitherto to have been in Hasted's orbit, and of Gabriel Thorne and his wife, who were Londoners, reflects a temporary move on Hasted's part to Throwley and his activities while there. In order to explain these it is necessary to go back a few years to try to uncover the roots of his fascination with history, as well as the promptings and encouragement which would set him on the path to becoming the historian of Kent.

e SOLD to the beſt Bidder,
ednesday the Fourth Day of *February* 1767,
Between the Hours of Eleven and Two of the Clock,

DEVIL TAVERN, TEMPLE BAR,

THE

on Houſe and Gardens called *Sutton Place Houſe*, the Wa
Woods in Hand, and ſeveral Meſſuages, Farms, and Land,
of *Sutton at Hone, Dartford, Darinth,* and *Wilmington,* in t
Kent, all Freehold, in the following Lots ; *viz.*

E Capital Meſſuage or Manſion Houſe called *Sutton Place Houſe,* with the Gar
round walled in (at the Bottom whereof runs a fine Trout Stream); alſo the
eral Parcels of Arable and Meadow Land thereunto belonging ; *viz.*

		A.	R.	P.
The Drift Way to the Land,		0	1	0
The Hop Ground, for ſeveral Years uſed as a Hop Garden,		2	1	30
The Hop Ground Piece,	A.	3	3	14
The Mill Meadow,	M.	6	0	20
The nearer Brook,	A.	2	3	9
The middle ditto,	M.	1	3	11
The little ditto,	M.	0	2	19
The nearer Mill Mead,	M.	1	3	32
The middle ditto,	M.	2	2	4
The further ditto,	M.	1	2	6
The Cloſe oppoſite the Houſe,	A.	1	2	20
Another Piece oppoſite ditto,	A.	2	2	10
Another ditto,	A.	2	0	12
The old Cherry Orchard,	A.	2	0	14
		32	1	1
The Land within the Walls,		10	0	6
	Total	42	1	7

he Meadows in the Pariſh of *Darinth,* Part of the above Premiſes, are cha
with the Payment of ſome ſmall Quit Rents to the Dean and Chapter of R
ſter, amounting in the Whole to   *per Annum* ; and o
Premiſes are many valuable Elms and Pollards.
he Fixtures and Brewing Utenſils, as alſo the Hop Poles in the Hop Garde
taken by the Purchaſor upon a Valuation to be made by proper Perſons fo

Chapter 4

The Lethieullier Chapter

Only a little further down the road from the remains of the old Commandery, which Hasted had succeeded in converting into an acceptable eighteenth-century residence, was the mansion house of Sutton-at-Hone's other manor, known as the manor of Sutton, and owned by John Lethieullier. The friendship which had formerly existed between the Lethieulliers and Edward Hasted (who was almost an exact contemporary of John Lethieullier) when he lived at Hawley was extended to Hasted the son when he in his turn came to settle in the area. The terms of the dedication which appears under the view of Lethieullier's house, in the first volume of the folio edition of the *History*, leave us in no doubt that the older man's friendship had meant a great deal to him. It reads:

> To the much respected memory of John Lethieullier of Sutton Place, Esq, this view of it is with much gratitude dedicated, in return for the generous and friendly welcome, which the author constantly received from the hospitable owner of it, during his residence in this neighbourhood.

This plate has the additional interest that it is perhaps the only one which was originally drawn by Hasted. One of his early commonplace books contains several sketches of local houses and churches, and he may have hoped initially that he himself would be able to provide the illustrations for his *History*.[151] But he realised fairly soon that a more professional touch was called for, and by the early 1770s we find John Bayly responsible in several instances for both drawing and engraving, as well as other artists engaged by those gentlemen (not, alas, as numerous as Hasted could have wished) who were willing to contribute and pay for illustrations of their own houses. A drawing of Sutton Place, apparently done by Hasted in 1766, had been given to Bayly to engrave as early as 1767, but a mishap occurred, and Bayly was obliged to redraw it. In December 1767 Dr Andrew Coltee Ducarel added a hasty postscript to some notes for the historian to the effect that:

> At this instant Bailey informs me that a day or two ago, he had the misfortune to drop a bottle of ink on your drawing of Sutton Place — that he has been at work ever since in making another which he will send you this week.[152]

It is quite possible that the rather stiff conception and composition of this plate remain those of Hasted himself.

John Lethieullier was the third generation of Lethieulliers to hold Sutton Place, since the time of Charles I a manor in its own right, but originally, with the smaller manor of St John's, forming part of the larger manor of Sutton-at-Hone. By the seventeenth century several Lethieulliers, descended from French Huguenot stock, were established in business in London, and an eighteenth-century directory lists them as Turkey merchants. Sir John Lethieullier, a liveryman of the Company of Barber-Surgeons, who was knighted on becoming sheriff of London in 1674, purchased a number of estates, both in Essex and in Kent in the parishes of Sutton-at-Hone, Wilmington, Beckenham, and Lewisham. The Kentish estates, with the exception of that of Lewisham, became in due course the property of Sir John's second son, William, and he in turn beqeathed them, when he died in 1733, to his eldest son John Lethieullier. The land at Lewisham and the Essex estates had gone to the sheriff's eldest son, also called John, and by the time Hasted came to live at Sutton-at-Hone these were held by a son of this John, Smart Lethieullier, who was thus a cousin of Hasted's neighbour.[153]

John Lethieullier of Sutton Place had been Remembrancer of the City of London, a position which he held from January 1727 to November 1743.[154] He must have been frequently down at Sutton during the 1730s, however, since he was among the social acquaintance of Hasted's parents at Hawley, and from 1743 he appears to have retired there for good. His first wife, Mary, died in 1748 at the age of forty-two and in 1752 John Lethieullier married again, taking as his second wife Ann Garret, who is mentioned in the *History* as coming from a London family, but who may well have been descended from the Thomas Garrett of Dartford, gent., and Ann his wife, to whom the wardens of Rochester Bridge leased a house and wharf on the Darent from 1693, a property which was only given up by the family in 1786.[155]

During his first years at St John's it seems clear that Hasted saw a great deal of Lethieullier. The older man, although twice married, had no children, and it may be that each man provided what the other lacked: the one, a father; the other, a son. Among Hasted's papers relating to St John's are to be found a few pages — possibly the only pages — of a diary kept for a few months by John Lethieullier. Quite why Hasted preserved these it is impossible to know: they relate only to trivial, day-to-day business connected with the Lethieullier lands and garden, with a single mention of himself — significantly, refusing to have anything to with with a former colleague of Edmund Browne, William Comber Kirkby. Perhaps they were kept simply because the brief entries reminded him of the voice of a

The Lethieullier Chapter

friend, a memento of a warm and happy relationship which ended abruptly with John Lethieullier's death in 1760.[156]

Nevertheless, the triviality of the entries which Lethieullier made between 9 March and 16 July 1756 has its own interest, for it shows the background to the urbanity of the eighteenth-century, the closeness to the soil of those same eighteenth-century gentlemen who at other times, bewigged and velveted, might be seen riding about London in their carriages. Lethieullier's diary shows briefly the effort required to urge on the digging of a pond or the levelling of a walk, while keeping an eye on one's barley, the sale of one's hops, and the timber to be allowed for repairs to a farm. At the same time there are difficulties with the men: surly or ill, it is the manual labour of which they are capable which slowly but surely carries the work forward. This is a far cry from the paintings of Gainsborough and Reynolds and the engravings of those elegant houses (now the mainstay of the National Trust) where ladies saunter in the park and gentlemen fish or ride.

When these pages were being written Hasted was ostensibly in Canterbury, but the enigmatic mention of him in Lethieullier's diary probably shows that he was in Sutton for at least part of this time. This was also the period of the grand rebuilding of St John's, and it is more than likely that Hasted rode over frequently from Canterbury to see how the work was progressing, particularly as he seems to have been his own architect: there would have been structural problems to discuss, the delivery of loads of bricks to supervise, and perhaps also labour difficulties to resolve. The garden, too, must have required laying out: one cannot think that Hasted, whose father had spent so lavishly on his own garden, would want to shame his parent's memory in this respect. The lease of St John's had also brought Hasted demesne lands to farm, and all in all it seems reasonable to see Hasted, throughout his occupancy of the Commandery, as a man who, like John Lethieullier, frequently had mud on his shoes.

* Diary of John Lethieullier Esqr of Sutton Place from March to June 1756[157]

March 9th   Bookham & Dunmoll ye carpenter have measured the timber for Northall's repairs allow'd him vizt 6 pollards, in the whole 57

---

* The Diary has largely been transcribed as it was written, with gaps, misspellings and absent-minded omissions as they occur. The letter y frequently represents th(e), as in yn = than, then, and yt = that.

foot, or 1 load 7 feet Order'd it to be brought down to my pit, to be work'd there. Order'd to come to morrow the 10th Dunmoll & servt to take up the pales yt part within the walls as far ye fountain garden corner, & lay it in to ye feild, & to remove that fence to ye back yard from Mrs Harris's gate slanting to the warren or hopgarden gate, & enclose yt part with ye hearth into the garden. The pollards were cut from Stevens' land as they were upon decay, & those on Northall's better, to be consider'd of.

10th   Dunmoll's men here taking up the pails

11   Dunmoll's men here putting up the posts by ye barn for the fence, rain, went home at four. Harry & mate carrying coal ashes etc to the dunghill. ½ a day

12   Dunmoll's at the posts & paling Do

13th   Dunmoll's men Do — & Bookham & Dunmoll about the pollards & in Stevens' & Northall's ground.

15th   Wm & gardener digging up the tory ground by the ponds & taking up ye turf by the river.

16   Dunmoll's men at the lime trees going down Darn Lane. Hired a stranger to dig by the ponds at 5pce pr rod. Levelling ye walk by the riverside; by ten a clock they had cut down 10 trees, & finish'd all by 4. 6 drawn into the yard. The digger reach'd 3 quarters of ye wall by ye mill. Order'd Harry to borrow Phocion's swing plow & to plow round the Great Pond to morrow; raked & levell'd the ground by ye gold fish pond, set the plants juniper etc.

17th   The boy gone to fetch Phocion's plow, Harry at the turnips picking them up. The man digging, gardiner gone to Dr Saunders for plants, Batt at the melon ridge, Harry drew in some of the limes.

18th   Harry & mate at ye limes. Digger at the ponds, gardiner levelling & laying down the turf in the walk, William helping, Johnson cleaning barley. 11 limes more to bring in, the whole 43.

19th   All beat off from work by the rain, so set to washing bottles. Johnson cleaning barley.

20th   Harry & mate drawing in the trees & then Harry to market, gardiner & Bat at the trees, man digging.

22d   Man & Wm digging at the ponds. Harry & mate gone to bring the timber home from Howman's Grove. Gardiner levelling.

The Lethieullier Chapter

23d   Harry & mate to bring home timber from Howman's Grove, Wm & ye digger at the ponds. Gardiner levelling ye walk. Draw'd the timber 9 peices home.

24th   Harry & mate at home removing wood, gardiner digging, the man at the ponds. Rain & snow.

25   Harry [&] mate at the trees. Man digging, gardiner levelling, rainy day & wind, put off.

26   Harry & mate to wood for bushes to bring home for the fences, digger at the ponds, gardiner digging & levelling. A letter from Lancaster & Filby Hop Factors in Southwark informing us our hops were sold vili pretio scilicet. — I apprehend 'tis only the fine bagging sold — ye course one No 10. £284 I apprehend is unsold from the letter sent.

27th   Digger here delay'd a little his wife ill of an ague, Harry & mate about home, gardiner levelling, Harry bought   quarters of oats at   but Nethercotte will quit him of ye remainder to come. Mr Stevens came in the evening to tell us he had bought some, & if we did not like them, he would have them; then Wm went & forbad Mr Nethercotte's; 2 persons have offer'd mony for ye limes, 7d per foot for what runs clear. To coal ye rest.

28th   Sunday, A letter from Mr Wilson copy'd & sent it to Sr C.G.

29th   Digger here, gardiner and boy levelling, Harry abt home. Oates quarter came in from Phocion's Sheerhall at   .

30th   Digger, William, gardiner laying the turf finish'd it, Harry & mate removed the coal ashes; Johnson new clean'd the barley, measur'd it 10 quarter good. 3 sacks tale sold to Mr Tasker brewer at Dartford at 15s.& 6.

31st   The team went with the barley to Tasker's, Harry to wood. A butcher sent by Waller's kinsman from Downe came to look on Waller's shop to take it; sent Wm with him to see it.

April 1st Harry to wood, gardiner, Joe mowing in ye court, digger at the ponds; Mrs Lethieullier & I went up to wood; made some observations; Harry with us. Dalton cut down some trees in the hedge as his, order'd to remove ym into the wood, some were carry'd in while I was there — 3 in all — his houses still empty.

2d   Harry & mate levelling & spreading the mold in the walk down to the ponds, the digger here finish'd round the Great Pond. Gardiner planted Indian corn; in the afternoon roll'd within ye walls agn. Wm with

85

Bookham to Forty Acres against London road to take notice how they dig down the bank for land.

April 3d Harry about home levelling, digger here. Mrs L. & I went to Dartford, dined at Brother Scrimpsour, came home late. Souldier stood in the pillory yre for abusing a girl, an attempt of rape; very quiet — thought an odd story — Feilder accepted ye draught on hop factors.

4th   Sunday

5th   The digger, Harry & mate to wood, gardiner in the garden, Stephens brought ye mony from Tasker for the barley being 10 quarter 7.5 — at 15.6. & pd him for 2 quarter of oats at 12s. — (l.4) & 5 quarter at 13s. £3.5.

6th   The digger & Wm at the ponds, Harry and mate & gardiner at the hops dressing them, at 12 ye digger went to them.

7th   All hands at the hops, Wm finish'd. Planted some wheat my self can't hold stooping long; Harry finish'd the hops, & round the pond was finish'd by Willm. Bookham hedging.

8th   Bookham hedging; digger, Wm, sowing India wheat, rain put off; yn picking it, Harry & mate to wood.

9th   Digger here.

10   Digger here, Harry to Sr Wm Calvert's to leave the Barking sow there.

11   Sunday

12th   Harry to wood & Sr Wm Calvert's for ye sow, digger here, the gardner mowing etc. Fry's post boy kill'd by two officers going up Shooters Hill.

13th   Harry to wood; digger, a letter from Sir C.G. will be here Easter Monday. Digger finish'd. Measured his work.

14th   Digger finish'd, gardiner in ye garden, ye fountain, turn'g gravel etc. Pd the digger in ye whole £2.2.

15th   Harry & mate at plow, finish'd one peice now before the house for lucern; gardner in ye fountain garden cleaning it up, etc.

16   Good Friday.

17th   Wood cart, Harry at Dartford collecting small debts, no success, mony short.

18th   Easter Day.

The Lethieullier Chapter

19th Two men lopping trees in Waller's feild bringing ye wood home to make it up in ware for sale, & pimps.

20th Ploughing within the walls, carpenters taking up Brown's path, cross'd the garden from the fountain garden wall, & then sowing it.

21st Ploughing & sowing within the walls, the carpenters sawing the lime trees sawing the butts of.

22d Sr Crisp examin'g, ye feild over ye way a 2d ploughing, very foul, a fishing, no great success, floods out, Dorman sulky. New tenants here to talk with Sr Crisp, carpenters at the, & woodman & son at the trees and prim hedge.

23d Carpenter at the limes. Harry sowing within the walls, & rolling wt he can, got the harrow by the ponds but can't get the roll in, nor any hay seed to sow it, pick'd up some from the loft & sow'd it, & yn measured some of the limes, girt   length   . In the afternoon Sr Crisp went on horse back to Eryth will return soon. Willmington Fair, all off.

24th Harry plough in the butcher's feild, & William to market to enter the chair.

25 Sunday. My spare man Joe ran away, & Swift's man.

26th Monday, at home, rain, no work, confusion, a little mowing, too wet.

27 Teusday William with Harry to the wood etc.

28 Gardiner nailing up the wines, & in the garden.

29 Wednesday Harry & gardiner to plough, Waller's feild, etc. Wm for chickens. Got 6, a shilling each.

30th The new man came, but no letter from Mr Colebrook, but a note from a neighbouring, send to Harry to plough, & order'd the gardiner home to work with Bat at ye asparagus bed. Johnson & his boy here, he cutting wood, & ye boy picking up the stones. A letter from Fowler about the lime trees, will come & view them next week.

May 1st Johnson & boy at the wood, & picking up stones, Bat & gardiner planting the asparagus beds, Harry & mate ploughing.

2d Sunday

3d Gardiner in the fountain garden, Johnson at the rubbish wood cutting it up. Harry & mate bringing the loppings home & ploughing. Sister P. came.

4th	Gardiner in the fountain garden. Johnson at the rubbish wood, Harry & mate to plow in Waller's ground. Mr Fowler here to look upon the lime trees, they are not his mind, will give 6d pr foot as they are & 7d if cut to his length for wt he takes.

5th	Tenants' Day. Johnson & boy at the rubbish wood piling it up. Harry sowing etc Waller's field. The chair to Eryth for Sr Crisp. He then went up to Durling Farm to view the repairs necessary to be done, & took the estimates both bricklayer & carpenter's with him.

6th	Marking Day. Sr Crisp to the wood.

7th	Harry & mate ploughing next to Mrs Harris's barn field, Johnson at the rubbish wood his boy at the stones & yn Harry in returning home bringing in the loppings from the feild.

8th	Biggs here again about ye stackwood — Harry & mate ploughing Waller's orchard.

9th	Sunday. Work men paid.

10	Fishing. Harry and mate to Rochester for coals return'd by two wth a chalder & 1/2 at 28d pr chalder.

11th	Strippers begun, Harry there, his mate brings home a load of bushes. Poling hops 2 men.

12th	Poling hops, 2 men; Harry & mate carry'g last load of birch.

13th	Poling hops. 2 men. Harry hedging, mate harrowing, gardiner cleaning. Ladies throwing stones into ye pond most clean'd round them. Mr Mumford borrowed a horse to Barming now even. No more of yt.

14	Harry to wood. Pimps to Garret.

15th	To wood, Harry & mate; talk'd with Mr Faunce abt the tythes, can get no direct answer. Carry'd pimps Garret.

16th	Sunday.

17th	Harry & mate to wood carry'd pimps to Biggs, Biggs made him too happy; team came home by chance, no accident thank God, his mate taken with the ague; Harry Non. Com.

18th	Harry & mate to wood, Wm & gardiners bottling 1111 of wine.

19th	Harry & mate to wood. Gardner in the garden — Wm to Dartford.

20th	Harry & mate to wood, a load to Biggs's of 1500 or 2000.

The Lethieullier Chapter

21st   Harry & mate to wood (several errors in goods fetch'd, wch must be rectifyed by those yt fetch'd them out of the wood) To London with bark.

22d   Team return'd

23   Sunday — Sent over to Barking. Harry's mate wants more wages.

24th   Monday — Ploughing over the way in the morning, yn Harry & mate to London with bark.

25th   Wm rolling ye barley round the ponds with the stone roller, looks better, and when wet will try it again.

26th   Ploughing over ye way in the morning; sent the sheep to Stevens, clean'd & mark'd ym — sent Wm to Mr Cleever, hearing he was sueing his pond for some Storiers carp — some difficulty tho' promised, got but 20 brace. Memdum: he had what turf he pleas'd — shilling Hungary water.

27th   The stack wood done, 4 stack 3/4 pd £1.1.6. Small digging ye hop ground, tyers a woman & children, bark carrying.

28   Harry & mate digging clay for ye penstock, Small digging the hops, tyers here. Wrote to the Insurance Office to renew Mrs L's policies on the houses in Foster Lane No. 14008 & 14009.

29th

30th   Sunday.

31st   Harry & mate harrowing over the, hop diggers & tyers in the garden — then with bark.

June 1   Hop tyers & diggers return'd from London.

2d   Harry & mate burning rubbish over the way. Hop diggers at night to town with bark last load return'd. Lilly cow, & one of the Barking cows to bull, Nethercote's bull.

3d   Pd Jennings & Bookham in part for hedging & ditching in Forty Acres. Tale 107 rod at 8d pr rod — right measure 111.

4th   Dunmoll's man at the ponds, Harry & mate to wood, wrote to Sr Crisp abt ye roguery in the woods etc.

5th   To wood. The pond cleaning.

7th   To wood. Saker's boy making pimps of the limes. Wm not satisfy'd not measured for a livery.

8th   Saker & boy at ye pimps at home, Harry to wood. Kirby came to view affairs Hasted won't shew him.

9th   Wm inclin'd to part. Sr Crisp came over.

10th   Sr Crisp settled Mr Barrell's account of tythes, total £ . Sr Crisp sold Dorman a load of wheat, at £10.5. pr load certain, & if it weighs well a crown more left to his option. Settled Mr Barrell's account of tythes.

11th   Pimps making at home, Harry ill, boy turning grass in the walk.

12th   Harry ill, Wm & gardiner to wood. Bavins to Mr Clarke & 1 stack of flaw'd wood to Barham.

13th   Sunday. A person here about the spokes, likes them, the price not fix'd but not so much as last year. A suckler, quere wt to do with it. Nothing grows, stock short of feet, & forward peas cut off.

14th   Harry still ill. Woodmen here at ye pimps, still cold & raw.

15th   Harry still ill. Can't get any body to go with the team. Sent William to enquire hop tyers; Mun's account unsettled, Harry borrow'd mony of him in my absence. Woodmen at the pimps here.

16th   Beat off. No body to go to wood, Harry ill; after some words the gardiner went; carry'd bavins.

17th   Harry still ill, gardiner & Wm to wood; the man at the pimps, Bookham mowing within ye walls, ye Boy in the garden.

18th   Harry still ill. Gardiner & Wm to wood, the man at the pimps, Bookham mowing wthin ye walls. The crop better yn expected. He finished one side in 2 days.

19th   Wm to wood, woodmen at ye pimps at home, Bookham mowing. Warning etc. Dunmoll's girl at ye hay. He & Bookham measuring Northall's timber, a load.

20th   Sunday — Wm to Barking.

21st   Bookham mowing, woodmen here, a new man to wood, wth Will ye gardiner. The new man a days man.

22d   Wm to the wood, gardiner & boy haying, Harry walks about. Woodmen here, two women haying.

23d   Bookham mowing, woodmen at the pimps.

24th   To Wm & man, Bookham haymaking, & all hands wth Harry.

25   Ploughing over the way, woodmen, & haying.

26   Woodmen, haying, & plowing over the way.

The Lethieullier Chapter

27   Sunday.

28   To wood a small load home yn Mrs L. & I to town.

Business or pleasure in town for the squire and his lady lasted only a couple of days: they were back by the 1st July, when Lethieullier resumed his diary for another two weeks, breaking off abruptly on the 16th.

John Lethieullier died in 1760, and was probably buried in the church of St John the Baptist at Sutton-at-Hone, a mere stone's throw from his house. His funeral hatchment, with its three parrots' heads, still hangs in the church, and in the churchyard stands a neat and rather elegant monument, consisting of a cubic base surmounted by an obelisk, originally railed round. It was erected to John Lethieullier's memory, although it also commemorates his first and second wives, Mary and Ann. The details on the obelisk relating to Lethieullier's life have been obliterated by the weather, but on the south face of the cube the following epitaph can still be read:

> This monument is erected by his afflicted widow Ann Lethieuller. The sincere friend, The accomplish'd gentleman, The universal scholar, The good Christian, An affectionate husband, Happily united in him and form'd one of the most amiable characters.

Hasted would undoubtedly have concurred in these sentiments, and indeed is very likely to have had a hand in the composition of the epitaph, particularly as it mourns above all the loss of a cultured friend and concludes with two lines of Latin, now barely legible.

By his will, 'In testimony of the great love and affection I bear unto my dear wife Ann Lethieullier', John Lethieullier had bequeathed to her:

> All those my several manors of Sutton at Hone Roughill otherwise Rowhill and Grandison otherwise Wilmington situate in the county of Kent together with all and singular the lands tenements hereditaments and appurtenances to the said several manors belonging.[158]

But by this time there was a considerable question-mark over whether there was in fact anything at all to leave to Ann Lethieullier.

Hasted, who must have had some knowledge of the transactions and lawsuits prior to 1760, contents himself with saying:

> John Lethieullier, esq, the eldest son, on his father's death, in 1733, became possessed of this manor and seat. He married twice, but had issue by neither of his wives; and dying in 1760, gave, by his will, all his estates and effects to his wife, Anne, who survived him; and she after some litigation in chancery, together with Mary Browne, who had contested her right to these manors and estates, but had compromised the same by their deed, in 1766 conveyed them to Nathaniel Webbe, esq, of Taunton in Somersetshire.[159]

Litigation over the estates occurred not only after John Lethieullier's death, but had already been taking place for several years before that. Indeed, it is quite possible that it was anxiety over his financial position which contributed to his demise at the relatively early age of 57. In 1760 the newly widowed Ann Lethieullier exhibited a bill of complaint in Chancery which continued or replaced one previously presented by her husband and not settled by the time of his death. From this it appears that as early as 1755, after the death of Edmund (or as he is sometimes referred to, Edward) Browne, John Lethieullier was accusing him of fraud. In the first place he appears to have converted to his own use £1000 which Lethieullier had settled on his wife on their marriage. This had been paid into the hands of Sir Crisp Gascoyne and Edward Browne, lent out by them on the instructions of Lethieullier, and then received back by Browne, with the interest, without the knowledge of Sir Crisp Gascoyne. In addition, continued Mrs Lethieullier's bill,

> The said Mary Browne as heir at law to the said Edward Browne did insist upon the benefit of a pretended deed or conveyance purporting to be an absolute conveyance from the said John Lethieullier to the said Edward Browne of the reversion of all the said John Lethieullier's manor of Sutton at Hone, Roughill otherwise Rowhill and Grandison otherwise Wilmington ... after his the said John Lethieullier's death.

And Mrs Lethieullier's complaint charged that this deed had been

> clandestinely and wickedly obtained by the said Edward Browne from the said John Lethieullier by fraud and imposition and without any consideration whatsoever and that the said Mary

The Lethieullier Chapter

Browne and William Comber Kirkby well know that such pretended conveyance was wickedly and fraudulently obtained by the said Edward Browne without any consideration and ought to be given up to be destroyed.[160]

How had things come to this pass? During the course of Lethieullier's suit, when hearings were still going on before his death, Thomas Harris of Barming (who reappears in the Hasted story and who had formerly rented some land from Lethieullier) made a deposition which shows how landowners' debts were passed from hand to hand, growing larger, as one might expect, each time this happened. When he inherited the Sutton-at-Hone estate Lethieullier inherited also a debt or incumbrance on it in the shape of £6000, which his father had left in trust for the purpose of dowries and fortunes for his younger children. Lethieullier had been able to pay off £2000 of this on his first marriage, and had apparently obtained the other £4000 with a mortgage on his property to his brother, Manning Lethieullier. In 1744 Lethieullier had told Harris that Manning was threatening to bring ejectments to get possession of the mortgaged premises, and accordingly Harris had advanced the sum of £4000 to Lethieullier to pay off Manning. There was of course interest to be paid on this, and at the same time Lethieullier received a straightforward loan from Harris, on bond, for £450. By 1747, in order to pay off the interest on the £4000, Lethieullier needed to borrow more money, which Harris lent him, plus an additional sum which, together with the £450 on bond, meant that a further mortgage of £1000 had to be placed on Lethieullier's property. The following year it was Harris who wanted his money back, and Manning who was prepared to make a fresh loan to his brother. In March 1748 Manning Lethieullier virtually 'bought' John's debt for the sum of £5222.9s.2d., which was what he then owed Harris in full, principal and interest. It appears to have been at this point that John Lethieullier, in some desperation, and reduced to little more than an empty money-bag being tossed back and forth between Harris and Manning, became acquainted with Edmund Browne.[161]

As far as Harris could remember, Browne had been introduced to John Lethieullier in that year 'when he was in necessitous circumstances'. There is no doubt that Lethieullier quickly entrusted Browne with the close conduct of all his private affairs. Among the letters and papers presented to Harris so that he could swear to John Lethieullier's writing and signature were two items which bore the words, 'Inclosed is my will to be opened in the presence of my wife and Mr Edward Browne of Lincoln's Inn'[162] — although this was not the will subsequently proved in

1760, which was dated 1755, a year after Edmund Browne's own death. How Browne used his 'insider' knowledge seems clear from the specific accusations which were laid at his door. Sir Crisp Gascoyne, a former Lord Mayor of London, who certainly became involved in some way with the Lethieullier estate in Kent — and possibly also with the Aldersbrook one, as he is referred to in a letter by Smart Lethieullier — seems to have cleared himself of any intent to defraud in the case of the £1000, but Browne, who appears to have been guilty on this count, also stands accused of having got the Lethieullier Sutton-at-Hone estate into his own hands for nothing.[163]

The case dragged on for some years, as Chancery cases had a habit of doing, and it would appear to have been exhaustion, perhaps both physical and financial, which finally compelled the two litigants in 1766 to sign a deed of compromise and together sell what remained of the estate before legal costs devoured it completely.

Neither Edward/Edmund Browne nor his heir was able to reap any reward from the attentions which the attorney had begun to bestow on the Hasted fortune, but it could well have been Browne who fed the young man's imagination with encouragements to live in the grand manner once the gavelkind settlement had been set aside and he controlled all the Hasted estates. Was it perhaps at Browne's suggestion that Hasted took the lease of what was almost a derelict property, the neighbouring manor of St John's, in 1755? Browne had died suddenly, 'of a short and violent fever', in 1754, but, 'cunning and ensnaring', would certainly have had plans snaking out into the future. If Hasted, like Lethieullier, became enmired in debt, the attorney, in coming to his assistance, would have been able in due course to acquire both estates, magnificently reuniting the two formerly undivided manors. There is no evidence from Hasted's later life that he was naturally spendthrift or even careless with money, and the outlay on St John's, which was held only on lease, and on a certain style of living to accompany it, seem to have been the sole extravagances of a long life.

Writing about his time at St John's fifty years later Hasted took all the blame for his expenditure there on himself. It was in character for him to do so: the unfinished *Anecdotes* are an anguished 'mea culpa' from beginning to end. But the heir to the Hasted patrimony was as impressionable as young men are apt to be. Edmund Browne did not die before he had mapped out for Hasted a path the dangers of which were not to be apparent for some years. The flight to Canterbury, in 1768, was an attempt to staunch the flow of blood which had been begun by a skilful cut administered many years earlier.

The Lethieullier Chapter

While it is possible that it was the Hasted family's friendship with the Lethieulliers which brought them into contact with Edmund Browne, there seem to be stronger grounds for asserting that the Lethieullier interlude may also have had a formative influence on the historian's career. For it is highly probable that it was through his intimacy with the Lethieulliers of Sutton-at-Hone that he entered, as a junior member, the antiquarian circle of Smart Lethieullier of Aldersbrook in Essex.

Smart, the eldest surviving son of John Lethieullier's uncle John, had inherited Aldersbrook on his father's death in 1737, and he was soon welcoming to it many of the learned men of his day, particularly those with an interest in antiquities and in art. C.H.I.Chown, the historian of *The Lethieullier Family of Aldersbrook House*, gives the following list of those who were frequently in Smart's company: Dr Charles Lyttelton, Sir Charles Frederick, MP for Queenborough and Surveyor-General of the Ordnance, Dr Mead, Dr Ducarel, Dr Borlase, Dr John Ward of Gresham College and Francis Wise of Oxford. This list is interesting as containing the names of several men whose lives impinge on that of Hasted — albeit in the case of Sir Charles Frederick at one remove.

A scientist of some standing, as well as keenly interested in history, Sir Charles Frederick had become Comptroller of the Royal Laboratory at Woolwich in 1748, and shortly after that had been promoted to Surveyor General of the Ordnance. An accompanying post was that of Comptroller of the Fireworks, where he had Edward Wilks as his clerk,[164] and it may well have been through Frederick that Hasted was introduced to Wilks, who was subsequently to be placed in charge of the government gunpowder works at Faversham; certainly Hasted and Wilks became very close friends.

Two of the men in Chown's list, however, not only became friends, but exerted a strong influence over the direction Hasted's life was to take. In the Preface to Volume I of his folio edition the historian was to express his gratitude for the early encouragement he had received from Dr Charles Lyttelton, a particular friend of Smart Lethieullier, in Smart's time Dean of Exeter but later becoming Bishop of Carlisle, and from Dr Andrew Coltee Ducarel, Commissary of the City and Diocese of Canterbury and Keeper of the Library of Lambeth Palace. 'In all probability,' wrote Hasted,

> this History would have remained unattempted by me, had I not in my literary pursuits become known to the amiable Dr Littleton, late Lord Bishop of Carlisle, and President of the Antiquarian Society, and to Dr Ducarel, and Mr Astle.

The letters from Smart Lethieullier to Dr Lyttelton, preserved among Lyttelton's correspondence at the British Library, are clear proof of the friendship and the identity of interests which existed between the two men. Both were Fellows of the Society of Antiquaries, although Smart had resigned from the Society on the grounds that its meetings were too frivolous. In 1751, however, he was noting with pleasure Lyttelton's news that the Society was to be incorporated by charter: while feeling that ' 'tis too much for a renegado to expect to be again receiv'd into any communion', Smart was prepared once more to 'embrace the honour of being admitted a member ... should the Society be establish'd on any footing beyond that of a tavern meeting'. In the same letter he wrote: 'I am glad to hear that men of fortune and abilities are engaging in any of our provincial histories', mentioning in particular Dr Milles (who was to follow Lyttelton as Dean of Exeter) and Mr Rowe Mores as likely to put the counties of Devon and Berkshire under 'great obligations' to them.[165]

Hasted, it is true, was himself to become a Fellow of the Society of Antiquaries, where he would have met both Lyttelton and Ducarel. But given that the recommendatory testimonial, as it was called, which he presented in November 1763 when he stood for election to the Society, stated that he was already engaged in writing the history of Kent (something which was not yet common knowledge), and that Dr Ducarel was one of its eight signatories, he must already have known Ducarel and have received encouragement from him. An earlier acquaintance thus seems to be indicated, and since there are proven Lethieullier links on all sides it seems reasonable to suggest that Hasted was introduced to both men by the antiquary, Smart Lethieullier, quite possibly at Aldersbrook House. Smart Lethieullier, who died, like his Kentish cousin, in 1760, did not live to see the publication of most of the county histories for which he had so ardently hoped, although the Revd Philip Morant's *History and Antiquities of Essex*, to which Smart had contributed, came out in 1768. The projects of Milles and Rowe Mores remained no more than projects. Alone of this group of men the 'young antiquary', as someone was later to dub him,[166] was to have the stamina and the command of his subject to undertake and complete a multi-volume history of his county. Its inception may well have been due in part to the promptings and encouragement which its author received from the circle of the lively Essex savant and host, Smart Lethieullier.

Chapter 5

Hasted and the History of Sequestrations

Hasted tells us in the Preface to his *History* that he had followed 'literary pursuits' before beginning his major work. While there may of course have been one or two projects of which we know nothing, the Index to his MSS, which he prepared for the auction of his papers many years later, lists two such, one of which has come down to us, and one which has not.[167] The one of which we know only the title is 'An Attempt towards the Life of Abraham Hill Esq., FRS etc'. The other, which exists in the form of an uncompleted manuscript, was given the title of 'The History of Sequestrations'. Both projects stemmed from the same source, and it is likely that some of the material from the 'Life of Abraham Hill' saw the light of day in the Preface to a small volume of letters which Hasted was to bring out around 1767, under the title of *Familiar Letters*. There is no preface to tell us how the 'History of Sequestrations' came to be written, but a reference in the Preface of *Familiar Letters* to the 'curious manuscripts, which some years ago fell into the hands of the editor' is perhaps clue enough.

When Hasted took the lease of St John's, in 1755, the massive furniture of the time was more likely to remain with a house than to be removed from it, over roads as yet, for the most part, unimproved by the turnpike trusts. It is quite possible that Hasted's new property contained beds, tables, chairs — perhaps those very black leather-covered chairs which John Lethieullier's brother-in-law, Thomas Scrimsour, gave him a recipe for polishing — presses and chests. The house itself, uninhabited for many years, must have been full of cobwebs and mouse-droppings, and Ann, if she was present on this first visit of inspection, would have held her skirts round her in disgust. But Hasted, excited at the prospect of turning it into a gentleman's 'seat', explored every corner, looking into all the rooms, making a quick inventory of what each contained, picturing to himself how they might be improved. We can imagine him tugging open the doors of some of the old carved presses and lifting the heavy lids of several ancient chests — who knows, there may well have been dresses and suits laid away there which had belonged to the previous owners: he a treasurer of the Royal Society in the time of Pepys and Newton, she the number of whose years, when she died, 'had taken very little from the comeliness of her person, less from the vivacity of her parts'[168] — until he came upon a large chest with several locks. Later that day he would bring one of his men to force it open. And when, towards evening, the last lock gave way and the lid could be raised, we can perhaps see the eager young squire, a raised candelabra in his hand, gazing down on a mass of parchments, bundles of folded papers, and vellum-covered ledgers. At that moment, without knowing it, Hasted was looking at the genesis of his future self as the historian of Kent.

He must have realised fairly soon that he had come into possession of the muniments of the former occupants of St John's, the Hills — at least, the London-based branch of the family. As he turned the documents over, trying to decipher the unfamiliar hands, he found that many of them pre-dated the Hills' time at the Commandery. One of the books contained the merchant's accounts of Richard Hill, who had dealt, among others, with Thomas Hollis, an earlier owner of the house, and who had traded for large sums of money in Bengal silks, Colchester and Bocking 'bays', Alicante wine, and Barbados 'shuger'. Noted down, too, were Hill's overseas investments, here termed 'adventures': 'Adventure in the orange trees £958.2s.6d.', and 'Adventure in the united joint stock of the E. India Compe'. 'Household implements', perhaps intended for his own use, accounted for smaller sums, such as ten baskets of Genoa soap, a bay nag, three pictures, and 'a bilyard table'.[169] But the accounts covered only the years 1654 to 1659 — at which point, as Hasted was to discover later, they were cut short by Richard Hill's death. For Richard Hill had been rather more than just a wealthy merchant.

The major part of Hasted's find did not consist of the usual type of family papers — terriers, leases and indentures. Other than some letters addressed to Abraham Hill there seem to have been relatively few personal papers among them. Initially, given the proliferation of accounts and ledgers, the chest must have appeared to Hasted to contain only the business books and ephemera of a London merchant — until he managed to make out the superscription on some of what were often no more than folded scraps of paper: 'To the Right Honourable Treasurers for Sequestrations sitting at Guildhall, London'. The papers of Richard Hill, which he had found in his own house, were the papers of an important committeeman of the time of the Civil War and the Commonwealth. It was these papers which would form the nucleus of Hasted's own collection of manuscripts and notes, those manuscripts and notes on which his life's work was to be based.[170]

In the Preface to *Familiar Letters* Hasted gives a brief outline of the life of Richard Hill:

> Mr Richard Hill was designed by his father to be bred a merchant, and accordingly he afterwards became one of the most eminent in that profession. He was chosen an alderman of the city of London, and was appointed by the parliament their chief and public

1. *Katherine Walker, mother of Katherine Yardley, and the historian's great-grandmother.*

*2. Joseph Hasted, the historian's grandfather
(the year of his death wrongly given as 1732).*

3. Katherine Yardley, wife to Joseph Hasted
(wrongly called John) and grandmother of the historian.

4. Edward Hasted, aged about eight, only son of Joseph and Katherine, and father of the historian.

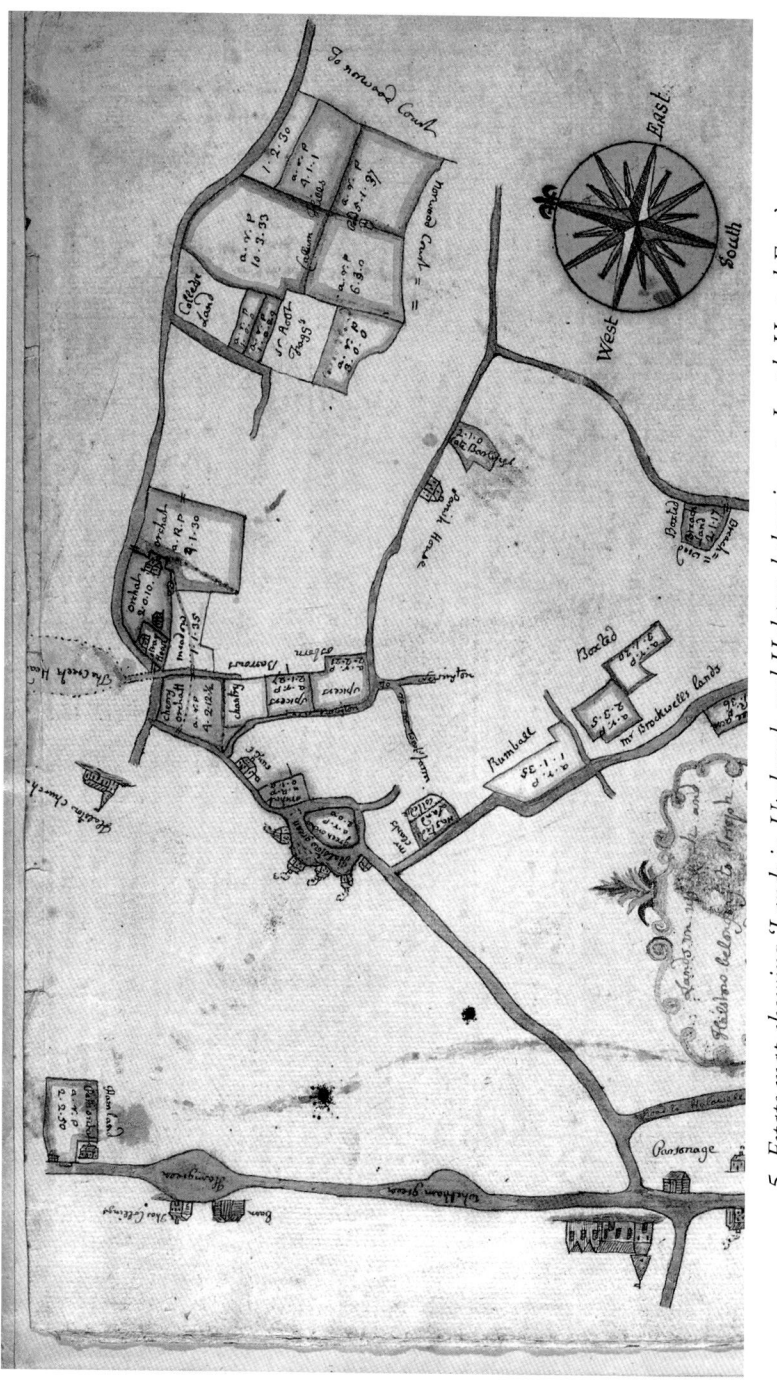

5. Estate map showing 'Lands in Upchurch and Halstow belonging to Joseph Hasted Esqr'.

*6. A Hasted hatchment, almost certainly painted for the
funeral of Joseph Hasted in 1733.*

7. *The historian's wife, Ann Dorman.*

8. *Ann Hasted's sister, Mary Dorman.*

treasurer, and he was accordingly employed by them as such, from the summer of the year 1642, the time the parliament began their war against king Charles the First, until the year 1649; and during that time, and afterwards, he was much courted and employed by the chief managers of the state, and in particular by the protector Cromwell himself, as appears by their many letters to him, now in the hands of the editor.[171]

We know in addition of Richard Hill, born at the beginning of the reign of James I, and clearly a man of many parts, that he came from an old-established West Country family and that he sat in the Long Parliament as a member for Truro, a Parliamentary descendant of that Richard Hill, a merchant taylor, who was one of the four Aldermen of London elected to Parliament in 1559.[172] The interests of the seventeenth-century Richard Hill were also mainly in London. He was a merchant of Lime Street, and, as a member of the Cordwainers Livery Company, was elected an alderman of the City of London for Candlewick Ward in 1654. In 1652 he became joint commissioner for the sale of prize goods and ships taken in the Dutch War — Hasted's papers contain his original commission. He also, on occasion, acted as a contractor to the government. The Hill papers show that Parliament was indebted to Hill and William Pennoyer, during the 1640s, for 'pistolls, carabines, musketts and corsletts', and 'armes at Dublin', and also include the articles of an agreement drawn up between the Committee of Parliament for the Navy and Richard Hill and Richard Henman, 'part owners of the ship called the Morning Starr of London, whereof Mathew Henman is Master'.[173]

Richard Hill's star was clearly in the ascendant in the 1640s and 50s, when his wealth and industry on behalf of Parliament obtained for him a position very close to the centre of things. Around 1658 he had the pleasure of seeing his son, Abraham, marry Anne, one of the numerous daughters of Sir Bulstrode Whitelocke, the Parliamentary lawyer and friend of Oliver Cromwell. Abraham was to be the purchaser of St John's Jerusalem at Sutton-at-Hone in 1660, and of his two children it was to be Frances, the elder, who, outliving her brother Richard, was to be the last inhabitant of St John's before the Hasteds moved in. Hill's success brought him under scrutiny, however, and in 1659 accusations of dishonesty were 'exhibited', as the phrase was, by one Robert Turner against the Commissioners for the Sale of Prize Goods, although there is no note here of the outcome of this.[174] It was perhaps a politic moment to leave the stage: Richard Hill died early in 1660, to be followed by his wife some six weeks later. In his account of the family who owned St John's for one hundred and twenty years, Hasted describes the obsequies of Richard Hill at St Dionis Backchurch in London as having been carried out 'with much pomp' — and he was, not surprisingly, one of the very few parishioners to be designated esquire in the register at this time.[175]

Richard Hill's papers had clearly come down to his learned and illustrious son Abraham, who had added to them letters from his own, more personal correspondence. But it was the documents relating to the time of the Civil War, or the Grand Rebellion, as it was then often called, which held the greatest fascination for Hasted. For what he had found, on that memorable day in 1755, were enough official papers relating to the Committee for Sequestrations, an organisation which functioned briefly in the 1640s, for him to contemplate writing a history of the subject.

Sequestration, or the confiscation of estates, was one of the many devices used by Parliament in the 1640s to raise money with which to prosecute its struggle against the King. Anyone who supported the King, either directly, by sending him money or arms, or indirectly, by helping others who did this, was termed by Parliament a delinquent, whose property, both real and personal, was then taken over for the benefit of the state. Owners of large estates were deprived both of their land and of the rents due from their tenants. Goods were inventoried, for the purpose of being sold. Hasted's Hill papers contain lists, both of tenants in arrears, and of the 'treasures' — particularly plate, gold rings, and money, although sometimes no more than plain household items — belonging to those unfortunate enough to suffer sequestration. Possessions with a hint of popery about them, such as religious pictures or books, were more likely to be burnt than sold.

But sequestration was a cumbersome system to administer. The management of the estates thus taken over ate into the funds which it had been intended to release, and an Act of early 1650 abruptly terminated, as from December 1649, the Sequestration Committees in each of the counties where they had been set up, ordering that sequestered delinquents should now compound, or pay a fine, for their estates, and have them restored.[176] The papers found by Hasted, therefore, which date from between 1643 and 1649, quite accurately mirrored the period over which sequestration was in force.

It is unlikely that Hasted's decision to write a 'History of Sequestrations' was taken immediately. Amazed at his find he probably began by opening papers at random, but he must soon have realised that their contents had been preserved in good order, and that many of the bundles represented the various counties which had contributed to the Guildhall treasurers' funds. In order to make it easier to read and study them he decided to put all the documents in a book, carefully pasting them up under the names of the counties in alphabetical order. In the event there were so many items that two large folio volumes were needed for them, Bedfordshire to Lancashire filling the first, and the remainder, Leicestershire to Yorkshire, being placed in the second. In all, Hasted found that he had documents relating to thirty counties, which were in fact those in which the Parliamentarians had been strongest, and where sequestration committees had been set up.[177]

Not unnaturally, there was an uneven spread of material over these thirty counties, with only a few items for Hampshire (then known as Southamptonshire) and Rutland, and not very much for Lancashire and Leicestershire. Essex, on the other hand, staunchly Parliamentarian, had sent in a beautifully penned book containing details of all its delinquents, who were listed under their parishes, arranged by Hundreds. And all these accounts, inventories of goods, lists of tenants in arrears, letters and miscellaneous papers had but a single end in view: to find and send up to the Guildhall sums of money, however small, which might help Parliament in its armed struggle with the King. The section on Middlesex opened with a resounding example of casuistry, dated 11 June 1644:

> Att the Committee for Sequestrations of Papists' and Delinquents' Estates within the County of Middlesex.
>
> Forasmuch as Informacon hath been given to this Committee that Mr Crane a delinquent hath due to him and in the hands of the Committee for the Navy three thousand pounds which being liable to sequestracon Mr Alexander and Mr Squire Bences Commissioners for the Navy (and members of the Common house in Parliament) being this day present att this Committee (and being requested to make knowne the true state of the said business) acknowledged that there is due for the said Mr Crane the said somme of £3000, but that the many charges of the Navy disable them from paying the same out, Itt is therefore ordered that the said moneys still remayne in the hands of the officers of the Navy, since therein the same publique end is promoted.[178]

Included among Richard Hill's Guildhall papers was a large ledger, labelled 'Account delivered in by Samuell Averie, William Hobson, Thomas Barnardiston and Richard Hill, Treasurers appointed by ordinance of Parliament dated the 19th August 1643 for all Sequestracons Monies by them receaved and paid to the 13th March 1643 as they were required'. The book does, however, contain accounts, although these are incomplete, for all years up to 1649.[179] The entries made in it show the money received from the various Parliamentarian counties via their

Solicitor-General and his collectors, or the (more humble) receivers. The sums coming up from Kent, usually paid in by Thomas Dyke, who was the county's Solicitor-General at this time, ranged between £11 and £450, and beside each sum was a note of the collector from whom Dyke had received it — William Woolfe, Thomas Bradley, Ralph Watts, Thomas Burges, or Edward Boys. Canterbury had its own collector in the person of John Cogan, assisted by William Reeve and Walter Dobson. And the amounts received were cross-referenced under the names of the counties, so that one can see that the total sent up from Kent for the incomplete year of 1643 was £4136.18s.7d., and for 1644, £15,638.4s.3d.

The 'Account' also shows payments made from the sequestration funds, particularly high ones between 1643 and 1646 going to 'His Excelency Robert Earle of Essex' (£30,000) and the Earl of Manchester (£13,768.2s.9d.), both of them leaders of Parliamentary forces in the early years. There are a few, but only a few, entries which seem to be of the fifth of an estate allowed (after supplication) to the wife of a delinquent: Mary Coltman got £60, and Mary Chichester £150, the latter sum including £26.11s.10d. against 'Tres at Cambden House' — presumably a fifth of some inventoried goods ('treasures') which had been removed to Camden House and there sold. Payments are also noted to the Assembly of Divines, which received £100 on two separate occasions, as well as to various lesser figures, including a certain 'Collonell Croomwell' who was in the process of making his mark and who, by order of Parliament, received three payments, totalling £1453.11s.6d., between 1643 and 1646.[180]

In addition the Hill muniment contained a series of ordinances and orders, or instructions, numbering well over a hundred items, which had been sent to the Treasurers at the Guildhall. And finally there were numerous miscellaneous letters and notes dealing with those termed delinquents, with the discovery or sending in of 'treasures', and with the forwarding to the Treasurers of sums of money of varying amounts.

There is no doubt that much time and thought was required on Hasted's part to decipher and understand the documents he had found relating to the time of the Civil War in England which led up to the execution of Charles I in 1649. It is very likely that he turned for clarification, in the first place, to the Earl of Clarendon's account of the period in his massive *True Historical Narrative of the Rebellion and the Civil Wars in England*, which had not seen the light of day until the eighteenth century, when it had appeared in three volumes between 1702 and 1704. And *The Life of Clarendon by Himself*, which appeared only in 1759, must have provided further stimulating background reading for someone about to embark on a 'History of Sequestrations'. There were also the many pamphlets which had been fired from all quarters over the whole of the disturbed period, and it seems quite reasonable to suppose that Hasted read a number of these, finding some, perhaps, among the papers he had himself unexpectedly acquired, and others in the libraries or presses of his many friends. It seems clear that he could not have made sense of the Hill papers without considerable study, and in his Introduction he does indeed refer to 'some authors', a rather sweeping manner of giving references, which he would later learn to detail for the benefit and reassurance of his readers. Among those 'authors', however, was no historian of the sequestration aspect of the troubled decade, and it was this that Hasted, with so much material at his disposal, now proposed to become.

His 'History of Sequestrations' was to be written in two parts. The first would contain both ordinances and orders which had been sent to the Sequestration Treasurers from Parliament — the ordinances being the virtual Acts of Parliament at this time, while the orders were more specific instructions, as for example, orders to pay money to Lord Fairfax for his troops, or to the Assembly of Divines for their expenses.[181] The second part was to be a detailed transcription of many of the documents relating to the counties, arranged alphabetically, with occasional comments interspersed by Hasted. The title was long and explanatory:

> The original Papers, Letters and Accounts of the Committees of Sequestration in the several Counties of England during the grand Rebellion and of the moneys received from them by the Public Treasurers at Guildhall in London. In which is contained not only the names, but a particular of the estates real and personal of the several delinquents and papists att that time seized by the Parliament of England. With the several ordinances of Parliament anyways relating to the same and many other particulars from the year 1642 to 1648 inclusive.

And the work was given a general Introduction, which begins with a splendid orotundity:

> Corruption and superstition, the fruits of a long peace, and increased by the discontinuance of Parliaments, had over run the Kingdom, when his Majesty King Charles the first was necessitated to call that Parliament, in which such contests arose between his prerogative and the laws and liberties of the people, as kindled the unhappy civil war, which at last cost the one his life

and crown and the others those very laws and liberties they contended for.

The Introduction then outlines the organisation of the various committees which were to contribute so largely to the Parliamentarians' success:

> Money being the sinews of war it is no wonder the Parliament should do their utmost to raise all they could, and according to some authors during the civil war they raised forty millions of money on the people, they imposed from time to time numerous taxes by several Ordinances of Parliament for the collecting and managing of which they appointed several committees, at the head of these was a committee in the House of Commons, who were to peruse all money grants passed by the House and to allow them before they could be paid at the proper offices, and under this Committee the following and in short the whole branch of their revenue were subject. Those called the Money Committees, were next, who sat at Goldsmiths', Haberdashers' and Guildhall. These had the immediate management of the Country Committees from whom all accounts and proceedings were ordered to be regularly sent up and from hence to the Committee of the House to be finally examined.

And the Introduction concludes:

> The transactions of these men are the subject of the following sheets and are transcribed from their own papers, wherein it will be seen how much they abused their trust, how difficult it was to bring them to account, how often they were changed; what immense estates most if not all of them acquired by this plunder and the whole of their iniquitous proceedings will be laid open.[182]

Hasted's Introduction was to be followed by Part I, consisting 'for the reader's benefit' of 'ordinances of Parliament, relating chiefly to the sequestrations, and the money ordered by the Parliament to be paid out of that branch of the revenue'. These were chosen by Hasted out of the instructions which had been received by the Treasurers at the Guildhall, Samuell Averie, William Hobson, Thomas Barnardiston and Richard Hill. A few of these were in the form of printed ordinances; many were no more than letters containing orders for payments to be made from the sequestration revenue, or were simply instructions detailing the action to be taken with regard to various 'delinquents'. The original collection numbered well over a hundred items: of these Hasted used some ninety-eight.[183] A great deal of work must have gone into his transcriptions: the simplified italic writing of the eighteenth century was far removed from the version of secretary hand which persisted into the late seventeenth century, and Hasted must frequently have puzzled over a word.

The young historian could not resist ending Part I with a successful petition from William Hill — undoubtedly a relative of Richard's (and there seem to have been several of them active on the Parliamentary side) — for payment of a bill for stores, which was ordered to be repaid in the form of permission to purchase land taken from the church:

> The humble petition of William Hill of London, merchant, was read, setting forth, that there is a debt of £602 due unto the said William Hill, for stores delivered in at Dublin. Ordered that the said sum of £602 be admitted as due unto the said William Hill upon the Publick faith.

And as a result of his petition Hill was permitted to become a privileged purchaser of sequestrated Dean and Chapter lands:

> Ordered that the said William Hill and his assignees be admitted to come in as purchasers of Dean and Chapters lands by way of doubling of the said sum of £602, and that he have the like benefit as others who come in by way of doubling, by the Act for Abolishing Deans and Chapters, have, or may have.[184]

With Part I completed, Hasted set to work on Part II, dealing with the counties in alphabetical order, and transcribing for this purpose many of the documents which had so surprisingly come into his possession. Whenever possible he opened the section on a county with a few items of correspondence. Thus Bedfordshire, the first county dealt with, begins with two letters, the first a business-like covering letter of September 1648 for some schedules of estates, real and personal, of all delinquents and known papists in the county, and the second a brief note without date or address, informing the Treasurers at Guildhall that in the writer's town the only persons sequestered were 'a barber, and little could be had from him, and two little prebends — yeilding thirteen pounds and six shillings a year'.

A SCHOLAR AND A GENTLEMAN

The details relating to Bedfordshire cover both sides of nearly forty folio sheets in Hasted's manuscript. Then come Buckinghamshire, Cambridgeshire, Cheshire, Cornwall, Devonshire, Essex, Gloucestershire, Herefordshire, Hertfordshire and Huntingdonshire, each with an average of some ten folio sheets.

Hasted's account of the sequestrations in Kent opens with a letter of May 1643 announcing that several hundred loads of faggots belonging to the Earl of Thanet have been seized at a wharf in Upchurch, 'to the use of the King and Parliament' — a phrase frequently made use of by the Parliamentarians. Next comes a statement of the appointment in June 1643 of Thomas Dyke as Solicitor of Sequestrations for Kent, and of Mr Peter Greenstreet, of Ospringe, as High Collector of the Hundreds of Milton, Teynham, Faversham and Boughton, followed by a loose transcription of a letter of the same year sent by Dyke 'to his honored friends Mr Hobson, Mr Averie, Mr Barnardiston & Mr Hill Treasurers for Sequestration Money at Guildhall London', informing them that,

> You shall receive from Mr Peter Greenstreet the sum of four hundred and seven pounds four shillings and six pence which is of subsidy money as you may perceive by the copy of the order of the House of Commons under my hand and likewise you shall receive from Mr Francis Romney one of the Collectors for Sequestrations the sum of two hundred pounds — I have sent you several sums and have appointed several persons to pay you in sundry parcels of money which I hope is and will be performed accordingly. I have used all my industry to supply our present occasion for Sir Wm Waller: and we have not only provided money, but now have drawn almost 4000 men up to the confines of Surrey to oppose Hopton's forces; and this for [the] present is all you shall receive from, Your affectionate friend and servant, Tho. Dyke.[185]

Thomas Dyke's hand is admittedly a difficult one to read, and Hasted was not yet the expert palaeographer he was to become. Like many of the letters relating to counties previously dealt with, that of Thomas Dyke is given in a very abbreviated form.

The Kentish Solicitor-General's letter is followed by a lengthy account of the annual rents of the archbishopric, now under sequestration and payable to the state, and of various other properties in the city which had been similarly taken over, including St Augustine's Palace, as the former abbey was now known, which had been in the hands of a papist family. But it is at this point that Hasted's manuscript suddenly breaks off:

the section on Kent was not completed, the other counties on which he had material, from Lancashire to Yorkshire, were never written up.

In spite of the wealth of material he possessed, Hasted never resumed work on his manuscript. Only the occasional correction of a word or phrase in his later hand shows that he ever looked at it again. In his great *History* he was to make but limited reference to the Civil War, and this mostly in footnotes, saying of Sir Roger Twysden simply that he 'suffered greatly for his loyalty during the great rebellion, and was forced at last to compound for his estate for the sum of £1300', and summarising as follows the trials of the owner of St Augustine's, Lady Margaret Wotton:

> During the time of Lady Wotton's residence at this palace, it was twice broke open and plundered; her effects in it, to the amount, by appraisement, of £330, were taken away and sold by order of the state; and one large picture ... of The Passion of Christ, valued in the appraisement at £20 was taken away by the authority of the mayor and publicly burnt; at which time the palace and the adjoining lands belonging to her were of the value of £500 per annum, out of which she was paid for her support one third part, after deducting all charges of the committee of sequestration out of it.[186]

And Hasted gives as his reference for this, 'Original papers of the sequestrators of the state'. But the sequestrators themselves remain faceless.

What happened to make Hasted abandon his 'History of Sequestrations'? It was well founded and had been carefully planned and ordered, but comes to a sudden end in the middle of the section on Kent. Hasted himself nowhere provides an explanation for this, and we have to look at the context in which it was being written for any leads which might help us to solve the mystery.

Another break in Hasted's life occurs at about the same time that work on his 'Sequestrations' was given up. For a number of years he had been an active magistrate at the petty sessions at Dartford as well as a member of the more important bench at the general quarter sessions, held, for West Kent, four times a year at Maidstone. In 1761, however, his activity on both benches suddenly ceased: he was to sit on the bench at Maidstone only once more, in 1764, and did not resume his duties at Dartford petty sessions until 1765.[187]

A general explanation could be that he simply gave up writing the 'History of Sequestrations' in order to write a history of Kent, and that his voluntary duties were relinquished at the same time so that he could concentrate on this. Such an explanation does not quite fit all the known facts, however, since Hasted still retained a number of administrative duties: he continued to act as a bridge warden, for example, and as a commissioner of sewers. And he also, in 1761, took on an additional duty, as a Deputy Lieutenant for the county. It is this last fact which can perhaps be made to reveal a more probable reason for the extraordinary switch from a 'History of Sequestrations', already more than half written, to a totally new project, the history of his county.

The likelihood is that, with so much of his 'History of Sequestrations' completed, and particularly now that some of the Kentish material had been written up, Hasted began to show his project around and possibly even to speak of looking for subscriptions, as was commonly done at the time, to help pay for its publication. News of this must have circulated among his local friends, in a small ripple which broadened, as ripples do, to come in time to the ears of some of the leading families in the county: the Honywoods, the Oxendens, the Finches, the Stapletons, the Dykes and the Hart-Dykes, the Tuftons, the Scotts, the Brooks or Brook-Bridges, as well as to various other well-to-do members of Kentish society: the Warings, the Bunces, the Boys and the Springetts among them. These were all names which were about to appear in Hasted's 'History of Sequestrations' — not, for the most part, borne by those who had suffered sequestration, but by those responsible for ordering it and implementing those orders: men who had, as it were, in the eyes of subsequent history, chosen the wrong side. For many prominent county families the deeds of their ancestors were about to be laid bare.

It cannot have been something which they were likely to welcome; indeed, the more they considered it, the less they must have liked it. Hasted, throughout his life, had a passion for the truth, and it may well be that the first mutterings of discontent which reached him only left him, as a young man sure of his facts, boldly determined to push on with his project in the face of opposition. If he was to be stopped, something more had to be done. The county consulted, and decided that, as a member of the magistracy, he should be spoken to by that august personage, the chairman of the West Kent bench, Charles Whitworth.

Whitworth was himself by way of being a historian. He had put together several works of Parliamentary reference, and he, if anyone, would be able to throw the book at this presumptuous unveiler of the past. Which is probably what he did. In particular, Whitworth would have been able to draw Hasted's attention to a certain Act known as 12 Charles 2, c.xi, or, An Act of Free and General Pardon, Indemnity and Oblivion, which Charles II had had the wisdom to pass in 1660, in order to avoid the bloodshed of recriminations and to prevent Royalists, now in the ascendant, from taking revenge for the treatment received from Roundheads over the past eighteen years. All was to be forgiven and forgotten — except with regard to royal estates and regicides — and to Sir Henry Vane in particular, who was excluded from the pardon in a special clause devoted to him alone.

Under this Act it was intended,

> That no crime whatsoever committed against his Majesty or his royal father, shall hereafter rise in judgment or be brought in question, against any of them to the least endangerment of them, either in their lives, liberties, estates, or to the prejudice of their reputations, by any reproach or term of distinction,

and also,

> That no person or persons, who by virtue of any order or warrant ... by virtue of any Act, ordinance or order of any or both houses of Parliament ... or any committee or committees acting under them ... have seized, sequestred, levied, advanced or paid to any publick use ... any goods, chattels, debts, rents, ... shall hereafter be sued, molested, or drawn into question for the same.

A penalty was payable for even so much as 'words of reproach' which might tend in any way 'to revive the memory of the late differences'. The penalty, admittedly, was only enforceable for the space of the next three years, but the Act itself was still very much in force in Hasted's time — and was not to be repealed until 1948.

What, in the face of such opposition, could Hasted do? It is true that Clarendon's *Narrative of the Rebellion* had appeared in the early years of the century, but Clarendon, who had, after all, been the grandfather of two queens, Mary and Anne, was himself dead by that time. The county of Kent was determined that Hasted's inflammatory material should not be made public, quite possibly breeding dissension once more, and the young magistrate's interview with his chairman must have left him in no doubt that he risked total ostracism throughout the county. Perhaps Hasted himself offered to resign from the bench. Perhaps Charles Whitworth suggested that it might be prudent to leave it temporarily. Certainly the upshot was that for the next three years Edward Hasted appeared neither at Maidstone quarter sessions nor at Dartford petty sessions.

Further proof of what has to be seen as Hasted's humiliation over the 'History of Sequestrations' may lie in the fact that in the same year, and virtually at the same time, that he ceased attending the sessions, he became a Deputy Lieutenant for the county.[188] For some time notices had been appearing in the press requesting the gentlemen of the county to come forward to act as Deputy Lieutenants, that is to say, to take on responsibility for the local militia, which it was thought might well be called into action in the course of the ongoing war with France. Hasted, although an excellent horseman, had ignored all these appeals — quite possibly because the original members of the County Committee of Kent, at the time of the Civil War, most of whom were also members of the County Committee for Sequestrations, had mainly been selected from among the county's Deputy Lieutenants — a fact which may have led him, with his inside knowledge of what had gone on at that time, to speak disparagingly of the position of Deputy Lieutenant. By 1761, however, the war was drawing to a close, and appeals for gentlemen to take on the duties of a Deputy Lieutenant were dying out. By coming forward — albeit at this late stage, which is exactly the moment when there is a crisis of some sort in his life — to accept a Deputy Lieutenancy, Hasted was able to show solidarity with the body of men, the gentry of the county, whom he had, on paper and in their ancestry, been about to attack. Even so, he seems to have found it necessary to keep a low profile for several years.

But that was not quite the end of the story. Disaster though it must have seemed at the time, it offered for Hasted a new beginning. As a historian himself and a man of culture, Whitworth could appreciate Hasted's grasp of his material and his skill in handling it. Why did not Mr Hasted turn his attention to another, less contentious area? Mr Whitworth had himself been contemplating updating Thomas Philipott's history of 1659, *Villare Cantianum, or Kent Surveyed and Illustrated* — perhaps Mr Hasted would consider co-operating with him on that? Mr Hasted might well dispose of more free time than Mr Whitworth — MP for Minehead, Lieutenant-Governor of Gravesend and Tilbury Fort, Vice-President of the Society for the Encouragement of Arts, Manufactures and Commerce, Major of the West Kent Militia, etc, etc,[189] — would be able to give to the project, and would be a most valuable colleague ...

There was indeed an attempt at a collaboration between Charles Whitworth and Edward Hasted on a revised version of Philipott, although it scarcely needs to be said that Whitworth, with so many other calls on his time, contributed hardly anything towards it. In 1763 he passed over to Hasted a box of items which he had collected for the purpose ('little more than rubbish', muttered Hasted to a friend at the time), and the future historian of Kent was launched on his own.

Hasted's 'History of Sequestrations' would not by any means have been a complete account of this aspect of the Great Rebellion. There was other material in existence, in particular that which is now in the Public Record Office.[190] But it would have broached a subject which, in Kent at any rate, was to remain untouched for another century, until 'Sir Roger Twysden's Journal' was edited by the Revd Lambert Larking for the yearbook of the newly-founded Kent Archaeological Society.[191] This account of the treatment suffered at the hands of the County and Sequestration Committees by a man of considerable independence of thought, whose writings show him to have been aware of the faults on both sides, serves only to confirm the denunciation which Hasted would have made of the activities he had uncovered in the papers of the Guildhall treasurers.

There can be little doubt that the Twysden Journal would have been incorporated into Hasted's 'History of Sequestrations'. The Hasted collection of papers and manuscripts was not bought in its entirety by the British Museum when it was sold by auction at the end of the century. Two of the items which were rejected, and of whose existence we know only from the Index which Hasted prepared for the sale, consisted respectively of 'A Quarto entitled Twysden 1 — being a collection of matters collected by the learned Judge Twisden wholly relating to the County of Kent' (and apparently consisting mainly of legal niceties), and 'Another Quarto entitled Twysden 2: Part 2 of the aforesaid collection, containing Kentish Petition of 1642, etc, etc.'.[192] Clearly, not every Kentish family of note would have sided with Whitworth. As the subsequent correspondence relating to the *History* shows, Hasted was always on remarkably good terms with the members of the related family, Sir Roger Twisden of Bradbourne, bt., and his son.

LONDON, Nov. 17.

YESTERDAY, about 12 at noon, a duel was fought in Hyde-park, between John Wilkes, Esq; Member for Aylesbury, and Samuel Martin, Esq; Member of Camelford, and late Secretary of the Treasury. At the first attack their pistols missed fire; at the second Mr. Martin's did so, upon which Mr. Wilkes generously retarded discharging his pistol, and offered Mr. Martin the choice of either of his pistols, which Mr. Martin refused: they then turned back to back; upon turning about again, Mr. Martin discharged his pistol, and the ball went into Mr. Wilkes's belly, about half an inch below the navel, and sunk obliquely on the right side of the belly down towards the groin. Upon which Mr. Wilkes said, Mr. Martin take care of yourself, for you have done for me. Mr. Martin replied, he would get him what assistance he could; and perceiving a chariot at a distance, ran up to it, and told the person in it that a gentleman lay wounded on the grass, and begged they would drive immediately out of the Park, and get a chair; which was done, and Mr. Wilkes was brought to his own house; and a Surgeon being immediately sent for, the ball was extracted, and the Surgeon was of opinion, that as it had not penetrated the abdomen, it would be attended with no bad consequences.

Mr. Wilkes was in great spirits during the operation, declared his antagonist had behaved himself like a Gentleman.

It is said the above affair was occasioned by ————— declaring that the Author of No. 45, ————— cowardly Traitor.

We hear that the North ————— hands of the comm————

...or repairing and widening several Roads ...ng to the Town of Dartford, in the ...ounty of Kent.

WHEREAS the Road leading *Preamble.* from the Cock and Lion Back Gate, in the Town of Dartford, in the County of Kent, into and through a certain Street called Lowfield, in the said Town of Dartford, to Sutton Place, in the Parish of Sutton Athone, in the said County; and from thence, through Sutton Street, to the Turnpike Road at the West End of E————ingham, in the said County, and from ————at the East End of Farni————
Eynsford S—————

Chapter 6

Throwley: The Preparation of the *History*, I

Before deciding to settle in Sutton-at-Hone, Hasted seems to have given some thought to establishing a family seat in the Eastling area where Joseph Hasted had originally purchased part of the demesne lands of Huntingfield manor. Joseph's son, Edward, had added considerably to this by becoming the possessor of that third part of the manor in which stood the mansion of Huntingfield Court. This had probably been reduced by time to little more than a farmhouse, although Hasted was to note, from the old flint and stone foundations which were sometimes dug up around it, that it must once have been considerably larger. That Eastling was indeed the family's most prestigious holding, and the one where it ought perhaps to have established itself, is shown by Hasted's choosing to set down under this parish, rather than under any of the others where he owned land, a brief history of his family.[193]

The Hasted property lay in the south-east corner of the parish of Eastling, bounded on the east by Throwley and on the south by Stalisfield, but it is quite possible that it may have extended into Throwley. Alternatively, Hasted may, at a time when he was pondering the feasibility of settling at Huntingfield, have purchased a property in the adjoining parish of Throwley which he kept for some years and subsequently sold. He certainly seems to have preferred Throwley to Eastling, which he describes as 'cold and forlorn', while of Throwley he says:

> It is a more pleasant and open country than that [Eastling] last described, for though wild and romantic among the hills and woods, it is not so dreary and forlorn, nor the soil so uncomfortable, being much drier. Besides it has a more chearful and brighter aspect from the width of the principal valley which leads through it, from north to south, whence the hills rise on each side, with smaller delves interspersed among them.[194]

In the early 1760s Hasted clearly had a property at Throwley, for the end of 1763 and the first half of 1764 were to see him using his house there as a refuge from the stream of visitors and other calls on his time that were constantly interrupting his work at Sutton-at-Hone.

The Throwley period brings to the fore two of Hasted's close friends, already mentioned in passing, Edward Wilks and Thomas Astle, both of whom may have been introduced to him at Smart Lethieullier's, Wilks as a protégé of Charles Frederick, his superior at the Ordnance

Office, and Astle under the wing of Dr Andrew Coltee Ducarel. Astle, three years younger than Hasted and a native of Staffordshire, has come to assume more importance than he actually had in Hasted's life, due above all to the survival of a number of Hasted's letters to him.[195] That these were preserved is probably due to Astle's collecting mania, plus a shrewd hope on his part that they might one day have some value. What the letters in fact reveal is that Astle let Hasted down on a number of occasions, while his much-vaunted assistance at the end of Hasted's life seems to have consisted of no more than the occasional five-pound note, from a very wealthy man, when the aged historian was *in extremis*.

Astle had originally been articled to an attorney, but had left home at an early age to seek his fortune in London. There he seems to have fallen on his feet very quickly by obtaining the patronage of the Rt Hon. George Grenville, chairman of the trustees of the newly founded British Museum. Astle was probably indebted to Grenville for the work he was given on the preparation of an index to the catalogue of the Harleian MSS, and he was subsequently appointed as the junior member of a small commission — the others being Dr Ducarel and Sir Joseph Ayloffe — which was responsible for superintending the public records at Westminster. Astle was to make a surprisingly lucrative career from the profession of archivist. This was probably aided more by a judicious marriage with the only daughter and heiress of the Revd Philip Morant, the Essex historian, and an uncanny knack of attracting to himself priceless manuscripts, than by the posts he acquired as joint editor of the parliamentary records, or chief clerk, and eventually Keeper, of the Record Office in the Tower. His reputation as a palaeographer resulted in the publication, in 1784, of a single work on the subject, *The Origin and Progress of Writing*, which is not particularly informative. Overall, one is left with the impression of a somewhat slippery character whose abilities did not match up to his ambitions.[196]

Edward Wilks inhabited a very different milieu. He seems to have trained initially as a surveyor, but we find him in 1749 at the Ordnance Office, where he was clerk to Charles Frederick as Comptroller of the Fireworks. Frederick's principal post, however, was that of Clerk of the Deliveries to the Board of Ordnance, and when, in 1751, he rose to become Surveyor-General of the Ordnance, second only to Sir John Ligonier, its Lieutenant-General, Wilks rose with him, becoming Clerk of the Survey at Chatham dockyards and storekeeper at the government magazine at Upnor Castle. He was promoted again in 1759 when, on their purchase by the government, he became storekeeper at the gunpowder mills at Faversham.

Throwley

The Royal Gunpowder Mills lay dispersed in the parishes of Faversham, Ospringe, Preston and Davington, and Wilks's duties on his appointment in May 1759 had included making an exact inventory of the mills and all they contained and seeing what repairs were necessary. The following month brought the Surveyor-General down to Faversham, with two other officers of the Board of Ordnance, the Principal Storekeeper and the Clerk of the Deliveries, to inspect the site. Wilks was granted an imprest of £300 to defray various expenses at the mills, including the cleaning and drying of mouldy stove cases, and a thorough overhaul of the hoy and other boats used for the transport of their dangerous product to the government magazines at Upnor, Greenwich and, a little later, Purfleet in Essex. Wilks and Mr Hall, the foreman, were also ordered to purchase 100 cords of alder or willow, to be made into charcoal — one of the three major constituents of gunpowder, along with saltpetre and sulphur. Perhaps there were old stores of charcoal at the mills which the government preferred not to use, for in August of that year Edward Wilks is to be found in the pages of the *Kentish Post*, advertising for sale several lots of charcoal, 'now lying at his Majesty's Powder Mills at Faversham'.

The following October Wilks was advertising not only 'several hundred sacks of charcoal, now lying in H.M. warehouses at the Powder Mill, Faversham', but also greenhouse plants and shrubs, which the warmth of the works may have enabled him to bring on exceptionally well. Given the gunpowder works' charcoal requirements, the storekeeper was expected to be knowledgeable about arboriculture, and Wilks seems to have had a passion for trees. At this time he had only the house and garden provided for the storekeeper at the gunpowder works, but in 1769 he was to build himself a 'seat', a substantial red-brick house, known as Belmont, on some land at Throwley. Here he enclosed a large garden which he planted with trees and shrubs. Hasted, too, loved trees, and this may have been one of the shared interests on which the friendship between the two men was based. That this continued for many years is shown by the fact that from 1770 if not before Wilks was one of Hasted's tenants, leasing from him what must have been a sizeable farm, with a rental of £113 a year.[197]

Wilks had been given what was perhaps his first taste of landownership in 1762, when, with money supplied by the Treasury of the Ordnance, he was enabled to purchase three acres of land near Faversham, to be held in trust by him for the use of the mills for ever. It was here that rose much of the water which was essential to the operation of the mills, and the purchase was meant to ensure that the Ordnance Office would command a permanent source of water.

A SCHOLAR AND A GENTLEMAN

In 1766 the Surveyor-General, by now Sir Charles Frederick, made use of Wilks by sending him to make a survey of his Lincolnshire estates at Brothertoft, Wyberton and Frampton prior to their enclosure, and the storekeeper was subsequently to become involved in the riots which ensued when enclosure actually took place three years later. It would seem to have been as a result of these extraneous duties imposed on him by Frederick that Wilks became, like his employer, deeply involved in debt, the full story of which did not come to light until the 1780s. A statement made by Wilks at that time includes the following graphic description of events in Lincolnshire when Frederick's land was enclosed:

> In 1769 by an Act for dividing Holland Fenn Sir Charles became intitled to for Brothertoft 757 acres of land which he offered to his tenants at 15s. per acre, which, with the old inclosed land would have amounted to £719 a year, but they being riotous almost to a man, and would not take it, Mr Wilks let it at the same rent to a Mrs Rinder, who, on account of the threatenings of the rioters, gave it up, and Messrs Edward and Thomas Wilks engaged at the hazard of their lives to subdue the rioters, which they did, and by dint of perseverance restored the owners of 21,000 acres of land to the peaceable possession of it, though Mr Thos Wilks was shot as he sat by his fireside and lost one eye and nearly his life, and Mr Edward Wilks let the Brothertoft estate on lease for 21 years at £930.

Wilks was to claim subsequently that he had received no remuneration from Sir Charles for his assistance over a number of years and that he had himself borne a portion of the expenses attendant on enclosure, including taxes and the cost of drainage and a new windmill. Thus, while Frederick himself had netted over £13,000 from the business, Edward Wilks and his brother had been left some £4000 out of pocket. The story was only to come out in 1783 under Thomas Pelham, who followed Sir Charles Frederick as Surveyor-General, when Wilks was found to owe a similar sum to the Board of Ordnance. This financial embarrassment did not lead to Wilks's dismissal — he was ordered to repay the money at the rate of £100 a quarter — but almost certainly contributed to his early death in 1784.[198] Frederick himself died the following year, having very narrowly avoided imprisonment for debt.

In 1763, however, both Hasted and Wilks were relatively young men, with Wilks perhaps a few years the older, the world smiled, both had prospects and projects, and neither could know the disgrace which awaited them. Hasted must already have been friendly with Edward Wilks for some time, for at the end of the summer of that year Wilks went to Sutton-at-Hone to stand sponsor at the baptism of Hasted's third son, George, where his co-sponsors were Hasted's brother-in-law Gabriel Thorne, a customs officer and already well known to Wilks, and Ann Hasted's sister, Mary Dorman.[199] Perhaps the notion of an extended stay at Throwley was born, like George, in the summer of that year, in discussion with Edward Wilks.

Nevertheless, even before this, Hasted seems to have been in the habit of spending time there. On the occasion of an earlier visit to Throwley in that same year he had become embroiled in a legal agreement for the purpose of rendering his brother-in-law a service. In this he played the part of a willing go-between, but it was, in the end, to cost him dear.

The neighbouring town of Faversham was at that time a fairly busy port, with a regular trade in corn and coal, as well as some seasonal carrying of wool and fruit and exportation of oysters, while ships came from the Baltic countries with timber, deals, tar and iron. There was accordingly a collector of customs at Faversham, who was also responsible for the customs at Milton, Whitstable and Herne. The holder of this important post was a certain Edward Beckwith, esq., who in the spring of 1763 was apparently letting it be known that he might soon think of retiring.

One day in May Hasted, who was then at Throwley, received a visit from Gabriel Thorne, who had gone on there after visiting his wife's sister Mary Dorman, now living with Thomas Harris at Barming. Harris appears to have been well-disposed towards all the Dormans, and he had expressed his willingness to 'do something' for Gabriel Thorne, who was a customs officer in London. Edward Wilks was another visitor at Mr Hasted's that morning, and it was probably he who mentioned the possibility of the post of customs officer at Faversham falling vacant. Thorne immediately asked Hasted and Wilks to call on Beckwith, presumably to check this, while he himself went posting back to Barming to lay the matter before Harris. Harris proved agreeable to pursuing the matter on Thorne's behalf, and Hasted, who like his father was happy when he could be of service, was deputed to act for Harris and treat with Beckwith for the handing over of the post. Beckwith was ready to part with it for £300, which the enormously wealthy Harris appeared willing to pay, and wrote to the Lords of the Treasury applying for permission to resign the position of collector of customs at Faversham in favour of 'my near friend and relation Gabriel Thorne'.

The wily Thomas Harris seems to have decided, when negotiations were already under way, that in the event of his obtaining the position Thorne should repay him the £300; but he was prepared to underwrite it initially, confident that his political connections would enable him to pull the necessary strings. Matters did not work out as he had expected, however, and a few days later they all read in the papers that Carless Franklin had been appointed to the Faversham collectorship. Hasted, as the intermediary, now stood bound to Beckwith for the £300 in the event of his relinquishing the post, money which Thomas Harris had promised to pay in the expectation that he would be reimbursed by a successful Thorne. But when Hasted applied to Harris for the money for Beckwith he refused to pay it, saying that 'if he could possibly find a flaw in the agreement, or a hole to creep out at, he would'. However, he eventually offered £150, if Mr Hasted would then cancel the whole £300.

Unwilling to be a loser in an affair in which he had intended to do no more than be of friendly assistance, Hasted sought a legal opinion, and the matter was finally passed to Charles Yorke, an eminent lawyer and member of a Kentish family who in 1770 was to be very briefly Lord Chancellor. Yorke's opinion, which he noted down on the case on 31 December 1763, was that the bond which Hasted had given would be found void in law, so that no one had a claim on him. This, in Yorke's view, was for the good of the public, 'that the channels for these appointments may be kept free from scandal and corruption'.

In spite of the implication of an office being for sale, it cannot be said that there had been any corruption in Thorne's attempt to obtain the collectorship, or in the efforts of any of those concerned with him. One cannot know how Carless Franklin came by his appointment, or who had suggested his name to the Lords of the Treasury. Yorke's rebuke is levelled rather at the suggestion that the Lords of the Treasury might in any way have found their hands tied in advance in the matter of making the appointment. The sufferer would appear to have been Edward Beckwith, who on the face of it had resigned his 'office of profit' without compensation. Or had Franklin merely offered him more?[200]

There is no doubt that financial deals and wrangles of this kind were part of the web and woof of the lives of many eighteenth-century gentlemen. All the participants in the present case were known to each other: Hasted was — and remained — very friendly with Samuel Fullagar, Harris's attorney; Thomas Harris, when he died in April 1769, left Edward Wilks £400 in his will; Edward Wilks continued to be a close friend of Edward Hasted for many years. Nevertheless, such an affair could not pass off without exciting some animosity. Harris's will, which was drawn up in October 1765, exceedingly generous to Mary Dorman, and forgiving debts to the husbands of her sisters Elizabeth and Margaret, Gabriel Thorne and John Pope respectively, as well as to her mother Mrs Dorothy Dorman, makes no mention of the husband of sister Ann: and it may well have been due to his friendly intervention in the matter of the Faversham collectorship that Hasted forfeited a place in Thomas Harris's will.[201]

Certainly, Charles Yorke's opinion, which is undoubtedly where the matter rested, must have been very welcome when it came at the end of the year. By then Hasted was again at Throwley — indeed, he had been there since some time in October.

Eighteenth century provincial newspapers are an unfailing source of interest, constantly revealing facets of life which might otherwise remain unsuspected by later generations. Here, for example, is a small personal advertisement which appeared in the *Kentish Post* for 27 August 1763:

> Wanted in a month or two, A servant, that can blow a French horn tolerably well, his wages 15 guineas with a livery, or 22 without. He must perfectly understand waiting at table; and as no other man servant is kept, he must not be against doing any thing that is required of him to do in the house. If he can shave and dress hair, the more agreeable. Such a one who can bring an unexceptionable character from the last person he lived with, may be informed of the advertiser by applying to the printer of this paper.

This is something of an oddity, not only in the requirement to play the French horn, but also in the amount of detail it gives about wages and the conditions of service, which might have been thought more appropriate to private discussion at interview, than announcement in public. Indeed, the conditions seem to be calculated to deter, rather than encourage, possible applicants. That the first advertisement was not wholly successful is proved by the appearance of a second one, two months later:

> Wanted directly, A man-servant, whose chief business will be to drive a chariot, and take care of three or four horses, to attend his master and wait at dinner every day, and on particular occasions help the footman in the house. He must have a good character for his honesty, and especially for his sobriety.
>
> NB A good cook wanting at the same place.[202]

A third advertisement, just under three weeks later, reveals the not immediately apparent link between the first two, and also, in its urgency, goes straight to essentials:

> Wanted immediately, A good cook who can have a good character from her last place; also a footman, whose business will be entirely within doors to wait on a large family. If he can dress hair and shave, or blow a French horn, he will be the better liked of; and he must have a good character, especially as to his honesty and sobriety.
>
> NB As his place will be a very good one to him, he must answer well in every particular.[203]

It is noticeable that the requirement for expertise in three or four branches of learning is now toned down to 'either/or'. And the most desperate need is for a cook! Both the second and third insertions name the advertiser: 'Enquire at Edward Hasted's, esq, at Throwley near Faversham'.

It seems clear that the move to Throwley was undertaken in order to secure the peace and quiet which Hasted now felt were essential for his research. As he explained to Thomas Astle in one of the letters dating from this period, he had too many visitors at Sutton — the price he paid, perhaps, for his sociability, and the accessibility which he seems always to have encouraged. One of his principal aims, at this stage, was to form a manuscript collection of all the heraldic arms in the county, and it is understandable that interruptions, particularly when he was engaged in the delicate and demanding task of copying what were in effect hundreds of tiny pictures, must have been very frustrating.

Nevertheless, as often with Hasted, there was an element of impulsiveness in the move. Throwley, then as now, may have been a parish, but it was hardly a village — Hasted himself describes it as having none 'excepting the few houses in Abraham Street may be so called, the rest of the houses, which are mostly cottages, standing dispersed throughout it, either single, or built round the little greens or fostalls, of which there are several in different parts of the parish'[204] — and it must have offered, together with all the advantages, all the drawbacks of a secluded spot. Other locations seem to have been tried, but to have been found wanting.

Before going to Throwley, for example, Hasted seems to have migrated briefly to a cottage at Sutton, most probably the one near Sutton

Throwley

Place in which he had lived before his marriage. Writing to Astle in November 1763 he commented:

> One thing I enjoy much here, which induces me to stay at Throwley, I enjoy my time and leisure without the interruption of too many visitors, with which I was pestered at Sutton cottage.[205]

Obviously, in an adjacent cottage Hasted had been far too easily flushed out by the gentlemen of the neighbourhood, when the civility of the age — which Hasted took great pleasure in practising — would have dictated an immediate abandonment of one's own pursuits in favour of entertaining one's visitors. The same thing may have happened with the house at Farningham. As we have seen, from the beginning of that year (and perhaps even from Michaelmas 1762) Hasted was renting what seems to have been a house newly built by the late landlord of the Bull inn, John Pratt, and known as Mrs Pratt's house. But the house at Farningham, like the cottage at Sutton, may have proved to be too close to his old haunts, and too accessible to his many friends and acquaintances, to serve the purpose of an ivory tower. For this, Hasted was forced to look further afield: an extended stay at Throwley must have seemed to offer the ideal solution.

Hasted's wife was perhaps the unintended victim of the simple life which was at once the allure and the limitation of Throwley. Only two months after the birth of George Ann had become pregnant again — and there were already two toddlers to attend to, Edward, now nearly three, and Francis, who was about eighteen months old. The early pregnancy after a birth perhaps points to the use of a wet-nurse, which would have been in keeping with the style in which the Hasteds lived, but nevertheless it probably began too soon for Ann to have recovered properly from the birth of her third child. Before her confinement was over, and probably before the new pregnancy was suspected, her husband had decided on the move to Throwley, and was advertising for the single man-of-all-work (and French horn player to boot) who he felt would be adequate for the small establishment, withdrawn from the world, which he planned for Throwley. Within a couple of months Ann had been whisked off to east Kent, where not only was there no French horn player, but there does not seem to have been even a cook!

The family chariot, bearing Ann Hasted, the wet-nurse with George, and the children's nurse in charge of Edward and Francis, must have set out around the middle of October. Hasted almost certainly accompanied them on horseback. He was a very accomplished horseman — there are several references in the correspondence to his skill and endurance in the saddle — and a long day's ride through the autumn colours of Kent's undulating countryside would have been a joyful prelude to the period of seclusion which he planned at Throwley. Other men went to town for the season: he was doing exactly the opposite, and with far more reason. The family chariot was loaded not only with the cumbersome trunks and travelling chests of those days, but also with a box containing several books on which Hasted proposed to work while he was away, including the *Monasticon Anglicanum* of William Dugdale, the much admired seventeenth-century author of the *Antiquities of Warwickshire*.

Hasted had perhaps intended to take care of his horses himself at Throwley, but it must have quickly become clear to him that the simple life could be as demanding as too many visitors, and that if he was to have the undisturbed hours of leisure of which he dreamed someone had to be engaged to attend to the machinery of civilised living. Accordingly, the single man-servant visualised in August had, by October, turned into two men and a cook. It may have been easier to meet the demands of the stable than the house: by mid-November the want of a cook and a footman were pressing: Mrs Hasted, feeling increasingly unwell, must have coped as best she could with the aid of the children's maid and the wet-nurse. In one of his first letters to Thomas Astle, written on 4 November, Hasted makes use of the metaphor of Robinson Crusoe and Man Friday, and although he is here describing an archaeological dig undertaken with another friend, Bryan Faussett, it was probably no less applicable to the first few weeks at Throwley, characterised by a resolute makeshiftness which was no doubt great fun for the chief, but trying for the Indians.

It was not quite the life of a hermit, although, apart from Edward Wilks and the Revd Bryan Faussett, a reluctant clergyman but a keen archaeologist and noted antiquary, Hasted intentionally saw little company over this time.[206] But the newsman carried letters as well as the *Kentish Post*, so he was in no danger of losing touch with the world. There were occasional rides, too, to be made to the Roebuck in Ospringe, to pick up parcels delivered by the post-coach, or, as it was also known, the Canterbury and Dover machine, which passed that way. Hasted sat down there once to write a letter of thanks to Thomas Astle for some material that Dr Ducarel had brought into Kent for him, ending, 'I shall trouble you with another letter very soon for at present I write in the midst of pipes, tobacco, on bad paper, worse pens and ink, and every inconvenience of a tavern.' The paper was indeed poor, the pens scratchy — both no doubt supplied by the inn.[207]

It is from the first of the sequence of Hasted-Astle letters that we learn that Hasted had not been long in east Kent when, with his usual impetuosity, he was off on a visit to Bryan Faussett at Heppington — a visit which was perhaps justified not only by their common interest in antiquities but also by the need for a respite from the primitive conditions of living at Throwley where the Hasteds still had no cook. It is not surprising that Hasted's first letter to Astle apologises for not writing earlier because in effect there was nothing to write about but his work. However, the visit to Heppington seems to have been very enjoyable and must have done them all good — Mrs Hasted was undoubtedly of the party, since Hasted refers to 'the ladies'. Long hours were spent in Faussett's study, discussing books and papers, pots and bones, but there was also time for several archaeological excursions. Hasted proceeds to give Astle a long account of one particular morning's dig, when Faussett and he, resembling, as he said, Robinson Crusoe and his Man Friday, investigated a Roman camp not far from Heppington, as well as a tumulus.[208] The speed with which they worked was probably typical of eighteenth century archaeologists — gentlemen to a man, and able to summon teams of 'hands' to do the navvying for them — but who nevertheless laid the groundwork for the slower, more painstaking excavations of later generations.[209]

Hasted's detailed letter was to have an unfortunate repercussion for which he was in no way to blame. Astle took it upon himself to have his friend's account of the excavation read out at the Society of Antiquaries in the absence of Faussett, who took great objection, when he heard about it, to the premature revelation by another of an excavation which he looked on as his.[210] The flurry of ill-feeling which this caused quickly subsided, but it must have cast a temporary cloud over the tranquillity which Hasted had thought to secure for himself at Throwley.

Surprisingly, that tranquillity seems to have registered also something of the surge of national events. In a letter from Astle dated 19 November which has survived among Hasted's papers and which is almost certainly Astle's reply to Hasted's first letter from east Kent, the news of the day is mentioned in such a way as to make one feel that Hasted had a personal interest in it. The subject opens with a reference to events in the House of Commons:

> I presume you have the paper regularly; therefore it would be impertinent in me to give you the news of the town. I have attended the House every day since the Session began.[211]

In common with most provincial newspapers at this time the *Kentish Post* carried far more national than local news, and in the issue of 19 November, which Hasted may or may not have seen before he received

Astle's letter, the first item, taken from a London paper, dealt with the latest development in the long Wilkes saga, which had begun earlier in 1763 when Wilkes, in No.45 of his political paper, the *North Briton*, (almost certainly acting at the behest of a certain faction in the government) had denounced the speech with which George III had opened Parliament. This had continued with Wilkes's appeal against the use of general warrants of arrest, and the latest news had been of a duel between Wilkes and Samuel Martin, fought with pistols in Hyde Park on 16 November. The *Kentish Post* was now able to report that 'This morning Mr Wilkes was much better, quite chearful, and is imagined to be entirely out of danger', that he had, when in danger, returned the letter containing the challenge to the gentleman who had sent it, 'that it might not be of any prejudice to him after his decease', and that Mr Wilkes and Mr Martin were now 'entirely reconciled'. Astle's letter, too, contains a reassurance: 'Mr Wilkes is not in any danger from his wound, tho' his fever is increased today. Last night he dictated a North Brit.'

While this may have referred only to an earlier interest displayed by Hasted in Wilkes's championing of liberty of the subject — with which, as the son of a man with close City connections, he undoubtedly concurred — the closing lines of Astle's letter contain the following:

> Last night Sir Jos. the Doctor and I attended at the Society of Antiquaries ... The old knight hath never been at a loss for a toast since he saw Miss Wilkes; he speaks of her in raptures ... However, (joking apart) pray make my compliments acceptable to that most amiable lady. After mentioning Miss W. I have not one idea of antiquity.[212]

'Miss W' can only be the aforementioned Miss Wilkes, who, it is generally agreed, was exceedingly charming and, although only thirteen at this time, probably already accustomed to appearing in public at her father's side and to holding her own in conversation. The letter makes it very clear, however, that she is in the vicinity of the Hasteds — it is hard to imagine that she can actually have been staying with them, although this has to be borne in mind as a possibility. What, in this case, was she doing at Throwley near Faversham? The question poses itself, of whether Edward Wilks of Faversham was in any way related to John Wilkes. The slight difference in the spelling of their surname is of minor importance: different branches of a family frequently changed the spelling of their name for one reason or another. Polly Wilkes was supposedly finishing her education in Paris at this time, but could easily have crossed the Channel for a visit to her father, who might have hustled her out of the way of his London troubles by sending her to stay with a relative in Kent; her mother also had had Kentish connections. However, the subject of John Wilkes does not crop up again in the Hasted-Astle correspondence; we are left with an intriguing puzzle, and the suspicion of an answer.

Astle's present post at the Augmentation Office, which Hasted himself might have envied if his future as a country gentleman had not seemed to lie so clearly mapped out for him, gave him easy access to sources which the historian was obliged to petition for the loan or sight of. The letters between the two men show that one such door which now stood open for Astle was that of Surrenden Dering, the Pluckley home of the Kentish baronet Sir Edward Dering, where there was a renowned library and a fine collection of Anglo-Saxon charters. Hasted was exceedingly eager to see these, and an opportunity seemed about to present itself. Astle, in his letter of the 19 November, says casually, 'I hope to see you at Surrenden at Xmas' — it sounds as if the invitation which he has received has been mentioned before. Hasted, eager not to let the occasion slip by, replies only four days later, spelling out more definitely his intention of riding over to Pluckley if Astle is there:

> I shall be very glad to wait on you, if you come to Surrenden at Xmas. Besides the pleasure I shall have in seeing you I shall have an opportunity of seeing the Surrenden Library, for tho' I was very well acquainted with the late Sir Edwd Dering, I am not at all known to the present gentleman.[213]

But Hasted saw neither Astle nor Surrenden that Christmas. Nursing his hopes, he waited until the 17 January before writing: 'I had some hopes of seeing you in Kent this Xmas, but I find the time is now past without it, which is no small disappointment to me'.

The New Year was clouded also by the receipt of a letter from Bryan Faussett, criticising Hasted's account of their joint excavation, for the making public of which Astle was entirely responsible. Hasted was clearly very upset at this turn of events, which seemed to him to have gone as far as accusing him of lying: 'I would sooner forgive any man's accusing me of almost anything whatsoever rather than of an untruth', he wrote in January, but there is no hint of any accusation levelled at Astle for his part in this, and later in the same letter his mood is once more one of hope and plans for future work.[214]

In March Hasted saw another possibility of meeting up with his friend. He proposed to attend the Lent assizes at Maidstone, which always terminated with a ball on the Wednesday night, and he thought that Astle might like to come too. At the end of his letter of the 11 March, which deals mainly with antiquarian matters and also the little worry of how he should pay his entrance money as a newly elected member of the Antiquarian Society, Hasted adds:

> As it is impossible to be an antiquarian, without having a particular attachment to the ladies, at least I judge so, from those I have the pleasure of being acquainted with, and you are a young man, why cannot you take a ride to our assize ball, Wednesday sennight; if you are fond of dancing, you will have an exceeding good one, and in all likelihood your flame will be there. I would induce you if I could, in the first place for your own sake, and in the next, that I may have the pleasure of meeting you there.[215]

One has the feeling, however, that Astle, yet again, may have failed to turn up. Long after Hasted's return from Throwley, he was to send Astle another invitation, to an assembly ball at Dartford in March 1765, 'next Monday, where I hope you will be, and indeed I claim a promise of it from you, made soon after your disappointing me at the last'.[216] Did Astle make an appearance this time? Alas for his Kent 'flame'! The following December was to see him married to the daughter of the Revd Philip Morant. Another refusal came in 1766, when Mrs Astle declined to act as godmother to the Hasteds' second daughter, Katherine. And Thomas Astle himself never became sponsor or godfather to any of Hasted's children, although it is highly unlikely that he was never invited to do so.

Nevertheless, the first part of the Hasted-Astle friendship, with Astle clearly in the ascendant, lasted until 1767 and included a small publication in which both men, although principally Hasted, had a hand. The last letter from Hasted from this period, dated 23 April 1767, was to make a reference to some important Dering MSS, of which Hasted, to his great pleasure, had now had a sight: 'I have wrote Sir E. Dering a letter of thanks for his MSS, and letting him know that I had sent the whole of them to you.'[217] It does not appear that Sir Edward was ever to see them again.

In spite of the limitations imposed on life at Throwley, the stay there clearly answered the purpose for which it was intended. Hasted was able to devote himself to his self-imposed task and to get a great deal of enjoyment from it, whether this involved archaeological excursions with Bryan Faussett, or quiet work in his study with pen and ink, and sometimes colour, on his collection of armorial bearings. His progress frequently formed the subject-matter of a letter to Astle:

> I do assure you I work very hard from morning to night, and I have the good luck to have some very valuable MSS pour in frequently. I have just finished the materials Dr Plot left for his Natural History of Kent, and am now about those which Warburton, Somt Herald, had collected for a history of this county. (23 November 1763)

> I work so hard at my favorite design, morning, noon, and night, that I know nothing of the world, but what my correspondents and the newspapers inform me of. I hope to do so much this winter in the transcribing part that when the fine weather comes in summer I shall have nothing to prevent my visiting every parish in the county without which I can never compleat my work. (17 January 1764)[218]

Part of that same January day had been spent in copying a pedigree and the arms of the Wilsford family from a document which Hasted seems to have been lent by his friends the Faunces, for they, as well as Bargraves and Derings, had married into it.[219] This had probably been among the materials which had been transported to Throwley, to be dealt with at leisure in the dark winter days before a good fire in the room Hasted had commandeered as his study. The pages of coats of arms were mounting up, with the shields ruled out in advance, twelve or twenty to a page. The tiny drawings of griffins, lions, boars, unicorns and other heraldic beasts cost Hasted, as he said himself 'some pains and trouble' — although some of the animals, less fanciful and more down to earth, seem drawn from the eighteenth-century country life which surrounded him at Throwley or Sutton-at-Hone, like the three little round-eyed owls on the Webb coat of arms, or the honking geese on that of Wiburn.

By the 11 March Hasted felt able to say that he had something to show for all his hard work:

> I have lately been very laborious in heraldry, and have collected 3 volumes with pretty good authorities, and about 2000 coats of arms, which, though at first it cost me some pains and trouble as well in the blazon, as colors, yet I go on now tollerably well and quick.[220]

In spite of a certain shadow which must have lain over the whole area due to the proximity of the gunpowder works — and there was a nasty explosion that February when one of the mills at Faversham blew up, fortunately without loss of life — the attractions of Throwley probably grew stronger with the coming of spring. However, two further advertisements in the *Kentish Post*, for 17 March 1764, seem to bear the Hasted mark, and, if they do, show that the secluded idyll was still beset by staffing problems:

> Wanted, as soon as possible, A sober lad to drive a gentleman's post chaise, and has been used to horses. He must have a good character for sobriety and honesty from his last place, and must not be too heavy.
>
> Wanted, A chamber maid, one who has been used to children, and understands something of housekeeping.

Both advertisements, which referred would-be applicants to the printer of the paper, appeared twice, the one for a driver for the post-chaise being slightly amended, adding 'civil behaviour' to the desired qualities of sobriety and honesty, and continuing to appear until the end of March. The signs are that Hasted's independent views made him a lenient, perhaps somewhat unusual, employer, of whom ill-educated servants found it easy to take advantage.

Nevertheless, with or without someone to drive his small post-chaise, and in spite of having told Astle in March that he intended to leave Throwley by the middle of April or the beginning of May, Hasted could not be persuaded to return to Sutton-at-Hone until the end of the latter month or the beginning of June. By then there seem to have been some worries in connection with Mrs Hasted's pregnancy, which perhaps made it imperative for her to be under her regular doctor and to rest at home: she was no longer in a condition to play Man Friday to her husband's Robinson Crusoe.

Although Hasted spoke in one of his letters to Astle of the need to spend four or five months in London in order to make use of the quantities of material which Astle was finding in the Augmentation Office, a visit of this duration seems never to have taken place. Indeed, it was to be many years before Hasted would again be away from home for quite so long at a stretch as he had spent at Throwley. The break in 1763 was a good one for him, however. Here he was able for once to indulge the studious side of his nature to the full, with interludes of just the kind that appealed to him, spending hours out in the sun and the wind with his old friend Bryan Faussett, digging trenches, finding flints and disturbing the 'bones of the old Romans on Chartham Downs near Canterbury', as he put it in a letter of April — the slight upset with Faussett of earlier in the year forgotten.[221] In the end the antiquities of the county were to play a smaller part in Hasted's *History* than he had at first expected, but he was at present only feeling his way, and everything which related to the past of the county was grist to his mill.

The heraldic bearings of Kentish families were similarly to be allotted a minor role, being given in blazon (description) only and not illustrated, although at this time they were engrossing much of Hasted's attention. The folio volumes which he numbered in his library D.IV and D.V, now respectively manuscripts Add.5479 and 5480 in the British Library, contain some of the work dating from this period. In his letter to Astle of 11 March Hasted had spoken of having copied some 2000 coats of arms. Add.5479 contains over 1700, and Add.5480, over 500. There is little doubt that this is the work on which he was engaged while at Throwley. The second volume, Hasted's D.V, is actually dated 1764 by the historian in several places. On the page which he numbered 19, he has written:

> The following coats of arms were taken from the Book of Picard Herald Painter of Canterbury, being those which he received instructions at different times to paint in achievements, by several families for their deceased relatives; it is now in the hands of B. Picard Herald Painter of Canterbury 1764.[222]

John and Valentine Picard had advertised their services in the *Kentish Post* (in conjunction with a coach harness maker) in April 1763, when as well as 'Coats of Arms painted in oil, or water colours on vellum, altar pieces, and sentences for churches, hatchments, shields and escutcheons, etc.' they offered the painting of arms and crests on coaches, chariots and post-chaises. Hasted may well have taken the family chariot in to Canterbury to have his arms painted, or repainted, on the doors while he was at Throwley. He certainly paid a visit to Canterbury during his time there, since his letter to Astle of 11 March mentions some observations he made on the monument of the Black Prince. But whether or not he availed himself of the Picards' services, this was probably the time when he was able to borrow from them the book in which they recorded the various funeral hatchments and bearings they were asked to paint. Hasted perhaps had to return the book before he had finished with it, borrowing it again on a later occasion to complete his series of Kentish armorial bearings: Add.5480 has some seven pages from Picard's book near the beginning and another ten copied from it towards the end, after some more precisely dated Hulse and Jacob entries.[223]

This means that Hasted was probably still engaged in copying arms from Picard's book when he was obliged to return to Sutton-at-Hone, since both Hulse and Jacob entries seem to have been made at St John's. Add.5480 contains, as well as coats of arms, a number of descents of families, or genealogies, a path that was to prove more fruitful to him in compiling his *History*. On his return to Sutton he seems to have been lent a pedigree by Richard Hulse, his near neighbour at Baldwins, for there are ten pages of carefully coloured work, containing drawings of knights-at-arms as well as heraldic bearings, in which Hasted copied out a pedigree 'of the Antient and worthy familye of Hulse ... by John Taylor living at the Lute in Fleet Street' — a piece of work which was itself undated. Hasted, however, has written at the end of it: 'I began copying this pedigree of the Hulse's June the 20th 1764 and finished it the 22nd instant following' — a very creditable achievement. On another manuscript, apparently lent to him by the Faversham historian (and doctor), Edward Jacob, which he must have brought back with him from Throwley to Sutton, and which filled thirty pages of Hasted's volume with coats of arms, he noted: 'I began copying this MSS about one at noon on the 30th of June 1764 and finished it about the same time the next day'.

Hasted was to be described by Sir Samuel Egerton Brydges as a man of quick movements, and the speed and dexterity with which he could copy manuscripts are a clear illustration of this.[224] It is no wonder that, when asking Astle for any further arms he could find for him to copy, Hasted added, 'You know I am not long in going thro' them, and will return them within any limited time'. In this letter, an early one in the series, dated 23 November 1763, Hasted wonders whether perhaps a Mr Edmondson may have some Kent arms, and Astle in fact seems to have obtained a manuscript from Joseph Edmondson — the former barber's apprentice, renowned for his skills in heraldry and genealogy, who was shortly to become Mowbray Herald Extraordinary — and to have sent it down to Throwley, marked, as Hasted had suggested, to be left for him at the Roebuck in Ospringe by the Canterbury machine where he could send to have it collected, for Add.5479 begins with a copy of a manuscript headed, 'Notes taken of Arms, Monuments etc. in several Churches in the County of Kent ... communicated to me by Joseph Edmondson Esq'.[225]

There can be no doubt whatever that Hasted's long stay at Throwley was made for the sole purpose of obtaining the peace and quiet he needed for what he saw as essential preparation for his *History of Kent*. As well as the copying of heraldic arms, there were probably long periods of reading and the entering of many snippets of information in one of his great folio commonplace books, in which all the Kentish parishes are listed alphabetically, each being given an appropriate reference from

Domesday Book. We cannot know whether there was ever a complete solution to the servant problem, or whether he had, regretfully to abandon his hope of finding someone who could blow the French horn tolerably well. Had this been required to fill a vacancy in a small church orchestra? This seems the most likely explanation, for Hasted was a steady supporter of his local church — although the church at Throwley seems, with or without its French horn player, to have been a relatively poor exchange for that at Sutton-at-Hone, diligently served for half a century by the Revd Edmund Barrell and recently reinvigorated with the installation of a new vicar, Hasted's friend (and Barrell's grandson) the Revd Edmund Faunce.

Hasted took up the cause of Throwley church with his usual directness, for among the correspondence relating to his *History* are two letters which he received during this time from the Archbishop of Canterbury, Thomas Secker, dealing with the lack of services in the church, of which Hasted had obviously complained. Although the complaint and the answers it received are, on the face of it, somewhat routine, both men come rather well out of the exchange. Hasted was clearly genuinely concerned that the church was so poorly served, and the Archbishop just as clearly felt some responsibility for the well-being of those appointed under him: Throwley's vicar, the Revd Johnson Lawson, is not forced to live in a place which has, he says, many unpleasant memories for him, and, on the understanding that his income is not £100 a year, is allowed to put in only a part-time curate, Mr Dawney, 'with a salary of £25 a year: and the rather, as I understood, that Mr Dawney could not easily get another curacy, and yet stood in need of one':

> Mr Lawson represented to me that Throwley disagreed with his health, and that the death of his brother there had made it insupportable to him, and for these reasons I allowed him to serve Pluckley.[226]

Items in the *Kentish Post* in 1762 and 1763, which Hasted had doubtless read and noted, had shown that the Revd Johnson Lawson was in Canterbury at this time, acting as a steward at the anniversary meeting of the King's School in August 1762, and deputed as a surrogate for granting marriage licences and the dispatch of business in the city and diocese the following February.[227] Hasted probably did not know all the details of the case: Johnson Lawson's brother had been Throwley's previous vicar and had died after only a year there, and Lawson had himself been very ill, spending time in Tonbridge, and then performing lighter work in Canterbury, with the Archbishop's permission. The churches of Eastling and Leveland were within easy reach of the parishioners of Throwley, and in his second letter to Hasted the Archbishop went gently on the attack with the hope 'That you, who set so good an example in all other respects, will not set the bad one of absenting yourself from the public service'.[228]

Hasted took advantage of this correspondence to ask permission to use the library at Lambeth for his researches, permission which was readily granted. The request is interesting, for it seems to be one of Hasted's earliest along these lines. Emboldened by the reception which met his very polite, almost timid, requests for information whenever he mentioned his purpose, his correspondence was to develop into the avalanche of letters, the answers to which today fill several boxes in the Kentish archives.

Edward Wilks and Gabriel Thorne were again called on to act as godfathers, with Thorne's wife Elizabeth as godmother, for the new baby, another boy, who was born at Sutton-at-Hone on the 25 July, and duly christened Charles.[229] The occasion of Charles's birth, which must have been a time both of worry and of relief to Hasted, was overshadowed by the threat of a rift with Astle, who, although he must have been aware of Mrs Hasted's condition, was annoyed at having received no answer to one of his letters. The humble way in which Hasted pleads for forgiveness shows the ascendancy which the younger, and in many ways less cultivated, man had acquired over him. Six days after the birth of his son, he was writing as follows:

> How often I have intended thanking you for your last kind favour I need not tell you. I will not think that you suppose me so void of gratitude, or even common civility, not to have acknowledged it, had I not been prevented by many concurring circumstances. I have expected every week to have made myself happy with you in London. This Mrs Hasted's condition has prevented and kept me confined at home. I received your kind note from Rochester, and did think I should have seen you in your return. I own, as I did not, I thought you were still at Surrenden, till yesterday, when I heard of your return and that you are angry with me. You must not be angry with me — you shall not — when I have never intended a cause for it, but day after day, week after week, has stole on, not one without uneasiness to myself in not having wrote to you, and still thinking I should get to you almost as soon as my letter. As it has run on to this length of time, I am convinced (tho' not intended) it is wrong and deserves your anger. As such I submit to your friendship, and know your generous sentiments will not let me long be in suspense, that you forgive me.[230]

That Astle viewed their relationship in the same way is shown by the curt comment which he made at the bottom of this letter, choosing Greek characters for the p and the m: 'His peace is made'.

Astle appears to have given Hasted to understand that he would like to settle in Kent. One can deduce from the mention in Hasted's letter that he had been attracted by a Kentish young lady, and as yet he was without an establishment of his own. Bryan Faussett's mother had died at Heppington in 1761 and in 1764 Faussett decided to let the house at Street End, where he had been living near her, and move to Heppington. An unnamed friend of Hasted's, who seems very likely to have been Astle, expressed an interest in taking Street End, but by the middle of July Faussett was writing to Ducarel with some anxiety: 'I have as yet seen neither Mr Hasted nor his friend, whom he promised to bring hither to take my farm'.[231] Once more Astle would appear to have let Hasted down. The farm was perhaps bigger than he could take on at this time — or his attention was turning from his Kentish 'flame' to the Revd Philip Morant's daughter. Street End was subsequently advertised in the *Kentish Post* at the beginning of August as a 'Capital messuage or mansion house, fit for a genteel family', with 'a good and well planted garden, walled in, two coach houses, and stabling for twelve horses, a good barn, two Dutch barns, a granary, and about 50 acres of land', although Faussett still retained hopes that Hasted's 'friend' might materialise to take it.[232] The matter is mentioned again in a letter of 2 October to Dr Ducarel: 'I have not seen Mr Hasted since; nor have I heard from that friend of his, who he was so sure would hire Street End'.[233] It must have been a trying time for a man like Faussett, rendered habitually short-tempered by the gout.

In the late summer of 1764, however, Hasted, now back at Sutton-at-Hone, was pursuing his work for the *History* as well as he could, amid an enlarged family, a bigger establishment of servants — with, one hopes, a greater propensity to stay than had been shown at Throwley — and renewed visits from the gentlemen of the neighbourhood. At the end of August he wrote to his old friend Dr Ducarel, with his usual enthusiasm and a pressing invitation:

> The fine weather makes me wish to see you down soon, whilst it lasts. I have been looking out for amusement for you, and have found two or three Roman tumuli within a mile of St John's. These we will open; and as I have served a regular apprenticeship to such labours, I fancy I can amuse you very agreeably ... You must afford me a day or two for this work, as you seemed to promise, when I saw you last, and let us be once more happy together.[234]

There is a considerable intimacy in the letters which Hasted sent to Dr Ducarel. After the death of John Lethieullier Ducarel may have come to represent for Hasted the fatherly figure which his life lacked. He certainly knew he could rely on Andrew Coltee Ducarel's discretion, for he is very blunt in this letter about the worthlessness of Charles Whitworth's collections, put together for the purpose of collaborating with Hasted on a revision of Philipott's *Villare Cantianum*:

> I received last Saturday from Mr Whitworth a large box of papers, etc. which he had collected for Kent; but of all the rubbish I ever saw in my life, I never met with anything so trifling. Indeed I can hardly think it possible that a man could undertake such a work as this, be four years about it, and at the end be just where he first set out; all that he has collected being comprised in three or four sheets of paper at most, besides the printed books that his box is filled up with.[235]

Whether or not Dr Ducarel was able to accept Hasted's warm invitation that autumn — and as Commissary General for Canterbury he was quite often in Kent — Thomas Astle appears to have stayed with the Hasteds some time in late November or early December of that year, for in December 1764 Hasted was to describe the visit in glowing terms in a letter to Ducarel. He had obviously taken Astle over to see John Calcraft at Ingress, and they had followed this up with a day of archaeological discoveries:

> I have no doubt but Mr Astle has told you how happy he made me in a visit here; of our antiquarian entertainment at Ingress, and our sallying forth in search of further antiquities the next day; of the Saxon arch; Roman bricks; tumuli and entrenchments; and of the Roman mile-stone, which, since he went, I have purchased, and have got home, and I esteem it as a singular and invaluable monument of antient times.[236]

The visit had probably been too short for Hasted's liking, and they had not had time to do half the things he had planned, for he appears to have continued his investigations on his own after Astle had left. He goes on to say that he has discovered more tumuli on Dartford Brent, and hopes that Dr Ducarel will come down to join him in opening them:

I wish I could have you down at the opening of some of these. I will not touch those on the Brent before summer, when I shall make a whole day of it, and then perhaps you may give me the pleasure of your company.[237]

Toil in his study now alternated, for Hasted, with administrative duties. In a letter of February 1765 to Ducarel he mentions that he has been at Rochester, possibly in connection with Rochester Bridge, of which he was still an assistant warden, or for a meeting of the commissioners of sewers, and that he was shown a brass plate found among the refuse filling an old wall which some workmen were demolishing in order to make a gateway. Small discoveries such as this linked pleasure to duty, but to his old friend he confessed that there was a good deal of wearisome work involved in preparing his *History*,

> which I labour much at, and in a no very agreeable part of it, which is making references and comparing authors, and running over a multiplicity of books, some of which are so very dry, and pass over so heavily, that they almost make me weary of this sort of work; but I go on, in hopes of getting through some time or other.[238]

And with typical generosity, Hasted promised to make Ducarel a present of the heraldic MS which Joseph Edmondson had recently bought for him, 'when I have done with it in reference to my History'.

Edmondson had probably bought this for the historian at one of the many book and library sales which were held in London: Hasted himself was unable to go up there as often as he would have liked. The four or five months he had originally spoken of spending in London have now dwindled to 'six weeks or two months' which, Hasted tells Ducarel, he hopes to be able to spend there in the summer of 1765. Even this may have been curtailed, since other things had a habit of claiming Hasted's presence, but he certainly spent most of the month of June in London during this year, staying as usual with his mother. We know that he attended two meetings of the Society of Antiquaries on the 6 and 20 June, but he was soon back in Kent, where he attended Courts of Sewers at Rochester on the 8 and 29 July, while his daughter Anne was to be born on the 15 August — on which date also he seems, now perhaps with a sigh, to have resumed his duties as a Kentish magistrate.

—I have nothing more to add to this but the compliments of the season to yrself & family & my hearty wishes
of happiness to you all who remain
&c. yr friend & humble servt
And: Colten Ducarel

Mr Faussett joyns with me in the Compliments of the Season &c. &c. &c. to you
& yrs, and little Ones — I am, Dear Sir,
I am, Dr Sir,
yr faithful & much obliged Servant
Br Faussett.

Yours very sincerely
St Denne

humble Servt
Ducare

I am, dear Sir,
Yours most sine
Wm Boys

I remain dear Sir
Your obliged & obedt
dutiful Nephew
Thos Astle
most humble Servt
R Bathurst

excuse me, my dear friend,
it is but a pleasure to serve
owing to my mean abilities; and am w.
Complmts, & Respects to you, & yrs
I am Dear Sir, yr most faithfull humble
Servt J. Thorp

your Obedt humble Servt
W. Boteler

Chapter 7

Hasted in London

London, for the first few years of his married life, seems to have meant very little to Hasted, immersed in Kentish life and continually adding to the administrative duties which he took on there. The disagreement between mother and son, marked by Hasted's preferring to live with the family's former housekeeper Mrs Aldridge rather than with his mother, had deepened to become an open rift with his decision to marry Ann Dorman, the descendant of an old Kentish yeoman family whose ancestor, John Dorman, had figured in the Kentish Hearth Tax of 1662 for Sutton-at-Hone with a respectable four hearths.[239] Marriage to Ann had served to underline both his break with his mother and his allegiance to the county of Kent, his father's country.

In the Anecdotes Hasted admits that at least two years went by after his marriage before he again saw his mother, and relations appear to have been strained between them for some time. She was invited down to Sutton-at-Hone with her daughter when the house of St John's was finished, but appears to have refused for several years to stay at the house itself — 'my mother not brooking to be a visitor to my house where my wife was mistress of it' — nor was she willing to renew her links with Hasted's neighbours, many of whom had in the past been close friends of herself and her husband:

> Whilst with us they never visited any of the neighbours, not even Mr Barrell and his family, who lived but a field from us, and who had been vicar of the parish and as such visited her and my father so many years before whilst they lived at Hawley. My mother, poor woman, had an excessive pride, which predominated on every occasion and made most people rather disgusted with her acquaintance, which they of course in future rather avoided than otherwise.[240]

And Mrs Hasted's visits to her son were to remain for some years on this footing: she would accept an invitation to go down into Kent in the summer with her daughter for the sake of a change of air, staying in the vicinity of Sutton-at-Hone — Hasted remembered that she stayed once in Wilmington, and another time in the small cottage near Sutton Place where he had lived before his marriage — but not at St John's itself.

Writing the Anecdotes in his old age Hasted seems to have felt that he had been lacking in filial duty to his mother over these years, although she herself would appear to have borne a good deal of the responsibility for the differences between them. However, the arrangement whereby the mother was now dependent for her income on her son was not an easy one to maintain without some friction. The annual rental from the Hasted estates amounted at this time to close on £1000, but Hasted himself admits that his rebuilding of St John's and the style in which he lived there swallowed up the whole of this sum without leaving anything over to meet the cost of his mother's annuity, and there is no doubt that this period saw the beginnings of those entanglements in debt which were to culminate so disastrously thirty years later.

It was not until after his sister's death, in the spring of 1762, that relations between Hasted and his mother improved, although even this sad event seems to have done little to soften the old lady's attitude towards her daughter-in-law. Hasted, as we have seen, was renting a house in Farningham from around the beginning of 1763, and it is likely that this was taken for the benefit of his mother, so that she could escape for a while from her London house where everything spoke of the daughter she had lost. But she eventually resigned herself to staying at St John's: Hasted recollects in the Anecdotes that she had got into the habit of spending up to two months of the year there, usually in the summer, before the family moved to Canterbury. Perhaps it was the presence of the children which finally made her cross the long-despised threshold of her daughter-in-law's house.

That the grandchildren had great appeal for her is shown by the fact that around 1765 she took Edward and Francis to live with her in London, where she was to care for them for the next two years, sending them to a day school in Charles Street, Westminster.[241] Such a move would by itself have increased Hasted's commerce with the capital, but two years before that he had forged some additional links of his own with London's intellectual life.

For in 1763 he had set in motion the procedures necessary for election as a Fellow of the Society of Antiquaries. This required the obtention of a suitable number of testimonials from those who were already Fellows, which would be kept on display for several weeks and then read out to all before a ballot took place. The Society was now a little over half a century old. Founded in 1707, it had obtained its Royal Charter in 1751. Prior to this we have noted Smart Lethieullier's objection to it as a 'tavern meeting', and it was not until 1753 that it had obtained its own premises in a house in Chancery Lane, when it gave up its old meeting place at the Mitre in Fleet Street. However, the Society's increased gravitas did not prevent it from celebrating its anniversary on St George's day every year with a dinner at its old haunt.

The Society was in recess from July and did not reconvene until November. Hasted's name was first brought before the Society at the opening meeting which took place on Thursday 10 November 1763. It was a well-attended meeting, with twenty-two members present. The minutes note:

> Testimonials were presented and read, recommending Edward Hasted of Sutton at Hone, in the County of Kent Esqr who is now writing the History of that County, and is well versed in English Antiquities, to be elected a Member of this Society; of which Honour he is desirous, and is certified to be a Person every way qualified to make a useful Member.
>
> Signed by J. Ayloffe, A. C. Ducarel, T. Astle, T. Birch, E. M. Da Costa, T. Tyndall, M. C. Tutet, C. Lowth.[242]

It is likely, therefore, that Hasted had canvassed his sponsors earlier in the year, making a call on each in turn, perhaps in the company of one to whom he was already well known. This would probably have been either the jovial Sir Joseph Ayloffe, or Dr Ducarel — very busy, as usual, but kindly willing to spare a little time for his protégé. It is less likely to have been 'Mr' Thomas Astle (noted thus when he became a member, where the more usual title was esquire, at the very least), since Astle's membership dated only from April of that year. Andrew Coltee Ducarel, on the other hand, had been a member since 1737, while Sir Joseph's membership dated back to 1731.

Ducarel had been born in 1713 in Caen, Normandy, to French parents who came to England and settled at Greenwich while their family was still young. Andrew was sent to school at Eton, where the roughness for which it was notorious resulted in his losing an eye at the age of fourteen. In spite of this he developed into a stout, athletic man, able to work hard and play hard, whose life was a resounding academic success. A Doctor of Common Law, he became in 1743 a member of Doctors' Commons, the association or college of ecclesiastical lawyers, serving in due course both as librarian and as treasurer. In 1757 he was appointed Keeper of the Library at Lambeth Palace and, in 1758, Commissary of the City and Diocese of Canterbury. Praised for the detail and accuracy of his indexes and catalogues and for his attention to the duties of Doctors' Commons, he was also well known as a keen antiquarian. Biographers of the eighteenth century enjoyed recounting his summer forays into the countryside when he would go exploring with a friend, travelling incognito and armed with Camden's *Britannia* and a set of maps. He lived to be the oldest officer in the Palace of Lambeth, and seems to have been quite a bon viveur, an excellent host and often heard to say that as an old Oxonian, 'he never knew a man till he had drunk a bottle of wine with him'.[243] Hasted's path might have done no more than simply cross that of Ducarel on some occasion soon forgotten: that they visited and corresponded, although inhabiting very different worlds, shows that there was considerable warmth and feeling on both sides. Praise for Andrew Coltee Ducarel's achievements is sometimes tempered by criticism of a certain meanness and snobbishness: kindness, however, seems to have been all that Hasted, a regular visitor at Doctors' Commons when he managed a trip to town, ever received from him.

Sir Joseph Ayloffe, another elderly friend, born in 1709, had succeeded to the family's baronetcy in 1730. He was now the last of his line, for his only son had died of smallpox at Cambridge in 1756.[244] The grief which this must have caused him had been laid aside by the time Hasted became acquainted with him, and from the mentions which we have of him he seems to have divided his time between antiquities and good living. Writing to Thomas Astle in March 1764, in an attempt to persuade him to come to the assize ball in Kent, Hasted was to add:

> I don't question if you were to give Sir Joseph two or three items of our Kentish lasses, if he would not leave even the charms of the British Museum for those of a beautiful lass of seventeen.[245]

And the herald John Charles Brooke, writing to his antiquarian friend Richard Gough in 1777, noted that,

> Sir Joseph Ayloffe is still jollifying at Brander's at Christchurch. He writes to Mr Topham most florid accounts of their Elysian manner of living; and I can believe it true.[246]

Ayloffe's own antiquarian pursuits did not, finally, bear very much fruit. Like Hasted, he was interested in county history and in 1764 published a lengthy prospectus for a 'Topographical and Historical Description of Suffolk', for which he had been collecting materials for some fifteen years, but the project came to nothing. Nevertheless, his enthusiasm gave encouragement to others. When in 1769 Hasted's friend John Thorpe published his father's collection of the records of Rochester under the title of *Registrum Roffense* it was to be dedicated to Ayloffe, 'one of the Vice-Presidents of the Society of Antiquaries ... in token of friendship and esteem'.

Of Hasted's other sponsors, most belonged to the same generation. Dr Thomas Birch DD, one of the original trustees and benefactors of the recently founded British Museum and a noted historian and biographer, while considered rather dull as a writer, had the reputation of being a lively talker, with the distinction of being labelled by Samuel Johnson 'as brisk as a bee in conversation'.[247] Mark Cephas Tutet was an eminent London merchant in Pudding Lane, and linked, most probably, to the family which gave its name to Cephas Street and Cephas Avenue in Stepney. He was described by John Nichols as uniting 'to the integrity and skill of a man of business the accomplishments of a polite scholar and an intelligent antiquary', and also as possessing 'the rare secret of collecting only what was truly valuable', although no indication is given of the area in which he specialised. Both he and Dr Thomas Tyndall were close friends of Ducarel, Tutet being named in Ducarel's will as one of his executors.[248]

Emanuel Mendez da Costa came of a family of wealthy London merchants who were of Portuguese extraction. It seems possible that Hasted may have known him from the Smart Lethieullier days, since da Costa corresponded for many years with Lethieullier, and as an ardent conchologist and fossil collector must frequently have gone down to see the fossils which Smart Lethieullier housed in the small private museum known as The Hermitage which stood in his grounds. A somewhat mercurial character, da Costa performed a number of services for the Society of Antiquaries, but had the ignominy of being expelled from it for fraud in 1768, and also spent some time in the King's Bench prison for debt. Before that, however, in 1766, Hasted was to have a brief correspondence with him when da Costa expressed a desire to see a Hebrew inscription said to exist at Canterbury, and Hasted offered his services to help him do so.[249]

The last name in Hasted's list of sponsors, that of Charles Lowth, belongs to a family which he seems to have known very well over a number of years. There are several letters in the correspondence relating to the *History* from the Revd William Lowth, vicar of Lewisham and also of St Margaret's Rochester, and the warm greetings at the end of these, including the writer's compliments to Mrs Hasted, show that the two men were on visiting terms.

Hasted's name came up for election to the Society at the meeting of the 15 December 1763, when the minutes record that,

> The recommendatory testimonials of Edward Hasted and Ralph Willett Esqrs having hung up the usual time, were read, and their

Elections ballotted for, and they were thereupon severally declared from the Chair duly elected Fellows of this Society.[250]

Hasted, who was now at Throwley, was of course not present on this occasion, but if he had had any intention of making an early appearance at his Society he was given little encouragement to do so by a sudden storm which threatened at the very meeting at which he was elected. It centred on the excavation which he had recently helped Bryan Faussett to carry out and which he had described to Astle in lively detail in a letter. At the previous week's meeting, on the 8 December, Astle had taken it on himself to communicate the contents of this letter to the Society — tidying it up slightly in the performance, and bundling out of the way both Robinson Crusoe and Man Friday, as well as Bryan Faussett's 'hollow trowel and tools' and all mention of any manual labour performed by the two friends.[251]

It so happened that Faussett himself, a recently elected member of the Society, was present on the 15 December and was astounded to learn from the Secretary, reading out the minutes, of the premature publication of the details of 'his' excavation. He was soon on his feet, to 'desire the President to pay no further regard to it' — entered more staidly in the Society's minutes as, 'There were some things to add to, as well as correct in, the account given by Mr Hastead (sic) of the Roman camp, tumulus, etc. communicated to the Society at their last meeting'. And Faussett promised the Society that he would 'favour the Society with a more exact particular thereof; for which thanks were returned to him'.[252]

No blame can be laid at Hasted's door for this, since not only had he not intended his account to be accurate in every detail, but he could not have dreamt that Astle would make his letter public. This was fully recognised by Bryan Faussett, whose subsequent kindly letter to his young assistant at the excavation was by no means the sharp rebuff one might have supposed from Hasted's heated reaction a few days later in a letter to Astle.[253] The newly elected antiquary seems to have felt that his accuracy, both as an archaeologist and as a person, was impugned:

> There is no doubt, but had I thought that letter would have been read at the Society I should have put it in a better dress, but as I think Mr Faussett's behaviour has attacked the truth of it, it is incumbent on me to assert the truth of the facts there mentioned, and to declare there they are literally and minutely true. As to the conjectures they are but conjectures, but are such as he or myself then made, and both acquiesced in at that time. I may perhaps have mistaken his words, but as you were present [i.e. at the

meeting] I hope you will let me know your thoughts of it, and if there is occasion, that you will vindicate it at your meeting ... for I would sooner forgive any man's accusing me of almost anything whatsoever rather than of an untruth.[254]

Astle assured Hasted that he would immediately inform the Society that he knew him to be 'incapable of asserting an untruth'.[255] But the Society's minutes are a model of decorum, and the antiquaries did not perhaps relish arguments being pursued in public. There is no further note of the matter nor any amended account of the excavation, and the members' attention soon passed to other things. But the small incident must have cast something of a shadow over Hasted's entry into the Society, which he had no doubt been looking forward to with considerable pleasure. The rupture with his old friend at Heppington seems to have been no more than momentary — indeed, the same letter in which Faussett recounts his dismay at hearing about the premature publication of details of the dig contains a pressing invitation to Hasted to come over to Heppington again, accompanied once more by his wife ('And I have a far better opinion of Mrs Hasted's goodness, than to think she will stand so much upon form, as not to accompany you') and by the end of April Astle was to receive details of yet another excavation in which Hasted had taken part, presumably again carried out with Faussett.[256] Nevertheless, Hasted did not put in an appearance at any of the Society's meetings that season. At Throwley, of course, he was too far away to think of making frequent trips to London, but it is possible that without this unfortunate incident he might have taken his place among the Fellows somewhat earlier than he actually did, in November 1764.

In his Anecdotes Hasted suggests 1763 as the year when he spent nearly two months in London, making use of the various 'public offices of record and other places for obtaining collections for my History of Kent'.[257] However, this is qualified by his own 'about the year 1763', as well as by the general title of the Anecdotes, which were, Hasted warns us, 'drawn up to the best of my recollection & to the best of my remembrance'. In fact, it seems more likely that this extended stay in London took place either in 1764 or 1765. George had been born in the late August of 1763, and Hasted specifically mentions that his wife accompanied him. She would have needed at least a month to recover from her confinement, during which time, of course, there was George's baptism to be arranged, with visits from Uncle Gabriel and Edward Wilks for the purpose of standing sponsor to the baby. Immediately following this Hasted must have thrown himself into organising the family's departure for Throwley, which took place some time in October — no doubt after such small postponements as frequently happen, to the vexation of the impatient traveller.

The June and July of 1763 seem relatively blank in the Hasted calendar, but Hasted would hardly have made enough progress with his *History* at this time to know the areas in which research in the London repositories could help him. 1764 seems altogether a better candidate for Hasted's stay of 'near two months' in London. On returning from Throwley he had settled down to a mixed routine of administrative duties and a continuation of the copying which had been begun at Throwley. From dated work in his MSS we know that he was copying a Hulse pedigree between 20 and 22 June, and another, lent him by Edward Jacob of Faversham, from 30 June to 1 July. Relieved by the safe passage of his wife through the ordeal of Charles's birth at the end of that month, he felt free to go out and pursue his researches beyond the house: some 'Observations' on Sutton church (and elsewhere) were dated September 1764 by him in one of his folio commonplace books. The long visit to London could well have taken place from the end of September through to the beginning of November: we know that he was in London on 8 November, as this was when he attended his first meeting as a Fellow of the Society of Antiquaries.

Further proof of a visit to London of some duration at this time seems to lie in the fact that there are no letters to Thomas Astle between 31 July 1764 and 6 March 1765, and that when the correspondence is resumed on the latter date the two men are clearly on a closer footing: instead of using the formal 'Dear Sir' at the head of his letter, Hasted now opens with 'Dear Astle'.[258] For this transition to have taken place the intervening months must have seen a closer intercourse between them. We know from one of Hasted's letters to Dr Ducarel that the elusive Astle actually paid Hasted a visit at Sutton towards the end of 1764, and again, for this to occur, it seems reasonable to deduce that they had recently developed a habit of doing things together.[259] There is no evidence that such a visit on Astle's part was ever repeated.

It is also possible that there was a long visit to London in the summer of 1765. In a letter to Dr Ducarel written in February 1765 Hasted hopes for 'the pleasure of spending six weeks or two months in London this summer', and such a visit could have taken place in May and June.[260] Ann Hasted was again pregnant, as she was to be virtually every year now until 1770,[261] but her baby was not due until the middle of August, and we know that Hasted, somewhat unusually, attended two meetings of the Society of Antiquaries in June of that year, on the 6th and the 20th.

In 1764 his only visit to the Society had been at the opening meeting of the season on the 8 November, and distance naturally prevented his ever putting in a regular appearance at the weekly meetings, which took place on Thursdays from November to June, although with breaks for Christmas, Easter and Whitsun. Nor was he, over this period, ever present at the April election of officers, which was followed by a dinner at the Mitre — a tavern which frequently hosted also, around this time, Samuel Johnson and James Boswell. But he was able to go to five meetings in 1765, and another five in 1766. 1767 saw him there only once, although he attended four meetings in the first half of 1768, before the move to Canterbury. From 1769 the names of those present are no longer given in the minutes, but we can probably assume that it was now only very rarely that Mr Hasted was found in attendance.[262]

He was by no means always a passive participant. In November 1765 it was noted in the minutes that,

> Mr Hasted being engaged in writing the History and Antiquities of Kent, borrowed, with leave of the Society, a MSS book in folio, containing, among other things, Inquisitiones post Mortem, capt. Temp Regis E. Filii Regis H. for that county

— a volume which Hasted duly returned the following January.[263] And at the meeting of 12 May 1768 he himself made a small contribution to the items on the agenda when he 'exhibited an old vellum MSS almanack, illuminated with a variety of figures of saints and other matters ... supposed ... to have been written about the year 1554'.[264]

There can be little doubt that Hasted's circle of acquaintances included far more people than those names we are accustomed to associate with him. He had a talent for friendship, stemming from a lively and seemingly open and hospitable disposition. Thus we find him at the Society of Antiquaries in April 1768 among those introducing guests, the gentleman entered against Hasted's name being none other than Joseph Banks's future colleague, the natural philosopher Dr Daniel Carl Solander, who was then employed at the British Museum.[265] And Solander was indeed to be a subscriber to Hasted's *History of Kent*.

In January 1766, at the meeting at which Joseph Banks of Revesby was himself proposed for membership, we find Hasted's name among those sponsoring the testimonial of 'Mr George Perry, of Aldgate, a gentleman well versed in English antiquities'. His co-sponsors were Sir Joseph Ayloffe, Dr Ducarel, Thomas Astle, M. C. Tutet, T. Tyndall, M. Duane and J. Letch. Matthew Duane, another of the older generation of antiquaries, was a lawyer by profession, and a keen antiquary, with a special interest in numismatics, in which Hasted also seems to have had some interest, although knowing himself to be without the funds to start a collection.[266] Duane, who collected particularly Syriac and Macedonian coins, and who became a trustee of the British Museum in 1766, makes an appearance in the same year as one of Hasted's own sponsors for election as a Fellow of the Royal Society, when on the 6 February two recommendations for election were received by that august body.

One of these was for 'Mr Dionysius Williams of Senear near the Lands End Cornwall a Gentleman who has devoted much of his time to the Study of Mathematicks and natural philosophy'. The other referred to:

> Edward Hasted of Sutton at Hone in the County of Kent Esquire, Fellow of the Society of Antiquaries of London, a gentleman well versed in natural history and other branches of literature, being very desirous of the honour of election into the Royal Society.

And he was recommended as 'a gentleman highly deserving that honour and likely to prove a valuable and useful member'.[267]

The Fellows putting their signatures to this were Sir Joseph Ayloffe, Andrew Coltee Ducarel, Thomas Tyndall, James Parsons, Matthew Duane and Henry Baker — Parsons, like Ducarel, a member of Doctors' Commons, and Baker being something of a polymath and probably a very lively personality. He had developed a system for teaching deaf-mutes, wrote and translated verse, and shared with Daniel Defoe — whose youngest daughter he had married — the writing of a weekly journal, the *Universal Spectator*. He published work on the use of the microscope and on experiments carried out with it on the crystallisation of saline particles, thereby acquiring the affectionate nickname of 'Microscope Baker'.[268]

The Journal Book of the Royal Society records that Mr Williams's and Mr Hasted's certificates 'were ordered to be fixed up in the Common Meeting Room', where they would be displayed for the next ten meetings — the usual procedure for anyone desirous of becoming a Fellow. And in due course the minutes were to note that on the 8 May,

> Mr Williams and Mr Hasted, formerly proposed according to the Statute, were elected into the Society; and Mr Hasted also having paid his admission fee and given the usual bond for contributions, signed the Obligation in the Charter Book and was admitted Fellow.[269]

It was more common to complete the formalities on a future occasion, but Hasted's visits could only be infrequent, and he probably requested special permission to pay his admission fee of twenty-five guineas while he happened to be in London.

Among the signatures immediately preceding that of Hasted in the Charter Book is that of Thomas Astle, and among subsequent ones are those of Joseph Banks, Thomas Pennant and the Hon. Daines Barrington. Banks had in fact been recommended for election just a week before Hasted's name came up. His certificate of election signed, among others, by the Bishop of Carlisle (Hasted's friend, the former Dr Charles Lyttelton), recommended him as 'versed in natural history, especially botany and other branches of literature and likely (if chosen) to prove a valuable member' — a not dissimilar recommendation from that of Hasted himself. There can be no doubt, however, that Joseph Banks's knowledge of natural history far exceeded that of Edward Hasted even at this early date. By the time his election came on, on 1 May 1766, Banks was at sea on the *Niger*, having set sail on the 22 April for Newfoundland and Labrador where he was to botanise to much purpose. He would not return until the following January, and he did not appear at the Royal Society, to be admitted a Fellow, until 12 February 1767. Eleven years later, at the age of 35, he was to follow Sir John Pringle, a distinguished medical man, as the Society's President.[270]

In the Preface to the first volume of his folio edition Hasted was to admit that he was 'but little acquainted with the study of botany', but he seems, as a landowner with many acres given over to timber, to have been knowledgeable about trees. They figure largely in the lease of 1754 of Great and Little Huntingfield Farms, with special stipulations protecting both timber and fruit trees, and it was in connection with trees that Hasted's name was to appear once, in 1771, in the printed *Philosophical Transactions* of the Royal Society. In a paper which had appeared in the *Transactions* two years earlier the versatile Daines Barrington, a keen naturalist as well as lawyer and antiquary, had stated his belief that the chestnut was not an indigenous tree.[271] This had obviously aroused lively discussion in Kent between the three friends, Ducarel, Hasted, and John Thorpe, of Bexley, who felt that there was enough evidence from the past to provide a vigorous counter-argument. Accordingly, Ducarel sent the Society a detailed and learned reply to Barrington, and appended to his contribution letters from Hasted and Thorpe — Hasted's being actually written from Huntingfield. Hasted joined with Ducarel in putting forward much archaeological and written evidence from the past, although he also, like Thorpe, was concerned to show the frequency with which such trees were found in this country, particularly in Kent.[272]

In the event Daines Barrington, who had evidently been given sight of the letters before they were read out to the Society on the 8 March 1771 so that he could respond, remained unconvinced. It appears that the tree in question was the sweet chestnut, although it has to be admitted that one cannot be sure the argument does not stray to the horse chestnut as well.

Hasted must have known that he would have little to set beside the learned disquisitions and contributions on astronomy, physics, mathematics, chemistry and medicine which dominated the Royal Society's transactions. One of the reasons which persuaded him to allow his name to be put forward may have been that membership would give him access to yet another library. The Society of Antiquaries provided a more natural ambience for him, and he probably felt more at home there than at the Royal Society, where his predecessor at St John's, Abraham Hill, in spite of the small fire which Hasted was to kindle before his shrine, provided only a very faint glow for him to bask in. It is impossible to tell from the records how often Hasted attended, but the lack of references to the Royal Society in any of the surviving correspondence must lead one to conclude that he was only rarely to be seen at its meetings.

There is only one letter in the Hasted-Astle correspondence for 1766. Domestic changes had in the meanwhile occurred in the lives of both men. Astle, in December 1765, had married the daughter of the Revd Philip Morant, the Essex antiquarian, and was now employed at the Treasury; Hasted's family, increasing yearly, now numbered six, four boys and two girls, and his two eldest sons, the one nearly six years old, the other soon to be five, had gone to live with their grandmother in London. It sounds, from Hasted's letter of the 1 September 1766, as if he had been up to town briefly ('I was but a few hours in town') for the purpose of collecting his sons for a short stay in Sutton, so that they could see the new baby sister, Katherine, who had been born on the 15 August. Astle, Hasted learns with dismay, has recently been ill, and Hasted makes a charming offer of his chariot to bear him away for a week's rest at Sutton-at-Hone:

> Was I your physician I should advise you change of air at some small distance, an easy journey, and should prescribe a week at least at Sutton. My chariot will be in town on Wednesday evening next, and return home on Thursday; you would make us both happy if Mrs Astle and yourself would fill it hither, it should be at

your command at any hour by leaving a line at my mother's before that time.²⁷³

It is in this letter that Hasted asks whether Mrs Astle will consent to be godmother to the new baby, and from the friendly greeting at the foot of the letter it is clear that both wives have had an opportunity to become acquainted — it is quite possible that the Hasteds had been among the guests at the Astle wedding the previous December.

The business of the letter, however, concerns a publication on which Hasted and Astle were then jointly engaged. This was to contain a collection of letters received from various correspondents by Abraham Hill, the former owner of Hasted's house of St John's. Hill had been a scholar of some repute in his day, and Hasted had already given him some attention, putting together what he called 'An Attempt towards the Life of Abraham Hill Esq., FRS etc'.²⁷⁴ Hill's connection with the Royal Society was in fact of prime importance, for he had been a founder-member of the Society in 1660, subsequently serving it for many years as treasurer, as secretary and, in 1698, in company with Sir Christopher Wren and John Evelyn, as one of its vice-presidents.²⁷⁵

Left to himself, as has been suggested, Hasted would probably have hesitated to apply for membership of the Royal Society, whose 'Obligations', signed in the Charter Book, bound new members to promote and improve 'Natural Knowledge', and with whose largely scientific and medical luminaries he had very little in common. He knew himself to be an antiquary, and although he tended to be modest about his own attainments, he could hold his own in discussion with other members of the Society of Antiquaries on most aspects of English history. He does not seem to have been in the mould of a large number of gentlemen at this time, for whom FSA dangled like a ribbon without a medal if it was not followed up by FRS.²⁷⁶ It was otherwise for someone like Thomas Astle, whose career was proving the means of a meteoric rise through the ranks of London's intellectual society, and it was probably Astle who suggested to Hasted that he too should apply for membership of the Royal Society at the same time as they collaborated in bringing out a collection of the letters of that founder which had so fortuitously come into Hasted's hands. Such a book could be promoted as a humble late centenary offering by the two new members.

Astle's role in the publication seems to have amounted to little more than acting as a liaison — and not, it would appear, a very successful one — with the publishers, while Hasted anxiously pored over Abraham Hill's letters, endeavouring to choose those which might seem the most interesting without being in any way political, and worked on the

Introduction, basing this, there is no doubt, on the notes he had already made for a life of Abraham Hill. Preparations were well in hand by the middle of 1766 since it appears from Hasted's letter of the 1 September that part of the book was already in proof stage:

> I corrected the sheet you sent me and told the printer to send the others to me, but I have not heard from him since; by what you sent me I think there remains much of the letters unprinted. There is a paragraph in the first 10 lines of the Life, which I must alter before it is printed off, if I can do it in the proof sheet.[277]

However, there was obviously some trouble with the publisher. From Hasted's next letter, written more than six months later, it is clear that publication of the Hill letters had stalled. Astle would seem to have made the mistake of offering the small volume to one of the most prestigious publishing firms of the time, founded by Robert Dodsley earlier in the century and now continued by his younger brother James; and what had perhaps been a somewhat high-handed letter from Astle had resulted in a sharp reply from Dodsley. Astle seems now to be in need of practical advice as to how to proceed, which Hasted crisply gives him, after first offering sympathy for the snub he has received. But Hasted's letter, dated 16 March 1767, also makes it clear that Astle's share in the publication was limited to action at the London end:

> I received the favor of yours on Sunday, with a very impertinent letter to you from Dodsley on the back of it. I have no great opinion of the merit of the Letters myself, and yet I think I have seen more insignificant than these published, trifling as they are. He must be a most impudent puppy to offer to write such a one to you, a stranger to him. I am very sorry you have had so much trouble in managing of it ... The least trouble I think would be to let Griffin have it, clearing himself every expense, and if any profit should accrue from it, he should have the half of it; if he thinks that too much, then let him take the whole. In either case, that we should have 6 or 7 copies apiece half bound gratis, and that the title shall be approved by us before it is printed, and neither of our names mentioned in or about it, as editors or otherwise. And if you will be so obliging to see this done, the sooner we get rid of it the better — for the time for the sale of such things wears off apace.

And Hasted wisely urges Astle in a postscript: 'Whatever you agree with Griffin make him sign his name to it'.[278]

The new publisher with whom it was now proposed to deal would appear to have been the W. Griffin of Garrick's Head in Catherine Street who in November 1768 was advertising 'No. 1, price 6d., of a new pamphlet, to appear every Saturday, The Gentleman's Journal' — which was clearly intended to compete with the well-established and very successful *Gentleman's Magazine*. Among Hasted's MSS is a numbered list of seventy-one letters, with the address underneath, 'Mr Griffin Printer, Catherine Street, Strand, London'.[279] This consists almost entirely of the letters which he proposed to include, but given a slightly different order. At this stage it seems to have been planned to begin the book with ten letters from John Newman and Alexander Travel, although Hasted, perhaps worried about their political sensitivity, was later to omit those from Travel and to place Newman's contribution more discreetly towards the end. But it may well be that Griffin was too busy with preparations for his *Journal* to take on the Hill book, for in the end *Familiar Letters* — its full title *Familiar Letters which passed between Abraham Hill Esq., Fellow and Treasurer of the Royal Society, one of the Lords of Trade, and Comptroller to his Grace the Archbishop of Canterbury; and several eminent and ingenious persons of the last century* — was to be published by W. Johnston, of Ludgate Street, one of the publishers, with Strahan and Dodsley, of Samuel Johnson's *Rasselas*.

The book bears date 1767, but given the delays it was encountering in the middle of that year it probably did not appear until some time in 1768, when, on the 29 July, a copy was presented by Thomas Astle to the British Museum. The centenary of the Royal Society was long past; the book's appearance can have caused hardly a ripple. It was not thought to merit a mention in the *Gentleman's Magazine*.

There can be no doubt at all that any literary or editorial work which *Familiar Letters* required was done by Hasted, and he certainly wrote the Preface. Only he could have had the intimate knowledge both of Sutton-at-Hone, where Abraham Hill, one of the sons of that Richard Hill who had served the Commonwealth, spent his last years, and of the company Hill knew there — most notably the Revd Edmund Barrell, vicar of the parish since 1705 and prebendary of Rochester Cathedral, whose long life had made him a contemporary of Hasted also. The Preface begins with a brief description of the discovery of the letters — 'The following letters were found among many other curious manuscripts, which some years ago fell into the hands of the editor', — and the purpose of the publication is declared to be twofold: to entertain the public, and to show the editor's 'reverence and esteem for the memory of Mr Hill, whose public and private virtues were such as deserve the remembrance ... of posterity'.[280]

The letters themselves, of which there purport to be seventy (although one, No. 63, is missing), all date from between 1652 and 1699, and for the most part avoid any reference to things political. Some, such as those of John Toft and Captain Nicholas Lucas, were written at sea, and recount movements of the fleet or battles. Two are from the MP John Pollexfen, Hill's colleague at the Board of Trade. And there are a number of communications from other distinguished Fellows of the Royal Society, such as Isaac Barrow, of whom Hill himself wrote a brief biography, Dr William Aglionby, John Brooke, Edmond Halley, Peter Pett and Sir Joseph Williamson. A foreign scholar, Nicholas Witte, corresponds (by no means perfectly) in both French and Latin — and in his Preface Hasted mentions that Abraham Hill himself knew Latin, Greek, French, Dutch and Italian. Most of the letters had been received by Hill, although the book also contains one or two which were written by him.

The arrangement is a loose one, letters being grouped by writer, and then for the most part chronologically within that group. It is noteworthy that although the correspondence covers a period of considerable political agitation in England, they pointedly avoid any English topic which might seem to be of a controversial nature. Letter No. 63, which is missing alike from the list of Contents and from the sequence of epistles, belonged among several sent to Hill by a merchant friend, John Newman. Letters Nos. 62 and 64, from the same correspondent, sent respectively from Pera of Constantinople and Paris, are dated 1 April and 19 August 1659, and it seems a reasonable guess that No. 63 was written between those dates, and that it was removed by Hasted at a late stage in the book's production because he feared that it might be considered politically suspect. The closest we are allowed to come to political comment is in Newman's letter of 19 August, when he adds cautiously: 'It is here said, there has been much shuffling and cutting in England, and we do not understand what or who is turned up trump'.[281]

In fact, however, Hasted had grasped the nettle in the Preface, when he summarised what he saw as Abraham Hill's views on the matter by saying:

> His principles in regard to politics were imbibed from his father, and from the powers then in being, both the very reverse of those which prevailed on the restoration of King Charles the Second; yet he had seen the bad effects of the former, and the confusion and destruction they had brought on this country; and therefore, though he had much of the republican system rooted in him, yet

he was convinced that a monarchical government was the only state that could bring happiness to this kingdom, so long as the prerogative was curbed and restrained within the severest bounds; and the liberties of the subject kept sacred and inviolate.[282]

A letter to Abraham from his brother Thomas, who, like their father, had become a merchant and an alderman of the City of London, shows the extent to which an English merchant of those days was very much a Renaissance man, hungry for the arts of which a puritanical state had long deprived him. Writing from Lucca on 1 October 1657 Thomas Hill gave Abraham a detailed account of the music which he had been hearing in Italy:

> Since my arrival in Italy, I have missed few opportunities of hearing what music has been publickly performed, especially in the churches; and I wish I could give you a satisfactory account of it: I would attempt it, could I but say half so well as they can sing. ...What they excel us so much in is the eunuchs, whose voices are very rare and delightful, and not to be compared but with one another; the other voices not so good as we have in England. The instrumental music is much better than I expected. The organ and violin they are masters of, but the bass viol they have not at all in use; and to supply its place they have the bass violin with four strings, and use it as we do the bass viol. In short, it would be worth any one's while, who is fond of music, to travel to Italy; he would find such sweet recompence for his trouble in it. Next month we have a concert of music at the chusing a new prince of forty voices with several instruments. I am using my endeavours to collect music for a single, or two or three voices, in which I have had good success.[283]

This letter has a particular interest, since it was written by the Thomas Hill whose friendship Samuel Pepys was later to covet as someone who 'hath travelled and I perceive is a master in most sorts of musique'. And Hill, described by Pepys in 1664 as 'a pretty gentile, young and sober man', did indeed become a close friend of the Secretary of the Navy, sharing musical evenings with him for many years.[284]

But it was to be over fifty years before any of Pepys's diaries were published. Most of the correspondents now brought before the public, including Abraham Hill himself, were names barely remembered, and *Familiar Letters* made little impact. As Hasted had wished, no editor was acknowledged, and the little book would probably have sunk without trace if Thomas Astle had not presented a copy to the British Museum. There, due no doubt to the appearance of his name on the flyleaf as donor, it has been catalogued for many years as edited by him. As has been shown, however, he seems to have done little more than liaise, not very successfully, with publishers in London, and the person who should now be acknowledged as editor is Edward Hasted himself.

The book had indeed taken an inordinately long time to appear. There is only one more letter in the Hasted-Astle correspondence, written some five weeks after that of 16 March 1767, before a gap of almost seven years is closed by a letter from Hasted dated January 1774, a letter in which both style and content indicate that a coolness had existed for some time between the former friends. It seems not unreasonable to guess that Astle's lack of any real help in getting *Familiar Letters* into print, and possibly also too great a readiness on his part to take credit for the book when it finally saw the light of day, may have contributed to this.

Chapter 8

A Tradition of Service

Before he was twenty-one, and long before his literary inclinations became apparent to himself or to anyone else, Hasted was being claimed for public duties as a member of the county's landowning class. In the summer of 1753, six months before he would come of age, he was named as a trustee of the New Cross turnpike road in place of Richard Manning, a former magistrate from Farningham who had recently died. There was nothing unusual in this: sons were frequently co-opted by fathers as tyro trustees at this age, and Hasted's father, had he lived, would by now have been introducing his son to the intricacies of turnpike road trusteeship. Among sons following fathers in this trust in the mid-eighteenth century we find Peter Burrell, Edmund Stevens, David Papillon, John Savary and Jacob Hagen, all marked 'junior', to distinguish them from fathers of the same name who were still active on the trust, while among Hasted's particular friends Edmund Faunce (later to become vicar of Sutton-at-Hone) attended occasionally with his father Thomas Faunce. Such family links, piecemeal as they were, helped to ensure the continuity of these very loosely constituted bodies. As was customary, although already named as a trustee, Hasted did not put in an appearance until after he had turned twenty-one, at a meeting of March 1754.[285]

The New Cross trust, which was to become the largest turnpike trust in Kent, responsible for the first section, of varying length, of all four principal roads into Kent from London, had come into being in 1718. Kent had had a turnpike road as early as 1709, when the Sevenoaks, Woodsgate and Tunbridge Wells road had been converted to one, but things had moved slowly for a while. However, enthusiasm for turnpiking the country's principal roads — which meant in effect removing them from the control of the parishes through which they ran and using money obtained from tolls for their rapid improvement — was at its height in the 1750s and 1760s, which saw the greatest number of turnpike trusts being set up in the country as a whole.

Trust meetings were, accordingly, very well attended at this time. Hasted was one of twenty-five gentlemen present on 16 March 1754, and on 29 June of the same year one of thirty-six. His next meeting, that of 28 June 1755, was similarly well attended. But he himself was never to be as assiduous an attender as his father had been. In view of the extent of road covered — some forty miles — the New Cross turnpike trust formed itself into a number of committees, including the Deptford, the Stones End, and the Lewisham committees, and it is very likely that Hasted was co-opted on to the Dartford committee, where Thomas Faunce, his Sutton-at-Hone neighbour, was active. The minutes of the committees do not appear to have survived, so it is possible that Hasted may have put in some work of which we know nothing. His move to Canterbury in July 1755, immediately after his marriage, constituted a natural break in his relations with the trust, and on his return in 1757 he seems to have had little inclination to resume the duties of a turnpike trustee. If it was suggested to him by his friends the Faunces and others that he should continue his trustee work, he resisted their suggestions until April 1759, when we find him present at a single meeting.[286]

It may well be that by the late 1750s the first flush of enthusiasm for turnpike road-making was over, particularly as concerned the long established New Cross trust, and that it was no longer so fashionable to be a trustee. By then, too, the trust had achieved many of its aims, and the matter of road improvements, in that area at least, had lost much of its urgency. After 1759 there is a long gap before we again find Hasted present at one of the trust's meetings, and in the meantime many general meetings had no more than one or two trustees present. On 25 January 1766, however, we find him attending a meeting in company with a number of other gentlemen from his neighbourhood, including Sir John Dixon Dyke, Francis Leigh, John Tasker, Thomas Faunce, James Chapman and John Calcraft, as well as over twenty others. So large a contingent from the Sutton-at-Hone/Dartford/ Swanscombe area makes one suspect that local interests were at stake, although there is nothing to this effect in the minutes — which do, however, reveal the embers of national controversy with the mention of a public house or inn near Greenwich called the Crown and Boot.[287]

With this meeting Hasted's work as a trustee of the New Cross road came to an end. It seems clear that he initially nursed a project to be a worthy successor to his father in this field: we can see from the Anecdotes how much he admired his father's public service, and he was probably flattered, as a very young man, to be welcomed as a replacement for a former magistrate. But by 1759 he was himself a justice of the peace, and it is likely that, of the two, he preferred to devote his energies to the administration of the law rather than to road maintenance. As has been suggested, the atmosphere at the trust may well have changed with the years: it is possible that it had come to be dominated by the older trustees, and that there was no longer the public enthusiasm (or, as might have been the case, his father) to carry a young man along to the trust's meetings. Hasted was to give more than thirty years of service to voluntary work in the public sector, but from now on this would lie outside the domain of turnpike trusts.

Nevertheless, in 1760 he appears to have allowed his name to go forward as a trustee of the Chalk turnpike road. The Chalk road was a continuation of the New Cross turnpike road, leading from Dartford to Northfleet and Gravesend, and on into Chalk and Strood. The first two meetings of 1761, on the 17 April and 1 May, held at the George inn in the parish of Chalk, saw Hasted among the trustees present. But these would seem to be the only meetings of the trust which he ever attended. Subsequent meetings were held at the Crown in Rochester, and we look in vain for a mention of Hasted among those present. He can hardly have felt a disinclination to follow the trust to Rochester: it was a place he knew well, and there were other matters to which he devoted himself which required his presence in the city. But he had probably come to feel that turnpike trust work was not his métier. Among the signatures at the bottom of the minutes for the meeting of 1 May that of Edward Hasted is unusually prominent. Perhaps he felt that he was signing off.[288]

Six years later, however, his name was to appear among those of the trustees of the new Dartford-Sevenoaks road, which had just obtained its turnpike Act.[289] This road ran right past St John's, in Sutton-at-Hone, and for the purpose of straightening its course there may even have been proposals to cut across some of Hasted's land. It was always in the best interest of gentlemen whose lands abutted on to the line of a turnpike road to take part in the trust's deliberations. The minutes of this trust, where Thomas Williams was one of the joint treasurers, do not appear to have survived, and we cannot know the extent to which Hasted was an active participant in its meetings. He certainly kept a lively eye on its doings, for in May 1767 he gave Dr Ducarel an account of some finds which had been made by the men working on the new road:

> In the making of our new turnpike road between Dartford and the town of Sevenoke, they have been widening of it for the most part of the way; and in digging down the chalk banks near Eynsford Castle the workmen with their tools disturbed the bones of many skeletons, which, before I could hear of it, they had laid among the chalk rubbish at the bottom of the road, so that before I could get to the place there were not many of them to be met with together.[290]

Although Hasted was present as one of the seven trustees who were busy assigning the tolls on mortgage on the morning of 6 April 1768, he himself did not become a mortgagee: it had probably been borne in on him by then that he would soon be obliged to give up St John's.[291]

His career as one of the thousands of voluntary administrators who at this time carried the burden of English local government had taken off in 1757 with his return to Sutton-at-Hone. 1757 was the year in which he was put on the Commission of the Peace.[292] It was also the year in which it was proposed, at the September meeting, to add his name, along with thirty others, to the new Commission of Sewers for the Limits extending from Gravesend Bridge to Sheerness and thence to Penshurst.[293] It was just twenty years since the same name had first appeared on a Sewers Commission. Accordingly, at the next meeting of the Court of Sewers, held on 14 April 1758, we find Hasted present to take his oath as a commissioner, under the writ of Dedimus Potestatem issued to Sir Roger Twisden and others, which gave them authority to administer and receive the oaths of those named in the commission of February of that year. This was to be a short-lived commission, however. With the death of George II in October 1760 it was assumed to have lapsed, as did the Commission of the Peace on such occasions, and a new one was immediately obtained, to which were added another eleven names, including those of Charles Whitworth and two of Hasted's neighbours, John Tasker and Edmund Faunce.[294]

It is not surprising to find Hasted involved in this work. As a landowner, the major part of whose lands were in the Medway area, he clearly had a vested interest in matters relating to drainage and water levels. He was a relatively frequent attender at the sessions, or courts (as the meetings were sometimes termed), and was to take up the work again in East Kent when he moved to Canterbury. In the meantime, while he lived at Sutton-at-Hone, he was able to make the Sewers Courts the occasion of a pleasant ride to Rochester in the company of his friends, the Faunces. Four Courts were held each year, and we usually find the historian present at the spring meeting, which was the most important one. Here, a review was made of the past year's work on the various Levels which were under the superintendence of the commission. Arrangements would be made to inspect the Levels during the coming weeks, so that the work of the ensuing year could be planned accordingly. At the meeting of April 1758, for example, the following Levels were the subject of discussion: Cliffe, Higham Abbey, High Halstow and St Maries, Stoke and Allhallows, North West Level in Grain, South West Level in Grain, and Chalk and Denton. Hasted, as well as being present on this occasion, also attended the spring meetings of 1759, 1761 and 1762, but after that we do not find him present again (as far as we can tell from his signature after the minutes) until 1765, when he made four attendances. He was also present twice in 1767, and again at the spring meeting of 1768.[295]

Meetings such as those of turnpike trustees or commissioners of sewers combined business with conviviality. As such bodies disposed of no funds of their own, and therefore usually had no business premises, it was customary to take a suitable room at an inn for the purpose, and the dinner which the gentlemen ordered when business was done provided a very pleasant increment to the income of mine host. The favoured hostelry is frequently noted in the minutes. The principal meeting place of the New Cross trust was the Green Man at Blackheath, while the Dartford committee of the trust usually met at the George in Dartford, or at the Catherine Wheel and Star on Shooter's Hill. The Court of Sewers from Gravesend Bridge to Sheerness was held regularly at the Bull inn in Rochester in the 1750s and 1760s, although in 1767 it seems to have moved to the King's Head, which was perhaps offering a better room, or better fare.

Not surprisingly, a number of Hasted's friends were drawn from this background of local meetings, and acquaintances were made here which were to be very useful to him in later years as he scoured the county for information for his *History*. The Revd William Lowth, vicar of Lewisham, a frequent attender at the meetings of the New Cross turnpike trust, was to answer Hasted's queries on several matters in later years, as did John Cator, father and son, of Beckenham Place, trustees of the same road. John Thorpe, of Bexley, the son of the historian of Rochester, whom Hasted may also have come to know at the New Cross trust meetings, was later to be one of the historian's closest friends.

A small but important body on which Hasted was to give some years of service was that of the Wardens and Commonalty of Rochester Bridge, responsible for the upkeep of the great bridge across the Medway. Unlike most of the voluntary bodies on which Hasted served, the bridge wardens, called into being at the time of the building of the stone bridge in the fourteenth century, had their own premises, the Bridge Chamber, or Audit Chamber, over the Crown Inn Yard — John Thorpe's own work on Rochester, *Custumale Roffense*, preserves a small illustration of this. It was used for the wardens' weekly meetings, although the more numerously attended Easter elections, when the commonalty were also present, were held in the larger premises of Rochester castle. Hasted explains in his *History* how the elections were effected under the Act which governed the administration of the bridge:

> For the more convenient assembling of the commonalty at the elections above-mentioned, it was further enacted that two householders at least, from every parish contributory within seven miles of Rochester bridge, in which there were four householders,

should be present at such elections under penalty of ten shillings.[296]

During the 1730s and 1740s the parishes thus summoned were Aylesford, Birling, Chatham, Cliffe, Frindsbury, Gillingham, Halling, Hoo, Meopham, Milton, Northfleet, and Snodland.

Hasted's father had begun a connection with Rochester Bridge, although only as a member of the commonalty, when he had been summoned to attend the election of April 1740.[297] The historian's name does not appear among the commonalty. Instead, we find him elected in 1761 as one of the twelve assistants to the two new wardens, Heneage, Earl of Aylesford, and John Longley. The following year saw his own election as one of the two wardens, and as such 'bound to the present Wardens in a Separate Bond of One thousand Pounds Penalty to execute the Office of Warden for the year ensuing as the Statutes require'. Hasted was to remain among the bridge wardens for another eleven years, serving throughout that time as an assistant warden and, on several occasions (in 1764, 1768, 1769 and 1771) as one of the four auditors. His fellow warden, in 1762, was Robert Wilkins, of St Margaret's, Rochester, the assistants being the Earl of Aylesford, Lord Romney, the Hon. Robert Fairfax, Sir Roger Twisden, John Longley, James Best, Thomas Faunce, Thomas Fletcher, Francis Child, Isaac Wildash, Charles Whitworth and John Page.[298] Here again, Hasted is useful in explaining the basis on which the wardens were chosen:

> That the business of the bridge may never be prejudiced by the want of attendance, the wardens and assistants are usually chosen one half of gentlemen who live in the adjacent country, and the other of the same in Chatham and Rochester. The latter meet weekly for this purpose at the Bridge-chamber, in the Crown-Inn yard, (where all the business relating to the bridge is transacted) but the former very seldom attend these meetings, though they are almost always present at the two annual meetings at Easter and Whitsuntide, to which matters of greater moment are deferred, at which times they inspect and deliberate on what has been and ought to be transacted at those weekly meetings in this intermediate time, and in future.[299]

The book containing the 'Orders of Wardens and Assistants' shows that Hasted, as one of the 'adjacent country' gentlemen, was a very regular attender at the two principal meetings, rarely missing either an election, which took place on the Friday in the week following Easter, or, the other main meeting, the audit, held on the Thursday of Whitsun week. By far the great majority of these wardens' meetings, as noted in their Order book, were concerned with the assigning and signing of new leases for the considerable amount of property belonging to the bridge estate, both in the Rochester area and in London, although the fabric of the bridge itself had to be considered from time to time. In 1765 it was ordered that the bridge rails should be painted, and that the bridge clock should have a new dial. Occasionally one can see worries surfacing about the structure of the bridge, as in 1765, when a proposal was made that the bridge should be surveyed — the preference being expressed for 'a skilfull Surveyor from London'. Two London men, Joseph Constant and Nicholas Love, actually reported on the bridge in 1769, although as far as one can see no action was taken on this.[300]

The business of the election was followed by a meeting of the wardens and assistants only, during which were noted the penalties to be levied on those of the commonalty who had failed to respond to the summons to attend. These, however, were frequently waived. On the occasion of the election in April 1763, presided over by Robert Wilkins and Edward Hasted as retiring wardens, it was deemed unjust to proceed with the penalties incurred by non-attending electors, in view of the poor turn-out on the part of the wardens themselves. It was felt that those who were likely to be (re-)elected should also acknowledge a duty to be present. Accordingly, it was ordered that the following letter should be written by Mr Thomas Tomlyn, the bridge's attorney, 'to the several Assistants who are absent at this present meeting':

> The Wardens and Assistants of Rochester Bridge Observing that only ffour Persons out of all the Contributory Lands attended at the Election this day, Think it not reasonable to Levy any Penalty upon the Electors unless the Attendance of the Elected is likewise enjoined. Therefore having Ordered Summons's to be sent to the Parishes to shew Cause why the Penalty shall not be levied for not appearing at this Election, They hope you will be so Obliging as to send your Reasons whenever hereafter it may not be in your Power to be Present at the Publick Meeting.[301]

The recipients of this letter were the Hon. Robert Fairfax, who had been elected warden with John Page, the Earl of Aylesford, Lord Romney, Sir Roger Twisden, Thomas Faunce, Thomas Fletcher, and Francis Child. Such an outspoken entry is most unusual in the minutes, but it seems in keeping with a marked strain of frankness in Hasted's character, a belief in an Englishman's right to free speech, which makes itself apparent from time to time. A better attendance was indeed achieved at subsequent elections, and while we should in fairness allow that the wardens as a body probably saw the justice of the gentle reprimand, we must credit Hasted himself with having had the courage to point out to them the dangers of low waters.

The Hasted-Wilkins wardenship was not particularly noteworthy for anything else, although a decision had to be taken during their year of office to raise more funds, since we read in the minutes that,

> The Expences of Carrying on the Repairs of the Bridge, the Wharfes and the other the Necessary work being at present much greater than the Annual Rents and Revenues are sufficient to bear and Discharge, It is Ordered that part of the Capital Stock of 3 per Cent Reduced Bank Annuities belonging to the Wardens and Commonalty of the said Bridge not exceeding in the whole the Capital Stock of £600 be sold out,

— a note of caution being introduced by the proviso that the sale was to proceed by no more than £100 at any one time, 'at discretion of the Committee'.[302]

Hasted does not appear to have had any very close friends among the other wardens, apart, perhaps, from Thomas Faunce, his near neighbour at Sutton-at-Hone. The name of Robert Wilkins, of St Margaret's, appears frequently alongside that of Hasted, as well as being put forward with his for the wardenship in 1762, and if we assume that the two principal wardens each year were generally men who could be relied on to work well together, we may be justified in thinking that Hasted was perhaps as friendly with Wilkins as with any one else attending these meetings. And it is likely that Wilkins shared Hasted's growing interest in the past of the county, since we find him listed as one of the subscribers to John Thorpe's edition of his father's *Registrum Roffense* in 1769. But Wilkins's name does not crop up in the correspondence connected with the *History*, and in fact he was to die in 1771. The *Kentish Gazette*, announcing this in April of that year, was to note that Robert Wilkins had left estate worth £30,000,[303] considerably more than that of many a landed gentleman, Hasted included.

Hasted made his last appearance at a bridge wardens' meeting on 1 May 1772, when he may have announced that he was not offering himself for re-election. This attendance had been preceded by an absence of two years — his previous attendance had been at the election of 1770 — and it brought to a close a wardenship which, between 1761 and 1770

9. St John's Jerusalem at Sutton-at-Hone, former Commandery of the Knights Hospitallers of the Order of St John of Jerusalem, and Hasted's home between 1757 and 1768.

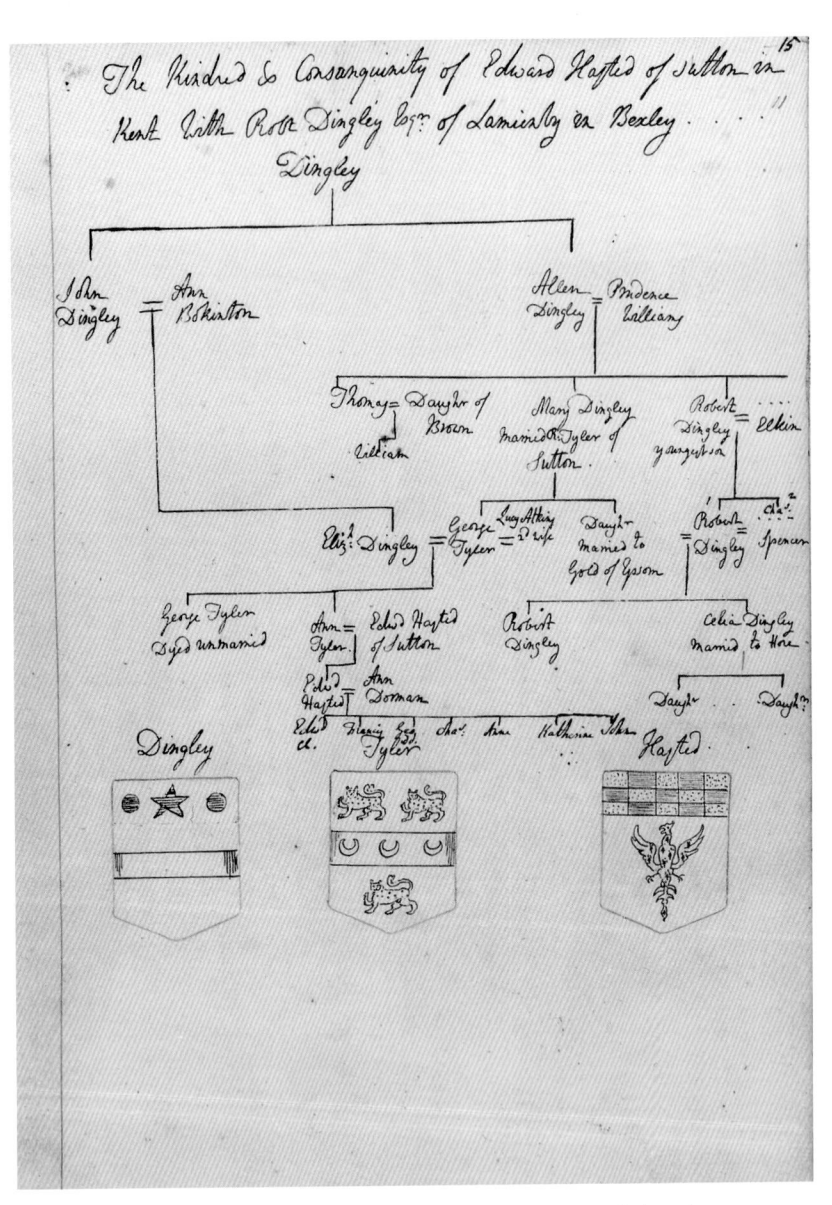

10. Pedigree of Hasted and Dingley, in Hasted's hand.

11. *Franks at Horton Kirby, near Sutton-at-Hone: a drawing by Hasted.*

12. and 13. Canterbury in 1800.

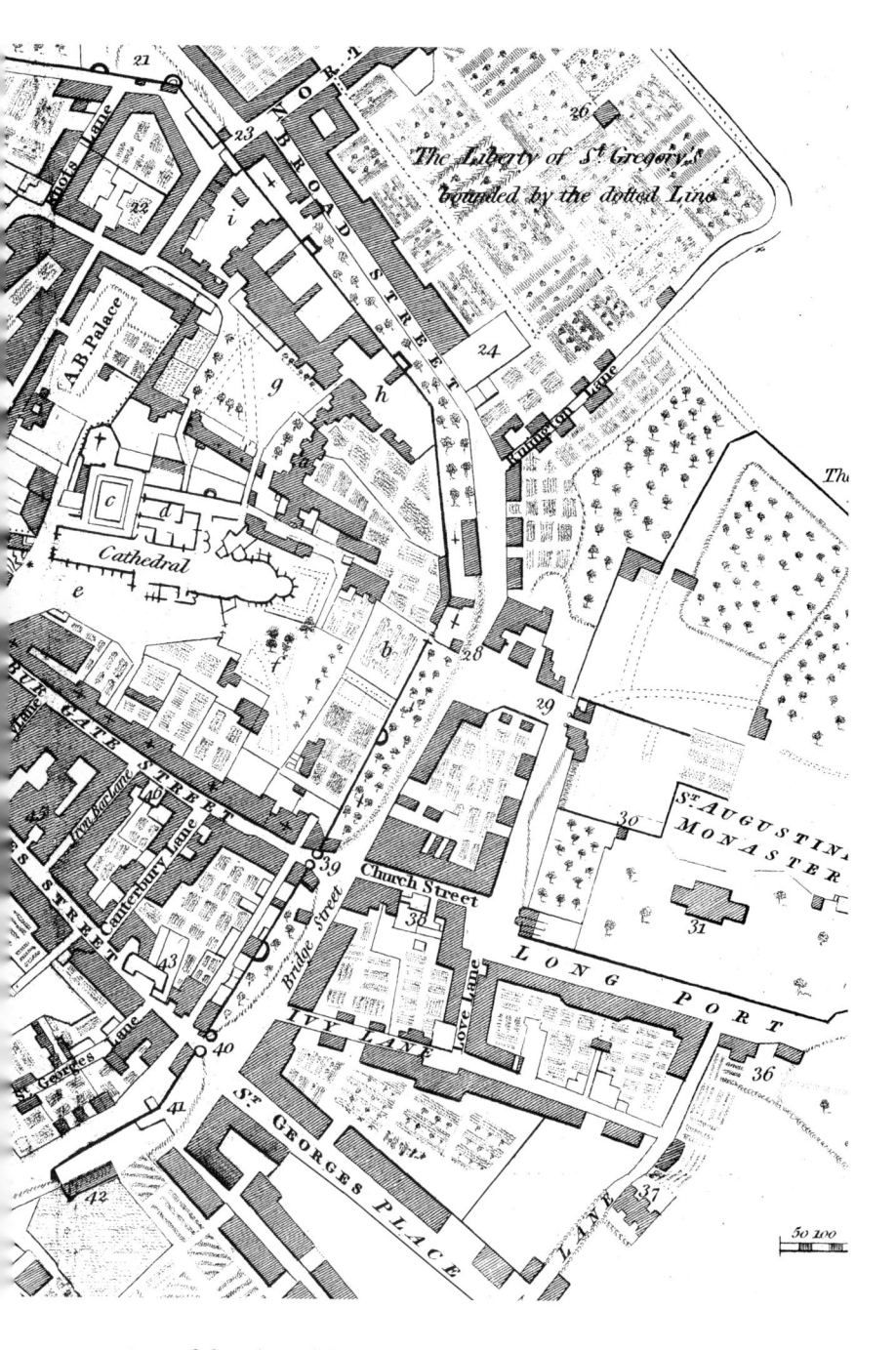

Part of the Plan of the City and Suburbs engraved by John Barlow.

14. *Dr Andrew Coltee Ducarel.*

IOHANNES THORPE,

A.M. OXON. &S.A.S.

Ætat. LXXII.

15. *John Thorpe, of High Street House, Bexley.*

16. Thomas Astle.

at least, may well have surpassed in diligence that of several of his colleagues.

As has been mentioned, Hasted's name was placed on the Commission of the Peace in 1757, and we know that he took out his writ of Dedimus Potestatem in 1758, although he does not appear to have become an acting magistrate until 1759.[304] In that year we find him present on both the petty sessions bench for the division of Upper Sutton-at-Hone, which sat, usually once a month, at Dartford, and on the quarter sessions bench at Maidstone, which drew on county justices from all the divisions of West Kent, and was held four times a year, at Epiphany, Easter, St Thomas and Michaelmas, that is to say, in January, March or April, July and October. It was in the magistracy that Hasted was to make his major contribution of voluntary service to the county.

As someone who had received legal training — and he had of course spent two years as a student at Lincoln's Inn — Hasted became at once a recognised member of the Kent quorum. There is plenty of evidence for his activity at petty sessions, although this has to be drawn from several sources, and does not constitute a single record. It is, however, sufficient to show that he took up the work of a magistrate with enthusiasm, and that he was frequently present on the Dartford bench, where he sat with either the vicar of Dartford, the Revd James Harwood, or the somewhat older Richard Hornsby of Horton Kirby, who had been sheriff of Kent in 1749. We find his signature in a number of parish rates books, which were taken to petty sessions for the accounts to be signed.[305] An assortment of official orders which have survived also attest to his presence there. In January 1760, for example, sitting with both Harwood and Hornsby, Hasted signed a removal order on a certain Edward Warde, who was adjudged to belong to Hurley, in Berkshire, and sent back there from East Wickham, while in May and June, with Richard Hornsby, he signed removal orders for, respectively, a family of eight, and a little boy aged five years. John and Mary Gibson and their six children, whose ages ranged from ten years to four months, were removed from Dartford to Foots Cray — an unalarming move, which left the family intact, and almost certainly sent them back to a place they knew. Five-year-old William Groves, on the other hand, was removed on his own from Dartford to Shropshire, following an examination of his mother, Ann Groves, a single woman. William had clearly had the misfortune to be born in Newport, Shropshire, to a mother who had subsequently come back into Kent, where she evidently belonged. While the authorities recognised Ann's right to assistance in her Kentish parish, William, by his birth, had a Shropshire parish of settlement, and had no claims to maintenance anywhere else. One is left to imagine the effect on both mother and child of legal separations such as this.[306]

More humanely, a settlement certificate of April 1761, signed by Hasted and Harwood, recognised William Tomlyn, his wife Mary and son William, as legally settled in Longfield, leaving them undisturbed, although the considerable certifying and counter-certifying which were necessary reflect the difficulties in the way of obtaining such recognition. The second part of the certificate concluded:

> We whose Names are hereunto subscribed, two of His Majesty's Justices of the Peace for the County of Kent ... do allow of the above-written Certificate. And we do also certify, That Richard Glover, the Witness who attested the Execution of the said Certificate, hath made Oath before us, That he did see the Church Wardens and Overseers, whose Names and Seals are to the said Certificate subscribed and set, severally sign and seal the said Certificate, and that the Names of the said Richard Glover and James Tufnail, whose Names are subscribed as Witnesses to the Execution of the said Certificate, are of their own proper Hand Writing.[307]

It must of course be remembered that orders such as these, whether of removal or settlement, do no more than reflect the course of the law at this time, and cannot be taken to show leniency or harshness on the part of the justices concerned. A request for removal was initiated by the churchwardens and overseers of a parish, and the justices' role was to enquire into the facts of the case and to sign an order accordingly if these were found to be proved.

It is probable that Hasted took the oaths as a magistrate in January 1759, when we find him present for the first time at a quarter sessions meeting in Maidstone.[308] He did not attend the following Easter meeting, but was present at the two remaining meetings of that year, in July and October, and in 1760 he attended all four quarter sessions. At Maidstone he was in company with a wider (and wealthier) selection of the county gentry: Abraham Tilghman, of Frinsted (who also sometimes sat on the bench for Upper Sutton-at-Hone); Sir Philip Boteler, of Teston; James Best, of Boxley; the Hon. Robert Fairfax, of Leeds Castle; Thomas Fletcher, of Chatham; Benjamin Hatley Foote, of Linton; Charles Whitworth, of Leybourne Grange; Sir Roger Twisden, of Bradbourne, Larkfield; Nicholas Haddock, of Wrotham; William James, of Ightham; Dr George Kelley, of Tunbridge Wells (who was to be knighted during his shrievalty in 1762); and some well-appointed clerics: the Revd Francis

Hender Foote, the Revd Pierrepont Cromp, the Revd Pierce Dixon and the Revd Thomas Curteis. When Hasted joined the quarter sessions bench Abraham Tilghman was acting as its chairman, a position which he had filled for some years, and it was perhaps he who had been responsible for inviting Hasted to sit at Maidstone, although from January 1760 Charles Whitworth appears to have taken over from Tilghman.

Various quarter sessions documents stemming from this time bear the arabesqued Hasted signature: on 17 January 1760, with two other justices, he was signing a licence for a Hucking man, Thomas Gilbert, to become a higgler or travelling market dealer and also, with three other justices, an order discharging an apprentice from his indentures. Another higgler's licence, this time for John Ransley, of Hothfield, was signed by Hasted in January 1761.[309]

Hasted's signature also appears, with those of two other magistrates, at the foot of several coroner's accounts: in March and July 1761, with Abraham Tilghman and William Parry, he was signing those presented by John Kirby, who was regularly called on at Greenwich to preside over a number of inquests on death by drowning, most of them caused by falling into the Thames. Fourteen of the seventeen cases contained in his July account came into this category. In marked contrast was the account presented by the Goudhurst coroner, Matthew Pope, which revealed considerable unrest in the now peaceful acres of Sissinghurst, at that time holding French prisoners of war. One of the bodies which Pope had been called on to view was that of a turnkey, William Bassack, murdered by a prisoner, while another was that of a Frenchman, Bastien Ballie, who had been killed by an English soldier for disobeying orders. Other papers bearing Hasted's signature relate to less disturbing matters, such as carpenters' and bricklayers' bills for work done 'att the Jaile and the Bridewell', the Maidstone doctor's bill for medicines and surgery at the gaol, and a baker's bill, made out appealingly for 'threepeney Loves' delivered to the prisoners.[310]

The justices at this time formed the principal administrative body in the county, charged with handling the county rate, or stock, collected from the ratepayers in every parish and paid in to the county treasurer. Much of this was expended in the payment of bills for authorised work of the type noted above, such as building repairs at one of the gaols, and bread or medical attention for the prisoners. Larger bills were scrutinised by what appears to have been a small finance committee, and although Hasted had only come on to the quarter sessions bench in 1759, we find him acting on the finance committee as early as July 1760. In April 1761, for example, with Abraham Tilghman and Thomas Fletcher, he was examining and allowing the bill of John Stevens, the Maidstone gaoler, which totalled £63.3s.1d., and included such items as brooms of various sizes to sweep out the wards, and gunpowder, brimstone, frankincense and tar which were used to fumigate them; the carriage of two men thirty-two miles to put them in the pillory at Greenwich (where their offence must have been committed); attending the execution at Sissinghurst of the Frenchman found guilty of the murder of Bassack; and conveying a French prisoner, who had escaped from Sissinghurst, back to base.[311]

Hasted, indeed, seems to have shown considerable interest and perhaps even flair in the financial business of the bodies on which he served. As we have seen, he was repeatedly invited to serve as an auditor for Rochester Bridge, and almost as soon as he joined the magistracy he became one of those involved in the reimbursement of those who had had several regiments of Hessian troops quartered on them — apparently for some time. In January 1759, which was the occasion of Hasted's first appearance at quarter sessions, the high constables of the Hundreds had been ordered to report in writing on the number of troops and the length of time over which they had been billeted in Kent, and to bring this information to the next general quarter sessions,

> In order to their settling and apportioning the payment of the sum of £390.11s.7d. ordered by his Majesty to be paid to the Clerk of the Peace for the innholders and other publick housekeepers in this county in consideration of the great expence they had been put to by the Hessian Troops having been so long billetted at their houses.[312]

The bundles of paper emanating from the Maidstone sessions show that at an adjourned session, at which were present Charles Whitworth, Sir Philip Boteler, and Edward Hasted, it was decided to allow £90.13s.1½d. to the innkeepers of the eastern division of the county, and £299.18s.5½d. to those in the western part. An accompanying minute from the quarter sessions for the eastern division of the county, held at Canterbury on 10 October 1760, apparently accepted this as equitable, and ordered that the sum allotted to East Kent should be shared out between those innkeepers of Canterbury and Faversham who had had troops billeted on them. There is a sheet of calculations in Hasted's own hand relating to the numbers of troops who had been quartered in West Kent, and dividing the money allotted to it between sixteen towns and Hundreds.[313]

The year 1761 would appear to have opened no differently from 1759 and 1760 for the young magistrate. He was among those attending each of the first three sessions. Significantly, however, his presence at the July sessions virtually concludes his appearances on the West Kent bench, and with a final attested presence at petty sessions towards the close of the year his activity as a justice comes to an abrupt end for the best part of four years. Not until Easter 1764 do we again find him present at Maidstone, and then only on this single occasion. As far as we can tell he was never to reappear at a meeting of quarter sessions while he lived at Sutton-at-Hone.

The explanation, as we have seen, seems to lie in the offence which may have been given by his 'History of Sequestrations', an outspoken condemnation of the activities of the forebears of too many of those who now wielded power in the county. Certainly, there is no other activity in Hasted's life which seems remotely likely to have caused such a break in his activities as a justice. It cannot have been due to the preparation of his *History of Kent*, since that was something on which he had not yet embarked. The signs all seem to point to the 'History of Sequestrations' as the cause of the disruption — and to his becoming a Deputy Lieutenant immediately afterwards as a way of proving that in spite of appearances his heart remained in the right place: that is, with King and country as then constituted.

On the surface there was nothing unusual about a decision on Hasted's part to become a Deputy Lieutenant for the county of Kent. A number of his fellow justices, such as Charles Whitworth, William Dalison, William Deedes, Sir Narborough D'Aeth and Thomas Best also held this postion. But there is no doubt that if Hasted had really wanted to serve his county (and country) as a Deputy Lieutenant, one of those responsible for the militia, England's home forces, he had left it rather late in the day. Urgent calls for gentlemen to serve as Deputy Lieutenants were no longer appearing in the Kentish press, as the war with France began to show signs of drawing to a close. It seems reasonable, therefore, to look for an underlying motive for his action.

Local gossip also expressed some surprise when it learnt of Hasted's latest move, which it saw as out of keeping with his commitments at home and in the locality. Miss Sally Williams of Dartford, who was almost certainly related to Hasted's attorney Thomas Williams, wrote in November 1761 to her friend William Perfect, the West Malling surgeon:

> Have you heard that Mr Hasted has accepted a Lieutenancy in the Militia? A married man with a fortune I think is simple for doing it. As to a single man, it is not very material whether he's at home or at Dover or elsewhere.

To which Perfect, in the course of one of the rhyming replies to which he was much given, and viewing it as merely an accretion of offices, made the rejoinder:

> Hasted accepted a commission —
> Nick! sink the justice to perdition!
> Enough I thought it was for him
> Of Quorum bench to be a limb.[314]

William Perfect could not know, of course, that the quorum bench was not to see Hasted again for some years.

Hasted qualified for the position of a Deputy Lieutenant of the county as the owner of an estate worth at least £400 a year, and his name was enrolled as follows:

> I Edward Hasted do declare that I am seized or possessed in law or equity for my own use and benefit of a freehold estate in possession for life or for some greater estate in messuages lands tenements or hereditaments lying and being in the parishes of Cliffe Linstead Tenham and Chatham in the County of Kent of the yearly value of four hundred pounds and do hereby certify the same as my qualification for a Deputy Lieutenant of the County of Kent and City and County of the City of Canterbury pursuant to the direction of the Statute in that behalf provided. Dated the thirty-first day of July 1761.[315]

As has been pointed out, this response to the country's need for Deputy Lieutenants came remarkably late in the day. Since 1756, when war had broken out in Europe in the wake of conflict in America and Canada, and when an invasion by France was a possibility not infrequently envisaged and discussed in England, considerable pressure had been brought to bear to persuade suitably qualified men to come forward to serve as Deputy Lieutenants or officers of the militia. Hasted was well qualified for such a post, both as regards the financial standing required, and, just as importantly, his abilities as a horseman. Had he been interested in the work, it is likely that he would have put himself forward much sooner. As it was, however, he had remained immune to the appeals of the Acts of 1757, 1758 and 1759. By 1761 the sense of urgency relating to the militia seems to have died down, and the work of the Deputy Lieutenants was not onerous: they were meeting at irregular intervals, mainly to decide on the months of exercise for the men, to whom was occasionally allotted a duty, although this was not always performed with conspicuous success. The militia from various counties was employed in Kent to guard the French prisoners held at Sissinghurst Castle, whose numbers were frequently swollen by the guerilla tactics which were engaged in with some zeal on both sides of the Channel. On the occasion of a tour of duty of the West Kent Regiment of Militia at Sissinghurst in July 1759, for example, it was reported in a London paper, and duly relayed by the *Kentish Post*, that 'Last Thursday morning about 10 o'clock about a hundred French prisoners broke out ... by undermining and have not been heard of since'![316]

As a newly sworn Deputy Lieutenant it is probable that Hasted attended the meetings called for the 12 January and 25 May 1762 at the Bell inn, in Maidstone, but by April 1763 peace had been proclaimed with France and Spain, the Seven Years' War was at an end, and with it the need for frequent meetings of the county's Deputy Lieutenancy.

It may have been Hasted's friend John Calcraft, the radical MP, who drew him back on to the petty sessions bench at Dartford. The historian seems to have been a not infrequent visitor at Ingress, the north Kent estate at Swanscombe which Calcraft, a former army agent and now Member of Parliament for Rochester, had purchased from the Earl of Bessborough. There is praise in the *History* both for Ingress and for its erstwhile owner (Calcraft was to die in 1772 at the early age of 45), who 'extended the plantations and gardens which Lord Bes(s)borough had begun, and continued making such additions to it that, had he lived, Ingress would, most probably, have been one of the greatest ornaments of this county'.[317]

Whatever the reason behind his return to the local bench, certain it is that at the monthly sitting of August 1765 we once more find the historian engaged in the work of a justice, acting at Dartford in company with John Calcraft.[318] Had Calcraft already agreed to become godfather to the child that Mrs Hasted was daily expecting that August? Or was it in the midst of the healths drunk to Hasted as father, to the baby's mother, and to the first girl in what was already a family of four boys, which greeted Hasted's announcement of the birth on the very morning of that sitting of the 15 August, that Calcraft generously offered to become her sponsor?[319] Whatever the course of these small events, we know that Hasted was friendly with the radical MP, a man quite close to him in age as well perhaps as in political outlook and with whom he probably shared an admiration for John Wilkes, and that, together with Richard Hornsby, Calcraft was a regular member of the Dartford petty sessions bench when Hasted once more resumed his duties there as an acting magistrate.

For the next three years Hasted was to remain an active member of the Dartford bench, sitting sometimes with Calcraft, sometimes with Hornsby, and leaving it for good only when he moved from Sutton-at-Hone to Canterbury in 1768. This is mainly attested by his signature at the foot of overseers' accounts, but we also find one or two committals by him. In January 1767, for example, he committed a Crayford man, Thomas Jones, to quarter sessions for refusing to indemnify the parish of Crayford in respect of no less than six bastard children which he had fathered; while in January 1768 he was responsible for committing to Dartford House of Correction three women who had been charged with stealing rags from the rag-house of William Quelch, a local paper-maker. As far as we can tell, one of the historian's last appearances on the Dartford bench was on 18 May 1768 when, again sitting with John Calcraft, he signed the accounts presented, among others, by the Dartford overseers.[320]

A person of Hasted's education — and Eton and Lincoln's Inn provided a most suitable recommendation in this respect — was a welcome addition to the body of gentlemen of the county, upon whom devolved so many unpaid judicial and administrative duties. Chief among these was that of a justice of the peace, which demanded regular attendance on a bench of magistrates, as well as a willingness to act as a single justice at any time should an emergency arise. However, after the first step in this direction had been attained, that of being placed on the Commission of the Peace, a gentleman might decide to let matters rest there, and, by not proceeding to take out his Dedimus (although such gentlemen were certainly in the minority) render himself unable to act as a magistrate. But there was an important occasional duty, that of service on the grand jury at the county assizes, which was not so easily evaded.

The assizes, which were held twice yearly, were the principal courts in each county and heard those cases known as felonies which were deemed too serious to be dealt with at quarter sessions, including murder, rape, burglary, robbery and arson. Assize courts could pass the death penalty, and it was rare for an assize to rise without leaving several unfortunate miscreants for hanging, although, in Kent at least, it was equally rare for several of those so condemned not to have their sentences commuted to transportation — seldom for life, and often for no more than seven years. It was the duty of the grand jury to make a prior examination of each case, and to allow into court, where they would be heard before the trial jury, only those cases which the grand jury felt able to pronounce 'a true bill'. Cases which were not felt to stand up to scrutiny were marked 'not a true bill', and the defendants would be discharged. Between fifty and sixty gentlemen were summoned for the grand jury each time, and out of this number a jury of between fifteen and twenty-three was selected. A fine of £20 seems to have been levied on non-attenders unprovided with an adequate excuse.

Non-attendance does not seem to have been much of a problem, however. In spite of the gloomy cause of their being held at all, the assizes were invariably an occasion of considerable social brilliance. The high court judges who travelled round on circuit to preside over them would be met some way outside the town or city where the assizes were to be held by the sheriff and his officers with accompanying pikemen and trumpeters, as well as some of the county gentry, and escorted in procession into the town. The assizes lasted from Monday to Wednesday and there was much entertaining during the course of them, the occasion usually terminating on the Wednesday evening with a ball. Clearly, many a grand juror, 'attached' as the phrase was, for the assizes by the traditionally named sheriff's officers, John Doe and Richard Roe, came to Maidstone or Rochester (where the Kent assizes were held alternately until 1764, when Maidstone became their permanent home) accompanied by his lady and perhaps one or two of his older children besides.

This was the society which Hasted was first summoned to join for the Lent assizes at Rochester in 1757, the year in which his name was put on the Commission of the Peace, although he had not yet been sworn as a magistrate. Summoned by William Russell, the Hundred bailiff responsible for his area, Hasted was also one of the fifteen gentlemen who, under the Hon. Lewis Watson (later Lord Sondes) of Lees Court, were asked to form the grand jury on this occasion and 'to enquire for our sovereign Lord the King and the body of the county' into the truth of the cases which it was proposed to bring before the court. His fellow-jurors were Sir Thomas Farnaby, of Kippington; William James, of Ightham; Abraham Tilghman, of Frinsted; James Best, of Chatham; Charles Petley, of Riverhead; Richard Hornsby, of Horton Kirby; Richard Coosens, of Deptford; John Fletcher, of Chatham; George Gordon, of Rochester; Thomas Faunce, of Sutton-at-Hone; Henry Wraight, of Ospringe; Thomas Pym Hales, of Bekesbourne; and John Cannon, of East Greenwich. Of these fifteen men, nine were already justices of the peace, and only two of them, Thomas Faunce and John Cannon, seem never to have aspired to be placed on the Commission of the Peace.[321]

It was at these assizes, somewhat unusually, that Hasted also served on a trial jury. Special juries were sometimes summoned to hear civil cases, and on this occasion a case had been brought by the clergy concerning the payment of tithes at Stonar in the Isle of Thanet. Hasted's papers contain the following account of what seems to have been a second hearing of the case, the first not having resulted in a satisfactory verdict:

However, the clergy resolved not to be browbeat by this, especially as they thought they had gained somewhat by it, and moved the Lord Chancellor for a new trial, which came on at the Lent Assizes 1757 before Chief Justice Willes; and a special jury was summoned on that occasion, of which but 3 appearing, they took 6 out of the grand jury and made up the deficiency with 3 farmers. The jury were Sir Thomas Farnaby, foreman, Hon. Mr Watson, James Best, Thomas Pym Hales, William James, Edward Hasted, John Cannon, Thomas Faunce, — Wraight and 3 farmers. The trial came on about 9 in the morning, and lasted till 3 o'clock, when the jury, after being shut up in court about a quarter of an hour, went to the Chief Justice's lodgings and gave a verdict for the defendant, upon which his Lordship expressed much pleasure, saying he was thoroughly convinced in the same opinion before he left the court.[322]

It is likely that Hasted was also summoned for the Lent grand jury the following year, although the list of grand jurors for these assizes is missing. He was certainly summoned again in 1759, being ordered to attend on Monday, 19 March, when the assizes were to be opened before Sir Thomas Denison and the Hon. Heneage Legge, esq. Here again, he was one of those who were required to act; and among those cases which must have received his consideration, and which the grand jury permitted to come into court, were two which received sentence of death, one for burglary and one for highway robbery. Another case, of attempted rape on a child of five, received the sentence of six weeks in gaol, and an hour 'in and upon the pillory at the town of Gravesend' on a market day. The following Lent assizes, for 1760, with Hasted again summoned and acting on the grand jury, had before it a case which had been committed by Hasted himself — a matter of sureties not having been found for an appearance at the assizes on the part of two men accused of an assault on the Revd Vincent Hotchkys, vicar of Sutton-at-Hone's neighbouring parish of Horton Kirby.[323]

The Lent assizes of 1761, when Hasted was again present and acting on the grand jury, saw some interesting cases. The most serious was that of the French prisoner, Jean Baptiste Francis Picard, charged with the murder of William Bassack, the turnkey at Sissinghurst prison. Picard was found guilty, and the heavy sentence was passed on him of hanging followed by dissection, 'pursuant to the Statute'. A man found guilty of forging two acceptances to bills of exchange was also sentenced to be hanged, although without subsequent dissection, and another man, convicted of sending a letter threatening to burn a house down, received sentence of transportation to the American colonies for fourteen years. There was also the case of a polygamist who had married two wives, whose mixed sentence was perhaps intended to show the severe moral obloquy with which such a crime was regarded: burning in the hand, ten calendar months in gaol, and subsequent transportation. And there was the curious case of one John Dalrymple, esq., who had been committed the previous January by the two Chatham justices, James Best and Thomas Fletcher. Dalrymple was charged with stealing a total of ninety-one books from the shop of John Townson, a Chatham bookseller, including six volumes of Dodsley's poems, eight (in French) of Labat's *Voyages*, two of Gravesend's *Mathematicks*, and ten volumes of Pope's *Homer*. Unless Dalrymple had had thoughts of setting up a school, it seems unlikely that this was a straightforward case of theft for the purpose of gain. But we do not have enough evidence to decide whether Dalrymple had simply not paid for books which had been delivered to order, whether he was a kleptomaniac with a passion for books, or whether the books were perhaps removed in retaliation for some supposed debt on the part of Townson. Dalrymple's counsel made a skilful application to the court, respecting the need for material witnesses to be present before the case could be tried, and Dalrymple was released on bail. Proceedings seem thereafter to have been dropped.[324]

Although summoned for grand jury service in 1762, Hasted was not called upon to act that year. In 1763, however, we find him both summoned and acting at the Lent assizes. Subsequent assize records then appear to show the same complete break with all judicial business on the part of Hasted that is revealed by the quarter sessions records. He was not to be summoned again for service on the grand jury until the spring of 1768, well after his resumption of duties at petty sessions, although we know from a letter which he wrote to Thomas Astle that he attended the Lent assizes of 1767.[325]

Nevertheless, despite whatever awkwardness may have arisen on the quarter sessions bench, Hasted had no intention of making a complete break with the tradition of service on which he had entered. As we have seen, throughout this period he continued to serve as an assistant warden of Rochester Bridge. There is no doubt, too, that, like his father before him, he very much enjoyed the socialising and conviviality which accompanied such meetings. By some chance or oversight, as he may have thought, he was not summoned to the Lent assizes of 1764, but he had every intention of going, as we learn from the postscript which he added to a letter to Astle written at the beginning of March of that year, inviting him to the ball which would close the assizes on the Wednesday night:

Why cannot you take a ride to our Assize ball, Wednesday sennight ... I would induce you if I could, in the first place for your own sake, and in the next, that I may have the pleasure of meeting you there.[326]

We cannot know whether Astle accepted this invitation, but Hasted duly attended the assizes, presenting himself to the sheriff's officers and having his name added, as was quite common, as a non-summoned attender for the grand jury. Exceptionally, however, it was later crossed out. The officers may have been unacquainted with any personal disputes and dissensions among the justices, and in any case would have had no authority to demur at a name. But one can imagine a senior member of the bench, although Charles Whitworth himself was not one of those summoned, scanning the brief list of additional attenders, and expressing a distaste for Mr Hasted's presence among the jurors. In the ensuing confusion the name of another justice, William Gordon, of Rochester, which had been likewise added, was similarly struck out, but immediately restored with a 'stet', and the number 12 put against it: Gordon, as was usual for unsummoned attenders, was therefore included among the acting grand jurors.[327]

Following this, Hasted's name is missing from the list of the grand jury for some years, as it is missing from the list of those attending West Kent quarter sessions. As we have seen, he made a single subsequent appearance at the quarter sessions at Easter 1764: perhaps he was invited to do so by some who felt that, whatever the reason, he had been treated somewhat shabbily. But the warmth of some may not have compensated for the coldness of others, and he did not again, during his remaining years at Sutton-at-Hone, sit on the West Kent bench.

He did, however, return to the petty sessions at Dartford. Possibly his friend John Calcraft was instrumental in coaxing him back — or in proving to the powers that be that the local bench needed the assistance of a willing and able magistrate such as Hasted undoubtedly was. He finally came in out of the cold in March 1768, when he once more received a summons to attend for the grand jury at the Lent assizes, and was numbered among those who were to act. Eager to show his disposition to serve, he attended also, as one of those who came unsummoned, at the following summer assizes which opened on the 25 July, although he was not, on this occasion, required to act.[328]

It seems unlikely that Mr Hasted was accompanied to these summer assizes by his wife. She must at this very moment have been in the throes of the family's move from Sutton-at-Hone to Canterbury, and less than a month later, on 17 August, at their new address in St George's Street, she was to give birth to her seventh child, aptly christened John Septimus.

hath come to inhabit in the said _____ not having gained a legal Settlement there, nor produced any Certificate owning _____ where, and that the said _____ to be settled elsewhere _____ of _____ likely to be chargeable to the said Justices upon due Proof made thereof, as well upon the Examination of the said Ann Grover otherwise, and likewise upon due Consideration had of the Premises, do adjudge the same to be true; and we do likewise adjudge, that the lawful Settlement of _____ the said _____ is in the said Parish of Newport _____ in the said County of Salop _____: We do therefore require you the said Churchwardens and Overseers of the Poor of the said Parish of Dartford _____ one of you, to convey the said William Grover _____ from and out of your said Parish _____ or some, or to the said Parish of Parish of Dartford _____ to deliver to the Churchwardens and Overseers of the P— _____ and to some or one of them, together with this our O— _____ thereof And we do also hereby require _____ and Overseers of the Poor of the _____ _____ to receive and _____

the Church-Wardens and Overseers of the Poor of
the Parish of Dartford _____ of Kent
in the County
or to any or either of them.

WE whose Names are hereunto subscribed, two of His Majesty's Justices of the Peace for the County of Kent aforesaid, do allow of the above-written Certificate. And we do also certify, That Richard Grover the Witness who attested the Execution of the said Certificate, hath made Oath before us, That he did see the Church Wardens and Overseers, whose Names and Seals are to the said Certificate subscribed and set, severally sign and seal the said Certificate, and that the Names of the said Richard Grover and John Tufnail whose Names are subscribed as Witnesses to the Execution of the said Certificate, are of their own proper Hand Writing. Dated the 7th Day of April in the Year of our Lord 1761.

Sam Harwood
Edward Hasted

Chapter 9

'The more the antiquarian toils, the more he sees beyond him to encounter'[329] :

The Preparation of the *History*, II

By the summer of 1763 word had spread round the county that Edward Hasted was collaborating with Charles Whitworth on an updated edition of Thomas Philipott's Kentish history of 1659, the *Villare Cantianum, or Kent Surveyed and Illustrated*. Several friends wrote to wish him well. Among them was the Revd John Potter, rector of Wrotham, who in July 1763 expressed the hope that

> your conferences with Mr Whitworth will enable you together to make a perfect continuation and a good new edition of Philpot; I think the method of publishing it alphabetically as soon as you have a few of the first letters complete will be attended with ease and satisfaction to yourselves and the publick, and perhaps it may induce some of those whose names or properties are concerned under each letter to send you further instructions.[330]

Before another twelve months had passed, however, the joint project was no more. Hasted, as we have seen, was very dismissive of the contribution made by Whitworth towards it, but it has to be said that its brief existence provided a springboard for his own great work, as well as serving to introduce him to the county as its historian. Not unnaturally, the impression that Hasted and Whitworth remained literary colleagues lingered on in some quarters. In October 1764 Charles Carter Petley, writing to Hasted to offer his own assistance with 'a work you have for some years taken so much pains about and have so nearly compleated as that of a General History of the County of Kent', ended his letter, 'You will need no better nor a more judicious assistant than my friend Mr Whitworth'.[331] But closer friends were better informed. Anna Ward, penning a letter a few days later from St Lawrence House, near Canterbury, on behalf of 'my sister Rooke', wrote:

> My sister Rooke desires me to acknowledge the favour of your letter and is very glad that you will oblige the public with a more perfect History of Kent than has as yet appeared. Many of the errors may be owing from one historian copying after another

without applying to the principal persons that could enable them to give true accounts, but by the caution you take there is reason to believe the History you are about will do honour to your self and much oblige the public.[332]

Hasted had clearly written to Mrs Rooke, whom he would seem to have known well (probably from the time of his two-year stay in Canterbury), with a request for information, but with his usual diffidence he hesitated to approach people with whom he was not acquainted, and the great avalanche of correspondence that was to bring him the details which, as Mrs Rooke rightly said, only those directly concerned in a matter could know, was not to be set in motion until 1767. Where he felt it was in order to do so, however, he ventured to request permission to look at material prior to that date. In November 1763, for example, when writing to the Archbishop of Canterbury, Dr Secker, to complain of the poor service Throwley church was getting from its vicar, he accompanied this with a request that he might be allowed to use the library at Lambeth Palace.[333] A year later he was to write to Lord Romney, of The Mote, at Maidstone, receiving the brief reply that Lord Romney had ordered his stewards 'to give you all the information in their power'.[334] For the next two years, however, the historian's main work was to be the annotation of secondary sources, and the copying of any manuscripts which he felt he needed to have to hand.

Already at the time of his collaboration with Charles Whitworth he had begun a commonplace book, laid out very much in the manner of Philipott's *Villare Cantianum*, with the bulk of the book devoted to the parishes of Kent in alphabetical order. Although this was not to be the plan which Hasted eventually adopted, he found it an easy format under which to make notes, and retained it for much of the preparation of the *History*. There are several sequences of such notebooks, of varying size, but the principal series is that of three large folio volumes, two of which are now in Canterbury Cathedral Archives. A third one was bought by the British Museum in 1796 at the sale by auction of his manuscripts.[335] In these, his large commonplace books, and more particularly in the two now at Canterbury, Hasted was to make notes on all the secondary material he could find which had any bearing on Kent. Thus, for example, he had told Astle in March 1764: 'My next labour will be to attack Dugdale's Monasticon and carefully to extract out of him whatever relates to Kent'.[336]

The first of the great commonplace books, which must have lain open beside him as he read — and was perhaps often carried around by Hasted for note-taking on the spot during the course of a 'parochial visitation', since it shows signs of much wear and tear — was begun around 1762, that is, as a result of his agreement to work together with Charles Whitworth on the new edition of Philipott's work. It is possible to date the book with some accuracy, as it contains several lists of holders of offices which were clearly written out at a single sitting by Hasted as far as 1761 or 1762. Thus the same pen and ink have been used to list the sheriffs of Kent down to Sir George Kelley, who occupied that position in 1762; while the names of sheriffs for subsequent years down to 1773 are obviously later additions. Similarly, the list of members of parliament elected throughout the county in March 1761 is only partially completed in the original ink: although Hasted knew who were the members for the county he did not, at the time he first made out this list, know the names of all the members for the boroughs, and these, too, were inserted later.[337]

The second commonplace book was begun, as some of the pages of the first began to fill up, around 1767.[338] Again, this date can be stated with some certainty. The holograph letters from Hasted to Astle show that 1767 was the year in which he changed a small characteristic of his handwriting, the form of his ampersand. From something like a figure 8 lying on its side, Hasted adopted a form frequently found in legal documents, a kind of open letter e which was much quicker to write, and once having adopted it he used it to the end of his life. This second book contains only parish material: to find out more about his preparation for writing the history of a county we must turn back to the first of the commonplace books.

From quite early on Hasted had been aware that there were many lines of enquiry which he would have to pursue in order to cover all aspects of this most varied of counties. On one or two of them he already had a good start: as a justice of the peace he was familiar with the administrative organisation of the county; as a warden of Rochester Bridge he knew a great deal about the bridge and the river it crossed, the Medway; as a commissioner of sewers he could appreciate the drainage problems encountered in the marshes. He was already quite well travelled in both the eastern and the western divisions of the county, so he possessed at starting a reasonably extensive knowledge of eighteenth-century Kent, which it could only be a pleasure to explore further. Nevertheless, wide reading was essential.

This would include not only books on Kent, but books covering as many aspects of England as possible, both historical and topographical. Hasted realised that events in the county could not be separated from the wider, national scene, and the lists of books which he drew up for himself included many of this kind: Horsley's *Britannia Romana*, Sammes's *Britannia*, a *History of England by Divers Hands*, Strype's *Stow's Survey*,

Brady's three-volume *History of England*, Thomas Cox's *Magna Britannia et Hibernia, Antiqua et Nova*, and the *History of England* by the Scotsman David Hume, are among those which he set himself to study.[339] If his commonplace books make little mention of national events or previous reigns, it is because this was familiar ground to him already. He says in the Preface to the first folio edition that he had always had a great interest in history, and we may believe him. Nowhere does he give us a full list of the books in his study (he very seldom used the more pompous 'my library' — in great contrast to Thomas Astle, who seems to have used the phrase on every conceivable occasion), but we can be sure that it contained more than one of the histories of England which the eighteenth century was producing in some numbers, and to which both Goldsmith and Smollett, as well as many lesser names, contributed. Fairly early on in the course of this preparation, however, Hasted drew up for himself the following list of 'books in my study to be particularly referred to':

> Camden's Britannia, article Kent
> His Preface, Introduction and Britons, Saxons and Romans in Britain
> History of Canterbury Cathedral — folio
> Burton's Monast[icon] — his history of the church — of monastic orders — and at the end his proposals and Quaeries for a Genl. history of a county
> Minshew's Dictionary (sic)
> Chambers' Dictionary
> No 433 — to be perused very carefully — Harl. Mss.
> Poll books for 1734 and 1754 for owners of Lds and difft states of the parishes in each year[340]

This was followed in the commonplace book by a very much longer list, consisting of over seventy items, which began with the following:

> Nicholson's Historical Library
> Decim Scriptores
> Tanner's Monasticon
> Journals of the Lords and Commons
> Rymer's Foedera
> Madox's Exchequer
> Dugdale's Baronage
> Sandford Genealogical History
> Barrington on Antient Laws

'The more the antiquarian toils, . . .'

Horsman's Britannia (sic)
Hickes's Thesaurus
Godwin, De Praesulibus
Wharton's Anglia Sacra
Dugdale's Hist. of Imbanking
Dugdale's Origines Juridicales (sic)[341]

Most of these are referred to in the footnotes to Hasted's work, and we may assume that he was able either to borrow them or to read them in a library. He could never afford to be other than a careful purchaser. Books which he would have liked to possess, but which were not essential or which he could easily borrow, were not added to his shelves. Thus his name does not appear among the list of subscribers to the rather nice little *History of Rochester* which was brought out anonymously in 1772, but this was, as a foreword makes clear, based on some of the source material which he was himself using, and in any case he would have been able to borrow a copy from his friend John Thorpe, who was a compulsive purchaser of books on Kent, being unable, as he once told Hasted in a letter, to 'forbear taking in these kind of antiquarian publications'.[342] But friendship could override pecuniary considerations, and Hasted does appear as a subscriber for two copies of the *Registrum Roffense*, John Thorpe's edition of his father's collection of Rochester records, which came out in 1769.

There were of course some works of reference which Hasted needed to have to hand all the time and we find a mention of some of these in his letter to Dr Ducarel of 18 February 1771, on the occasion of the sale, after his death, of the library of Philip Carteret Webb:

> I have marked a few lots in Mr Webb's Catalogue, which I should be much obliged to you to look at for me, and settle the prices with Baker to buy for me. They are, No. 36, Willis's Not.Parl; 55, Blount's Tenures; 1014, Alphabeti et Diplom. etc; 1530, Dugdale's Baronage, 2 vols.; 1635, Heraldi Adversari, if wrote by Ludovicus Herault, Prebendary of Canterbury, not otherwise; 482, British Curiosities — much wanted, if written by one Burton; 1008, Du Fresne, 3 vols, if the best edition.
>
> I am in great want of Sir William Dugdale's Baronage, but still I must not go beyond the market-price; and if I do not have this, I hope Baker will pick up one for me somewhere, as soon as he possibly can. Pray give me, or desire him to write me, a line of the

prices he puts to them before the sale, that I may have time to write him my mind, if I disapprove of any of them.[343]

A brief glance at a few of the authors mentioned by Hasted will show something of the depth and breadth of his reading in preparation for his great undertaking.

Sir William Dugdale, much admired by Hasted, as by many others, was a seventeenth-century writer whose *Antiquities of Warwickshire* had first appeared in 1656. It had been reissued in 1730. While Dugdale, like Hasted, works through his county by Hundreds, the treatment meted out to each place is very different from what we find in Hasted. Apart from anything else, the fact that there were only four Hundreds in the whole of Warwickshire means that the structure of Dugdale's work differs considerably from that of Hasted. Dugdale's *Baronage of England, An historical account of the lives and most memorable actions of our English nobility*, a two-volume folio work like his *Warwickshire*, appeared in 1675. The same writer's *History of Imbanking and Drayning of diverse Fenns and Marshes*, which came out in 1662, and his *Origines Juridiciales, or Historical Memorials of the English Laws, Courts of Justice, etc.*, of 1666 — both of which were used by Hasted — were so highly thought of in the eighteenth century as each to receive a new, revised edition in 1772 and 1780 respectively, some years after Hasted made out his lists of requirements.

Thomas Rymer, the editor of the *Foedera*, had held the position of Historiographer Royal from 1692, appointed by Queen Mary 'to transcribe and publish all the leagues, treaties, alliances, capitulations and confederacies which have at any time been made between the Crown of England and any other kingdoms, princes, and states, as a work highly conducing to our service and the honour of this our realm'. The resulting work was the *Foedera*, which covered all such material between the years 1101 and 1654, and which came out in twenty volumes between 1704 and 1732. Anyone wishing to consult it today has the benefit of the *Syllabus to Rymer's Foedera*, the three volumes of which were published between 1869 and 1885, but Hasted, of course, who makes not infrequent references to it, was obliged to sift these out of the original multi-volume edition.

Thomas Madox was a scholar of the first part of the eighteenth century who wrote exhaustively on the history of the exchequer: his *History and Antiquities of the Exchequer of the Kings of England* was published in two parts in 1711 and republished in 1769. Madox, who had followed Thomas Rymer as Historiographer Royal in 1714, also wrote *Firma Burgi, or, An Historical essay concerning the cities, towns and buroughs* of *England*, a work which appeared in 1726; this too was used by Hasted, as a number of footnotes make clear.

Thomas Tanner's *Notitia Monastica, or An account of all the abbies, priories and houses of friers, heretofore in England and Wales, and also of all the colleges and hospitals founded before AD 1540*, which first appeared in 1695 and was reprinted in 1744, was to be a work to which Hasted made frequent reference. Another edition was to appear in 1787. Francis Sandford's *Genealogical History of the Kings of England from the Conquest ao 1066 to the year 1677* was a one-volume work which had first appeared in the latter year, and then been continued and brought up-to-date with another edition in 1707. Daines Barrington's *Observations on the more ancient statutes* was a recent work which had come out in 1766. Hickes's *Thesaurus* of 1705, like Spelman's *Glossary* of 1664, which was also used by Hasted, offered, among much else, elucidation of archaic Latin law terms. The use of either, like many of these late seventeenth- or early eighteenth-century tomes, required brawn as well as brain, being weighty as regards both erudition — they were written in Latin throughout — and avoirdupois.[344]

This very brief survey of some of the hundreds of books and manuscripts to which Hasted refers for his authority shows several of the main areas which he researched. Ecclesiastical history, given that Canterbury was and remains the seat of the primate of all England, the importance of church foundations and institutions down to the time of Henry VIII, and the still very considerable extent of ecclesiastical lands down to Hasted's own time, had to occupy a great deal of his attention. Treaties and laws were of equal importance in directing the development of the county, and were also studied by Hasted. The descent of land through families, with the descent of those families themselves, was another of his major preoccupations, requiring much original research and forming a large part of his contribution to the history of the county.

An area not reflected in the short lists of books quoted was that of the agriculture of the county: William Ellis's *Practical Farmer* of 1732, his multi-volume *Modern Husbandman* of 1744, and the same author's *Shepherd's Guide*, of 1749, are only three of the titles Hasted felt it important to look at, in relation to a county where agriculture was gaining yearly in importance. Of considerable interest also at the time were the mineral waters found in various parts of the country. Kent had several spas of chalybeate water, and books or pamphlets on the subject are also found in Hasted's list of required reading. Another Kentish subject, on which he became very learned, was that of gavelkind: this he studied both in Somner's *Treatise* of 1660, which had been reprinted in 1726, and in Robinson's thorough analysis, *The Common Law of Kent, or the Customs of*

Gavelkind, which had first appeared in 1741 and was to have a fifth edition as late as 1897. He delved, similarly, into the works of naturalists, such as the beautifully illustrated Johnson's *Gerard's Herball*, and Merret's *Pinax*, in order not to neglect the natural history of the county, and he knew and read a great deal about Kentish antiquities. If neither of these subjects was to occupy much space, finally, in his *History*, this was to be the result of decisions taken consciously, and with a modest sense of his own limitations. Both, he felt, were subjects which required the attention of a specialist — and he undoubtedly had in mind here the work of Dr Solander and Joseph Banks on the one hand, and of men such as the Revd Bryan Faussett on the other.[345]

The references in his own volumes show that he pored over virtually any county or local history which came his way. Such references are legion, particularly of course to Kentish works — not only the older ones, such as Lambarde's *Perambulation*, Kilburne's *Survey of Kent*, Philipott's *Villare Cantianum* and Harris's *History*, but contemporary ones too, among them *A History of Maidstone*, Lewis's *History of Thanet*, Boys's *Collections for Sandwich*, and Gostling's *Walk in and about Canterbury*. And they also include Morant's *Essex*, Chauncy's *Hertfordshire*, Burton's *Leicestershire*, Borlase's *Cornwall*, Blomefield's *Norfolk*, Aubrey's *Antiquities of Surrey*, and Bentham's *Ely Cathedral*.

At the back of the first great commonplace book is a list which is far longer than those at the front. Here, Hasted has made a note of the abbreviations he was using in his footnotes. And it is in the footnotes themselves that we find confirmed the full extent of Hasted's reading, as well as of his research.[346]

For the purpose of having adequate material to hand, Hasted put into his study quite a number of books of his own making. This was by no means so questionable an exercise as it may seem. There were at this time still a large number of manuscript books in circulation, copies of copies, particularly of items which had never gone into print, such as the heralds' visitations, in which the historian had a special interest. By making a copy of such manuscripts himself, therefore, Hasted was not merely taking notes for future study, as we would see it today, but adding to the common store of such books. Where he was able to add something from his own later knowledge he was, he felt, making a contribution along the lines which these early mentors, particularly the heralds, had mapped out. Thus for example we have the 'Copie of the Visitation Book of the County of Kent as taken by John Philipott Rouge Dragon Annis 1619, 1620 and 1621' with which one of Hasted's manuscript books begins.[347] Lambarde, similarly, in his *Perambulation*, had added to 'The Names of suche of the Nobilitie, and Gentrie, as the Heralds recorded in their visitation, 1574' with 'suche as I called to mynde, and have set a starre before ech of them, that they may be knowne from the rest'. Lambarde's amended list, from the quarto edition of 1576, was another copy made by Hasted into the same folio manuscript volume.

In order to add to the value of his copy of the 1619 Philipott visitation for future users, Hasted indexed it — but was later to find that Bryan Faussett had borrowed (and presumably copied) a manuscript of this same visitation belonging to the Canterbury heraldic painter Picard, and that this copy did not correspond in pagination to his own. Accordingly, he cross-referenced between Faussett's copy and his own, and added an explanation of what he had done.[348]

The copying, therefore, which played a large part in Hasted's original moves towards preparing a history of the county, and which provided many of the volumes which were beginning to fill his study, had, in the eyes of an eighteenth-century historian, a value in itself. Much of this copying, as we have seen, was being done in 1763 and 1764, that is, during Hasted's stay at Throwley, and shortly thereafter. It was perhaps on the occasion of his 1768 move to Canterbury that Hasted gave his manuscripts shelf or press marks, from A to Z, accompanied by a running Roman numeral, for in 1769 he prepared a 'General Index to all my Manuscripts relating to the County of Kent'.[349] The manuscripts had perhaps by then acquired familiar positions in his study, Hasted knew where they were, and wanted to re-establish the same order at Canterbury, although this might have been the occasion to undertake a finer classification. In order to maintain the order he was used to he seems to have gone through them as they stood or lay, on shelves or in presses, beginning with A.I, A.II, A.III, up to Z.CXVII. They were manuscripts of all kinds, among them parchment rolls which he had been given, books of his own notes made in various locations, libraries and offices of record, all the Hill papers on which he had based his ill-fated 'History of Sequestrations', visitations of Kent, and numerous folios of assorted genealogies or pedigrees.

Some time between 1764 and 1767 was begun what was to be described in the Index as 'A large port folio entitled MSS Pedigrees ... of families of Kent' and numbered X.CIII (now in the British Library's collection of manuscripts as Add.5520). This originally contained one hundred and twenty-one pedigrees — Hasted himself later removed the three which were of the most importance to him personally — the first twenty or so mainly reflecting the families and acquaintances with whom he was surrounded prior to his move to Canterbury. No.1 is that of the Chiffinches of Northfleet, whose ancestor, Thomas Chiffinch, born in 1600, became Keeper of the King's Jewels on the restoration of Charles II, his wife Dorothy being given the position of the King's Laundress and Sempstress. The second pedigree is that of the Fortryes, of Wombwell Hall in Northfleet, and the fourth that of the Leighs, of Hawley. The pedigrees of the Dormans (No.7), and of the Chicheleys (No.13) — to whom Hasted was apparently related through his grandmother — are two of those which he was to remove, together with that of Dingley (No.66). Nos.14, 15, and 16 are those of Leigh, Bargrave and Smythe respectively, all families either living locally, or, like the Bargraves, with local connections. No.17, a parchment sheet, has been endorsed by Hasted, 'Pedigree of Godfrey & Faussett in the late Revd Brian Faussett's own handwriting', and was undoubtedly given to him by his friend, perhaps on the occasion of one of his visits to Heppington, when the two men would spend long hours deep in discussion of antiquarian matters.[350]

This portfolio was to be added to over the years, as is clear from the dates contained within some of the pedigrees. No.106, a pedigree of Gibbon of West Cliffe, was 'Communicated to me by Saml Egerton Brydges Esqr', and contains dates of 1780 and 1784, while No.111, a pedigree of Bridges of Goodnestone sent by Sir Brook Bridges, Bt., goes down to 1784, so was probably received by Hasted after that date. Pedigree No.120, of Solly of Ash and Sandwich, in the handwriting of Mr Joseph Solly of Sandwich, has several members of the family marked 'living 1789', while a few pedigrees noted as communicated by William Boys or William Boteler, two men who were to prove of great assistance to Hasted in the final years of preparation of the *History*, contain even later dates.

There are other manuscripts which bear dates later than 1769, but virtually all such dates refer to short entries made subsequently, in volumes or portfolios which had been begun in the earlier years. Thus the British Library's Add.5512 (Hasted's L.LX), which contains notes on a large number of Kentish parishes entered alphabetically and is a supplement to an earlier volume that (somewhat inconsistently) was not bought by the British Museum, was in use before 1767, as can be deduced from Hasted's writing, and re-used, possibly in that year, when Hasted seems to have made a stay of a few weeks in London. This was the commonplace book which he took with him on visits to both Lambeth Palace and the British Museum itself, as can be seen from the series of entries made from the archbishops' Visitation Returns or, as he termed them, the Lambeth Queries, and from the Harleian catalogue.

It is therefore possible to state definitely that by far the greater part of Hasted's collection of manuscripts had been put together by 1769, and also — where the MSS consisted of full-scale copying by Hasted himself, rather than simply note-taking — that the greater part of this had been done before 1767, much of it having been carried out in 1763 and 1764. The fact that Hasted's 'General Index' is clearly stated as 'taken by me Edwd Hasted 1769' (BL Add.5536), confirms this as the date by which his collection was virtually complete.

Briefly, the historian dreamed of employing an assistant. In a letter to Astle of 17 January 1764, when he was relaxing after copying out the Wilsford pedigree, which was finished on the same day, Hasted says:

> I find that I must next summer get a young man somewhere to live with me [as] amanuensis, for I shall have full employment for him, and myself too.[351]

There are indeed two manuscripts in the Hasted collection which were almost certainly written out by someone else under Hasted's direction. These are Add.5514 and 5515 (Hasted Q.LXXXIV and R.LXXXV). Both of these relate to Wye College and were made from the collections of Dr Nicholas Brett of Wye. They consist mainly of an abstract from the statutes of the College, of its surrender under Henry VIII, and subsequent grants of it, all of which have been copied out in a clear and probably younger hand, with the occasional insertion of a word or two in Hasted's handwriting in places where his junior scribe had perhaps been unable to read the original. In addition, Hasted has himself made a number of footnotes and directed where space should be left for these, and has also copied several pages of rentals which were in Latin and probably easier for him than for his assistant to cope with. A brief note on Wye Abbey, taken from Browne Willis's *History of Mitred Abbies*, was probably dictated by Hasted.

All in all, the close attention which was necessary when a manuscript was being copied by someone else did not, perhaps, save Hasted very much time in the long run, and the Wye College documents seem to be the only example of Hasted actually employing someone else to do his copying for him.

In the case of at least one other manuscript, however, he commissioned the copying, very probably through Thomas Astle. This was the 'Compleat Copy of Doomsday', shelved by him as A.II (now Stowe 851 in the British Library), and noted in a duplicate Index as 'A Copy of Domesday for the County of Kent, being attested by Mr Farley the Keeper of it, who received 16 Gns as a composition for his Fees for it'. Abraham Farley was the respected keeper of the Chapter House records, who made or attested transcripts from Domesday Book for a number of scholars in the eighteenth century, and who was to be the editor responsible for the text of the first official printing, in 1783, of the complete book, the expense of which was borne by the Treasury. Astle would seem to have been a useful intermediary, since Hasted was apparently charged only a third of the normal rate for his copy.[352]

At the time that Hasted was embarking on his *History* Thomas Astle was employed in the Augmentation Office, which looked after all the records pertaining to the dissolution of monasteries and chantries by Henry VIII and their subsequent disposal. Astle appears to have whetted Hasted's antiquarian appetite on a number of occasions with the mention of documents he had come across relating to Kentish families, and constantly promised help. He may well have been responsible for supplying Hasted with one or two other items, including an 'Abridgement of the Patent Rolles of King John, Henry 3, Edw.1 and Edw.2 by Mr Bowyer Keeper of the Records in his handwriting'.[353] This was perhaps the 'Extract from the Rolls' for which Hasted thanked Astle profusely in his letter of 19 May 1764, and which Dr Ducarel had brought down to Throwley for him. From Astle, too, may have come some old charters taken from among the records for which he was responsible, relating to Horton Priory, Holy Sepulchre at Canterbury, and the Priory of St Martin at Dover, which Hasted shelved in his study at T.XC (BL Add.5516). And Hasted's manuscript T.XCII contains what was perhaps received in answer to a request to Astle of March 1765 for assistance in establishing a friend's kinship to William Wickham, the founder of New College, Oxford:

> I have a near friend, whose interest I have much at heart, who would reap great benefit from Founder's Kin at New College. I think I heard you say you had a descent to Sr Edwd Dering from Wickham.[354]

Astle would appear to have sent Hasted, in answer to this, a judgment given 'in the Matter of Controversy between Humfrey Wickham of Swacklist Esq. and Sr Richard ffines, Knt, touching their right to have their children admitted to the New Colledges in Oxford and Winchester of the ffoundacon of William Wickham', which can hardly have been of very great use.[355] And Astle was almost certainly the source of an 'Antient Roll of Parchment, once belonging to the Augmentation Office — about 70 leaves of Parchment' which appears at the conclusion of the duplicate Index, BL Add.5537, as a.II.

Surrounded as he was by old documents relating to the sale and disposal of land and estates, Thomas Astle naturally came across frequent references to Kent, and it is not surprising that Hasted expressed eagerness to see anything and everything that might turn up:

> You judge very right that the MSS and drafts you mention will be very acceptable, indeed they will, there is no satisfying an antiquarian's appetite, the more you feed him, the more ravening he grows.

Hasted was not, however, thinking in terms of Astle giving him such items, but is speaking in terms of loans and copying:

> Those or anything you can procure for me, I shall receive with many thanks to you, and any little matters (if any should fall in your way that cannot be procured for a small time) I shall gladly pay the expence of, if you will be so kind to trouble yourself to get ym copied for me. (23 November 1763)

And again, the following year:

> I do not overlook your very kind promises of assisting me, as to Kent. I shall gladly thank you for every little trifle you will put down on paper for me, and I shall very willingly return it with any thing in my power. (29 April 1764)[356]

It is fairly obvious from Hasted's letter of April that Astle's help, even well into 1764, still consisted chiefly of promises. Finally, Astle seems to have done little more towards Hasted's *History* than provide him with a few very miscellaneous items from among the records nominally under his care.

From time to time the historian would allow himself to make a few purchases at sales. Among these were several folios of heraldic MSS, which he apparently commissioned Joseph Edmondson, Mowbray Herald Extraordinary, whom he seems to have known quite well, to buy for him. In a letter to Dr Ducarel dated 13 February 1765 he mentions a coloured heraldic MS which Edmondson had obtained for him, promising to give it to Ducarel when he had made use of it for his *History*.[357] In addition, he also owned two very fine MSS, signed and dated 1765 on the back pages, which he numbered together I.XL (BL Add.5504) and described in his Index as 'Baronage of Robt Cooke Clarencieux ... from the Conquest to the year 1572'. The first part shows 'sundry coats of arms' in trick and blazon, four to a page, while the second has only one to a page. It is perhaps an augmented copy of a Clarenceux visitation of 1572, as it contains both this date and another of 1595.

Hasted's purchases also included a rather lovely volume full of hand-written pedigrees, with many illustrations, which had formerly belonged to Tom Martin (Hasted X.CIX, BL Add.5524). This the historian has noted as bought in 1777 at the sale of the collection built up in a few years by John Ives, a young East Anglian antiquary who had fallen a victim to tuberculosis at an early age the year before. And several old folios, all containing pedigrees, came from the collection of the somewhat eccentric Edward Rowe Mores, sold at auction in 1779 shortly after his death.

Hasted made at least five purchases at this sale, usually noting inside the front cover their provenance and what he had paid for them, sums which varied between 2s.6d. and £4.0s.0d. The first of these, BL Add.5526 (Hasted Z.CXIII) contains yet another copy of Philipott's visitation of Kent in 1619, with an index, and fifty-four pages of pedigrees written out by Rowe Mores. For this Hasted paid £1.11s.6d. BL items Add.5527-5529, 5532, and possibly also 5531, also came from this sale. All contained pedigrees, to which further additions or notes were made by Hasted himself. BL Add.5528 (Hasted Z.CXV), described on its title-page as containing 'Pedigrees of Kentish Familys collected by Edward Rowe Mores', actually contains far more material in Hasted's hand than in that of Rowe Mores, whose pedigrees fill only nineteen pages. Indeed, Hasted, in purchasing this book, was neatly killing two birds with one stone, as he rather liked to do: at the same time that he acquired a few pedigrees which might be useful to him, he also obtained an almost empty folio volume of close on 400 pages. It was in this book that William Boys was to have his 'Stemmata Boysiana' copied out for Hasted, some time after 1782, and here that Hasted, a year or so later, was to make some 'Memdms from the Wills in the Prerogative Registry of Wills at Canterbury' — mainly short seventeenth-century pedigrees established on the basis of the wills he examined. BL Add.5529, (Hasted Z.CXVI) which obviously aroused little interest at the auction, and went to Hasted for no more than 2s.6d., was a quarto volume of pedigrees in the County Palatine of Chester in 1630. Hasted's attention was clearly caught by the names of families such as Bostoke, Hatton, Hill, Legh, Stringer and Tatton, all of whom had branches in Kent.

On the whole, however, Hasted's manuscript collection grew little after 1769. Very probably he could not bring himself to repeat the tremendous feat of copying which he had carried out in 1763-4 — nor, indeed, did he need to — and it was his collection of printed books to which he now added when he was able. This should not be taken to mean, however, that the records were neglected from this point on. Far from it. It was his intention from the first not to repeat the mistakes of past

'The more the antiquarian toils, . . .'

historians by merely copying from them, and he did not deviate from this: his references are, above all, references to sources, and seldom references to earlier Kentish historians. This attitude found expression as late as 1793, when Hasted wrote:

> It is impossible for us to observe without a degree of astonishment what errors, inaccuracies, and fallacious accounts disgrace our historical accounts of places, especially when we reflect that the writers had such an abundant store of valuable records and authentic resources in the numerous public repositories to which they might resort for information.[358]

Nevertheless, as he worked on his material, it became clear to him that in order to bring his *History* fully up to date he would have to consult, not only the records, which might not be available until an owner or a whole family had been laid low, but also the living. This, for him, was always a delicate matter, particularly when he was not known to any of the family. Initially he probably addressed his enquiries only to those whom he already knew well, and this in quite a general way. As we have seen, when friends knew of his project, especially if this was also a subject in which they, too, had a particular interest, as was the case with Mrs Frances Rooke and her sister, offers of help were immediately forthcoming. John Street, of Dartford, appears to have been another early helper.[359] But it was soon clear that random assistance of this kind was inadequate, and that a more systematic approach would be necessary.

Increasingly, he turned to his wide circle of acquaintances, in West Kent, in Chatham and Rochester, and in Canterbury. These were gentlemen in various walks of life, although it is not surprising that they usually came from those areas in which Hasted himself was involved. Thus the Revd William Lowth, of Rochester and Lewisham, may have first met Hasted at the Society of Antiquaries, where they became close friends and apparently on visiting terms. Samuel Fullagar, an attorney, came of an old Chatham family which had long been friendly with the Hasteds — and was incidentally also of Huguenot descent — and he and Hasted shared legal interests and discussed cases at the West Kent quarter sessions, of which Fullagar was treasurer. George Gipps, originally an apothecary, but who was to rise, via hop-factoring, to be both banker and MP, seems to have been known to Hasted in Chatham as well as in Canterbury, where Hasted's two-year stay following his marriage must have reinforced the friendship. These three gentlemen are broadly representative of the three groups of people who were to provide Hasted with much of the information he needed: clerics, attorneys, and the well-to-do, particularly when these were landowners.

In making use of the clergy as informants for his *History* Hasted was tapping an excellent source. The eighteenth-century incumbent, even were he a pluralist, was expected to be fully conversant with his parish. Incoming archbishops were likely to send each vicar in his diocese, which covered the greater part of Kent, a set of queries, known as Visitation Returns, relating to the size of his parish, the number of houses and parishioners it contained, and whether it had any schools, hospitals, almshouses or charities — and to expect an early reply. Among Hasted's clerical correspondents were the Revd Andrew Burnaby of Greenwich, the Revd Thomas Hey of Wickhambreux, who was related to Hasted's friends the Faunces, and the Revd Francis Fawke of Hayes; while in later years there were the delightfully named Revd William Wing Fowle of New Romney, a Romney Marsh man by birth who was to spend all his life on the Marsh, and the Revd William Disney of Pluckley, with both of whom the historian was on very friendly terms. The kindly William Disney, in particular. concerned as much with the world of the present as with that of the past, (or indeed, as a clergyman, with that to come) did not desert Hasted in his adversity.

The Revd Samuel Denne of Wilmington, on the other hand, although a near neighbour of Hasted when he lived at St John's, was very much the antiquarian, concerned as much or more with what had been, rather than what was, and maintaining a somewhat garrulous correspondence with several who were eminent in the same field, including Richard Gough.[360] He was inclined to be offended if his proffered items of information were not incorporated in the *History*, and was later to mingle criticism of Hasted's work with criticism of his life. Hasted seems overall to have made only limited application to other antiquarians and historians, although he had some correspondence with Edward Jacob, of Faversham, whom he probably knew quite well from his sojourns at Throwley. Jacob, who was by now an old man, responded courteously — 'you may command me' — although most of his own 'collections' (as these gentlemen tended to call their notes) appeared in his own *History of the Town and Port of Faversham*, published in 1774.

On the whole Hasted was prepared to be his own antiquarian, although feeling it wiser to leave the early period of the civilisation of Kent to those who specialised in it. What Hasted's correspondents were asked to provide was a kind of eighteenth-century oral history, concentrating on families and their ownership of the land. To facilitate their replies, particularly where busy attorneys were concerned, he would frequently draw up a questionnaire, containing precise questions to which he needed the answers.

This was nothing new where county histories were concerned. In 1755 the *Gentleman's Magazine* had reprinted a set of questions originally circulated by the Society of Antiquaries and 'proposed to gentlemen in the several parts of Great Britain, where they reside, with a view of obtaining from their answers a more correct account of the antiquities and natural history of our country, than has yet appeared'. Such a result would undoubtedly have been obtained had all the gentlemen approached been omniscient enough to answer all the questions. Question 28, for example enquired as to the 'Present and former price of provisions'; Question 29 desired to know what were the day wages for labourers in husbandry, and what for carpenters, bricklayers, masons, tilers, etc., and Question 34 asked: 'Are there any Roman, Saxon or Danish castles, camps, altars, roads, forts or other pieces of antiquity in your parish?' There were ninety-six such questions to be answered, forty-seven of a more general nature, thirty-eight on natural history, plus an additional ten if your parish lay on the coast, and a final poser which asked anyone living in a city to provide an outline history of it![361] But the questionnaire had been tried out even before this. According to the article which opened the first number of John Nichols's *Bibliographia Topographica Britannica* in 1780, questionnaires had been distributed in 1736 by the Revd Francis Blomefield for his modestly titled *Essay towards a topographical history of the county of Norfolk*, and in 1739 by John Hutchins for his *History and Antiquities of Dorset*. Rowe Mores, always a favourite of John Nichols, is here praised for having 'circulated a set of queries through Berkshire in 1759, in order to facilitate his perambulation previous to his design of writing a history of that county', a design which does not, however, seem to have reached even the perambulatory stage. But a failure of purpose could be imputed to either side: Nichols records that the Physico-Historical Society at Dublin received only 40 answers to 4000 sets of queries, a return of precisely 1%.[362]

The questionnaire, therefore, as an aid in the compilation of a county history was by no means unknown, and may well have been recommended to Hasted by a number of friends. And its use was probably welcomed particularly by the attorneys of the time, who were mostly very busy men indeed, and yet who seem to have accepted without demur this new duty of making a brief report to the county's historian on the estates and manors they serviced: it became simply one more voluntary duty in an age which expected many.

Hasted's initial approach to Lord Romney, as the lord of a number of manors, had shown him that requests to those with very large estates would be unlikely to elicit much information directly (although in later years a number of titled gentlemen, including Lord Romney himself, Lord Dacre, the Earl of Radnor and the Earl of Darnley, were to be very helpful). The attorneys who collected the tenants' manorial quitrents, however, were intimately acquainted with the ownership of lands, and accordingly, quite early on in his first great commonplace book, Hasted drew up a list of 'Names of Attorneys who Collect Qt Rents'. Of the names which follow only two or three do not seem to figure in the correspondence:

>Dine at Milton
>Hind at ditto
>Messrs Franklyn and Pattenson at Ashford
>Richard Halford, Canterbury
>John Jeken, Town clerk of Canterbury
>Young Jeken of Canterbury
>Mark Thomas of Canterbury
>John Middleton at Deal
>Wellard, Town Clerk of Dover
>Sampson Farbrace of Dover
>Westfield, Attorney in Dover
>Jordan, Folkestone
>Samuel Simmons, Town Clerk of Sandwich
>Solly of Sandwich
>Mr Geo Geree Elwick of Ashford, who collects the Qt Rents of many manors
>Tournay in Hythe
>Rolfe of New Romney.[363]

Not mentioned here are several attorneys who were so well known to Hasted as not to require noting down. Thomas Tomlyn, of Rochester, was to be of great help to the historian, as, too, was Francis Austen, steward to the Duke of Dorset, and a near neighbour of Hasted at Sutton-at-Hone. Austen's old-fashioned hand and spelling are to be found in several letters and questionnaires which he returned to the young historian, whom he clearly liked and who, indeed, was apparently distantly related to him through his grandmother. An early questionnaire addressed to the duke's steward covered the parishes of Shoreham, Kemsing, Seal, Sevenoaks, Chevening, Sundridge, Chiddingstone, Penshurst, Cowden, Leigh, Speldhurst, Westerham, Edenbridge and Brasted, and contained the following typical questions, to which answers were given as shown:

'The more the antiquarian toils, . . .'

Brasted Place: Q. if not the same as was formerly called Crow Place, alias Stockets, owner, Ld Willoughby of Brooke. Q. if now?

It is the same, and belonging to ye present Lord Willoughby of Brooke.

Delaware late Mr H. Streatfield. Q: Whose now?

The present Henry Streatfeild Esqr. of High Street House, Chiddingstone.

Q: Has there been 2 branches of the Hyde family, and how are they distinguished in their property?

John Hyde Esqr of Sundridge Place long since dead had several sons, his eldest son who is also dead many years ago removed to Bore Place in Chidingstone and Savil Hyde the youngest continued at Sundrish, but he and all ye famely of ye Hydes .. (illegible)

Q: Etonbridge Manor late Mr Ward's. Q. Whose now?

No Manor of this denomination that ever I heard of nor has Mr Ward any manor here.[364]

It is of course possible that Hasted sent out a number of questionnaires which were not sent back, but his sheet of queries, brief and to the point, permitting the correspondent to answer with the minimum of words and accompanied by a polite covering letter, probably resulted in a good return. He was writing to gentlemen to whom, as a justice of the peace, his name would not have been unknown, with a request for information which lay within their competence, and failure to respond, in the polite society in which they moved, would have been regarded as ill-mannered. Replies were frequently slow in arriving — respondents struggled with ill-health, such as agues, rheumatism, gout in the hand, or an apoplexy which, in the case of W. H. Solly of Sandwich, nearly resulted in his 'going off the stage',[365] or they were delayed by the unsatisfactory answers which they, in their turn, received from others in prosecuting Hasted's enquiries — but arrive they eventually did.

Many of Hasted's friends entered with enthusiasm into his project. Of no one was this truer than of John Thorpe. Thorpe, an MA of University College, Oxford, was the son of Dr John Thorpe of Rochester, whose collection of the records of that city he brought out posthumously in 1769. And Thorpe the younger was himself to appear in print in 1788, four years before his death, with a companion work at which he had laboured long, called *Custumale Roffense*, and containing attractively written accounts of most of the churches in the Rochester diocese as well as the Rochester Custumal.

Some eighteen years older than Hasted, John Thorpe lived in Bexley, his house, like that of Henry Streatfeild at Chiddingstone, known as High Street House, and described by Thorpe as one of the five 'principal and antient seats' in the parish: 'All the gay things which have started up of late years were only cottages'.[366] Hasted's cousin, Robert Dingley, occupied Lamienby, another of Thorpe's five 'antient seats', and it is possible that Hasted and Thorpe had been first introduced at Lamienby, although their friendship may have developed as a result of their membership of the Society of Antiquaries. They already had more in common than simply a Kentish background: Thorpe's first school had been that of the Revd Stephen Thornton, at Luddesdown, where Hasted's father had earlier been a pupil, and where Dr John Thorpe, as the headmaster's medical man, must also have doctored the boys when they were unwell. Certainly, by the mid-1770s there was a very close friendship indeed between the Hasted and the Thorpe families: they usually spent a few weeks of the year at each other's house, and the children in each family — John Thorpe had two daughters, Catherine and Ethelinda — were on equally good terms with their parents' friends. On the occasion of Catherine's approaching marriage in 1779 with Thomas Meggison, a London attorney, Thorpe passed on his daughter's thanks for the Hasteds' good wishes: 'my daughter's compliments for your obliging and sincere wishes for her wellfare in the matrimonial state. Nothing can add more to her happiness than the good wishes of her friends, among whom she justly esteems Mr and Mrs Hasted'; while Ethelinda, in March 1781, was daily expecting a letter from Mrs Hasted. Hasted's third son, George, was perhaps a favourite with the Thorpes, for in September 1777 John Thorpe added a postscript to his letter at his wife's bidding — although quite what was being referred to we cannot know: 'Mrs Thorpe is not unmindfull of our good friend little George, when an opportunity offers, and will let you know the result'.[367]

The warmth of the Thorpe/Hasted friendship comes out particularly in John Thorpe's greetings at the end of his letters: in the winter this might be, 'With our best respects to you and fireside, I conclude, dear Sir', or 'Our joint compliments of the season and many happy returns attend yourself and family'. Thorpe was willing to intercede, too, to heal a breach which occurred in 1777 between Hasted and his old friend Dr Ducarel: 'Friends should never suffer their tempers to be ruffled by heats and animosities. We are to forget and forgive one another's faults'[368] — a successful intercession, since there is evidence of later correspondence between Hasted and the Doctor. The genial Thorpe must have been dismayed when relations deteriorated between Hasted and his wife and the historian set up a separate establishment, but he seems to have remained in touch to the end: a note in Hasted's writing records that Mr Thorpe visited Cobham in 1787 to see the stately mausoleum of the Earl of Darnley, a snippet of information which he is only likely to have had at first hand.

Thorpe's encouragement of his friend ranged from his own informative letters to chasing up neighbours for details to which they might have access:

> I have been fishing among the N. Cray folks, who cannot inform me of the name of the gentlemen married to two of the Miss Brokes. Mr Moore tells me, the only person who can give any light in these matters is Mr Haranc of Foots Cray Place [who] is expected down tomorrow, when I will directly apply to him'.[369]

There was also a memorable visit which Thorpe paid to the Roman camp at Keston on a June day in 1775 with the engraver John Bayly for the purpose of measuring, recording and drawing it:

> the day excessive hot and broiling, and the tops of the trenches so high and slippery, that I got two or three tumbles among the furzes. We had two men to assist us, and with a running box-line with a winch containing 50 links, or 2 poles, we made the quicker dispatch. ... The cold bath, the source of the Ravensbourne, was a high regale to slake our thirst.[370]

Bayly's drawing and engraving of Keston Camp, a generous double-page spread, was to be John Thorpe's contribution to the plates for Volume I of the *History*, while a charming drawing by Catherine, 'A view of the Manor House called The Temple, in Stroud', which was again given to Bayly to engrave, provided another small illustration for the same volume.

It was Thorpe who urged the diffident historian to approach the owners of distinguished seats in the county with a request for an engraving to grace his work. As Thorpe said, 'They can but refuse, if not agreeable, and ... it is paying them a compliment', which was undoubtedly true.

Thorpe was full of cheerful encouragement with regard to Hasted's initial choice of engraver, John Bayly, who had perhaps been his own recommendation — it was Bayly who had engraved the portrait of Thorpe's father, Dr John Thorpe, which appeared as a frontispiece to the

Registrum Roffense. Bayly's great merit lay in not being too expensive, his great defect in being very slow. Hasted seems to have proposed originally to entrust all his engraving work to Bayly. 'I believe he will do them much cheaper than any other person', commented Thorpe, writing about the maps in October 1775, although earlier that month he had been obliged to agree with Hasted that 'Bayley is certainly a most dilatory creature, and requires a good spurring, which I will give him as you desire'.[371] Thorpe seems to have provided Hasted with a useful link with the engraver: living as he did at Bexley he was little more than a morning's ride away from London which the historian, now in Canterbury, could visit only rarely. One can understand Hasted's decision to have the printing of his work done locally where he could be in regular touch with the printer — he had undoubtedly learnt from his lengthy experience with *Familiar Letters* — in spite of Bayly's warnings, passed on by Thorpe, that a local printer might prove more expensive and do the work less well than a London one.

The letters from John Thorpe are particularly interesting for their comments on the maps, for they show some of the difficulties of establishing these, with the engraver having almost equal responsibility for the final outlines. In June 1775 Thorpe writes that he has lent Bayly his copy of Kilburne,

> for though he is an able artist, yet we may say with Horace, he is abnormis sapiens, in matters of this kind, not having the Kentish historians, etc., to direct him. He has got my Kilburne, which he says is of great service to him, as to the names of the parishes, and proper division of the Hundreds.[372]

Similarly, in September of the same year, Thorpe reported excitedly that he had just bought from Jasper Sprange, the Tunbridge Wells bookseller,

> an accurate map of all the roads, gentlemen's seats, etc., within fourteen miles of that place. It is a new thing, and I was so well pleased with it, that I purchased it, the price 2s.6d. I should think this map would assist Bayley in correcting the Hundreds of Somerden, Watchlingstone and Codsheath.[373]

By choosing to provide large-scale maps of the Hundreds Hasted gave himself a particularly difficult hurdle to leap. Since the text was to deal with the county by Hundreds, it seemed a relevant form to choose. But it appears never to have been attempted for Kent before (although the Hundred was, and was to remain for many years, an acknowledged administrative unit) and the boundaries of each one proved to be very difficult to determine. Once embarked on his plan, however, Hasted could not turn back. He appears to have prepared the initial sketch himself, on the basis of maps already in existence, subsequently sending them out to various gentlemen who he felt had the knowledge and expertise to make the necessary alterations, or who might be in touch with such men. Thus Thomas Clout, the Sevenoaks bookseller, who was already busy taking subscriptions for the *History*, and who, like Sprange at Tunbridge Wells, had a vested interest in maps, was approached in the autumn of 1777, replying on 26 November as follows:

> I have endeavored to communicate the maps of the Laths sent me to all who could be thought at all capable of judging of them, but cannot find any persons acquainted with the geography of this part of the county. There is a trifling correction or two, and I have examined the situation of the Roman Camp on the spot, and the roads about it, and find them erroneous there, and the more so as there is a new turnpike road on Ightham Common or Chart.[374]

The correspondence which relates to the maps of Marden and Eyhorne Hundreds provides a good illustration of the pains Hasted took to have them corrected. On the 31 May 1775 Mr J. Taylor wrote to him from Staplehurst as follows:

> At my return from London, I found your favor of 16th with the Map of the Hundred of Marden inclosed, which is not free from errors ... But what renders it difficult, and indeed impossible, to ascertain the bounds of Marden Hundred, is, that from the west end of Hockingbury Bridge, perhaps Holkenbury Bridge, part of the Lower Half Hundred of Eyhorne, stretching along the western side of the parish of Stapleherst, and the eastern side of that of Marden, extends itself thro' Goudherst as far as Kilndown. It increases almost every year. For the inhabitants on each side are desirous of crowding into it, that they may seldomer be obliged to serve as Peace Officers ... Not many years ago, a farmer was indicted at the Qr Sessions for refusing to serve the office of Constable. His plea was, he liv'd in the H. of Eyhorne. The prosecutor failing in his evidence, the defendant was acquitted ...
>
> Your milestones are right, and the cross roads and rivers are as nearly so, as an enclosed country, and a very irregularly inclosed country, will admit.[375]

The Revd Richard Bathurst, who had apparently been sent the same maps to look over, wrote from Finchcocks at Goudhurst on 6 June 1775:

> There were some very considerable mistakes in the maps, which I have therefore made very free with, as you desired; and I am of opinion that they are now tolerably correct.[376]

Edward Belcher, of Ulcombe, a fellow justice of the peace, returned the map of Eyhorne Hundred on 19 June with only a few adjustments and corrections to the spelling of names, commenting as he did so:

> These are the few remarks I have been able to make with regard to the correction of the map you are pleased to think we are in some measure capable [of]. I wish it had been in my power to render you considerable service to your great and useful undertaking.

And Belcher added the following PS:

> Mr Hogben of Doddington, who, with the help of his father late of Smarden, has survey'd a considerable part of the land in the Hundred of Eyhorne, above the hill, cou'd give assistance to you, were he [to] spend one day in viewing that part of the country; but wou'd expect something for his trouble, probably.[377]

Nevertheless, in spite of these corrections and suggestions, the map of Eyhorne Hundred was still found very faulty by the Revd Pierrepont Cromp in January 1781 when it was sent to him for last-minute revision:

> It is so amazingly incorrect, and more particularly so in the Upper Half Hundred, that I scarce see how it can be rectified; the roads are excessively wrong, and what is very extraordinary, the bounds of the Hundred are not observed, as Lenham Heath, Shelve, and Cobham are omitted, all which are in the Hundred of Eyhorne, and Pett, in Stockbury, inserted, which is in the Hundred of Middleton.[378]

Hasted has humbly headed Pierrepont Cromp's emendations, 'Memdms Concerning Errors in Map of Eyhorne Hdd from Mr Crompe'.

'The more the antiquarian toils, . . .'

In just a few cases was he able to entrust his maps to someone who was a more than competent surveyor. John Tressé, of Brompton, who seems to have been well known to Thorpe, and who took over responsibility for the map of Nonington, appears to have worked at Chatham as a surveyor, for in his letter of March 1779 he mentions 'an actual survey I made last summer of the road from Room Lane to Horsted, and from thence to the 3-mile post in the road to Maidstone, for the purpose of improving it'[379]. But for the most part the preparation of the maps remained uphill work.

The late eighteenth century saw a proliferation of maps, none of them perfect, which was why the Board of Ordnance, alarmed at the very real threat of an invasion by France, commissioned the Trigonometrical Survey of the county of Kent in 1791 under the direction of Captain William Mudge. The first steps towards a more accurate survey had been taken in the 1780s, when base-lines (the first stage in triangulation) had been measured for Hounslow Heath and Romney Marsh, and from Greenwich to Dover. But even had it been available to them this preliminary material would not have been of very great use to Hasted and his gentlemen surveyors, and the maps accompanying Hasted's *History* were, therefore, to be almost the last products of the old school of map-making.

The detail of Hasted's preparation for his *History* is preserved in the surviving notes and files of correspondence. It is unfortunate that there is no parallel source for the detail of his personal life. Nevertheless, the correspondence which we have frequently contains personal references, and other sources, too, can be combed to flesh out the man whose brief autobiographical Chronology, appended to the Anecdotes, provides a useful skeleton, if rather roughly drawn. Hasted was far from being a cloistered antiquarian, and there was always a great deal going on in his life while he worked on his *History*. The decade up to 1770 witnessed the birth of his seven children, the performance of a variety of civic duties, undertaken in the spirit of the age which pointed propertied men in the direction of public service, and much more. Of particular importance in his life, when the *History* was still in its early stages, was the decision in 1768 (erroneously noted in Hasted's Chronology as 1776) to move to Canterbury.

Glaisbrooke

Glassenbury Dutchess of St Albans owner — Sr Tho: Roberts young[er]
Thomas Roberts Bart: from Ireland a descendant of Sir [son] to him by [Duchess] of St Albans
Sir Thomas Roberts who died in 1627 & had escaped to Ire- the present
troublesome times & now continues the Title which sometime
in the late Sr [Walter] St Albans Mr Cha[rle]s N
Plashinghurst, about a mile N from Glassenbury.
milkhouse decd owner his Widow — Mrs

Frizley Borough — a mile E of Plashinghurst. Mr
lately purchased by Mr John Collens ?

Anglie Manor — in N. part next Staplehurst
Angley Mannor belongs to the Heirs of Mr Henl[ey]
present possessor & Resident at little Angley which

Hattridge, Sipinghurst (scite of Milkhou[se]
Horse Mill all those are about this

Hockridge 3/4 mile N.E. from church — and Ho[...]
Milk-House street have their late Mr Cha[rles]
White-Well — belongs to Mr Ro[berts]
Bettenham Mr Henley of Otham decd. no[w]

Chapter 10

Hasted in Canterbury

Perhaps the most unexpected move in Hasted's life is his decision, in 1768, to give up St John's at Sutton-at-Hone and to become a city gentleman in Canterbury. From his expenditure on the old Commandery it is clear that he had intended St John's for his permanent home. This was the part of Kent to which he had come with his father as a little boy of two, in which he had been brought up, where the family had established itself, and where the Hasteds had close friends. Situated almost mid-way between London and the town of Maidstone, it could have enabled the historian with similar ease to pursue his antiquarian researches in the libraries and record offices of London and to sit on the magistrates' bench at Maidstone. Something had happened to sour his relationship with the controlling powers on the West Kent bench. Time might have healed that breach — but time was what he did not now have. Faced with a demand for £836 by the 20 December 1767, it was probably only by parting with St John's that he could meet that demand: the alternative, to organise the sale of several outlying parts of the Hasted estate, was simply not feasible in the time at his disposal. In buying Oakleys/Homefield House — prompted to it perhaps by what must have seemed the sensible plan of starting to concentrate the Hasted holdings in one place, instead of having them scattered over the county, and, there is no doubt, encouraged to it by his attorney Thomas Williams — Hasted had quite possibly over-reached himself, and it may have been necessary to sacrifice St John's in order to stave off a greater disaster.

The new occupant of St John's was Robert St Paul, related through his sister to the Petleys of Riverhead. A church rate made at Sutton-at-Hone in October 1768 shows him installed by then, and the Hasteds' actual move to Canterbury appears to have taken place in the early summer of that year.[380] Such a removal was not the affair of a day, however, and some months had to elapse while arrangements were made and the lease transferred, probably at midsummer. It is noticeable that in April 1768, when subscriptions were being received for the initial outlay on the new Dartford to Sevenoaks turnpike road which had recently obtained its Act of Parliament and which went right past Hasted's property in Sutton, Hasted acted as one of the trustees assigning the tolls on mortgage, but unlike many of his neighbours — Sir John Dixon Dyke of Lullingstone Castle, Francis Leigh of Hawley, John Calcraft of Ingress, Richard Hulse of Baldwins, John Tasker of Franks and Nathaniel Webb, the new owner of Sutton Place, all of whom subscribed sums between one and three hundred pounds — did not himself become a subscriber.[381]

The meeting of the Dartford-Sevenoaks turnpike road trustees was held on 6 April, and there were several other meetings which Hasted attended that month. On 15 April he was at Rochester for the annual election of the bridge wardens, when he was re-elected an assistant warden and also became one of the four auditors for the year, with Roger Twisden, James Best and William Gordon, and he went to Rochester again on 22 April for a Court of the Commission of Sewers.[382] A day or two later, however, found him in London: a letter from Peter Eaton, dated 26 April, had to be re-addressed from Sutton to 'Princes Court, near Great George Street, Westminster'.[383]

While it is likely that Hasted had some business to attend to in connection with his proposed move, he made use of his time in London to attend three meetings of the Society of Antiquaries, on 28 April and 5 and 12 May,[384] and he may well have made arrangements with Thomas Astle and Andrew Coltee Ducarel to work on records in the Augmentation Office and Lambeth Palace Library on the same occasion.

In Princes Court with his mother there were social visits to be received and paid. Mrs Hasted must always have been delighted to be able to present her son, the magistrate and Kentish landowner, to her acquaintances, and no doubt several small receptions were held by her friends in return at which Mr Hasted was the guest of honour: there is at least one letter in the correspondence relating to the *History* which mentions that the writer had had the pleasure of meeting the historian at Mrs Smyth's (a neighbour of Mrs Hasted in Princes Court) 'but did not then know you was engag'd in a work of this nature'.[385]

By 26 May, when we again find him present at a meeting of the bridge wardens in Rochester, Hasted must have been back at Sutton-at-Hone, and it is probable that the month of June was given over entirely to the removal to Canterbury. Ann Hasted was by now in the seventh month of another pregnancy, and it is hardly likely that the move could have been put off any longer if it was to take place that summer. John Septimus, the Hasteds' seventh child, was to be born on 17 August in the house in St George's Street which Hasted had taken in Canterbury. The baby's sponsors on his baptism in St George's church were to reflect both Sutton-at-Hone and Canterbury. Of the two godfathers, one was Andrew Coltee Ducarel, who, as Commissary General of the City and Diocese of Canterbury, also had a house in Canterbury, and the other was John Tasker, a wealthy brewer and landowner in Sutton-at-Hone and the neighbouring parish of Horton Kirby, whose wife was the sister of Sutton's vicar, the Revd Edmund Faunce, while Mrs Elizabeth Faussett, the wife of

Hasted's noted antiquarian friend, the Revd Bryan Faussett of Heppington, consented to become the baby's godmother.[386]

Hasted clearly felt that the reductions in establishment and outlay effected by the move to Canterbury justified his taking an elegant residence in the city, and the house which the family now occupied was one of the largest on the south side of St George's Street. It was equipped with commodious stables and a coachhouse. A tithe account book of 1770 shows Edward Hasted, esq. paying an annual tithe of £1 on his house and 10s.6d. on his 'offices', where the average for the better houses in the street stood at around 12s., with 2s.6d. or 5s.0d. paid for the offices. The Hasteds' neighbours were Mrs Papillon, Dr Roussel and Mr Le Grand (names which reflected the still considerable Huguenot element in the city), Mrs Loftie, Mrs Bridger and Mrs Webb on one side, and on the other Mrs Lushington, Mrs Harrison, Mr Rock, and a certain 'Jumper esq.' — who is probably the William Jumper who was sheriff of Kent in 1761. Of these only Mr Jumper, with tithes of £1.2s.0d. on his house and £1.0s.0d. on his outhouses, was rated higher than the historian.[387]

Nevertheless St George's Street, which took its name from the old Norman church standing on its northern side, was very much part of the city's busy commercial life. Here, for example, were the premises of Mr Kidder the cabinet maker, of Thomas Roch an upholsterer and appraiser (and also author of several pamphlets criticising the actions of the Canterbury Burghmote), and of Benjamin Smith a watchmaker. Thomas Sankey, the street's grocer and tallow-chandler, advertised his 'tobacco and snuff manufactured at Canterbury' and the street also had a post-office. Mr Williamson, surgeon, apothecary and man-midwife, had taken over Alderman Hayward's practice at about the same time that the Hasteds moved in — was it perhaps he who was called on to deliver John Septimus? In his *Walk in and about the City of Canterbury* of 1774 Gostling mentions that the Shambles, the butchers' market, was a little lower down on the same side of the street, and that the smells of a fish-market were nearby:

> Here also is a fish-market, lately established, where they who bring their fish to town, may sit and sell them toll free. Just by is the public engine for weighing loads of hay, and near this, at the same side, and the corner of Butchery-lane, is the corn-market, with a granary over it.

This commercial bustle was not confined within the city walls. Next to St George's Gate and facing the cattle market Joseph Gofter had a warehouse for men's and boys' clothes, while in May 1769 Mrs Price from London was advertising that 'having engaged the house next door to Mr Hatcher, carpenter, without St George's Gate,' she intended opening a school 'for the education of young ladies, boarding and day scholars, in English, French, and all sorts of needlework, with proper masters engaged for writing, arithmetic, and dancing'. In St George's Street itself Mr Kidder's son, who had in the meantime moved to the post office, was to announce in June 1770 that he too would shortly be opening a school, where boys would receive instruction 'in reading, writing, arithmetic and merchants' accompts'.[388]

The cabinet-maker, Mr Kidder, was to retire shortly after the Hasteds arrived, his premises being taken in October 1768 by James Simmons, who had recently emerged victorious in his struggle to introduce a new newspaper in Canterbury, the *Kentish Gazette*. It was here that Simmons, together with George Kirkby, opened the King's Arms Printing Office, with a bookshop and stationer's attached, to which, a little later, a circulating library would be added. As was common among printers at this time, Simmons and Kirkby also kept a large medicine warehouse, where they sold not only a variety of patent medicines, but also beauty products such as milk of roses, recommended for preserving and clearing ladies' skin and as an after-shave for gentlemen, soap, lavender water, tooth-pastes and powders, tooth-picks and tooth-brushes, as well as hair-restorers 'for making the hair grow thick and fast and preventing it from falling off or turning grey', and plain or delicately coloured hair-powder — most of these items, with the possible exception of the hair-powder, still available today.[389] Hasted's acquaintance with Simmons, which was to result in his choosing him as the printer for his *History*, may have begun when Simmons opened his printing office in St George's Street, although the two men may not have known each other particularly well until some years later, since an item in the *Kentish Gazette* in 1772, relating to the committal of a man to gaol in St Dunstan's on violent suspicion of theft, named the justices who acted in the matter as John Lade and, erroneously, 'William' Hasted.

To Hasted's wife, the move to a more bustling environment may have been not unwelcome: to the children, it probably felt more like being driven out of Eden, with the loss of woods, fields and their own small, cool river. School, of course, occupied most of their days, but holidays and weekends must have changed immeasurably for them. Hasted himself must have been all too keenly aware of his altered situation, from country squire to city gentleman, but perhaps found some compensation in fitting out a new and more spacious room as a study, no doubt taking the opportunity to provide himself with more shelves and presses than he had been able to squeeze into the tiny room which had served him at St John's, to cope with his ever-increasing rows and piles of books, printed and manuscript, and the folders in which he carefully placed the letters and returned questionnaires which he was now constantly receiving. A general settling-in, followed by the birth of the new baby, must have occupied most of the summer of 1768, and in fact domestic affairs seem to have loomed large during the next two or three years, and perhaps account for the fact that there is very little correspondence dating from this time in the files relating to the *History*. John Septimus was to be the last of Hasted's children to survive. The following year (Hasted mistakes the date in his brief Chronology, giving it as 1770) another son, Joseph, born at the end of November, was to live only a few days. He was buried in the south aisle of St George's church in December 1769, and commemorated with a small white stone in the shape of a heart.[390]

1769 also saw the death of an elderly and very wealthy acquaintance of the Dormans, as a result of which Ann Hasted's sister, Mary Dorman, became a figure of some importance in the family and also in her own right. The previous August Samuel Fullagar, in closing a letter to Hasted with the usual greetings to his friend's wife, had been reminded to add: 'I was on Saturday last to visit Mr Harris who is very well considering he has lived altogether in one room above stairs for 9 months or more. Miss Dorman is likewise pretty well considering'.[391]

Samuel Fullagar, of Maidstone, was Thomas Harris's attorney, who had acted for him in 1763 on the occasion of the unfortunate Gabriel Thorne's failing to secure the collectorship of Faversham, and who in 1765 assisted him in drawing up his will. It would appear that Mary Dorman, one of several Dorman sisters, had then already been living with Harris for some time. Harris had had links with Sutton-at-Hone much earlier — in his will, besides small bequests to be laid out in bread for the poor of Barming and East Farleigh, he was to leave £5 a year to the poor of Sutton-at-Hone for the purchase of linen for shirts and shifts — and it was probably at Sutton that Mary had first come to his notice. When he died, towards the end of April 1769, the *Kentish Gazette* noted:

> On Monday last died, far advanced in years, Thomas Harris esq., of Barming, near Maidstone, worth £150,000. He has left the bulk of his fortune to Mr Mumford, of Sutton, near Dartford, in Kent.

This was substantially correct, but at the same time Mary Dorman had been left £5000, and by a codicil, which had been added on the same day that the will was made, Harris also left her, for the term of her natural life, his house and all the land belonging to it at Barming, together with barns, stables, and outhouses, his chariot and horses, cows and other cattle, a farm at Barming and another at Maidstone, as well as two cottages at Coxheath. The £5000 was not to be paid to her until two years after Thomas Harris's decease, but in April 1769 Mary Dorman became, nevertheless, mistress of a seat at Barming, The Homestall, and a very wealthy woman overnight.[392]

Her position in the Harris household, whatever it was, had already been of some use in obtaining loans for her Dorman relatives: Thomas Harris's will cancelled any debts which were owing to him by Gabriel Thorne, whose wife Elizabeth was another of Ann Hasted's sisters, or by John Pope, who had married Margaret, also one of the sisters, while Mary's widowed mother, Mrs Dorothy Dorman, was forgiven a debt of £142.10s. for which Harris had held her note of hand. Unfortunately for the Hasted finances Mary's sister Ann was not a legatee — the Dorman involvement with Thomas Harris may only have come about after Ann's marriage in 1755, so it is possible that she was not so well known to the wealthy old man. But it is clear that he knew Hasted and that they had friends in common: Edward Wilks of Faversham, with whom Hasted was very friendly, received a bequest of £400. Any claims which the Hasteds may have felt they had to be remembered in Thomas Harris's will, either through friendship or through Ann's relationship to Mary, seem to have been totally ignored.

The Dorman connection was therefore not so totally 'without fortune' as it might seem from Hasted's Anecdotes. There was no reason, of course, for Mary Dorman to underwrite any of Hasted's debts, nor does she appear to have done so. But the Hasted children seem to have had in her a kind and caring aunt, who certainly had her nephews and nieces to stay with her, and who probably enjoyed being in a position to make them frequent presents of gowns, bonnets or waistcoats. On the Hasted side, the children's only relative was their unbendingly snobbish grandmother, whose attitude to their mother does not seem to have been softened by Ann's acquisition of a wealthy sister at Barming.

The Hasted calendar for 1770 was dominated by the removal of old Mrs Hasted from London to Canterbury.[393] Hasted had made his own sacrifice in 1768, when he had given up St John's and with it the life of a country gentleman. It is likely that he had wanted his mother to leave her expensive London residence at the same time — the income of both of them was dependent on the same source, the rents from the Hasted lands — but it took another two years, and perhaps many heated exchanges, to bring the old lady, who was herself approaching seventy, to the point where she was willing to abandon her London life.

Before Hasted's mother could give up her London house, however, came the business of disposing of the lease. The London housing market was probably less sluggish than the Kentish one had proved in 1757, when Hasted had wanted to give up his Canterbury house Without Riding Gate. At all events, Hasted and his mother soon had an eager purchaser. In April 1770 John Wilkes, just released from the King's Bench prison, where he had been sentenced to spend twenty-two months for his part in publishing No.45 of the *North Briton* and the scurrilous *Essay on Woman*, was looking for a new house for himself and his daughter Polly. In the meantime he was living in Fulham and, when in town on aldermanic business, lodging at a Mrs Henley's, only a few doors away from Mrs Hasted in Princes Court. Hasted himself mentions in passing that his mother's house was taken by Alderman Wilkes, but fortunately for us Polly happened to be on holiday in Paris at this time, and in several of the many letters which passed between father and daughter Wilkes recounts the details of his search for a house.[394]

Wilkes and Polly had both initially favoured a house in Berners Street, but the negotiations for this fell through, as 'the title to the house in Berners Street cannot be cleared', and 'Mrs Macauley bought-in herself the house in Berners Street, where I visited her yesterday'. The Mrs Macauley concerned, her name more usually written Macaulay, is almost certainly the historian Catherine Macaulay, sister of John Sawbridge who was a close friend of John Wilkes — and incidentally the owner of Olantigh, not far from Canterbury. Whether it was through the Kentish grapevine or the London one it is impossible to know, but having learnt that Mrs Hasted's house in Princes Court was on the market Wilkes announced to Polly that he was now 'in treaty with Mrs Kent for a house in Princes Court, the last house next to the Birdcage Walk'. 'Mrs Kent' was probably a slip of the pen for Mrs Hasted, now preparing to move into Kent, for that it was indeed her house Wilkes had in view is confirmed in a letter of 5 June, when he tells Polly: 'I cannot have my new house in Princes Court till midsummer-day, for Mrs Hasted's brother does not come to town till the 20th' — another slip here, when Wilkes mistakes son for brother.

In spite of these errors, however, it seems very likely that Wilkes and Hasted were known to each other. Hasted's father had had strong connections with the City of London, where Wilkes's father, like his son, had been based, and Hasted probably shared the common support of Wilkes in his struggle against repressive authority. There is in addition the reference to Miss Wilkes in Astle's letter of November 1763 which clearly indicates that she was in the vicinity of the Hasteds at that time.

Wilkes's letters to his daughter provide us with some details of the house in which Mrs Hasted had lived for sixteen years and where her son had often stayed. It was, wrote Wilkes, 'small, but exceedingly pleasant. The rent is to be fifty guineas a year. There is an excellent hall. I mean to furnish two print-rooms: one for you, the other for myself'. Like most houses which have had the same occupant over a number of years, it was now in need of refurbishment: 'After I have the house, there must be a thorough repair, as I am to have a lease for fourteen years: and in all cases I prefer it; for the excellence of the situation ensures me a tenant if ever I quit it, which I should only do for a house six times as large'.

In another letter, when passing on to Polly a request from 'Dr Wilson ... to bring an umbrella for him', Wilkes suggests that she bring two, 'as the house in Princes Court is at a little distance from the street'. And we learn also that Mrs Hasted's house had a secluded garden full of rose-trees, which Hasted, on his visits, must often have tended for his mother, and which may well have been planted by him:

> I returned here [to Mrs Henley's] last night from Fulham, my dearest Polly, in order to settle every thing for the new house. I was a gardener there, in compliment to you; for I cut off all the rose-buds of the trees in our little garden, (which is a secret) to make them blow at the end of the season, when I hope to enjoy your company there after our tour.[395]

The business with Hasted was evidently completed to everyone's satisfaction, for on 22 June Wilkes wrote from his lodgings:

> This will be the last day, my dearest Polly, of my being here; and therefore, you may suppose me not a little hurried in the removing all my books and furniture. I like the appearance of the house more and more every day,[396]

while Mrs Hasted, in Princes Court, was probably similarly engaged in watching the last of her belongings being packed up, in preparation for her move to a house in the Precincts of the cathedral at Canterbury.

This was an area of which her son was to say in his *History*:

> At present, the several houses within these precincts are, for the most part, large and handsome; many of them have been rebuilt, and others have had great improvements and additions made to them within memory, sufficiently convenient to accommodate the

owners, who, in general, are men of large preferments, as well as good private fortunes, and when they are not resident here, let their houses to genteel families, who form a very respectable neighbourhood within these precincts, which are kept remarkably clean and neat, and being gravelled and well planted with rows of trees, make a most pleasant and desirable residence.[397]

The Hasteds, from 1770, were to become part of that 'very respectable neighbourhood'. An advertisement of 1763 in the *Kentish Post* gives some idea of the Precinct houses of the time, when one was offered to let, being described as a brick house, with four rooms on a floor, plus closets, a large kitchen, very good cellars, a large wash-house and brewhouse, and 'well supplied with good water, which comes in every day from seven o'clock in the morning till seven in the evening'.[398] The house Hasted took for his mother was close to the Green Court, a name which probably reflected its use, since it had in it what Gostling called 'the great reservoir', which supplied the Precinct houses and from which a great deal of water ran waste every night when it was not being used. Hasted describes the house as lying between that of the second prebend and the cathedral, 'up the flight of steps leading from the Green Court to the church ... a comfortable, convenient house'. It seems not to have had its own garden, but there was a garden behind it belonging to the neighbouring prebendal house owned by Dr Barford, and Hasted was able to rent this for his mother for an extra £1 a year. Mrs Hasted was charged poor rates on a rental of £6 when she first went there, but this probably represents the £5 which we find mentioned in the lease plus the extra £1 for the garden.[399]

There is a set of leases in the cathedral archives, dating from 1776, 1785 and 1792, which relates to the Hasted occupancy of this house, confirming, as Hasted says in his Anecdotes, that it was near the stone steps leading up to the cathedral, and had previously been in the possession of the Turner family. The leases describe the property as a house, woodhouse and other appurtenances, and give the impression that it was relatively new. The lease was for no more than £5 a year, but as was the custom a fine would have been levied at the time of purchase, to compensate for depreciation in the real value of money since the lease had been fixed — probably in line with other Dean and Chapter properties. When the lease was relinquished in 1792 a sum of £400 was paid, and we can suppose that Hasted on taking the lease paid a similar sum.[400]

Mrs Hasted's would appear to have been rather less grand than the prebendal houses in the Precincts, which were rated on a rental of £10, although it was by no means the smallest house there, since the poor rates also note rents of £4 and even £2. However, her rent increased to £8 in 1773, and there may have been other increases, since Hasted, who was eventually to move in with his mother, later remembered it as being £12.

Hasted was to record in his Anecdotes that his mother's furniture and belongings were 'sent down by water in the hoy to Whitstaple, and thence by land carriage to Canterbury' where they were eventually 'set to rights in her new habitation'. Before the move was complete, however, Mrs Hasted and her granddaughter Anne, who seems to have gone to live with her permanently a year or so earlier, were accommodated in St George's Street. In a letter to Dr Ducarel, written on 10 July of that year, Hasted was to refer to 'all our bustle and confusion here, as you may imagine at present',[401] and one can indeed picture the constant coming and going between St George's Street and the Precincts, the orders and counter-orders given to carpenter and decorator alike, before the elderly widow's 'new habitation' was arranged to her taste and liking.

Hasted's account of the Hasted family ceases abruptly with the installation of his mother at Canterbury, but not before he has mentioned how much more comfortably she was able to live there than she had done in her expensive London house. Her establishment, which there had been reduced to two maids only, was here composed of two maids and a footboy in livery, and she was able to live, says her son, 'tho' in a private and oeconomical way yet with a genteel appearance and with much credit and respect'.[402] Much of that respect was due to the esteem in which her son was himself held, as a justice of the peace, a Deputy Lieutenant, and a man who filled several of the voluntary roles to which both local government and numerous public institutions were indebted for their smooth running at that time.

Nevertheless, in spite of the air of 'a gentleman of fortune' which Hasted was able to maintain outwardly, it soon became clear to him that even more stringent economies would be necessary. Accordingly, in 1772 the Hasted family moved yet again, although this time to within walking distance of their former home. The house which Hasted now took was another house in the Precincts, that of Dr Bennett Storer, who had been presented to the second prebendal stall in the cathedral in 1769. Those prebendaries who did not choose to reside in the houses which fell to them with their prebends were free to let them, with the proviso that they themselves spent at least twenty-one days' continuous residence there in the year. Persons leasing such accommodation therefore found themselves under an obligation to take an annual holiday of the same duration, which could perhaps place a burden on family and friends. Hasted probably felt that it would provide little inconvenience for those of his family who were at home to move in with his mother (who was not in a prebendal house) for a short while, although in letters of the later 1770s we find several references to summer visits to John Thorpe at Bexley, which probably offered a happier and more relaxed alternative.

It may well have been possible for Hasted to maintain, in defence of his second move, that a house in the Precincts would provide a quieter environment for his work than St George's Street, which was undoubtedly true, although the Precincts at that time contained a number of workshops and yards serving the cathedral — Gostling mentions 'pieces of ground made use of for carpenters' and masons' yards', and there was also a plumbers' workshop, 'where sheet lead is cast for the repairs of the church'. But it could also be that Hasted was drawn by the ancient features of the second prebend's house, as he had been drawn by the old chapel of the Knights Hospitallers at St John's. Gostling describes it as near the Dark Entry, and

> mostly of modern structure, but the hall of it was that of the old infirmary, a large and handsome room, open to the roof, built (according to Mr Somner) about the year 1342, and still in good repair. The free-stone arches over the door and windows of it are strengthened by others just above them of flint, curiously cut, so as to resemble bricks set on end.[403]

Like all the prebendal houses, it paid poor rates on a rental of £10. Among Hasted's neighbours, similarly housed, were the Revd Osmund Beauvoir, Dr Barford, Dr Benson, Dr Berkeley, Dr Lynch, Dr Tatton, Dr Dering, Gilbert Knowler and Richard Hopton. In smaller houses, with rentals of only £5, were the Revd Francis Gregory, rector of the parish of St George, and the Revd Joshua Dix, who were both minor canons of the cathedral.[404] These were the gentlemen who now formed Hasted's 'neighbourhood', almost all 'men of the cloth', whom Hasted, although himself a practising Christian, seems to have regarded, like not a few of his contemporaries, with some reservations. In his Anecdotes he was to say of the Precincts and their inhabitants:

> The Dean and Prebendaries are accounted the superior gentry of the place, and may be said to carry themselves by far too haughty and proud to every one else.[405]

John Thorpe was clearly in agreement with this, confiding to Hasted in a letter of 1778: 'You know I look upon Deans and Chapters in the same light that you do, and wish that Government would lay a good tax upon them and ease the laity'.[406] Nevertheless, Hasted could not help making friends, and while perhaps having little in common with many of the upper clergy, there were several among the members of the cathedral with whom he became very close.

The Revd Osmund Beauvoir MA, headmaster of the King's School, was very probably a man of a wider outlook than some of the more narrowly focused clerics whom Hasted disliked. A fellow of St John's College, Cambridge, he had been the third son of the Revd William Beauvoir MA, chaplain to the embassy at Paris. He was appointed to a number of livings, first at Calne in Wiltshire and then in Kent. He had himself been educated at the King's School in Canterbury, and returned to become its headmaster in 1750. He was also one of the Six Preachers of the cathedral. Athough now generally referred to as Dr Beauvoir, he was, during most of the years of Hasted's friendship with him, no more than the Revd Osmund Beauvoir: his DD was conferred by the archbishop in 1782, when he resigned his headship, married again (his first wife had died in 1762), and subsequently, on account of ill-health, moved to Bath, virtually severing his links with Canterbury. He seems to have been popular with many, and was generally given a good character although perhaps not altogether universally liked. To Hasted, however, he was a man 'whose great abilities brought this school to the highest degree of estimation; who united the gentleman with the scholar', and 'whose eminent qualifications and courtesy of manners gained him the esteem and praise of all who knew him'. Sir Samuel Egerton Brydges remembered him as 'an excellent classical scholar of fine taste, and some genius'; and Cole, in his 'Athenae Cantabrigienses', called him 'a cheerful companion, who sang a good song and understood music well'.[407]

Although noting in his diary that 'Faussett called Beauvoir an impudent, shewy, pushing, bossy, florid man', who was 'too expensive for him', the unmarried, unadventurous, somewhat waspish Revd Joseph Price, Faussett's curate at Monk's Horton, confided to that same diary that he longed 'to be intimate with Beauvoir'.[408] This, Edward Hasted undoubtedly was — perhaps entering the world of music for the first time under Osmund Beauvoir's genial tuition, and certainly sharing with him his own passion for Kentish antiquities. Many years later, writing to another friend, William Boteler, Hasted was to remember collecting seals of coats of arms with Beauvoir: 'I have a number collected by myself and Dr Beauvoir with the names written at the backs of them — being those of the noblemen and gentry we have corresponded with'.[409]

Beauvoir was ten years or so older than Hasted. The Revd Joshua Dix, minor canon of the cathedral and vicar of Brookland on Romney Marsh, was younger by about the same amount. As a minor canon, inhabiting a smaller house, he undoubtedly fell outside the circle of 'haughty' churchmen. From a reference to him in one of John Thorpe's letters 'friend Dix' seems to have accompanied Hasted on a visit to Bexley, and to have enjoyed with Thorpe the fishing in the river Cray which ran through the grounds of High Street House. Dix and his wife Martha were just beginning their family when Hasted's was virtually complete: Ann Hasted and Martha Dix were both pregnant around the same time in 1773 and both chose the name Mary for the little girl to which each gave birth. On the evidence of friendship between the families it seems likely that Hasted became godfather to Dix's second son, born in September 1778, who bore his own name of Edward.[410]

There were, of course, plenty of children of an age with those of the Hasted family living in the Precincts at this time. The cathedral register shows numerous children born in the 1760s in the families of the Revd John Tucker, undermaster at the King's School, of the Revd John Duncombe, of Edward Thurlow, and of the cathedral barber, John Abbott. The Hasted boys were to be at school with several of them.[411]

One of the advantages of living in the Precincts of the cathedral was that boys who did so might receive their tuition at the King's School free, as King's Scholars. The records show that Hasted's two eldest sons, Edward and Francis, were both sent there in 1769, Edward staying until he was seventeen, when he left at Christmas 1777 to go to Oriel College, Oxford, and Francis leaving shortly before his fourteenth birthday, at Christmas 1775, to go into the army. Neither of them was able to take advantage of the King's Scholarships as the family lived outside the Precincts until 1772. George, however, who went to the school in 1771, was young enough to be admitted as a King's Scholar the following year, holding the scholarship, as was usual, for five years. Charles, similarly, sent to the school in 1772, was a King's Scholar for five years, from 1773 to 1778. John Septimus, the youngest son, also benefited from the scholarship, and was a King's Scholar from 1778, when he entered the school at the age of ten, to 1783, when he left.[412] These scholarships, which covered tuition fees, and also provided £4 a year towards a scholar's expenses, must have been of considerable help to Hasted in what appear to have been increasingly straitened circumstances.

Osmund Beauvoir is often credited with having improved both tone and discipline at the school, and with having made it more attractive to 'the leading county families'. While this may have been true in the long run, the class list for Edward's year shows a preponderance of tradesmen or farmers among the parents, with 'county families' in a very small minority. Only John Lade, who, like Hasted was a county magistrate, and William Weight, are described as esquires, in a list which includes an attorney, a cleric (the Revd William Delves), a surgeon and an apothecary, as well as two farmers, a merchant, a bricklayer (i.e. a builder), a grocer, a distiller, a mercer, a victualler, a draper, a shipwright and a tobacconist. The parents of George's year were similarly mixed, and included a butcher, a baker, and three surgeons, as well as a draper, a distiller, a mercer and three gentlemen in holy orders: the Revd John Tucker, who was the school's undermaster, the Revd Francis Gregory, and a prebendary, the Revd Dr Berkeley. Samuel Chambers's father was a banker, and esquire was written only against the names of the parents of George Carter and George Hasted.[413]

The year 1772, however, when Charles Hasted became a scholar there, in company with another young Lade, also called Charles, was something of an annus mirabilis for the school. While Charles Abbott and William Lane were both sons of barbers, William Tatton, William Hassell and William Gregory were the sons respectively of the prebendary Revd Dr William Tatton, the Revd William Hassell, of Chislet, and the Revd Francis Gregory; Thomas Kite's father was Thomas Kite of the Custom House at Sandwich, Cowper Willyams's father was John Willyams, esq., a captain in the navy, Richard Barry's father was the Hon. John Smith Barry, Mark Thomas was the son of an alderman and chamberlain of Canterbury, while Charles Thurlow's father, himself educated at the school, was soon to be attorney-general, rising to become Lord Chancellor in 1778. But perhaps the most remarkable career of all was to be that of one of the boys, Charles Abbott, second son of a barber and wig-dresser, who in 1818 became Lord Chief Justice and in 1827 the first Lord Tenterden.[414]

Then, as now, parents were sometimes called on to support the school with their presence: speech-days, prize-givings and Founders' Days might all be occasions when parents were summoned to appear. The sociable Hasted was very willing to play his part. One of the big days in the school calendar at Canterbury was that of the School Feast, held in August, described as the 'Anniversary meeting of the gentlemen educated at the King's School, in Christ Church, Canterbury'. This began with a sermon in the cathedral in the morning, followed by a dinner in one of the city inns. In 1770 this was advertised for the 30 August at the Fountain tavern, 'Where the company of any gentleman, who is willing to encourage the Charity (tho' not educated at the school) will be very acceptable'. The stewards on this occasion were the Revd Dr Tatton, John Willyams and Edward Hasted.[415]

There must have been an equal care on the part of the historian to educate his daughters — there were a number of schools in Canterbury to which they could have gone — but unfortunately we know little of the activities of Katherine and Anne during these years, apart from being told by Hasted that Anne went to live with her grandmother when Edward and Francis returned from spending two years with her in London.

For rather less than a year the family consisted of five boys and three girls. Two weeks before Christmas 1773 Mrs Hasted had her ninth, and, as it was to prove, her last child, a little girl who was baptised at home on 14 December by the names of Mary Barbara Bennett. The private baptism probably shows that the baby was a sickly one, and that there were fears that it might not live, but on Saturday 8 January Mary was well enough to be taken to the cathedral, when she was received into the church and given the godparents after whom she had been named: for godmother, Mrs Barbara Knowler, the wife of Gilbert Knowler, another Precincts inhabitant and Hasted's colleague on the county bench, and for godfather, the Revd Bennett Storer, the prebendary in whose house the Hasteds lived.[416]

The day seemed a propitious one. The ceremony was undoubtedly followed by a dinner at the Hasteds', to which the Knowlers and the Storers were invited — the historian always took great pleasure in extending hospitality to his friends — and after their departure Hasted retired to the quiet of his study to pen a letter to Thomas Astle. There had been a coolness between the two men for some years, but Astle had recently — and apparently quite unexpectedly — obtained a royal favour for Hasted, and in the mellow mood engendered by a happy day Hasted now wrote warmly, both to thank Astle and to suggest a resumption of their friendship:

> What return further than my thanks I can make to you I know not. I can only assure you that should you, as I know you make excursions in summer into the country, favor us with a visit at Canterbury, I shall do all in my power to make this place and its environs as agreable to you as I possibly can, and Mrs Hasted will be happy to see Mrs Astle and renew her former friendship with her; and I hope you will believe this to be really meant, and not designed as an empty compliment without the hopes of its being put in execution.[417]

But Astle's star was in the ascendant: not only had his former friend chosen an obscure country life at Canterbury, but the socialising which that permitted fell far short of the wide circle of London acquaintances now cultivated by the Astles. In Thomas Astle's eyes Hasted's position had become something akin to that of a poor country cousin, and it is in this manner that he appears to have conducted himself towards the friend of his younger days on the few occasions when he reappears in the Hasted story.

The warmth of Hasted's letter was not reciprocated, nor did the other event of that day in January have a happier outcome. Little Mary was to live only a few months, and on the 17 September her burial took place in the cloisters of the cathedral.[418]

As at Sutton-at-Hone, public affairs occupied much of Hasted's time in Canterbury, where he soon resumed several of the duties which he had been happy to perform in West Kent. The East Kent bench was to acquire in him a very active acting magistrate. Early in October 1770 the *Kentish Post and Canterbury Journal* reported two men taken before Hasted and committed to St Dunstan's gaol to await trial, and also mentioned his presence on the local petty sessions bench at the Old Castle with the Revd Francis Hender Foote. He appears to have joined the Canterbury quarter sessions bench at the last sessions of that year, the Michaelmas one. By 1789, when he sat for the last time, he had been present at a total of sixty-five sessions out of a possible seventy-six — an impressive record. His name was soon being written second or third on the list of attenders, which denotes considerable standing, and on two occasions, in the absence of the chairman, William Deedes, it is clear that Hasted was asked to act in that capacity: at Michaelmas 1779 and at St Thomas (the July sessions) in 1782.[419]

William Deedes was one of the East Kent justices with whom Hasted became particularly friendly — both had taken out their Dedimus at the same time, in 1758 — and their correspondence continued through Hasted's darkest days. The frequency with which the signatures of both men occur, for example, in the rates books which overseers were obliged to present before the magistrates, with the previous accounts sworn to, in order that a new rate might be allowed, shows that both were regular attenders on the petty sessions bench of the Home Division of the Lathe of St Augustine, together with John Lade, Gilbert Knowler, Charles Webb, and the two clerics, John Duncombe and Osmund Beauvoir, as well as one or two others. It was on the petty sessions bench, too, that the justices signed removal orders and settlement certificates, which allowed people to work outside their settled parish, their own churchwardens and overseers having agreed to accept liability should they fall on hard times and need parish support. A batch of such certificates, carefully preserved by the parish of Chislet, reveals Hasted's presence on a number of occasions, along with that of one or other of the justices mentioned above.[420]

We also find a number of cases being committed for trial by the historian, both at quarter sessions and at the assizes. Typical of the cases dealt with by the quarter sessions bench was that of John Miles, committed by Hasted in April 1775 as the father of a 'male bastard child ... likely to become chargeable' to the parish of Minster in Thanet. A maintenance order was usually the outcome of such cases, but here Miles was discharged, so it is probable that the child had died shortly after birth. Thomas Gore, committed to quarter sessions by Hasted in June 1776, was charged with being 'a rogue and vagabond, on his own confession, by lodging in out-houses and barns at different places, and having no visible way of maintaining himself'. Gore was sentenced to one week's imprisonment and a private whipping, after which he was to be passed to his parish of settlement.[421]

Gore seems to have turned up in Canterbury by chance. There were those who lived in the parish who could be a similar, and more frequent, nuisance. Mary Emptage had already been convicted more than once, both as a 'loose, idle and disorderly person' (in 1770) and as a 'rogue and vagabond' (in 1775), when she was committed by Hasted in March 1776 as 'being convicted upon his own view of being an incorrigible rogue, having on the 13th of this instant, and at several times before, placed herself and gone about in places and passages, in the parish of Christ Church, Canterbury ... where she dwells, to beg and gather alms'. On this occasion, Mary Emptage was sentenced to six months in the House of Correction, and a private whipping before being discharged. Turning up again in 1777 for the same offence, she was this time merely labelled a rogue and vagabond, although her sentence in the House of Correction was doubled to twelve months. Hardly released, in 1778 she returned to her old ways, which brought her a further six months' sojourn in the House of Correction, enabling her to come up before the court again in 1779, this time to receive a sentence of two years. When she appeared before petty sessions yet again, in 1781, where Hasted was sitting with John Lynch, it was discovered that her parish of settlement could be proved to be St James, Westminster, which meant that Christ Church, Canterbury, was at last free of someone who was by now a 65-year-old widow.[422]

Another case committed by Hasted to quarter sessions was that of John Benskin, charged by the overseers of the parish of Chislet in 1777 with running away and leaving his wife chargeable to the parish — quite a common misdemeanour — which earned him a whipping at the public whipping post, an ugly and disagreeable fixture in most towns that confined the culprit's arms and legs while he underwent his punishment. The last committal by Hasted to quarter sessions at Canterbury appears to be that of 31 August 1789, when Edward Stone was kept in gaol until he could find sufficient sureties to keep the peace towards his wife Hannah.[423]

These were of course smuggling days, and few people's lives at this time can have remained untouched by the trade — did the Revd Wing Fowle, Hasted's friend at New Romney, never offer him a glass of run spirits, one wonders? — but the evasion of taxes in this way did considerable harm to the revenue, and on the coast the Prevention Service worked hard to live up to its name, frequently assisted on its sorties by dragoons enlisted from the neighbouring camps. Any romance attaching to smuggling has come to it with the patina of time: the gangs, when tackled, could be vicious, and not infrequently left their pursuers seriously wounded or dead. There was an affray of this kind on Bostal Hill near Whitstable in February 1780, when two of the 4th Dragoons who had been called in to assist in escorting a seizure of uncustomed goods from Whitstable to Canterbury were shot dead, and another two dangerously wounded. Two weeks later Hasted, acting on information received, was the justice who committed a Whitstable man to St Dunstan's gaol to await trial for his part in the murder.[424]

Serious cases such as this were heard at the assize court, to which Hasted was now not summoned for some years. With his move to a street address in Canterbury he could no longer be considered as one of the county gentlemen seated in the country, although he still remained the possessor of a quite extensive estate. Not until the summer of 1785 was he again called for grand jury service, at the somewhat lighter assize which followed fairly closely on the heels of the heavy Lent one, when 'Edward Hasted of the Precincts Esq.' was both summoned and chosen as one of those required to act and to 'enquire for our sovereign Lord the King'. He was, however, present at the Lent assizes of 1780, his name written in as an unsummoned attender, when the usual courtesy was then extended to him of picking him for service on the grand jury.[425]

The Lent assizes for 1786 had two serious cases before it, in both of which Hasted was the committing justice. Thomas Bax was charged with causing the death of George Morgan on the road outside Canterbury by stabbing him with a hanger, or short sword, and Manley Williams was accused of raping Sarah Lucas. Williams was hanged for his crime, but Bax was convicted of manslaughter and gaoled for only a year. Hasted does not appear to have been present at these assizes, but he was again summoned as a grand juror and asked to act in the summer of 1786, when there were two committals by him: of John Williams, charged with the murder of Mary Savin at Minster in the Isle of Thanet, and of Richard Fright, charged as an accomplice in her rape and murder. Williams was sentenced to be hanged, but Fright was discharged.[426]

Hasted also received a summons to attend the grand jury in the summer of 1787, although he was not this time picked for jury service. Here, Edward Ellison, the defendant committed by him in a case of theft, was found guilty and sentenced to six months' hard labour. The following Lent assizes again had before it two cases in which Hasted was the committing justice: Elizabeth Hatton, charged with 'feloniously murdering her bastard child' was discharged; but William Capsell, charged with theft in Whitstable, was found guilty and sentenced to be transported for seven years.[427]

The name of Edward Hasted was now regularly appearing in the list of those summoned for grand jury service at the summer assizes: we find it there in July 1788, in 1789 and in 1790, although on none of these occasions was he required to act. Indeed, in the summer of 1790 it would have been impossible, for he was not there to answer to his name. During the time he lived in Canterbury, however, it is likely that 'justice business' of one kind or another occupied him for several days a month.

This included acting in his own home as a 'single justice' in those cases which could legally be settled in this way. A conviction of 7 June 1787, for example, required Thomas Thornhill to appear before him 'at my dwelling house in the Precincts of Christ Church Canterbury in the said county on Monday the eleventh day of June instant at four o'clock in the afternoon' to pay the penalties incurred for selling bread of an inferior quality.[428]

As a former commissioner of sewers in West Kent, where he had served for the area known as the Limits extending from Gravesend Bridge to Sheerness and thence to Penshurst, Hasted, on moving to Canterbury, was soon placed on the Commission for the Sewers for Several Limits (an area which covered virtually the whole of the northern part of East Kent, from Whitstable down to Sandwich). His name appears among those of the twenty or so commissioners, along with the Revd Osmund Beauvoir and the Revd Bryan Faussett, who were 'sworn by virtue of a Dedimus Potestatem before William Long' on the 16 May 1771.[429]

Over this date in the minute book is written 'Dinner at the Red Lion', and the minutes are quite informative about the conviviality which followed the Commission of Sewers meetings here. The meeting of 27 May of the same year was followed by a dinner at the Fountain, that of 11 June by dinner at the King's Head; and throughout the time of Hasted's activity as a commissioner of sewers for the Several Limits these remained the preferred dining places.

Hasted made five appearances at the commissioners' meetings in 1771, attending on 1 August and 7 September in addition to the dates mentioned above. 1772 saw him at only three, two in February and one in June, and his average attendances each year remain around three or four. The commissioners were responsible for initiating an Act to drain part of their area known as the General Vallies, an area that provided much of the water for Sandwich harbour, and one of Hasted's manuscript volumes now in the British Library contains a number of printed documents which he received as a commissioner, including *A Report of the state of the River Stour, in the County of Kent, in July 1775*, submitted by Thomas Yeoman, FRS, which dealt also with the preservation of the port of Sandwich. Hasted was rarely at the meetings which discussed this matter during 1775, however, perhaps preferring to leave the decisions here to those more closely connected with the area. It was a contentious matter. The Corporation and inhabitants of Sandwich were firmly of the opinion that the new cut proposed by the commissioners of sewers could have only a deleterious effect on Sandwich haven and harbour, and sent a printed petition to Parliament in support of their case.[430]

With the single exception of the year 1784, the 1780s show even greater activity on the part of Hasted as a commissioner of the Sewers for Several Limits. While he appears to have attended only three meetings in 1779, those of April, June and December, one finds him at nine in 1780, now clearly one of the senior commissioners: his name is frequently written second, after that of the chairman, William Carter, and on at least one occasion, that of 11 January 1783, Hasted himself was to be asked to take the chair. However, his name is also to be found at the end of the list of commissioners present. Unlike most of the other commissioners Hasted lived a bare ten minutes away from the Old Castle, where the Commission's Courts were usually held, but one can deduce from the way in which his name sometimes appears as a later addition that, as frequently happens, a short journey was no guarantee of an early arrival, and on more than one occasion the two Precincts residents, Hasted and Osmund Beauvoir, seem to have put in a late appearance together.[431]

The Commission of Sewers and its leisurely dinners at the Fountain or the Red Lion, as well as the occasional rides through the Kentish valleys to view marshes, drains and sea walls, which the commissioners' work entailed, perhaps served to cement several more friendships which were to be important in Hasted's life. It could well have been on the Commission of Sewers that he first met William Boys, of Sandwich, a fellow-commissioner in 1771, and, through him, William Boteler, of Eastry. Both Boys and Boteler were surgeons, and they were also brothers-in-law, each having married one of the two daughters of

Thomas Fuller of Statenborow, Jane and Sarah — who were co-heirs to their uncle, John Paramor of Statenborough. Boys's first wife, Elizabeth Wise, had died in 1761, after giving birth to a son, William Henry, and Boys had then married Jane Fuller, who was to present him with five sons and three daughters before her death in 1783. William Boteler, considerably younger than Boys, had married Jane's younger sister Sarah, although by the time he was brought on to the Commission of Sewers in 1781 he, too, was a widower, his wife having died at the age of only thirty following the birth of a son in 1777.

1781 was also the year when the list contained the names both of Edward Hasted senior and of twenty-one-year-old Edward Hasted junior. As has been mentioned, it was common throughout the eighteenth century for sons to follow their fathers on to public bodies at an early age, serving a virtual apprenticeship before their views would be deemed to carry much weight, and Hasted was obviously very keen that his son should maintain the tradition of service established by the family. Edward took his oath as a commissioner in May 1782, but as he was at that time a student at Oxford his attendances could only be infrequent, and he was not to be present again until 14 April 1784. By the time of his next attendance, on 17 March 1785, he had taken orders, and is entered as 'Edwd Hasted Clk'. He was to make two more appearances in 1785, on each occasion attending with his father, who made a total of seven attendances in that year. But after that Edward is not found at a meeting of the commissioners until 1790, when he put in two appearances in May. His father, however, continued to attend meetings from time to time each year until June 1789, when he made his last appearance at a meeting of the commissioners for the Sewers for Several Limits held at the Bell inn in Sandwich.[432]

A further voluntary office undertaken by Hasted was that of commissioner of the land tax. The historian's signature appears at the foot of the land tax assessments for Christ Church, Canterbury for 1782 and 1784, together with those of George Gipps and John Cantis (in 1782) and of Osmund Beauvoir and John Cantis (in 1784).[433] What cannot be disputed is that Hasted took very seriously the duty of the propertied man to be of service to the community, entering wholeheartedly into the fabric of local government, sitting regularly on the benches of both petty and general sessions, and actively involved in decisions which concerned the Kentish countryside and the environment. It is not surprising that her son's civic virtues should have gained for old Mrs Hasted 'the acquaintance of the best families of the clergy and gentry within the Precincts'.[434]

Minor duties also figured in his life. He seems to have been a regular attender at the secular vestry for his small parish of Christ Church when the accounts were audited in April; and as someone who held land in the manor of Teynham he was elected for the year 1771 to act as reeve, the office which had been held by his grandfather in 1717.[435] Friendship, too, sometimes brought with it obligations that had to be honoured. His old friend Bryan Faussett, crippled and rendered often bad-tempered by the gout, died of it in 1776, naming Hasted in his will (together with the baronet Sir William Fagg and Johnson Macaree) as overseer or assistant to his wife Elizabeth, who was executrix.[436]

To lighten these many calls on his time there must have been visits to friends, dinners, social occasions, and perhaps sometimes tickets taken for a concert or the theatre. The company known as Their Majesty's Servants performed frequently in Canterbury around this time: in May and June 1769 their repertoire included *Venice Preserved, Tamerlane the Great with the Fall of Bajazet Emperor of the Turks, The Provoked Husband*, the ballad play or comic opera *Love in a Village, Richard III*, and *The Country Wife*. In 1770 they offered the chance of seeing *Macbeth*. In 1773 they brought with them *Cymon, The Beaux' Stratagem*, another comic opera called *The Padlock, The Anatomist, Lionel and Clarissa*, and a revival of the perennially popular *Love in a Village*; while *Tamerlane* was toured again in 1774. Another touring company which appeared in Canterbury came from the London spa of Sadler's Wells, bringing dancers, tumblers, tight-rope walkers and musical interludes.[437] Events such as these, if they were taken to see them, may have compensated the Hasted children to some extent for the loss of the freedom of the fields at Sutton-at-Hone.

Although he took up many of the same duties in Canterbury that had claimed him at St John's, the move must have made a considerable difference to Hasted's life, and during the first two or three years here the *History* was perhaps frequently relegated to second place in his list of priorities. That he did put in some very hard work on it from time to time, however, there is no doubt, and around 1773 and early 1774 several other literary events in Kent seem to have spurred him on to envisage its completion. When his great project was first conceived, at the beginning of the 1760s, there was little more for the reader of Kentish topography than the by now dated histories of Lambarde (first edition 1576), Kilburne (1659), Philipott (1659), and Harris (1719). By the time the four-volume *History* was complete the scene had changed out of all recognition. Over the period of its gestation, and particularly during the 1770s, a number of other Kentish topographical works were to appear, and Hasted began to be jostled by the competition.

In November 1771 the *Kentish Gazette* carried the 'Proposals for Printing, by subscription, The History and Antiquities of the City of Rochester and its Environs', an anonymous work, printed and apparently published by T. Fisher of Rochester. This subsequently appeared in 1772, extended with 'A Description of the towns, villages, gentlemen's seats, and ancient buildings, situate on or near the road from London to Margate, Deal and Dover', in an attractive small octavo format, embellished, as the title-page had it, with some copper-plate engravings, and quite well referenced. From the length of the list of subscribers (swollen, in particular, by the names of several young gentlemen from 'Mr Hawkins's school') it would appear to have found a ready market.

1772 also saw the appearance of *An Historical Description of the Metropolitical Church of Christ, Canterbury*, which was advertised in the *Kentish Gazette* in May, while during the summer of 1774 both Edward Jacob's *History of the Town and Port of Faversham*, and the Revd William Gostling's *Walk in and about the City of Canterbury*, were in process of being printed. Hasted was well aware that the two latter items were in preparation, since he was a subscriber to the Gostling, and appears to have donated Plate XIV, which was respectfully inscribed to him, to the Jacob history, a plate showing Roman medals and traders' tokens found in or near the town.[438]

While it may well have occurred to Hasted that he was in imminent danger of losing his chosen historical ground, he received a spur from an unexpected quarter. As we have seen, the friendship with Thomas Astle appears to have lapsed after the publication of *Familiar Letters*, and the two men seldom saw each other, since Hasted, now at Canterbury, could no longer make frequent excursions to London to attend the meetings of his two Societies. However, a possible word of greeting from Hasted towards the end of 1773, undoubtedly including some account of his continuing labours on the *History*, may also have mentioned a perplexity as to the choice of dedicatee. Dr John Harris's 1719 *History of Kent* had been most flatteringly dedicated to George I — most flatteringly, and somewhat pointlessly, since George I spoke no English. There would be more logic in dedicating a county history to his great-grandson, since George III was the first of his line to be thoroughly and happily British. Such may have been Hasted's comments, lightly penned, with little thought of being able to dedicate his own work at so high a level. His friend, however, rising in his career, now had connections which could be made to stretch as far as the court, and the upshot was that, much to the historian's delighted surprise, Astle was able to obtain permission for this new history of Kent to be likewise dedicated to the king. It is highly unlikely that Hasted would have sought this out for himself, and in his letter of 8 January 1774 we find him asking Astle how such an honour is to be acknowledged:

I cannot omit the first opportunity of returning you my best thanks for the honor you have been so kind to procure for me, which I assure you I receive with all due respect and gratefullness. If there should be any letter written, any notice or other kind of acknowledgment taken of it by me, you will be so kind to instruct me in it, and I shall be happy in the doing it.[439]

This, for Hasted, was more than simply permission to dedicate his work to the king. It was as if he had received a royal command: come what may, the *History* now had to appear — and soon, rather than later.

The following August, therefore, a rather lengthy advertisement appeared in the *Kentish Gazette*, which began:

Mr Hasted thinks it a duty incumbent on him to acquaint the nobility and gentry of the county of Kent, and his friends in general, that his intended HISTORY AND TOPOGRAPHICAL SURVEY OF KENT is now great part of it finished, and ready for the press.[440]

The historian goes on to explain that as a result of his examination of various offices, records and libraries, deeds, rolls, and private papers, his notes now fill more than a hundred volumes, which have had to be 'digested' and given a suitable order. He is profuse with his thanks to all those who have taken the trouble to answer his requests for information, and he ends with a note to the effect that, 'It is proposed to reduce it to the size of three small folio volumes'. This appeared in some of the London papers as well, and certainly caught the eye of at least one person who was to become a friendly supporter of the project. On the 3 September 1774 the Earl of Radnor wrote to Hasted from Longford Castle:

Till I saw your advertisement in the London Evening Post, I knew nothing of your intention to publish an history of Kent, or I should have sooner become your correspondent. By your mention of three volumes, I imagine your plan is an extensive one. I think I can enable you to give a better account of the antient Barony of Folkestone and some of its neighbourhood than appears either in Philpot or Harris.[441]

Clearly, the advertisement was put out in something of a hurry, and Hasted had not yet sufficiently studied the costs of the project, although he does seem to have enquired of printers from time to time what these were likely to be. An undated, but certainly much earlier, note in one of his commonplace books shows that he had originally envisaged only a single-volume work:

> Mr Richardson the printer says the 200 sheets folio printing and paper and 750 copies will come to £650 or thereabouts, and that he can print off 6 sheets a week but very well 4.[442]

Set beside this the Canterbury printer's quotation for a two-volume work was to look very attractive. While the historian probably abandoned the idea of a third volume with some regret, James Simmons came up with a suggestion which was intended to leave the writer comfortably in pocket and must have seemed the very least Hasted could hope for, after the years of unpaid labour which he had already put in. In effect, the cost to Hasted for 750 sets of a two-volume History was to be £816.10s.0d., including printing of the Proposals, insertion of advertisements in both Kentish and London papers, and half-binding; which, assuming 750 sets sold at £3.3s.0d., and deducting booksellers' discounts at 15% and incidentals, including carriage at 1%, would result in a net return of £1982.8s.0d., or just over £1000 profit. Simmons's rate of printing, however, did not match that quoted by Richardson, since he could offer no better than ten sheets per calendar month.[443]

The Canterbury printer's quotation having been accepted, probably during the month of September 1774, it was announced on the 1 October that:

> Next month will be published, Proposals, for printing by subscription in two volumes, The History and Topographical Survey of the County of Kent, by Edward Hasted, of Christ Church, Canterbury, Esq., one of his Majesty's Justices of the Peace, and Fellow of the Royal and Antiquarian Societies.[444]

Advertisements for the *Proposals* appeared in the *Kentish Gazette* for the 13, 16 and 23 November 1774. Notice of them was also given in the *Canterbury Journal* for the 15, 22 and 29 November and the 6 and 13 December, as well as in some London papers.

The *Proposals* themselves were issued as a single folio sheet printed on both sides. The manner in which they are set out is typical of the orderly way in which Hasted's mind worked, and must certainly have inspired confidence, in those in any way likely to be interested in it, in his ability to handle such a large project. A modest introduction leads into a list of the sources used: the various offices of record which have been combed for references to Kent, the old manuscripts, many of them heraldic, borrowed or purchased, which have been perused, the correspondence with the gentlemen of the county. And Hasted mentions also, and justifiably, his own extensive knowledge of Kent both as a private individual and through his activities in the public sphere. He then goes on to explain the two-part plan of the work itself, the first to contain a general description of Kent, and the second dealing with places, arranged under their Lathes and Hundreds.

Potential subscribers were also told what the new *History* would look like: it was to be 'handsomely printed (on a new Pica letter, cast by Mr Caslon) in two volumes folio, containing about 500 pages each, and illustrated with maps and copper-plates'. And Hasted took the opportunity to encourage those who might be willing to provide a plate or map for the work to get in touch with him, 'and they will be waited on for that purpose'. The whole work was offered to the public at a subscription rate of £3.3s.0d.

Hasted, it should be noted, was prepared to accept all costs, and was therefore his own publisher. In his *Proposals* he announces this with a flourish, but it signalled in effect a considerable error of judgment, both of the expense which his personal fortune would be able to bear, and of the support which could be expected from the public in an undertaking of this kind:

> The editor has been much importuned to make this History the property of the booksellers, as a means of greater and more certain profit to himself. But notwithstanding the great expence the publishing this work will be attended with, he has rejected every offer of this kind, which he knew by example would be an additional burthen to the public, and he is determined to rely wholly on the countenance and support his labours may meet with from the gentry of the county. He thinks this a compliment due to them, and the only desirable method he can take of making this History public.[445]

This was to prove too large a gesture: Hasted was to pay for it by years of imprisonment for debt; the public, preserved from harm by Hasted's naive trust in it, was also to pay, indirectly, by its long wait for the completion of the *History*. Publishing by subscription was a standard — and clearly, in Hasted's eyes, a gentlemanly — way of bringing out works of this kind: it almost certainly guaranteed that the gentleman-publisher would end up out of pocket.

The *Proposals* were not, as was often done, published in the Kentish papers themselves, but could be obtained, free of charge, at certain booksellers up and down the country: in London, Oxford, Cambridge, Bath, Canterbury and Rochester — a surprisingly limited list of names, to which subsequent advertisements added J. Hall at Tenterden, R. Walker at Maidstone, and J. Hogben at Rye, as well as, more generally, 'the other booksellers in this county'.

A countrywide distribution of the *Proposals*, and the insertion of advertisements in London as well as country newspapers were essential, as the gentlemen of the time seem to have been in almost perpetual motion. Lord Dacre, for example, was to write to Hasted both from Belhouse in Essex and from his house in Bruton Street, Lord Radnor from Longford Castle, from London and from Folkestone, Lord Darnley from Cobham Hall and Berkeley Square. We have seen that Hasted's initial advertisement had caught the eye of Lord Radnor in London; the Revd William Lowth, vicar of Lewisham and a close friend of Hasted, wrote to him on 1 February 1775 from Winchester, where he occupied a canonry: 'I saw by an advertisement that you intended publishing your book by subscription; as soon as I am at home I shall desire Mr Dodsley to put me down as a subscriber'.[446] Ten thousand copies of the *Proposals* were printed, but it is hard to think that a half or even a quarter of these found an outlet. However, they were not a major item of expense.

Intriguingly, there seems to have been some counter-activity going on at the same time. Hasted's insertions in the *Canterbury Journal*, the rival newspaper to the *Kentish Gazette*, were accompanied on each occasion by proposals for printing a revised edition of Philipott's *Villare Cantianum* — the project which Hasted, seeing no reason to hide his feelings about it, had abandoned with some disgust around 1763 — which was to be published by subscription at a third of the cost of Hasted's two-volume set. This edition of the *Villare Cantianum* cannot have been solely the initiative of its Norfolk printer, W. Whittingham, of Lynn Regis: Thomas Smith, the printer of the *Canterbury Journal*, and T. Fisher, of Rochester, appear also to have had a hand in its re-appearance.[447] It was Fisher who had brought out the *History and Antiquities of Rochester* in 1772; in 1777 John Thorpe was to tell the historian:

> I hear Fisher, the bookseller of Rochester, who answers to his name, is again angling for fresh matter, and is assisted therein by two parsons, who are fond of scribbling for him, in a work entitled 'Chronological Events for Kent', which is to make its appearance

in May. My assistance has been desired; which I have declined; and I hear likewise he intends a 2nd edition of Rochester; but waits till your work is published.[448]

Hasted's *Proposals* received no more than a passing mention in the *Gentleman's Magazine*. The issue for November 1774 carried a review of Jacob's *Faversham* which contained a brief reference to them, as well as to the forthcoming edition of the Philipott:

> As a laudable thirst for topographical knowledge seems at present to prevail, glad are we to see as laudable a desire of gratifying it no less prevalent, especially in the county of Kent, this being the fifth work of the kind, which we have lately announced from that part of our island; and, in addition to these, a Norfolk bookseller is reprinting Philipott's Villare Cantianum; and Edward Hasted, Esq., of Canterbury, FRS, has just published Proposals for printing a new Topographical History of Kent.[449]

The second edition of Philipott in fact came out in 1776, and in 1776 appeared also another general work on the county, Charles Seymour's *New Topographical, Historical and Commercial Survey of the Cities, Towns and Villages of the County of Kent* — a long title for a very perfunctory dash through the county, which was perhaps undertaken for no other purpose than to show that such a survey could be done overnight, as it were, as against Hasted's years of laborious and patient study.

Hasted, it is obvious, found himself embarked amidst a competition of authors and booksellers with which he had not calculated, all of them striving for the public's ear and pocket. It must have been with considerable relief that at the beginning of May 1778 he was able to announce the *History*'s imminent appearance. The following insertion appeared in the *Kentish Gazette* on the ninth of that month, apologetically revealing at the same time the almost inevitable story of escalating costs and insufficient subscriptions:

> History of Kent. Mr Hasted's respects wait on the noblemen and gentlemen, who have favoured him with their subscriptions to his History of Kent; and he acquaints them, that the first volume of it will be published the beginning of next month. He is sorry that the great expence of this volume, which is much beyond what he has received from his subscriptions, obliges him to call on them for

the payment of the remaining guinea and an half for the second volume on the delivery of the first. Subscriptions will continue to be taken in at the usual booksellers ... The second volume is ready for the press, and will be forwarded as expeditiously as the nature of the work will admit of.[450]

The printing of a subscription work was a very slow process; the likelihood is that Hasted's manuscript of Volume I had been with Simmons for the best part of two or three years. Volume II, which is here stated to be ready for printing, was not to make its delayed appearance until the middle of 1783. But it is quite possible that the text relating to several of the Hundreds which were eventually to comprise the second volume were indeed deposited with Simmons in 1778, since by the autumn of that year Hasted had realised that two volumes were not going to be enough. Volume I contained around 600 pages, Volume II was to have over 800: even for folio volumes, they were very big and heavy; there would, after all, have to be a third volume. On the 25 November 1778 John Thorpe wrote to Hasted welcoming the news:

> I am glad to hear by your kind favor of the 16th instant that you have begun printing your 2nd volume, and will favour the public with a 3rd, which will enable you to treat more fully of your City and its districts, for Gostling has slovened over the other religious houses, etc., confining himself chiefly to the Cathedral and its environs.[451]

Again, there would be the long wait while Simmons printed off a few sheets at a time, interspersing them with his own inevitably more pressing matters which had a deadline to meet: the *Kentish Gazette*, twice a week, and, for two or three months in the year, the almanacs, journals and day books which constituted a large part of a printer's and bookseller's trade. But perhaps Mr Richardson would not have been very much quicker.

PRECINCTS of CHRIST-CHURCH,
CANTERBURY.

MR. HASTED thinks it a Duty incumbent on him to acquaint the NOBILITY and GENTRY of the County of KENT, and his Friends in general, that his intended

HISTORY AND TOPOGRAPHICAL
SURVEY of KENT

is now great Part of it finished, and ready for the Press. He takes this Opportunity of returning them his sincere Thanks for the Trouble they have given themselves in the repeated Informations they have favoured him with, as well in relation to the Descent of their Families, as their Manors and Estates.——He hopes they will not think he has delayed the Publication of this Work longer than has been necessary for so extensive and difficult an Undertaking, in a County, with which almost every Family of Note in the Kingdom has been connected; where Property always has been, and still is so continually separating, and changing, and where the religious Foundations have been so numerous, and opulent; especially when they take into the Consideration the Length of Time, and Labour, it has required to inspect, and search through the several public Offices, Records, and Libraries, and the Deeds, Rolls and private Evidences of Families, and after all the digesting these numerous Materials, which have already (well) to upwards of 100 Volumes, into that Order, and small Compass necessary to make them acceptable to the Public. He assures them that he intends to continue his Endeavors and to spare no Expence whatsoever towards the completing this Work, in hopes that it will then have the Honor of their Support and Approbation, and in the mean Time the Favor of any further Information will be thankfully received by him, directed to his House in the PRECINCTS of CHRIST-CHURCH abovementioned.

∗ It is proposed to reduce it to the Size of three single

Chapter 11

The Route to Calais

Hasted's agreement with James Simmons had referred to two volumes, to be supplied in the half-bound state. This was common practice, and left the purchaser free to have his books bound as he chose. The plates or illustrations would be supplied separately — and often later, which accounts for the presence, in books of the period, of a small rubric to the binder (i.e. the purchaser's binder), instructing him where to position them. Hasted's agreement of 1774 with Simmons covered only the printing, but not the making, of his plates. The two volumes were intended to contain a total of fifty illustrations, and it was Hasted's hope that these would be donated by friends and supporters. In this he was to be sadly undeceived, and it seems to have been the cost of the plates, coupled with unremunerative sales of what in the end became a four-volume work, which finally made of the *History* a financial mill-stone round Hasted's neck.

The closer the work approached to publication, the more pressing became the question of illustrations. It is of interest that an early reference to a plate for his work mentions an artist and engraver who later became a very close friend, John Barlow. Barlow had obviously been engaged by the Earl of Radnor, a keen supporter of Hasted's work and the donor of two plates, to make a drawing of Folkestone: a footnote to the earl's letter of 12 October 1775 says, 'The name of the person who took the drawing of Folkestone is Barlow, the engraver's name is Sherlock'.[452]

At that time, however, Hasted was making use of the engraver John Bayly for his illustrations and maps. He seems to have cast about among his friends for drawings, and may even have thought initially of providing some himself. A careful drawing of Southfleet parsonage which he made in 1768 in one of his commonplace books, and another of Franks in Horton Kirby, may well have been considered as possible illustration material, although later discarded as not being of enough interest to justify the expense of engraving.[453] But it certainly sounds as if he was responsible for the drawing of Sutton Place, which was to be inscribed to the memory of John Lethieullier — or, at least, as if he made the original sketch. As early as 1767 Andrew Coltee Ducarel was reporting Bayly's accident with an ink bottle, adding in a postscript to a note sent to Hasted from Doctors' Commons: 'At this instant Bailey informs me that a day or two ago, he had the misfortune to drop a bottle of ink on your drawing of Sutton Place — that he has been at work ever since in making another which he will send you this week'.[454]

Hasted clearly discussed the problem of obtaining plates with all his friends, and in a letter of June 1775 we find two of them putting their heads together over the matter. Thorpe wrote to Ducarel from Bexley:

> When I had last the pleasure of seeing you in town, you desired I would turn my thoughts relative to Mr Vyse's plate for Hasted's History. I have therefore maturely considered that matter, and think there can be no subject so proper as Penshurst Place, the noble and superb antient seat of the Sydneys, Earls of Leicester. ... There is no building so grand, except Knoll, in that part of Kent, nor more proper for Hasted's work, or will embellish it more.[455]

Dr Ducarel was able to obtain for Hasted the offer of another plate, writing one of his hasty notes from Doctors' Commons in March 1776 to tell him that Mr Derby, chaplain to the late Bishop Pearce, was willing to give a plate of Bromley College, 'provided the giving the said plate is considered by Mr H as a full payment of his subscription'.[456]

Thorpe cast around for any other means of obtaining illustrations. In a letter of January 1776 he has several suggestions to make:

> Now I am upon the chapter of plates, when we were in East Kent my daughter took a drawing of Wye College ... now converted into a school. It would make a beautiful print ... The Duke of Dorset is fond of pictures; and perhaps would contribute Knoll. Cobham Hall, likewise, would be a noble print; but who has interest with Lord Darnley I know not.[457]

Fifteen months later, however, the vexed question of a suitable number of plates — which Hasted simply could not afford himself — had still not been resolved, and Thorpe suggested a more direct approach:

> The best and surest way to obtain plates for your History is writing to the gentlemen. They can but refuse, if not agreeable, and in short it is paying them a compliment. ... The writing to gentlemen, as I said before, would probably please and engage many who have handsome seats and like to have 'em introduced in a County History: at least they can't frame an excuse that they were not asked.[458]

Thorpe was himself happy to donate a double-sized plate to the *History*, and in May 1776 was able to send Hasted a proof of it. It was to show Keston Camp, scene of Thorpe's 'tumbles among the furzes' on a hot June day, 'which I think does Bayley credit; and as it was your choice for me, so I hope [it] will meet with your approbation'. The same letter notes that Thorpe had been in town last week, 'and saw at Bayley's ten of your plates of the hundreds quite finished, except inserting the titles'.[459] And one of the plates appears to have been contributed by the engraver himself: an 'ichnography', as Hasted was fond of calling them, the 'Ground Plot of the Antient Palace of Eltham', which appeared in Volume I, was inscribed to Edward Hasted by J. Bayly.

Perhaps Bayly felt some compensation was due for the inordinate length of time he was taking to complete the plates entrusted to him. The years were slipping past, and Hasted was still unable to put any of his *History* before the public. In March 1777 Thorpe tried to soothe the fraying nerves of his friend, engaged in such 'arduous and laborious work':

> Indeed, I am very sensible what a great fatigue it must be, and the no small share of patience that is requisite to comply with the humours and tempers of persons, and dilatoriness of workmen. Of the latter sort, Bayley, as you justly observe, stands foremost in the list of engravers. ... I shall be in town in a few days, and will then give him a smart spur. He requires now and then a good jogging; and if he don't mend, as soon as he has finished your maps, the other plates may be carried on by hands not so desultory.[460]

Of the twenty or so plates in Volume I, Bayly was to have a hand in about half of them, some engraved from others' drawings, some both drawn and engraved by him. It cannot be said that he was a brilliant artist. Acting on Thorpe's suggestion of approaching some of the owners of 'handsome seats' Hasted had written to the Earl of Darnley, who had initially proved very enthusiastic, responding in March 1777:

> Cobham Hall has, both wings and front, been new cased with brick, and sashed; which, with the Grand Avenue and striking approach to it ... would make a most noble print, if executed by a good artist.[461]

Later that year Bayly must have gone down to Cobham to make a drawing of it, for 'Cobham Hall. The Seat of the Rt Hon. the Earl of Darnley' is one of the plates noted as both drawn and engraved by him.

However, a letter from Hasted to Lord Darnley makes it clear that his noble patrons did not always donate the whole cost of their plates. In the present case, it seems that Lord Darnley stipulated what should be spent on his illustration, and then offered to pay no more than a portion of it. Hasted's response of the 9 November 1777, a rare item, contains the following:

> I return your Lordship my most respectfull thanks for your kindness to me, in relation to the engraving of Cobham, and your kind intentions in it. The engraver can certainly do it well, and your Lordship's price, which you have fixed, demands it to be done in [the] best manner an artist is capable of executing it. The remaining part of that price is more than I know well how to afford, considering the great and many expences I am continually disbursing in the prosecution of this work. However, I must rely on your Lordship's kindness and generosity to extend it towards me, as you please, and I have no doubt I shall not be disappointed.[462]

It seems highly unlikely, however, that any further generosity was forthcoming from Lord Darnley, who found nothing to his liking in Bayly's work and let Hasted know it the following February:

> Your engraver (Bailey) brought me very lately a print of his plate, which he calls Cobham Hall. But it is so miserably executed that I can scarce own it for such. He has preserved no proportion ... the windows are square, and look more like the windows of a prison, than the just proportions of Inigo Jones. However, if you think it fit to be placed in your work I shall fullfill my engagement with you.[463]

Given this reception of the Cobham plate, Hasted must have accounted himself fortunate to receive any assistance at all towards the cost of it.

Another plate in Volume I, also drawn and engraved by Bayly, was donated by Dr Ducarel: it shows the tenth-century Queen Edyve (now more usually written Edgifu or Eadgifu), mother of the future kings of England Edmund and Edred, 'from an original picture in the library of Canterbury Cathedral'. Thorpe's offer of his daughter's drawing of Wye College does not seem to have been taken up, but Catherine Thorpe's small drawing of 1767 of the Manor House in Strood known as The Temple was used as a vignette to open the section on the Lathe of

Aylesford; this, too, was engraved by Bayly and stands up well alongside the work of more professional artists. And Volume I contains several plates, at least one of them drawn and engraved by Richard Godfrey, which were donated by the elderly Lord Dacre, who took a great interest in Hasted's work.

The name of Richard Godfrey, who had engraved many of the plates for Gostling's *Walk in and about the City of Canterbury*, occurs on a number of plates in Volume I: he was also responsible for the drawing and engraving of Mrs Burrell's Langley Park, of Sir Sampson Gideon's Belvidere, of Sir Richard Betenson's Bradborne Place, of Sir Timothy Waldo's Hever Castle, and of Knole Park, so it is clear that Hasted finally lost patience with Bayly and turned some of his work over to Godfrey. There is a single surviving letter from Godfrey in the correspondence which shows that the offending plate of Cobham Hall was given to him to alter, 'agreeable to his Lordship's and your request'.[464]

It was Godfrey who was to be used for almost all the engravings in Volume II, and Bayly's work for the remaining volumes of the *History* was to be limited to some of the maps and one or two plates which had been done in advance. In November 1776 William Boys was writing to Hasted from Sandwich to let him know that 'I have at last finished my drawings of the three sides of Richborough Castle, which I beg you will forward with the letter to Mr Bayley. I have taken so much pains to be accurate …'. Two and a half years later Mr Boys' drawings had been turned into an engraving, although Boys was not particularly gratified with the result:

> Mr Bayley has not perfectly pleased me with the engraving; I told him I was but an indifferent draughtsman, and should depend on him to soften those defects, which an unlearned pencil must necessarily create.[465]

The matter of the royal dedication was to cause Hasted more trouble than he privately thought it was worth. In March 1778 Thomas Astle had sent Hasted a draft dedication, together with a suitable covering letter to accompany the first volume. Of his proposed wording Astle wrote:

> You will observe I have used the word 'Sir', which I think more proper than 'Sire', for the latter word would in my opinion be improper unless you was writing in French or speaking of a stallion.

And he added, somewhat patronisingly, since the dedication, after all, would come from Hasted: 'I shall be glad to know if you think any alterations necessary'.

Hasted did not quite copy Astle's draft word for word, and gave it two additional lines of his own, although he rather timidly hoped 'they will meet your approbation'.

On June 8 he was able to tell Astle that the book would probably be ready for publication by the middle of the following week, but once more there were difficulties. It sounds from Hasted's letter as if Astle wished to be present when a copy was donated to the royal library, and the two men seem not to have been free at the same time: 'If you think it will be any advantage for me to come to town purposely to carry it to his library, I will, tho' inconvenient at present, certainly come up on Monday 23d just for it, and will with your leave wait on you the next morning as you shall please to appoint, but I must of necessity return before the end of the week'. Could Astle perhaps deliver the book in Hasted's place? And the general publication would be held over until after the royal library had received its copy.[466]

In the event it was indeed Astle who took charge of the presentation of the royal copy — which was one of only six printed on extra large paper — a service he could hardly refuse, since it seems to have been he who in the first place had wished on Hasted all the attendant trouble of a royal dedication; and he was also a beneficiary of one of the precious large paper copies which Hasted could so ill afford. But this was not to be the end of the matter.

Distribution of the work, once it was published, does not seem to have been a problem, since 'Simmons's newsmen' covered the county, and a 1% distribution charge had been included in the contract. Nevertheless, there was a great deal of administrative work involved in this, all of which Hasted seems to have handled himself. On the 15 August 1778 we find the Sevenoaks bookseller, Thomas Clout Junr, writing a business letter to the historian, and taking the opportunity to pass on a few small corrections at the same time:

> Sir, I take the liberty to acquaint you that the money is all paid for the books you sent me, so that if you please to order the payment of it, I shall immediately make it good....
>
> Mr Charles Polhill Esqr has issue by both marriages: by the first a daughter Penelope; and by the second several children. ... The Mr Allen who has Ridley living was only curate of Seal. I thought you would like to have anything of this kind noted, lest you might

have opportunity in future to correct it and it might again escape you.[467]

Orders for the work came through various channels. John Tressé, the Chatham surveyor, who was also apparently a bookseller, wrote to Hasted on the 8 March 1779 that he had received 'an order for another copy of your work'. And gentlemen sometimes sent orders via their attorneys, whom they seem to have been in the habit of using to transact their business in their frequent absences: thus a letter received by Cyprian Rondeau Bunce, a Canterbury attorney, and passed on by him to Hasted, asked Bunce to subscribe 'for two sets of Mr Hasted's intended History of Kent'. Thomas Williams, Hasted's Dartford attorney, also collected subscriptions and provided a useful distribution point, writing after the appearance of the second volume: 'After I receive the books they shall be delivered to the gentlemen whose names you have — and I will receive the subscriptions of those who shall chuse to continue them for the 3rd volume'.[468]

With publication came exposure to criticism. The first raps, not surprisingly, came from those who found fault with the account of their families. The loudest voice here was that of Lord Dacre, who wrote to Hasted several times in August and September 1778, calling for a total reprinting of pages 107 and 108, 'for Errata's people never look into; and the errors in the present sheet are fundamental'.[469] Lord Dacre's shower of rebukes obviously caught Hasted off balance, and he was panicked into having the two offending pages reprinted. This, however, meant also having six sets of them reprinted for the six large paper copies, a not inconsiderable expense. By the middle of November these were ready, and two sets then had to be sent up to London, for the royal copy and for Astle's. Somewhere en route — and it seems to have been at Astle's office — these were mislaid. Hasted was frantic:

> I duly received your last kind favor and immediately wrote to Mr Johnson, St Paul's churchyard, to know what he had done concerning the reprinted sheets I sent to him, directed for you at the Paper Office, Treasury, Whitehall, to which I received for answer, that the parcel for Mr Astle was sent agreeable to the direction some time since. As this is the case, I must beg the favor of you to send someone to investigate this matter, both at the Treasury, and at Mr Johnson's, and to find whom it was carried by, and by whom delivered. There were in the parcel 2 sets of the reprinted sheets, Large Paper, put between 2 thick paper boards, and then inclosed in a covering of paper tyed up, and directed as

> above. Dr Ducarel and other gents had parcels of a like nature, which all went safe. I would not put you to this trouble could I replace them for you, but I printed but 6 sets of these sheets <u>on large paper</u> answerable to the <u>6 copies</u> of the volume, so that I cannot replace them again.[470]

The missing sheets were eventually found and inserted as Hasted wanted.

It transpired after all this that Lord Dacre had not expected the historian to have fresh sheets printed for more than his copy. However, there was the occasional small recompense for Hasted and his family from Belhouse:

> I will take up no more of your time at present, only to beg your acceptance of half a buck, which I shall take the first opportunity of sending you by the Canterbury Coach, and of which I will give you timely notice by a line.[471]

In spite of the nervousness which Lord Dacre's criticisms had aroused in him, Hasted actually encouraged his correspondents to let him know of any mistakes they found. Thus Francis Tressé, sending some information for Volume II from Brompton in November 1778, ended his letter: 'I have inclosed agreeable to your request, a paper pointing out some few errors I discovered in reading the first volume of your excellent work'.

The Revd Samuel Pegge, writing from Whittington in Derbyshire in June 1779, had only had

> a transient view of your first volume, and therefore could not make many remarks. The following enlarged, tho' not complete list of the rectors of Sundridge is, however, at your service, and I rely on your candour to take it in good part.[472]

The History and Topographical Survey of the County of Kent was noticed in the *Gentleman's Magazine* in July.[473] An ample review recognised the time, labour and expense which its author had bestowed on it, and welcomed it as a replacement for the works of Lambarde, Somner, Kilburne and Philipott, all with their merit, but 'some of them local, others imperfect, and all now obsolete; and one more modern, Dr Harris's History of Kent, 1719, though it promised much, has performed but little, and that in a very erroneous and superficial manner'. The writer was probably Dr John Duncombe, at this period the *Magazine's* reviewer, a Canterbury man and an acquaintance of Hasted. The review is both friendly and objective: Duncombe praises the solid achievements of the *History* — its clear well-drawn plan, the plates, the maps, the indexes — and finds the execution of it, as far as it has gone, very satisfactory. He does, however, voice a reservation as to whether 'the succession of property, and genealogies, however proper in such a work' will be of interest to 'those who are not possessed of them'.

All in all, it was a good review, and Hasted was probably very satisfied with it. Not so, apparently, a young man of thirty-three whom a legacy had just enabled to become part-owner of the *Gentleman's Magazine*. This was John Nichols, a printer turned editor, with both literary and antiquarian pretensions, whose own *History of Leicestershire*, entering the fray some years after the major topographical writers of the eighteenth century had retired from the scene, was to be reputedly the work of many hands. Unable as yet to influence the reviews appearing in the *Magazine*, Nichols seized the opportunity to make known what appear to have been his personal views on Hasted's *History* when in 1780 he brought out the first number of the *Bibliotheca Topographica Britannica*, a periodical for which he was solely responsible and which was to appear at irregular invervals for ten years. No.1 was devoted to the antiquities of Kent and Sussex, and opened with an account of a small parish near Sittingbourne, the 'History of Tunstall', by the late Edward Rowe Mores, who had recently died. A pompous preface by the editor concluded with the following words:

> So much may suffice for the original design of this little history. In its execution Mr Mores may be fairly presumed to have exerted all that the *dulcedo natalis soli* calls forth. He professes to have drawn his materials chiefly from printed books. Had the compiler of the general history of that county, of which Tunstall makes so small a part, confined himself only to those sources, how much would he have improved that long-expected and voluminous work! But had he penetrated more intimately (for, notwithstanding the profession of his preface, scarce any such appear among his authorities) into the *keimelia* of records, inquisitions, chartularies, registers, and that fund of materials which are open to every diligent investigator, what a history of KENT, that county of Britain to which her first invader pays such a compliment, would have arisen under the pen of Mr HASTED![474]

This was a positively vitriolic attack, not only insinuating that Hasted had made poor use of his secondary sources, but attempting to wrest from him the grounds on which he based the claims of his *History* to be more accurate than its predecessors, namely, the use of those very records, inquisitions, chartularies and registers which Rowe Mores patently has not used!

If Hasted did not see this as soon as it appeared, he must quickly have been made aware of it. By early February 1781 John Thorpe was writing to him:

> Notwithstanding More's Hist. has such merit, which may be easily undertaken for any single or separate parish; yet to pursue his plan in a large County Hist. Good Lord! how voluminous would it be, and what few could purchase it, or indeed, what man's life or pocket is adequate to it? Therefore the editors might have spared their severe censure on your Hist. in the last page of their preface.

And Thorpe goes on to discuss the value of printed questionnaires, as advocated by the writer of the preface:

> The parochial queries towards forming county histories, which have been put out at different times, by the parsons which they enumerate and which they themselves now offer to the publick, have scarce ever been answered, or attended to, nor ever will be, on so large a plan. I only mention the above, that you may, if you think proper, vindicate yourself, and give these carpers a good dressing, in your next preface.[475]

But Hasted had soon decided on his response and a month later Thorpe was writing, 'As to the criticks, I think you judge right, to take no notice, and despise them'.[476] Hasted may have been hurt, but his silence was perfectly justified: any comparison between the history of a single parish and the history of a county, with its four hundred and fourteen parishes, was simply fatuous.

There were, on the contrary, many who, like the Revd Thomas Austen, vicar of Allhallows in Hoo and a former minor canon of Rochester cathedral, realised the extent both of Hasted's erudition and of his patient labour. A few months after the first volume's appearance Austen wrote to its author:

> Your work astonishes me at the sight of your infinite number of authentic vouchers, the regular detail of pedigrees, accuracy of dates, variety of interesting and entertaining matter, expressiveness and compact run of the style, without the least tautology, the

elegant and regular form of your method throughout, and most ample indexes, etc. [477]

Hasted had indeed given the county the first volume of a history which was, as Thomas Austen noted, better researched and better presented than any that had gone before. It was also, when complete, to be a noble work, of four large folio volumes, which, suitably bound by its subscribers, would grace many a gentleman's library. It is one of the charms of the practice of leaving the binding to the purchaser that when one comes across these volumes today each set looks unique, bound in red, green, brown or black leather, frequently embossed and sometimes bearing the monogram of the original owner.

In the event the matter of the dedication seems to have gone off, for Hasted, like a damp squib. November 1778 found him writing to Astle:

> I don't know much of the custom of dedicating books to his Majesty, but I wish to know if what has already past is all the notice I am to expect he will take of me, or my book. If it is usually so, I am quite content, but in that case, I think I could have found out a more gracious patron.[478]

Astle had clearly implied that the permission to dedicate the work to the king could be a prelude to greater honours, and even now he could not resist fuelling Hasted's hopes, suggesting that a knighthood might be expected. In a letter of late December, dealing with the missing replacement sheets, the historian replied to this:

> I thank you for your information relating to my expectations from the King, pecuniary ones I never dreamt of — I only wished to know if there might not be usually some notice taken on this occasion more than has been — as I fare the same as others I am quite content. You are quite mistaken as to Mrs Hasted's not being surprised at my receiving the honor of being dubbed, nor should I receive it at any rate till I had consulted my good friend, apothecary, and mayor of Maidstone, now the worshipfull Sir Thos. Bishop, Knight, which I shall take the first opportunity of doing, as I expect every postboy that I see to find him a messenger to fetch me up for this glorious purpose. I hope you have not deceived me by flattering tales — if you have, *Heu quanta de spe decidi.*[479]

Hasted's hopes or expectations, which seem to have been created wholly by Astle, were of course unrealised. The special wider-margin paper, not infrequently used for the dedication copies at this period but a lavish gesture from Hasted, went unremarked, and because it had to be repeated for every ensuing volume, would constitute yet another drain on his limited resources. That his *History* would prove such a financial burden Hasted, when he embarked on it, had never dreamt.

Nor could he suspect that the state of his finances would one day force him to fly the country. The first steps on the road to Calais, that haven of English debtors, were, however, taken long before April 1790, when Hasted found himself travelling with all speed down to Dover. In his long 'Statement of Mr Hasted's transactions with the late Mr Thos Williams concerning the conveyance of his estates', the historian was to speak of 'upwards of 30 years' as the period over which Williams, acting as both attorney and accountant, had begun to ensnare him financially. Nevertheless, the slow draining away of the value of his estates, through mortgages and sales, although it must clearly have resulted in a shrunken legacy for his heirs, need not have terminated in such a devastating manner as came about in 1790. Hasted may have spent more in some years than the estates brought in, but he never spent more than they were worth, as is shown by the sums which they fetched when they were finally disposed of after his death. There were several causes which contributed to the debacle of April 1790.

One of these was the initial overspending when, in his early twenties, he took and refurbished, indeed, partly rebuilt, St John's at Sutton-at-Hone. It is hardly surprising that once he was installed there the young squire, still only twenty-four, should have proposed to lead the life of a gentleman of ample means. Becoming known as a generous host he had continued to allow his annual expenditure, particularly in this direction, to outstrip his annual income. There can be little doubt that Hasted was encouraged in this by Edmund Browne, who very possibly envisaged a scheme of the kind which was to be put into operation by Thomas Williams, which entailed encumbering the young man with debts, lending him money to pay them, and being ultimately in pole position to take over what had become a heavily mortgaged estate. Hasted had been given a reprieve from Browne's machinations by his early death, but the purchase of Oakleys had been another costly blunder. In spite of the sacrifice of St John's he was never able to throw off the weight of those early debts, and Williams found himself at last in a position to take over the whole of the Hasted property, offering the small loophole of a six months' bond, of which he knew the historian would be unable to take advantage.

The second cause was very definitely, as Hasted himself maintained, the enormous expense of bringing out his *History*. This is underlined again and again in the prefaces to the folio edition. It is difficult to imagine that if he had not occupied himself with this he would have sought a government post which might have brought him a lucrative salary. Many men saw the advantage of doing this, as the Treasury's pay ledgers show. That Hasted preferred to devote his time to the voluntary service of his county seems unquestionable. But without the *History*, he might well have been able to give greater attention to the management of his estates, which, in the absence of expenditure on his great work, would have been sufficient to maintain the Hasted family's position in the county. As it was, not only did the *History* absorb most of his money and attention, it seems also to have encouraged a will-o'-the-wisp existence, when he would be elsewhere for days together as he explored yet another remote parish or examined a bundle of old family papers. It is significant that it is not remarked on as unusual that their father was not at home — he appears to have been staying at Belmont with Edward Wilks — on the night of the great storm about which Anne wrote to her brother Edward in 1779.

Edward had now been at Oxford for a year, and it is probably chance that this single letter survives. His sister may have sent him many such, as she obviously tried unsuccessfully to correspond with Francis and later kept in touch with her other brothers, but this is the only letter of hers we have, with its marvellously clear picture of the Hasteds at home in early January 1779.

> Dear Brother, Grandmama received your letter with pleasure and wish's you a happy new year. I hope you have not received any damage from our late violant hurricane of wind rain and snow which was very frightful. We did not get up but most people did they thinking themselves in danger of losing their lives. Mama and George got up and had some plumb cake and cherry brandy, they had a fire in Mama's room. Charles was too lazy to get up, Jack never heard anything of it and Kitty had old puss to bed.
>
> Canterbury and the adjacent places have suffered much but our house is very little damaged. Papa has lost above an £150 in the country and said tho Mr Wilke's was a new built house he was rock'd as if it was a cradle and the sea came up to the back door.
>
> You said in your letter you had made Frank a good correspondent. I wish I could do the same for I cannot make him write but very seldom and then he writes about half a dozen lines which is not

fair for I always write him very long ones. I shou'd be very much obliged to you if you wou'd let him know in your next letter that I shall be very happy to hear from him and am very much disapointed in not having a parcel or letter from him but hope when he has anything to spare and any time to write he will not forget he has a Sister who will think herself very much obliged to him for all his favours.

As for news there is very little, Miss Bridges was married to Mr Lefroy last Monday and Miss Gipps yesterday to Mr Bolland. I believe Canterbury is as dull as Oxford: there are no routs nor anybody to make them. Tomorrow is twelfth day and Kitty and I go to choose king and queen at the Duncombes. There will be Mrs Blomer Miss Willyams's and three or four more. I was there last year and was queen. Mrs Blomer was there likewise and took the largest piece of cake she could find and the piece of paper upon [it] was Goody Greedy Guts which was a very proper name for her. We met as usual on Christmas day. We were very merry and the Celestial Gothic din'd drank tea and supp'd with us, play'd Pope Joan and sung two songs.

I am afraid you will not find my letter so entertaining or well wrote as I could wish but hope you excuse all faults. Grandmama desires her love to you and I hope you will accept of the same from your ever Affectionate Sister, A. Hasted.[480]

A delightfully informative letter, although it leaves one wishing that the 'Celestial Gothic' — Osmund Beauvoir? — had been identified!
Anne was clearly conversant with all that went on in the other Hasted home in the Precincts, but at the time of writing was still living on her own with her grandmother: 'we did not get up'. This was soon to change. The Canterbury land tax returns show that by June 1780 Hasted had given up the prebendary house and moved his whole family into the house he held in the Green Court, occupied for ten years only by his mother and Anne.[481] This rather less than ideal arrangement must have been forced on Hasted by his worsening financial position. Nevertheless, an account of the rents due to him on Lady Day 1780 from freehold and leasehold property show that he should have received no less than £936.6s.8d., and that this was a slight increase over previous years when the amount had lain between £920 and £901.[482] One can only assume that some of this had to be paid out as interest on loans.
Anne's letter reveals that five of the Hasted children were still at home in 1779. George, sitting up with his mother during the storm and

enjoying a small midnight feast with her of plum cake and cherry brandy, was now the oldest of them. Edward, as we have seen, was at Oxford, and Francis, who was perhaps the most difficult son, and who had been the first of the Hasted children to leave school, appears to have been in the army. George himself had by now left school and would shortly be going to live in Tonbridge, where he was to be articled to the attorney William Scoones, and it is probable that Hasted, envisaging further reductions in family numbers in the near future, felt that separate establishments for himself and his mother had become an unnecessary luxury. Since they were both resident in the Precincts the move itself was a minor one and can have caused little disruption in Hasted's life.

The house in the Green Court, described as 'his now dwelling house', is undoubtedly the one which, together with its contents, Hasted insured with the Sun Fire Office in December 1780.[483] Described as brick, timber and tiled, the house itself was insured for £425, while a separate building, containing washhouse, brewhouse and loft was insured for £75. Of the contents, it was Hasted's books which were insured for the highest sum — £200 — which should give us some idea of the extent of his library; the Hasteds' household goods were covered for the sum of £175, the family plate for £100, and the utensils in washhouse and brewhouse for £25. Also covered by the same policy was a brick and tiled house at Chatham, in the tenure of a labourer, John Live, which was insured for £200. The total sum insured by Hasted, £1200, represents a fairly average figure at this time, when sums insured could be as low as £60 or as high as £10,000.

A visit to the Thorpes at Bexley was still almost an annual fixture. A torn and undated letter from John Thorpe, apparently written towards the end of 1780, refers to one such occasion — as well as to a change of heart on his part towards what may have been another annual event: a summer encampment by the military on neighbouring Bexleyheath, which was obviously the subject of much banter between the two families:

> Mrs Hasted will laugh when she hears that I was, at last, quite a convert to camp amusements. I din'd at their messes, had several of them to dine with us, went to their balls and assemblies, which were very brilliant. In short, Miss Thorpe will write soon to Mrs Hasted, and give her a budget of camp news, etc. After so gay a summer, and the military being gone into winter quarters, make this season appear the more dull and gloomy to us. ... We are very happy to find that yourself, Mrs Hasted, and son, received any pleasure at Bexley: I do assure you, that you and yours will, at all times, meet with a sincere and hearty wellcome under our roof.[484]

The all-important thing now was to complete the *History*. As is evident from John Thorpe's letter of November 1778, Hasted had soon realised that it would run to more than two volumes, and the part which would now form the second volume was very near completion. Hasted set to work on it with a will, feeding pages to his printer as they were ready. Again, there was the search for plates, although some had been prepared earlier, and the Hundred maps were well in hand. Once more the correspondence built up, as Hasted worked through the Rochester, Chatham, Tonbridge, Maidstone and Faversham areas: the file of letters and papers relating to this volume was to contain some two hundred and five items, carefully numbered by Hasted, and occasionally renumbered, as later sheets of information were inserted in their proper place — the correspondence is ordered along the same lines as the Hundreds and parishes in the book. Following the publication of his first volume those whom he approached for information were even more ready to assist him, frequently concluding with a sentiment such as that expressed by James Whatman in 1779 in a letter dealing with the parish of Boxley:

> It will always give me particular pleasure to have the honor of seeing you here, and I hope the next time you come into this part of the county you will favor me with more of your company, and be assured I shall be happy in an opportunity of paying my respects to you at Canterbury.[485]

As before, vicars frequently proved a useful source of information: the Revd George Burville was also applied to with regard to Boxley (Hasted seldom relied on a single correspondent for any one place if he could help it), the Revd Peter Wade sent information about Snodland, the Revd Richard Husband about West Malling, the Revd Ezekiel de la Douespe about Loose, Barming, Farleigh, and Linton. Mr de la Douespe would have supplied more, had he been able, but was hindered due to 'the want of my horse, which has been lame these five weeks, and an unusual variety of interruptions'. Clearly already a friend of the family, he ended his letter on a personal note:

> If I can be of further service, I beg you will command me. Miss Dorman return'd from Sutton last Friday, very well; and desires her loves to you, and Mrs Hasted; who will also kindly accept my respects.[486]

Five years later the Hasteds' eldest son, Edward, now the Revd Edward Hasted, was to become curate to Mr de la Douespe in East Farleigh.

The Revd Richard Bathurst, sending 'Respects to my Aunt and cousins' in the Spring of 1780, was happy to supply information about Goudhurst and Finchcocks, the country house which he had inherited, but regretted that Hasted had not found time to call on him — 'I should have been very glad of the pleasure of a visit from you'[487] — and indeed, the historian seems now to have been in demand from all quarters.

Attorneys were equally obliging: Thomas Durrant Punnett returned Hasted's sheet of queries about Maidstone in February 1779, and Francis Austen, of Sevenoaks, his writing showing even greater signs of age than when he had corresponded with the historian in the sixties, sent him information the following month about Boxley and Boxley Abbey. Thomas Tomlyn in Rochester and William Scoones in Tonbridge were also useful correspondents. From 1780 Hasted's son George was working in the Tonbridge attorney's office, and was usually given the opportunity of adding a short personal note to any communications intended for his father. In January 1783 there was a parcel to acknowledge:

> GH desires to add his kind remembrance to all. He had the pleasure of receiving Mr H's parcel safe by the newsman yesterday eveng and hopes soon to repeat his packet. He sent per post on Sunday.[488]

The promised 'packet' may well have been a sheaf of notes for his father. George, perhaps alone among Hasted's sons, seems to have entered into his father's passion for the minutiae of Kentish history, and there are a number of sheets in George's neat hand among the papers relating to the Lowy of Tonbridge, Capel, Hadlow, Southborough, Leigh and Edenbridge. At the bottom of a long account of a lawsuit George has written: 'I hope you will be able to understand something of the decision from the account I have given you ... you must remember I am but a novice in the law.'[489]

It had apparently been intended that the second volume of the *History* should appear at the end of 1782, but something seems to have happened to prevent this. Early the following May an insertion in the Canterbury papers announced that 'The second volume of the History of Kent having been unexpectedly delayed beyond the time proposed for the general publication of it, will certainly be ready for the subscribers, together with the map of the county, on or before the 24th instant', and on the 20th of that month both book and map were announced as ready for delivery or collection.[490] Curiously, however, review copies appear to have been available and sent out, as planned, at the end of 1782.

It was exactly five years since the first volume had appeared, in May 1778. This was to be the shortest interval between publication of the four books: seven more years were to elapse before Volume III would appear, and another nine before Volume IV completed the work. Other events were to intrude and to be partly the cause of these long delays. Between 1778 and 1782, however, there is no doubt that Hasted spent every minute he could in trying to bring his work to completion and that by the time Volume II eventually appeared he was exhausted. This is abundantly clear from his Preface, written in November 1782:

> This volume has been about three years in hand, during which time hardly a day has passed, the greatest part of which has not been spent in close application towards the prosecution of it, almost to the destruction of an exceeding good state of health.

And for the first time he admits to a reluctance to continue:

> Here I had made a resolution of finishing my labours, and of leaving the completing of this History to the industrious pains of some future continuator; but many of my subscribers, whose good will to me I can have no doubt of, have, within these months, on being told my design, so strongly urged my being bound in honor, as well as honesty, to complete it in a third volume, that I own, I hardly know how to refuse it. The two chief obstacles to my compliance are, — my declining health, and the great expence which I have already been at, and which of consequence must increase, in the further prosecution of it. The former I must trust to Providence to establish; the latter must be left to the option of the purchasers of these volumes to enable me to undertake it, or not, at their pleasure; for without their approbation I certainly shall not risque the hazard of it.[491]

The reviewer of the second volume in the *Gentleman's Magazine*, who must have obtained an advance copy of the work, since the appearance of his review in the May issue coincided with the general publication of the book, was not ignorant of the expense and labour which the *History* was costing its author, and took the opportunity to wish him 'the success he deserves, as all he can expect to receive will by no means compensate the time and expence bestowed on such an elaborate undertaking'. As before, the review was a good one, although the *History*, originally promised in two volumes, would now run to three: 'Though his first subscribers have not, at present, a complete work, more pages than were promised have been given them'. Readers of the *Magazine* were entertained with two extracts from the new volume: a brief biography of Sir Joseph Banks, contained in a footnote on Provenders, the country house in the parish of Norton of which Banks had become joint owner by marriage, and an account of finding sweet-water and sinking a well at Sheerness, in the Isle of Sheppey, an area notoriously destitute of that element. The review concluded with a couple of small queries 'amidst the entertainment and information this work has afforded us'.[492]

It is no surprise to find the historian making a plea for support in his Preface. The subscriptions were already proving insufficient to cover the cost of bringing out the work and Hasted seems to have resigned himself to bearing a considerable part of it, but some subscriptions, which he was quite willing to take in at his own house, he must have! In December 1783, still confident of completing his work in three volumes — and in a short space of time — he placed a modest insertion in the papers under the heading 'History of Kent': 'Those gentlemen who intend to subscribe to the third volume of the above History (which concludes the work) are requested to pay their subscriptions for it to their respective booksellers during the course of this month, soon after which the book will be put to the press, and then no further subscriptions can be received'.[493]

Already by the early 1780s Hasted appears to have been hard pressed for money. The Court Book of the manor of Teynham shows that in October 1782 he transferred or sold three of the properties there which had been in his family since the time of his grandfather, Lewson going to Henry Pratt, Cambridge to Philip Chapman, and lands at or near Barrow Green, known as Hays, to Nicholas Gilbee.[494] Other records throw light on the state of his finances in 1783/4. A sheet in his own handwriting among the Rochester Guildhall papers shows that he had 'lands in hand', that is to say, which he was farming himself (and which seem to have been planted with timber) at Halstow, Lower Halstow and Upchurch, and that rents due to him at Lady Day (25 March) of that year amounted to £734.[495] That this was insufficient to carry him through the next twelve months we know from the fact that on the 12 March 1784 he negotiated a bond with Richard Gibbs, a yeoman of Ickham, for £1100.[496] The bond refers to a mortgage, drawn up between Hasted and his wife of the first part, his mother of the second part, and Richard Gibbs of the third part, so it is clear that both wife and mother were fully aware of Hasted's financial difficulties. The mortgage, doubtless one of many, must have provided a temporary solution to these. The state of the historian's health, however, was something which could not be improved so quickly.

In the files relating to the *History* there are no more than five letters dating from 1783 and 1784, and it would appear that Hasted was now in need of a complete break from it. 1783 is marked by an almost total dearth of documentation, although we do know that he put in an appearance at all four quarter sessions, in January and July, and at Easter and Michaelmas. Work in the public sector may have been a relief after the close application which bringing out the first two volumes of his *History* had entailed. And there was always a background of family matters which demanded attention.

Francis had been the first of Hasted's sons to leave school. The King's School register notes that he left at Christmas 1775 and went into the army. But it is likely that he tried a number of things before finally settling down. John Thorpe's light-hearted letter about camp amusements, probably dating from the end of 1780, had earlier dealt with a more sombre subject, although, since the top of the letter has been torn away, we have to guess at the person Thorpe is talking about:

> And should Dingley, or any one, mention it, I shall only say, that young men nowadays prefer the Army, or Navy, to serving in a shop. I am glad you go on with your History; and pray, keep up your spirits, and trust to Providence: so I shall dwell no longer on this unpleasant subject.[497]

Since there was never any question of Edward, George or Charles entering the army or navy, and John was still at school, some escapade or rejection of a good opening on the part of Hasted's second son would seem to have been the subject of Thorpe's remarks.

Edward, the eldest son, was by now already at Oxford, and throughout his time there his father kept a careful tally of his expenditure. In 1778, when Edward first went up, Hasted made out a careful list of the clothes and items of linen which were to accompany him. Among the 'other items' we see the young undergraduate providing his own sheets, pillow-cases, towels, table-cloths, napkins and tea-cloths, much as he would today, but the list of clothes shows us also an elegant student of the second half of the eighteenth century, who, as well as having two cloth coats and waistcoats, a pair of worsted breeches, and five pairs of worsted stockings, also had black satin and white breeches, which could be partnered with a variety of waistcoats — pink, green striped, or spotted Manchester — and with one of his several pairs of silk spun, white silk or white thread stockings. In addition Edward took with him a pair of leather breeches and a pair of boots and spurs for riding, as well as thirteen stocks, six pairs of ruffles and three neckcloths. Slippers and dressing-gown offered relaxed wear for his evenings, and two night-shirts and six night-caps conduced to his repose. No doubt Edward was given a copy of this list, with instructions to check that everything came back from the laundry.[498]

His first year's expenses had totalled £121.13s.3d., and a warning from his father that this must be kept down had resulted in the slightly lower figure for 1779 of £112.13s.11d. However, expenses for the next two years came respectively to £144.3s.4d. and then the astronomical £219.15s.7d. The Hasted income could not support such a sum, especially as the second volume of the *History*, with all its attendant expenses, was about to come out: Edward, in 1782, was obliged to get by on £65.2s.3d. In 1783 his expenses had again totalled three times this sum, but there were probably some unavoidable costs in a final year. Overall, keeping Edward at Oxford for six years cost Hasted what was virtually a whole year's income from his estates, £829.0s.2d.[499]

University was clearly a financial impossibility for any of his other sons, but Hasted seems to have taken care to let them enter the professions of their choice. John Septimus, in 1783, was apprenticed to Dr Thomas Fitzgerald of Deal for the sum of £105, an average premium for the profession, although it would have been possible to find a doctor asking a lower one. Father and son travelled down to Deal together at the beginning of July, when John's indentures were signed on the 3rd of that month, and he began a new life within sight and sound of the sea.[500]

A few days in Deal probably made a pleasant break for his father, too, but such short vacations — and even a rest of a whole year away from the close application which had been necessary to bring out Volume II — were not sufficient to re-establish the historian's health. He was ill throughout most of 1784, and may possibly have suffered a near breakdown, solely as a result of the demands of his *History*. The evidence shows that, in spite of putting in an appearance at the Canterbury quarter sessions for January, July and Michaelmas, Hasted spent most of this year in Tonbridge, under a Tonbridge doctor, and it seems to have been as a result of this long absence from home that his life took another direction altogether.

It is quite possible that Hasted chose to go to Tonbridge because from there he could ride to the Wells to take the waters — it was undoubtedly cheaper to stay in Tonbridge than Tunbridge Wells — and there was the added attraction that he would also be near George. And he probably had no thought initially of staying away from home for so long. As it turned out, a bill from a Tonbridge doctor, John Fuzzard, shows that

Hasted was being attended on a regular basis from 17 February to 24 December 1784, with frequent prescriptions for purging, and saline draughts and alterative pills, commonly used together at this time to treat bilious complaints. Indeed, between May and September the doctor seems to have been an almost daily visitor. Fuzzard's final bill, for £16.5s.0d., was submitted on the 18 October 1785, when Hasted received it with an accompanying note:

> Dear Sir, I received your kind letter, and am heartily glad to hear your complaint diminishes. I have received five guineas of Mr Scoones on your account, which I have applied as you directed to the discharge of the first bill and personal applications for which I return you sincere thanks.
>
> I have (as you requested) herewith sent the account remaining for medicines — am sorry we are not likely to see you at Tonbridge — when an opportunity occurs shall be happy to pay my respects to you in town.
>
> I am Dear Sir your much obliged and humble servant, John Fuzzard.[501]

This was addressed to Hasted at No. 7, Grange Court, Carey Street, London, which must have been the 'lodgings in London' where he was now, on his own admission, keeping a young mistress.

On the 6 January 1785 a removal order was served on a young unmarried woman at Sutton Valence. She had no claim on parish welfare there and possibly no visible means of support either, and since she was now known to be six or seven months pregnant, the parish authorities thought it prudent to ensure that she returned to the parish where she had an acknowledged settlement, in case of future claims for support of her illegitimate child. The parish to which she was removed, Linton, acknowledged its responsibility, and noted in its vestry book:

> Jany 6th, 1785: An Order of Removal Mary Town from Sutton Valence to ye Parish of Linton.[502]

Two months later a son was born to Mary Town, and on the 27 March he was christened Edward in Linton church, the minister, in his entry in the register, adding the information that the child was base-born.[503]

In the only reference Hasted makes to his young mistress by name he calls her Mary Jane. However, double given names were less common in the eighteenth century than they became in the nineteenth, and the Kentish registers cannot be made to reveal a single Mary Jane Town at the time when she is likely to have been born, although Town is a relatively common surname in the county. Whatever the source of the name Jane, whether added by Mary herself or by her amoroso, its presence or absence does not seem a serious stumbling block to a possible identification of the historian's young mistress with Mary, the third daughter of Philip and Elizabeth Town, who was born in Hunton in 1763,[504] or a more definite identification of her with the Mary Town who gave birth to little Edward in 1785. It is true that Hasted himself only admits to having become acquainted with her in 1785, but he is out by a year or two in the case of several events in his brief Chronology, written when he was well into his seventies, including the move from Sutton-at-Hone to Canterbury and the flight to France, errors which are more probably due to lapses of memory than to any wish to falsify the record.

Apart from this evidence, we know very little about Mary Jane. On the back of an appeal which William Boys was to send to Thomas Pennant some years later on behalf of a by then penniless Hasted, Pennant noted that the historian had 'left his old wife and ran away with a young girl'.[505] Boys, in the course of that same appeal, attributed the whole affair to Hasted's 'poverty', which implies that Hasted had not been looking for an adventure when he took up with Mary Jane, and might also explain his prolonged stay in Tonbridge as a need to escape from the tensions of home life in Canterbury, where his wife and his mother now shared a house, and where his wife, over the years, had probably come to reciprocate the dislike which her mother-in-law nursed for her. The fact that Mary Town's place of settlement was acknowledged to be Linton, and not Hunton where she had been born, makes it likely that she had been in service there and that she had occupied her position for at least a year. In after years the historian seems to have regretted the escapade: the entry in the Chronology, under 1785, notes simply that he 'Unfortunately became acquainted with Mary Jane Town'.[506] Was it love on both sides, or was Mary Jane something of an adventuress, eager for the more elevated lifestyle that a gentleman would provide for her? Perhaps both elements came into it: it was certainly more than a brief infatuation, since Hasted and Mary Jane Town were to remain together for more than twelve years, years that were the most fraught of the historian's whole life.

There is a single clue in the records to Hasted's experience of love, and it comes, not in his own words, but in the translation of a sonnet by the Portuguese poet Camoens, printed in an issue of the *Kentish Gazette*. When Hasted came across it, he cut it out and pasted it into the back of one of his small notebooks. It reads as follows:

> Whoever says that love is like the wind,
> Fickle, ungrateful, full of fraud and lies,
> That wretched man has sure deserved to find
> From love all rigour and all cruelties.
> Gentle, benignant, merciful is love,
> Believe not him who says love is not so;
> Let the false slanderer live, by men below
> Despised, and hateful to the Gods above.
> If ever love works misery in me
> Let men the sum of all his evils see,
> Me, whom he seems delighted to oppress,
> The utmost rigour of his power I prove,
> Yet would not change the miseries of love
> For all the world beside calls happiness.[507]

And yet an enigma remains, since this appeared in the *Kentish Gazette* for 14 January 1800, several years after he had parted from Mary Jane 'for infamy and wickedness'. But it may well, for Hasted, have epitomised his years with her.

Mary Jane Town certainly did not become the single object round which Hasted's life revolved. That was, and remained, his *History*. And although an entry against 1786 in his list of dates states: 'Took her into keeping and hired a house for her first at Sheldwich, and then at Boughton under Blean and then in lodgings in London and then at Dover',[508] they did not, at this time, set up house together: Hasted continued to use his house in the Precincts as his base, riding out from there to his work as a justice of the peace and Deputy Lieutenant, as well as commissioner of sewers and of the land tax.

We know nothing else about the child, and the probability is that it died. Thereafter the pair were a little more careful: some notes dating from the late 1780s contain several unpleasant-sounding recipes or prescriptions 'to procure a miscarriage', and 'for a slight accident'.[509]

It could be that Hasted gave himself up the more easily, in 1785, to a liaison which provided him with an alternative to the serious discords of the house in the Green Court at Canterbury — which must also have made concentration on his *History* difficult — because all his sons were now launched on their careers, and such an irregularity on his part was unlikely to disrupt their lives, although relations were always to be strained between the historian and his eldest son, who had now entered the church. Francis, in the army, was at last provided with a commission. John Thorpe, writing to Dr Ducarel in October 1781, had mentioned a letter received from Hasted two months earlier in which the historian had told him that Lord Amherst had 'given his son Francis an ensigncy in an old regiment now in Minorca; so that his History has produced some good effect'.[510] George was happily settled with the attorney William Scoones at Tonbridge, where he apparently formed part of the Scoones household; Charles, who seems to have been quite content to enter commerce, was working as a mealman, perhaps already in Dartford; and John Septimus (Jack to his family) was at Deal, studying to become a surgeon.

Hasted was occasionally engaged, during the 1780s, in helping William Boys with his *History of Sandwich*, answering queries and checking sheets for him.[511] He could be elusive, however, as his Eastry friend William Boteler found, chiding him gently with sometimes promising visits which did not materialise, and, in March 1787, writing lightly that it was so long since he had heard from the historian that 'I began to doubt if you breath'd vital air, and was not a little pleas'd to be inform'd of your existence by your handwriting'.[512]

There was a reason, however, for Hasted's silence in the spring of 1787, and the tone of his reply is unlikely to have been as lighthearted as William Boteler's. George had fallen ill during the winter, and already there must have been fears that he might not have long to live. He seems to have been exceptionally bright, and was perhaps the closest of all five sons to their father. Edward and Francis, it will be remembered, had spent two or three formative years away from home, living with their grandmother, when little George must have taken the place of the eldest son, his happy temperament making him everyone's favourite — even the snappish Samuel Egerton Brydges spoke well of him. There was certainly time then for a closer relationship to have built up between Hasted and his third son than either Edward or Francis was able to enjoy. Edward seems to have been reserved by nature, and Francis to have had no difficulty in detaching himself from everyone in his family — with the possible exception of his elder brother — at a very early age. Only George, of the whole family, seems to have been willing to lend his father a hand in his Herculean task, and may well have acted as a young amanuensis on several occasions while still a boy.

By February George's condition had already become serious. In a letter dated the fifth of that month Hasted's old friend, Dr Osmund Beauvoir, himself now an invalid and living at Bath, was to say in a letter to him: 'I hope poor George will receive benefit'. But wherever it was that George had been sent, or whatever it was that was being done for him, there was no improvement, and Hasted's third son died, a month before his twenty-fourth birthday, on the 17 July of that year. His death took place at his Aunt Dorman's, at Barming. The *Kentish Gazette* for the 20

July carried an obituary notice for one 'whose amiable disposition and goodness of heart endeared him to all who knew him, and makes his death universally lamented'. George was described as 'of Lincoln's Inn', which probably meant no more than that his father had hoped to send him there in due course, since his name does not appear in the Lincoln's Inn registers. His death was also announced in the *Gentleman's Magazine*, although the brief notice contained several errors of fact, and was probably based on details supplied by a friend rather than by a member of the family.[513]

Hasted spared no expense for his son's funeral at Newington: the bill, from the Maidstone undertaker Finch Hollingworth, totalled £50.2s.4d. There were items covering the hearse, a coach and four, ostrich feathers, refreshments for men and horses at both Barming and Newington, and payments to the sextons of Maidstone and of Barming, where Hasted probably had the bell tolled as well as at Newington. George's body was laid in the family vault which had been built on the occasion of Hasted's sister's death in 1762. It was to be the last time the vault was used.[514]

Only a week after George's death there was a bereavement in William Scoones's own family: the death of his second daughter, Frances, aged 12, was announced in the *Kentish Gazette* for the 31 July. It is of course possible that the disease which had killed George was the cause of her death, too; but it could also be that her death was hastened by grief at the loss of someone who had been her favourite no less than everyone else's.

Hard work on his *History* may have helped Hasted to cope with the loss of his son. There is a great deal of correspondence relating to Volume III on which he was now working, most of it dating from the three years 1786 to 1788, with the writers of it coming largely from the same groups as before, namely landed gentry, clergy and attorneys.

The most unreliable of these groups was perhaps that of the landed gentry — unreliable, both because they were capable of not providing very much information, or not the kind of information which Hasted required, and because they not infrequently turned the tables on the historian by requesting help with their own genealogical researches. In 1766 Anna Ward, one of Hasted's earliest correspondents, had been eager to have a copy of a terrier which Hasted had come across and which must have related to some family lands; while Lord Radnor, in August 1787 and again in March 1788, was asking Hasted to obtain for him a copy of 'the schedule of the deeds in the public offices you mention having relation to Folkestone'. In 1785 and 1786 Thomas Heron of Chilham Castle seems to have set Hasted to work on his family pedigree, which was to appear as a plate in Volume III, along with a view of Chilham Castle. This was probably the starting point for the *Genealogical Table of the Herons* which appeared in 1798. This considerably extended pedigree with copious notes seems to have been solely the work of Sir Richard Heron, Thomas Heron's youngest son, and there is nothing to support the suggestion which is sometimes made that it was drawn up by Hasted; the historian is briefly referred to in a footnote.[515]

Nevertheless, in spite of other calls on his time, work proceeded steadily on the third volume. In place of the two large commonplace books which he had taken on his earlier 'parochial visitations', Hasted was now using some small notebooks, which were much handier to whip from his pocket and use for jotting down on-the-spot observations on a church and its monuments, or the location of a house or a village. This series of notebooks, which finally numbered sixteen in all, he later entitled 'Itinerarium Parochiale Cantianum, being the Parochial Itinerary of Edwd Hasted, made by him thro' the several parishes of the County of Kent for the collecting of whatever was worth notice local or personal, any ways relating to that county, begun in the year 1764 and continued on to the year 1788'.[516] A typical entry is that for Biddenden, on which, in a notebook bearing the date 1783, Hasted commented:

> It is a large well built church with a handsome square tower having a beacon tower at NE corner. The church stands on an eminence, having the town eastward of it. Next the N side of the churchyard (a small close only between) stands the Parsonage House, being a modern building of brick and sashed. On the other side of the road SE of the church-yard is the school house, a brick building of the time of Q. Elizh, seemingly adjoining to it about 1/2 an acre of land said to be given for a playground for the children. The lower part of this parish next Cranbrook is very pleasant, the upper part next Smarden and that towards Bethersden very much otherwise.

And on Cranbrook itself, which he loved, and visited more than once:

> Has a market on a Saturday for hops and corn. There was formerly a great trade of cloathing carried on in this and the neighboring parishes, from which many families of the rank of gentry, and in good estimation now, took their rise, as the Bathursts, Courthopes, Tempests, Westons, etc. There are only 2 houses of it remaining now in this parish, but there is some little woolstapling

carried on ... The church consists of 3 isles and 3 chancels, has a square tower with clock and chimes and 6 bells now and 2 more making. The church is large and remarkably handsome, and beautifull from the slightness of the pillars on each side the middle isle.

And Hasted also noted that 'There are 3 meeting houses in the parish, 1 for Presbyterians, 1 for Methodistical Baptists, 1 for Calvinistical Baptists, and a 4th for Independants'.[517]

In August 1786 Hasted made a tour which took in Crundale, Wye, Boughton Aluph, Elham, Acrise, Paddlesworth, Lyminge, Stelling, Swingfield, Hawkinge, Folkestone, Capel, Alkham, Lydden, Postling, Saltwood, Newington, Cheriton, Poulton, Seasalter, Whitstable, Swalecliffe, Harbledown, St Dunstan's, Thanington and St Stephen's. September 1787 saw him in what were mainly Romney Marsh parishes, and later the same year he visited various parishes to the east of Maidstone, among them Leeds, Lenham and Ulcombe.[518]

The information which he noted down on these occasions — sometimes enlivening his notes with a brief sketch — would subsequently be collated with findings from his research and information from his correspondents. In 1788, for example, he was writing up his Romney Marsh material, and corresponding at the same time with the Revd William Wing Fowle, rector of New Romney. Mr Fowle wrote to him on the 18 May in answer to two letters which he had received from Hasted via 'the newsmen', ending his letter: 'I believe I shall be at Canterbury on Wednesday or Thursday sevennight, when I will call on you'. Hasted's reply was dated only four days later:

> I am very much obliged to you for your last letter, which has in some measure enabled me to go forward ... I am ashamed of the trouble I give you, but I am travelling fast thro' the Marsh, and hope the sooner to get thro' it, that I may not trespass so heavily on your patience. I hope when you do come to Canterbury you will do me the favor of spending your evening with me. I will keep myself disengaged at your service, both Wednesday and Thursday, in hopes of it one of these days, and I have engaged my neighbour Dix to meet you, when I hope in person to acknowledge my best thanks to you for all the kind services I have received from you throughout my work.[519]

The file of letters and papers relating to Volume III is the thickest of all, numbering three hundred and twenty-one items. As usual, these mingle attorneys' answers to Hasted's queries with letters from friends and relatives which sometimes contain also more personal details. One such came to Hasted early in January 1789, bearing New Year's greetings from an old school friend, Sir Robert Wilmot of Chaddesden, as well as some details about the Wilmot pedigrees. It begins humorously — Hasted's eldest son was obviously a guest at Chaddesden at the time:

> Your son Edward about five hours ago gave me your letter dated Decr the 16th. I can contribute (sic) his forgetfulness to arise from no other cause but his head being loaded with divinity, as he has promised to preach to morrow, and his cargo of sermons are not yet arrived, nor his shirts, etc.

After giving Hasted the information for which he had asked — apparently a clarification of the two Wilmot baronetcies — Sir Robert continues, 'My son and yours are now drinking their bottle by me, and plaguing about pedigrees, however, I will conclude, and drink your health and all your family, wishing you a happy new year'.[520]

There was a convivial meeting with his two surgeon friends, William Boys and William Boteler, early in the August of 1789, heralded by a letter from Boys — 'Boteler will be glad to see you on Monday. His dinner will be ready at three, and I will endeavour to be of the party' — but as it progressed the year was to be anything but a happy one for Hasted, culminating in an accident, which seems to have occurred when he was away from home on one of his fact-finding missions and which resulted in a broken leg. Boteler wrote to him on the 29 December:

> The news of your misfortune did not reach me till some days after the accident had happened, when I was assured of your being in a fair way to do well, or I should have sent to enquire after you.

As a doctor, of course, Boteler took a cooler view than the patient himself of a tumble of which he had heard no bad reports:

> That you at present remember it with horror is not to be wondered at, but I can by no means admit that the remembrance will never wear away, and that a final period is to be put to your parochial visitations in consequence of it![521]

Nevertheless, Hasted's spirits remained low, and his friends at Eastry and Sandwich were forced to accept that he might be unable to make the remaining tours which were needed to complete the *History* as it had been planned. Nobly, they divided out between themselves the parishes which remained to be visited, and in a letter of March 1790 Boteler sent a sample of what he was proposing to collect for a historian whose riding days were now apparently over:

> I send with this what I have collected relative to Betshanger and Northbourne as a specimen only of what I mean to glean in every place as far as I can; when you have read it you may if you please return it with observations and if I have omitted any thing necessary for your information within my power minute it down ...

and Boteler even went so far as to beg Hasted to allow him and Boys to check the material on their localities before it finally went to press:

> Promise me only, my dear Sir, that Eastry and every contiguous parish to it shall not be finally done till Boys and I have seen them. Don't censure my presumption in making this request, locality will give opportunities for information that cannot be procur'd at a distance.

The tone of Boteler's letter seems to imply that the subject had been raised before and had encountered some unwillingness on the part of the historian to delegate that labour which, until now, had been his alone.[522]

But it was on the financial front that matters were now looking blackest. For many years Hasted had been in the habit of leaving the management of his income to his attorney at Dartford, Thomas Williams. Williams had been empowered to raise mortgages on various parts of the scattered Hasted estates, finding clients who were prepared to make loans, and, when these had to be repaid, arranging for the sale of parcels of land in settlemement of them. Hasted was later to estimate that these transactions had amounted to not less than £20,000, and that the business had been very lucrative for Williams, who, 'having the whole management and business of the conveyances, and percentage from both parties, on all moneys advanced ... made a triple profit from the whole. This lasted for upwards of 30 years'.[523]

During the course of such transactions, probably in the later 1780s, Williams had been asked to raise a second mortgage on some properties, and claiming that they were not an adequate security for a further loan he had added another estate to them as collateral security. This appears to have been the large Horsham manor estate, held on lease from All Souls College, Oxford, which Hasted may have intended initially to preserve from financial encroachments of this kind. His financial troubles did not decrease, however, and knowing that the value of this property far exceeded that of the security required against the mortgage obtained by Williams, he himself, acting without his attorney's knowledge, took out a second mortgage on it, borrowing £2000 from a certain Joseph Davies, and another £2200 from Robert Rugg. There was a limit to the extent to which the estates could be milked in this way, however, and early in 1789 everything began to come to a head.[524]

It was apparently on Thomas Williams's advice that in the March of that year Hasted was persuaded to assign all his estates over in trust to a certain William Pennington and John Williams, Thomas Williams's nephew, for the purpose of selling them, on the death of his mother, in order to clear all his mortgages and debts. The existence of his mother's annuity, dependent as it was on the Hasted estates generally, prevented their being sold immediately, but Williams appears to have prevailed on Hasted a few months later to release the property from this claim, in order to make an earlier sale possible. Accordingly, on the 23 October following, the trust of the 12 March was amended, with Ann Hasted being joined in the first part with her husband, and old Mrs Hasted being named of the second part in order to extinguish her annuity. The dividend and interest of the residue of the surplus money arising from such a sale were to be paid by the Williamses to Hasted himself and to his wife and mother; while one third of the principal of the trust monies was to go to Hasted to be left to whoever he should name in his will. As amended, the trust was clearly intended to ensure some financial security, whatever happened, for Hasted's dependants.[525]

Hasted had himself realised by now that only the sale of his estate in its entirety would clear off the debts and mortgages with which it was encumbered, and had already taken the step of having it valued. The valuation figure of around £12,000 which he was given was, he felt, sufficient to satisfy all his creditors, and would also allow a little over for his family to survive on. It was at this point, however, before anything was done under the trust, that Williams suddenly announced that the clients he had been representing all required their money to be repaid immediately. Hasted had some suspicions that Williams, who had built up a very lucrative practice, had in fact been lending out his own money, and represented no one but himself. In the event this appears to have been true. Williams had bought up several of the mortgages obtained by

Hasted, so that of the £8685 which was now due, £3035.12s.6d. represented debts to him, while a debt of £4439.7s.6d. standing in the name of Darcy Tancred, of Lincoln's Inn, was in fact in trust for Williams himself. The remaining £1210 was owed to two local gentlemen, George Godden and John Colyer, both of Southfleet. It seems to have been at this juncture that the historian's own creditors, Davies and Rugg, hearing perhaps by a side-wind that the Hasted credit had become shaky, took out a writ for his arrest. If the estate could not be disposed of immediately, Hasted was cornered, and Williams must have known it.[526]

It thus became a relatively easy matter for Williams to enter into possession of the Hasted estates. Claiming that no other purchaser could be found, he was able to drive the desperate historian to the limits of despair and then to present himself as the saviour who would take the otherwise unsaleable property off Hasted's hands. Although Hasted had not told Thomas Williams that he had borrowed further sums on those estates used by Williams as collateral security, the fact that he was now menaced by a writ for imprisonment for debt from another quarter must surely have alerted the experienced attorney to the fact that such a loan might be involved. In spite of this, however, Williams would offer no more for the whole estate than the amount of the debts due to himself and his supposed clients, namely, £8685. Hasted had no choice. The sale was agreed to, with a douceur of £100 for Hasted himself, and the conveyance was rushed through by Williams, worried lest the distraught historian should fly the country before it was completed. Hasted was allowed just the faintest glimmer of hope for the return of his estates by the bond to which the attorney agreed, under the terms of which the estates would be reconveyed to their former owner if they could be sold at a better price within a twelvemonth and all demands due to Williams and his clients fully satisfied.

Now, as a fugitive before the law, or at least before a sheriff's officer with a writ in his hand, the luckless historian had to arrange meetings with his attorney or Thomas Williams's representatives in a furtive and clandestine manner. The 'Statement' which he was to set down on paper ten years later vividly recalls this period, when he was abruptly stripped of the property which his grandfather had put together piece by piece at the beginning of the century.

At an unhappy meeting held at Sittingbourne at the beginning of April 1790 with Thomas Williams's nephew and partner, John Williams, Hasted put his signature to the contract. Williams, however, who was to have brought the bond to the meeting, came without it, excusing this on the grounds that his uncle 'had not settled in his mind in what manner he should draw it'. This was clearly duplicitous, as the terms of the bond had already been agreed.

Four or five days later there was another meeting, this time with Mr Williams's clerk, Mr Bedell, at the Fountain inn in Canterbury. Here Hasted was required to hand over all the maps, terriers, and papers relating to his estates, and to sign various documents instructing his tenants to accept Thomas Williams as their new landlord. In return Bedell brought Hasted his bond. But it was now drawn up with very different terms from those which had been originally agreed. The penalty for its non-fulfilment had been reduced, as had the term of twelve months for the sale of the estates, which was now cut to six, Williams's covering letter explaining that he feared he might not live so long, and that he wished such a reconveyance, if it ever took place, to be carried out in his lifetime.[527]

The 'Statement of Mr Hasted's transactions with the late Mr Thos Williams concerning the conveyance of his estates to him and the bond Mr Williams gave him to reconvey them' from which the above details are taken, continues as follows:

> Vexed at this usage so very unfair, Mr H. on his return to his own house threw the bond into his bureau among a heap of confused papers and being in the utmost perturbation of mind and almost mad with the thoughts of leaving his family in distress and misery and with the fear of being laid hold of by his numerous creditors, he took no further notice nor gave himself any further trouble or concern about the bond nor was the whole of the transactions above made known by him or communicated to any person whatever. Mr H. at the same time knew well that he dared not stay to investigate the dishonesty of Mr Williams in thus drawing the bond, who knew well equally with himself that he could not stay in England for that purpose, and he knew equally too that Mr H. must remain a fugitive abroad much beyond the 6 months stipulated in the bond, most probably for years, which would wholly prevent any steps that could be taken to recover the estates from him either by suit on the bond, or by any other means of law, and therefore that he would rest in safe possession of his ill acquired bargain.
>
> Mr H. left Canterbury for France on the next Sunday sennight (being the 25th) after the above meeting.

Only a month before, on the 23 March, Hasted had sat in his study at Canterbury and penned a graceful dedication of Volume III of his *History* to the Archbishop of Canterbury. Amid the ruins of his position and the recriminations of his family, the hasty consultations and the forced sale of his estates, he probably had no time, and no heart, to respond to the letter which came a few days later from the devoted Boteler:

> I send with this what I have collected relative to Betshanger and Northbourne as a specimen only ... if I have omitted anything necessary for your information within my power, minute it down ... In short, arrange for me systematically every point of enquiry, and if you will give me a few places in the order you next want them I by that means can allow a little more time to each and yet keep before you ... If I knew when you might be found at home, I think I would steal over and pass a long day with you.[528]

Chapter 12

'Monsieur Ested'

Volume III, when Hasted left the country at the end of April 1790, was on the point of appearing. Throughout the month he had had the satisfaction of seeing the following small advertisement appear in the *Kentish Gazette*:

> The third volume of Mr Hasted's History of Kent, being finished, will be ready to be delivered to the subscribers at the latter end of next month, or the beginning of June. Those gentlemen, therefore, who have neglected to pay their subscriptions, are requested to pay them to their respective booksellers, or to Messrs Simmons & Kirkby in Canterbury, before the end of next month, that their books may be sent for them accordingly.[529]

Before any of the subscribers had the book in their hands, however, its author had crossed the Channel with his mistress and was facing a new life in France.

The French coast at this time offered a haven for Englishmen in danger of imprisonment for debt. Indeed, both before and after the French Revolution there seems to have been a two-way traffic across the Channel, when English and French alike were able to escape their creditors by taking up residence in the other's country: even during the Revolution the French émigrés in England were not wholly composed of political exiles, but contained among their number several who were in flight from financial disaster.[530] The use made of Boulogne in this way by the English was commented on in 1787 by the agricultural writer Arthur Young:

> It is well known that this place has long been the resort of great numbers of persons from England, whose misfortunes in trade, or extravagance in life, have made a residence abroad more agreeable than at home. It is easy to suppose that they here find a level of society that tempts them to herd in the same place. Certainly it is not cheapness, for it is rather dear.[531]

The benefits of the Acts passed from time to time during the eighteenth century for the relief of insolvent debtors were available also to those who had fled 'beyond the seas' to avoid the rigours of a debtors' prison. It was a 1774 Act of this kind which had induced several Kentish debtors to return to England from Calais or Dunkirk — Samuel Golding, of Chatham, gentleman; Stephen Bean, of Ashford, brewer; John Catt, of Newington, yeoman; James Thorley, of Greenwich, joiner — their names appearing in the *Kentish Gazette* only a month before Hasted's first public announcement in it of his forthcoming *History*.[532]

It cannot have been easy for the historian, justice of the peace, Deputy Lieutenant, commissioner of sewers and of the land tax, fellow of both the Royal Society and the Society of Antiquaries, to 'herd' with great numbers of other English outcasts. He was undoubtedly not the first, and he was not to be the last, justice of the peace whose affairs had become entangled to this degree. But it was certainly not an extravagant style of living, at least after the Sutton years, which had reduced this Kentish magistrate to the condition of a fugitive.

His destination now was not Calais or Boulogne, but St Omer, a town some thirty miles inland. Had Hasted and Mary Jane merely been intent on putting the Channel between themselves and Hasted's English creditors they would probably have found lodgings in Calais or Boulogne. Hasted tells us himself, however, that they went to St Omer, and it seems reasonable to assume that they were heading for a definite address. Like the small coastal towns of Calais, Boulogne and Dunkirk, the cathedral town of St Omer was used to the sight of impoverished English gentlemen in its streets, but with a population of around 17,000 it must have been able to offer rather more sophisticated society than would have been found in the ports. John Byng, the eighteenth-century English traveller and diarist, erstwhile army colonel, latterly a commissioner of stamps in the government offices of Somerset Place and destined, for the last fortnight of his life, to become the fifth Viscount Torrington, set out on one of his tours with a certain Mr P, 'whose acquaintance I procured in my exile at St Omers, when my heart softened by calamity was ready for impressions'. And Byng, noting in Llandaff church when on a tour of South Wales in 1787 'many fine stone figures that did belong to monuments of the Matthew family', is reminded to add that 'the present possessor is (the well known) Mr M. living at St Omer'.[533]

By the late 1700s St Omer, a place of great antiquity, had had close links with England for some two hundred years. Occupying a promontory surrounded on three sides by marshland, it had once been protected by ramparts boasting seventy towers with four great land gates and four water gates. Its importance as a centre of Christianity dated back to the seventh century when the abbey of St Bertin was founded there, and over the years other religious orders, some of them English, had chosen to settle in the same spot. In the sixteenth century, in particular, the town had provided a refuge for persecuted catholics from several of the Reformation countries, and its increasing importance as a religious centre was reflected in the foundation of its bishopric in 1561. With the final establishment of a reformed church in England by Elizabeth I, English Jesuits, forced to take their institutions elsewhere, had set up a school in St Omer in 1593 for the children of English catholics. This took its place in a strong educational tradition which included a French Jesuit college founded some thirty years earlier, the Collège de St Bertin which came into being at the beginning of the seventeenth century, and the Collège de St Omer which trained young seminarians for the catholic priesthood. It is not surprising that by 1750 St Omer had become one of the most important centres of learning in northern France.

The English school, known to the French as 'le collège anglais' and in England as 'Saint Omers', was much patronised by English recusants among the aristocracy and had an excellent reputation in France, although Arthur Young, again in the area in 1788, commented sourly: 'Why are Catholics to emigrate in order to be ill-educated abroad, instead of being allowed institutions that would educate them well at home'? — a view which was at one and the same time enlightened and biased, since it was prefaced by the statement that 'St Omers contains little deserving notice', a crude dismissal of a fascinating town.[534] In 1760 the 'collège anglais', perhaps then at its zenith, had been permitted to add the word 'royal' to its title, but the following year it suffered a serious setback when the Parlement de Paris forbade Jesuits to teach in France. Secular teachers were found to replace them, however, and the Royal English College continued its function of educating the sons of English catholic families.

As happened in England at this time, the master of a school might seek to augment his income by taking private pupils, or even simply boarders, as we can see from the following advertisement which appeared in the *Kentish Gazette* in February 1778:

> St Omer. Mr Boudeille, Writing Master and French Professor in the Royal English College, has taken a large convenient house in St Bertin's Street and fitted it up for the accommodation of twelve English boarders on the following terms ...

For 25 guineas a year young gentlemen were offered genteel accommodation, which included tea in the morning, firing, candles, paper, pens and ink, as well as lessons in writing, arithmetic and the French language. Visiting masters were engaged to teach dancing, fencing, music, drawing, the classics and mathematics. And the advertisement added:

There are a few large apartments in his house, in which English gentlemen, of a more advanced age, may reside on the foregoing terms, paying only a trifle for extra accommodations.

It is unlikely that by 'English gentlemen, of a more advanced age', Mr Boudeille had in mind mature students, a concept which did not then exist. On the contrary, there seems every likelihood that this part of the advertisement was addressed to gentlemen whose necessitous circumstances would remove any objections they might have had to sharing the house with a school — just such men, in fact, as Edward Hasted, obliged by the pressure of their debts to seek shelter abroad. But the advertisement of 1778 is doubly interesting in that it ends:

Mr Boudeille has permission to refer any one, for further information, to Mr Boys, at Sandwich, in Kent.[535]

The Mr Boys in question, who, it is quite probable, had one or more sons at that very time spending a year or two learning French in Mr Boudeille's establishment, which may not necessarily have been catholic, can only have been that prominent man William Boys the surgeon and jurat, mayor of Sandwich in 1767 (and again in 1782), and a gentleman who was on very friendly terms with Edward Hasted. It is quite possible, therefore, that after landing in France Hasted made his way to the address in the rue St Bertin mentioned in the advertisement of 1778, assured of some sort of reception as a gentleman, in spite of his position as a fugitive.

He would not have been unaware of recent events in France, leading up to the fall of the Bastille in July 1789 — there was reasonably good coverage of French news in the English papers — but for most Englishmen, as indeed for many Frenchmen at the time, this event marked the culmination of a revolution, and was seen as a not inglorious act, a symbolic cleansing of the old feudalities from the body politic of France. Few could guess at the years of turmoil which were to follow. The historian's personal distress demanded the solution of a sojourn in France, where he could not be touched by his creditors, and clearly overrode any forebodings which he might have had of troubles to come there. He took a room, or rooms, in St Omer, and perhaps soon made the acquaintance of other English gentlemen who were similarly placed. Mary Jane Town, there is no doubt, had the dual occupation of companion and housekeeper, herself considerably reduced from the gentility in which Hasted had been keeping her in England. It seems doubtful whether her education would have included any French, but she was probably quick-witted enough to pick up some of the language, which would enable her

'Monsieur Ested'

to go about the maze of hilly streets around the rue St Bertin, making the couple's daily purchases out of what must have been a very slender purse. Arthur Young had commented on the mixture of French and English women's attire in Boulogne in 1787 — and St Omer was probably no different — observing that the English were 'dressed in their own fashion, but the French heads are all without hats, with close caps, and the body covered with a long cloak that reaches to the feet'.[536]

In the brief Chronology of his life up to the year 1807 Hasted gives 1791 as the year of his flight to France. The document of 1801, however, the 'Statement of Mr Hasted's transactions with the late Mr Thos Williams', written with more care, shows that he went there the year before this. If further proof were needed, we have the letter of the 3 December 1790 sent by the vicar of Wilmington, the Revd Samuel Denne, to the antiquarian Richard Gough, and subsequently printed by John Nichols in his *Literary History of the Eighteenth Century*. Concluding a long letter on antiquarian matters with a touch of gossip, Denne wrote:

> In a catalogue of books as advertised for sale by Bristow, a bookseller at Canterbury, there is notice of there being among them the valuable library of a gentleman who lately left this county; for county perhaps might be read with propriety country, as I rather suspect the valuable library of the Historian of Kent is alluded to, and to him the motto in his third volume is truly applicable, 'Quo me cunque rapit tempestas, deferor hospes'. A stranger in a foreign land is he, as it is generally believed, likely to remain for ever and aye, because he has deviated from the Poet's rule in the preceding verse, 'Quod verum atque decens curo et rogo, et omnis in hoc sum'.[537]

Denne was wrong, however, in his supposition that the library now offered for sale by Bristow was Hasted's: this was not to come on the market for another five years.

While the Hasted finances remained in confusion, the outlook with regard to the *History* was not quite so bleak as it must have seemed to many of the historian's acquaintances, for this had at least reached the point of publication of Volume III. Hasted's part in it was definitely complete, and the book perhaps only needed its half-binding, for which the printer was responsible, to be ready for distribution. Simmons and Kirkby, left on their own, could do no less than notify the public when it was finally ready in July, at the same time clarifying arrangements with regard to the price:

271

History of Kent. Third Volume. The subscribers to the third volume of Hasted's History of Kent are desired to send their receipts to the respective booksellers, to whom they have paid their former subscription of one guinea and a half, and the third volume will be delivered to them on the farther payment of one guinea.

If any of the subscribers or purchasers of the first and second volumes have omitted to pay their subscription to the third volume, they may now purchase it for 2$^1/_2$ guineas, being the subscription price till the end of October next; or any person not having the two former volumes, desirous of purchasing the third volume only, may have it for three guineas at the time above-mentioned, or the three volumes compleat may be had for 7 guineas.

The booksellers who have received and paid their subscriptions may have the third volume immediately delivered to them or their order, on paying the remaining subscription to Simmons & Kirkby.[538]

As we shall see, the historian remained in close contact with his printer, and the wording of this notice probably had his approval.

The Preface to Volume III began with two apologies. The first was for the long gap which lay between the appearance of Volumes II and III. The other concerned the fact that the *History* had not been completed with this volume, as had been promised, but would now run to a fourth. It seems that the historian had seriously considered letting Volume III cover the whole of the remaining parts of the county — the very fact that it is dedicated to the Archbishop of Canterbury can be taken as additional proof that this volume was originally planned to include an account of that city — but had been deterred both by the additional months which would have been required for the printing and by his accident of 1789, although there can be little doubt that the crisis in his financial affairs was a contributory cause also. It is certain, however, that the section on Canterbury was already written, and probably most of that on Thanet and the Hundred of Ringslow also, and that the Hundreds which remained to be dealt with, and which were to give him a great deal of trouble to put together in France, could have been despatched fairly rapidly had he been able to remain in Kent, so that an enlarged Volume III was, in terms of its execution, something which might have been envisaged under other circumstances. Nevertheless, it would have been weighty to the point of being almost unusable, and in spite of the additional expense most of the subscribers, faced with the seven hundred and sixty-five pages of Volume III, must have accepted Hasted's decision to let the *History* run to four volumes as a realistic solution to this problem also.

There was no longer any question of the work not being concluded. Hasted had promised the county a *History*, and he would honour that promise, in spite of the lack of inducements to continue the self-imposed task:

> The continued fatigue and expence, much to the detriment of my private fortune, and the ill state of my health, increased by the dreadful accident I met with in the course of this undertaking, would surely induce me to finish here, both prudence and reason say, *Solve senescentem mature sanus equum*, and I ought to acquiesce in the propriety of this advice; but my engagement to the subscribers of this and my former volumes, to complete the History of the County, and include in it that of Canterbury, a place which well deserves, and would almost fill, a volume of itself, I cannot with honour get rid of, for I can have no other inducement to it, as past experience has banished all expectation of profit, though surely such a series of time, devoted to it, might with justice claim some recompence. To perform my promise, therefore, I intend, if [I] am encouraged and supported in it, to complete this History in a fourth volume.[539]

The preface, written at Canterbury, bore the date 23 March, and just a month and two days later Hasted was on his way to France, where there was every possibility, as the Revd Samuel Denne had observed, that he might be obliged to spend the rest of his life. In this respect also the prognosis did not seem very good. Hasted's health had been poor for some time, and the accident, in which he may have been lucky to escape with no more than a broken leg, had clearly unsettled him. A very kind letter from William Boys, written on the 17 March in obvious ignorance of the historian's planned flight, confirms that he had been unwell and proposes a visit to Sandwich to recuperate:

> Your indisposition, most likely, is the consequence of your long confinement. Change the air and use exercise, and all will be right again. I would recommend the air of Sandwich to you in the summer, and some of the pigs and poultry of Statenborow and Goshall by way of restoratives.[540]

Dr Boys' recommendation of a change of air was to be followed, although in a more radical way than he had anticipated.

The need to abandon friends and family, as well as Kent, the very subject of his writing, could have proved the breaking point for a less resilient man. But Hasted was both optimistic and stubborn, with a historian's natural curiosity thrown in, and these characteristics combined now to endow the French episode with something of the sparkle of the unexpected. The air was different, the atmosphere was lighter. Divested of the numerous duties which always awaited him in Kent, Hasted was also free here to walk the streets openly with Mary Jane without the fear of arrest which had restricted his movements during his last weeks in England to a furtive scuttling. In the Preface to Volume III he had expressed the hope of being able to re-establish his health during the coming months, but the likelihood is that that first summer in France gave him the bohemian holiday which he had never had, restored his health to the point where he could forget about it completely, and thoroughly rejuvenated him.

Buoyancy was in the air in the France of 1790. The poet Wordsworth, on the first lap of an intended walking tour in the Swiss Alps, crossed the Channel in the selfsame year.[541] He landed in Calais on 13 July, and the following day was able to witness the town's own version of the splendid Fête de la Fédération which was being held in Paris to celebrate the first anniversary of the Fall of the Bastille; he could well have been thinking of events experienced in Calais when he wrote:

> Bliss was it in that dawn to be alive,
> But to be young was very heaven! — Oh! times
> In which the meagre, stale, forbidding ways
> Of custom, law, and statute, took at once
> The attraction of a country in romance!
> When Reason seemed the most to assert her rights,
> When most intent on making of herself
> A prime Enchantress — ...
> What temper at the prospect did not wake
> To happiness unthought of?[542]

The historian of Kent, schooled in reason as he was, was quite likely to have shared this enthusiasm. The poet was to tell his sister, in a letter written some time later, that this had been a time when 'the whole nation was mad with joy in consequence of the revolution'.[543] One can only think that Hasted, with his family background among the freemen of London, possible acquaintance with John Wilkes and friendship with

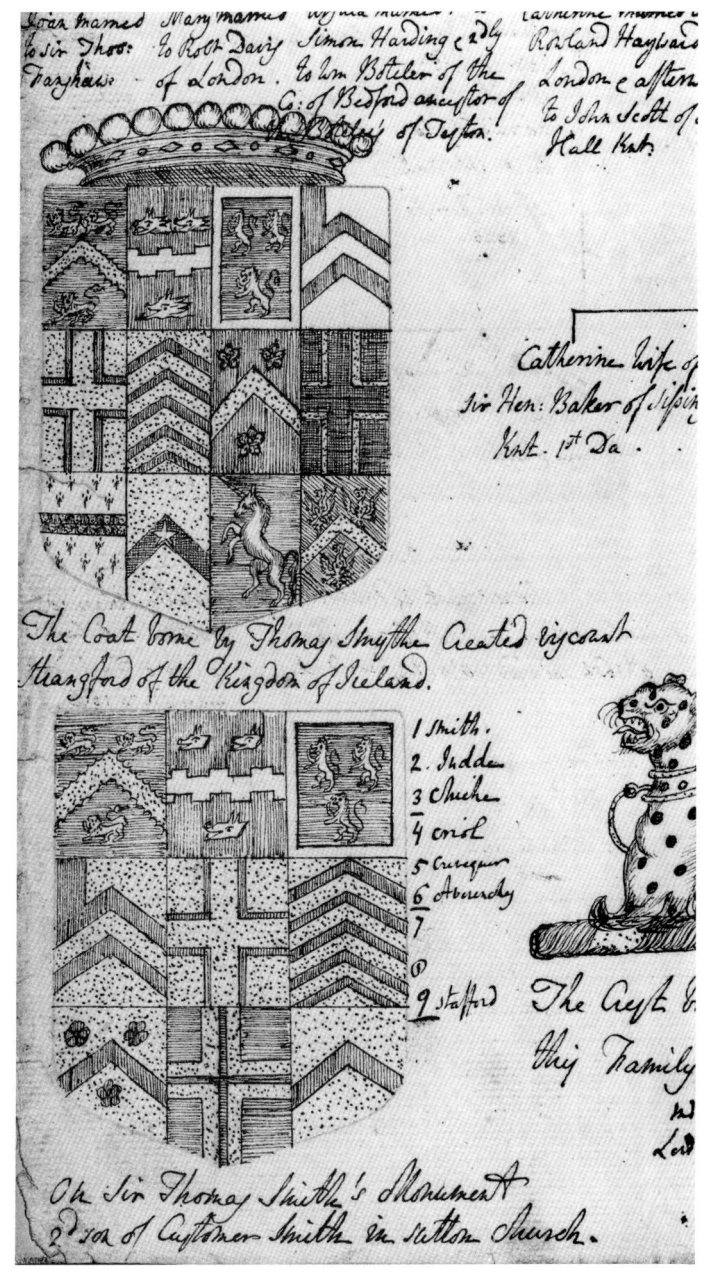

17. Part of the pedigree of Smith or Smythe of Westenhanger, drawn up by Hasted in one of his folio manuscript books.

18. *'Edward Hasted at sixty-nine'* – probably the work of a fellow-prisoner in the King's Bench.

THE
HISTORY
AND
TOPOGRAPHICAL SURVEY
OF THE
COUNTY OF KENT.

CONTAINING THE

ANTIENT AND PRESENT STATE OF IT,

CIVIL AND ECCLESIASTICAL;

COLLECTED FROM PUBLIC RECORDS,

AND OTHER AUTHORITIES:

ILLUSTRATED WITH MAPS, VIEWS, ANTIQUITIES, &c.

THE SECOND EDITION,

IMPROVED, CORRECTED, AND CONTINUED TO

THE PRESENT TIME.

By EDWARD HASTED, Efq. F. R. S. and S. A.

LATE OF CANTERBURY.

" *Ex his omnibus, longe funt humaniffimi qui Cantium incolunt.*"
" *Fortes creantur fortibus et bonis,*
" *Nec imbellem feroces progenerant.*"

VOLUME III.

CANTERBURY:

PRINTED BY W. BRISTOW, ON THE PARADE.

M.DCC.XCVII.

19. Title-page of Volume 3 of the octavo edition.

20. 'Templa quam dilecta': vignette by John Barlow for the dedication to the Revd Edward Hasted in Volume 10 of the octavo edition.

21. 'The North View of the Ruins of St Augustine's Abbey at Canterbury', engraved by John Barlow, the figures perhaps representing Hasted, his wife, and his daughter Anne.

22. *Lady Margaret Hungerford, from the painting by Cornelius Johnson, 1631.*

23. *Lady Hungerford's Almshouses at Corsham in Wiltshire.*

24 Undated pencil drawing of the historian.

the radically disposed John Calcraft, would, like Wordsworth, like Charles James Fox, like many another Englishman of the day, have felt considerable sympathy with what was going on in France at that stage. Among the French aristocracy, too, there were many who were equally enthusiastic about the initial reforms — and indeed throughout the Revolution former members of the nobility were to be found participating in events.

With the exception of the taking of the Bastille, the major upheavals of the first year of the Revolution were administrative. Thus Calais and St Omer, which lay respectively in the Boulonnais and the Artois, found themselves designated after February 1790 as principal towns in two of the eight districts which now made up the newly formed département of Pas-de-Calais. The old Parlements of the provinces were abolished, and local officials now had to be elected, instead of being appointed from above. In place of the old magistracy, each town now had a mayor and supporting municipal officers, with new justices of the peace, all posts being subject to election. But understandably, the structure of power in the villages changed very little, and even in the towns elections frequently confirmed in office those who under the old regime had been or would have been appointed.

These reforms did not mark the end of the turmoil, however, and St Omer was to be particularly affected by subsequent events. Three months after Hasted and Mary Jane had set foot in France the 'Civil Constitution of the Clergy', passed by the Assembly in Paris, decreed that both priests and bishops should also owe their positions to election. This was not a measure likely to be accepted without demur in so traditional a catholic centre as St Omer, and from this point on there was increasing unrest in the town. In November, as a result of clerical resistance to the 'Civil Constitution' throughout the country, it was proposed that all clergy should swear an oath of loyalty to the constitution. Out of a total of one hundred and fifty-nine members of the clergy in St Omer it is recorded that only twelve took the oath. The bishop, who seems to have spent much of his time in Italy, was deposed, and in April 1791 a humble priest, Nicolas Porion, was elected in his place and declared Bishop of the Pas-de-Calais, with his seat at St Omer. All the occupants of the town's convents and monasteries were now ordered to leave, with a resulting evacuation of one hundred and forty-eight monks and over twice as many nuns. Their lands and their buildings, already stripped of their bells, were declared state property and were being sold off before the year was out. 1792 saw the closure of all religious teaching establishments in France, so that almost at a stroke St Omer lost the four schools which had made it pre-eminent throughout the region. Two of these were made use of as prisons, while the seminary became a hospital for soldiers suffering from scabies. The English College managed to survive until July 1793, when it, too, underwent conversion into a military hospital.[544] By then, however, the months spent in St Omer were only a memory for Hasted and Mary Jane.

The disruption of the town's clerical life had led to civil disturbances. In the general alarm many of the well-to-do had fled, seeking asylum in England or Germany as early as 1791. Hasted and Mary Jane may well have wished themselves among this first wave of emigrants, but Hasted dared not, at this stage, return to England. The mass unemployment which now engulfed St Omer was dealt with by the setting up of public workshops, offering employment for fifteen hundred people. But the low wages brought strikes and increased unrest in their wake, and the workshops were soon discontinued. Towards the end of 1791 there was rioting due to serious food shortages, with scenes of insurrection along the canal where it was rumoured that barges laden with grain, passing daily for Dunkirk, were intended for foreign destinations. St Omer was no longer a safe place for foreigners, and it was probably during the course of this year that Hasted and Mary Jane moved to Abbeville, a town nearly sixty miles away, which was much less disturbed.

Abbeville, with its streets of old wooden houses, still presented the appearance of a medieval town, and there must have been a great deal here to interest a historian. But was there also, earlier in the year, a more extended journey in France, to the French capital? In the brief Chronology of his life which Hasted was to jot down shortly before his death, the only places mentioned in connection with his flight to France are those in which he made an extended stay, St Omer, Abbeville, and Calais. Half a century later, however, genteel conversation over the teacups in the vicarage at Hollingbourne was to turn on the former presence of a member of the family at the great educational centre of St Omer, someone who had also been in Paris at the time of the two funerals of the Comte de Mirabeau — Mirabeau's heart having been deemed worthy of a place in the Panthéon of Sainte-Geneviève, while his body was interred elsewhere. Such a one was certainly not the vicar of Hollingbourne, as a diarist mistakenly noted down, but could indeed have been the vicar's father, Edward Hasted the historian, who was in France over this period, and must have been an involuntary witness of many extraordinary events.[545]

It is hardly surprising that against this background of disturbances there is virtually no correspondence relating to the *History* stemming from 1790 and the first half of 1791, which probably means that Hasted did little or no work on it during these months. In the first place, as we have seen, he was in need of the complete break from it which his move to another country offered, and in the second, his life in St Omer undoubtedly registered some of the riots and confusion which led to his departure for Abbeville.

And thirdly, in spite of the initial relief which Hasted must have felt when he first set foot in France, and the infectious excitement of the events going on around him, there was unquestionably an element of trauma in the imperative necessity to leave England and escape to France, a shock which must have registered more strongly as the months went by and Hasted realised all that he had lost. Not only had he parted with the estates which had bonded him and the name of Hasted to the county of Kent, but with his flight he had relinquished the position which he had maintained worthily for more than three decades among the active members of that county's gentry.

And he was also separated from his family — something which he may have felt more than he had anticipated. It must have been particularly bitter to him that he would not now be present in July 1790, when Edward was inducted as the vicar of Hollingbourne. He had taken great pains over his eldest son's education, had tried, like many fathers, to give him what he himself had not had, and had hoped, above all, that his son would become an eminent member of that line of Hasteds begun by his own grandfather. The choice of a career in the church had probably been Edward's, not the historian's, and it perhaps underlined outwardly how deep were the differences between father and son. Nevertheless, until the events of April 1790 Hasted had had every hope and expectation of being present at his son's induction in July to the vicarage of Hollingbourne with Hucking annexed.

Like all vicars at this time, Edward expected to receive a large part of his income from his tithes — the tenth part of the produce of his parish which was assigned to the maintenance of the incumbent of a church. The tithes varied enormously from parish to parish and in some places were divided into Great and Small tithes, the Great tithes going to the rector, and the Small falling to the vicar's share. So it should have been in Hollingbourne, where the rector, the Revd John Cautley, held a purely sinecure office, but Edward, to his alarm, seems to have discovered that the vicarial tithes did not automatically make their way to him, but were also claimed by the rector. This had perhaps not mattered when the vicar had had his own private source of income, but Edward was not so placed and was dependent on his tithes. In such a dilemma his father, as a former close friend of Dr Andrew Coltee Ducarel, who had been an expert on such matters, and with his own extensive knowledge of local administration, both civil and ecclesiastical, was the obvious person to turn to; and the fact that Edward appealed to his father for help shows that in spite of their differences the Hasted family still remained very close.

Plunged as he was into a new life and a totally unexpected set of circumstances, Hasted must have spent some time coming to terms with his own situation, but he gradually became aware that Edward's letters — brought with all his other mail by the packet boats which plied regularly between England and France — continued to show that he was in great difficulties over the question of his tithes. The young vicar clearly needed all the advice he could get, and some time in the early months of 1791 his father finally sat down to write him a long letter, suggesting where he should look for the document which would prove the vicar's right to the tithes — 'If the original instrument is anywhere, most probably, and I suspect it strongly, the rector has it in his possession' — setting out succinctly the steps which needed to be taken to recover them, and, perhaps in the light of his own experiences, cautioning Edward in his dealings with some of the people involved in the affair, whom Hasted had obviously met:

> Take care what you say if you write or ever see the steward, for he is a crafty, wary man, and will draw things from you before you are aware. Be very circumspect in your words to all, especially your parishioners concerned in it — and be sure to avoid promises in any shape whatever, for advantage will always be taken of them.[546]

In spite of all that was going on around him, Hasted seems not to have wavered in his intention of providing a proper conclusion to the *History*. In the Preface to Volume III he had claimed to be in possession of all the information he needed for that purpose, and while this was to prove something of an exaggeration, a letter from James Simmons to William Boteler shortly after his flight from England confirms that a large quantity of notes and manuscripts had indeed accompanied the historian to France:

> The fate of a fourth volume is yet undetermined, but should I have any principal concerns therein, I shall be most happy in the assistance of yourself and Mr Boys. The return of Mr H. is very uncertain, but he has such materials with him that were they digested and methodically transcribed, I should not despair of procuring such essential help as would render the 4th at least equal

to the preceding volumes, but what may be the event, it is at present impossible to say.'[547]

Simmons was clearly privy to Hasted's flight, which Boys and Boteler seem not to have been. The printer's letter was written in answer to one offering corrections to two Hundred maps, in which a slightly aggrieved Boteler had allowed some criticisms of his friend to escape him. Simmons was in agreement:

> Your remarks on Mr Hasted's conduct are too true, in numberless instances he might have made his work much more correct, but he was frequently too late in making application to his friends, and having made it, much too precipitate in printing off his sheets without waiting for it.

In fairness to Hasted, however, one must remember the numerous long delays which had often occurred before he received the information he had requested — as well as the length of time Simmons himself took over the printing, which William Boys was also to experience, to the extent of declaring in 1798, 'I am resolved, when I publish two more quarto volumes, he shall have nothing to do with the matter'.[548] However, where others doubted, Simmons seems to have retained confidence in Hasted's ability to finish his work. The historian and the printer and bookseller, who was by now a founding partner of the Canterbury Bank and an increasingly important man in the small world of Canterbury, must have developed a close working relationship over the many years that the printing of the *History* had been in hand, and the Preface to the third volume in fact contained an appreciation of Simmons, whom Hasted called 'my printer and much respected friend, to whose liberal and unremitted assistance throughout the whole course of this undertaking I am under the greatest obligations' — a graceful acknowledgment which seems, however, to have had little effect in lessening Simmons' final bill some years later.

Secrecy was obviously of the essence if one proposed to escape a sheriff's writ by going abroad, and most of Hasted's friends must have been kept in the dark about it, but contact with his printer was essential, not only with regard to Volume IV, but also in connection with the third volume, which was left, as it were, in suspension — almost, but not quite, ready to be launched on the world. Simmons probably made himself responsible for sending a copy to the *Gentleman's Magazine*. It was duly noticed in October 1790, in a somewhat impatient review which began, 'The two former volumes of this History have been reviewed in our vols.

XLVIII ... and LIII ..., and we trust the reader's patience has not been wearied out by the long interval between the publication of each volume'. After a brief summary of the contents the reviewer drew to a snappish close: 'It cannot be expected that we should make extracts from a work of this kind'.[549] The review had a slightly spiteful tone throughout and cannot have cheered the exile in France.

There were also the large-paper copies to be distributed. These were not always acknowledged as they should have been, but Hasted was willing to blame this on his absence from England. In the August of 1791 he was obliged to write to Thomas Astle as follows:

> By Mr Simmons, printer of Canterbury, I understand you have received from him my 3rd volume, L.P. copy, which I directed him to send to you. My 2 first volumes of the same size I presented to the King for the permission you so kindly procured of dedicating my work to him, and had not some very unpleasant circumstances happened in my affairs since, I should certainly have done the same by the present 3rd volume. But, though I would not deprive the Royal Library of it, I cannot, in my present situation, afford to give it. May I request the favor of your friendship to inform the Librarian of this, to make the proper application for me, that he may send for it to White in Fleet Street (where I will order it to be sent the beginning of next week) and to pay the same price for it that has been paid for the 2 others, L.P. copies, which I have sold, viz., five guineas and a half, the price fixed by Payne, newsagent, on it, as he will inform you.[550]

Hasted added two postscripts to this letter, which was dated 17 August 1791 and probably written from Abbeville. The first requested 'the favor of a line from you in answer to the above directed to me at Dover, Kent, which will be sent to me here', and the second added, 'I have finished great part of my next and last volume, which I hope to put to print this winter'. Simmons' confidence in Hasted's ability to complete the *History* in France was clearly not misplaced.

There can be no doubt that Boteler and Boys performed a valuable service in pressing their offers of help on a somewhat reluctant Hasted. Boteler, it will be remembered, had suggested that they should be allowed to check the sheets relating to their area before they were printed off, when it seemed likely that Hasted's accident was going to prevent any more 'parochial visitations', and in November 1791 we find William Boys returning to the same theme, and urging it with considerable tact:

'Monsieur Ested'

I think it may be of advantage to your work to let all the manuscripts relating to this neighbourhood pass under the view of Boteler and me before it be printed off. So far from its being any trouble to us, we shall be highly gratified by the confidence you repose in us; and you will find us anxious to acquit ourselves to your satisfaction.[551]

It is difficult to know whether Hasted availed himself fully of this generous offer, but he leaned heavily on his two friends for the collection of material in their locality, the Hundreds of Bewsborough and Cornilo, and a third member was soon added to the duo in the person of the Revd John Lyon, vicar of St Mary the Virgin, Dover. Described by the critical Samuel Egerton Brydges as 'self-educated, uncouth, and in some respects illiterate', Lyon was nevertheless admitted to be 'a good sort of man'. He had developed wide interests, was a keen student of natural history and physics who wrote several treatises on electricity, and as an antiquarian was later to publish a two-volume history of Dover. Most of Hasted's correspondence of the second half of 1791 seems to have been with John Lyon. The first letter of Lyon's which we have, dated 21 September 1791, referring to some queries despatched two months earlier but not received by him until well into August, underlines some of the difficulties under which Hasted was now working.[552]

The Revd John Lyon's letters have a very friendly tone — the need for Hasted to flee the country had clearly not forfeited for him the respect of everyone in Kent — and one wonders if it was perhaps at the Dover vicar's house that the historian had found shelter for a night or two while he waited for a boat to France. Nor was the flow of information all one way: Lyon both imparts information and requests help for his own work from Hasted, 'when you are at leisure'.

Letters from John Lyon were occasionally transmitted by William Boys, showing that the trio of assistants in East Kent often combined their efforts to further the ends of their unfortunate friend in France, Lyon's information relating more specifically to Dover and the Hundred of Bewsborough, Boys's and Boteler's to the Hundreds of Bewsborough, Cornilo and Eastry. Taking the place of the historian in making personal enquiries of local inhabitants they discovered, as Boteler told Hasted in February 1792, that,

The ignoramus's, if you will allow the word, that we must get information from, generally mistake the tenor of two questions out of three; at least, I have often found, like Dr Johnson in the

Highlands, that the answer to the second has frequently nullified the first.[553]

Hasted did not need to be told: 'I am very sensible,' he replied, 'of the many difficulties you meet with in obtaining any accurate knowledge in your enquiries. It is what I have too often met with myself in my parochial progresses, and in leaving a place, I have frequently remained in greater doubts and uncertainties, than when I entred it.'[554]

In the same letter, Boteler is given a list of various items of information which are needed, and instructed to forward them under cover to Latham & Co. 'If you would favour me with part of them as you finish them, I should be much obliged to you as I can then be still jogging on to the end of my thirty years' journey'. And Hasted adds that he has also written to Mr Boys, 'to beg his joint assistance, which I hope he will not refuse me the continuance of'.

It is perhaps worth commenting on the way Hasted wrote 'entered' in the above letter. Eighteenth-century spelling was still mildly idiosyncratic, and this spelling of the word, more French than English, is occasionally encountered, but coming now from Hasted's pen it may well reveal that the writer, immersed in French and French culture as he now was, was quite possibly speaking and reading the French language with some fluency. Undoubtedly, he himself foresaw a lengthy exile in France, and, like most of those who were now his compatriots, could not imagine the darker days to come.

The correspondence for 1792 shows that throughout the year both Boteler and Boys worked hard to help the historian fill in the gaps which had remained when he left England, sometimes writing him joint letters — some information from Boys on Stonar and Worth has a note added by Boteler to the effect that, 'The soil of Worth is in general exceedingly good, and may be properly stiled the Garden of this part of the county', with a final paragraph from Boys, showing him fully enjoying the pleasures of the antiquarian chase:

> I will not delay this paper; but I have within this half hour conceived a notion, that the whole of Sandown manor is within the parish of St Clement. I shall be able to ascertain this point tomorrow. Mr Boteler has nearly finished Eastry.[555]

Hasted was well aware of the burden he was placing on his friends. Their profession as surgeons could leave them little time for antiquarian pursuits, although the demands made on them by his *History* were to a large extent offset by the fact that both men proposed to use the material they were collecting — in more detailed fashion than Hasted actually required — in topographical works of their own, something to which Hasted had no objection whatever. In July 1792 Boys was writing:

> I send you the production of the last fortnight. Boteler is indefatigable, and I have not been idle. If it is less than you expect, consider that we are bound to consult our own credit as well as your wishes for dispatch. We are resolved, that the information you give the public by our means shall be as accurate as possible; and we need not tell you what a deal of time is required to ascertain facts, names and dates with precision. We beg the favor of you to preserve our manuscripts, and to return them to us when you have extracted from them what may be useful to you. The minutiae which you reject will be valuable to us.[556]

Both Boys and Boteler entertained hopes of making their own contributions to Kentish history. They were fully encouraged in this by Hasted, who in a later letter was reassuring Boteler that he was in no danger of being thought to have 'plundered' from his, Hasted's *History*. Only Boys, of the two men, was to have any succes in his aim, bringing out his *Collections for a History of Sandwich*, which were printed for him by James Simmons, although at what Boys considered an infuriatingly slow pace, in 1792.

The French interlude is well documented, as far as Hasted's work is concerned, since all his information now had to be gleaned from correspondence, and Boteler, as well as Hasted, kept the letters he received. Both Boys and Lyon wrote fairly frequently to Hasted over this time, particularly when there was research to be transmitted to him, but the greatest number of letters came from William Boteler, always eager to be of help to someone whom he seems to have considered — and with reason — as his master in the field, although impeded in this desire occasionally by ill-health and, in the autumn, not infrequently by the demands of visitors and the shooting season. The slightly more personal nature of Boteler's letters seems to reveal also a more personal side of Hasted at this time: the Eastry surgeon's letters often close with warm wishes for Hasted's happiness — which it would surely have been out of place to mention had Boteler not known that the historian was indeed happy, openly enjoying his new life in France in the company of Mary Jane Town.

Hasted, on his side, was torn between a wish not to place too great a demand on his friends and the need to meet his business engagement with James Simmons. It was probably because he was, in the end, unable to comply with the terms of this, mentioned to Boteler in a letter of August 1792, that there was such a delay in the appearance of Volume IV, for which the printer was obviously responsible, and which Hasted, although not so his friends, seems to have accepted in silence. Hasted's August letter began:

> I duly received your kind favor with the papers which yourself and Mr Boys have taken so much trouble to collect for me, for which I return you my sincere thanks. I am very sorry to ask so much of you, but your kind friendship in it gives me a certainty of your not deserting me in it. I am sorry I am forced to be so impatient with you for the dispatch of them, but I am engaged to deliver up the MSS of my next volume to Mr Simmons in the beginning of next month, and it will cost me some time to arrange what you send me, which again obliges me to intreat you to send me the remainder you have for me by the end of this month.[557]

And Hasted, feeling that some recompense is due to his friend for the time and trouble he is spending on his behalf, diffidently mentions a box of impressions of seals which he and Osmund Beauvoir had formerly amused themselves with collecting at Canterbury, and which, though 'these are too trifling to offer you, and will hardly be worth your while to incumber your house with' Boteler may like to have since he is interested in heraldry — a touching offer, coming as it does from someone with little left to give.

As far as the manuscript of Volume IV was concerned, however, both Hasted and Simmons were obliged to wait. It was not until 12 December that Boteler was able to write:

> Herewith you will at last receive the completion of my engagements for the use of your last volume. To have procured the materials sooner would have added as much to my own satisfaction as your own. The business, ever since your last pressing letter, has hung upon my mind as a dead weight; and it has been a matter of infinite regret to me that avocations, of a much more disagreeable nature, have prevented me from using a diligence that would have gratified my own inclinations in a favourite pursuit, and have answered your wishes at the same time.

Boteler's life, no less than Hasted's, had had its own complications during the year, although of a very different kind. William Boys had already told Hasted in April that his brother-in-law was buying Marley, in Northbourne, for four thousand guineas. Boteler's letter continued:

> I will not tire you with explanations that cannot mend the matter: suffice it to say, that, altho' I have quitted the profession I was bred to, my time has been in a much greater degree arrested in fitting out my vessel for other ventures. Figure apart, I am become farmer, grazier, hop planter and hop merchant, too.[558]

The greater part of this correspondence was now being sent to Hasted at Calais. The historian would appear to have survived in France on a small income which he must have received regularly from England via the Dover bank of Latham, Rice & Co., who, as merchants in Dover, also owned packet boats which made regular crossings to France. His correspondence was routed through the same channel. In the disturbed climate of early 1790s France, however, it was next to impossible to ensure that money orders or letters would travel safely within the country, and it was probably the difficulty of maintaining contact with Latham's, as his bankers and forwarders, that made Hasted leave Abbeville and move back to the coast. It was from Calais, in March 1792, that Hasted wrote to Boteler to thank him for passing on the news that a relative had noticed his name among the proprietors of unclaimed dividends of 3 percent Consols:

> My best thanks to Mr Bargrave for the knowledge of it. Would you be so kind as to intercede with him, the next time he has an opportunity of enquiring for me, what it is that is remaining unclaimed, and to advise me what method I can use to obtain it to be paid into the hands of Latham & Co — for let it be more or less it will be of much service to me.[559]

The sum due did indeed turn out to be less rather than more, amounting only to £1.10s.

A more satisfactory sum could be expected from the sale of a leasehold property in Chatham which Hasted still owned. This was probably the brick and tiled house which had been insured in 1780 for £200. In December 1792 his son Edward was negotiating the sale with the tenant, Mr Cemp, who eventually agreed to buy. Hostilities in the

Channel were to cause a hitch in proceedings, however, when the boat carrying the engrossment of the deed of sale, which required Hasted's signature and had been despatched to him at Calais, was captured by the French.[560] Another engrossment was prepared in its place, but the events of the next few weeks must have decided whether this was signed by Hasted in France or in England.

Calais was to prove a reasonably good choice as a refuge, since it was to have a rather smoother passage through the Revolution than St Omer, and here Hasted was able to concentrate on his *History*, as is shown by the number of letters dating from 1792. The newly instituted elections of 1790 had brought to the post of mayor a man from the upper echelons of Calais society, Jacques Leveux, a liberal royalist whose long mayoralty — he retained the position until 1797 — ensured stability in the town. It was due to his intelligence and skill that Calais managed to pass through these years, including the Terror of 1794, without bloodshed. In place of internecine strife the town opted for greeting the various stages of the Revolution with loud and enthusiastic demonstrations of loyalty held in the old town square, the Place d'Armes. It was there that the anniversary of the Fédération was celebrated on the 14 July 1791, there, in October of the same year that to the sound of cannon the Constitution accepted by the King was read out to the people. From March 1792, if not a little earlier, Hasted was a resident on the Place d'Armes and, with Mary Jane, must have been a spectator at some of the demonstrations which took place in it.

Calais is the only town for which we have a known address for Hasted in France. His correspondents were usually told to send their letters care of Latham, Rice & Co, in Dover, and it was probably as an extreme measure, prompted by the declaration of hostilities between France and England and fearful of delay, that in February 1793 William Boteler sent a letter direct to 'Edwd Hasted Esqre, Chez Mons Herbelot fils, Sur la Place, Calais'.[561]

It is likely, in an age when introductions were of great importance, that each time Hasted moved to another town he went to a family or an address which had been recommended to him. The Herbelots, who seem to have been a family of some dignity, since a branch of it lived on the principal square in Calais, appear to have had connections in St Omer, whom Hasted may have come to know when he was staying there. During the later months of 1793, then known as Year 2 of the Republic, by which time it had become impossible to move about France without documentation, several of the Calais Herbelots obtained a passport or laisser passer for the express purpose of travelling to St Omer. As we have seen, Calais was less disturbed than St Omer, and it can perhaps be assumed that it was family matters that caused the Herbelots, described in their passports as domiciled in Calais, to go to the inland town. Thomas Herbelot père, an old man of sixty-seven, noted unusually in the records as 'portant perruque', and three Herbelot women, are recorded as having obtained passports for travel to St Omer, while the passport of 'Herbelot fils', aged thirty-four, qualified him unreservedly to travel 'dans la république'.[562]

In spite of the relative calm which was maintained in Calais itself, the desperate displays of solidarity which took place there must have reflected the increasingly ominous tone of events now unfolding elsewhere. A day of carnage in Paris paved the way for the announcement, on the 10 August 1792, of the fall of the French monarchy. On the 14th of the same month elections for the new Convention saw Thomas Paine (who, ironically for Hasted and other fugitives from Kent, was a former resident of Sandwich, feted now as the author of *The Rights of Man*, a document which had become a manifesto in France) chosen as one of the eleven deputies for the Pas-de-Calais; another was Maximilien de Robespierre, the terrible disciple of purity through bloodshed. In November, in place of a column which had borne a bust of Richelieu, the citizens of Calais planted a liberty tree, one of thousands up and down France. Towards the end of 1792 there were riots in Calais itself against grain shortages, and also against Englishmen coming to France, to the extent that the municipality thought it prudent to extend a combination of protection and surveillance towards them. At the same time there were heady celebrations of French military victories — war had been declared against the emperor of Austria the previous April — and the 4 November saw a civic celebration of successes against the Germans, with the firing of cannon and the singing of the new popular song, 'La Marseillaise'.[563] Alarm must now have been widespread among the English exiles. With December came news of the trial of the French king Louis XVI and, in January, of his execution. A bare ten days afterwards, amid arguments over the French right to proclaim the Dutch river Scheldt open to all shipping, war was declared on the King of England.

This must have been the event which triggered Boteler's letter of the 15 February, alarmed for his friend's safety. War had been declared on the first of the month, but it was not made public in Calais until three weeks later, when it was announced on the Place d'Armes on the 24th. The delay was probably intentional, to allow the large numbers of English living in the area time to embark for another destination. Aliens were not immediately required to leave France, but Hasted and Mary Jane had probably experienced enough to feel that imprisonment for debt, if it had to come, would now be the lesser of two evils.

*Please to pay to Monsieur Frayal or Bearer the
of Five Guineas & place the same without farther
advice to the Acct of Gentn
Your obliged humble servt
Edward Harlock*

£ 5 : 5 : 0

Calais
March 30th
1792

*Messrs Latham Rice & Co
Bankers Dover*

PROPOSALS
For an Octavo Edition of the
HISTORY OF KENT,
In Eight Volumes:
WITH THE MAPS, VIEWS OF SEATS, ANTIQUI-
TIES, &c.
TO BE PRINTED AND PUBLISHED BY
W. BRISTOW,
PRINTER, BOOKSELLER, STATIONER, AND PRINTSELLER,
PARADE, CANTERBURY.

MANY Gentlemen having been averse to purchase the Folio Edition of the HISTORY OF KENT,
as well from the largeness of the Price as the size of it; and
having repeated their wishes to obtain it at a more reasonable
price, and of a SMALLER size; the Author has been induced
to accommodate the Public with an Edition of it in Octavo,
at a reasonable price; in which the History is considerably
abridged, by omitting numberless repetitions and unnecessary
matter, the subjects will be new arranged, the present
state of parishes enlarged; and to render it more pleasant and
agreeable in the reading; the bulk of the Notes (excepting
quotations of authority) will be added to the Text; the
families and Estates will be continued to the present time, and
the whole will be corrected and amended in every part, by
other improvements in it too numerous to mention.

The Public is therefore respectfully acquainted, that this
Publication will be executed on an elegant wove DEMY paper,
and new Types by Caslon. The first Volume to be published
in January next, and the remaining Volumes successively at
the end of every five months afterwards. Each Volume at
the moderate price of 7s. 6d. in boards, with the Maps of

Chapter 13

In the King's Bench

The truce for aliens in France was to be only temporary. By a law passed in September 1793 all foreigners were placed under arrest, and their property confiscated; exceptions were made only in the case of those who had come to the country before 1789 and who earned their living there. Hasted was wise to leave when he did.

The flow of aristocrats escaping through the port of Calais had now all but ceased, and the boatloads of émigrés which continued to set sail for England were composed increasingly of those in trade and the professions. It was probably not difficult for Hasted, after nearly three years in France, to take his place among them as a Frenchman fleeing with his mistress. Did he retain the disguise once he was back in England? Perhaps the persona of a Frenchman would have attracted more attention than he wanted, but it is quite possible that he travelled now under an assumed name. He was still wanted for debt: a sheriff's warrant had been issued for his arrest and was liable to be enforced the moment he was found to be on English soil.

Although in his 'Statement of Transactions with the late Mr Thos Williams' Hasted says only that after re-entering England he stayed for some time in Cirencester, the brief Chronology which he jotted down towards the end of his life tells us that this was preceded by a tour through England with Mary Jane.[564] We are given no clues to their itinerary apart from the mention of that one town. Initially there must have been considerable interest for Hasted in discovering more about his own country and noting comparisons and contrasts with Kent. But he was no longer a young man, and the constant moving, packing and unpacking must have been tiring in the extreme. It was probably with growing relief that he found an extended stay in Cirencester gave him no cause for alarm. So far did he seem from discovery, indeed, that the possibility of actually settling in London began to cross his mind. It was a daring move, but there were probably several factors which encouraged him to it.

Chief among these was the greater ease with which he would be able to work on the still unfinished *History*. It seems almost miraculous that he should have spent years wandering as a fugitive in France and England, encumbered with much of the material for the production of a tome of encyclopaedic proportions, and mislaid little or none of it on the way. A reminder from William Boys in November 1791 that 'Mr Boteler ... desires me to say, that you have already from him everything he can collect respecting the parishes of Betshanger and Norbourn, and therefore he hopes you will not expect him to go over that ground again' and that Boys, too, had sent Hasted 'about the time you left England a full account of the farms along the coast belonging to the Leiths and Pointers, which must be either with you or at Canterbury', seems to have been one of the few occasions when the historian's orderly mind was at fault.[565] From a settled London address it would be easier to maintain the correspondence so necessary for the completion of his work. And he may have had other, more personal reasons, for wanting to be within closer reach of Kent. Although he still remained estranged from his wife, and while Edward, and perhaps Katherine, too, highly disapproved of their father's conduct, he had not broken his ties with the whole of his family: Charles and Anne, in particular, appear to have been more understanding, and to have offered what support they could. But he would not see his mother again: old Mrs Hasted had died, at the age of nearly 90, when he was in France in 1791. A dignified announcement in the *Gentleman's Magazine* had let the world know that the relict of the late Edward Hasted, barrister-at-law, and mother of Edward Hasted, the Kentish historian, had passed away on the 3 March of that year in the precincts of Christ Church, Canterbury; and her body now shared the grave in the cathedral cloisters where his baby daughter had been buried nearly twenty years before. An inscription had been commissioned for little Mary Barbara, but her grandmother lay uncommemorated, which is perhaps why, in a footnote on the cloisters in his fourth volume, Hasted was to give her a full obituary, as the only memorial which it was now in his power to erect.[566]

By the late summer of 1794 the decision to come to London had been taken, and Hasted and Mary Jane were in lodgings in Camden Town near Tottenham Court Road where, as Hasted noted in the 'Statement', he 'hoped to have remained unknown too and forgotten'. The earliest letter which we have for the ensuing period is one from William Boys, dated 31 August 1794 and carefully addressed to Hasted 'at the Somerset Coffee House, opposite the New Church in the Strand, London', a poste restante address which was to serve him, although he could not know it at the time, for many years to come.[567] It was from his London lodgings that he was now able to arrange for the sale of his books. There had been an awkward occasion, after he had been in France for nearly eighteen months, when he had learnt that Edward was about to sell some of them to William Boys. Facing an indefinite future in a foreign land the historian knew that his library would have to be sold at some point, but he knew also that it would attract less interest when put on the market if some of the more valuable items had already been removed. Boys, somewhat huffily, was obliged to retreat:

I acted by advice in treating with your son for your books. There were some of them which I wished much to have, but I shall be better pleased to hear you have parted with them for a sum near your estimate of their value, than to have had them fall into my hands at mine.[568]

The sale was handled by the Canterbury booksellers, Flackton, Marrable and Claris. Giving his friend Richard Gough gossip from Kent in November, the vicar of Wilmington, the Revd Samuel Denne, was to tell him that he had seen in the *Kentish Gazette* that the sale of Hasted's books was being advertised in the booksellers' catalogue for 1795.[569]

In London, there is no doubt, Hasted again applied himself to the task which had remained unfinished when he was obliged to leave France, and it is almost certain that it was during this time that he finally brought it to a conclusion. Volume IV was to be dedicated to William Pitt, since 1783 first lord of the treasury and chancellor of the exchequer — the equivalent of prime minister. This was neither so surprising nor so political as it might seem, since Pitt was both Lord Warden of the Cinque Ports and a resident of Kent, his father having purchased Hayes Place near Bromley in 1756. The dedication would eventually bear the same date as the Preface, 24 January 1799, but Hasted's notes contain a copy of his letter to Pitt, requesting permission to make the dedication, and this is dated London, 8 December 1793.[570] It is impossible to know whether the historian was living in London as early as this, or whether he made sporadic visits there while wandering about England with Mary Jane.

But he certainly seems to have had the temerity, once he was based in London, to make one or more excursions into Kent. On the 29 October 1794 we find William Boys writing to him: 'I shall be happy to see you again at Sandwich, and shall hope to be favored with your advice in arranging my books and curiosities in my new room.'[571]

Boys' letter, as before, was sent to the Somerset Coffee House in the Strand, an address which was clearly intended to provide Hasted with some cover, since he was still in hiding. The Somerset Coffee House, taking its name from the imposing residence built in the Strand for Lord Protector Somerset in the sixteenth century, was one of the London coffee houses with an importance almost equal to the inns for the variety of activities carried on there. Not only did they have reading rooms supplied with newspapers, and provide a venue for clubs and debating societies, sales and auctions, but the largest ones also functioned as stage coach stops and handled parcels and letters. Most of the mail coaches coming up from Kent used the George and Blue Boar in Holborn as their terminus, and after crossing the river at Westminster probably came up Whitehall and along the Strand before turning north up what is now Kingsway for their final destination. The Somerset Coffee House would have been the main stopping place in the Strand, perhaps the last one before the George and Blue Boar was reached. Virtually all Hasted's mail from Kent — and certainly all that coming from Dover, Sandwich and Thanet — would have travelled up to London in these coaches, which also took up en route the mails from Maidstone and Queenborough. To have his correspondence dropped off here and left to be called for was something which would have attracted little notice, and certainly helped to make it possible for the historian to live undetected in London for the best part of a year.

Nevertheless, it was a very restricted life-style which was now forced on him. Not only were contacts with friends difficult to maintain, but circumstances had contrived to debar him from any share whatever in the public debate concerning national safety and the war with France. It is unlikely, of course, that he would have had any prominence in this, but as a Deputy Lieutenant and an acting justice of the peace for the county of Kent, he would have had a voice in the many meetings which were held to consider the crisis. William Boys' letter of August 1794, which appears to have been written in answer to a request from Hasted for news of himself after a silence of some months between the friends, must have brought home forcefully to the fugitive the fact of his own social exclusion. Boys' letter began:

> I rise every day at seven and ride, and work, and write till eleven, allowing the shortest time possible to the necessary, tho' now troublesome, recruit of the body. The hospital at Deal demands all my time and attention, and an addition of 283 soldiers, women and children from the Schelde on the 21st instant has deprived me ever since of all recreation whatever; and what is worse, (as to fatigue, I mean) I hear today that I am to expect another freight of 50 at least.[572]

From the summer of 1794, therefore, if not earlier, Mary Jane Town was slipping into the Somerset Coffee House once or twice a week, asking quietly over the bar for Mr Hasted's mail. But an astute sheriff's officer probably only needed to linger in a corner of the room to overhear from time to time a name which was on his list. All he then had to do was to follow the bearer of this mail to discover where the person in question was living, and to keep the house under observation, in order to be able to perform an arrest on one of the infrequent occasions when that person ventured into the street — an arrest could not be made in a house. There was perhaps something like nine months' peaceful seclusion for Hasted in his Camden Town lodgings before this was to happen to him. Then, in the words of his own 'Statement': 'After a few months he was discovered there and arrested at the suit of Mr Rugg's executors and after being in the sheriff's custody for about a month he was removed by Habeas to the custody of the Marshal of the King's Bench'.[573]

The folio book of Commitments to the King's Bench prison in St George's Fields gives us the precise dates for these events:

> Edward Hasted Esqr Committed etc. 12th June 1795 for want of bail upon a Writ of Hab.Cor. directed to the Sheriff of Middlesex. And by the return it appears that on the 16th May 1795 he was taken and under the said Sheriff's custody detained by virtue of a Bill of Middx retble before the King at Westminster on ffriday next after the morrow of the Holy Trinity to answer Robert Rugg and John Rugg in a plea of Trespass. And also to their Bill as Exors of the last Will and Testament of Robert Rugg their late ffather decd for £4400 debt according etc. to be exhibited. Oath £2660 and upwds Gregory for Rolfe and Slatter.[574]

The King's Bench Abstract Book of Commitments for 1791 to 1796 confirms that Edward Hasted was indeed committed to the debtors' prison on 12 June under a writ of Habeas Corpus signed by Lord Kenyon. It also shows two further debts owing to a man named Josiah Stanley: these are for £65.2s.0d. and £4.11s.8d.[575] A sheet of paper listing items of expenditure for the years 1778-1781 which probably relate to Edward's time at Oxford shows the names of two tailors, Friend and Stanley, and it is possible that the more complaisant of the two had allowed some of his bills to mount up unpaid to the point where, losing patience, he added his own writ to that taken out by the Ruggs.[576] The alteration in Hasted's circumstances was now radical, and, it would seem, final. Most committals for debt lasted no more than a matter of months. Edward Hasted was to remain a prisoner for seven years.

Immediately on committal there were fees to be paid. These went to swell the enormous salary of the Marshal of the prison, at this time a certain William Jones, esq. The philanthropist James Neild, who was carrying out an investigation into prisons, particularly debtors' prisons, around this time, gives the Marshal's annual salary as £2300, although unofficial sources seem to have suggested that he received more than double this amount.[577] Like every other debtor, Hasted probably managed his fees as best he could, and would then have received his 'Chummage', the ticket which assigned him to a particular room in the prison —

although whether, when he got there, he would find himself the sole occupant, was another matter: there might be another person in the room, or even two, depending on how full the prison was. During the time Hasted was there the prisoners in the King's Bench seem to have numbered between 400 and 600, and as the total number of rooms, according to James Neild's very detailed account of it, was 224 (including eight better apartments, known as the state rooms), the likelihood is that Hasted was never, or very seldom, the sole occupant of his room, which, from 1795 to 1799, was known as No.1 in 7. Neild's description of the prison building makes it clear how this should be understood:

> The residence of the prisoners is in a large brick building, about 120 yards long, with a wing at each end, and a neat uniform chapel in the centre. ... The building is divided into sixteen staircases, with stone steps and iron railings. No.1, at the further wing, contains 21 rooms; and on each staircase the ranges of rooms are divided by a passage, or gallery, about two yards wide. In the staircases No.2, 3, 4, and 5, there are four rooms on each floor, making 16 in each staircase, separated from each other by a passage of about a yard wide. The staircase No.6 contains 12 rooms, besides two small cabins. No.7, 8, and 9 contain eight rooms each. No.10 contains thirty rooms ... The whole number of rooms, including the eight state rooms, is 224; the size of them, in general, is 15 to 16 feet by 12 or 13 feet; some few are on a larger scale.[578]

The imprisonment itself was in no way intended to be punitive — debtors' prisons merely being places in which creditors, if they were so minded, could have their debtors confined until they settled up — but it must have reduced most of those held in this way to a level of existence which, in their more affluent days, they could not have imagined possible. It was the Marshal's business, out of his colossal salary, to maintain the prison, but this seems to have been taken to refer to the fabric of the building only: the level of cleanliness in the prisoners' rooms seems to have depended wholly on their inmates, with the mixed results one would expect, while cleaning of the public areas appears to have been non-existent, for Neild comments that 'the staircases and lobbies are in the most filthy state imaginable'.[579] In such surroundings, the few women among the debtors were probably able to make shift to look after themselves. For the great majority of male debtors, however, life must have looked bleak indeed if there was no woman — wife, daughter, servant or mistress — to care for them in the way of cooking and cleaning, and washing and mending of clothes. Hasted at least had Mary Jane. When he went into the King's Bench, he tells us, she went with him.[580] However, in view of the fact that there was a regular call at 9.30 every night of 'Strangers, women, and children out!', and given also the pressure on living space within the prison, this may have meant only that she had a room somewhere in the vicinity of the prison, in the area known as the 'Rules', which formed a circle around it of some three miles in circumference. From here she would have come in each day, lightening Hasted's incarceration by her presence, caring for him, still taking his letters and occasional parcels of proofs to and from the Somerset Coffee House which he continued to use for his post, and perhaps even, on occasion, as the evidence of a neat hand suggests, serving him as an amanuensis.

Mary Jane's daily presence probably prevented Hasted from sinking into utter neglect during the first year or two of his imprisonment. However, the situation must have appeared as hopeless to her as it did to Hasted — he seems eventually to have despaired of ever being released — and it is not really surprising that she should finally have sought her fortune elsewhere. Hasted felt bitter over this betrayal: 'I parted with her for infamy and wickedness', says the entry relating to this in his brief Chronology, obviously referring to unfaithfulness on her part. They had been through a great deal together, and perhaps been very much in love, but the days of exciting escapades were over for both of them. Hasted himself was nearly sixty-five, and Mary Jane, considerably younger and with no real tie, must have found the stagnation of prison life depressing in the extreme. She perhaps left the King's Bench in the company of one of the more fortunate prisoners who was able to obtain his discharge after only a few months. Hasted's dismissal of her in 1797 brought their liaison of thirteen years to an end.[581]

The ageing prisoner does not seem to have had too much difficulty in finding someone to replace her. The Chronology notes: 'Harriet Brewster then came and lived with me' and adds 'as my servant' by way of making the relationship clear. There is no way of knowing how Hasted found her: there may well have been a ready supply of servants in the locality willing to accept the lottery of a King's Bench prisoner as a master — many of them had been, and might be again, when their affairs had been sorted out, wealthy men. Harriet may not have been in her first youth, and was perhaps a member of one of the Brewster families of whom there were several at that time trading in and around the City. Subsequent events were to reveal that she was literate, sharp, and perhaps one of those who had an eye to the main chance.

Now, however, Harriet was to take over, probably more willingly than Mary Jane of late, the duty of looking after the elderly prisoner in No.1 on staircase No.7, preparing his food, and trying to keep respectable the clothes which had once graced the back of a Deputy Lieutenant and a justice of the peace — and of someone who still remained a Fellow of the Society of Antiquaries and of the Royal Society. And Harriet must also have now become his link with the outside world, fetching and carrying his post from and to the Somerset Coffee House.

Postage for his correspondence could have constituted a heavy drain on Hasted's meagre finances: it was fortunate for him that letters, at this time, did not have to be prepaid. The historian's existence in the King's Bench prison seems to have been utterly hand to mouth, and there were many occasions when if he had not solicited a little help he would have starved. It is likely that Charles and Anne, at least, did what they could for him, but Anne, at this time, probably had no money of her own, and Charles's fortunes were never buoyant. From time to time there was nothing for it but to beg assistance from his friends and acquaintances — perhaps the greatest punishment which the King's Bench could inflict on him.

For it was altogether impossible to exist in the prison without money. 'No places in the universe,' says the *Debtor and Creditor's Assistant*, published in 1793,

> abound so much with character as the King's Bench and the Fleet. Of the prisoners, some have a property, or an income, to subsist upon; some a regular allowance from their friends; some are obliged to feed like moths upon their clothes, and some have to depend wholly on chance, or accident, to lengthen out a miserable existence.[582]

Rent even had to be paid for the room one occupied. Those possessed of an adequate regular income were able to take one in the so-called State House, at 2s.6d. a week. Hasted would seem to have had one of the 'master's side' rooms, for which 1s. a week had to be paid. Only those without a penny to call their own lived rent-free. Reduced to living on prison charity, which was known as being 'on the box', they slept seven or more to a room on the 'commonside', in the shadow of the prison wall, or on a makeshift bed in the tap. Food was another item of expenditure, as the King's Bench did not cater for its prisoners; however, service of a kind was provided by the public kitchen, where prisoners could have their own food cooked free of charge every day — so long as they were prepared to dine before three o'clock: after that hour the service was no longer free.

Fees were also due to those who performed essential duties there, such as the scavenger and the crier, although these seem to have been paid out of the initial 'inside fees' or 'garnish' claimed from each newcomer by what was known as 'the college'.[583]

Was Hasted, one wonders, ever able to frequent the coffee house within the prison, the meeting place of the (formerly) more well-to-do among the prisoners? The likelihood is that he was seen there very seldom. His position, after all, was not that most commonly found among the prisoners of the King's Bench, although this had nothing to do with social status, for a glance at two lists of prisoners, drawn up in 1797 and 1801, shows that he would not have wanted for polite company. In 1797, among the 287 prisoners who were held at this time were Francis Bateman Dashwood, esq., François Henry de Lambert, commonly called the Count de Lambert, Paul George Elers, esq., Sir Thomas Hope, Bt., George Parkyns, esq., James Bradshaw Peirson (among whose creditors was Sir John Honywood), the Revd Henry Rowe, Francis Keate Reeves, esq., Charles Granville Wheler, esq., the Revd Robert Thorpe and Sir John Thomas Wheate, Bt.[584] Indeed, Thomas Borrett, of Shoreham, another Kentish landowner, of whom Hasted would almost certainly have heard, was committed to the King's Bench in November 1799, although removed to the Fleet prison almost immediately. In fact, the 'better' type of prisoner was in the majority, and it was they who formed what was called 'the college' — a kind of corporation or guild of prisoners, which existed to promote harmony among the prisoners and a certain level of well-being among themselves, formalised to the extent of having officers and a rule-book. The existence of this 'college' appears to have been of considerable support to the small official staff of the prison, and was in many ways conducive to its smooth running. The permanence of the 'college', however — which sometimes resulted in the prison being called King's College (Hasted himself was quite often sent letters with that superscription) — disguises the fact that the membership of it must have been fluid in the extreme. The majority of the people held in the King's Bench prison in 1797 had only been committed in 1795 or 1796, and most of these were discharged under the Act of 1797, under which the list in question was drawn up. Hasted's singularity lay in the long duration of his confinement.

An examination of committals to the King's Bench shows that the majority of prisoners were discharged very quickly. Of the three other people whose names appear on the same sheet of committals as Hasted's, i.e. committed around the same time, two were discharged in 1795 and one in 1797. On the next sheet, all those committed were released in the same year that they were taken, that is, 1795.[585] The King's Bench was not intended for the indefinite internment of debtors, but rather as somewhere they could be put by their creditors in a final and frequently successful attempt to obtain repayment. Credit and debt were common features of the eighteenth-century commercial scene, due partly to a shortage of ready money, and partly to the fact that there were few financial institutions at this time able to organise and oversee loans. A creditor's powers extended to a right to bring about imprisonment, but the mere threat of this was frequently enough to oblige a debtor to come to some arrangement to pay.

The initial imprisonment, under a writ, was on what was known as mesne process only, because the debtor was unable to put up bail. It was at this point in the proceedings that many debtors managed to settle with their creditors, whose suits therefore did not come to trial. Suits were also sometimes abandoned at this stage by creditors who realised that no more would be forthcoming from their debtors. A suit which came to trial under final process, as the second part of this procedure was called, usually resulted in the imprisonment of a debtor for a longer period, until the next Act for the Relief of Insolvent Debtors gave him the opportunity to apply for his discharge. Under such an Act, the justices of the peace in each county were required to form special commissions to which all debtors, imprisoned on mesne or final process, could present schedules of their assets. Where these appeared to have been honestly drawn up, the justices would consent to the release of a debtor. Creditors could then proceed against the property of a debtor, such as it was, but were not allowed to return him or her to prison again for the same debts.[586]

Situated as he was, Hasted could name no assets. His estates were in the hands of Thomas Williams, and to have listed any smaller items still remaining to him, such as furniture and other moveables, would probably have deprived various members of his family, wherever they were now living — the house in the Precincts had been sold in 1792[587] — of some of their household goods. Nevertheless, one way out of the prison was by making an accommodation with one's creditors, and this Hasted was apparently able to arrange on more than one occasion. His efforts in this direction seem to have been blocked by Thomas Williams, however, since on the 30 June 1796 Hasted was to tell William Boteler in a letter:

> Tho I have more than once entirely satisfyed my plaintiff, and obtained his good will for my release hence, yet a malicious attorney has ever stepped between, and rendered this agreement void, so that unless providence interferes by his removal in some measure or other I fear my doom will be to languish here in misery and want.[588]

It is hardly surprising that Hasted, in prison, could be morose and obliged on occasion to apologise for his ungracious reception of a rare visitor. 11 October 1795, for example, found him writing an abject letter of regret to William Boteler for what had occurred between them that very day:

> My good sir, I cannot omit an hour to throw myself on your goodness, to pardon my strange behaviour to you today, but the sudden surprise, totally, as you might well see, deprived me of all recollection, not only of yourself, but of whatever I might and ought to have mentioned to you, it deprived me of expressing the sincere and grateful sentiments of my heart, for the many acts of friendship I have so often experienced from you, especially the last of late, at a time when I stood so much in want of it.[589]

Clearly, the insouciant gaiety of the King's Bench coffee room was not for Hasted, even had he been able to afford it, and whether or not those he would have met there were on his own social level. Men such as Samuel Evans, esq., who came in in 1799, Sir John Thomas Southcott, Bt., admitted in 1800, Ralph Thrale (1801), George Brooke, esq., (1800), Terry Pierce Crane, esq., (1799) and Thomas Dyke (1800), all these, with the exception of Sir John Thomas Southcott, the justices were able to discharge in 1801 under the Act of that year. It was only a minority of the prisoners whose cases could not be resolved in this way. Hasted was one of these. He remained a prisoner in the company of Andrew Robinson Bowes, committed in 1787 for debts totalling more than £20,000, George Joseph Pedley, committed in 1785 with debts over £10,000, Dame Elizabeth Pryce, committed in 1787 with a debt of just over £1000, Timothy Topping, committed the year before Hasted, with a debt of some £1100, and Nicholas Hoskins, a Cornish gentleman, the son of a surgeon, who had come in in 1785 in respect of a disputed debt of £340, which he had vowed never to pay.[590]

Hoskins had become one of those who made a small livelihood within the prison itself. For a number of years he acted as its postmaster, in an office which seems to have been run very much like any other London post office, with set hours for sending out the twopenny post, the general post and the penny post. The postmaster would receive the letters for all the inmates, and then display a list of the fortunate recipients, who could claim them on payment of the postage, plus a small fee of a half-penny which Hoskins charged for his services.[591]

Like Hoskins, many of the old-timers in the prison turned their hands either to their old trade or to a new one, dictated by their changed circumstances. A few became racket-masters, in charge of the games of rackets and fives which were played against one of the prison walls. Tailors and bootmakers were always assured of work, while some earned a living by valeting for those who could still afford such services. Other prisoners kept the small shops which were to be found at the foot of the staircases. At the bottom of No.1 staircase, for example, were to be had boiled ham, pork, butter, candles and shoe blacking. Rather later than Hasted's time, the shop at the foot of No.7 staircase was described as kept by

> a ci-devant captain in the West India trade, who now instead of his hogsheads retails with a good humored smile, his quarter of a pound of brawn, his penny-worth of butter, and half a penny loaf. He whistles "Cease, rude Boreas" while he deals out his farthing's-worth of sand, and hums out "Ye gentlemen of England" while snipping for a customer his penny candle from a string.

And the same source comments:

> It is no unusual thing, to see men who have moved in the highest sphere of life, waiting with patience at one of these humble counters, jostled about at the pleasure of the rude and vulgar, and content on being served, to carry away his penny rasher of bacon, his roll and his potato, and happy in the meal thus produced, at a cost less than he was wont to give as a tavern waiter's fee.[592]

The gentleman in what was known as No.1 in 7, from 1795 to 1799, was Edward Hasted, and while the captain who had formerly been in the West India trade and been obliged to turn grocer may have come after Hasted's time, there is no doubt that he would have had a predecessor, whose shop Hasted must have known well — as well, that is, as his meagre funds allowed.

For the Kentish historian had no trade or profession that could be followed in the King's Bench. He had worked all his life, but always in a voluntary and unpaid capacity. Had he been an attorney or a doctor he would probably not have lacked for employment. Carpenters, joiners, hairdressers, plumbers, bricklayers, all could find some work within the prison community — sometimes, particularly if they were carpenters or builders, in the employment of the prison authorities themselves. The elderly Hasted could offer nothing that was wanted, and, unable to supplement his pittance, seems not infrequently to have been on the verge of starvation. William Boys bluntly said as much in a letter of August 1795 which he wrote to Thomas Pennant:

> Mr Hasted, after whom you enquire, I am sorry to say is in the King's Bench and in the greatest distress. I have lately relieved him, when he assured me he had not money for three days' further subsistence. His MS History of Kent is in the hands of Mr Simmons, a bookseller and printer at Canterbury, who will, I believe, very soon put it to the press. In the mean time the author is starving. I cannot solicit for an unworthy man; but having lived in a habit of intimacy with him formerly, and having received a number of civilities from him in my early antiquarian pursuits, I must own, it would be a satisfaction to me to learn that persons, who wish well to literature, would contribute a little matter to prevent the Historian of Kent from being starved in a jail. He has labored hard in the service; and perhaps his close attention to his History may have exposed him to temptations to which his poverty, at first, rather than his will gave way.[593]

Thomas Pennant was equally blunt. He scribbled on the back of the letter:

> Mr Hasted at the age of seventy left his old wife and ran away with a young girl. He absurdly apologizes for it in his motto to vol.III.

— but he also noted: 'I sent him 5 Guineas'.[594]

There is no doubt that Hasted was becoming desperate for money. His horses, the family postchaise and chariot, had probably gone long ago; a small collection of seals was sold to John Nichols, through Thomas Astle, for £5 in 1795.[595] He had recently disposed of his books. Now it was the turn of his manuscripts. 'The fate of a fourth volume', as James Simmons had put it, had become submerged under the more tumultuous happenings of recent months, but it is clear that it was finished and that the text was in the printer's hands. Hasted had now no real need of his notes and manuscript collection which, ironically, could be used to raise some of the cash for which he had hoped from the sale of his completed work. Once more a slight awkwardness arose over this with Boys, who would have liked to take some items prior to the sale. Again Hasted was afraid of spoiling the impact of the auction if some of the best pieces were taken out in advance, and he was obliged to tell William Boteler:

Could I have separated those Mr Boys selected without entirely ruining the sale of the others, I should with pleasure have complyed with it, notwithstanding which, should any change of circumstances happen by which I can separate them from the rest, or give him an opportunity of purchasing them I shall gladly do it and give him advice of it accordingly.[596]

The circumstances of the unfortunate writer were to remain unchanged, however, and it could well be that the slight rebuffs which Boys encountered, both now and previously on the occasion of his attempted purchase of some of Hasted's books, contributed to his outburst of ill-temper when he discovered a few months later that one or two of his own letters had formed part of the sale. The auction, as Hasted told Boteler early in February 1796, was scheduled for the end of that month or some time in March: 'I don't suppose so trifling a matter can bring you to town, but should you have other occasion to come to town, you may take the opportunity of taking this sale at the same time' — and Hasted, hoping that if Boteler comes to the auction he may find time to visit him, is again obliged to add an apology, 'for the last unaccountable reception I gave you, when I last saw you here, after the trouble you had taken to come so far to me in such a place'.[597]

The catalogue came into a number of hands, including those of the epistolist vicar of Wilmington, who on 26 March, writing after the sale had taken place, and ignorant of the fact that Hasted had already brought the *History* to a conclusion, told Richard Gough, in a sentence lightly embellished with a quotation from *Othello*:

> On a cursory perusal of the MS articles at the end of the catalogue, which by your direction Mr Deputy dispatched to me with haste, post haste, I was convinced that the substance of these had been incorporated into a History of Kent, though I frankly own it did not occur to me that they were conveyed from Mr Hasted to the hammer of Leigh and Sotheby, not having a suspicion that he would dispose of his materials before his work was completed.

And Denne went on to express surprise at some of the prices mentioned in the catalogue:

> For I should not have been willing to have given half the money ask'd for the whole previous to the sale, even in better days; ... Not but there are some of the MSS I should have wished to have

picked up some gleanings from, had a sufficient time been allowed for so doing.[598]

Nevertheless, although Denne was clearly not present, the sale probably brought together a number of Hasted's friends. The historian had drawn up two indexes of his manuscript collection, so that we know exactly what he possessed. The British Museum showed its discernment by being the principal bidder: it secured sixty-two, or a little over half, of the items on offer, including the quarto volumes of indexes, although it seems regrettable that Hasted should have benefited by no more than £63 from its purchases.[599] Some of the other manuscripts which were bought have been lost to view. However, Thomas Astle acquired three items: the certified folio copy of Domesday Book for Kent, for which Hasted had paid Abraham Farley 16 guineas nearly thirty years earlier, and Hasted's own transcription, in two quarto volumes, of charters and deeds belonging to the Hospital of St Nicholas, Harbledown, near Canterbury. It was probably Astle who had the two latter volumes bound under one cover, since it was certainly he who wrote on the flyleaf: 'T. Astle purchased Tuesday March 15th 1796'. These were among the manuscripts left by Astle under his will to the Marquis of Buckingham, so that they too, as part of the Stowe collection, which was purchased in 1883, are now to be found in the British Library.[600]

A few of the items offered for sale, including Hasted's original folio commonplace books, and a series of small notebooks which had served the same purpose, found no takers, and seem to have been returned to Hasted in prison. Some years later he was to suggest to William Boteler that it might be worth his while, in connection with the latter's proposed history of Eastry, to consult those of his papers which were now at the Museum, and also the commonplace books which he still had with him: 'Should you like to peruse them here, it may save you a multiplicity of reading'.[601]

William Boys' discovery that some of his own letters had featured in the sale resulted in his breaking off all relations with the prisoner in the King's Bench. Letting an imagined affront to his dignity take on far greater importance and reality than the plight of someone incarcerated in a debtors' prison, he vowed never to correspond with him again. Hasted, who seems to have been completely innocent of any intention to let private letters form part of the sale, was overcome with grief at this behaviour of one of his oldest friends, and begged Boteler to try to win Boys' friendship back for him:

I dare say sir you have been long ere now made acquainted with it, and the cause of it — a cause which tho' it may have existed, I may truly say I was in fact innocent of, for, from my present situation, I was debarred months before of looking over the MSS. I was forced to trust to others to peruse and delete from them those which were unfit for the eyes of the public and I truly thought that I had myself in possession every letter of Mr Boys's either of a private nature or which could give any umbrage otherwise. Unhappy I am, unhappy indeed, that he thinks it not so, and that there were left, unknown to me, those, which have deprived me of his most valuable esteem, and friendship, a loss which has affected me more than imprisonment or any other misfortune from my birth to the present moment. ... Let me sir by every intreaty, by every appeal to your feelings implore you to intercede for me, for his forgiveness, for him to obliterate from his memory this unhappy break of our friendship, and to restore me to the same place in his esteem.[602]

Boys did not relent immediately, and another letter to Boteler written just over a week later feared that 'you have had no success in obtaining me a return of Mr Boys's friendship', and continued:

If he persists in blotting out from his memory all former kind and feeling sensations of it which he for so many years taught me to believe he had for me and which I have in every instance so continually experienced from him — if I cannot obtain his pardon for an involuntary fault, which I never intended to commit and was totally ignorant, that I had offended in it — I must submit to his pleasure in it, but I cannot say, but I think it rather a harsh and cruel resolution on so old a friend, as myself and this in the time of my adversity.[603]

The case was touchingly put, and exactly a month later Hasted was able to thank Boteler 'for your additional act of goodness, in regaining me the friendship of Mr Boys, who has at last written to me a most kind and friendly letter, a balmy comfort to me in my distressfull situation'. Hasted's letter continues:

This comfort indeed I have, and it is no small one, that in that fallen situation which in general causes the loss of every friend, I have found hardly one, who has not afforded me every assistance, and attention, among them none more essentially so than yourself and Mr Boys.[604]

It is clear from the crippling constraints under which Hasted was living that he was virtually never to be found in the prison's coffee house, or at the Brace, a public tap room which took its name from the fact that it had been kept originally by two brothers by the name of Partridge. The Brace would perhaps have been rather a lowly resort for one of Hasted's former standing. It was described in a pamphlet of the time as 'a sort of medium between the vulgarity of the common tap of the prison, and the tip-top of the coffee house, its frequenters are the semi-genteel, or the equi-distant between the canaille and what are familiarly and quaintly called the snobs'.[605]

Distinctions of rank, however, must have been of the most flimsy here, and there is little evidence that the historian of Kent was ever snobbishly inclined. His liberal inclinations, his wish to continue his father's tradition of service to all, had made of him a man who, rather than sharing, had suffered from his mother's 'excessive pride' in his happier days, and this attitude may well have rendered him here, in the levelling community of the King's Bench, someone who did not cling to former status. It could well have been a refusal to brood on the indignities of his present position which enabled him now to turn his thoughts to a second edition of his *History of Kent*.

It is probable that his friendship with the artist and engraver John Barlow, introduced to him many years before by the Earl of Radnor, was of considerable importance in leading to the decision to produce a second edition. In view of the similar nature of their occupations it seems not unlikely that John was a descendant of Francis Barlow, the seventeenth-century artist who lived and worked in London, who was the first English artist to specialise in drawing and painting animals and whose illustrations to *Aesop's Fables* went into many editions. Unexpectedly Barlow and Hasted appear to have met up again, if not in the King's Bench, at least in the King's Bench area. The name of John Barlow actually appears in the prison records in 1790 and 1794, and it is perhaps significant that his private address, in St George's Fields, lay within the area known as the Rules.[606] Barlow, as a professional book illustrator — now known mainly for his illustrations for Rees's *Encyclopaedia* and some engravings after Hogarth executed for Ireland's work in 1791 — would have been aware of the much greater appeal of a smaller, more manageable octavo edition, and perhaps encouraged Hasted in this direction with the offer of some vignettes. The new project must have helped to sustain the historian's spirits during many dark days and nights, as the century wore on to its close and there seemed no prospect of his release.

There was no question, this time, of Hasted being his own publisher, and someone had to be found who would publish as well as print. Hasted's first choice appears to have been John Nichols, now the editor of the *Gentleman's Magazine*. Thomas Astle was asked to approach Nichols, which he did on 1 January 1796, but Nichols, as we shall see later, was unlikely to wish to encourage such a scheme.[607] At all events, he declined to take it on. July 1796 found Hasted himself writing to Nichols, in a letter which is partly an attempt to persuade him to change his mind, and partly a request for professional advice:

> Sir, The liberal manner in which you received me when I last waited on you, and the kind assistance you offered me, in regard to the printing of my History, encourages me to apply to you again, for the favour of your advice in relation to my intended edition of it in 8vo. Happy should I have been, had you condescended to have printed it and published it for me. You have known me, Sir, many years in the habits of friendship with our mutual friends Mr Thorpe, Dr Ducarel, and many more, now long since taken from us; one of whom, and almost the only one left to us, Mr Astle, I requested to join his interest with you for this purpose; but you, though with much politeness, declined it, though, at the same time, had you but attended to my offers, you would have thought them well worth your consideration; indeed, you would not have rejected them. I am now in treaty, Sir, with Mr Bristow of Canterbury, to print it, and publish it for me; Mr Simmons, the printer of my folio volume, now in the press, not having sufficient presses to carry forward both at the same time.
>
> It is proposed, Sir, to print it in eight octavo volumes; each volume to contain the folio maps of the Hundreds, and the vignettes, as far as can be, of the folio volumes; a volume to be published every six months; the matter in them to be corrected, amended, and the subjects brought down to the present time, and new arranged, and the superfluous matter, tautologies, etc. taken from it; and, therefore, the work so far abridged, and brought to a smaller compass. The folio prints relating to each volume, being about ten on an average, to be stitched in blue paper, and delivered at a separate price, with the volume, should the purchasers wish to have them; but to be at their option.

This, Sir, is the plan which I beg the favour of you to give me your opinion of, and correct at your pleasure for me ... As to the prices, I beg the favor likewise of your advice. We have thought of about 7s.6d. a volume, and about 6d. (if not too much) for each folio print in each number. The allowance to the trade to be liberal, for the promoting the quick sale of the book. An agent in London has been proposed to me, who should have a like allowance with the trade; but it appears to me that an agent is of no kind of use, but merely to afford warehouse-room for the books, and will be only a kind of monopolist to rob the trade of their proper discount.[608]

William Bristow, as well as being a printer, bookseller and stationer, specialised also in the sale of prints. This accounts for the fact that each volume of the second edition, as it appeared, was accompanied by a set of folio prints — these were in fact reduced to six in number — which could be purchased separately, and which were mainly reproductions of the engravings that had accompanied the original folios. It may well be that Bristow, who had hitherto done little publishing on his own account, had asked Hasted to lay these proposals before the more experienced London publisher. Nichols does not seem to have suggested any amendments, for when Hasted told William Boteler in August that there was to be a second edition (in the letter which contained the glad news that William Boys had at last broken his silence and written to him again) the details given to Boteler were very similar to those outlined to Nichols:

I have within these few days executed an agreement with Mr Bristow of Canterbury, to print and publish an 8vo edition of my History, in 8 vols. It will be abridged of all tautologies, and uninteresting matters, the subjects will be new arranged, the present state of parishes enlarged, and to render it more pleasant and agreeable, all the notes excepting authorities will be added in the text, the families and estates will be continued to the present time and the whole corrected and amended, the parochial charities will be added compleat throughout, and the monuments and memorials in the western part of the county, omitted mostly in the 1st folio volume, will be added.[609]

Mentioning that Bristow's 'advertisement of proposals' was to appear the following week, Hasted hoped his friend would approve of the scheme. And he added, too, that the undertaking was intended, eventually, to be of some profit to himself, something which he felt obliged to emphasise, since he was reduced once more to begging for some money to live on. All of which makes it seem very unlikely that, without his confinement in prison to act as the spur, the second edition would ever have come about.

> I dread to ask a further favour of you, but I am now, and shall be, but for the assistance of my friends, in a state of unhappy necessity till the above time. Would you, Sir, befriend me with the loan of 5gns (I have not forgot your former liberal bounty nor shall I ever forget it) till January, the time of my lst volume's publication, when I will sacredly repay you on the first receipts from it. Indeed Sir, I am (at) in that crisis of want, nothing less than which should drive me to request so serious a mark of your friendship to me.[610]

It is of course true that Hasted no longer had many of his notes on the county, although he was still in possession of at least three series of commonplace books, as well as all the correspondence which he had amassed over the years in connection with his *History*.[611] However, most of the work which was required for the new edition entailed merely rearranging and abridging. New publications on the county were constantly coming out, and Hasted was probably confident of being able to obtain from these the slight additions of new material — complete lists of charities, present state of the parishes — which he wanted. Boys had spoken in 1794 of sending him the survey which had been commissioned from one of his relatives by the Board of Agriculture, John Boys' *General View of the Agriculture of Kent*, and he had seen, and made some notes on, Sir Frederick Eden's *State of the Poor*, which had come out in 1795.[612]

And so Hasted passed almost without a break from work on his first to work on his second edition. Correspondence for this, frequently channelled through the Somerset Coffee House although sometimes sent to him direct at King's College, St George's Fields, was exchanged with William Boys, William Boteler, John Lyon, Lord Guilford, Charles Small Pybus, John Springett Harvey and William Deedes among others. For Boys and Boteler, however, this was very much the second time round, and while time had, in a sense, stood still for Hasted, incarcerated in the King's Bench, it had carried both his friends into new areas of activity and interest. Boys had recently relinquished his practice at Sandwich in order to devote all his time to the Naval Hospital at Walmer, while Boteler, having exchanged a medical career for that of hop planter and farmer in 1792, was revelling in the outdoor life which came with it. 'This being the commencement of the shooting season, my time has been totally taken up in field pursuits', he wrote to Hasted in the middle of September 1796, and a week later, 'This being the shooting season, my time is so taken up in following the partridges and attending to some friends now visiting me, that I can only find a leisure hour on a Sunday to settle my debts with my correspondents, amongst whom, yours has hung on my mind'. Both letters, nevertheless, dealt with information for which Hasted had asked.[613]

The remainder of 1796 was probably employed in revising and rearranging the folio text for the new edition. There were also new dedications to be written. The first two volumes were given a suitable send-off with dedications to two noblemen having strong connections with Kent and seats in the county, Lord Romney, of The Mote at Maidstone, and Viscount Sydney, of Chislehurst. Thereafter the dedicatees, although distinguished, were chosen more particularly from among Hasted's friends. Volume 3 was dedicated to Sir John Henniker, his old friend from early Chatham days, now a very wealthy baronet, Volume 4 to Brownlow North, the former Dean of Canterbury and now Bishop of Winchester, Volume 5 to Charles Small Pybus, and Volume 6 to Thomas Astle.

Bristow seems to have been as businesslike as Hasted could have wished. His 'Proposals for an octavo edition of the History of Kent' were published in the county papers in October 1796, and Volume 1 was ready for distribution the following February:

> This day is published, price 7s.6d. in boards, printed on an elegant demy wove paper, with new types by Caslon — Vol.I of an Octavo edition of The History of Kent, in eight volumes, corrected, improved and brought down to the present time. To be continued in succeeding volumes at the end of every five months, and illustrated with maps, views of antiquities, etc. etc. By the Author of the Folio edition.[614]

More details followed, with regard to the folio plates, which were offered as a separate set of six at 3s.6d., and to the booksellers — and in spite of Hasted's initial reservations on the point, two London booksellers were named as agents, White's, of Fleet Street, and B.Law, of Stationer's Court, Ludgate Hill — while a postscript made it clear that the eventual appearance of Volume IV of the folio edition was not jeopardised by the publication of this new edition.

The historian was now seconded in his efforts by at least one of his sons. Charles was no George, who might have worked on the second edition with his father, but he was a willing messenger and publiciser of his father's work. Writing again to Richard Gough Samuel Denne noted:

Hasted's fourth volume goes on briskly, and his octavo edition of the History of Kent, ridiculous as the plan appeared to me, I find is likely to succeed much better than could in reason have been expected. To the account above given of the reduced History of our great County, I have to add, that a son of Mr Hasted, who is clerk to a brewer of Dartford, has lately circulated his father's proposals, and solicited subscriptions, not without success, as I am told.[615]

Bristow was even better than his word: the first three volumes of the new edition appeared in 1797, and the next four in 1798 — Volume 7 was being advertised in the local papers on the 25 December.[616] Hasted was worried that this might be too fast, although it must have been some relief to him that the actual publishing was now out of his hands.

The immediate reaction to the octavo edition seems to have been very favourable. In May following the appearance of the first two volumes William Boys was able to write, 'Your octavo edition of the History of Kent is much approved, and will answer your purpose, I believe, in every respect'.[617]

The Revd Samuel Denne was somewhat more measured: 'By the civility of Mr Peete, I had the first cut of the little dish of Mr Hasted's History of Kent, and the morsels of new matter were so few, that it was easy to digest them all without loss of time', he informed Richard Gough in June; and in September of the same year:

> Hardly can it be new to you, that the third volume of the diminutive History of a great County is published; and that printer Bristow has assigned his reasons for the unpleasant task he is under, of representing to the numerous subscribers the necessity of adding a shilling per volume to the first stipulated price. He, however, contends that the book at 8s.6d. in boards will be the cheapest of its kind, considering the size and engravings contained in it, of any at this time published;

to which he added a few days later:

> By the civility of Mr Peete, I have had the perusal of the third volume of the History of Kent in octavo; and sorry, though not surprised, was I to find that, notwithstanding there is an advance in price, the value of the performance is not increased.[618]

The reverend critic, who was able to make his perusals without paying for them — 'the civility of Mr Peete' clearly implying that the Dartford bookseller had allowed him to read the volume in the shop — seems to have been invited by Gough to review the octavo edition, a task which he refused for more than literary reasons:

> The commission of public censor of the diminutive edition of the History of our great County, I must be so free as to decline, for these among other reasons: first, that, though I address my letters to the author at a coffee-house in the Strand, I do not forget that he is an inmate in a large house trans Thamesin; second, that I cannot well become a criticiser without laying myself open to an imputation of betraying the secrets of a confidential correspondence; third, that the said octavo historian is incorrigible.[619]

Honour clearly preserved both Denne and Hasted.

Interest was still being shown in Volume IV of the folio edition. 'When,' Sir John Henniker had asked Hasted in 1796, 'are we to have the last volume of the folio book?'; William Boys, in 1797, knowing that Hasted was now deep in revisions for the second edition, admonished him, 'I hope you will not relax in your attention to the greater work, of which I hear nothing'; and William Deedes ended a letter of May 1799 with the words: 'I am glad to find your folio volume is to be published so soon'.[620]

Hasted's final worries over Volume IV concerned the plates. The text had been finished before he went into prison, but the plates which were to accompany it were far from ready — several of them perhaps barely thought of — so that the lapse of time before the publication of the final volume in 1799 allowed Hasted to present his public with a more worthy completion of his work than if it had actually appeared in 1794 or 1795.

We can see from the dates on some of the plates in this volume that they were being prepared throughout the 1790s. Plate 6, the 'Plan of Dover Harbour in the Reign of Queen Elizabeth', actually bears the legend 'Engraved by James Basire for Hasted's History of Kent 1797'. It was inscribed 'with much respect and gratitude by the author' to Charles Small Pybus, and in the Preface Hasted notes that 'to Mr Pybus, MP for Dover, and one of the Lords Commissioners of the Treasury, he has particular obligations for his very liberal assistance and much esteemed friendship throughout it'. The file of correspondence for Volume IV only shows Pybus corresponding with the historian, on the subject of Dover, in

1796, but one has to remember that Hasted's files relate solely to the subject matter of the *History*, and that personal letters were not included in them. We do not know when Hasted began corresponding with Pybus, but the Dover MP clearly crowned his support by donating for the *History* an interesting and very relevant plate which was specially commissioned from one of the leading engravers of the day.

For the rest, most of the plates seem to have been engraved by John Barlow, although quite a number of them, due to the financial stresses now bearing on the work, are no more than quarter-page sketches, and have no engraver's name. However, 'A Plan of the City of Canterbury and the adjoining suburbs, 1798' bears John Bayly's name, and shows that Hasted was still in touch with him, although he had not been used on a large scale after Volume I. The three Hundred maps here are unattributed, and from their style do not appear to be Bayly's work. They are, it has to be said, more interestingly presented than Bayly's maps, setting the Hundreds in context with names of places falling beyond their boundaries.

Barlow certainly engraved many of the Canterbury plates: the 'Plan of the Cathedral Church of Canterbury' is his, as are the engraving of the delightful 'Eadwin's drawing of the Cathedral and Priory', dating from the twelfth century, a view of the Castle, and another of Dungeon (now Dane John) Hill (the last-named a plate donated by James Simmons, who, as Alderman Simmons, had been responsible for laying out the hill with walks and donating it to the public), and several views of St Augustine's Abbey.

The last full-page plate in the whole work is a 'North View of the Ruins of St Augustine's Abbey, at Canterbury'. The foreground, as was frequently done, is enlivened with a small group of visitors, a man, a lady and a little girl. On this occasion, however, they are of more than passing interest. The man, a slim figure in a tall hat, with his hair in a queue, is holding a large book in which he is busily writing. There can be little doubt that this is Hasted himself, making an entry in one of the large common-place books which accompanied him on so many parochial visitations, the author finally made visible, taking a modest bow at the end of a lifetime's work. The lady, elegantly attired in a rather similar hat, is almost certainly Ann Dorman his wife, while the little girl must be Anne, his eldest daughter. The humour of showing Hasted thus engaged is probably that of both author and illustrator — Hasted's dry wit sparkles out at the reader from time to time from the text also.

A view of the Earl of Guilford's Waldershare House was drawn and engraved by Barlow, permission for this having been obtained through Hasted's friend Brownlow North, who was a son of Lord Guilford (and half-brother to the former prime minister, Lord North) and who, writing to Hasted on the 5 August 1796, informed him that Lord Guilford's answer had been: 'I shall be very happy to comply with Mr Hasted's request, if he will put me into a way of doing it. I cannot, however, but think this house will look ugly enough upon paper'. And the following January the Earl of Guilford was himself writing to Hasted to let him know that 'Whenever you please to send Mr Barton (sic) to Waldershare he will be welcome to take such a view as he thinks best'.[621] The plate is not actually inscribed to Lord Guilford, and it is possible that Hasted himself bore the cost of it, as he may have done of the engraving of Sir Narborough d'Aeth's Knowlton Court, prepared earlier and dated 1791.

    He was always aware that his maps might have been better, and circulated them as widely as he could, in the hope that an accretion of local corrections would result in a more perfect product. He was not always helped, however, when those to whom the maps were sent held on to them for too long. Even his friend William Boys could be guilty of this. 'As to these maps', wrote Hasted to Boteler on the 26 October 1798,

> I am sorry Mr Boys who in everything has been my good and experienced friend, was not so kind to return them earlier. He might well know his inability to serve me in it then, as well as now, when from the length of time he has kept them, I am precluded from requesting anyone else to assist me in them.

But he concluded with his usual good nature: 'However, I submit to this (which I am sure had he thought of it he would have done otherwise) with chearfulness: he has been too good a friend to me to be displeased at any inadvertent omission he may have been guilty of towards me'.[622]

    Once more, however, events — and these none of his making — were to break the fine thread of Hasted's industry. On the night of Saturday, 13 July 1799, the north-west wing of the King's Bench prison went up in flames. It was discovered at about nine o'clock in the evening. Several bodies of volunteers — readily available, as the war with France had called them into being — were quickly in attendance, coming from St George's, Bermondsey, St Saviour's, Lambeth, and Christ Church, Newington, together with a party of the Surrey cavalry, to prevent any of the prisoners from escaping (memories of prisoners breaking out of Newgate during the Gordon Riots were not yet twenty years old); but it was more than an hour before any fire engines arrived and began working. By then the fire had gained a terrible hold on the prison, with flames leaping to a great height, and destroying many of the prisoners' belongings. No lives were lost, but very considerable damage was caused to the prison itself. The *Gentleman's Magazine* for August 1799 carried a full report of it:

> How the fire was occasioned no one can with certainty tell. It broke out at No.10, in an upper room, in the farther corner of that part of the building where the tap is, just at the entrance of the prison. There was no fire in the room, nor was there even a fireplace. The person who occupied it was an old man, of the name of Adams, who at the time of the accident was drinking at the Brace ... The story he relates is, that his son had called upon him early in the evening, and had left him two £10 notes, which he was to call for again on Monday morning; for the better security of these notes, he put them in his trunk, and he supposes, at the time he did so, a spark from the candle fell into the trunk. ... There are between 80 and 100 rooms destroyed.[623]

One of the prisoners to lose his room was the ageing historian of Kent. The fire swept through No. 1 in 7, destroying as it did so some of the papers and records by which Hasted set most store, things which he had kept by him because they were personally dear to him. Among these was the Dingley pedigree, which he had removed from the manuscript book in which it had originally been placed before it was sold. There had been too much for him to carry out of his room in the short space of time before the fire attacked it: books, papers, records, in spite of the mean state in which he was now living, had been accumulating again over the years. It was perhaps a miracle that he did not lose everything. But he was to lament the loss of the family pedigree on several occasions after that, and one can imagine the old man in tears as flames, and smoke, and the lead boiling out of the stone staircase, made it impossible to rescue anything else.

In all, fifty-five rooms were destroyed. The prisoners themselves were at first suspected of having caused the fire in order to escape. None of them did so, and they were afterwards praised for their part in helping to bring it under control. Rebuilding of the damaged area was begun as quickly as possible and while this was taking place those who had lost their rooms were accommodated in shacks. Among them was Hoskins the postmaster. The *Description of the King's Bench Prison* says of him:

> He had been at the time so many years a prisoner, that ... the Bench was his world, and he surveyed its ruins with a pensive and a powerful feeling; as though the work of desolation had done its

worst, and robbed him of his home. In this state of mind he reared himself a shed, from the scattered fragments of the former one, and lived amidst the ruins seemingly content, sharing his meal with a poor mouse, who every morning visited him at the breakfast-hour, and was fed. Hoskins and the mouse found a home amidst desolation, and they sojourned together in unabated friendship, until the builder's hand disturbed their good harmony and good fellowship.[624]

It was perhaps the circumstance of the fire which ultimately brought the full horror of Hasted's position home to his friends. Without the stimulus of this event Hasted, too, might have been allowed to moulder away his final years in the prison, grown so used to it that it became home for him, as it had done for many other men: 'a happy and welcome asylum', where 'the unceasing persecution of relentless creditors' came to an end, providing for them 'a noiseless privacy, where they may commune with their own thoughts, and be in themselves the world which they have left'.[625] He had been reconciled with his wife after the break with Mary Jane Town, but it was possibly as a result of the fire that more thought was given by his friends to ways of securing his release.

But the historian himself, although he was probably informed of any efforts that were being made on his behalf, had been a prisoner for too long to harbour hopes of imminent freedom. By now one of the oldest prisoners, both by seniority and age, he was not expected to bivouac in a barrack for long, and was quickly installed in another room, No.6 in 1, where, as he told Boteler on the 5 October, 'By the help of good friends, I am tolerably well recovered from my losses by the dreadfull fire here, and indeed with much greater comfort than I was before'.[626]

Here he settled down once more to work on the second edition. The fire certainly caused an interruption to this: after three volumes in 1797, and four in 1798, only one was to appear in 1799. But the pause was perhaps providential, as it allowed the fourth volume of the folio edition to come on the market relatively untrammelled, and duly make its mark. For Hasted, its appearance was an occasion both for rejoicing and dismay. His October letter to Boteler, still on the theme of comfort, continued, 'And when I begin to taste the fruits of my 4th volume, I shall be made still more so.' But the next sentence contained the sobering information that, 'Mr S's charge for the cost of it is beyond all belief: no less a sum than £1100, all which, he must be paid before I can receive a shilling from it.' Publicity was not helped by the fact that the *Gentleman's Magazine* did not design to notice it.

There is no doubt that the friendship and encouragement of John Barlow became very important to Hasted over this time. Living locally, Barlow was able to visit Hasted frequently, popping in with a half-finished vignette in a manner which must have made it seem that they were merely two gentlemen living within a few streets of each other, and rendered the prison walls almost invisible. Visits, now, on the part of friends from his former life when they happened to be in London, which was not often, were clearly increasingly embarrassing events for both parties. The flow of correspondence between them, too, faltered, Hasted telling Boteler on one occasion that, in spite of the reconciliation between them after the differences of 1796, 'Mr Boys has almost ceased to write to me'. Virtually the only link between them now was the *History*. When Boys did write, it was from another world, one which Hasted, in his confinement, was precluded from sharing:

> I thank you for your kind enquiries after my family. I have four sons employed in the service of their country at sea; another is in France, superintending one of the four depots of British prisoners there and another is with me as dispenser of the hospital — all in health and doing well. One daughter married, another likely to be so; and another son at home. I am truly happy in what regards my family, and have scarcely anything to wish for, but peace.[627]

As had been the case with the folio edition, the second edition was to run to more volumes than the number originally envisaged. The likelihood of this occurring must have been apparent fairly early on, but it was not announced to the public until the eighth volume was being advertised in September 1799, with an apology and the hope that ten volumes would suffice.[628] In the event, of course, the second edition was to run to twelve books, and this must soon have become obvious to both Hasted and Bristow. In spite of Denne's strictures on 'the diminutive History', very little was being cut from the original, and additional material frequently compensated for its loss. Hasted was probably very reluctant to reduce the material on Canterbury, over which he had laboured long and lovingly, and it was finally decided to print this word for word as it had appeared in Volume IV of the folio edition and to make this section also available as a work on its own. Printed now with careful attention to spacing — which was Bristow's particular contribution throughout the second edition — it filled two further volumes, notified to the subscribers with a small 'NB' at the end of the advertisement for volume 10: 'NB: The History of the Church and City of Canterbury, now in the press, in two volumes, will form the completion of this work'.[629]

It would be unfair to suggest that there was any attempt on the part of Hasted and Bristow to mislead their subscribers. The volumes were only paid for as they were collected, and purchasers were obviously at liberty to decide not to take any more of them, something which both men would have been most anxious to avoid. The increase in size of the second edition was simply due to a miscalculation — perhaps on the part of both men: Hasted over-estimating the number of excisions he would want to make, and Bristow over-estimating the space he could save by running paragraphs together and cutting out headings.

Like Volume 3, the seventh volume had been dedicated to a former school friend who had become a patron of Hasted's work, in this case Joseph Musgrave, now living far from Kent; and Hasted had probably decided in advance that the proposed final volume on Canterbury should be dedicated to Archbishop Moore. With the dedications to books 8 and 9 he was to acknowledge the two men who had been among the closest to him in helping to bring the *History* to a successful conclusion, William Boys and William Boteler. Only then did Hasted feel at liberty to remember his own family, and perhaps more particularly those members of it who had stood by him in the difficult times of the recent past. They were too many to name: in the wording of the dedication to Volume 10 the vicar of Hollingbourne, as the eldest son, had to stand in for them all. But the charming vignette designed by John Barlow (who drew and engraved vignettes for all twelve dedications) makes graceful reference also to George, Anne and John as well as Edward, with the symbols of a church window for Edward, an anchor for John, a memorial for George, a girl for Anne — and an angel: whether as guardian spirit overall, or a symbol of the good-natured Charles, or even as a peace offering to his wife, one can only guess.

Of the two volumes on Canterbury, which appeared both as nos. 11 and 12 of the complete *History* and as 1 and 2 of a *History of Canterbury*, the first was dedicated to Archbishop John Moore, and the second to Canterbury's Dean and Chapter.

One can sense the relief in Bristow's advertisement which announced, in August 1801, the appearance of Volume 12. His foray into county publishing seems to have proved expensive. Like Hasted, he had found that costs have a tendency to escalate along the way: from 7s.6d. per volume, at which the work had originally been offered, the price had risen with volume 3 to 8s.6d., and despite a promise then that the whole work would continue at this price, Bristow found himself obliged to ask 10s.6d. for the final volume:

This day is published, price 10s.6d. in boards, Vol.XII and LAST, of the 8vo edition of the History of Kent.

After a list of the illustrations it contained, and the usual announcement of an accompanying set of folio prints, which purchasers might or might not wish to take also, the advertisement continued, as had several of the preceding ones:

> The many flattering commendations bestowed on this work by some of the most exalted literary characters in the kingdom, and by the subscribers in general, at the same time that they are highly gratifying to the undertaking, cannot fail of being a sufficient recommendation of it to a discerning public.

And it concluded with an offer of the two final volumes as a separate work:

> As the two last volumes of the foregoing work wholly relate to the History of the City and Metropolitical Church of Canterbury, the press has been so arranged as to enable the Printer to offer them to the public as a complete history of that respectable and ancient city; such gentlemen as are desirous of being furnished with this work are requested to apply without delay to Mr Bristow, the printer and publisher, at his house, on the Parade, Canterbury; or to the booksellers before-mentioned.[630]

However, Bristow was not the first in the field here. Simmons and Kirkby had already seen the advantages of a separate work of this kind, and extra sets of the second half of Volume IV of the folio edition, with its own title-page and pagination, had been printed by them as early as 1799, under the title of *The History of the Antient and Metropolitical City of Canterbury, Civil and Ecclesiastical*, by Edward Hasted, of Canterbury, Esq., F.R.S. and S.A., with Hasted writing an entirely new Preface for it.

Although the historian, as 'Edward Hasted, Esq. F.R.S. and S.A., late of Canterbury', was given his due as author on every title-page of the second edition, his name appeared in none of Bristow's advertisements, where he was described only as 'the Author of the Folio Edition' or, in connection with the *History of Canterbury*, as 'an Inhabitant'. Later editions of what became known as *The Canterbury Guide, or Traveller's Pocket Companion*, a mangled and abbreviated version of the Hasted, were to appear until the 1830s. In 1805 it was being printed and sold under this title by Cowtan and Colegate, William Bristow's successors, at the Kentish Chronicle Office. It was clearly very successful, and perhaps helped Bristow to recover some of the cost of the publication of the *History* itself. But it was not for the sake of a Canterbury guide only that Hasted had spent the greater part of his adult life on original research.

Naturally there were times when he thought of other things. On one occasion he made a translation of some Latin lines he had come across in a Harleian MS, copying it out into one of his notebooks, and signing and dating it, 1800. The wise prescriptions it contains must have caused him to smile wryly, since a healthy style of living had to be followed perforce by those confined without an income in a debtors' prison:

> Would you be well and means of health pursue,
> Avoid dull care, and frantic passion too;
> Of wine be sparing; suppers e'er refuse;
> Rise after meals, and midday sleep disuse;
> Your water ne'er withhold by frequent stay,
> Nor your digestion stop by long delay.[631]

Even in the King's Bench the turn of the century must have given rise to a certain amount of celebration among the prisoners, and it is not impossible that the above lines were dashed off, as such things often are, as part of a game played among a group of the more scholarly of the inmates, forgetting their individual worries in the conviviality of an evening spent toasting the new century. But it was also a time for looking back, and Hasted, reflecting on all that had passed since he had been a little boy playing in his father's garden at Hawley, felt moved to make a record of his own family history, as far as he knew it. He was to entitle it 'Anecdotes of the Hasted family, drawn up to the best of my recollection and to the best of my remembrance in the year 1800 by me Edward Hasted'. And he chose for it two Latin mottoes, the first referring to the family's fortunes, and the loss of them, and the second a more personal one: 'Nos quoque floruimus, sed flos erat ille caducus, faeciniis periit flebilis ille dolis', which translates as 'We also flourished, but that flowering decayed; it perished lamentably through base trickery'; and the second, written twice, first as 'P.P.O.', and then in full as 'Peccavi, paenitui, oblivio', relating to a chapter in his life for which he could blame no one but himself, and meaning, 'I have sinned, I have repented; the past is expunged'.[632]

The Anecdotes were begun in a small notebook, and provide us with valuable information about Hasted's early years. The first notebook was filled, and 'Book the Second' started, but the initial impetus to tell the family story seems to have worn off — perhaps there were too many painful episodes to recount — and the second notebook went no further than page 13, breaking off with his mother's move to Canterbury in 1770. Hasted valued what he had written, however, and the two small notebooks were specifically left to Edward in his will.

But the Anecdotes were not Hasted's only literary production of the year 1800. It is almost certain that by then revision of his *History* was complete, and he was again in need of something with which to occupy his mind. Whether the commission came as a godsend, or whether it was something that had been requested earlier and promised by Hasted when he should have finished work on his second edition, certain it is that in 1800 he was able to present the Earl of Radnor with a four-hundred-page manuscript, containing 'The History and Account of the antient Barony, Honor, and Lordship of Folkestone in the County of Kent. Taken from records in the public offices, and libraries, muniments, and other authorities, both manuscript and printed. Collected and digested by Edward Hasted Esqr, F.R.S. and S.A. at the desire of the right Honble Jacob Bouverie Earl of Radnor, Viscount Folkestone etc. etc. the present lord and possessor of it'.

Donated by a later earl to Folkestone library, the work echoes Hasted's original pages on the town, but with much new material incorporated. It is beautifully written out, in his own hand, with several of the engravings which had appeared in the printed *History* inserted as illustrations. There are also nine pedigrees of the families connected with Folkestone since the time of the Conqueror — that for the Bouveries, not surprisingly, being particularly detailed. And Hasted is punctilious in giving his sources, not only in brief footnotes, but also in an appendix. The volume's vellum binding, with its gilt ornamentation, was almost certainly provided by the Earl of Radnor — the son of Hasted's early patron, and thus the second of his line to interest himself in the historian.

In spite of the reconciliation with his family, the occupation provided by work on the second edition and the Folkestone history, and the pleasant collaboration, in the matter of illustrations, with his friend John Barlow, as well as a steely determination to survive, Hasted remained in the greatest penury. It does not appear that his hopes of considerable financial gain from the second edition were ever realised. A cheerful letter to Boteler in 1800 seems to show him enjoying (if such a word is not out of place) some measure of financial independence, but this was probably only temporary, and was certainly insufficient to cover a crisis.[633] Friends, when such occasions arose, were better placed than family to help him, but the crisis had to be extreme for Hasted to bring himself to appeal to them. One such occurred in the summer of 1801, when the ageing historian sent a desperate appeal to Thomas Astle, the friend of his youth, whose career, marked by the acquisition of wealth through marriage to an heiress and a steady progression of lucrative posts, had been the exact inverse of that of Hasted.

In the brief correspondence surviving from this period, dealing mainly with place-name or genealogical queries put by Astle, Hasted is constantly at pains to thank his friend for his liberality, although in 1798 this seems only to have taken the form of 'the friendly manner in which you mention my debt to you' — money obviously lent on a former, but not on the present occasion — while in 1800 the historian is grateful for 'the liberal manner in which you have cancelled my note'. There is only one other letter to Astle which refers to financial assistance, or to Hasted's need for it (and there were perhaps no others, since the correspondence appears to have been carefully preserved by Astle himself). This was written in July 1801, and seems to have been wrung from Hasted by a wholly unforeseen circumstance: from his mention of an affliction, he had probably fallen ill, and there was no provision for medical care in the King's Bench — 'neither pity nor relief', as James Neild put it, 'for sickness accompanied with poverty'.[634] The letter summarises the historian's situation so lucidly and so touchingly that it deserves to be quoted in full.

> Dear Sir, I sit down with no small reluctance to write this letter to you. I feel my presumption in it, and yet I trust to your feelings, and the friendship that has for so many years subsisted between us. I have been near 7 years within these walls, during the latter part of which I have struggled against adversity, and by the help of many noble and generous friends who knew me in the days of prosperity, among whom yourself stands foremost, and by the labours of my pen I have till now borne myself up from sinking under it. My property has been torn from me and kept possession of by the villainy of an attorney, and the profit I hoped for from my History is locked up and useless to me, from the balance due to the printer, and the copies, upwards of 260 remain, an unsaleable pledge for it with him. These were all my hopes, and they are frustrated, and I am now come to a state of distress and woe, and I feel it still more severe from the want of those necessaries which my age, and what I have formerly known, require for my comfort. You have at all times, sir, shewn your friendship most liberally to me, I feel the weight and gratitude of it, it has never been from my mind, and my firm hope was never to have trespassed on you again; but tho' I struggled against it and

delayed it for this week past, yet I am at last, at last compelled by urgent necessity, hard fate — that is so — to request you once more to assist me in the hour of my distress.

You have known me, sir, when my heart has been open to all my friends, and my hospitality equal to my heart, a bitter and yet not an unpleasing remembrance, and I am far from repenting of it — that has long been passed by, never to return.

With much diffidence I request the kindness of your assistance in my present unexpected crisis of affliction, for it has come on me suddenly and unexpectedly, when I had no idea of the so hasty approach of it. I am no spendthrift here, sir, I live secluded from everyone, almost a hermit, on hard scanty fare, and only know the plenty and luxuries of life by distant remembrance. I think from all your past kindness to me, that you will not refuse my request in the hour of my distress, and be assured it will be ever remembered by me with a heartfelt gratitude.[635]

What Astle's response was we do not know, but it seems clear that had Hasted not been discharged the following year, with permission to draw a small income from his estates, he would soon have succumbed to the combined weight of the life he was being forced to lead in the King's Bench prison, and the need to approach his former friends in the vein of a beggar.

Chapter 14

The Scholar in the Garret

It was, as Hasted had told Boteler, a 'malicious attorney' who constantly baulked his efforts to come to an agreement with his creditors, but it seems, in the end, to have been an attorney who hit on the way to secure Hasted's release from prison and enable him to reassert his ownership of the estates which Thomas Williams was dishonestly holding. Hasted's creditors were not unwilling to come to some accommodation with him, but Williams seems to have been able to counter whatever was proposed with a move of his own. It had become a macabre game of chess, with the Dartford attorney able to put his opponent in check to the end of his life. And Hasted, without going so far as to wish for Williams's death, had begun to feel that only if he outlived the attorney would he have any chance of regaining his freedom.

Any worries he may still have had over the future of his family, and in particular his daughters Anne and Katherine, now in their mid-thirties, had been laid to rest early in 1800 with the death of his sister-in-law, Mary Dorman.

Mary, it will be remembered, had become a wealthy woman under the will of Thomas Harris, who had died in 1769. Together with property in Barming, bequeathed to her for life only, she had also been left a considerable sum of money, much of which had been invested in the 'public funds', and at her death she left interest or dividend from such stock to her two surviving sisters, Mrs Margaret Colyer (formerly Mrs Margaret Pope), and Mrs Ann Hasted, stating specifically that their receipts alone should suffice for the trustees, who were named as her nephews Edward and Charles, and that the sisters' legacies should not 'be subject to the debts, controul or engagements of their present or any after taken husbands'.

Mrs Ann Hasted, the sole executrix, was also the main beneficiary, the interest from one thousand pounds-worth of stock going to Margaret, and interest from the residue, which seems to have been considerable, to Ann. Small amounts of stock were to be transferred to Mary's nieces, Anne and Katherine Hasted, the difference in the amounts — one hundred pounds-worth going to Anne and two hundred pounds-worth to Katherine — probably revealing where the two girls' sympathies lay between their divided parents. Mrs Hasted was to benefit also from the interest left to Margaret, if she survived her, and after the death of both surviving sisters Mary's money was to go to her Hasted nephews and nieces, although all did not benefit equally. Edward and Charles were to share between them the £1000 of stock the interest on which had originally gone to Margaret Colyer, while Anne was to receive £1000 and Katherine 'all the rest and residue of my stock'. John, the ship's surgeon, was to receive £200. Edward and Charles, as the trustees, were responsible for transferring the estate as their aunt had directed. Only Francis, who had been out of the country now for some years, received no mention in his aunt's will. Apart from Hasted's second son, however, all the historian's children were clearly much indebted to their Aunt Mary both during and after her life.[636]

Hasted himself remained in the direst penury, fortified only by a faint hope of one day securing his release and being in a position to pay off his creditors. His existence was utterly hand to mouth, dependent on what visitors pressed on him as they left or correspondents sent him. Boteler is thanked in a number of letters for his kindnesses, and seems to have provided continual, if perhaps irregular, support. More distant friends might send something when the thought crossed their mind. Joseph Musgrave, sending him in 1799 'a bank bill for five pounds — an emblem of the times', added the hope that 'if I prove the least of your benefactors, you will not consider me the least of your well wishers' — which although clearly kindly meant was tantamount to suggesting that the historian might exist on the breath of goodwill!'[637] There can be no doubt that members of his family helped also when they could: Anne and Charles seem to have been the most sympathetically disposed towards him, and the Revd Edward Hasted of Hollingbourne, too, may have assisted from time to time, though racked on a Procrustean bed, the four corners of which pulled variously in the direction of duty to a parent, a natural antipathy to his father, the charity and forgiveness directed by his holy calling, and the individual Christian's horror at adulterous sin — all of which perhaps left him with the feeling (which seems to have been shared to some extent by the historian himself) that retribution was being justly exacted.

Crises could still occur — indeed, Hasted could have little hope that there would be much improvement in his personal situation even were he to be released — and at such times there was nothing for it but to beg for help, as he was forced to do in his letter to Thomas Astle of July 1801.

By then, nevertheless, providence had shown that it might be on Hasted's side, for Thomas Williams had died towards the end of 1800, leaving his extensive property, in which were included the Hasted estates, to his brother Richard, vicar of the neighbouring parish of Horton Kirby. The Revd Richard Williams now had to become the focus of Hasted's attempts to obtain his release. One might have supposed that he would prove a less intractable adversary of the imprisoned historian. However, on his death, only a few months later, the Hasted estates were again passed on within the Williams family, the main beneficiary being the attorney John Williams, nephew of both brothers, who had been in partnership with his uncle Thomas. Once more an approach was made to the attorney, Mr Rolfe of Maidstone, who was acting for the principal creditors, the Ruggs, with a request for terms to be agreed for the release of the unfortunate prisoner.

There can be little doubt that 'the Hasted case' had by now become notorious among legal circles in Kent. There was increasing dissatisfaction in the country generally with the way debt was being handled, and numerous articles and pamphlets pointed out the flaws in a system which incarcerated debtors, putting it out of their power to improve their position, and sometimes even resulting in their death in jail from starvation. In spite of this, major reform of the system was over half a century away — arrest and imprisonment for debt was not to be abolished until 1869[638] — and until the law was changed it was necessary to work within the antiquated framework and find a legal channel for the release of a prisoner so held.

Mr Rolfe, who according to Hasted had been informed very early on of the existence of the bond which provided for the reconveyance of the estates if they could be sold for a better price within six months of Williams's coming into possession of them, suddenly began to urge the production of this document. Hasted himself, from the moment when it had first been handed to him, seems to have dismissed all thought of the bond ever being of use, and now could hardly remember what he had done with it. However, another firm of attorneys was also involved, that of Simmons and Scudamore, and Mr Simmons, too, was insistent that the bond must be found:

> Soon afterwards Mr Simmons called on Mr H and having gained likewise knowledge that there was such a bond, but that it had been for a length of time mislaid, he likewise pressed anxiously for the search after it. Accordingly Mr H wrote to his son the Revd Mr Hasted at Hollingborne to request him to spare no pains to search among the chests of confused papers belonging to his father which he had brought from Canterbury. After some days' search the bond was at last found, and copies of it were taken and sent both to Mr Rolfe and Mr Simmons.[639]

Thus Hasted describes the momentous finding of the document which was to be used as the basis for his release. It comes from a statement of the events immediately preceding his flight to France which Hasted was asked to provide in December 1801, and which resulted in the long, ten-page document that he completed on the 15th of that month, heading it 'A Statement of Mr Hasted's transactions with the late Mr Thos Williams concerning the conveyance of his estates to him and the bond Mr Williams gave him to reconvey the same'. Most of this had to be written from memory, for, as Hasted mentions at the end, fate had dealt him a further blow in the loss of many personal papers in the fire at the King's Bench prison two years earlier.

The 'Statement' deals mainly with Hasted's meetings with Thomas and John Williams prior to his flight to France, the agreement by Thomas Williams to take the Hasted estates at a price only sufficient to repay the loans arranged by Williams himself, and the giving by the attorney of a bond, or promise, that in the event of a better sale proving possible within a limited time the estates would be reconveyed to Hasted. Williams, cool and reflective in the presence of a panicking Hasted, had had the upper hand at each encounter, and when Hasted finally received the bond, after having been made to wait for it, he found that the attorney, who had initially suggested a validity of twelve months, had reduced this to six.

It is no wonder that Hasted tossed the bond into a chest of papers in angry frustration, knowing that it would be impossible for him to return from France and take advantage of it within so short a period. As Mr Rolfe and John Simmons now saw, however, extenuating circumstances existed which might make a court willing to override the limitation on time. The temporary sale to Thomas Williams would continue to be held as such, and Hasted would be able to demand the resale of his estates for the purpose of satisfying the still outstanding creditors. Thus would be resolved the stalemate which had kept those creditors unpaid and Hasted in prison all these years.

Legal advice concerning the bond was sought from John Springett Harvey, a Master in Chancery, and a relative of William Boteler. Although Harvey felt that the length of time which had elapsed since the giving of the bond had weakened Hasted's case, he considered that it might still be won:

> There are strong circumstances in addition to what appears on the face of the bond why the conveyance to Mr Williams should be considered in a Court of Equity only as a mortgage; and I think that Court would have compelled Mr Williams to reconvey the estates to the Trustees, to whom Mr Hasted had previously conveyed them in trust for the payment of his debts, on being paid

the several sums of money due to him, if Mr Hasted had applied for that purpose within a reasonable time after the date of the bond, tho' after the time specified therein. ... It appears to me to be a case, which under all circumstances, if they can be proved, affords expectation of success.[640]

Mr Harvey emphasised, however, that there were three important questions which would have to be answered. The first related to the length of time which had elapsed before the bond was brought forward; the second to the value of the estates; and the third to the extent of Thomas Williams's knowledge of 'Mr H's distressed situation at the time of his conveyance to him of these estates'. To each of these there was a satisfactory answer. The bond had not only been mislaid, but Hasted, first as a fugitive, and then as a prisoner, had been unable to make use of it; the greater value of the estates than the sum given by Williams was not difficult to establish; and there was no question of Williams, as Hasted's lifelong 'confidential attorney, adviser and the sole director of all Mr Hasted's law and money business', not being aware of the extent of his financial distress at the time he took possession of the estates.[641]

This, in the event, was to be the view taken by the courts. The slow course taken by the law, and particularly by cases in Chancery, which was where Hasted's case was heard, meant that it was only after the historian's death that the sale of the Hasted estates actually took place. Nevertheless, the fact that such a process was about to be set in motion resulted immediately in Hasted's semi-release. On the 24 February 1802 he received permission to live outside the prison and within 'the Rules'[642] and on the 13 May of the same year came the order signed by Lord Ellenborough, in the matter of Robert Rugg and John Rugg, executors of Robert Rugg, deceased, against Edward Hasted, 'that the defendant be discharged out of the custody of the Marshal and as to this action the debt and costs being satisfied'.[643] After seven years Hasted was at last a free man, free, that is, to institute litigation for the recovery of his estates and the repayment of his debts.

The first step towards the repayment of the outstanding creditors was the recovery of the estates. The bond played an important part in this, and it was due to its existence that a case could be brought against John Williams, Thomas Williams's nephew, and against other members of the Williams family who had benefited from the old attorney's will and, subsequently, that of his brother Richard. It was not possible for Hasted, in his penniless situation, to bring such a case himself, and it was for this reason that rights to the bond and its benefits were assigned to Simmons and Scudamore, the attorneys acting for the families of Davies and Rugg, who had remained as Hasted creditors when Thomas Williams took possession of the whole estate. The case was instituted in Chancery in 1803 as Davies v. Williams. It dragged on for several years. Hasted himself, and subsequently all the surviving Hasted children, including John Septimus, serving as a surgeon on the high seas, and Francis Dingley, now thousands of miles away in India, were named in the suit as defendants. Not until 1808 was a decree to be obtained, when Lord Eldon's decision, as had been expected, went against the Williamses, the conveyance of 1790 being ordered to stand only as a security for the sum given for it at that time.[644]

The whole miserable business might never have happened had Hasted used another attorney, or had he kept a closer watch on what was going on over the years. As he realised later — too late — it was indecent how much money Williams had made on the transactions which he had handled for the historian: in his 'Statement' Hasted underlined that he had probably made a triple profit on each of them. The choice of Thomas Williams as his attorney had probably been quite fortuitous: Hasted, living at the time on the outskirts of the village of Sutton-at-Hone, would naturally have sought an attorney in the neighbouring town of Dartford to handle the variety of business resulting from his position as a gentleman and the owner of a very dispersed estate, and Williams was probably recommended to him by a friend. The young squire already had some experience of attorneys and was inclined to be wary of them — remembering how his mother had become entrapped in some way by Edmund Browne soon after his father's death, and how the family fortunes had only been saved from the London attorney's clutches by his own sudden demise. Thomas Williams, from an established Dartford family and much the same age as Hasted himself, must have made a very different impression. Hasted had continued to use him even after the move to Canterbury, and over the years Williams had become the historian's trusted legal and financial adviser.

Hasted could have exercised some control over what Williams was doing, checked facts and figures with him. He was no novice in the law, although he had not completed his law studies, and the figure-work entrusted to him as a justice shows that he was perfectly competent in this field also. But two factors conspired to make him disdain to do the necessary auditing. It has already been suggested that Hasted, pursuing his genealogical enquiries on his own behalf, had discovered a distant relationship between himself and Williams. That in itself would have inspired an implicit trust in the Dartford attorney. In addition, however, Thomas Williams was, or became, exceedingly wealthy. Actively engaged in a profession as they were, attorneys could not normally expect to be addressed as esquire, but there is no doubt that Williams, with an income several times larger than that of Hasted, earned the title as many times over. In addition to the various estates that came his way, he had also become the patron of the living of Horton Kirby, to which, in 1770, he presented his brother Richard. Hasted, there is no doubt, had trusted Thomas Williams, both as a distant relative and as a gentleman. The code of honour in which he fervently believed would not allow him to suspect that another gentleman might be capable of a dishonourable act.

How deluded he had been in this belief his long retention in the King's Bench prison had given him but too much leisure to reflect. Now, after seven years, justice was at last to be done, and the Chancellor's decree had paved the way to the settling of his debts and the clearing of his name. In the meantime he appears to have been allowed to draw a small income from his property which did little more than ensure his independence. But at least he was partially free, and the slur and taint of imprisonment in the King's Bench were things of the past. On being released into the Rules in February 1802, as he tells us in his brief Chronology, he had found lodgings first in Clarence Place, and then in Greenhouse Row, and it was there that he received the happy news that he was once more a totally free man.

He could now, in theory at least, have returned to Kent and to his wife, who must have been living in comfort since the death of her sister two years earlier. But it was probably much too late for both of them: it was nearly twenty years since they had become estranged, and despite their reconciliation in 1798 the likelihood is that now, both around seventy, they had little in common. And Hasted would have found himself in the humiliating position of dependence on his wife, too reminiscent of his prison dependence on charity. Many friends had remained kind to him at a distance, but that kindness would not hold — he may well have made the trial of it — at closer quarters. And so he remained where he was, living in the St George's Fields and Blackfriars area, frequently changing his lodgings, but never moving far away: in 1803 he was lodging with a Mrs Marks, opposite the Magdalen Hospital for Repentant Prostitutes; in 1804 he moved to Belvidere Place; and then he went back again to Greenhouse Row. It was an area which, from being originally considered beyond the pale, had in recent years undergone considerable redevelopment, with the laying out of the Royal Circus, ornamented with an obelisk, at the meeting point of five roads, chief among them Great Surrey Street which led straight up to Blackfriars Bridge. And it had besides particular attractions for Hasted. It was cheap, his friend John Barlow lived nearby, and it was easy to walk from there into the centre of London, a never-failing source of interest. The elderly historian was probably often to be seen browsing in one or other of the many booksellers' shops there. A letter of November 1803 to his friend Boteler ends with the following PS:

> There are two most superb collections of books now on sale. I think I never looked over two such in any auction catalogue before; the one Sir Horace Mann's library, to be sold among his other effects in Conduit Street on Monday next, the other a still more curious one at Richardson's Print Shop in the Strand. Among the books are all the local English Histories, some of them the most scarce, many of them on large paper, and all in the most excellent preservation. I cannot but think it would have highly gratifyed you, at least to have looked them over. I was highly entertained for some hours in looking them thro'. The sale begins on Monday and lasts all the week. I cannot learn whose they were, but they are certainly of great value and will fetch a large sum if the dreadfull crisis of the time and the general want of money does not depreciate their value.[645]

Freed from the isolation of prison, he was now encountering another, that of old age. A number of his former friends had already, in the words of William Solly, left the stage, and others were soon to follow them. Dr Ducarel, a stout, strong man, who had had every expectation of being able to 'take a peep into the next century', had died suddenly in 1785, on hearing a report — erroneous, as it turned out — of his wife's death. The Revd Dr Osmund Beauvoir had succumbed at Bath in 1789. John Thorpe had lost his wife Catherine in the same year, and had had her remains placed in a vault in Bexley churchyard, excavated next to the wall of his own grounds, with a large fossil as the keystone, which he had intended should serve also for his own memorial. But marrying his housekeeper, who had been the widow of an old college friend, he had moved soon afterwards to Surrey and then to Wiltshire, leaving behind the house in Bexley, with the garden he had landscaped and the fishing in the river Cray which ran through it, all of which had been so much a part of his persona, to die at Chippenham and be buried at Harden Huish in 1792. The very first year of Hasted's release was darkened by the deaths of three of those who had formerly been closest to him. 1803 brought him news of the death of William Boys, whose life had begun to draw to a close in 1800 when he suffered the first of a series of strokes, of Thomas Astle, who died of dropsy, and of his wife Ann.

Ann Hasted, who may have been living in Dartford at the time of her death, was not given long in which to enjoy the legacy left her by her sister. She was buried at Sutton-at-Hone, in the same grave as her sister Mary. A proposed epitaph for her, intended to be inserted on the decorated headstone which commemorated 'Mrs Mary Dorman', would have noted that she 'married Edward Hasted formerly of St John's in this parish Esqr, Deputy Lieutenant and a Justice of the Peace for this County, by whom she left surviving four sons and two daughters and died September 16th 1803 aged 71 much respected and sincerely lamented by all who knew her'.[646] Mary Dorman's gravestone still stands in Sutton-at-Hone churchyard, alongside the carved memorials to her mother, Mrs Dorothy Dorman, and her father, John Dorman, but the words which should have commemorated Ann Hasted were never to appear. Was her husband among the mourners at her funeral? It seems quite possible that he was: the two had been reconciled for some time, and as his will shows, his 'late wife's gold wedding ring' passed into his possession and was one of the items ultimately bequeathed to Edward.

In many cases the families who had been known to Hasted were now represented by another generation, and it was to this second generation that he was obliged to turn in the hope of possible assistance — not in the form of money, but of a recommendation to some employment, the income from which might supply a few comforts for his declining years. An early supporter, and a very keen one, had been the first Earl of Radnor, who, dying in 1776, had not lived long enough to see the publication of even the first volume of the *History*. To his son, the second earl, Hasted wrote now, wondering if he could recommend him to the position of a schoolmaster. Old Lord Romney, whose longevity appeared to have rendered him an immovable part of the Kentish scene — he had inherited his title in 1724, well before Hasted's birth — had died in 1793, and it was to his son, now the Earl of Romney, that Hasted addressed the following letter, which was sent from his lodgings at Mrs Marks's in December 1803:

> My Lord, The many repeated instances of friendship, which I have received for such a series of years past, both from yourself, and from your late honorable, and much respected father, encourages me to take this liberty, which requires but too much your Lordship's pardon for my presumption in it, but that generous feeling, which you have always held forth toward me, will I hope be extended once more in my present interesting crisis. I have, My Lord, after 8 years unhappy restraint cleared myself of all my embarrassments by a sacrifice of all I was possessed of, within a trifle, and am now left at a very advanced period of life, to the wide world, to look for almost wholly a subsistance, after having

devoted 40 years, as your Lordship well knows, in the compiling of my History of Kent, for the service of the public in general, and of the county itself in particular. I wish not, My Lord, to sit down in idleness, but to earn my livelyhood in any station I may be so fortunate to acquire, be it ever so humble, for I must banish all other thoughts, and a very moderate addition to the trifle I have left, would make me most happy and comfortable.[647]

The letter continues with a query as to whether Lord Romney might perhaps be able to recommend the writer to some lowly post in the government offices at Somerset House, or any other public office. And Hasted ventured to hope that if such a post could indeed be found for him, 'it might be such, as may not be uncomfortable for my time of life'. Clerical positions of this kind, however, were not always available, or were perhaps unsuitable, for a man of seventy, and Hasted's applications, although they did not always fall on deaf ears, were unsuccessful in this direction. Lord Romney, in particular, was unlikely to have forgotten what he may have seen as the pointed irony of a book being dedicated to him, the president of the Thatched House Society, otherwise the Society for the Discharge and Relief of Persons imprisoned for Small Debts, by someone who was himself a prisoner for debt, and beyond the help of the Society.[648]

However, there was another avenue to explore, and this was to prove, for a while, more fruitful. It was perhaps as the result of a modest note, posted at the Society of Antiquaries, offering help as a researcher or an amanuensis, that he came into contact with the Revd Richard Yates who was, like himself, a Fellow of the Society. Yates was at the time chaplain to His Majesty's Royal Hospital at Chelsea and rector of Ashen in Essex. He was also a native of Bury St Edmunds, and inheriting his father's interest in the antiquities of the place had set out in 1802 his *Proposals for publishing by subscription ... an Illustration of the Monastic History and Antiquities of the Town and Abbey of St Edmund's Bury*. He had brought out a first volume on this subject in 1805 containing most, although not all, of what was intended to be Part I, and a single chapter of Part II, of which another thirty-three were projected. In addition there was to be an Appendix, consisting of 'An Accurate Transcript of the present Bury Charters'.[649]

The premature publication of some of this material was undoubtedly due to Yates's desire to establish himself as a man of letters, and he was rewarded in this in 1806 by being appointed as one of the Alternate Preachers of the chapel of the newly established Philanthropic Society. He continued working on the projected completion of his *History of Bury*, but, inundated by material and with ever less time to devote to it, realised that without expert assistance he would make little progress. Hasted was the archetypal scholar starving in a garret. He had unparalleled skills in deciphering and translating ancient documents, and was obviously the very person whom Yates needed.

The surviving correspondence seems to indicate that Hasted began working for the Bury historian in May 1806. The 7th of that month found him writing to Yates from 4 Greenhouse Row:

> Sir, I have been prevented from beginning your task till last Monday. Inclosed I have sent you what I have done in it — but being without a guide or any kind of instructions, I know not whether I have done it in that manner you wished. I have made it a kind of abbreviation of the MS, leaving out much of the superstitious and more trifling stuff in it. I observe in the poems at the beginning, especially the latter part of them, some circumstances relating to the Monastery of St Edmund which may perhaps have escaped you and be worth noticing.
>
> What I have done has taken up 2 days close application. The MS, from the numerous abbreviations, mostly 3 in each word, and those frequently of different meanings of interpretation (sic), requires much attention for that purpose. It is indeed a kind of short hand, and I don't know, among the many MSS I have had, I ever met with one more intricate or required more poring over it, and it has, even in this early part of it, almost made me purblind; and being without those glossarys and diplomatic books to refer to, which are so necessary for interpretations of these sorts of MSS, I am like a man going to battle without his arms to enable him to fight and overcome his adversary.
>
> You will be so good, Sir, to pass your judgment on what I have done and to let me know it and give me your future instructions in every particular.[650]

Hasted seems to have been asked to continue translating a manuscript where another hand, perhaps Yates's own, had left off. It appears to have dealt with the life of St Edmund, and to have been one of a number of manuscripts which Richard Gough had acquired from the antiquary Thomas Martyn and which, knowing his interest in the subject, he had made available to Yates.[651]

Not surprisingly, the Kentish scholar's work was found most satisfactory, and he was sent a number of manuscripts to translate. Initially, at any rate, he probably derived great pleasure from collaborating with another enthusiast. In July he was sent a piece of work which appears to be 'the business of the register' referred to in the second letter in the Hasted-Yates correspondence. Among the numerous sheets in the Yates archive in the British Library which, although not attributed, are clearly in the Kentish historian's hand, are some which Hasted has headed 'Extracts from the Register of the Abbey of Bury St Edmunds, entitled … the Black Register of the Vestry', although this has been crossed through and replaced with the heading 'Bulls of Alexander II and Urban III'.[652] The work seems to have been nearing completion by the middle of the month, and on Thursday 17 July Hasted scribbled a hasty note which caught the 8 o'clock post and went off to 'Revd Mr Yates, Chelsea College, Chelsea, Middx':

> Mr Hasted's respects to Mr Yates. He shall tomorrow have finished the business of the register which he intrusted him with. If Mr Yates will indulge him so far, he will gladly meet him at Mr Winchester's with the MSS on Saturday at 12 o'cl., or, if that is inconvenient to Mr Yates, any day next week, except Monday and Tuesday, when if he has any further commands for Mr H. he hopes to receive them there from him, with the MS for that purpose. Or if it is too inconvenient for Mr Yates to meet him there, he will wait on him at Chelsea any day excepting the Monday and Tuesday above mentioned, between 12 and one o'cl. Should he not hear in the meantime from Mr Yates, he shall take it for granted Saturday will be convenient to meet at Mr Winchester's, and will be there accordingly with punctuality.[653]

'Mr Winchester's' was very probably the stationer's shop kept by Winchester and Son at 61 Strand, which would have been a convenient place to meet and was something like mid-way between Greenhouse Row and Mr Yates's Chelsea address. The 73-year-old Hasted was retaining his health — who knows, the enforced meagre diet of the last ten years may have contributed to this — but wiry and active as he remained, he must have tired much more quickly than in his younger days, and was no doubt happy to avoid when he could the long trek to Chelsea and back, which he would almost certainly have performed on foot.

There must have been other letters in the correspondence, but only three survive, and they certainly do not refer to all the pieces of work which Hasted did for the would-be historian of Bury St Edmunds. The Yates MSS volumes in the British Library contain no less than ten pieces of work in Hasted's hand, all apparently translations from the Latin, and most of them averaging seven or eight sides of paper. One of them, however, headed 'Pleas of the Crown before H. de Bath and associates, Justices Itinerant in Co. Suffolk in the 29th year of the reign of Henry son of K. John', covers no less than forty-seven sheets. This was intended to appear in Chapter IX of Part I, 'Franchise', while seven pages beginning with a 'Writ of the Chancery of the King', plus another two pages, would have been in Chapter X, 'The Mint'. Further work by Hasted was to have appeared in Part II, Chapter X, 'Lord Abbot's Palace', and in Chapters XXII, XXVI, and XXIX, respectively 'Charnel House and Chapel', 'Town Gates', and 'Hospitals, Guilds, Chauntries'. The extracts from the register mentioned in Hasted's second letter to Yates covered thirteen sides, and would apparently have formed part of a revised Chapter IV in Part I.[654]

And there was more, written out in the firm and elegant hand which had changed little over the years. An undated list in the Kentish historian's writing of the lines he had recently translated from various folios gives some idea of the concentrated work that he was doing for Yates. It came to a total of three hundred and ninety, and the historian noted at the bottom that, '65 lines a day is for 6 days 390 lines, but I was some days more about them'.[655]

However, apart from the fact that Hasted was being paid very little for such work, Yates appears to have been reluctant to part with his money. The skills brought by the Kentish historian to the Bury manuscripts had been acquired through a lifetime of similar work, which was receiving no recognition in the puny sums he was forced to accept. And he was, in addition, finding the constant poring over manuscripts a great strain on his eyes. He was now wearing spectacles, but even so probably had difficulty in making out the lighter inks. At the end of Hasted's third and final letter to Yates we find him declining with dignity any further work at the rates of remuneration hitherto offered:

> It is now more than a month ago since I troubled you with a letter to request your leave to call on you, and informing you, that the business I had done for you had employed me together 12 days and more, hard labours, and that the least you could recompence me for it would be 15 shillings, and I hope you will think it worth more. Since which I have recollected that there were some pages of the MS I have now brought of yours with me, which cost me [much] toil to translate, being so very intricate, and which I sent to you by post for your approbation, but which you never returned to me, and I hope you will not think that one pound is too much to ask of you for the whole together.

I am at present much straightened for money, therefore I should be exceedingly obliged to you would you favor me with a note for it by post in the course of this week.

The MS I now return is so very intricate, that I fear you would think the satisfying my pains in it far beyond what you would wish to recompence me in. I have therefore returned it. Should you think otherwise, I am ready to receive your commands in that, or any thing else, if you will let me know it.[656]

This appears to have marked the end of Hasted's work for the Revd Richard Yates. In the event, the proposed history of Bury was to remain unfinished. Yates's later publications — which were not, finally, to be very numerous, three of them being no more than *Letters* addressed to Lord Liverpool — were all on religious subjects, including the popular theme of 'the church in danger'. Richard Yates became a Doctor of Divinity in 1818, and died in 1834 — by an irony of fate in Kent, at Penshurst, where he was then living. In 1843 John Bowyer Nichols brought out a second edition of the 1805 work, with a transcription of three Bury charters and some additional plates. Otherwise the text of the 1805 edition remained unaltered.

Hasted's work for Richard Yates, therefore, was never to appear in print. It had done little to improve his financial situation, and his eyesight may well have suffered as a result of it. The winter of 1806 saw him in low spirits, and on the 19 February 1807, feeling that time must be running out for him, he penned a sheet of detailed 'directions for my burial if I die in or near London':

I desire to be buried in the churchyard of Lambeth church in Surry, and if it may be close to the walls of the church on the west side of the small south-eastern door of it, adjoining to the east end of the burial place of John Ives there and on the west side of the said doorway in like manner as William Bacon is buried on the opposite or eastern side of it.

I desire my funeral may be by daylight and if it can suit on a Sunday as cheap as it possibly can, and as nice and decent — a neat hearse without plumes or trappings, and one coach in the same manner, with a pair of horses only to each. My coffin to be as plain as can be, of plain oak with iron nails, but without any covering to it, and a leaden plate on the lid with the following inscription cut deep on it:

Edward Hasted formerly Esquire, the Kentish Historian.

Dyed on ... day ... anno ... aged ...

And I wish that it might be entred in the register of my burial, with the leave of the Rector, my being the Kentish Historian. And I desire that no one but my executor and Harriet Brewster if she chuses it may attend my remains to the grave.

And I desire that the paragraph written on the paper inclosed with this, with my will and codicil, may (be) immediately after my death be sent to the publisher of the Gentleman's Magazine to be inserted in the Obituary of the next monthly publication of it, and I am certain my much respected friend, Mr Nicholls, of Red Lion Passage, Fleet Street, will kindly acquiesce in it.[657]

There was clearly an earlier will than the one which Hasted was to make in 1808, but the executor of this was almost certainly, as in 1808, his friend John Barlow. The warm dedication of volume 10 of the second edition of his *History* to the Revd Edward Hasted in 1800 had perhaps marked a temporary rapprochement between father and son, but the relationship between them had soon cooled again, to one of undoubted embarrassment on Edward's side, and perhaps of some bitterness on Hasted's that his son did not attempt to do more for him.

The only people on whom he felt he could rely were John Barlow and his servant Harriet Brewster. Harriet had now been with him for ten years, following her master on his release from the King's Bench to his various lodgings in the area. His friendship with Barlow dated back to the happier days of early work on the folio volumes, for which the Earl of Radnor had commissioned from the engraver views of The Park House and of the port of Folkestone — although by the time these appeared, in Volume III, Hasted could do no more than inscribe them, 'with much respect and gratitude' 'to the much lamented memory of the Rt Honble William Bouverie, Earl of Radnor, deceased, a kind encourager and patron of this History'.

It had been the second earl, recipient of the 'History of Folkestone' whom Hasted had ventured to address on being released from prison, in the hope that Lord Radnor might be able to recommend him to some minor position in the patronage of the family. Hasted's letter had probably been answered at the time, but with a polite negative. Now, however, four years later, Lord Radnor suddenly found himself with a position on his hands which required filling, and remembered the old scholar in his garret in St George's Fields.

THE HISTORY
OF
The ANTIENT and METROPOLI[TAN]
CITY OF CANTE[RBURY]
CIVIL and ECCLESIAST[ICAL]
OF THE
CATHEDRAL and PRIORY of C[HRIST]
AND OF THE ARCHB[ISHOPS]
WITH
The LIVES of the ARCHBISHO[PS]
OF THAT CH[URCH]
OF TH[E]
ARCHDE[ACONRY]
With the LIVES of the ARC[HDEACONS]
AND O[F THE]
MONASTERY of ST. AU[GUSTINE]

Collected from public RECORDS, and other good AUTH[ORITIES]
Both MANUSCRIPT and PRINTED

And illustrated with MAPS, CHARTS, and [&c.]

By EDWA[RD HASTED]
OF CANT[ERBURY]

[Inset advertisement:]

78. The History and Topographical Survey of the County of Kent; containing the ancient and present State of it, civil and ecclesiastical: collected from public Records, and other the best Authorities, both manuscript and printed; and illustrated with Maps, and Views of Antiquities, Seats of the Nobility and Gentry, &c. By Edw. Hasted, of Canterbury, Esq; F.R.S. and S.A. Vol. I. Folio. 1l. 11s. 6d. Simmons, Canterbury.

FOR this valuable addition to our county histories, and for the time, and labour, and expence bestowed upon it, the author deserves the thanks of his countrymen, particularly of Kent, and we hope will reap his reward. Lambard's Perambulation, Somner's Canterbury, Kilburne's Survey, and Philipott's Villare Cantianum, have their merit, but are some of them local, others imperfect, and now obsolete; and one more modern Harris's History of Kent, 1719, though it promised much, has perform[ed little]

[Manuscript note, diagonal:]

get him to go in for the purpose I hope you will give him all ... you in his way for your advice in his application there ... in excuse every liberty I have taken in this Letter Believe me it ... peated the friendship of it shall ever be acknowledged by Dear Sir

Your ever obliged & faithful servant
Edward Hasted

georges hills
Sept 9th 1796

[Footer:]
[CANTERBU]RY,
[SIMM]ONS AND KIRKBY.
MDCCXCIX.

Chapter 15

Corsham

Hardly more than a month had elapsed since the penning of the 'Directions for the Funeral of Edward Hasted Esqr, Kentish Historian' and Hasted was perhaps still in the same sombre mood, anticipating no more than an imminent dissolution, when, as is the way of things, he received a letter which made nonsense of his melancholy and shone an unexpected light on the future. Turning the letter over, he probably recognised the seal. It came from the Earl of Radnor, the son of his former patron, and on being unfolded it read as follows:

> Sir, You some time since told me you should like the situation of a school-master, if I could provide you such an employment. I have at this time vacant a situation, which has gone generally by that name, and at the foundation of the Charity was really such.
>
> The Charity is an almshouse for 6 old men or women over whom is a master; all in my patronage. I always appoint women. The Master was originally required to teach poor children, and he has sometimes had a considerable school of the sons of the gentlefolk of the neighbourhood. He has usually been a clergyman. Indeed, with a view to make you this offer, I have sought and have had some difficulty to ascertain, that he has ever been otherwise, one of his duties being to read prayers to the old women. I am considerably pressed in behalf of a clergyman at this time. The Master has a salary of £20 per annum, paid quarterly, and a house, which is kept in habitable repair by me. Constant residence is required, with a conformity to the Statutes, and superintendance of conformity to them by the old women.
>
> The situation is at Corsham about 90 miles from London, and about 10 from Bath. I require a bond for residence.
>
> If you think this will be a comfortable asylum for you, depending upon your performing the requisite duties, I offer it to you. It is a situation inferior to what you have borne in life, and for which I should not have thought of you, but for the intimation you as above gave me. You will see the propriety, if you accept it, of stooping to its character, and class. I wish an early answer.[658]

A SCHOLAR AND A GENTLEMAN

The letter was dated 21 March, and Hasted had not been at home when it arrived — he may have been spending a few days with Edward or Charles, or even with one of his surviving old friends. The emotion which swept over him now as he took in its contents, increased by the disturbing knowledge that several days had already gone by since Lord Radnor made his sharp demand for a quick decision, must have caused in him the same distressed state of mind which had resulted from unexpected visits when he was a prisoner in the King's Bench. He could not bring himself to write an immediate acceptance, and another day passed before he had decided how to reply. And then it was to ask for a little longer in which to ponder 'so great a change in my future condition of life'. For acceptance of the position of master of an almshouse demanded, in effect, a final abdication of all that had constituted Edward Hasted, esquire. He had been impoverished, but had remained genteel. His standing had been shaken by his imprisonment for debt, but it was an ordeal which many gentlemen, in the eighteenth century, were forced to undergo, and if their debts could be settled they remained gentlemen on their release. Lord Radnor's letter had been sent to 'Edward Hasted, esq'. As the master of Corsham almshouse he could not expect to continue to be addressed in that way.

Until he accepted the post, however, he remained, as he had always been, Edward Hasted, esq., the former friend of Lord Radnor's father, and in that capacity he felt able to request a few more days in which to make up his mind, answering on the 27 March:

> My Lord, Having been from home for some days, I did not receive the favor of your Lordship's letter till yesterday, and I take the earliest post to acknowledge it. I cannot, my Lord, sufficiently express my thanks for your kind remembrance of me. The asylum you have been so good to offer me, I have a due sense of, and the pleasing prospect it holds out to me in future. I by no means slight the acceptance of it, but it has come so sudden on me, that I request of you to indulge me with a few days' respite, to bring my mind to my final resolution, in relation to so great a change in my future condition of life. Your Lordship will I hope indulge me in this and pardon the liberty I take in requesting it, and in the course of next week I will do myself the honor of troubling you with the result of it.[659]

By the 4 April Hasted's mind was made up. His letter of that date to Lord Radnor has a firm tone, although it seems to hint at opposition encountered from members of his family:

> Since I had the honour of troubling you with my letter, I have been constantly employed in overcoming the many obstacles, which might prevent my accepting your Lordship's kind offer to me, for my mind is, and has been fixed, to avail myself of it.

And Hasted went on to hope that he might be allowed to call on Lord Radnor when he was in town at the end of the month, in order to be more fully informed of 'the nature of the Statutes, and the residence required of me, and such other particulars of the duty required of me, as your Lordship may condescend to inform me of'.[660]

But time had run out for calls of this kind. It was enough that Hasted had taken his decision. He was informed by post that he would be expected to take up his duties on the first of May. Nine days later, not only had he been sent and returned the Statutes in question (of which there were some forty-five), but he had already been down to Corsham, to see, as he put it, when his predecessor's belongings would be removed — and whether, perhaps, any of them were to be left for his own use. There was to be a slight delay in clearing the master's house — usefully, from Hasted's point of view, since he needed to make some arrangements with his 'friends' — a term frequently used to refer to one's relatives, and probably, in Hasted's case, meaning principally his son Edward. Hasted wrote to Lord Radnor again on the 13 April:

> I return you my thanks for the favor of the Corsham Statutes, which having looked over, I again returned them to your Lordship's house the next day, and I am happy to find there is nothing in them (as your Lordship is so very indulgent to me, not to insist on my keeping on the school, which at my present advanced state of life, I fear I should feel too much the labour of) but what I can with cheerfulness perform to your Lordship's satisfaction, at least I can answer that my best endeavors shall be exerted for that purpose, and I with my most sincere thanks accept the liberal offer you have made me of this situation ....

> I hope I shall not have offended your Lordship, when I inform you, that wishing to gain intelligence in what state Mr Page's effects were continued at Corsham, and when they would be removed, I thought it would not displease your Lordship, if I went down there. I found there were none of them removed, that a sale of them was intended, which from the circumstance of the administrators living in London, and some variance between them, could not be effected, and the goods wholly cleared away,

before the end of this month at soonest. The first of May is on a Friday, and I hope as this is the case, and from the great difficulty I find in gaining the fixed time of my pecuniary assistance from my friends, so necessary for my removal, that your Lordship will indulge [me] in my removal thither, with a very few days only beyond the first of May, and I will punctually be there, in the course of the week after it. Tomorrow I am necessitated to go down into Kent, to sollicit some further assistance from my friends, and purpose to return by the end of the week, when I hope to receive your Lordship's directions and commands, in whatever you may please to favor me with previous to my going to Corsham.[661]

Hasted's letter concluded by mentioning that he had pointed out to Lord Radnor's steward, Mr Heath, that there was no schedule of the fixtures which should remain in the master's house, and that the steward had agreed to attend to the matter — and added the hope that Lord Radnor would not disapprove of his having taken this step.

The visit to Kent which Hasted made in April 1807 was probably the last time he set foot on Kentish soil — there would be no holidays for the master of the almshouse. The journey was almost certainly made for the purpose of obtaining from Edward the money needed for the removal of Hasted himself, his clothes, remaining books and papers, and quite possibly some items of furniture, as well as of Harriet Brewster and her belongings, to their new home in Wiltshire. It was probably more embarrassing now for Lord Radnor than it was for Hasted, after his years of privation, that such penury had to be alluded to.

On the 30 April a bond was drawn up relating to Corsham almshouse, endorsed, 'Mr Edward Hasted to The Earl of Radnor: Bond for performance of Covenants on Appointment to Mastership of Corsham Almshouse'. Under the terms of the bond, Hasted was bound in the sum of five hundred pounds to perform the duties incumbent on the master, 'which Rules and Orders are put up in the School Room of the said Almshouse for the better direction of the said Master how to govern and manage the said Almshouse and poor People therein'. And on the resignation of the master, or on his death, the almshouse and premises were to be handed over in a peaceable manner to the earl or his heirs. As in most cases of this kind, there was little likelihood of any need for the bond to be enforced. Hasted put his name to it with the simple, unobtrusive signature which was now habitual with him; the counter-signature of Lord Radnor's steward, John Heath, was marked by the curlicues and arabesques of a man whom life had not yet humbled.[662]

Somehow the money for the move was got together, and Harriet Brewster probably went down in advance of her master to make the place habitable. It is quite likely that Hasted on his previous visit had managed to secure some of the late master's furniture, for he must have had little of his own — it was perhaps purchases of this kind which had been the subject of dispute between Hasted and his son and made another expedition to Kent necessary. A few days later, in the first week of May, Hasted left 4 Greenhouse Row, Westminster Road, for the last time, caught the coach which went to Bath via Sandy Lane and Lacock, and settled into his seat for the five or six hour journey which would take him to his new home at Corsham.

He was heading for a bustling market town, with an important clothing industry that probably found a good outlet in the spa city of Bath. The world had moved on, now, from the conjectures of the eighteenth century into which Hasted had been born to the certainties of the nineteenth. There is no need to guess at the population of Corsham, which the census of 1801 had ascertained to be 2402 persons, with a much smaller percentage employed in agriculture than was to be found in most inland towns in Kent.

The turnpike road ran past the almshouses, and it is likely that the coach made a special stop outside them for the purpose of setting down the person and boxes of an elderly passenger with a determined chin. One of Lord Radnor's 'old women' filled the position of porter, and it was no doubt she who now stood ready under the heavy, late Renaissance porch to open the door to the new master, essaying a curtsey learnt when she was a girl and the master a boy, and then standing aside for him to pass into what, for the first time in seventeen years, he could call his own house.

What was it like, this master's lodge, which Hasted had so surprisingly acquired? It was ironic — or was it a small recompense on the part of fate for all that he had been made to suffer? — that after having begun the wreck of his fortune by over-extending himself on the conversion of a historic house, in the shape of the Commandery of St John at Sutton-at-Hone, Hasted's final home, which came to him gratis, should have been a small gem of Restoration architecture.

Corsham almshouse was the endowment and charity of an eminently sensible-faced woman, who had herself reached old age, and knew that it was a time of life which demanded some creature comforts. Built in 1668, it lay in the shape of the letter L at the junction of two roads, the Lacock road and the Melksham road. One arm of the L, that facing north, comprised six small almshouses, each with a court in front, and connected by a cloister at the back. The master's lodge filled the angle of the L, while a splendid porch, and, beyond it, a schoolroom-cum-chapel, formed the west arm of the building. Under the unbelievably high porch gable — which is decorated with a coat of arms, and does in fact form the outer wall of a small parvis — is a plaque, with the following inscription:

> This freeschoole and almshouse was founded and endowed by the Lady Margaret Hungerford relict of Sr Edwd Hungerford Knt of the Honble Order of the Bath Daughter and Coheire of Willm Halliday Alderman of London and Susan his wife Daughter of Sr Henry Row Knt and Alderman and Lord Major of London.

The Hungerford arms were repeated in the centre of the north wing — a suitable memorial to a family which had held land in Corsham since the fifteenth century. And Lady Hungerford herself was both granddaughter and great-granddaughter to two lord mayors. The charity was supported by rents from the manor of Stanton St Quintin, and it was with the purchase of this manor by Lord Radnor's family in 1718 that responsibility for the almshouse had devolved on them.[663]

The interior of the house, kept in repair by Lord Radnor, had apparently been renovated shortly before Hasted's time, and its panelled hall and stairway, although small, were considerably more than decent, indeed, almost elegant. The living room, with the bedroom above it, lay in the angle formed by the two wings of the building, and with windows on two sides was pleasantly light and airy. The Revd Charles Page, during his occupancy of the house, seems to have had an eye to making it as convenient as possible. The house had a cellar, with its own well, and Page had been at the expense of erecting a pump over this. There was a considerable amount of space upstairs, and Hasted must have felt that a reduction in status was a reasonable price to pay for the luxury of a house of his own, after twelve years spent cooped in prison or in the shabby gentility of lodging houses. The parvis over the porch, a particularly charming little room, with Venetian-style windows facing north and south along the Melksham road, he most probably used as his study. From here, he could see the approach of his occasional visitors, much as he had been able to look down on them from his study window at St John's.

The duties entailed on him by the Statutes were not onerous. Lord Radnor had indicated in his letter that Hasted, as master, would be required to read prayers for those living in the almshouse, and this may perhaps have been a nightly custom which had taken the place of the Statute directing that the master should 'instruct them in point of religion especially in the articles of our Christian faith', something for which

Hasted was hardly qualified. It was a further part of his duty to be concerned for the wellbeing of the almsfolk, visiting them when they were sick, and reading the Statutes over to them twice a year, either in the chapel or the schoolhouse, 'to the end', as the beneficent foundress had said, that 'ignorance may not excuse the said poor people or cause them to go away that are willing to live in order'. Most of the regulations related to the behaviour expected of the inmates, for whom drunkenness, swearing, idleness and quarrelsome behaviour were forbidden. As Lord Radnor had indicated in his letter, the almshouses, although designed originally for either men or women, now contained only women.

The ground behind the almshouses seems to have been intended for cultivation by the inhabitants as their garden, but under the previous master an amicable arrangement had been entered into, whereby he himself cultivated this, paying the almswomen an agreed rent for it. A statement signed by five of the women in 1791 notes that 'the plot of ground allotted for our garden, when the oldest of us came to it, was in a state little better than the common highway', that on being encouraged to dig it up 'several trials were made in the most likely spots', but that these had been unsuccessful due to the shallowness of the soil and the want of manure. It is reported to have been 'with unanimous desire and satisfaction' that the Revd Charles Page had then taken the management of the plot into his own hands, resulting in 'its present creditable condition'. In addition, with the help of a willing relative, the old woman who acted as the porter of the almshouse was able to earn almost as much again as her stipend from the charity by keeping the plot free from weeds. This arrangement, satisfying to all parties, seems to have been disturbed by the advent of a newcomer to the almshouse, 'who by threats to some and different management with others, hath been continually endeavouring to diffuse her own turbulent spirit amongst us'. Thus it was that the five older residents of the almshouse set out the matter — or had it set out for them: the writing may well be that of Charles Page — for Lord Radnor to settle, and appended their signatures or marks to it: Martha Belcher, Betty Pritchet the porter, Betty Hambleton, Sarah Brinkworth and Sarah Fry.[664]

It is not recorded what became of the horticultural arrangements under Hasted. But he was no doubt happy to have a garden to supervise once more, and probably had little difficulty in finding someone to keep it under cultivation. The atmosphere fostered in the almshouse by the late master seems to have been a peaceable one that did not welcome troublemakers, and Hasted, who was no stranger to the differences which could arise between those obliged to live in close proximity to each other, doubtless did all he could to maintain this. Were any of the almswomen of 1791 still in residence when Hasted took over, one wonders? Of one thing we can be certain: the porter who opened the door to him was no longer 'Betty Pritchet': the statement of 1791 had extolled the Revd Charles Page's 'lenity and moderation', but even he had had his limits, and in 1794 it had been necessary to expel Elizabeth Pritchard for 'irregularities'.[665]

The outcome of the suit Davies v. Williams was still awaited when Hasted went to Corsham, and another year had to pass before the Lord Chancellor's decree finally settled the matter. Only on the 24 May 1808 was Hasted finally vindicated, when the Hasted estates were adjudged to have been fraudulently retained by Thomas Williams, and ordered to be restored under the bond. In the words of the decree:

> His Lordship doth declare that the conveyance to the said Thomas Williams in the pleadings mentioned ought only to stand as a security for what (if anything) shall be found due on the taking the account herein after directed and doth order and decree that it be referred to Mr Stanley one of the Masters of this Court to take an account of what is due to the defendant John Williams for principal of the sum of £8685 mentioned in the deed bearing date the 7th day of April 1790.[666]

To the sum of £8685 was to be added money laid out by the Williamses on 'lasting repairs and improvements'; from it was to be deducted what had been received in rents and profits over the time that they had held the Hasted lands. All deeds, books, papers and writings which might be needed for the purpose of drawing up this account were ordered to be produced, as the Master might require. John Williams was to bear the plaintiffs' taxed costs.

While the day on which he learnt of the Lord Chancellor's decree must have been one of the happiest of Hasted's old age, there could be no immediate change in his situation — indeed, he was not to live long enough to see the account finally made up and the estates sold for well above the amounts for which they had been mortgaged. As so often happened with cases in Chancery, a supplementary bill had to be brought to settle a subsidiary issue. This was concerned with the rights of Hasted's children, under the 1789 trust and settlement, to whatever might remain after the bond had been made use of to the benefit of the mortgagees. Only in 1822 was the last Hasted suit to disappear from the Chancery records.

The Kentish historian remained, therefore, a gentleman in reduced circumstances, but one who was not ashamed to earn his living as the master of Hungerford almshouse. In former days he could have expected an invitation to visit the owner of Corsham Court, Paul Methuen, esq.; now he occupied a position which might bring him no more than a passing acknowledgment from such levels. However, the house was regularly opened to the public, and he is unlikely to have missed an opportunity of taking advantage of one of the Tuesdays and Fridays when visitors were welcome to view the considerable collection of paintings which Methuen had assembled, including works by Michelangelo, Castiglione, Bruegel, Rubens, Veronese, Titian, Giordano, Claude Lorraine, Tintoretto, Lely, Holbein and Salvator Rosa.[667]

At other times, if he wanted it, he probably did not lack for company among the professional gentlemen in the town. Although the fact that he was not required to run it may indicate that the school was defunct when Hasted was appointed (the Revd Charles Page had noted in a Visitation Return of 1783 that 'the better sort of people are above the charity and the lower unable to afford the loss of their childrens labour') it would appear to have been restarted during his time there, since two of the witnesses to the historian's will, made just over a year after he went to Corsham, were George Turner, a schoolmaster, and his assistant, H. Weaver. The large schoolroom which formed part of Lady Margaret Hungerford's almshouse offered excellent premises, and it is unlikely that anywhere else in Corsham could provide similar space. On the Monday in August 1808, when Hasted had finally settled the matter of his will to his satisfaction — and it seems likely that he had been moved to draw up a new one as a result of the Lord Chancellor's decree — Turner and his assistant were probably called in at the close of the school day to take a glass of wine with the master of the almshouse, whom they found in conversation with the vicar, the Revd Mr Lewis: the historian's will, dated 8 August 1808, bears the signature of all three men.

Mr Lewis, shortly after that, seems to have become too ill to take the services in his church, and the clergyman who was put in to do his duty, the Revd J.C.Meffre, appears also to have become friendly with the aged historian. Meffre was of French origin, and a convert from Roman Catholicism. Hasted's years in France gave them much in common, and both men may have enjoyed the occasional opportunity to speak French together. We know that they were well acquainted as it is from Monsieur Meffre's hand that we have an account of Hasted's last days.

In London and Kent the slow business of disentangling his affairs continued. Hasted must frequently have been agitated that he was not there to oversee what was happening, although he was no longer legally concerned in it. He was now at leisure to ponder on his former estates and to consider, at greater length than when he was in possession of them, what might be the annual return on them. He remained in touch with one of the lawyers in the case, Mr Clarkson, and plied him with anxious letters, apologising for trespassing on his time, yet eager to make suggestions and discuss various points.

He still saw the *Kentish Gazette* occasionally, perhaps sent on to him by Edward, and from this he would make entries, arranged, as in the old days, alphabetically by parish, in a new commonplace book which he was now keeping.[668] It was a book of Kentish origin — many of the pages bear the watermark 'Buttanshaw 1804', with the figure of Britannia in an oval surmounted by a crown, and must have come from the papermill of that name at West Peckham. Perhaps it had been a parting gift from someone when he left Kent for the last time.

The entries made in the Corsham commonplace book frequently refer to changes in ownership of houses or estates, something which for Hasted signalled the slow march of history through the countryside. Quite often there are cross-references to an earlier notebook which he clearly still had to hand, F.XVII, 'Particulars and advertisements of estates and houses in Kent, chiefly to be sold or let' — although he calls it, erroneously, F.XVI. A few parish entries began by noting something which had occurred in the intervening years since the publication of his *History*: thus, under Denton near Elham: '1796 July 31st dyed at Exning in Co. Suffolk Mrs B. wife of S.E.Bridges, aet. 29; she dyed of a broken heart for his neglect of her and the attachment to his 2d wife'; and under Pluckley, '1798, Decr: dyed Sir Edwd Dering Bt'. Such items must have been copied from other notes made earlier. Apart from these occasional backward glances the Corsham entries, although relatively sparse, cover all the years which Hasted spent in this small Wiltshire town, from 1807 to 1811, with a single entry made in the year of his death, 1812. Thus the entries for Denton, after the one record for 1796, are dated 1808, 1810 and 1811, and those for Pluckley, after one for 1798, fall between 1807 and 1811.[669]

The keeping of a new commonplace book in Corsham seems to show that Hasted was quite happy there, whiling away the time with the small items of fact and news on which his life's work had been built — but without the need, now, to check and verify each one, or to embed them in their context, as he had taken such pains to do when writing his *History*. It also shows that he retained his interest to the last in what was happening in Kent. There are quite detailed entries for several parishes, such as Shoreham, only a few miles from his house at Sutton, including the recording of a 'Mistake in Hasted's Kent relating to Waring and Humphrys' which had been noted in 'Mag.p.796' — his abbreviation for the *Gentleman's Magazine* — in 1793, and several comments on Thomas

Borrett, the former owner of Shoreham Castle and Preston and Filston manors, whose financial difficulties, as well as landing him temporarily in a debtors' prison, had forced him to sell his lands and leave Shoreham. The new owner was hardly happier in his possession of them. Hasted noted against 1811 that on 10 June of that year an Act was passed for repealing an Act passed only a year earlier, a Local and Personal Act of 1810, obtained for the purpose of repairing and maintaining the road from Eynsford turnpike in Shoreham to the turnpike road in Farnborough leading from Sevenoaks to Bromley. In consequence of this reversal of a project which had been dear to him, the prime mover of the new turnpike road had sold up in disgust:

> Sir Walter Stirling has sold his Shoreham estate, the road appertaining to which cost so much ill blood, for the round sum of £100,000. Mr Alex Baring is said to be the purchaser. County Gaz.[670]

And of course, as someone who was himself to live to the age of 79, Hasted also had the mournful task of recording the deaths of many of his old friends:

> Jan 22 1807 dyed Jas Simmons Esq MP for Canterbury in his 66th year, buried 30th January in a vault in St Mildred's churchyard, Canterbury. A handsome quadrangular monument, with a Grecian pedestal, has been erected to his memory since.
>
> 1807 March 27 at Pluckley Revd Wm Disney DD, near 30 years Rector, rich in good works and highly respected by every [illegible] connection.

The last commonplace book contains entries relating to many of those whom Hasted had known, particularly from his Canterbury days. Robert Legeyt and Johnson Macaree had died in 1798. 1800 had seen the deaths of the Revd John Loftie, a member of a well-known Canterbury family, and of two Canterbury worthies, John Cantis, mayor in 1770, and Allan Grebell, a local landowner, of whom Hasted noted that he had died at Bath, aged 67, and that he had been Treasurer and Secretary to the Kent Agricultural Society. The death of the Canterbury surgeon, William Loftie, aged 76, was noted down in 1811; two years earlier, in December 1809, had occurred a death which must have recalled many scenes to Hasted's mind as he entered the name, that of the Revd Joshua Dix, who in former years had been one of a merry party invited to enjoy the fishing in the river Cray from John Thorpe's Bexley grounds.

Also commemorated, under the heading 'School', was Dr Osmund Beauvoir, the Canterbury headmaster, who had been one of those whose final years were spent in Bath, in search of a recovery that was not to be. Bath was only ten miles from Corsham, and it would not have been incompatible with his duties as master of the almshouse for Hasted to go there from time to time. It was probably after one such visit that he made the following indignant entry, betraying much affection for his old friend, Precincts neighbour, and colleague on the magistrates' bench:

> Dr Beauvoir dyed in 1789 and was buried near the west end of the south aisle of the Abbey Church of Bath, but there is not any memorial or even a gravestone over him, and no one but the sexton woman, as she herself informed me, knows in which spot he lyes. Indeed, there is a small tablet of marble to his memory against the south wall near where he lyes, which is a blemish to the church, and the inscription on it, which describes him as of Stanhope Street, seems rather to misinform the readers of it, what Dr Beauvoir it was, and to gratify the vanity of those who placed it there, from whom, surely, he deserved better treatment of his memory.

There was much for the master of Hungerford almshouse to ponder and reflect on as he sat in his tiny study over the porch. It was perhaps there, shortly after he had moved to Corsham, and remembering that the 'Anecdotes of the Hasted Family' which he had begun in 1800 had gone no further than 1770, that he jotted down a brief chronology of his life up to the year 1807. But if he ever contemplated continuing the Anecdotes, it was a plan which remained unfulfilled.

One of the mottoes, which in its Latin form had headed the Anecdotes, 'I have sinned, I have repented; the past is expunged', shows that he felt he now had little on his conscience. Indeed, so severe had been the repentance demanded of him, in the long years of confinement in a debtors' prison, that the failing which he seems latterly to have felt he most needed to guard against was bitterness. This was alluded to in his last letter to Thomas Astle from the King's Bench, when he had briefly compared his former generous hospitality to his present condition of a beggar: 'You have known me, sir, when my heart has been open to all my friends, and my hospitality equal to my heart, a bitter and yet not an unpleasing remembrance, and I am far from repenting of it — that has long been passed by, never to return'.

And yet there was something which remained on his mind, if not on his conscience. It related to his friend Astle and concerned a nastly little bit of trickery which Astle had played on Sir Edward Dering; and in 1810, shortly before the end of his life, he committed it to paper for whoever might find it. Astle had already been dead for some years, and Hasted's statement of what had occurred one night could not now harm him. The Dering library at Surrenden, in Pluckley, had had an unparalleled collection of ancient charters and registers, which had been in the family, itself an old Saxon one, for generations. Both Hasted and Astle had been eager to see them, and it seems to have been Hasted who had first gained access to the library when Astle, in 1763, had failed to turn up to meet his friend at Surrenden at Christmas. However, from Hasted's account both men appear to have gone there later, when they had been allowed to take away a number of items which Hasted no doubt wanted to make use of for his *History*. For greater security, he made a list of everything they were borrowing, and gave a copy of it to Sir Edward. We know from the rapid use which the historian made of other borrowed documents that he was always punctilious in returning them as quickly as possible. But Sir Edward was never to see his Surrenden material again. Going through some of his old papers one day at Corsham, Hasted came across the list which he himself had written, and added the following note to it:

> A list of the MSS brought by Mr Astle and myself out of the Surrenden library, all which I copied and then sent the originals to Mr Astle, and they were afterwards bought by him of the late Sir Edwd Dering for a hogshead of claret. They remained in Mr Astle's library till his death, and were then sold with the rest of his MSS library to the Marquis of Buckingham where they now remain. 1810.[671]

While Kent and things Kentish remained always in the forefront of Hasted's mind, he could not fail to find much of interest in the county in which he was now living. A loose slip of paper in his Kentish commonplace book relates to a feature of Wiltshire topography. It contains the 'Names of places in Wiltshire having the surnames of their former possessors annexed to them' — and here Hasted has made a collection of around fifty names, such as Somerford Keynes, Pool Keynes, Littleton Drew, Compton Bassett, Winterborne Bassett, Honington Odstock, and Lidiard Tregoze.

Corsham, it was clear, was to be his last home, and one day in October 1810, sitting in his small, light, parvis study, looking out along the Wiltshire roads, peopled by Wiltshire figures, Hasted took out the instructions for his burial that he had been writing in London only a month before he received Lord Radnor's totally unexpected letter and began to amend them accordingly:

> But in case I should dye at Corsham, of which I think there is the greatest probability, I wish that my coffin should be the same as I have mentioned above and the plate likewise on it, and I would have it a foot burial: two men with scarfs and staves before it, then my executor as chief mourner, and after him the undertaker, both with hatbands and scarfs, then two men with scarfs and staves as before following them, and no more of any sort. I would wish to be buried in the church of Corsham close to the wall of the south window next and southward of the font with a like gravestone so placed over my grave and tablet against the wall there — only after the word dyed on the coffin, gravestone, and tablet, I would have added, Master of the Lady Margt Hungerford's Hospital in this parish — and I would wish that my coffin as soon as I have been laid in it should be placed in the middle of the chapel of my house and that the six women of the almshouses should have black gowns, bonnets and handkerschifts against the day of my burial, and that when my coffin is carried forth they should respectively stand three on each side my front gate, but go no farther with it, and after my executor's return, that they should be paid half a crown each of them.
>
> I wish the clergyman who shall perform the burial service should be invited to the burial and if he pleases to walk before my coffin and immediately following the two men with staves before it, and have a hatband and scarf accordingly, and I wish that my executor should provide any other necessary matters at the funeral which he may think proper and decent, and which I may have omitted in the above directions, so that it be with a small expence farther and within the bounds of frugality and oeconomy.[672]

Frugality and economy seem now to have ruled all that Hasted did. Indeed, it had perhaps been his own secret rule ever since the heady days of St John's, when he had fitted up his gentleman's residence and his friends had benefited by his prodigality. But in the quiet of his study, that October day, he could not help his thoughts turning to what might have been:

I could have wished to have been laid in my family vault at Newington near Sittingbourne in Kent, but as I have no kind of prospect of being able to afford the expence of it consistent with the other bequests in my will I must think no further of it. Nevertheless I could wish that the same fees be paid to the parish there for my burial in the vault the same as if I had been laid in it, and one guinea to the clerk there for sweeping the vault out and making it and the coffins in it cleanly swept, and I could wish with the leave of the vicar there that an entry be made in the parish register as follows: That on such a day and year dyed and was buried at Corsham in the County of Wilts aged so and so Edward Hasted Esq. the Kentish Historian, Master of the Lady Margaret Hungerford's Hospital in that parish but formerly of Canterbury in this county. And I could wish that my son Edward should his circumstances permit him to afford it, that a small white tablet of marble against the wall by the side of my grandfather's monument should be placed there by him with my shield of arms at the top thus [and here Hasted sketched a rectangle laid on its side surmounted by a small semi-circle containing his arms] and this addition to the description on it after age, viz.: He was the only son and heir of Edward Hasted Esq. barrister at law and of Hawley in this county, and left surviving four sons and two daughters. And I could wish that if it should further suit my said son so to do, that he would cause my grandfather's monument to be repainted, and my father's gravestone, if it continues to lye unfixed on the pavement of the chancel, to be placed over the middle on the top of the vault, the sides of it cut even and the surface of the stone to be one half of its thickness above the pavement round it.[673]

Alas for Hasted's wishes! It was to prove impossible to carry them out with regard to his own memorial, and the stone intended for his father's grave was to continue unfixed, as it had been already for nearly seventy years. But it had nevertheless been Hasted who had been responsible for the family vault, in the south chancel of Newington parish church, and who had had deposited there, in a single coffin, as his statement continued,

the remains of Joseph Hasted Esq. and Katherine his wife, the same being removed thither when the vault was made. Also the remains of Edwd Hasted of Hawley, Esqr above-mentioned; of Anne his daughter who married Captn James Archer in the East India Company's service, dyed in ... and of Geo: Hasted Gent. son of Edwd Hasted of Canterbury and grandson of Edwd Hasted of Hawley Esqr who dyed unmarried in ...

The responsibility for carrying out these 'Directions' for his funeral was laid, in Hasted's will of 1808, on his executor, who was named as 'my worthy and much respected friend Mr John Barlow of St Georges Place, in Blackfryars Road, in Surry'. It is most likely that this will replaced an earlier one, made in London, where the choice of Barlow would have been less surprising. Barlow having agreed to act, however, Hasted was probably reluctant to replace him, and he was continued as the executor in the Corsham will — although not, as we shall see, without some later misgivings on the part of the testator regarding the rightness of his action. Under the will Barlow, as executor, was to receive £50,

> as a mark of my regard and the true sense I have of the many obligations I am under to him for his continued acts of kindness and friendship, to use and for the care and trouble he will have in the performance of this my last will, and I further will that all debts and sums of money due from me to my said good friend Mr John Barlow shall be with interest duly paid and discharged to him in the performance of this my last will.[674]

Friendship had always been an important element in Hasted's life, and he seems to have come to rely as on a brother on this friend of his last years, who had stood by him throughout the vicissitudes of his time in the King's Bench without any of the disapprobation, however veiled, which he sometimes felt he encountered in former friends. As a result, it was Barlow who was also charged under the will with responsibility for concluding the business of the recovery of the Hasted estates, and their subsequent sale. It is hardly surprising that the Hasted family should appear to have resented his introduction, as executor, into their father's affairs, but he seems, very fairly from all points of view, to have allowed the Revd Edward Hasted to act, as he undoubtedly wished to, as the principal in the recovery of the estates, and to have concerned himself mainly with settling the smaller matters entrusted to him. Even so, however, his actions under the will were probably always received with coolness by the Hasteds. He seems to have kept many of the historian's personal papers — to which, nonetheless, he had a perfect right, since Hasted had ordered that all his private letters, papers and pocket books of expenses were to go to Barlow, and, after he had destroyed those which he judged 'of no use to be kept' that these should 'remain in his possession and not be inspected or given up to any one else'. This put the Hasted family at a distinct disadvantage: even the directions for the funeral of the historian, which were eventually to be among the papers left at his own death by the Revd Edward Hasted, were in fact, as they were headed, only a copy of those directions 'now in possession of John Barlow Esqr, No.2, St George's Place, Blackfriars Road, Surrey'. However, one cannot help but feel that had those children, and Edward perhaps in particular, done more for their father in his hour of need such a situation might not have arisen.

To Barlow, as executor, all Hasted's estate, real and personal, was made over in trust, to be disposed of as the will further directed. This would, of course, involve the sale of all the Hasted lands and property, which had not yet taken place. Two-thirds of the sum realised by this sale, after all debts had been cleared, appears to have been settled on his children 'or such one or more of them as I shall give the preference to' by the deed of October 1789, and a tripartite division was now to be made of this sum, two-thirds of which was bequeathed to Edward, and the remaining third being shared equally among the other children. The third part of the surplus money arising from the sale, which Hasted had reserved to himself, to leave as he pleased, was to be used to bear the funeral expenses, small bequests, and the cost of his 'monument and memorial'.

As well as being the major beneficiary, Edward was also left his father's rings and seals:

> My old fashioned gold ring set with pearls being the wedding ring of my great grandmother Walker and my late wife's gold wedding ring, my stone seal with my arms on it, and my silver seal ring with my crest on it, all which are now in my possession.

To these was to be added the small pastel portrait of himself, which had gone with him to Corsham but which, on his death, was to hang with the family portraits already in Edward's possession at Hollingbourne. After Edward's death all these things were to go to Francis, and then to Francis's eldest surviving son. To Edward, too, were left the two small memorandum books, containing 'the account of the family of Hasted'. And both Edward and Charles were to keep all the furniture, goods, plate, books and other effects belonging to Hasted, but now in their respective houses at Hollingbourne and at Dartford or Sevenoaks — Charles's address changed quite frequently.

There was also a small literary estate to be disposed of. The historian's manuscript books, papers and letters 'anyways relating to the history of Kent', as well as the large folio Bible dating from the time of Henry VIII, in which Hasted had recorded the dates of births, marriages and deaths occurring in the family, were to be handed over to the British Museum, with a request that they should be deposited among those of his manuscripts which the Museum had acquired at the auction of 1796.

Apart from this fairly standard distribution of an estate which yet remained to be freed of its legal entanglements and realised, there were only two other personal bequests in the will. To Anne, the eldest daughter, was left the only item which had come down to Hasted from the Hawley days, which had perhaps meant more to him than any of his other possessions, and to which he had clung when everything else had been sold: his father's silver pepper-box. In addition Anne was to receive £10 for her mourning outfit,

> And likewise a ring or locket of the value of five guineas hoping she will keep it in remembrance of her father whose affection is great towards her and who gives her his blessing and prayers for her future happiness and welfare.

There could be no greater proof that Anne had remained close to her father throughout his years in the wilderness. There is no actual mention in the will of Katherine or of John Septimus, and it is likely that when the split occurred between their parents both children had sided with their mother. To this one may add that Katherine was now keeping house for her brother Edward, whose views on her father she undoubtedly shared, while for John, the ship's surgeon, the participants in that early drama had probably come to seem as unimportant as the grains of sand on the beaches from which his ship was forever sailing away.

The last legatee to be named in the will is Harriet Brewster. There can be no doubt that as his servant-housekeeper she had been the person, above all, who had made Hasted's final years comfortable. Not only had she seen to it that his rooms were kept clean and tidy — and latterly, at Corsham, she may well have been able to procure in this the assistance of one of the 'old women', as Lord Radnor loftily called them — but it had been she who had coddled the historian when he had a cold or when damp weather brought on an attack of rheumatism, she who met him at the door with a warm drink when he returned from a brisk walk on a winter's afternoon. Within the house, she was undoubtedly the staff he leaned on for all his personal wants, and Hasted made her his residual legatee. At first sight Harriet would appear to have been left no more than what remained when everyone else's bequest was satisfied. Specifically, she was to receive all the historian's household effects, the furniture, plate and money which were in his possession at the time of his death — with the exception of those items referred to earlier in the will. Harriet was thus provided at a stroke with everything which she might need to set up her own establishment.

Almost the last words in the will refer to Harriet Brewster, when Hasted makes an impassioned plea to his executor,

> That he will shew every kindness in his power to the said Harriet Brewster and protect her from every means that may be used to injure her and to soften as much as possible her forlorn and comfortless condition, and to give her such advice and assistance as may conduce to place her in that situation of life as may be most for her advantage, benefit and comfort.

Was this a plea to protect her from the world, or from his family? For Hasted, in naming Harriet as his residual legatee, had given her also 'all the rest and residue of my estates real leasehold and personal and the surplus of moneys arising from the sale of the same'. But there could be no surplus that was not already accounted for in advance, and such a bequest ran wholly counter to the previous content of the will, which dealt in such detail with Edward's two-thirds of two-thirds, and the one third which Hasted, under the settlement of 1789, had retained to dispose of as he wished. The historian undoubtedly wanted to favour Harriet Brewster, but his other dispositions show that he clung to the settlement of 1789 as salvaging from the wreck of his fortunes something that would be passed on to his family. It was an idle fancy to pretend that there would be any small sums left over here and there which could then go to Harriet, and unfortunately Hasted, as an old man, wrote that idle fancy into his will. It was to add to his eldest son's troubles in after years in bringing the affair of the Hasted estates to a successful conclusion. And subsequent events were to prove that Harriet was not altogether the 'lone, lorn creetur' which Hasted seems to have imagined her to be.

Two years later, on the 15 November 1810, Hasted was to add a codicil to his will, amending it in two important respects. A closer relationship appears to have been built up in the meantime with Edward and now, instead of his receiving only two-thirds of the two-thirds part of the estate which had been settled on one or more of the family in 1789, he was to receive the whole of it, plus whatever else might remain when the final third had been applied for the purposes stated. Francis, Charles, Anne, Katherine and John, named here only as Hasted's 'other children', were each to have ten guineas out of Edward's two-thirds with which to buy mourning and a ring in remembrance of their father. The enlarged bequest to Edward was intended not only to improve his standing as the eldest representative of the Hasted family, but also to be of some assistance, ultimately, to Francis, now so far away, but the only one of Hasted's seven children to have given him grandchildren. Edward's portion had been increased in the confidence that he would, in the words of his father's will,

> of his goodness assist his brothers and sisters with as much as he sees necessary of it from time to time and that he will at his death consider his brother Francis's children by giving and leaving them a good portion of it, my other children being all independently provided for and having none of them any issue.[675]

The fuller reference here to Francis, with the realisation that his were to be the family's only descendants, is perhaps indicative of an earlier rupture between father and son. Francis seems to have had difficulty in settling to anything, had got into trouble, perhaps more than once, and his departure for India, probably around 1790, may have been accompanied by his father's then washing his hands of him. But now the historian was getting old. The codicil, increasing Edward's legacy and expressing the hope that it would eventually be used to benefit Francis's children, appeared to Hasted to be the answer to what he saw as two new requirements: the first, to mollify Edward as the eldest son, who had not been named, as he might justly have expected, as executor, and the other, to make some provision for his grandchildren.

The other amendment dealt with the manuscripts, papers and letters relating to the history of Kent which were still in his possession. Revoking the bequest to the British Museum, Hasted remembered a younger friend, who had been proud to be called on to assist in the *History*, who had done much to help keep the work going when the historian was in France, who seems to have been able to withhold censure during the dark days of confinement in the King's Bench, and who now, as the passing years laid in the grave so many of those he had known, was one of the few old friends who were left. William Boteler now became the legatee of all these papers, 'as a small mark, and the only one in my power, of my grateful remembrance of the many favors I have received from him'. Excepted from this bequest were the pedigrees of Hasted, Dingley and Dorman, the two small memorandum books containing an account of the Hasted family (the Anecdotes) and the Henry VIII Bible, all of which were to go to Edward.

In his codicil Hasted also gave some additional directions for the disposal of the family portraits, originally willed to Francis after the death of Edward. If Francis had not notified his acceptance of them after the space of twenty-four months — a time-lapse which would allow for a dilatory correspondence with India — the portraits were to go to Charles, and if Charles did not want them they were to be destroyed, 'to prevent their coming into the hands of brokers and exposed to a sale for a few shillings'. John, on the high seas, would have seemed an unlikely recipient, and Hasted probably knew that Anne did not have the space for a gallery of portraits.

Hasted's concern about his belongings coming on the market extended also to his clothes. It probably shows that during his long period of incarceration, and afterwards, in considerable poverty, he had been forced to frequent the second-hand shops known as slop shops, where he may well have come across items belonging to men he had known whose fortunes, like his own, had suffered a reverse. If it was necessary for his clothes to be sold, Hasted now asked that 'they should be disposed of to some clothes shop in London, where it shall not be known to whom they have belonged'.

Otherwise, the will remained unaltered, with a final plea, framed as a somewhat rambling 'dying request', that Edward would not take offence at not being named as executor, something which Hasted suggested might save him from 'many inconveniences and disagreeable circumstances'. George Turner the schoolmaster was again called on, to witness the codicil, together with William Ricketts and James Harcourt.

Hasted continued to interest himself in the proceedings which were taking their slow course through Chancery. On the 26 November 1811 he sketched out a letter to the attorney, Mr Clarkson, only a short time after sending a previous one: 'Tho I fear much that you will think me troublesome in trespassing on your time so soon again, yet so anxious am I ...' His anxieties would have been allayed could he have known that, in the event, his estates were to be sold after his death for something in excess of £26,000 — far more than enough to repay the mortgages which had been taken out on them.[676]

In his spare time he still made entries in his Kentish commonplace book whenever he received a packet of Kentish newspapers, noting that on 30 June 1811 Sir Edward Dering Bt had died suddenly in his 55th year, and that on 17 July of that year a new chapel had been opened in Margate, its combined name and address, St John's, Hawley Square, recalling early Kentish memories for him. At the same time he noted down an account of the Sea Bathing Infirmary in Margate.[677]

On the occasion of his birthday at the end of December — he was now entering his eightieth year — Hasted must have received a Kentish newspaper, or perhaps a letter from Edward containing some clerical gossip, because he made an entry under Cuxton, dated January

1812, to the effect that the Revd R.H. Chapman, MA, had been presented to that vicarage by the Bishop of Rochester.[678]

Only a few days later, on the Monday morning of 20 January 1812, Hasted's friend Mr Meffre sat down to write to Lord Radnor from his lodgings at No.1, Wood Street, Bath, setting out his own qualifications for the now vacant post of master of Lady Margaret Hungerford's almshouses:

> The occasion of my troubling your Lordship with this line, is in consequence of the death of Mr Ested at the almshouse, Corsham; which I was informed of yesterday upon my going to do the duty of Corsham Church.'

The Kentish historian had died quite suddenly the previous Tuesday, on the 14 January, and the Revd Mr Meffre's letter contains a brief description of his end: 'Mr Ested was but a short time ill, having been at church very lately, at which place he was a very constant attendant.'[679]

It is some satisfaction to know, after all the suffering and indignities which had been heaped on Hasted during his life, that illness did not bring a recurrence of these at his end, and that death came quickly for him. John Barlow was a dutiful executor of his old friend's wishes, and the small solemnities which Hasted had requested for his final rites seem to have been observed, the old ladies of the almshouses standing in their black at the gate of his house as his coffin was borne out for its short journey down the road to the church of St Bartholomew, and receiving their half-crowns when the funeral was over. But the gravestone and tablet for which Hasted had hoped were never to be erected: there simply was not enough money for them and Hasted's place of burial was always to remain unmarked. It may well have been, as he had wished, within the church itself. It is generally believed, although there is no evidence for this, that his son Edward would have conducted the funeral service, which took place on the 21 January — there had been no expectation on the part of the historian, when he wrote out his 'Directions' for his funeral, that Edward would be the officiating minister. And Edward is unlikely to have made the entry in the parish register which noted, with a slight inaccuracy that must have been due to ignorance of the month in which he had been born, that

> Edward Hasted Esqr formerly the Kentish Historian died Jany 14th 1812, aged 80 years.[680]

Mr Meffre was unsuccessful in his application for the post of master of the almshouse, Lord Radnor preferring to appoint someone who, like Hasted, had become the victim of circumstances beyond his control. The new master was to be John Slade, a considerably younger man and a former clothier, who had been bankrupted by the failure of a wool broker in London.[681]

The obituary of Edward Hasted which appeared the following month in the *Gentleman's Magazine* was on the lines which he had himself suggested. It read as follows:

> Jan. 14. At the Master's Lodge of the Lady Hungerford's Hospital in Corsham, co. Wilts, at the advanced age of 80, Edward Hasted, esq. the Kentish Historian F.R.S. and S.A. His laborious History took him up more than 40 years, during the whole series of which he spared neither pains nor expence to bring it to maturity; and the reputation which it still maintains in the judgment of the publick, is the best proof of its merits. Notwithstanding his attention to this his favourite object during the whole of the above time, he acted as a magistrate and a deputy lieutenant for the county of Kent with uncommon zeal and activity.
>
> He was the only son of Edward Hasted, of Hawley, in that county, esq. barrister at law, was descended paternally from the noble family of Clifford, as he was maternally from the antient and knightly family of the Dingleys of Woolverton, in the Isle of Wight. By Anne his wife, who died in 1803, Mr Hasted left four sons and two daughters, of whom the eldest son is now a respectable clergyman, vicar of Hollingborne, with the Chapel of Hucking annexed, near Maidstone, in Kent, and in the Commission of the Peace for that county.
>
> In the latter part of his life he felt the pressure of adverse fortune, which obliged him to quit his residence in Kent, after which he lived in obscure retirement, and for some time in the environs of London, noticed by a few valuable friends, from whom he received constant tokens of benevolent friendship, as having known him in more fortunate circumstances, several of whom are of the rank of nobility, and of high estimation in life. A few years ago, his honourable and highly respected patron and friend, the Earl of Radnor, presented him to the Mastership of the Hospital at Corsham in Wiltshire (a most desirable asylum), to which he then removed; and having obtained, a few years ago, the Chancellor's decree for the recovery of his estates in Kent, of which he had been

defrauded, it enabled him again to enjoy the sweets of an independent competence during the remainder of his life.[682]

The obituary summarised his life and, modestly, his achievements. Had it been written by one of his sons or daughters it would have been little different. Hasted probably wrote it himself to lighten the load of his executor, who was, after all, a friend of his later years, and unacquainted with most of his earlier life. An explanatory note had been attached to it for Barlow's benefit and in the rush of activity following the historian's death was sent off with the obituary notice to the *Gentleman's Magazine*. It is unlikely, however, to have been simply printer's incompetence which resulted in the notice being printed within inverted commas, as though unsubstantiated, with Hasted's instructions to his executor appearing as a footnote:

> I request my executor to cause the following insertion, immediately after my death, to be sent for that purpose to the publisher of the Gentleman's Magazine to be inserted in the Obituary of the next Magazine after my death; and I am sure my much-respected friend Mr Nichols will have the goodness to consent to it. Edward Hasted.[683]

There seems, unquestionably, to be an element of spitefulness in this presentation of the obituary. The bad taste of the inclusion of the footnote is compounded by its attempt to pour scorn on the great historian's style, particularly in the folio *History*, where the many annotations are integral to the text. Was this simply poor judgment on the part of the editor of the *Gentleman's Magazine* — for by now John Nichols had the reins firmly in his hands, and only he can be blamed for this — or was it intentional malice? Hasted seems to have been deceived in one or two of his friends, and it is quite possible that Nichols, who was a competitor in the field of topographical history, and whose work on Leicestershire was far from being, like Hasted's, a single-handed product, did not reciprocate the friendship which the Kentish historian imagined existed between them.

A brief obituary appeared in the *Kentish Gazette* a week after the funeral:

> Lately, at Corsham, in Wiltshire, in the 80th year of his age, Edward Hasted, esq. F.R.S and F.A.S. — a classical scholar, a polished gentleman, and a sincere Christian. His 'History of

Kent', his native county, will be a lasting record of his learning and industry'.[684]

The same notice was placed in the *Kentish Chronicle*, appearing on the 31 January. This was a shortened version of an obituary notice which had appeared in the *Bath Herald*, and which was repeated in full, to its credit, in the *Maidstone Journal*. Whose hand wrote it we cannot know, whether that of John Barlow, Monsieur Meffre, or another. It seems more likely that it was written by a friend rather than by a member of his family. Edward's final words on his father may have been those contained in a letter to Lord Radnor written two months after his father's death. The letter concerned some of his father's MSS, and ended with Edward thanking the earl 'for the many distinguish'd tokens of benevolence shewn by your Lordship to an unfortunate, but highly-respected parent'.[685] There was nothing apologetic about the obituary which appeared in the *Bath Herald*, and which provided the departed historian of Kent with the words that could have been carved as his epitaph:

> Died,
>
> Last week at Corsham, Wiltshire, much lamented in the 80th year of his age, Edward Hasted, esq., F.R.S and S.A. — A man, in whom were combined the classical attainments of a scholar, without pedantry; the refined and polished manners of a gentleman, without affectation; and the piety of a sincere Christian, without bigotry. His 'History of Kent' will be a lasting record of his learning, and his indefatigable researches into the history and antiquities of his native county. — It is a work which will bear comparison with the valuable labours of Dugdale, Thoresby, Blomefield, etc. in the same department of literature.[686]

These are surely the words which should linger in the folk-memory of the county to which Hasted devoted himself: they give a fair assessment of the man and his work.

As for the Hasted estates, the final task of disentangling the confusion into which they had fallen was now shouldered by the Revd Edward Hasted, as the eldest son and the one who was to inherit whatever remained after their sale and the clearing of all debts and mortgages. At the time of his father's death the account by the Master in Chancery relating to the amount now due ('if anything', as the decree had stated) to John Williams, in respect of the land and property which the Williamses had been holding since 1790, was still awaited, and might still have been long in coming. With this in mind, and in order to avoid the delay and expense of a further suit in Chancery, shortly after Hasted's death all the parties concerned in the matter agreed to accept John Williams's own accounts. There were six parties to the agreement, which was drawn up on the 23 April 1812: John Williams and John Tasker, representing those who had benefited under the wills of Thomas or Richard Williams; Joseph Proud Davies and John Blaxland, the executors of Hasted's original mortgagee Joseph Davies; Robert and John Rugg, executors of the original mortgagee Robert Rugg; the attorneys John Simmons and William Scudamore; the Revd Edward Hasted; and Hasted's own executor, John Barlow. Williams's account, when presented, showed that his family had not let the Hasted lands lie fallow, and that they had undergone considerable development and improvement, for the amount now owing to him, supported by relevant vouchers, and accepted by the other parties, was £13,931.[687]

Two firms of attorneys — or, as they were coming to be called, solicitors — Messrs Clarkson of Essex Street, Strand, and Debary, Scudamore and Currey of Gate Street, Lincoln's Inn Fields, were retained to handle the sale of the estate. On Friday and Saturday the 25 and 26 September 1812, at the Crown inn at Rochester, the whole of the Hasted property was put up for sale in forty lots under the hammer of a London auctioneer, Thomas Dawson. In spite of the inroads which earlier sales of some of it must have made, it was still a very sizeable estate, consisting of three hundred acres of freehold lands, in the parishes of Cliffe, Newington, Halstow and Upchurch, and the leasehold manor farm of Horsham, which covered some thousand acres of various types of land — meadow, pasture, wood, salts and marsh — lying in a number of parishes, including Upchurch, Halstow, Newington, Hartlip and Rainham. As in the days when Joseph had first taken it, nearly a century earlier, the lease of the manor of Horsham still required, on paper at least, payment in kind as well as in money — 'Also to pay 1 firkin of Melton oysters every year, and to pay 20s. per annum and a bushel of wheat to the poor of Halstow'; 'Also to 1 Bushel of good well fed oysters, or in lieu thereof 10s. to be paid at Christmas yearly' — although most of these may have been commuted by now to money payments only.[688] The good-tempered Charles came in from Chatham each day to act as the family's representative at the auction, writing to Edward immediately after the close of business on the second day to let him know that that day's sales had brought in £7180: 'Dr Brother, the above is the amount of the sale of Lots today. Yr affectionate Brother, Charles'.[689]

The total amount raised by the two-day auction was £15,867.15s.0d. Hasted's friend and executor, John Barlow, who had been a tenant of three lots of arable land totalling some twenty-one acres in the parish of Cliffe — Globe Field, The Five Acres and Knowles — now became their purchaser for the sums of £270, £230 and £360. Another five acres of arable land, Lot 7, the delightfully-named Jinglings, went to George Comport, of Cooling, for £230. Lots 20 and 21, consisting of some twenty-two acres of pasture, including Hither Mill Bridge Marsh, Water Half Acre, Island One and a Half Acre, and Breeches, were bought for the Earl of Darnley by Richard Knight for a total of £937.15s.0d.[690] Only the manor of Horsham, offered as lot 25, remained unsold, and private contracts were subsequently arranged for this. The sum finally realised by the sale of the Hasted estates was something in excess of £26,500.

There seems however to have been considerable delay in getting in the money raised by the sale — the historian was by no means alone in having cash-flow problems — and the executors representing the two original mortgagees, Davies and Rugg, do not appear to have been paid until 1816, by which time the sums due to them had been increased by interest over the intervening years, to say nothing of the mounting legal costs.

At this point the fifty-six-year-old vicar of Hollingbourne would appear to have reached the limits of his patience. Compromise was forgotten. Instead, together with his Chatham bankers, the firm of William Budgen, William Jefferys and John Gurr, he instituted a new suit in Chancery, alleging that the two firms of solicitors of Clarkson and Debary, as well as the executor John Barlow 'and his confederates' had large sums of money in their hands which they had not handed over, and also that they had shown negligence in calling in the various sums due to the estate. Among those called to put in an answer to the Revd Edward Hasted's Bill of Complaint were all the solicitors acting in the case, which included Richard Debary, George Clarkson, John Simmons and William Scudamore, as well as the Ruggs and Joseph Proud Davies, as executors, John Barlow, and Harriet, erstwhile Brewster, and her husband Samuel Taylor.

The solicitors produced accounts to show that sales of the property had realised £22,816.5s.1d. to date, and claimed that the sums owing to Williams (£13,931) and the mortgagees' executors (£2,200 to the Ruggs, £2,000 to J.P.Davies) had been paid off, but that interest on these sums, plus legal fees, had left a balance owing to the trust of a mere £53.4s.5d! Private sales were still in hand for some of those lands which had not gone at auction, and were likely to bring in a further £3,500, although here again, in connection with one of the sales, completion was held up by 'the embarrass'd state of Mr Ludgater's affairs'.[691] Inevitably, time added its complications — John Simmons died while the case was pending, and his wife Sarah became answerable in his place — as well as its simplifications: by 1818 the amount owing on the Rugg mortgage was admitted to have been fully paid off, and Robert and John Rugg asked to be dismissed from the suit, with costs.

Harriet Brewster was listed in the suit as a 'confederate' of John Barlow. She, it will be remembered, had been named as Hasted's residuary legatee, and with what might seem almost indecent haste had married Samuel Taylor at the church of St Marylebone, Marylebone Road, London, on the 13 April 1812, exactly three months and a day after the death of her benefactor. In the joint answer which Samuel and Harriet Taylor put in to the suit, the terms of the will are recited. Neither of them had been a party to the agreement of 23 April 1812, and they therefore claimed, in right of Harriet, to be 'absolutely entitled to one third part of the said testator's real estates comprised in or affected by the said indentures of 11th and 12th day of March, 1789 and of the monies arising from such estates', and to all other benefits given to Harriet by the will.[692] Such a claim must have seemed somewhat offensive to the Hasted family, but there is no doubt that their father's will had laid the way open for it.

There was a counter-claim against the Revd Edward Hasted for £537.19s.6d. by the firms of Clarkson and Debary, which he was refusing to pay because he felt that they were withholding money from him, as the beneficiary of the trust set up in 1789.[693]

The case dragged on for some years. Certainly it was clear that no fortune was to be forthcoming from the Hasted estates. Harriet Brewster's claim to be considered along with the other members of Hasted's family to the benefits of the trust established in 1789 was probably annulled by the codicil, and only Edward stood to benefit by it. By the time an agreement was reached even the few thousand pounds which, on the showing of the solicitors in 1816, were due from the final sales of the estate, must have been further reduced by legal costs. It seems unlikely that Edward was in pocket by more than about £2000, when, a little over ten years since his father's death, it was recorded in Chancery on the 19 February 1822 that 'the matters in difference between the parties have been accommodated', and the case was finally dismissed, without costs.[694]

In the answer which he put in as one of the defendants John Barlow had given evidence that he had received from the auctioneer who sold the estates the sum of £116 only, all of which had been expended in paying for the probate of Hasted's will and codicil, his funeral expenses and sundry small debts, and that Barlow himself was still owed £360 in respect of his own legacy and money which he had advanced on behalf of the estate.[695] Whether this sum included the amounts proposed to be spent on Hasted's gravestone and tablet we cannot know. In the event, however, we can understand why it was that the grave of the master of Hungerford almshouses remained unmarked and uncommemorated. Only towards the end of the twentieth century were latter-day historians moved to remedy the omission, when the Kent Archaeological Society obtained permission to have a small plaque placed on the wall of the church at Corsham, where Edward Hasted lies.

AND THE CONDITIONS OF SALE,
OF
A Valuable Freehold Farm,

And 178A. 3R. 0P. *of Arable, Meadow, and Pasture*

LANDS,

In the Possession of Mr. RICHARD EDMONDS, whose Lease will expire at Michaelmas, 1812,

SITUATE AT CLIFFE

NEAR ROCHESTER;

Also 112A. 0R. 7P. of FREEHOLD LAND,
AND SEVERAL GOOD HOUSES AND BUILDINGS,
AND THE

MANOR FARM of HORSHAM,

AND UPWARDS OF

One Thousand Acres

OF

Meadow, Pasture, Arable, Wood, Salts & Marsh Lands,

Held of ALL SOULS COLLEGE, OXFORD;

On Lease renewable every Four Years,

Situate at Upchurch, Halstow; Newington, Hartlip, Rainham, &c.

NEAR SITTINGBOURNE, IN KENT,

N.B. THE WHOLE OF THE LAND TAX REDEEMED;

IN THE POSSESSION OF

William Ludgater, James Ayres, James Barley, John Stunt, Richard Mitchell, & others,
at Will, and on Leases which expire in 1814, 1815, and 1819;

Being the Estates of EDWARD HASTED, Esq. deceased;

𝕎hich will be 𝕊old by 𝔸uction,

BY

MR. DAWSON,

AT THE CROWN INN, ROCHESTER,

On FRIDAY and SATURDAY, the 25th & 26th Days of SEPTEMBER, 1812, at Twelve o'Clock.

THE TENANTS WILL SHEW THE LOTS.

Jan. 14. "At the Master's Lodge of the Lady Hungerford's Hospital, in Corsham, co. Wilts, at the advanced age of 80, Edward Hasted, esq. the Kentish Historian, F.R.S. and S.A. His laborious History too

Chapter 16

The Kentish Legacy

A number of reviews and notices, probably more than are now extant, greeted the appearance of Hasted's first edition. We still have, however, those reviews which were published in the *Gentleman's Magazine*, and in the *Monthly Review* and the *Critical Review*, all journals of some standing and longevity. None of these appears to have noticed the fourth volume which triumphantly completed the *History* — due, no doubt, to the embarrassing fact that its author was at the time a prisoner at his creditors' behest for debt — but reviews of the first three volumes were printed in the *Gentleman's Magazine*, reviews of the first two, in the *Monthly Review*, while the *Critical Review* seems to have noticed Volume I only.

The review which appeared in the *Gentleman's Magazine*, in the August of 1778, has already been mentioned.[696] It was followed, on the publication of Volume II, by a similarly appreciative notice in the May of 1783.[697] These two reviews appeared during the editorship of David Henry, who had taken over the *Magazine* on the death of Edward Cave, the founding editor, in 1754, and were probably the work of Henry's chief reviewer, the Revd John Duncombe. Duncombe, who lived in Canterbury, must have known Hasted personally. His reviews did not fail to underline the time, labour and expense which the historian was dedicating to his work, and he praised both volumes for their judicious mix of information and entertainment. Duncombe's reviews were rounded off with suitable extracts which might be calculated to whet the reader's appetite for more.

The *Critical Review* had also given Hasted's first volume a good review, concluding with the following paragraph:

> This volume contains a description of 87 parishes in the county of Kent, which are delineated with great accuracy, and rendered the subjects of such information as must not only afford pleasure to the antiquary, but entertainment to all who would acquire a topographical knowledge of the county. Mr Hasted has methodically arranged his materials on every article under distinct heads, which, though often treated copiously, are never swelled with any detail that is either uninteresting, or impertinent in a work of this kind. The extraordinary pains with which these materials have been collected are abundantly evident from the numerous references at the bottom of every page; and at the same time that the volume is ornamented with a great number of plates,

it is uniformly executed with a degree of judgement which has seldom been displayed by those who have prosecuted local researches.[698]

The writer of this review offered a perceptive comment on Hasted's achievement, acknowledging not only his scholarship and industry, but also his care to present this to his public in an acceptable and even graceful way. It was a review which the historian richly deserved, and must have done a great deal to offset the irritation he was undoubtedly caused by another review which had come out at the same time. The notice which appeared in the *Monthly Review, or Literary Journal*, regretted that Hasted had not written a quite different book. It began:

> This is a most laborious and expensive undertaking; yet it contains very little in proportion to its bulk, to gratify those readers who may be more inquisitive after the natural history and antiquities of the county, than the descents and family histories of the private landholders.[699]

After complaining of 'loads of dry tedious genealogical details' the first paragraph ended by concluding that such materials were 'proper ... to arrange in an appendix, or to compose occasional notes; but ought not to overwhelm and smother the general subject' — thus rather losing sight of the fact that the passing of ownership of the county of Kent, subdivided into landholdings, from generation to generation, or from family to family, was no more and no less than the history of Kent which Hasted had intended.

Hasted's years of labour were acknowledged with only a cursory nod at the end: 'and now comes Mr Hasted, furnished with many additional materials from the MSS collections of ... etc. etc., beside the various public respositories, which our author assures us in his preface, he has carefully consulted.' Even this churlish reviewer, however, has to admit that the numerous engravings are 'for the most part, very elegant', and the indexes good — although this is turned into a rather back-handed compliment by the insinuation that no work ever stood in greater need of them. And in spite of all his criticisms, one of which had been that the sections on natural history, antiquities, etc, were lost amongst the other material, the reviewer seems to have had no difficulty in finding such a section, 'for the entertainment of our readers', filling two and a half pages with Hasted's account of the natural history of Tunbridge Wells.

The *Monthly Review* had perhaps changed its reviewer by the time Volume II appeared. In the 'Supplement to the Monthly Catalogue' for

December 1783, the second volume of Hasted's *History*, 'likewise enriched with full and useful indexes' was given a cheerful welcome, and the brief notice concluded:

> The author's labours are not yet completed. A third volume was announced for the press in October. We wish Mr Hasted the success, which such 'toil and trouble' merit; and we hope, that the number and liberality of his subscribers will amply reward him, and not merely defray the expence of publication.[700]

The only review which now appears to be extant for Volume III, which was published in 1790, is that which it was given by the *Gentleman's Magazine*. A number of changes had taken place at the *Magazine* since the time of the second review. Over the last decade it had been moving out of the hands of David Henry and into those of John Nichols — although Nichols was not to be officially named by Henry as his replacement until 1791.[701] John Duncombe had now been dead for several years, and Nichols's chief reviewer was his great friend Richard Gough. It could well have been Gough — responsible for belittling the Herculean efforts and damaging the reputation of several other men engaged in similar fields — who wrote the waspish review which met Hasted's eye in the October following the third volume's appearance.[702] Contradicting the ease with which Duncombe had quoted extracts from the work, the present writer declined to do this, declaring it an impossible task, and, when at last forced to admit something in the book's favour, doing his best to rewrite the favourable reviews which Duncombe had earlier given the *History*.

> It cannot be expected that we should make extracts from a work of this kind. Suffice it that we observe, in its favour, that it appears to us, on a careful perusal, to have been executed with greater care and attention than the preceding volumes.[703]

The review ended by directing the reader, for a more ample discussion of 'several of the places treated of in this volume', to various numbers of the *Bibliotheca Topographica Britannica*.

The *Bibliotheca Topographica Britannica* was an occasional series which had then been running for ten years, bringing out a miscellany of articles on British topography, some of them reprints of old ones. It was printed and published by John Nichols, for himself, which does, of course, mean that he had overall control of the editorial material appearing in it. It was the first number of Nichols's *Bibliotheca* which had been responsible, in 1780, for the invidious comparison between Hasted's history of a whole county and Edward Rowe Mores's history of the single parish of Tunstall, and which had endeavoured to suggest, besides, that Hasted had made good use neither of his secondary nor of his primary sources:

> Had the compiler of the general history of that county ... confined himself only to [printed] sources, how much would he have improved that long-expected and voluminous work! But had he penetrated more intimately ... into the *keimelia* of records, inquisitions, chartularies, registers, and that fund of materials which are open to every diligent investigator, what a history of KENT ... would have arisen under the pen of Mr HASTED![704]

Such a dismissal of Hasted's years of research was both ignorant and spiteful. However, it was not the only attack made on the historian in 1780. In the same year apeared Volume 1 of a very similar compilation to the *Bibliotheca Topographica*, this time called *British Topography, or, An Historical account of what has been done for illustrating the topographical antiquities of Great Britain and Ireland*. Nichols, again, had a hand in it, and he was joined in the enterprise by two antiquarians, Richard Gough, who wrote the preface for it, and Francis Grose. Together the three men probably wrote most of the contents. Which, of these three, was responsible for the two pages which dealt with Hasted's first volume? — introducing the subject, in a manner that can only have been intended to stir up mischief, with a repetition of Hasted's own perhaps injudicious comment on Sir Charles Whitworth's abandoned attempt to put together a history of Kent: 'but the progress he made was so small, as hardly to be called an attempt'. The pages on Hasted's *History* take rather the form of an attack than of any measured criticism. There are considerable quotations from his Preface, managed in such a way that his fine acknowledgments of those who provided materials for him are turned against him, as showing that his work was negligeably easy. In particular he is stated to be indebted to 'the history of Kent corrected and compiled by Mr Austen of Sevenoke, who is well verst in every matter relating to this county'.[705] Such a 'history' is a total figment of the imagination of *British Topography's* writer, since Mr Austen of Sevenoaks, while always pleased to assist Hasted in whatever way he could — the family link between the Austens of Chatham and Hasted's grandmother should not be forgotten — was far too busy in his position as steward to the Duke of Dorset to have time to put together his own history of the county.

The illustrations are dismissed in a manner that can only have been intended to put Hasted out of favour with his patrons:

> The plates, which amount to twenty-five, are presents from his friends, whose liberality is disgraced by the engraving. Eleven, the work of Bayly, are below criticism ... The lesser plates interspersed are very inconsiderable; and of these the seal of Odo Bishop of Baieux is beyond description wretched.[706]

How well had the writer examined the work he was supposedly criticising? There is the same unjustified complaint which had appeared in the *Bibliotheca*, namely, that the *History* is 'too much of a compilation from printed books, without those authorities from record which the author so highly extolls in Dugdale'. And in spite of the fact that Hasted's work contains numerous quotations from Domesday Book, inserted where appropriate together with a translation, surprise is expressed that Hasted should have been deterred by the expense from printing 'the antient record of Domesday ... even in the easy type employed in Dorset' [i.e. John Hutchins' *History of Dorset*].

Here, particularly since the printing is singled out for what is intended to be crushing criticism, it is almost certainly correct to detect the voice of John Nichols, who was first and foremost a printer. The good-humoured Francis Grose, whose skills as a caricaturist were used on more than one occasion to undermine the earnestness of the antiquary, author also of *The Grumbler* and compiler of a dictionary of slang, who was to die in 1791 while at dinner with his friend Nathaniel Hone in Dublin, can almost certainly be exonerated of having had a hand in this — indeed, of all three men the name of Captain Grose is the only one which crops up in the working correspondence on the *History*.[707] Richard Gough, a very close friend of John Nichols, probably shared the printer's views and is, as has been said, a strong candidate for the authorship of the cutting review of Volume III.

By the time we come to 1812, however, and the appearance of the historian's obituary in the *Gentleman's Magazine*, Richard Gough had been dead for some three years, so that to Nichols alone can be imputed the malice which let the footnote appear, thus making it clear to all that the obituary was Hasted's own work. Nor, when the *Magazine* was obliged to print a more fitting tribute to the Kentish historian, based on the fine obituary which had appeared originally in the *Bath Herald*, could Nichols resist altering the text to bring himself into prominence. Whereas the obituary as printed in the *Bath Herald* and the *Maidstone Journal* had ended: 'it is a work which will bear comparison with the valuable labours of Dugdale, Thoresby, Blomefield, etc. in the same department of literature', the list of eminent writers was now expanded by three names to include that of Nichols himself. [708]

But these covert attempts to undermine Hasted's reputation were not felt to be enough. Before the year was out someone at the *Gentleman's Magazine* decided that a more open attack was called for. Readers of the August issue came upon the following letter, printed over the pseudonym 'Litterator':

> It does not appear to me that your Correspondents have yet succeeded, in giving an appropriate portrait of the literary character of the late Mr Hasted, the Historian of Kent. His great Topographical work has much merit. As an history of the property of the county, it is in my opinion a wonderful performance; as containing its genealogies, it is entitled to much, but not to unqualified, praise. But when we have said this, have we not exhausted all its claims to commendation?[709]

What was wanted, continued the writer, was 'the literary history of a county, or at least the history of its really eminent men' — a Johnsonian criticism which is rather beside the point, since that was not the book which Hasted had set out to write. But it is this demand which leads to the suspicion that the author of this letter may have been John Nichols himself, since it is a clear feed to a smug note at the foot of the column to the effect that 'This [i.e. a literary history of the county] has been given in the 'History of Leicestershire'. And the footnote was signed by the editor of the *Magazine*, who was of course none other than John Nichols, compiler, as frequently as he was author, of the *History of Leicestershire*[710] — and publisher of Samuel Johnson.

Even this, however, was not felt to blacken Hasted's reputation sufficiently, and 'Litterator' decided to return to the attack the following month, using the clumsy excuse of 'an accidental interruption' which had caused him 'to close abruptly my late article on the literary character of Mr Hasted'. The strong plug which this second letter again contains for Nichols's *Leicestershire*, when there were by now a number of county histories with which Hasted's *Kent* might have been compared, strengthens the impression that Nichols himself may have been Litterator — a pseudonym which does not appear to have been used by any of his regular contributors.[711] Certainly Nichols, if it was indeed he, was not unsuccessful in this final attempt to belittle the Kentish historian, for the words he used are still sometimes quoted today, by those who have never sat down to enjoy an hour or two of Hasted's company, letting his detail

— and it is by no means all genealogical — build up in parish after parish a picture of the Kentish families who have peopled the county through the ages.

> It is very true, [wrote Litterator on the second occasion] that that of which I complained as a deficiency in Hasted, has been supplied with uncommon industry and extent of research by the Historian of Leicestershire. No spot, no collateral aid, has remained unexplored: and it adds greatly to the value, that a large portion of the materials is in the very words of the originals .... The fault of Hasted is, that he has no variety: all is reduced to one dull narrative, consisting of little more than a dull deduction of the Proprietors of Manors in a kind of language, which forms nothing like a style, but savours most of the technicalities of an Attorney's office. Anything curious in Nature or Art, any traits of Manners, or Illustrations of the characters of individuals, never engage his remark or attention. With him, one man only differs from another by his name, the date of his birth, and death; and the family into which he married: unless we add his rent-roll, and the specification of the manors of which he was the owner.[712]

Dull, with no variety; and now the lowest jibe that 'Litterator' could think of: the historian of Kent — who had indeed spent some time as a youth studying law under an attorney — was no more than the product of an attorney's office. What had Hasted done to be the butt of such personal animosity? Could it be that in an unguarded moment he had once reminded Nichols that he was first and foremost a printer or even, more heinous still, been heard to mention that he was the son of a baker? The historian could on occasion be tactless, and it seems quite possible that Nichols nursed a grievance of which Hasted remained all his life blithely ignorant.

Of course, like all journals and periodicals, the *Gentleman's Magazine* was in the business of stimulating copy for subsequent issues, and the 'Litterator' letters were successful in provoking a sturdy and detailed defence of Hasted's work, which was printed the following November. It came from someone who had made his own small contribution to Kentish history with short accounts of Gravesend and of the Tufton family, someone who, without having known Hasted, appreciated the worth of his *History* for the county. This was Robert Pocock, an enthusiast in many fields, writing now as 'The Chairman of the Kent Natural History Society'. It is slightly unfortunate that the address of this (short-lived) Natural History Society was the Leather

Bottle Inn — although at Northfleet, not Cobham — since this has, for later generations, tended to cast a quirky, Pickwickian air over what are nevertheless the soundly based views of an educated admirer of Hasted.[713]

As Hasted said himself in his Preface to Volume I, his interest in the history of the county had stemmed from an early attraction to history generally. Allied to this was undoubtedly an interest in heraldry, a tradition which was very much alive in the eighteenth century and which is by no means dead today. When it became evident to him, after considerable persuasion from friends, that a better history of Kent was needed than existed at the time and that he might be the man to write it, he set out to read anything and everything that could possibly relate to the subject, had books bought for him at auction, and begged the loan of manuscripts and deeds, which he would set to work to copy straight away and always returned promptly. His friend Thomas Astle worked for a while at the Augmentation Office, which held all the records of lands taken from the dissolved monasteries in the sixteenth century; another friend, Dr Ducarel, was the librarian of Lambeth Palace, the London residence of the Archbishop of Canterbury. Both places held many records relating to Kent, and Hasted was able to make use of both. But he went further afield than simply to those offices to which he had an easy access. In the Preface to his first volume he also lists the Chapter House at Westminster, the King's Remembrancer's Office, the Tower, the Rolls-chapel, the King's Surveyor's Office, the Heralds' Office, the British Museum (only recently established), and the Priory of Christ Church, Canterbury, commenting, 'But few, very few indeed, are acquainted even with the names of the several offices, in which these records are deposited', and adding: 'so great is the store in them, that was the life of man extended to two, or even three times its usual period, it would not be sufficient for him, with his utmost endeavours, to search through one half of their contents'.[714] Many of these collections are now centralised in the Public Record Office, and one has only to visualise a fraction of that vast store to realise the accuracy of Hasted's statement. We are now more familiar with our hoard of records than were any but a tiny handful of men in Hasted's time, however, and those who criticised him for not using these sources would in fact have had little notion of the study and time involved. In addition, Hasted was able to examine the private papers and title deeds of large numbers of the Kentish gentry, which means that his researches also covered some of the material that now, neatly catalogued, forms part of the holdings of the county archives office.

The endeavours of his predecessors in the field and many useful works of reference were also acknowledged in the Preface, and references to these are to be found over and over again in his footnotes, as well as in various lists of material which he drew up in his commonplace books. 'Books in my study, to be particularly referred to', are noted in one memorandum, and this was followed by a longer list of 'books which I have not' — but which he clearly hoped to beg, borrow or buy for the purposes of his *History*. Other lists were drawn up from time to time. At the end of the correspondence for the fourth volume, for example, is a list of books, with the abbreviations to be used for them in the footnotes. Indeed, it is the footnotes in the first edition that confirm the depth and breadth of Hasted's preparation for the writing of a history of his county.

By the time his finances collapsed about his ears and he was forced to take refuge in France, there must have been few scholars of his stature in the county. He had become skilled in palaeography, he could read Latin and Anglo-Saxon, he was an expert genealogist, and more than proficient in matters of heraldry. Other areas of interest come through in his work also: the old jurisdictions in the county, the presence or otherwise of drainage in Kent's extensive marshlands — and any trees which stand out as a feature of the place under discussion: elm, oak, alder, or willow.

Modern histories of the county of Kent, benefiting from the many works on the same subject which have preceded them, as well as the development of 'history' into an academically formulated subject, do not lack for models, and can choose between a geographical or a thematic plan: a run along the roads of Kent, with an informative voice-over telling the reader what to look for, or a meander through the centuries, mentioning national highlights as and when they impinge on Kent. Both can result in highly readable books, both kinds usually aiming to present a selection of known and unknown facts. Or there is the guide, a thumbnail account of various locations, brief, or comprehensive.

Edward Hasted's massive four-folio-volume work does, at first sight, bear some resemblance to a guide. Abandoning the simple alphabetical format favoured by Kilburne, Philipott and Harris, he opted for a geographical framework, basing this on the old administrative areas known as Lathes and within these on the Hundreds, with maps of the Hundreds accompanying the work throughout. It is within this framework that each parish in the county is visited and discussed.

One of Hasted's great merits is the depth of his treatment. Another is his impartiality. And a third is that his manner of dealing with the descent of the land through the ages — painstakingly built up from what must have been the thousands of documents consulted, records transcribed and translated, and facts verified, from as early a date as possible — succeeds in building up a history of a county through the people who lived there.

A description of the descent of the manors and estates into which Kent was broken up gives us also, at one and the same time, details of the marriage settlements, of the sales and purchases, and of the divisions and sub-divisions of the land, which form a background to many of the names that still surround us today, in places, farms, houses, or on memorials or tombstones in churches, together with some knowledge of the people who once bore those names — and women are as likely to figure as men.

This is the main body of his text; but each parish also has all or most of the following subheadings: ecclesiastical jurisdiction; antiquities; botany; present state of the parish. Under this last heading Hasted has sometimes been accused of not giving enough attention to the social and economic changes which were taking place during the years when his *History* was being written. In Kent, however, little more was to be found of the Industrial Revolution at this time than a few hesitant (and often unsuccessful) beginnings. The county seems to have lain between a past that was becoming no more than a memory — there were still a few clothiers left in the Weald, for example, but the cloth industry that had thrived there in Tudor times was now virtually extinct — and a future that was slow to awaken. Hasted does indeed mention several new 'manufactories', but in more than one instance they vanished into thin air while he was writing about them — his 'Corrections and Emendations' contain proof of this. Nevertheless, what industries there were are given a mention, and the list is not inconsiderable: the production of muslins, brocaded silks and stockings at Canterbury; copperas works at Whitstable and Deptford; salt-making at Stonar in the Isle of Thanet and in the Isle of Grain; gunpowder works at Ospringe and elsewhere; iron-casting in the Weald near the Sussex border and iron manufactories at Dartford and Crayford, which latter town also had large works for the printing of calicos and bleaching of linens; a silk factory near Sevenoaks; paper-making at Boxley; a nascent resort industry at Margate, whose 'weather shore' and smooth seas were beginning to entice bathers. These, and other smaller, and frequently ill-fated enterprises, are duly given their places in the *History*.

Communications are not neglected, and turnpike roads, where these already exist, are noted. It must be remembered, however, that in Hasted's time not only was the system far from complete, but the putting in of turnpike trustees was seen as no more than an extension and improvement of the ages-old parish control of roads. Where a road through a parish was a good one, or had recently been improved, Hasted says so; the voluntary service provided by the turnpike trustees in order to bring this about was not the subject of his *History*. The other transport development which occurred during the early years of the industrial revolution, namely, the building of canals, had not yet affected the county when he wrote about it. The canal mania in Kent was to be short both temporally and geographically. In the 1790s James Simmons was to be one of the promoters of a canal from Canterbury to the sea at Reculver which, in the event, was never begun: the project, however was mentioned by Hasted, with an extract from the surveyor's favourable report on this in a footnote. The Royal Military Canal between Hythe and Rye, excavated as a second line of defence in the event of invasion by Napoleon, dates from 1804-9. The only commercial canal which was actually built in Kent, the Thames and Medway, begun in 1800, did not open until 1824.

It has sometimes been assumed that so much detail cannot be passed on in other than a dry style, and that 'Litterator's' jibe must, after all, be correct. But this is not so. It could hardly be expected that in the inevitably long accounts of the passage of a manor or estate from one family to another down through the ages — and who else has taken the trouble to give us these? — Hasted should be more prolix than necessary, or turn aside into numberless digressions. His *History* could not have supported a Laurence Sterne or a John Aubrey. It is quite erroneous, however, to suggest that it is written in the language of a legal document. And in passages which allowed freer rein to the writer he was perfectly capable of rising to the occasion. In the description of Kent eastwards of Adisham, for example, — a scene he must have gazed at many times on visits to his friends — the combination of fact with personal feeling results in a long, flowing sentence, that twists and turns agreeably among the features of the countryside it portrays:

> From hence over the Isle of Thanet northward to Sandwich, Deal, and Dover, on the sea shore eastward, and the extremity of Barham Downs southward, this part of the county, which has the name in particular of East Kent, is remarkably beautiful and pleasant, being for the most part an open champaign country, interspersed at places with small inclosures and coppices of wood, with towns, frequent villages and their churches, and many seats of the gentry, with their parks and plantations throughout it.

In the main, however, Hasted's is a straightforward style, plain but not uninteresting, and at times almost conversational, as when he tells us of the church at West Langdon that

> it has long been in a ruinated state. In 1660, Sir Thomas Peyton, bart. of Knolton, had a design to repair it, for which purpose he provided a quantity of timber, but in the night the country people

stole the whole of it away, and besides took away the pulpit, pews, etc, which had been left standing, out of the church; in which dilapidated situation it still continues. The ruins of it consist of a nave and chancel tolerably entire, excepting the roof. In the chancel is a gravestone, now covered with rubbish, for Sir Timothy Thornhill, once owner of this abbey.[715]

There is considerably more variety in Hasted than is generally recognised — the recounting of old customs, the odd rhyme, even occasionally the writer himself stepping up alongside his material to add a personal anecdote or corroboration. It is all arranged with considerable skill. And when one says 'all', how much there is! Professor Alan Everitt has drawn attention to the fact that several thousand local families are mentioned by Hasted[716]: a computation based on the indexes makes it possible to state that some seventeen to eighteen thousand individuals make an appearance in the pages of the *History*. Had Hasted not been methodical in his handling and presentation of such material, the result would have been chaotic. But method does not banish variety.

A further characteristic of Hasted's folio volumes is the footnote. Rare indeed is the page which does not have its accompaniment of small print at the bottom; and the letters *a – z*, which relate the footnotes to the text, are run through over and over again at a great rate. The lengthy footnote — and many of Hasted's notes are of considerable length — was not regarded with disfavour when he was planning his work. Apart from the service it provided in authenticating sources, the footnote offered the scholarly author a small podium from which to address more personal comments to the audience, the small print, as it were, embodying the lowered voice of an aside. Edward Gibbon, writing at around the same time as Edward Hasted, made much use of his footnotes in *The Decline and Fall of the Roman Empire* to carry the ironic comment which would have been out of place in his history. Hasted's long footnotes normally serve to impart additional information, which would have impeded the flow of the main text, although he sometimes made use of them, as in the case of the unhappy marriage of the vicar of Eastling, to make a personal comment.

It is the footnotes which confirm just how wide were Hasted's reading and preparation for his *History*: from Caesar, Pliny, Tacitus, Suetonius and Strabo, through Nennius, Ethelward and the Saxon Chronicles, to Strype's *Stow's Survey*, Rymer's *Foedera*, piles of books on heraldry and the peerage, shelves of legal books, collections of works on other counties, together with records in the various offices, and stray MSS, which had as yet found no editor, all these were read, studied, and, as

Hasted said, 'digested'. By 1790, with Volume III about to be published, and a considerable part of Volume IV already written, he was to say in his third Preface: 'I hope I may say without assuming too much, that when I look through the contents, I wonder myself how I ever collected and digested such a variety of reading, and have gone through the continued labour requisite for it'.[717] We, too, can only share this wonder.

The details of a few of his footnotes have been called into question — and how few these are when we compare them with the thousands the work contains! — but we must remember that we do not now always have to hand the editions which Hasted was using, and that when he worked in the offices of record he was using largely uncatalogued documents. The criticisms levelled at Hasted by Dr Henry Holman Drake, the editor of *Hasted's History of Kent: The Hundred of Blackheath*, which came out in 1886 and was the only part of Lambert Blackwell Larking's proposed revision of the *History* ever to appear, are so ill-founded as hardly to need refuting. Drake, a member of the Royal Archaeological Institute of Great Britain and Ireland who had previously co-edited a Visitation of Cornwall for the Harleian Society, was clearly seized on with enthusiasm by a grateful John Wingfield Larking, burdened by the mountain of papers and the uncompleted task which had come to him on the death of his brother Lambert Blackwell — although in taking on the task of editor Drake, a west-countryman, seems to have been actuated mainly by a desire to discover, as a descendant of Sir Francis Drake, 'why Sir Francis and his brethren became Kentish men'.[718]

Drake hastens to inform the reader that much in Hasted is secondhand. But Hasted himself acknowledges his secondary sources. He is far from incorporating them simply verbatim, as Drake suggests, or from being, as a later critic would have it, a scissors-and-paste historian. Assuming that the older historians were at least partially correct, there was no way in which some of the information already in Lambarde, Philipott, Kilburne, Harris and others would not reappear in a later history of the county. Drake's particular hard place, however, lay in the escheat roll references.

These rolls, which emanated from the exchequer, dealt with the reversion of a property to the lord of the manor or to the crown on the death of the owner in default of an heir. They went hand in hand with the so-called Inquisitiones post mortem, which established these facts, and seem to have been not infrequently confused with them. A further series of rolls, the patent rolls, which assigned crown property thus acquired in return for a fee or a service, was kept at the same time. All these rolls, in their plenitude and confusion, seem, by Hasted's time, to have come into the keeping of the Augmentation Office, set up in 1554 to keep the records of the Court of Augmentations, which was abolished in that year, and which had administered the lands and possessions of dissolved religious houses. There is no doubt at all that Hasted paid a number of visits to the Augmentation Office, where his friend Thomas Astle held the position of Keeper for some years, and that he used these occasions to make notes from original documents, some of which Astle had perhaps put aside for his perusal.

Drake's ignorance of Hasted's access to this material led him to conclude, without citing any evidence for this, that there had been a wholesale borrowing of escheat roll references by Hasted from another source, which he identified as the Lansdowne MSS in the British Museum.[719] However, 'the Lansdowne MSS' as such did not come into being until the purchase in 1807 by the British Museum of the papers of William Petty, second Earl of Shelburne and first Marquess of Lansdowne; prior to this it can be said categorically that the Marquess of Lansdowne's papers were on too high a shelf for Hasted to reach.

Drake's unsuitability for a task requiring patient and accurate research should have been apparent to all in his blithe acceptance of a statement that Hasted had been imprisoned in the Marshalsea.[720] In spite of this, however, a late twentieth-century writer, John Boyle, intent on proving that Hasted had made use of secondary sources in the matter of the escheat rolls, and obliged to admit that Drake's suggestion, that a collection made available only in 1807 could in any way have contributed to a *History* which was complete by 1798, was nonsensical, nevertheless propped Drake up as a witness to what were no more than his own 'suspicions', with the fact that 'over a century ago, Henry Drake had concluded that Hasted's 'Escheat Rolls' references were not based on first-hand knowledge'.[721] And Boyle finally felt that he had clinched the argument by seeming to note a confusion in Hasted between escheat rolls and patent rolls.

It is unnecessary to defend Hasted by pointing out that similar entries could appear in both rolls — and in the Inquisitiones post mortem. Anyone suggesting, as does Boyle, that Hasted 'did not even understand what the expression "Escheat Rolls" meant!' (at a time when escheat for want of an heir could still occur) is simply walking into a trap of his own making. Hasted gives a brief description of these rolls in his Preface to Volume I, while his MS 'History of Folkestone' contains a detailed, five-page account of how the escheat rolls and the Inquisitiones post mortem came into being.[722]

Since Hasted's time, the Augmentation Office records have come under several authorities: from the King's Remembrancer, to the Master of the Rolls, to the Public Record Office. On their way, they have been re-ordered and catalogued. We cannot, now, see them in the same way that Hasted saw them. But see them he undoubtedly did. His known visits to the Augmentation Office under Thomas Astle gave him the opportunity to make escheat roll references, and random checks show that these are correct. Modern lists and calendars, not surprisingly, reveal that there was much that he missed. How grateful he would have been for their assistance! The state of the records into which he dipped, some few in boxes, many of them loose, must at least have doubled the time needed to deal with each one. And the general conditions under which such records would have been seen were far from those maintained in the modern record office. A report by the Revd Joseph Hunter, assistant keeper of the newly established Public Record Office, disclosed around 1840 that there was a 'huge mass of unarranged Exchequer documents, filthy, crumpled, fragmentary or worse, contained in 751 sacks at Carlton Ride and the Augmentation Office'.[723] We should be grateful for all and every reference which Hasted was able to extract from documents in this condition.

Hasted's maps have also received criticism. They came out at a time when properly surveyed maps were just beginning to appear; and it has been suggested that Hasted should have been aware of these developments. On closer inspection, however, they are seen to be developments which did not happen fast enough for the historian to be able to take advantage of them.

From the section headed 'Mapp' in his first great commonplace book — he may well have thought originally only in terms of a single map of the county — it is clear that Hasted was aware of all that was available at the time of planning his work, including a *Map of the Kentish Coast*, *Map of 20 miles round London*, and, in particular, the great *Topographical Map of the County of Kent*, which was brought out in twenty-five sheets by John Andrews, Andrew Dury and William Herbert in 1769. There was no Ordnance Survey map of Kent available to the public until 1801, which was then too late for Hasted. While the trigonometrical survey carried out by Captain Mudge had been completed nearly ten years earlier, that part of the map which was done by surveying draughtsmen was attended to in fits and starts, and was not finished until 1799, by which time all Hasted's map-work had been completed. However, Hasted's maps are by no means as faulty as has been suggested, and complement the Ordnance Survey in numerous instances, as, for example, with additional names of places and the site of turnpike gates.

Hasted was unlucky in his need to offer maps of the county just at the time when professional map-making was coming in. The fact that he did so, however, marked a great step forward from earlier histories of the county, which had not mapped the county systematically. The method he adopted, of working from others' maps, seemed perfectly acceptable at the time. His were to be small, sectional maps based on the Hundreds which formed the framework of his *History*, and which, given the continuing administrative importance of the Hundred at the time he was writing, were intended to be particularly useful to the gentlemen and justices of the county. He could not foresee that one of the main difficulties would be the precise establishment of the boundaries of each Hundred.

Comparisons make it clear that Hasted's maps were closely based on maps already in existence, particularly the topographical maps of John Andrews, and it is likely that Hasted himself made freehand sketches from these of the parts he needed for his Hundred maps. This would account for the slight variations in scale of the Hasted maps (from 1 to 2 inches per mile) as against the 2 inches to a mile of the Andrews. But his maps are by no means simple copies of the Andrews: a particular — and limiting — feature of the Andrews maps, which does not reappear in those of Hasted, is the naming of owners alongside their houses. Nor did Hasted rely on his predecessors' maps for accuracy. Once he had put together a map of a Hundred he made every effort to have it checked on the spot — frequently by more than one person. Surveying and land-measuring, so necessary for the running of an estate, were considered an essential part of a gentleman's education at this time, and many gentlemen, while not professionally trained, acquired the reputation of being excellent surveyors, and not infrequently found themselves called upon to survey whole parishes where rateable values were in dispute. It was on gentlemen such as these that Hasted tended to rely: although professional surveyors were already to be found, they were not considered to be essential, in the first place; and in the second, Hasted could not have afforded their services.

As we have seen, in 1796 Hasted took the decision to bring out his work in a cheaper, less cumbersome form. But he did himself a disservice when he told his friend Boteler that the new edition would be 'abridged of all tautologies and uninteresting matters', for it is hard to find examples of either. It is clear, however, that the historian must have gone through his work with a blue pencil, and that small cuts were made where he felt items of information could be dispensed with. The four Prefaces to the four folio volumes were condensed into one, repeating Hasted's fine acknowledgments to his predecessors, but also explaining his motives in preparing a second edition:

> The present undertaking ... has been begun at the request of many, who though they approved much of the work itself, yet, from the

bulk of the folio edition, and the very high price it sells for, declined the purchase of it, though at the same time they wished much to obtain it in a smaller and more convenient size, and at a much more reasonable price.[724]

William Bristow, the printer and publisher of this edition, was undoubtedly of much service to the historian in suggesting where space could be saved in the layout. New sections, such as a new Hundred, are frequently begun here without any formalities, often in the middle of a page, forcing one to admire over again the excellence and beauty of the layout of the folio volumes, a design which was probably due partly to James Simmons and partly to Hasted himself.

In the effort to reduce the bulk of the work the relatively neat cut-off points for the folio volumes had more than once to be overridden. Thus folio Volume I is contained in second edition Volumes 1-3 and the first forty-five pages of Volume 4. Folio Volume II fills the remainder of Volume 4, together with Volumes 5 and 6. Folio Volume III is contained in Volumes 7 and 8, and three hundred and seventy-three pages of Volume 9; while the remainder of Volume 9 (another two hundred and thirty-eight pages) and all of Volumes 10 to 12 are devoted to the contents of the fourth folio volume. There is more logic to this than might at first appear. Volume 1 of the second edition had to contain both the Preface and the very important 'General History of Kent', which could suffer few cuts, and which took up well over half the pages. And both Bristow and Hasted had recognised that the history of Canterbury, left uncut, and given two volumes to itself, would serve as a good guide to Canterbury, offering in a cheaper and more modern format the very same history of the city which Simmons and Kirkby had put on sale in a folio version. There was no double-dealing or piracy involved in this, since Hasted had been his own publisher of the folio version, and therefore retained the right to issue or re-issue it as he pleased.

Throughout the second edition the text was shorn of almost all subheadings, and given the form of a more continuous narrative. In the introductory 'General History of Kent' the changing subject-matter is usefully indicated by the device of running headings at the top of the right-hand page. Under each parish, only an account of the charities, and the lists of church incumbents, which are here given in smaller type, retain their sub-headings. The material is re-ordered, so that the reader begins the section on, say, Deptford, with a description of that parish, instead of having to wait until near the end of the section to learn about the 'Present state of the parish'. There can be no doubt that this represents an improvement over the arrangement of the material in the folio, and it may well be that Hasted, gaining in hindsight as his *History* progressed, had realised that it could be otherwise presented, but kept to his original plan for the sake of consistency.

Two further casualties of the decision to bring out the *History* in a form which would be more 'user-friendly' were the original text of Domesday Book (which appeared now just in translation), and the lengthy footnote. Only those footnotes which referred to sources and authorities were retained; others were either cut altogether, or incorporated into the text. On the Lethieullier family, for example, there are in the folio volume no less than ten footnotes in the section on Sutton-at-Hone: in Volume 2 of the second edition most of this additional information has been cut, and the remainder skilfully incorporated into the text. The description (in heraldic terms, the blazon) of the arms of the gentlemen of Kent, originally always given in a footnote, now also became part of the text.

Books 11 and 12, however, containing the history of the city of Canterbury, present an exception to this selective pruning. Here, not only is the main text reproduced almost verbatim, but the footnotes, too, remain virtually intact. Only the fact that the occasional omission — or addition — meant that the footnotes had to be relettered; the deletion of the occasional word; and minor updatings, as in mention of the removal of Canterbury's place of execution to the use of a temporary scaffold between the gaol and the keeper's house, show that Hasted did indeed submit his account of the city to the scrutiny of revision. But he clearly felt that the subject-matter of this section was too important to be cut, and must have carried Bristow along with him in this.

Some of the correspondence which related to the second edition remains in the Hasted archive, and it can be seen that Hasted actively sought for updating of his information — numerous questionnaires were apparently sent out, headed as before, 'Parishes', 'Places', and now, 'Owners in 1792. Alterations since?' — and where he obtained a more recent detail, this was incorporated. Lists of office-holders, for example, including parish incumbents, were brought down to around 1796. New fortifications at Hythe constructed in response to the ongoing war with France, the forts of Twiss, Sutherland and Moncrieff, built only in 1798, received a mention in Volume 8 which appeared in 1799 — a detail which highlights also the greater speed with which Bristow was able to work compared with James Simmons.

It was obvious, however, that if, as was indeed the case, the original *History* was substantially correct, there would be little to add to it, and one wonders what the critical Mr Denne — who was gratefully and gracefully acknowledged by Hasted under his parish of Wilmington as 'a gentleman to whom literature in general, and the editor of these volumes in particular, is highly indebted for his liberal communications' — expected in terms of *nouveautés*.[725] Hasted's aim remained the same, namely, to show the history of the county in terms of the people who had tenanted its land. To this extent it is far more of a social history than it would have been had he concentrated either on antiquities, as Denne seems to have wanted, or on a few of the names already known through their contributions to literature, as 'Litterator' was perversely to insist.

The service which the engraver John Barlow rendered Hasted has already been mentioned. Where possible, some of the smaller plates or engravings in the first edition were re-used for the second, a folio quarter-plate for example here becoming a full-plate. But Barlow provided several new plates for most of the second edition volumes, as well as the charming vignette which accompanies each of the dedications. And it was probably his hand which touched up, or re-engraved, the several small engravings from the first edition which were made use of again in the second. His contribution to the last two volumes, those dealing with Canterbury, seems to have been less, although he had done some work for folio Volume IV. R. (?Richard) Pollard is the engraver whose name appears most frequently in the two final books, quite possibly a local man engaged by the Canterbury printer for the several drawings done by M. Thomas — again, possibly the Mark Thomas who had been in Charles Hasted's class at the King's School in the seventies.

Barlow was a further contributor to the second edition, however, in the adjustments which were made to the maps. Hasted, who took such pains to be accurate with the information contained in his text, had hoped for an accompanying accuracy in his maps. The correspondence relating to these shows how he agonised over their content, and there is no doubt that he received further comments and corrections from readers after the publication of each set of maps with the folios. The result is that, with the exception of the three Hundred maps which had accompanied the final folio volume, every one of the earlier maps received emendations and improvements. These, transmitted by the historian, can only be the work of John Barlow, Hasted's closest friend of the years between 1795 and 1807, and proven collaborator on both editions.

The first improvement which strikes the eye is that the maps of the second edition have a less barren appearance than those of the first. In particular, the physical features have been given more emphasis: woods and copses are thickened and darkened, and lines of hills are strengthened, marshland is given texturing, and turnpike roads are highlighted by being more deeply graved. The number of place-names is also increased, both within the maps, and, where it was easier to insert them, round the edges.

Boundaries have been altered, and, occasionally, the lines of roads also. Examples of such improvements can be found on almost every map. Thus the map of the Hundred of Bromley and Beckenham and the Hundred of Ruxley adds the name Shooters Hill in the north, and Penge Green, Elmours End and Notley in the west, at the same time amending the spelling of Aylmours Green to Elmours Green. Hills are added along the southern boundary, and the line of road through Crayford is straightened, with the consequent alteration of the position of the mile-stone marking thirteen miles from London.

The map of the Hundreds of Hoo and of Chatham and Gillingham, as published with the second edition, shows striking differences from that which had accompanied the folio edition. The boundary itself has been adjusted here, so that the map only just fits on to the sheet allotted to it. In the west, the words 'Liberty of the City of Rochester' have been added; in the east, the words 'The Isle of Shepey' (sic) make more sense of an outline which had been unexplained on the original map. An arm of the Medway, previously totally missing, has been drawn in, and the plan of Chatham Yard slightly amended, while Rochester Bridge, which had appeared on the folio map, now has 'and City' added after it, with tiny drawings of both castle and cathedral. The folio map's 'Gillingham Castle' is now more correctly named Gillingham Fort. The 'Isle of Grean' has been changed also, to Isle of Graine, a correction which is carried through into an 'NB' at the foot of the map. Minor roads, too, have been altered, with turnpike roads, following the amended pattern of the second edition, indicated by a darker line. And this is the first map on which Barlow has placed the Hundreds more firmly in the context of the county map by naming several of the surrounding parishes: Queenborough, Rainham, Bredhurst and Cowling (Cooling) are all marked by a tiny drawing of their churches, with spire or tower, although lying outside the confines of the Hundreds in question. This was a feature which the engraver was to continue for the rest of the maps, frequently indicating the position of a dozen or so of the surrounding parishes. Preeminent among them is the map of the Hundreds of Wingham and Kinghamford, in which no less than nineteen parishes, lying beyond the bounds of the Hundreds, are marked in this way.

No such changes were necessary to the three Hundred maps which had accompanied Volume IV, since they already incorporated the new features which Barlow now brought to the second edition maps — proof indeed that the same artist's hand was at work in folio Volume IV and the second edition. The map of the city of Canterbury, which had accompanied Volume IV, and which had been engraved by John Bayly, was re-engraved by John Barlow and actually signed by him. The Hundred maps, however, although subject to considerable revision, continued to show the name of the original engraver, where this had appeared — although many of them, even in the original, bore no attribution.

In the light of the work which Barlow did for Hasted, both on the fourth volume of the folio edition, and throughout the second edition — there is no way of knowing at what modest cost, or even if, as seems likely, the charge was frequently waived — it is not difficult to understand Hasted's affection for him, and the choice of the engraver as his executor. He was a worthy collaborator on the great project, and should be remembered by the county along with William Boteler, William Boys and John Lyon, who gave Hasted considerable assistance, particularly when he was obliged to live abroad.

But however much assistance his good friends provided, it was Hasted's hand which ordered and wrote up his information, his mind which conceived and carried through a plan that could encompass the history of one of the largest of English counties with a formality which is worthy of Domesday, and a grace which is the legacy of the eighteenth century. His was the reading, his the research, his the 'parochial visitations' — which brought him, as an unlooked-for reward, the friendship of perhaps more Kentish men and men of Kent than anyone else in the county enjoyed at that time.

The writer of *In Quest of Hasted* expressed disbelief that one man could have accomplished so much. In connection with the second edition, John Boyle claimed that alterations to the text could not have been the sole work of Edward Hasted, incarcerated in the King's Bench, and postulated instead a second editor, whose personality turned out to be so complex that Boyle eventually split him into two people, a 'more cultured man' and a 'cliché-monger', whom he christened Mr Cludge — adding, with reference to the latter: 'I have found that the giving of a name helpful in envisaging him as an actual person' (sic).[726] It would seem that these hypothetical personages, for Mr Boyle, were able to subdivide like amoebae, since the chapter in which he puts these notions before the reader ends with a reference to 'Mr Cludge' and his 'colleagues'.

There is, however, not a shred of solid evidence that anyone but Hasted was responsible for the alterations, or variants, in the second edition, nor is Boyle able to draw a stronger conclusion from what he calls the external evidence than that there is a 'general effect' of 'evasiveness, suggesting a determination by those concerned to avoid saying outright that Hasted will be personally responsible for the new edition'.[727] But care is seldom taken to spell things out for posterity. Boyle then goes on to discuss the financing of the second edition, about which there is no question at all: Bristow was the publisher of this, and as such accepted the financial risk. This, however, had nothing to do with the content of the second edition, for which Hasted was, and remained throughout, solely responsible.

Boyle tries to justify his charge by commenting on the amendments and additions to many parish descriptions in the second edition, particularly in the case of the parishes which made up folio Volumes I and II. As most writers will know, however, it is always one's earlier work which seems to be in need of correction: written years ago — and in Hasted's case this was of course many years ago — it seldom meets more recently held criteria, and any chance of revision is likely to be seized with alacrity. Hasted had himself recognised this, in the letter telling Boteler about the scheme to publish a second edition of the *History* in which he intended to supplement the descriptions of some of the parishes with more details about charities and church monuments. Readers of this study are unlikely to find it incredible that the general information which extends a few of the entries should have been added by Hasted himself: the parishes in question were the parishes of West Kent, where, man and boy, he had spent around thirty years of his life. Riding through the area year in and year out, as a landowner whose estates were parcelled out in a great number of separate holdings, as a voluntary administrator of the local government of the time, and as a topographical writer who made a point of 'parochial visitations' and who had moreover retained links with the area, it is not surprising that he should have been able to tell us something of interest in the second edition about parishes sometimes dismissed in the first as containing nothing worthy of notice.

But the overriding question must be, who would have been in a position to edit Hasted's work? Who, like him, knew the face of the county, and its families, inside out? His lifetime of dedication to the labour of accumulating this knowledge, by means of research and note-taking, by correspondence with literally hundreds of correspondents, and by personal visit and investigation, had contributed to ruin him. Anyone who knew the county as well as Hasted must have been similarly placed — and there are no candidates for the post.

Hasted, who as a man of private fortune had been able to take all the steps necessary for the writing and publication of a massive county history, was no less able, in the penury and the enforced leisure of the King's Bench prison, to wield the blue pencil, not only to make cuts, but to add details which had seemed to have no place in the folio volumes. Such, for example, as the greater emphasis now laid on the remoteness and dreariness of much of agricultural Kent — a fact which had perhaps been almost subconsciously played down before, with the aim of presenting a picture of the county which would be more pleasing to the subscribers. This time round there were no subscribers, for whom the text had to match the engravings, but an emerging public, for whom the honesty of hard facts was becoming important.

Boyle's suggestion of additional 'editors' at work on the second edition does not stand up to scrutiny, and is in fact a slur on the integrity of the Kentish historian.

The History and Topographical Survey of the County of Kent, as written and published, was in tune both with contemporary taste and with contemporary criteria. Samuel Ayscough, introducing in 1782 his *Catalogue of the manuscripts preserved in the British Museum*, wrote of 'the present favourite study of county history', laying emphasis on the importance of knowing 'the old land-owners, and the tenures by which they held their estates'.[728] The correspondence relating to the *History* is full of letters containing praise for the author's intentions, and eager enquiry as to when it will be completed. For later historians, benefiting from improved access to the records, the research contained in the four folios or the twelve octavo volumes has remained an invaluable jumping-off point. Thus Charles Elton's *Tenures of Kent*, while contesting some of Hasted's conclusions relating to the Kentish custom of gavelkind, nevertheless includes well over a hundred references to his work.[729] David Bates, in his *Bibliography of Domesday Book*, considers Hasted much sounder in his identification of domesday manors than his predecessor, John Harris.[730] And Professor Alan Everitt, in his major work, *Continuity and Colonization*, which deals with the evolution of Kentish settlement from the end of the Romano-British period down to the thirteenth or fourteenth century, found Hasted his principal standby in the reconstruction of the primitive jurisdictions of the county which, as he explained, 'often shed light on the course of settlement'. Hasted, he notes in his Preface,

> wrote at a crucial period in Kentish history when much of the ancient jurisdictional structure of the county still remained intact, or else was readily recoverable by a man of his inclinations and connexions. His systematic account of matters like these thus furnishes us with an unrivalled historical record in its own right, and one to which there is little parallel in most other counties.[731]

Edward Hasted was very much a man of his time, marked by and believing in the notion of honour, which he saw as embodied in the arms borne by a gentleman. To give the history of the county in terms of the families who had inhabited it was, in some measure, to act out this belief.

And in so doing he has left us with a detailed document which has to be consulted, along with Domesday Book, when undertaking the study of any village or parish in Kent. It is also a picture painted at the last possible moment of a mainly agricultural county, before the industrial revolution began to make its indelible mark. Elsewhere Professor Everitt has described Hasted's work as 'one of the finest of the great Hanoverian county histories of England'. With Sir Anthony Wagner, a former Clarenceux King of Arms, we should acknowledge the great 'honour ... due to the prodigious industry of those few who, with whatever shortcomings, completed histories of whole counties single-handed'.[732] There is no need to qualify the praise due to the historian of Kent: whether it is read in the first or the second edition, Edward Hasted's *History and Topographical Survey of the County of Kent* is a magnificent achievement.

Chapter 17

Epilogue

The historian Edward Hasted and his wife Ann had in all nine children, two of whom, Joseph and Mary, died shortly after birth, Joseph living no more than a few days, and Mary some nine months. On Mary's death in 1774, however, the bereaved parents could console themselves with the reflection that they were still left with seven healthy children, Edward, Francis Dingley, George, Charles, Anne, Katherine and John Septimus, and that the name of Hasted was likely to be borne by many generations in the future. Sadly, and for a number of reasons, this was not to be.

In 1787 came the first blow to such expectations, when George, the third son, became ill and died shortly before his twenty-fourth birthday. This was a tragedy for the historian in more ways than one, for George had been the only member of the family who had shown any inclination to help him in his massive project. The occasional mentions of him in the correspondence show him to have been lively and outgoing, and popular with everyone. His death was certainly a loss to far more than a small circle, for Samuel Egerton Brydges, who had been at school with him, rated George even higher than Charles Abbott, his schoolmate, who eventually rose to become Lord Chief Justice.[733]

His eldest brother, Edward, was very possibly more reserved by nature than George. It was no doubt in their best interests that Hasted let his mother take Edward and Francis away from home at an early age, to receive their initial education in London, but it probably widened the gap, which might have been there anyway, in the understanding between father and eldest son. In later life father and son were to be respectful to each other, and struggled to be dutiful. But Hasted could not bring himself to name Edward as his executor, and Edward, who must have received many letters, possibly hundreds, from his father, did not preserve a single one among the family papers.

Nevertheless Edward was given an excellent education. Like all the boys he was sent to the King's School, Canterbury, and he was to spend longer there than any of his brothers, entering it a few months before his ninth birthday, and leaving only at Christmas 1777, when he was 17. From the King's School he went to Oriel College, Oxford, where he matriculated in 1778, obtaining his BA, later to be converted into an MA, in 1781.

In 1784, at a General Ordination held on 6 June by the Archbishop of Canterbury, John Moore, Edward Hasted Jnr was ordained as a deacon. On the same occasion,

The above named Edward Hasted Jnr was also licensed by his Grace to serve the cure of East Farleigh in the County of Kent and peculiar jurisdiction of the Cathedral ... upon the nomination of Ezekiel Paul de la Douespe Vicar thereof, with a salary of £40 a year.[734]

Eighteen months later Edward, together with another young curate, William Lade, who had been serving St Paul with St Martin in Canterbury, had what were known as letters dismissory from the Archbishop, which allowed them to receive priest's orders from the Bishop of Lincoln. The priesting took place on the 18 December 1785, an occasion at which it is likely the historian was present. Edward appears to have remained as curate of East Farleigh until he became vicar of his own parish in the summer of 1790, when on the 10 June he was collated by the Archbishop of Canterbury to the vicarage of Hollingbourne, with the chapel of Hucking annexed.[735] The Revd Edward Hasted was to remain vicar of Hollingbourne for the rest of his life. He never married.

Edward was undoubtedly a conservative-minded member of the clergy: in 1828 he was one of twenty Kentish clerics who signed a declaration against Latitudinarianism.[736] He was, however, as conscious of the calls of public duty as had been his father and grandfather before him: he was placed on the Commission of the Peace in 1799, and served as a magistrate for fifty years, his signature frequently appearing on quarter sessions documents of the time. He seems to have inherited, too, his father's ability with figures, since as late as the summer of 1840, when he was nearly eighty, he was one of those signing the audited county accounts. He also served for many years as a trustee of the Savings Bank and Provident Institution for Maidstone and its Vicinity.[737] And it is hardly surprising to find him as a trustee of the Hollingbourne Charity Schools, set up in 1839, and of which the Earl and Countess of Jersey were patron and patroness.

As has been shown, Edward spent ten years in all in settling the matter of his father's estate. This was not wholly due to the intricacies of mortgages and debts with which the estate was encumbered, and which resolved themselves quite easily, in the final analysis, into three large sums. As the years passed the Revd Edward Hasted's own temperament became a factor in the proceedings, and the suit that he instituted against the solicitors, Clarkson's and Debary's — finally settled out of court in 1822 — probably slowed things down, as well as adding to the legal fees.

He was not, however, a man without friends, and their few surviving letters show that there was always a close bond between all the Hasted siblings. In 1841, under the will of Mr William Jeffreys, Edward received £63.16s.3d., and the main beneficiaries of his own will, drawn up in 1854, were to be members of the Best family of Chilston: Caroline Best, the daughter of his friend the late George Best and sister of his late friend Thomas Fairfax Best, and the latter's four daughters: Caroline, Isabella, Margaret and Frances.[738] Thomas Fairfax Best himself had died only in July 1849, his obituary notice in the Kentish papers describing him as the 'perfect gentleman', who never lost his temper and who, always eager to discharge whatever he deemed to be his duty, had held a prominent position among the leaders of his native county.

Nor was the Revd Edward Hasted ungenerous towards those who worked for him. To his manservant, William Collings, he bequeathed all his clothes, wages for the whole of the current year, and a legacy of £20, while Fanny Collings, William's wife, also received the whole of her year's wages, and a legacy of £20 — for which her own signature was to be a sufficient receipt. The housemaid, Elizabeth Hughes, received her year's wages and a legacy of £10. A codicil added in the year of his death left to the Collingses also the furniture of front and back parlours, as well as the implements in the washhouse. And all three servants were to be provided with mourning, 'the same as they respectively received on the decease of my said sister Catherine'.[739]

Edward's executors were his friend Joseph Oliver of Hollingbourne, and Joseph's brother William, of Maidstone, Joseph receiving £50 and his brother £5 for acting. And the Olivers must also have been left the Hasted family portraits, since it was from members of the Oliver family that most of these were to pass, in 1880, into the possession of Maidstone Museum. Edward was to die, the last and the longest lived of the historian's family, on 15 September 1855 at the age of ninety-four. He was buried in the chancel of his own church, where his body was laid beside that of his sister Katherine. It had perhaps been on the occasion of Katherine's death, in 1842, that all claim to the family vault at Newington had been given up, where the unpaid fees had in any case meant that the vault lapsed to the parish.[740]

While one may feel that the historian's financial difficulties, which caused his abrupt departure from England in 1790, left his eldest son with a difficult role to play, one should remember that Edward was then nearly thirty and, one would have thought, capable of shouldering some responsibility. By 1790 all Hasted's sons had been launched in the world, and it was his daughters who were to suffer the most, being unlikely to attract husbands, in those days of marriage settlements, with little more to their name than a subsistence allowance.

And so it was to prove. Neither daughter married, but equally, neither ended her life in want. When writing to his brother Edward in

1794 Francis, the second son, had expressed his fears that the two sisters would be 'forced to go abroad into the world to seek their living', apparently echoing anxieties to which Edward had previously given voice.[741] Inevitably, however, Francis, now in India, was answering letters written many months earlier, and the situation which he addressed could well have changed in the interim.

Katherine — or Catherine, as she herself seems to have preferred to write it — eventually made her home with her clerical brother. She receives not a single mention in the historian's will, and one may deduce from this a certain animosity between father and daughter. The Revd Mr Hasted and his sister seem to have been able to lead a genteel life at Hollingbourne, with quite a wide circle of well-placed friends, and among the family papers preserved by Edward are letters in which brother and sister are thanked for their kindness. But their old age seems to have been joyless in the extreme. A Hollingbourne parishioner, Mrs Louisa Thomas, noted in her diary in February 1840 that she had 'Paid a visit to Miss Hasted, whom we found with old Mr Hasted the portraiture of gloom and invalidism', while another visit in October of the same year 'found them both at home wearing on together their melancholy existence in their melancholy room — what a contrast to the sunshine of the Duppas' — and we must assume that Mrs Thomas in fairness was comparing like with like.[742] Catherine lived until 1842, dying at the vicarage in October of that year at the age of seventy-six. Her will, made only a month before her death, left everything to her brother Edward.[743]

Anne, on the other hand, probably had something of her father's mettle. She is remembered with affection in his will, and would seem to have remained on good terms with him, quite possibly siding with him when the split occurred between her parents. She seems to have led an independent existence, and eventually moved to Lambeth, an area which she may have come to know during her father's incarceration nearby, and where the terraces of small houses which were springing up at this period would have provided bright and pleasant accommodation falling well within her means. When she was buried at St Mary's, Lambeth, on the 21 March 1839 at the age of seventy-four, her address was given as Catherine Street, a street which had come into being around 1820.[744] Mary Dorman, their Barming aunt, would appear to have taken her nieces in (and very probably their mother, her sister, too) when the house in the Precincts was given up in 1792, and The Homestall, in Barming, may have become home to all of them until their aunt's death in 1800.

When this occurred, the independence of Katherine and Anne, as well as that of the three brothers who remained in England, was increased and confirmed by their legacies. No members of the Hasted family therefore — apart from the historian himself — ended their lives in penury: Anne was able to live on her own with dignity, and Edward and Katherine, combining their resources, seem to have been in a position to support their station in some style.

One should perhaps spare a thought here for Hasted's wife, the former Ann Dorman. It was not until 1791 that she was released from the ever-present burden of a mother-in-law who, by Hasted's own account, detested her. The eighties, when she lost her son George, learned of her husband's involvement with Mary Jane Town, and then saw him obliged to flee to France, must have been a particularly difficult decade for her. Francis, in his letter to Edward of 16 December 1794, wrote of his hope that he would shortly be in a position to remit some money 'to you and our dear mother' — although it is very likely that she was by then living with her sister Mary. And when by Mary's death in 1800 she finally became a wealthy woman in her own right, she had only three more years in which to enjoy her new position, since she herself was to die in September 1803 at the age of seventy-one.[745]

Only Edward, of all the Hasted children, was to emulate his grandmother's longevity. The next longest lived was John, his youngest brother, who was eighty-five when he died. On leaving the King's School at the age of fourteen and a half John had been apprenticed for five years to a Deal surgeon, Thomas Fitzgerald, who seems to have practised formerly in Milton, where Hasted had perhaps come to know him.[746] Deal may well have been chosen purposely for a boy already enamoured of the sea, for at the end of his apprenticeship John immediately entered the navy as a surgeon's mate, spending a total of three years in this position on five successive ships: the *Boyne*, the *Victory* (in 1791), the *Kingfisher*, the *Assistance*, and the *Stately*. Francis, in his letter of 1794, was to speak of John's recent 'good fortune': this probably referred to the latter's promotion to full surgeon, which had occurred in the autum of 1793, when he had left the *Stately* as surgeon's mate on the 29 October, to begin service the following day as surgeon on *Le Lutin* — a ship captured from the French, apparently off Newfoundland. John was to remain with *Le Lutin* for two years, and then went on to serve for a total of twenty more on the *Kangaroo*, the *Pearl*, the *Glenmore*, the *Boadicea* (six years), the *Plantagenet* and the *Gladiator*, with which ship he remained for five years, from 1810 to 1815. He must have seen a great deal of action, and lived to tell the tale. His career continued after the end of the Napoleonic Wars, when he served as a surgeon aboard several ships stationed at Portsmouth, including the *Rivoli*, the *Ramillies*, and the *Queen Charlotte*. He finally retired in 1824.[747]

John's wife, a Miss Clara Carrington whom he married around 1802, came from Kent, and appears to have been heir to a considerable amount of property. This was subsequently ceded to a friend of her family in return for an annual sum paid to her and her husband; and after his wife's death, early in 1834, John Hasted continued to receive £150 a year derived from her property, as well as his retired pay as a surgeon.[748] While this did not make him a wealthy man, he was able to continue living comfortably in his home at Farrington Gurney in Somerset, and in his will of 1835 he left £100 to Charles and £50 to his sister Anne, as well as arranging for the sum of £20, which he had been giving Anne each year, to be continued as an annuity. There were no children of his marriage, but the will also contained a bequest to a godson, George Hasted Ellis, the son of a naval friend.[749]

As was only too likely to happen, however, since Charles and Anne were older than John, both brother and sister predeceased him, and a codicil of 1843 revoked their bequests. By a second codicil of 1848 the bequest to George Hasted Ellis was also revoked — whether due to his death, or to the fact that he had in some way displeased his godfather, it is impossible to know. And the main beneficiary of the will, Thomas John Burgoyne, of Stratford Place, London, being now also dead, two other members of the same family, possibly sons, Thomas and John Charles Burgoyne, were named in his place.[750] John Hasted himself was to survive for another five years at Farrington Gurney, some six miles south-west of Bath, and only about twelve miles from Corsham, in Wiltshire, where his father had spent his last years. Two letters received towards the end of 1853 by Joseph Oliver, the friend of the now very elderly Edward, from Somersetshire friends of John, give a touching picture of the old ship's surgeon's end. In November Charles James was writing:

> I am requested by Mr J. S. Hasted to acknowledge and thank you for your kindness in giving him an account of his brother, as I am sorry to say that he is unable to reply to your letter himself. Mr J. S. Hasted is extremely ill, suffering perhaps unknown to his brother from the dropsy. His infirmities have in a great measure deprived him of the pleasure of reading, he is entirely confined to the house. He received a letter from his brother yesterday, perhaps he may make an effort to answer it. Between ourselves he is in a very precarious state.[751]

And on 14 December 1853 Mr Scobell wrote:

Epilogue

Sir, My much regarded and very old friend, Mr Hasted, departed this life about 10 cl. this morning. I am truly happy to gather from those who were about him that his end was peace and hope, and that he passed away without pain. I address you on this occasion because I find you are intimately acquainted with his still more aged brother, whom I fear to address directly, lest the shock might injure him.[752]

Of all Hasted's children it was perhaps John Septimus whose life was the most representative of the family traditions. He had felt the call of the sea which his great-grandfather old Joseph, as a ship's painter, must have known; he had continued the tradition of service instituted by his grandfather; and the mention by his friend of 'the pleasure of reading' as one of his characteristics probably indicates that he inherited also his father's love of learning. John was buried beside his wife in Farrington Gurney churchyard.

Charles, the fourth son, the one nearest to John in age, and with whom John was perhaps on the closest terms, given the mention of him in his will, seems to have been cast in a rather different mould. Like John, he left school before he was fifteen — not to be apprenticed, however, but to become a mealman, or dealer in meal. He does not seem to have had a regular career, but surfaces occasionally in the records, now in one job, now in another, usually having some connection with the brewing trade. For many years, from at least 1787, he lived in Dartford and in the late 1790s was clerk to the Dartford brewer Hussey Fleet. We find him first in Spital Street and then, from about 1800 to 1806, in Lowfield Street, where he had a relatively imposing house with a rateable value of £25.[753] By 1811 he seems to have been in business as a brewer himself in the Chatham area — Robert Pocock mentions meeting him at Gad's Hill in that year — but he later moved up to London, to Shadwell, east of the City of London, where in 1828 he was described as a seller of intermediate beer of Johnson Street, St George in the East.[754] He seems at that time to have been trying to dispose of a brewhouse, and was perhaps on the point of changing his trade for that of tobacconist, which is how he is described in Robson's *London Directory* from 1832 to 1834, when he lived at 11 Aylesbury Street in Clerkenwell.

We know no more of Charles's wife than that she was a Miss Harriet Warington, a name which echoes that of John's wife before her marriage; and Charles and Harriet, like John and Clara, were to have no children.[755] Seemingly a man without pretensions, Charles's brief appearances in the Hasted story are as assistant to other members of the family: soliciting subscriptions 'not without success' to the second edition of his father's *History*; dropping a quick note to Edward at the time of the sale of the Hasted estates in Rochester in 1812 to keep him informed of the sums they were fetching; brought in, by pure chance, to help his nephews in India obtain an inheritance. Although he may from boyhood have allied himself most nearly with John, his younger brother, he remained in close touch with Edward, Katherine and Anne, mentioning Anne in his letters (by the 1820s they were both living in London and may have seen each other frequently) and closing a letter to Edward in 1828 with the words, 'Should very much like to be sitting under your quince tree, but that cannot be this summer'.[756] Charles appears to have died in December 1839.[757]

Large families not infrequently have a black sheep, and it may have been Francis Dingley, the second son, who filled this role for a time. Francis left school in 1775 before he was fourteen and went straight into the army, where he perhaps had a few escapades. There is some evidence for this in the undated letter from John Thorpe, commiserating with Hasted on 'this unpleasant subject' which clearly refers to one of the historian's sons, who would seem more likely to have been Francis than any of the others.[758]

In 1781, however, Lord Amherst returned the compliment of Hasted's proposal to dedicate the second folio volume to him with a commission for Francis, who was thus enabled to enter the 61st Regiment of Foot as ensign under Colonel Staates Long Morris. When Francis received his ensigncy the regiment was said to be in Minorca, but Francis did not see service abroad with it. His name duly appears in the *Army Lists* for 1782 and 1783, but the regiment's complement of ten ensigns had been reduced to seven by 1784, and Francis was one of those who were not kept on.

The next few years in his life are a blank, but by the early 1790s he had begun a completely new life on the sub-continent of India — and was perhaps a totally reformed character. The letter which he wrote to Edward — 'my dearest brother' and 'my dear Ned' — from Malda in Bengal, dated 16 December 1794, fills in some of his most recent history. Not only had he acquired a wife — he had married Miss Sarah Powell on 27 June 1794 — but he had entered into business with two other men, and seems to have been doing very well:

> You are already acquainted with the concern I am engaged in with two gentlemen residing near Malda, this is the second year, and it has been productive beyond all expectation, we have this year, by a moderate computation, cleared a nett profit of thirty thousand

rupees, or three thousand pounds sterling, one third of which is mine. I have great hopes of doing still better this ensuing year.[759]

Sarah Powell had obviously not married a man without prospects. She herself was the daughter of a well-to-do cabinet maker of St John's Street, Clerkenwell with Welsh roots who had married a Miss Thomas of Fairford in Gloucestershire. All the family were keen Baptists. And it is at this point that Francis enters history in a capacity other than that of son to Edward Hasted, for Sarah Powell was a niece of the man, a doctor, who went to India with William Carey as one of the first two missionaries to be sent out by the Baptist Missionary Society.

The Revd Dr Thomas seems to have been a more mercurial character than Carey, occasionally tempted by a life of affluence and running up considerable debts, but, if not as brilliant as Carey, whose linguistic gifts were to gain him the position, in less than ten years, of professor of Sanskrit, Bengali and Mahratta in the newly founded college of Fort William, Thomas was certainly a man of many talents, undertaking the translation of several books of the Bible, and, as a doctor, responsible for saving the lives of many thousands of Indians. Thomas seems, in fact, to have begun missionary work in India on his own, before the formation of the Missionary Society. He was in India on at least two previous occasions, in 1783 and 1786, before going out with Carey in 1793, and it is likely that his niece and her brother Samuel had accompanied him there earlier. Francis, at any rate, must have met Sarah before the summer of 1794, when the Carey party first came to Malda. Samuel is mentioned by Carey in a letter as Mr Thomas's assistant. He was baptised by Carey in November 1795, and became one of the first four members of the Baptist church formed in that year by the missionaries in Malda.[760]

Francis, in marrying a niece of the Revd Dr Thomas, was almost certainly drawn in as one of the supporters of the small missionary outpost — the religious fervour of his letter to Edward shows this, were it not also that he writes of his 'kind and dear friend' Mr Udny.

George Udny, an indigo planter of considerable wealth and standing, had been friendly with Thomas on the latter's previous visits to Bengal, and an Udny family tragedy, (which Francis mentions in his letter) when a brother, Robert, was drowned with his young wife in crossing the river opposite Calcutta, was responsible for reuniting the two friends. Udny subsequently came to the financial rescue of both Thomas and Carey, by offering them positions as superintendents in two new indigo factories which he was in the process of setting up at Moypaldiggy and Mudnabatty, and he was to remain a benefactor to their mission. He later held high office in the colony, becoming first member of council and, in the absence of the governor-general, vice-president and deputy-governor. Udny seems also to have been an enlightened industrialist: he engaged Carey and Thomas at 200 rupees a month, with commission on all the indigo they sold, and a promise that the following year he would give them a share in the works. Carey quoted him in one of his letters home as saying, 'I always join the interest of those I employ in places of trust with my own'. It is very likely, from the way Francis Hasted speaks of him, that he, too, was equally indebted to George Udny, and that he was helped to set up in the indigo business in a similar way. Carey set out from Mudnabatty at the beginning of December 1794 to spend Christmas at Malda with Mr Udny 'and other European friends who are met together there', and it seems permissible to see Francis and his young wife as figuring among this Indian Christmas party.[761]

Francis and Sarah were to have six children, all born during the historian's lifetime: Francis, born in 1795, Sarah Anne (1796), Jonathan (1797), George (December 1798), Edward (1801), and John (1808), and the knowledge that he had six grandchildren may perhaps have contributed both to the serenity of the old master of the Hungerford almshouses and to his determination to regain something of the lost Hasted estates.[762] But the Indian climate was recreating for Europeans the hazards of an early death from which those who stayed at home now had some reason to hope to escape for a little longer. The Indian Hasteds appear to have prospered for some time, but Francis lost his wife in 1809, and on his own death ten years later was found to be bankrupt.[763] His eldest son, Francis, wrote a heart-rending letter to his uncle Edward on this occasion — clearly he did not know where to turn:

> My mind shudders at taking up my pen for the first time that I am writing to you, it should be to communicate the most melancholy and afflicting of news, the deaths of my very dear father, sister, and brother!!! Oh, how shall I explain to you the heavy afflictions that have fallen upon us, and of our forlorn state, my poor father's insolvency has left us pennyless in the world, the factories are entirely at the Agents' disposal, and will certainly be put up to sale soon, when we shall be cast upon the wide world without the means of support: finding employment in this country is become a matter of the greatest difficulty.[764]

It is possible that Francis Dingley's insolvency had been known about earlier, and had hastened his death. He had died on the 22 May 1819, after losing his son Edward on the 24 December 1818. Sarah Ann

Epilogue

died exactly a month after her father, on the 22 June 1819: she was twenty-three, Edward had been seventeen. One can understand the despair in Francis's letter. In addition to these terrible calamities, he himself had recently suffered an accident which would render him lame for life:

> On the 5th of January last as I was returning from shooting on horseback, and the servant with a gun on his shoulder before me, it went off (from a distance of about three feet) and the whole contents lodged in my right knee. It was [long] before any medical aid could be procured, and great apprehensions were entertained for my life. The wound is not yet healed, nor can I make any use of the limb, or leave my couch.[765]

The litany of disasters is almost unbearable.

Only three of the family of six now remained: Francis, who was twenty-four, George, twenty, and John, the youngest, who was only ten and who was, wrote Francis, 'growing up in ignorance and uneducated' — a mention which leads one to suspect that financial difficulties had been creeping up on the family for some time.

The vicar of Hollingbourne was a tardy correspondent, although hardly in a position to offer very much help — a fact recognised by his nephew in another letter, sent the following year.[766] By then George had obtained work as a clerk with Messrs Palmer & Co in Calcutta, who had apparently been the agents for his father's factory. However, a short note by the Revd Edward Hasted, dated July 1822, referring to 'the proper steps' which his solicitors were to take 'on behalf of my nephews' seems to indicate that his father's trust in him had not been misplaced, and that following the final settlement of the Hasted estates in Kent some provision was made for the Indian nephews, although the sum involved cannot have been a large one.[767] For a while the three young Hasteds seem to have got by, although John did not survive for long, dying in 1823 at the age of fourteen or fifteen.[768]

It was something of a counter to the terrible reverses they had known that in 1828 Francis and George became heirs to the property left in 1819 by their maternal grandfather, Mr Benjamin Powell, who had earlier retired to Hay near Brecon. This property consisted of some £2500, which was to come to them on the demise of an elderly uncle Benjamin, brother of their mother. Although it is likely that they would, in time, have learnt of their good fortune through the Calcutta newspapers in which advertisements were about to be inserted, the story of how the surviving children of Sarah Powell were traced is quite an extraordinary one. Advertisements had appeared in the *Times* for 12 May 1828, enquiring after the next-of-kin and any grandchildren of the testator, Benjamin Powell, formerly of St John's Street, Clerkenwell, and requiring them or their representatives to make their claim before Master Eden at his Chambers in Southampton Building, Chancery Lane, London. These were seen by one John Pearce, who worked for the Customs as a landing waiter at London Docks. Pearce had known the Powells well, and had corresponded for some years with Sarah Powell's brother Samuel until the latter's death in about 1801. Pearce's sleuthing on behalf of Sarah Powell's children would have been commended by Sherlock Holmes, and is best recounted in his own words in a letter subsequently received by the Revd Edward Hasted.

> I then lookt over my letters and did make out a rough sketch of the family and did as before stated began to learn something of the grand children. Proof no doubt must be produced of the marriage of Miss Powell and also her Baptism certificate etc etc. I here beg to state her parents was of the Baptist pursuasion perhaps did not christen at the parish church, if they did Saffron Hill I now think is in the parish of St Andrews, Holborn. The Meeting that Mr B. P. used to attend to was in Little Wild Street, Lincolns Inn Fields. The name of the Minister I forget — I once went there. I am of the Church of England, some branch of my family are otherways.
>
> No doubt you will be anxious to know how I found you out, all the Directories etc I lookt into. What gave the last chance was I saw a cart name of Hasted, Cooper, Wellclose Square, who I lost no time to see. He had no recollection of being related to the family in Kent, but he informed [me] that there was a person of same name selling intermediate beer in Johnson Street, St George in the East there. I got your direction.[769]

Before that the diligent Pearce had got a friend 'to enquire many parts of Kent, he found out that there had been a short distance from Chatham a brewer of that name, but had left and gone no one could tell [where]. The above proved to be the same'.

All this was set out in a letter to the Revd Edward Hasted at Hollingbourne, who, having been brought in to the matter by Charles, had written in some agitation to know the cause of 'the unjust silence of the executor' in the matter. Pearce assured Edward that Powell's executor,

Epilogue

Mr Fell, who was apparently also known to him, was 'lookt up to as an honest safe man', and that he would 'one day this week make a point of calling on Mr Fell to inform him that by perseverance I have discovered the names of the uncle and also the grandchildren of the late Mr Benjn Powell'. Fell, in fact, realising that the will would be a difficult one to administer, had handed over the management of it to Chancery, as was explained in a subsequent letter from Charles to Edward, in which Charles recounted the visit he had had from Pearce:

> About a fortnight ago a gentleman called here, when, as it generally so happens, I was unfortunately from home, saying he had accidentally seen an advertisement to discover where some grandchildren of a late Mr Benjamin Powell, by his daughter Sarah, were now living, as they would eventually be entitled to some property devised to them by their grandfather's will. He would not leave his name, but only said having been acquainted with Miss Powell from her childhood, and having always had a very great regard for her, as a most amiable young woman, he felt great pleasure in so far affording information likely to prove beneficial to her children.[770]

Charles, not surprisingly, was initially at a loss to know how his visitor had tracked him down, but having been left the name of the executor of the will in question, he had made it his business to call on him immediately and to have the matter put in hand on behalf of his nephews.

With this windfall inheritance Francis and George were able to establish themselves as indigo merchants, following the same trade as their father. The English branch of the family then seems to have lost touch with them, for three years later Edward was making enquiries about his nephews through some influential Kentish friends, the Lushingtons, one of whom was at East India House and who was eventually able to obtain a report from a correspondent that they were alive and well, 'respectable and worthy men', trading as indigo merchants in the Benares district.[771]

It seems likely that the indigo plantations throve. According to Bengal directories of the time, Francis and George had plantations at Jaunpore, Dooleypore, and Alleenugur.[772] There were hopes, in India, at least, although probably unknown in England, that there would one day be younger Hasteds to carry them on. The India Office records for Bengal note the burial at Benares on 15 April 1837 of a certain Mary Ann Hasted.[773] No other details are given. They also record the burial at Goruckpore on 7 November 1844 of Francis Hasted, grantee and planter, his age stated imprecisely as fifty-two.[774] But it is the quiet, business-like will of George, drawn up in November 1849, eleven months before his death in 1850, which tells the end of the Hasted story:

> In the name of God, Amen.
>
> I George Hasted of Doolypore Factory in the gellah of Benares an indigo planter, being at present of sound mind and disposable memory and in perfect bodily health and knowing the uncertainty of this transitory life, and to avoid controversies after my death do hereby make publick and declare this to be my only last will and testament in the manner and form following, that is to say:
>
> 1st And principally I commit my soul to Almighty God, hoping for the remission of all my sins and the eventual resurrection of my body, and as to my body I either commit it to the earth or sea, as it may please Almighty God to order. Should it please Almighty God to call me from my present habitation on earth, I will and desire that my body be decently buried in a Christian-like manner at Doolypore Indigo Factory, near and to the north of my deceased son George Henry Hasted's tomb.
>
> 2ndly I give and bequeath both my real and personal property to my favorite John Alexander Vincent Williams, at present about eight years of age; subjecting him at the same time to the payment of all my just and lawful debts.
>
> 3rdly I do hereby appoint my friend Moses Bellis Taylor Williams of Chuckeah in the gillah of Mirzapore to be my true and only lawful executor.
>
> 4thly Having no earthly connection with the exception of a nephew named Francis Hasted, the natural son of my late brother Francis Hasted of unsound mind, I therefore will and desire that my executor above-named will provide for his maintenance during his lifetime.[775]

A fifth clause provided for bequests to 'my faithful servants ... as a reward for their long servitude to me': one thousand rupees to go to Babou Doorgapersaud Singh, his sircar; one hundred rupees each to his moonshi, Bissa Surdial and his court mooktar, Shuk Jiaoolla; and to Bassowan his bearer and to Luckhan, 25 rupees each.[776]

George could not know that in England two uncles still lingered on, John Septimus at Farrington Gurney in Somerset, and Edward in Kent. But with the death of the vicar of Hollingbourne on 15 September 1855 the line of the Kentish Hasteds came to an end.

Appendices

Notes

List of Subscribers

Index

Appendix 1

The following entries appear in the registers of various Huguenot churches in London, and seem to show full integration of members of at least one Hasted family within the Huguenot community:

Hoguel. 1711, 1 Juli. Jean Philipe, f. de Charles et de Marie; bap. par Mr Laplace, min. P. Le père. M. Elizabeth Halstead. Né 5 Juin.
(Baptism of Jean Philipe Hoguel, 1 July 1711, son of Charles and Marie, by Mr Laplace, minister. Godfather, the father. Godmother, Elizabeth Halstead. Born 5 June.)
    Crispin Street Register, printed in *Registres des Quatre Eglises du Petit Charenton, de West Street, de Pearl Street, et de Crispin Street*. Edited for the Huguenot Society of London by William Minet and Susan Minet (Vol.XXXII, 1929, 79)

Casalar. 1739/40, 20 Jan. André, f. d'Etienne, et d'Elizabeth; bat. par Mr Jean Blanc, min. de cette ég. P. André Regnier. M. Judith Hasted. Né 11 Jan.
(Baptism of André Casalar, 20 January 1739/40, son of Etienne and Elizabeth, by Mr Jean Blanc, minister of this church. Godfather, André Regnier. Godmother, Judith Hasted. Born 11 January.)
    'Registre pour l'église de Lesterfilds' in *Registers of the Churches of the Tabernacle, Glasshouse Street and Leicester Fields, 1688-1783*. Edited for the Huguenot Society of London by William Minet and Susan Minet (Vol.XXIX, 1926, 157)

Du Jardin. 1757, 19 Juin. Suzane, ff. de Pier, et de Katherine Hasted; bap. par Mr E. Palairet, Past. P. Jacque Delport. M. Suzan Betanbo. Née 30 Mai.
(Baptism of Suzane Du Jardin, 19 June 1757, daughter of Pier and Katherine Hasted, by Mr E. Palairet, pastor. Godfather, Jacque Delport. Godmother, Suzan Betanbo. Born 30 May.)

Dujardin. 1759, 3 Fév. Anne, ff. de Pierre, et de Catherine Hasted; bap. par Mr Gédéon Patron. P. Pierre Dujardin. M. Anne Delporte. Née 15 Jan.
(Baptism of Anne Dujardin, 3 February 1759, daughter of Pierre and Catherine Hasted, by Mr Gédéon, patron. Godfather, Pierre Dujardin. Godmother, Anne Delporte. Born 15 January.)

Appendices

Register of the Church of Saint Jean Spitalfields 1687-1827.
Edited for the Huguenot Society of London by Susan Minet
(Vol.XXXIX, 1938, 66)

Appendix 2

Translations provided by Hasted for the Revd Richard Yates, intended for the continuation of Yates's *Illustration of the Monastic History and Antiquities of the Town and Abbey of St Edmund's Bury*

BL: Egerton 2370	ff.99-111: Extracts from the Register of the Abbey of Bury St Edmund. (Intended as an addition to Part I, Chapter IV, as Bull of Alexander 2nd)
BL: Egerton 2371	ff.38-84: Pleas of the Crown before H. de Bath and associates, Justices Itinerant in Co. Suffolk in the 29th year of the reign of Henry son of K. John. (Intended for Part I, Chapter IX, Franchise)
	ff.252-258: Writ of the Chancery of the King.
	ff.265-266: Suff: Memdm. (Intended for Part I, Chapter X, The Mint)
BL: Egerton 2372	ff.84-88: Agreement between the Lord Symon Abbat of St Edmund ... and the Lord Philip Basset. (Intended for Part II, Chapter X, Lord Abbot's Palace)
	ff.345-352: The Charter concerning the Chaplains serving in the Charnell. (Intended for Part II, Chapter XXII, Charnel House and Chapel)
	ff.443-451: Extracts from the Register of R. de Denham Sacrist of the Monastery of St Edmund of Bury. (Intended for Part II, Chapter XXVI, Town Gates)
BL: Egerton 2373	ff.118-126: St Nicholas's Hospital. (Intended for Part II, Chapter XXIX, Hospitals, Guilds, Chauntries, St Nicholas's

Appendices

Hospital without the East Gate)

f.151: Of the Guild of the Bakers.
(Intended for Part II, Chapter XXIX, Guilds or Corporations)

BL: Egerton 2374

ff.171-173: Continuation by Hasted of the translation of some folios containing a history of Bury Monastery.
(Intended to appear in the Appendix, under the heading, Other Curious Papers)

Notes

Abbreviations

Arch.Cant.	*Archaeologia Cantiana*, Yearbook of the Kent Archaeological Society
BL	British Library
BL, OIOC	British Library, Oriental and India Office Collections
CCA	Canterbury Cathedral Archives
CJ	*Canterbury Journal*
CKS	Centre for Kentish Studies, Maidstone
CL	Canterbury Library
CLRO	City of London Record Office
DNB	*Dictionary of National Biography*
FMM & L	Freemasons' Museum and Library, Canterbury
GLL	Guildhall Library, London
GM	*Gentleman's Magazine*
IGI	International Genealogical Index
KG	*Kentish Gazette*
KP	*Kentish Post*
LPL	Lambeth Palace Library
MALSC	Medway Archives and Local Studies Centre
MBSA	Minute Books of the Society of Antiquaries
ML	Marylebone Library, London
Phil. Trans.	*Philosophical Transactions*, Journal of the Royal Society
PRO	Public Record Office
RBT	Rochester Bridge Trust
RGM	Rochester Guildhall Museum
SRO	Surrey Record Office
VCH	*Victoria County History*
WRO	Wiltshire Record Office

[1] Anecdotes of the Hasted Family, *Arch. Cant.* XXVI (1904), 267-294 (hereafter Hasted 'Anecdotes'). This transcription contains a few minor errors. Original MS, CKS: U1823/94/F1.

[2] E. Hasted, *The History and Topographical Survey of the County of Kent* (hereafter Hasted, *History*) (2nd edn), Vol.6 (1798), 430-1.

[3] Hasted, *History*, Vol.II, 753-4(y).

[4] MS in the possession of Mr B. Gipps, of Egerton.

Notes

5. W.H.Long, ed., *The Oglander Memoirs: Extracts from the MSS of Sir J. Oglander, Kt., of Nunwell, Isle of Wight* (1888), 92-4; Isle of Wight County Record Office: IW.49/Fam/10. The presence of Hasteds in the Isle of Wight in the seventeenth century is well attested in the IOW Record Office, but there is no trace of a Revd John Hausted in the sixteenth century, nor of the birth of a Moses, Thomas and John being the predominant family names. A John Hasted lived in Shorwell in the seventeenth century, but too late to have been the John Hasted whom the historian describes as married to Jane Hacket and dying at the beginning of the reign of Charles I. The earliest references to Hasteds in the Island are to Thomas Hested, son of Thomas Hested of Shorwell, bap. 1631, and to John Hasterd, son of John Hasterd, bap. 1654.
6. CCA: U3/90/1/1.
7. J.M.Cowper, ed., *The Regyster Booke of Chrystenynges, Maryages and Buryalls of the Parish of St Alphaege in the Cyttye of Canterburye 1558-1800* (1889), 124.
8. J.M.Cowper, ed., *The Roll of the Freemen of the City of Canterbury from AD 1392 to 1800* (1903), 271.
9. RGM: Hasted family papers (G.211).
10. MALSC: RCA/A1/1.
11. See Appendix 1.
12. T.Colyer-Ferguson, ed., *The Marriage Registers of St Dunstan's, Stepney, in the County of Middlesex*, Vols. 2 and 3, 1640-1696 and 1697-1719, (Canterbury 1899 and 1901).
13. MALSC: RCA/A1/1.
14. CCA: U11/6/B. Cest = cessed.
15. CCA: U3/90/1/2.
16. CCA: AC/5.
17. CCA: FA/27.
18. CCA: FA/28.
19. Ibid..
20. Ibid..
21. CCA: U3/3/1/2. The suggestion by A.M.Everitt ('Kentish Family Portrait' in *Landscape and Community in England* (1985) 254) that Moses buried two wives in successive years and was married three times is not borne out by the evidence. The single register entry (CCA: U3/3/1/2) is quite clear: 'Mary wife of Moses Hasted Buried

ye l May 1678'. The Bishops' Transcripts, however, repeat for 1679 several entries relating to 1678, a confusion noted in J.M.Cowper, ed., *The Register Booke of the Parish of St George the Martyr* (Canterbury, 1891).

[22] CCA: U3/3/1/2.
[23] GLL: MS/5668.
[24] IGI: London; T.Colyer-Fergusson, ed., *The Marriage Registers of St Dunstan's, Stepney, in the County of Middlesex, Vol.3: 1697-1719* (Canterbury, 1901).
[25] Ibid..
[26] IGI: Kent.
[27] GLL: MS/5668.
[28] Hasted, 'Anecdotes', 272-3.
[29] CCA: AC/8 and FA/31.
[30] GLL: MS/5669.
[31] SRO: P11/1/3.
[32] MALSC: P85/5/3-6.
[33] MALSC: P85/5/7-9.
[34] Now in the possession of Maidstone Museum and Art Gallery.
[35] CCA: U11/6/2, no.2.
[36] CCA: U11/6/431.
[37] Hasted, 'Anecdotes', 272n.
[38] CKS: Q/RJf/2/1-34.
[39] CKS: Q/SB/30.
[40] MALSC: P85/5/5.
[41] MALSC: P85/8/2.
[42] CKS: U24/T9.
[43] CKS: U390/M20.
[44] C.T.Martin, *Catalogue of the Archives in the Muniment Rooms of All Souls' College* (1877), 70.
[45] RGM: Hasted family papers (G.198).
[46] GLL: MS 11936/31, policy no.51346.
[47] CKS: U390/M20.
[48] LPL: VP II/2/1.

49. Hasted, 'Anecdotes', 273n; C.M.Foust, *Rhubarb, the Wondrous Drug* (1992).
50. CKS: U1823/94/P1/1-4.
51. Hasted, 'Anecdotes', 273n. 'Being looked on at Chatham as very rich': the transcript printed in *Arch.Cant.*, XXVI (1904), 273, gives, erroneously, 'as very kind'.
52. Personal communication, 1993, from H.E.Paston-Bedingfield, York Herald, The College of Arms, London.
53. *Arch.Cant.* 27 (1905), 139, letter of 4 November 1763.
54. CCA: U11/6/1, no.40, letter of 18 May 1782.
55. PRO:PROB11/1530/75.
56. Hasted, 'Anecdotes', 271.
57. Ibid., 274n.
58. SRO: 2487/1/1.
59. John Aubrey, *The Natural History and Antiquities of the County of Surrey* (1718; repr.1975), Vol. 2, 303ff.
60. CKS: U1823/94/F3.
61. IGI: Surrey.
62. *Records of the Hon. Soc. of Lincoln's Inn, Admissions,* Vol.1 (1896), 438.
63. CLRO: Rep.129 and CF 1/444.
64. CLRO: Rep.129.
65. CLRO: Rep.129 (1724); Rep.142 (1736); Rep.145 (1741).
66. GLL: MS 9492.
67. GLL: MS 1002/2.
68. GLL: MS 7638 and MS 1002/2.
69. Under the Act 24 Geo.II, c.23.
70. CCA: U11/6/2, no.2, letter from Revd Thomas Austen of 2 December 1778.
71. Hasted, 'Anecdotes', 273.
72. CKS: U24/T9.
73. CKS: P265/8/1.
74. RGM: Hasted family papers (G.204).
75. Ibid.. Fruchard was a prominent member of the Huguenot community in London.

Notes

[76] RGM: Hasted family papers (G.204). Until 1752 the New Year in England began on 25 March.
[77] RGM: Hasted family papers (G.208).
[78] *Poll for Knights of the Shire to represent the county of Kent* (1734).
[79] The Million Bank was dissolved by Act of Parliament in 1796.
[80] CKS: U24/T9.
[81] BL: Add.5492.
[82] Hasted, *History*, 2nd edn, Vol.6, 430-1; CKS: U47/22/T40.
[83] Hasted, 'Anecdotes', 276; Indenture in the possession of Dr P.Draper.
[84] *Records of the Hon.Soc. of Lincoln's Inn, The Black Books*, Vol.III (1899), 311; J. Dummelow, *The Wax Chandlers of London* (1973), 104-5.
[85] C.B.Andrews, ed., *The Torrington Diaries*, Vol. 1 (1934), 31-2.
[86] Hasted, 'Anecdotes', 281n.
[87] Ibid., 282.
[88] Ibid., 276.
[89] CKS: T9/A1/15,16.
[90] CKS: T9/A1/16.
[91] Ibid..
[92] CKS: S/NK/SM3.
[93] Original Act 13 Geo.II, c.26.
[94] RBT: A4/33, Election register, 1734-1742, and A4/31, Election register, 1731-1811.
[95] CKS: T9/A1/16.
[96] Hasted, 'Anecdotes', 276-7.
[97] CKS: U390/M20.
[98] Hasted, 'Anecdotes', 280.
[99] Ibid., 280, 282.
[100] CCA: U11/6/2, letter no.146 of 24 May 1781.
[101] Hasted, 'Anecdotes', 284.
[102] Ibid., 285. Hasted (ibid., 277) erroneously gives the date of 1742 for his sister's elopement, although this is corrected (284) with the statement that his mother fled to London in 1747 to escape the scandal.
[103] ML: Marylebone Rates Books, Reels 4 and 5.

[104] Hasted, 'Anecdotes', 292; (CKS: U1823/94/F3); R.A. Austen-Leigh, *The Eton College Register, 1698-1752* (1927), 164.

[105] Hasted, 'Anecdotes', 292; E.Gibbon, *Autobiography* (Everyman edn, reprinted 1948), 33.

[106] Hasted, 'Anecdotes', 285.

[107] *Records of the Hon.Soc. of Lincoln's Inn*, Admissions, Vol.1 (1896), 404.

[108] ML: Marylebone Rates Books, Reels 4 and 5.

[109] Hasted, 'Anecdotes', 285.

[110] St Marylebone Rates Books, Reel 5.

[111] St Marylebone Rates Books, Reel 6.

[112] Hasted, 'Anecdotes', 285-6.

[113] Ibid., 286.

[114] Ibid., 285n.

[115] MALSC: P358/5/1.

[116] Hasted, 'Anecdotes', 278, 279n; BL, OIOC: L/MIL/9/85.

[117] CKS: U24/T9.

[118] Hasted, 'Anecdotes', 287.

[119] Westminster Poor Rates, vols. E405/1758 — E453/1770. (Here again there is a discrepancy, since after the first year Mrs Hasted should have been paying no more than £40 a year.) J. Almon, *The Correspondence of the late John Wilkes with his friends* (5 vols.,1805), Vol.4, 31-71.

[120] *The Poll for Knights of the Shire to represent the County of Kent* (1734 and 1754).

[121] MALSC: P358/1/1; P358/5/1.

[122] MALSC: P358/1/2.

[123] CL: Diary of Revd Joseph Price, May 1771, (MS transcription) 101.

[124] MALSC: P110/12/8; see Chapter 4.

[125] MALSC: P358/1/2.

[126] PRO: PROB11/982/391. BL: Add.5486 and 5520.

[127] Hasted, 'Anecdotes', 288.

[128] Hasted, *History*, 2nd edn, Vol.2, 347-8.

[129] CKS: U47/22/T40.

[130] The original advertisement, which appeared in the *Kentish Post* on 18 May 1757, was as follows: To be Lett on Lease, and Enter'd on at

Midsummer next, A Very good Brick House, four Rooms on a Floor, with a good Garden, Drying-yard, Wash-house, and a Stable, with Stalls for two Horses; neatly and conveniently fitted up; pleasantly situated near, and without Riding Gate, Canterbury. Now in the Occupation of Edward Hasted, Esq. For further Particulars, inquire at the House, or, of William Morrice, Esq., at the next House.

[131] Hasted, 'Anecdotes', 281.

[132] *Familiar Letters which passed between Abraham Hill ... and several eminent and ingenious persons of the last century* (1767), Preface, viin.

[133] CKS: U24/T9.

[134] Ibid..

[135] Ibid..

[136] Ibid..

[137] CKS: U1823/94/F3.

[138] CKS: U451/T40, T41.

[139] Indentures in the possession of Dr P.Draper, of Stansted (refs. 779, 780, 781, 782). Hasted would appear to have finally disposed of Oakleys in 1773, with the obtention of a further small sum against it.

[140] BL: Add.5480.

[141] BL: Add.5533.

[142] See e.g. CCA: U11/6/A.

[143] Hasted, 'Anecdotes', 279.

[144] RGM: Hasted family papers (G.208).

[145] RGM: Hasted family papers (G.204).

[146] Ibid..

[147] CKS: P145/5/1 and P145/12/1.

[148] C.B.Andrews, ed., *The Torrington Diaries*, Vol.4 (1938), 152.

[149] Hasted, 'Anecdotes', 293.

[150] J.H.Appleby, 'Robert Dingley, F.R.S. (1710-1781), Merchant, Architect and Pioneering Philanthropist', *Notes Rec.R.Soc.Lond.* 45(2), 139-154 (1991).

[151] BL: Add.5486.

[152] CCA: U11/6/3, no. 288.

[153] C.H.I.Chown, *The Lethieullier Family of Aldersbrook House*. (Reprinted from the *Essex Review*, Vol.XXV, Oct 1926, 203-220; Vol.XXVI, Jan 1927, 1-21).

Notes

154 *The Remembrancia. City of London. AD1579-1664* (1878), which contains a list of later Remembrancers.

155 RBT: E9/1/19-28.

156 MALSC: P358/1/1.

157 BL: Add.5488. Hasted heads this diary 'from April to June 1756' although it begins in mid March and continues until mid July, with two final entries made in November. John Lethieullier's spelling has been left unchanged, but punctuation has been regularised. Mr Northcote was a farmer and Sutton-at-Hone churchwarden, Mr Cleever a Dartford wine-merchant. 'Dorman' is probably Ann Dorman's brother, John.

158 PRO: PROB11/856/204.

159 Hasted, *History*, 2nd edn, Vol.2, 351.

160 PRO: C12/1859/43.

161 PRO: C12/2399/8.

162 Ibid..

163 PRO: C12/1859/43.

164 PRO: WO48/90-2 et seq.; see also Chapter 6.

165 BL: Stowe MSS 752, letter of 18 November 1751.

166 Revd Samuel Denne, Rector of Wilmington, as reported by Revd Joseph Price in his diary; see *A Kentish Parson*, G.M.Ditchfield & B.Keith-Lucas, eds., (1991), 125.

167 See BL: Add.5536: Hasted S.LXXXVI, not bought by the British Museum; Hasted G.XXIV, now BL: Add.5491.

168 From the ledger stone over the grave in Sutton-at-Hone church of Mrs Frances Hill, daughter of Abraham Hill, and great-granddaughter of Lord Willoughby of Parham, who died 28 October 1736.

169 RGM: Hasted family papers (G.206). Hasted himself catalogued this book as D.VII, 'Collection of seals', and he would appear to have used the blank pages for a collection of impressions of seals: see BL: Add.5536.

170 See BL: Add.5536 for a complete list of Hasted's MSS holdings and notes. The following BL items contain sequestration material: Add.5478, 5491, 5494, 5497, 5500, 5501, 5505, 5508.

171 Any letters from Cromwell to Richard Hill seem to have been abstracted from Hasted's collection at an early date.

Notes

[172] A.B.Beaven, *The Aldermen of the City of London*, Vols. 1 & 2 (1908 and 1913).

[173] BL: Add.5478; Add.5501.

[174] BL: Add.5500.

[175] Hasted, *History*, 2nd edn, Vol.2, 348; J.L.Chester, ed., *The Reiester Booke of Saynte De'nis Backchurch Parishe* (1878). (Publications of the Harleian Society, Registers, Vol.III).

[176] 'An Act for the better ordering and managing the estates of papists and delinquents' of 25 January, 1650; (see C.H.Firth and R.S.Rait, *Acts and Ordinances of the Interregnum*, 3 vols. (1911): Vol.II, 329-335).

[177] BL: Add.5494 and Add.5508.

[178] BL: Add.5508.

[179] BL: Add.5478.

[180] Ibid..

[181] In the 1640s an Ordinance was a declaration made by the two Houses of Parliament which had the force of law, although it had not received the assent of the King.

[182] BL: Add.5491.

[183] BL: Add.5497; Add.5491. Hasted's numbering here is a little awry at times, reaching no more than 95 instead of 98.

[184] BL: Add.5491.

[185] BL: Add.5494.

[186] Hasted, *History*, Folio, Vol.II, 276, note (f); Vol.IV, 662n (a).

[187] See Chapter 8.

[188] CKS: QROm.1.

[189] See *DNB*, Sir Charles Whitworth (?1714-1778). He was knighted in 1768.

[190] See e.g. PRO, Classes SP20 and SP28.

[191] 'Sir Roger Twysden's Journal', transcribed by L.B.Larking: *Arch.Cant.* 1-4 (1858-1861).

[192] See BL: Add.5536, where these two volumes of notes are listed as M.LXII and M.LXIII.

[193] Hasted, *History*, 2nd edn, Vol.6, 430-1.

[194] Ibid., 445-6.

[195] Hasted-Astle correspondence, *Arch.Cant.* 27 (1905), 136-66. The originals of these letters are in CKS: U1823/94/F2.

Notes

[196] *DNB*; T. Astle, *The Origin and Progress of Writing* (1784); BL: Stowe 1014 (Astle's small and apparently only commonplace book).

[197] RGM: Hasted family papers, rent-roll, 1751-1784 (G.212).

[198] PRO: WO48/90-100; WO48/127-129; WO47/53 & 58. CKS: U443/T7; BL: Add.33,116 (Pelham papers); Hasted, *History*, 2nd edn, Vol.6, 447.

[199] Hasted, 'Anecdotes', 293.

[200] RGM: Hasted family papers (G.215).

[201] PRO: PROB11/947/129.

[202] *KP*, 29 October 1763.

[203] *KP*, 19 November 1763.

[204] Hasted, *History*, 2nd edn, Vol.6, 446.

[205] Hasted-Astle correspondence, 140, letter of 23 November 1763. As printed the letter ends 'with which I was pestered at Sutton'. But Hasted originally wrote 'at Sutton cottage' ('cottage' crossed out): CKS: U1823/94/F2.

[206] The Revd Bryan Faussett's disinclination for the role of clergyman is made clear in some of his letters: see e.g. Faussett-Ducarel correspondence, J.Nichols, *Illustrations of the Literary History of the Eighteenth Century* (hereafter Nichols, *Illustrations)*, Vol.3, 556, letter of 16 July 1764.

[207] Hasted-Astle correspondence, 146: letter of 19 May 1764.

[208] Ibid., 137-9, letter of 4 November 1763.

[209] Hasted-Astle correspondence, 137-9, letter of 4 November 1763. Hasted was working here with one of the century's most eminent archaeologists, who perhaps combined in himself all the virtues and the drawbacks of the practitioners of the time. His enthusiasm was described as follows by his great-grandson, Thomas Godfrey Godfrey-Faussett: 'Tradition tells us of the state of almost boyish excitement in which he superintended the opening of his barrows; of the eagerness with which he sifted every crumb of earth taken from them; of his not unsuccessful endeavours to instil some of his own ardour into his labourers; of his good humour when they worked well; his anger when they flagged; and his rage and vexation when an unlucky pickaxe shattered a vase or a patera; of his even animating his men by seizing spade and axe himself; and, in spite of gout and infirmity, setting no mean example of activity. His good humour and good pay appear to have been more remembered than his occasional outbreaks of wrath; and his cottagers always rejoiced when an interval freer than

usual from gout gave the signal for another digging for 'the Squire'.' (B. Faussett, *Inventorium Sepulchrale* (1861), Appendix I, 204). Could Godfrey-Faussett be quoting here from a letter by Hasted, written after Faussett's death in 1776? The style is very reminiscent of that used by Hasted in his letter to Ducarel of 13 December 1764 (Nichols, *Illustrations*, vol.4, 643).

[210] CCA: U11/6/3, letter no. 297.

[211] CCA: U11/6/4, letter no.23.

[212] Ibid..

[213] Hasted-Astle correspondence, 140, letter of 23 November 1763.

[214] CCA: U11/6/3, letter no.297 of 9 January 1764; Hasted-Astle correspondence, 141, letter of 17 January 1764.

[215] Hasted-Astle correspondence, 143: 11 March 1764.

[216] Ibid., 147: 6 March 1765.

[217] Ibid., 150.

[218] Ibid., 140 and 141. Dr Robert Plot's materials for a 'Natural History of Kent' were apparently owned at this time by the Faversham doctor and antiquary, Edward Jacob.

[219] BL: Add.5480.

[220] Hasted-Astle correspondence, 142.

[221] Ibid., 145, letter of 29 April 1764.

[222] BL: Add.5480.

[223] BL: Add.5480, pp.19-31 and 214-232 (recto only).

[224] S.E.Brydges, *Autobiography* (1834), 51.

[225] M. Noble, *A History of the College of Arms* (1804), 444. Edmondson found his vocation on becoming a herald painter, employed to emblazon arms on carriages. Noble says of him: 'Mowbray was a respectable man, he had the skill to raise himself to a station, that in the outset of life he could not have believed possible; what is more to be prized, he had prudence to retain it; uniting the discordant avocations, science and trade.'

[226] CCA: U11/6/2, letter no.196, of 9 December 1763. Background to this case can be found in J.Gregory, ed., *The Speculum of Archbishop Thomas Secker* (Church of England Record Society, Vol.2) (1995), 141.

[227] *KP*, 28 August 1762 and 2 March 1763. The Revd Johnson Lawson had become vicar of Throwley in 1758. (E.H.W.Dunkin, *Index to the Act Books of the Archbishops of Canterbury 1663-1859*, Part II (1938),

13 — where, incidentally, there is no mention of Lawson's transfer to Pluckley.)

[228] CCA: U11/6/2, letter no.196, of 9 December 1763.

[229] Hasted, 'Anecdotes', 293.

[230] Hasted-Astle correspondence, 147, letter of 31 July 1764.

[231] Faussett-Ducarel correspondence, Nichols, *Illustrations*, Vol.3, letter of 16 July 1764.

[232] *KP*, 11 August 1764.

[233] Faussett-Ducarel correspondence, Nichols, *Illustrations*, Vol.3, letter of 2 October 1764.

[234] Hasted-Ducarel correspondence, Nichols, *Illustrations*, Vol.4, 642-3, letter of 26 August 1764.

[235] Ibid., 643.

[236] Ibid., 643, letter of 13 December 1764. Ducarel used an illustration of the mile-stone in his *Normandy*, and John Thorpe copied this in his *Custumale Roffense* (Plate XXXII). Thorpe's work also contains a description of Hasted's stone: 'It was two feet and an half long; two of its sides were sixteen inches each; the other two fourteen; its corners were chiselled, but its faces were very rustic; however, upon one of the sides there was a very fair X cut; which was undoubtedly to shew that it stood ten miles from some particular place.' *Custumale Roffense* (1788), 251.

[237] Ibid., 644.

[238] Ibid., 644, letter of 13 February 1765.

[239] PRO: E.179/129/702/33.

[240] Hasted, 'Anecdotes', 289.

[241] Ibid., 290.

[242] MBSA, Vol.9, 1762-5, 10 November 1763.

[243] *DNB*; Nichols, *Literary Anecdotes*, Vol.6, 380-405; A. Kippis, ed., *Biographia Britannica*, Vol.5, 398-410; G.D.Squibb, *Doctors' Commons* (Oxford, 1977). Doctors' Commons, in Knightrider Street, London, founded in 1511, was dissolved in 1857, following the Court of Probate Act of that year.

[244] *DNB*.

[245] Hasted-Astle correspondence, 142-3, letter of 11 March 1764.

[246] Nichols, *Illustrations*, Vol.6, 362.

[247] J. Boswell, *Life of Johnson*, ed. R.W.Chapman (Oxford, 1980), 116.

[248] Nichols, *Literary Anecdotes*, Vol.6, 403; Vol.9, 425; Nichols, *Illustrations*, Vol.4, 631.

[249] *DNB*; C.H.I.Chown, *The Lethieullier Family of Aldersbrook House*, [1927] 23-4; Nichols, *Illustrations*, Vol.4, 645-6; BL: Add.28,538, E. da Costa correspondence.

[250] MBSA, Vol.9, 15 December 1763.

[251] Ibid., 8 December 1763.

[252] Ibid., 15 December 1763.

[253] CCA: U11/6/3, no. 297, letter from Bryan Faussett of 9 January 1764.

[254] Hasted-Astle correspondence, 141-2, letter of 17 January 1764.

[255] CCA: U11/6/3, no. 298, letter from Astle of 26 January 1764.

[256] CCA: U11/6/3, letter no. 297; Hasted-Astle correspondence, 144-5.

[257] Hasted, 'Anecdotes', 290.

[258] Hasted-Astle correspondence, 146-7.

[259] Nichols, *Illustrations*, Vol.4, 643-4, letter of 13 December 1764.

[260] Ibid, 645, letter of 13 February, 1765.

[261] From Hasted's account of the birth of his children, 1769 was the only year between 1760 and 1770 when his wife was not at some stage in a pregnancy.

[262] MBSA, Vols. 9 and 10, 1763-1769, *passim*.

[263] MBSA, Vol.10, 14 November 1765; 9 January 1766.

[264] Ibid., 12 May 1768.

[265] Ibid., 28 April 1768.

[266] *DNB*.

[267] Royal Society, Certificate of Election no. 348.

[268] *DNB*; J. Boswell, *Life of Johnson*, ed. R. W. Chapman (Oxford 1980), 272.

[269] Journal Book of the Royal Society, XXV, 1763-1766, entries for 6 February and 8 May 1766.

[270] Journal Books of the Royal Society, XXV, 1763-66; XXVI, 1767-1770. P.O'Brian, *Joseph Banks* (1987).

[271] *Phil.Trans.*, Vol.LIX, 23.

[272] Ibid., Vol.LXI, 136-165.

[273] Hasted-Astle correspondence, 148-9.

Notes

[274] BL: Add.5536: Hasted MS S.LXXXVI (not bought by the British Museum).

[275] M. Hunter, *The Royal Society and its Fellows 1660-1700* (Chalfont St Giles, 1982).

[276] The letters FRS were usually given precedence over FSA.

[277] Hasted-Astle correspondence, 148-9, letter of 1 September 1766.

[278] Ibid., 149-50, letter of 16 March 1767.

[279] *KG*, 5 November 1768; BL: Add.5488.

[280] *Familiar Letters*, Preface, i.

[281] Ibid., 206.

[282] Ibid., Preface, viii-ix.

[283] Ibid., 16-17.

[284] R. Latham & W. Matthews, eds., *The Diary of Samuel Pepys*, (11 Vols., 1970-83), Vol.5, pp.12, 83, etc. It seems very likely that the 'Letter book of Thomas Hill', now among the Faunce-Delaune papers at the Centre for Kentish Studies in Maidstone, cat.no. U145/C1, came originally from the archive found by Hasted at St John's. It was probably lent to the Sutton-at-Hone Faunces and, for one reason or another, never returned. The political content of some of the letters, written around 1660, makes interesting reading today, but would almost certainly have been shunned by Hasted, after his probable experience with the 'History of Sequestrations'.

[285] CKS: T9/A1/1, New Cross Trust Minutes, 1745-1765.

[286] Ibid..

[287] CKS: T9/A1/2. The name was obviously a mild satire on the young King George III and his unpopular minister, the Earl of Bute.

[288] CKS: T7/A1, Chalk Trust Minutes, 1761-1809.

[289] 6 Geo.III, c.98.

[290] Nichols, *Illustrations*, Vol.4, 646.

[291] CKS: T22/F1.

[292] Hasted, 'Anecdotes', 292.

[293] CKS: S/NK/SM5.

[294] CKS: S/NK/c.6.

[295] CKS: S/NK/SM5 and SM6.

[296] Hasted, *History*, 2nd edn, Vol.4, 82.

[297] RBT: A4/33, Election Register, 1734-1742.

Notes

[298] RBT: A4/31, Election Register, 1731-1811.
[299] Hasted, *History*, 2nd edn, Vol.4, 82.
[300] RBT: A1/1, Minute Book, Orders of Wardens and Assistants, 1663-1819.
[301] Ibid..
[302] Ibid..
[303] *KG*, 20 April 1771.
[304] PRO: C193/45; CKS: Q/SMa/W8.
[305] See e.g. CKS: P145/12/1; MALSC: P110/12/8; P362/12/5.
[306] CKS: Q/SB 1760.
[307] MALSC: P110/13A/3.
[308] CKS: Q/SMa/W8.
[309] CKS: Q/SB 1760 and 1761. The level of importance of the document in question dictated the number of justices' signatures required to it.
[310] Ibid..
[311] Ibid..
[312] CKS: Q/SMa/W8.
[313] CKS: Q/SB 1760.
[314] FMM & L, Canterbury: MSS of Dr William Perfect.
[315] CKS: Q/ROm1.
[316] *KP*, 7 July 1759.
[317] Hasted, *History*, 2nd edn, Vol.2, 417.
[318] MALSC: P110/12/8.
[319] Hasted, 'Anecdotes', 293. Anne's two godmothers were Mrs Anne Leigh, wife of Francis Leigh, and Miss Jane Faunce, daughter of Thomas Faunce.
[320] MALSC: P110/12/8.
[321] PRO: ASSI35/197/5.
[322] CCA: U11/6/4, no.77.
[323] PRO: ASSI/35/199/5; 35/200/5.
[324] PRO: ASSI/35/201/5.
[325] PRO: ASSI/35/202/5 — 35/208/5.
[326] Hasted-Astle correspondence, 143.
[327] PRO: ASSI35/204/5.

[328] PRO: ASSI35/208/5 and 6.

[329] Hasted-Astle correspondence, 143: letter of 17 March 1764.

[330] CCA: U11/6/2, no.64.

[331] CCA: U11/6/1, no.75.

[332] CCA: U11/6/4, no.82, letter of 12 October 1764.

[333] CCA: U11/6/2, no.195.

[334] CCA: U11/6/5, letter of 18 November 1764.

[335] CCA: U11/6/A and B: these were probably Hasted's L.LIX and L.LXI. BL: Add.5512 (Hasted L.LX, noted in his Index as a supplement to L.LIX).

[336] Hasted-Astle correspondence, 143.

[337] CCA: U11/6/A.

[338] CCA: U11/6/B.

[339] CCA: U11/6/A.

[340] Ibid..

[341] Ibid..

[342] CCA: U11/6/2, no.158.

[343] Nichols, *Illustrations*, Vol.4, 649.

[344] George Hickes, *Linguarum Vett. Septentrionalium Thesaurus Grammatico-Criticus et Archaeologicus* (Oxford, 1705). Henry Spelman, *Glossarium Archaiologicum* (1687).

[345] Faussett's account of his principal excavations, *Inventorium Sepulchrale*, was not to be published until 1861. Richard Gough noted that 'both his collections of antiquities as well as his papers relating to them, and his transcript of the monumental inscriptions throughout the diocese, are locked up by his will, so as to be of no use to any one'. J. Russell Smith, *Bibliotheca Cantiana* (1837), 14.

[346] CCA: U11/6/A.

[347] BL: Add.5507 (Hasted K.XLVI).

[348] Ibid..

[349] BL: Add.5536. Add.5537 is a not quite identical, later, copy of the Index. Both contain errors in numbering, between Z.CIV and Z.CVII, which should be Z.CXIV – Z.CXVII.

[350] BL: Add.5520.

[351] Hasted-Astle correspondence, 142.

Notes

[352] E.M.Hallam, *Domesday Book Through Nine Centuries* (1986), 134. Hasted's copy of the Kent folios also contains a quotation for engraving Domesday Book, but 'Mr Bailey's estimate', undated, and for the astronomical sum of £18,443.12s.0d., using two-colour copper plates, is almost certainly a later item, collected and inserted by Thomas Astle, who owned the copy for a time, and has nothing to do with Hasted, who could not have contemplated such a project.

[353] BL: Add.5511 (Hasted K.LVIII).

[354] Hasted-Astle correspondence, 147-8.

[355] BL: Add.5538 (Hasted T.XCII).

[356] Hasted-Astle correspondence, 139 and 145.

[357] Nichols, *Illustrations*, Vol.4, 644.

[358] CCA: U11/6/1 (not numbered).

[359] CCA: U11/6/1, e.g. nos. 14 and 55.

[360] See e.g. Nichols, *Illustrations*, Vol.4.

[361] *GM*, Vol.25 (1755), 157-159.

[362] *Bibliotheca Topographica Britannica*, No.1 (1780), i-iv. Nichols follows up his brief history of the questionnaire with a set of his own queries, closely modelled on, although not identical to, those of the Society of Antiquaries, v-xiv.

[363] CCA: U11/6/A, p.316.

[364] CCA: U11/6/1, no.66.

[365] CCA: U11/6/3, no.259.

[366] CCA: U11/6/1, no.52.

[367] CCA: U11/6/2, nos. 162, 161; U11/6/1, no. 81.

[368] CCA: U11/6/1, no.52.

[369] CCA: U11/6/1, no.49.

[370] Ibid., no.18.

[371] Ibid., nos.54 and 99.

[372] Ibid., no.49.

[373] Ibid., no.104.

[374] Ibid., no.80.

[375] Ibid., no.2.

[376] Ibid., no.3.

[377] Ibid., no.4.

[378] Ibid., no.5.

[379] CCA: U11/6/2, no.142.

[380] CKS: P358/5/1. The Hill family retained ownership of St John's until 1780, when it was sold to John Mumford. (Hasted, *History*, 2nd edn, Vol.2, 348).

[381] CKS: T22/F1.

[382] RBT: A4/31, Election Register, 1731-1811.

[383] CCA: U11/6/4, no.16.

[384] MBSA, Vol.10.

[385] CCA: U11/6/1, no.64.

[386] Hasted, 'Anecdotes', 294.

[387] CCA: U3/3/3/2.

[388] W. Gostling, *A Walk in and about the City of Canterbury* (1774), 47; advertisements in the *Kentish Gazette, passim*, ca. 1768-1772.

[389] *KG*, 7 December 1768. The beauty products advertised were prepared by the firm of Richard Warren in Marylebone, possibly the original of the firm for which Dickens worked as a boy.

[390] Hasted, 'Anecdotes', 294; Folio edn, Vol.IV, 470.

[391] CCA: U11/6/3, no.68.

[392] *KG*, 29 April 1769; PRO: PROB11/947/129.

[393] Hasted, 'Anecdotes', 290-1.

[394] J.Almon, ed., *The Correspondence of the late John Wilkes with his Friends*, (5 vols, 1805), Vol.4, 'Letters from Mr Wilkes to his daughter during her residence at Paris in the months of April, May, June and July 1770', 31-56.

[395] Ibid., letter of 19 June, 1770.

[396] Ibid., letter of 22 June 1770.

[397] Hasted, *History*, Vol.IV, 586.

[398] *KP*, 5 March 1763.

[399] Hasted, 'Anecdotes', 290-1 and footnote; CCA: U3/100/11/2.

[400] CCA: DCc/BB64/38-39; 40-41; 42.

[401] Nichols, *Illustrations*, Vol.4, Hasted to Ducarel, 647.

[402] Hasted, 'Anecdotes', 291.

[403] W. Gostling, op.cit.,147.

[404] CCA: U3/100/11/2.

[405] Hasted, 'Anecdotes', 291, footnote.

[406] CCA: U11/6/1, no.58.

Notes

[407] Hasted, *History*, Vol.IV, 583; Sir Samuel E. Brydges, *The Autobiography, Times, Opinions and Contemporaries* (2 vols, 1834) Vol.1, 5; quoted in J.S.Sidebotham, *Memorials of the King's School, Canterbury* (1865), 68.

[408] Diary of the Revd Joseph Price, quoted in G.M.Ditchfield and B. Keith-Lucas, eds.,*A Kentish Parson* (1991), 46 and 90.

[409] CCA: U11/6/6, letter of 13 August, 1792.

[410] CCA: U3/100/1/3.

[411] Ibid..

[412] King's School, Canterbury, First Register of Admissions (instituted by Dr Beauvoir in 1750).

[413] Ibid..

[414] Ibid.; *DNB*; Sir S.E. Brydges, op.cit., Vol.2, 401-2.

[415] *KG*, 30 August 1770.

[416] Hasted, 'Anecdotes', 294; CCA: U3/100/1/3, 8 January 1774.

[417] Hasted-Astle correspondence, 151.

[418] CCA: U3/100/1/3.

[419] CKS: Q/SMa/E8.

[420] CCA: U3/100/11/2; U3/55/12/A4 and A5.

[421] CKS: Q/SB 1775; Q/SB 1776.

[422] CKS: Q/SB 1770, 1775, 1776, 1777, 1779, 1781.

[423] CKS: Q/SB 1777; Q/SB 1789.

[424] *KG*, 1 and 15 March 1780.

[425] PRO: ASSI/35/225/6; ASSI/35/220/5.

[426] PRO: ASSI/35/226/5; ASSI/35/226/6.

[427] PRO: ASSI/35/227/6; ASSI/35/228/5.

[428] CKS: U1823/94/F3.

[429] CKS: S/EK/SM1-4 (Minute Books, 1770-1792).

[430] Ibid.; BL: Add.5489.

[431] CKS: S/EK/SM1-4.

[432] CKS: S/EK/SM 3 and 4. Hasted's name continued to appear on the Commissions of the Sewers for Several Limits until his death.

[433] CCA: Q/RPL/61

[434] Hasted, 'Anecdotes', 291.

Notes

[435] CCA: U3/100/11/2, Poor rates, Christchurch, Canterbury; CKS: U390/M20, Court book of the manor of Teynham.

[436] CCA: U11/6/3, no.299.

[437] *KG*, 1768-1780 *passim*.

[438] E. Jacob, *The History of the Town and Port of Faversham* (1774), 108.

[439] Hasted-Astle correspondence, 151.

[440] *KG*, 20 August 1774.

[441] CCA: U11/6/3, no.165.

[442] CCA: U11/6/A, p.316. Richardson was one of the printers used by John Thorpe for his *Registrum Roffense*.

[443] RGM: Quotation, undated but signed by Hasted, pasted into Vol.I of his own copy of the folio edition of the *History*. (G.197).

[444] *KG*, 1 October 1774.

[445] Hasted, *Proposals for Publishing by Subscription the History and Topographical Survey of the County of Kent*. Extant in Grangerised copy of the *History* at CKS, Vol.1.

[446] CCA, U11/6/1, no.25.

[447] *CJ*, 15, 22, 29 November and 6, 13 December 1774. Whittingham, however, seems to have sought involvement in the reprints market: following the centenary of the appearance of Robert Thoroton's *Antiquities of Nottinghamshire*, the first part was reprinted by Whittingham in 1781.

[448] CCA: U11/6/1, no.121.

[449] *GM*, Vol.44 (1774), 521.

[450] *KG*, 9 May 1778.

[451] CCA: U11/6/1, no.58.

[452] CCA: U11/6/3, no.166. Barlow's engraving of The Park House, near Folkestone, was to appear in folio Vol.III.

[453] BL: Add.5486.

[454] CCA: U11/6/3, no.288, 29 December 1767.

[455] Nichols, *Illustrations*, Vol.4, 676, letter of 11 June 1775.

[456] CCA: U11/6/1, no.33.

[457] Ibid., no.35.

[458] CCA: U11/6/2, no.163, 9 March 1777.

[459] CCA: U11/6/1, no.43.

[460] Ibid., no.52.

Notes

[461] CCA: U11/6/2, no.163.

[462] CKS: U565/E241.

[463] CCA: U11/6/1, no.118, 28 March 1778. Cobham Hall was not in fact by Inigo Jones, although it seems to have been often attributed to him.

[464] Ibid., no.87.

[465] CCA: U11/6/3, nos.274 and 275, letters of 17 November 1776 and 16 March 1779.

[466] Hasted-Astle correspondence, 151-154, letters of 6 and 15 March and 8 June 1778.

[467] CCA: U11/6/1, no.84.

[468] CCA: U11/6/2, no.41; U11/6/1, no.62.

[469] CCA: U11/6/1, nos. 89, 69 and 90.

[470] Hasted-Astle correspondence, 156.

[471] CCA: U11/6/1, no.89, letter of 3 August 1778.

[472] CCA: U11/6/2, no.1O; U11/6/1, no.91. In the Preface to Vol.I Hasted comments humorously that readers may well prefer incomplete lists of incumbents, given the length to which complete lists would run.

[473] *GM*, Vol.48 (1778), 378-9.

[474] Preface to E. Rowe Mores, 'History of Tunstall', *Bibliotheca Topographica Britannica*, Vol.1, Antiquities in Kent and Sussex, eds. J.Nichols, R.Gough and F.Grose (1780), vi.
Dulcedo natalis soli: sweetness of the native soil; *Keimelia*: that which is stored or valuable, a treasure.

[475] CCA: U11/6/2, no.158, letter of 5 February 1781.

[476] Ibid., no.161, 8 March 1781.

[477] Ibid., no.2.

[478] Hasted-Astle ccorrespondence, 155, letter of 20 November 1778.

[479] Ibid., 156, letter of 28 December 1778. *Heu quanta de spe decidi*: Alas, how much hope have I killed.

[480] RGM: Hasted family papers (G.208).

[481] CCA: Q/RPL/61.

[482] RGM: Hasted family papers (G.212).

[483] GLL: MS 11936/289, policy 436378.

[484] CCA: U11/6/2, no.160.

485 Ibid., no.28.
486 Ibid., no.34, letter of 2 April 1779.
487 Ibid., no.94, 30 March 1780.
488 Ibid., no.73, letter from William Scoones of 29 January 1783.
489 CCA: U11/6/1, no.101.
490 *KG*, 3 May; 11, 13, [18 - missing at BL Colindale], 21 June 1783. CJ, 6, 20 May; 10, 17 June 1783.
491 Hasted, *History*, folio Vol.II, Preface, i.
492 *GM*, Vol.53 (1783), 421-2.
493 *KG*, 11 June (re subscriptions taken in at Hasted's own house), 10 December 1783.
494 CKS: U390/M20.
495 RGM: Hasted family papers (G.205).
496 CKS: U1823/94/F3.
497 CCA: U11/6/2, no.160.
498 RGM: Hasted family papers (G.205).
499 Ibid..
500 RGM: Hasted family papers (G.208).
501 RGM: Hasted family papers (G.215).
502 CKS: P229/12/2.
503 CKS: P229/1/2. Linton Register of Baptisms, entry for 27 March 1785: 'Edward, son of Mary Town, base-born'.
504 CKS: P197/1/3.
505 CKS: U1823/94/F3, letter of 23 August 1795.
506 Hasted, 'Anecdotes', 292.
507 CKS: U2083, Box 7, Notebook K.
508 Hasted, 'Anecdotes', 292.
509 RGM: Hasted family papers (G.208).
510 Nichols, *Illustrations*, Vol.4, 678, letter of 17 October 1781.
511 See e.g. CCA: U11/6/437, letters 62-64, of December 1786 and September 1787.
512 CCA: U11/6/4, no. 34, letter of 16 March 1787.
513 CCA: U11/6/3, no.238. *KG*, 20 July 1787. *GM*, Vol.57 (1787), 741: 'July: At Mr Mountford's, at East Barming, Kent, the second son of Edward Hasted, esq., author of 'The History of Kent'.' Mary

Dorman's house at Barming was to go to Mr Mumford after her death: Mountford probably represents a misreading or mishearing of this name. George was of course the third, and not the second, son.

[514] RGM: Hasted family papers (G.204).
[515] CCA:U11/6/3, nos.72 and 78. Sir Richard Heron, *A Genealogical Table of the Herons of Newark, heretofore of Northumberland and of Durham* [1798].
[516] CKS: U2083, Box 7.
[517] Ibid., notebook A.
[518] Ibid., notebooks F and G.
[519] CCA: U11/6/3, no.220.
[520] Ibid., no.240, letter of 3 January 1789.
[521] Ibid., no.281, letter of 31 July 1789; ibid., no.291.
[522] CCA: U11/6/4, letter no.36 of 27 March 1790.
[523] RGM: Hasted family papers, 'Statement of Mr Hasted's transactions with the late Mr Thos Williams' (G.211).
[524] Ibid..
[525] PRO: C33/558 and C13/1688/35.
[526] RGM: Hasted family papers, 'Statement of Mr Hasted's transactions with the late Mr Thos Williams'; copy of the bond of 7 April 1790; 18 points listed by Hasted relating to a submission by John Williams (G.211). PRO: C13/1698/8.
[527] RGM: Hasted family papers, 'Statement', and copy of bond of 7 April 1790 (G.211).
[528] CCA: U11/6/4, no.36, 27 March 1790.
[529] *KG*, 13, 16, 20 and 23 April 1790.
[530] Georges Saugnier, *Les Emigrés du Pas-de-Calais pendant la Révolution* (Calais, 1959).
[531] Arthur Young, *Travels in France during the Years 1787, 1788 and 1789* (1792; Everyman edition, [1915]), 8,9.
[532] *KG*, 20 July 1774.
[533] C.B.Andrews, ed., *The Torrington Diaries*, Vol.4, 93 (1938) and Vol.1, 282 (1934).
[534] Alain Derville, ed., *Histoire de St-Omer* (Lille, 1981), *passim;* Arthur Young, op.cit., 91.
[535] *KG*, 25 February 1778.
[536] Arthur Young, op.cit., 9.

[537] J. Nichols, *Illustrations*, Vol.VI, 614. The Latin translates as follows: *Quo me cunque rapit tempestas, deferor hospes*: Wherever the storm carries me, I am brought as a guest. *Quod verum atque decens curo et rogo, et omnis in hoc sum*: What is right and seemly is my study and pursuit.

[538] *KG*, 20 July 1790.

[539] Hasted, *History*, Vol.III, Preface, i-ii. The Latin quoted by Hasted translates as follows: *Solve senescentem mature sanus equum*: Release an ageing horse from service in good time.

[540] CCA: U11/6/4, no.67.

[541] F.B.Pinion, *A Wordsworth Chronology* (1988), 8.

[542] William Wordsworth, *The French Revolution*, lines 4-11, 18-19.

[543] P. Wayne, ed., *Letters of William Wordsworth* (1954), 4.

[544] Alain Derville, ed., op.cit., 153-164.

[545] Diary of Mrs Louisa Thomas, in the possession of Mr Bryan Gipps.

[546] Document dated by its contents, and its reference to 'July last 1790', in the possession of Anthony Whittaker, of Brenchley.

[547] CCA: U11/6/6, letter of 9 August 1790.

[548] CCA: U11/6/5, letter of 5 May 1798.

[549] *GM*, Vol.60 (1790), 926.

[550] Hasted-Astle correspondence, 158-9.

[551] CCA: U11/6/4, no.33, letter of 21 November 1791.

[552] S.E.Brydges, *Autobiography* (2 vols., 1834), Vol.1, 48; CCA: U11/6/4, no.3.

[553] CCA: U11/6/6, letter of 4 February 1792.

[554] Ibid., letter of 10 March 1792.

[555] Ibid., undated.

[556] Ibid., letter of 27 July 1792.

[557] Ibid., letter of 13 August 1792.

[558] Ibid., Boys to Hasted, 6 April 1792; Boteler to Hasted, 12 December 1792.

[559] Ibid., letter of 10 March 1792.

[560] RGM: Hasted family papers, bill to the Revd Edward Hasted from Budgen, Jefferys and Gurr, Chatham bankers (G.213).

[561] CCA: U11/6/6, letter of 15 February 1793.

Notes

[562] Ville de Calais, Archives Municipales, File of passports or 'laisser passer' granted to citizens of Calais ca. 1793, nos. 1512, 1513, 1514; 1300 and 1308.

[563] See for descriptions of Calais during the Revolution: Alain Derville et Albert Vion (eds), *Histoire de Calais* (Westhoek, 1985); Charles Demotier, *Annales de Calais, depuis les temps les plus reculés jusqu'à nos jours* (1856); R. Fonte et S. Reboule, *Calais sous la Révolution* (Calais, 1889).

[564] Hasted, 'Anecdotes', 292.

[565] CCA: U11/6/4, no.33, letter of 21 November 1791.

[566] *GM*, 61 (1791), 285; Hasted, *History*, Vol.IV, 576.

[567] CCA: U11/6/4.

[568] Ibid., no.33, letter of 21 November 1791.

[569] Nichols, *Illustrations*, Vol.6, 634.

[570] CCA: U11/6/5.

[571] CCA: U11/6/4, no.9, letter of 29 October 1794.

[572] CCA: U11/6/437, letter of 31 August 1794.

[573] RGM: 'Statement of Mr Hasted's transactions with the late Mr Thos Williams', 7.

[574] PRO: PRIS 4/14, Commitments, No.1135. The £4400 mentioned here is the combined debt to Joseph Davies and Robert Rugg.

[575] PRO: PRIS 5/9, 304.

[576] RGM: Hasted family papers (G.205).

[577] James Neild, *An Account of the rise, progress, and present state of the Society for the Discharge and Relief of Persons Imprisoned for Small Debts throughout England and Wales* (1802), 287. But see also his later account of the King's Bench Prison in *State of the Prisons in England, Scotland and Wales* (1812), 304-312.

[578] J. Neild, *Account of the rise ... of the Society ... for Small Debts* (1802), 292-3; reprinted in Neild's *State of the prisons*, 306.

[579] J. Neild, *State of the prisons*, 312.

[580] Hasted, 'Anecdotes', 292.

[581] Ibid., 293.

[582] Anon, *The Debtor and Creditor's Assistant* (1793), 42.

[583] *The Debtor and Creditor's Assistant*; Anon, *A Description of the King's Bench Prison* (ca. 1800).

[584] PRO: PRIS 10/141.

[585] PRO: PRIS 4/14.

[586] J. Innes, 'The King's Bench Prison in the later eighteenth century' in J. Brewer and J. Styles, eds., *An Ungovernable People* (1980), 250-298.

[587] CCA: DCc/BB 64/42: 4 September 1792 is given as the date of the sale of the Precincts property to William Baldock, in an indenture relating to its resale on 9 October 1792 to Mrs Susanna Duncombe for £400.

[588] CCA: U11/6/5.

[589] Ibid..

[590] PRO: PRIS 10/142.

[591] *Description of the King's Bench Prison*, 14.

[592] Ibid., 11.

[593] CKS: U1823/94/F3.

[594] Ibid..

[595] CKS: letter from Thomas Astle to John Nichols of 1st January 1796, in Grangerised folio edition of the *History*, Vol.I.

[596] CCA: U11/6/5, letter of 1 December 1795.

[597] Ibid., letter of 6 February 1796.

[598] Nichols, *Illustrations*, Vol.6, 669; W. Shakespeare, *Othello*, Act I, Scene 2, line 37: Cassio: The duke does greet you, general,/And he requires your haste-post-haste appearance.

[599] P.R.Harris, *A History of the British Museum Library 1753-1973* (1998), 23. The Hasted manuscripts are now BL Additional Manuscripts 5478 to 5539.

[600] BL Stowe 851 and 855. St.851 was originally Hasted's MS A.II. St.855 contains Hasted's MSS O.LXXII and O.LXXIII, now bound together. Hasted's pressmarks have been erased, but St.851 contains one line in Hasted's writing on the title-page, and a page of queries in his hand at the back, while St.855 is in his handwriting throughout.

[601] CCA: U11/6/5, letter of 24 March 1800.

[602] Ibid., letter of 30 June 1796.

[603] Ibid., letter of 9 July 1796.

[604] Ibid., letter of 9 August 1796.

[605] *Description of the King's Bench Prison*, 10.

[606] PRO: PRIS 4/12 and 4/14.

[607] CKS: Letter from Thomas Astle to John Nichols, in Grangerised folio edition, Vol.I.

Notes

[608] Nichols, *Illustrations*, Vol.4, 650-1, letter of 16 July 1796.

[609] CCA: U11/6/431, letter of 9 August 1796.

[610] Ibid..

[611] CCA: U11/6/A and B; CKS: U2083, Box 7, Books A-Q; CKS: U1823/94/Ql-Q4. Hasted in his will bequeathed all his remaining MSS to William Boteler, and all these manuscripts now stem from the Boteler collection. The correspondence (CCA: U11/6) also went to Boteler on Hasted's death.

[612] CCA: U11/6/4, Boys's letter of 31 August 1794. Eden had himself referred his readers to Hasted's *History* in his 'Parochial Reports' (*State of the Poor*, Vol.2 (1795), 285).

[613] CCA: U11/6/5, letters of 18 and 25 September 1796.

[614] *KG*, 25 October 1796; *KG*, 14 February 1797. Similar advertisements appeared also in the Maidstone Journal.

[615] Nichols, *Illustrations*, Vol.6, 686.

[616] Dates on which the twelve volumes of the second edition were advertised in the *Kentish Gazette* are as follows: 1: 14 February 1797; 2: 19 May 1797; 3: 15 September 1797; 4: 23 January 1798; 5: 22 May 1798; 6: 2 October 1798; 7: 25 December 1798; 8: 17 September 1799; 9: 7 February 1800; 10: 1 August 1800; 11: 12 December 1800; 12: 10 August 1801. The same advertisements appeared, around the same dates, in the *Maidstone Journal* also.

[617] CCA: U11/6/6, letter of 22 May 1797.

[618] Nichols, *Illustrations*, Vol.6, 703, letter of 5 June 1797; ibid., 713, letter of 25 September 1797; ibid., 714, letter of 4 October 1797; *KG*, 15 September 1797.

[619] Nichols, *Illustrations*, Vol.6, 705, letter of 17 June 1797.

[620] CCA: U11/6/3, (no.18), letter of 14 November 1796; U11/6/6, letter of 22 May 1797; U11/6/5, letter of 22 May 1799.

[621] CCA: U11/6/5, letters of 5 August 1796 and 8 January 1797.

[622] Ibid., letter of 26 October 1798.

[623] *GM*, 69 (1799), 708.

[624] *Description of the King's Bench Prison*, 16.

[625] Ibid., 3.

[626] CCA: U11/6/5.

[627] Ibid., letter of 5 May 1798.

[628] *KG*, 17 September 1799.

[629] *KG*, 1 August 1800.
[630] *KG*, 10 August 1801.
[631] CKS: U2083, box 7, notebook P.
[632] CKS: U1823/94/F1.
[633] CCA: U11/6/5, letter of 24 March 1800.
[634] J.Neild, *State of the prisons*, 304.
[635] Hasted-Astle correspondence, 165-6, letter of 12 July 1801.
[636] PRO: PROB11/1338/191.
[637] CCA: U11/6/5, letter of 26 January 1799.
[638] By the Act 32 and 33 Vict., c.62, An Act for the abolition of imprisonment for debt.
[639] RGM: Hasted family papers, 'Statement of Mr Hasted's transactions with the late Mr Thos Williams concerning the conveyance of his estates to him and the bond Mr Williams gave him to reconvey the same' 7, 8. (G.211).
[640] RGM: Hasted family papers, 'Mr Harvey's opinion concerning Williams's bond', letter of 10 November 1801. (G.211).
[641] RGM: Hasted family papers, 'Statement of Mr Hasted's transactions' 1, 8-10, (G.211).
[642] PRO: C33/558.
[643] PRO: PRIS 7/21.
[644] PRO: C33/558.
[645] CCA: U11/6/5, letter of 24 November 1803.
[646] MS in the possession of Mr Bryan Gipps, of Egerton.
[647] CKS: U1300/C5/15.
[648] The first volume of the second edition had been dedicated to Lord Romney.
[649] R.Yates, *An Illustration of the Monastic History and Antiquities of the town and abbey of St Edmund's Bury* (2nd edn, 1843, with 'Memoir of the author', by the publisher, John Bowyer Nichols, xix-xxiv).
[650] BL: Egerton 2374, f.308.
[651] Ibid., ff.169-173.
[652] BL: Egerton 2370, ff.99-111; see also Appendix 2.
[653] BL: Egerton 2374, f.313.
[654] For full details of Hasted's work for Richard Yates see Appendix 2.
[655] BL: Eg.2371, f.103.

Notes

656 BL: Egerton 2374, f.307

657 RGM: Hasted family papers (G.208).

658 WRO: 490/15, copy letter among the Earl of Radnor's papers, dated 21 March 1807.

659 WRO: 490/15, letter of 27 March 1807.

660 WRO: 490/15.

661 Ibid..

662 Ibid..

663 *VCH Wiltshire*: Vol.XIV, 216-7.

664 WRO: 490/18.

665 WRO: 490/19.

666 PRO: C33/558, ff.1494-1504.

667 John Britton, *An Historical Account of Corsham House in Wiltshire, the seat of Paul Cobb Methuen, Esq., with a catalogue of his celebrated collection of pictures* (1806).

668 CCA: U11/5.

669 Ibid..

670 Ibid..

671 CCA: U11/6/6.

672 RGM: Hasted family papers (G.208).

673 Ibid..

674 PRO: PROB11/1530/75.

675 Ibid., codicil of 15 November 1810.

676 PRO: C13/1688/35.

677 CCA: U11/5.

678 Ibid..

679 WRO: 490/16.

680 WRO: 1157/8, Corsham parish register.

681 WRO: 490/16.

682 *GM*, Vol.82 (1812), 189.

683 Ibid..

684 *KG*, 28 January 1812.

685 WRO: 490/16, letter of 3 March 1812.

686 *Bath Herald*, 25 January 1812; reprinted in the *Maidstone Journal* 4 February 1812. There is no copy of the Bath newspaper extant for this date, but the attribution in the *Maidstone Journal* is clear.

687 PRO: C13/1688/35.

688 RGM: Hasted family papers, 'A Particular and the conditions of sale of ... the estates of Edward Hasted, esq. deceased.' (G.198).

689 RGM: Hasted family papers (G.215). Charles made a slight error in his calculations: the first day's sales made £8712.15s.0d., the second day's £7155.0.0d.(G.198).

690 RGM: Hasted family papers, 'A Particular and the conditions of sale of ... the estates of Edward Hasted, esq. deceased' (G.198).

691 PRO: C13/1688/35.

692 PRO: C13/1678/23.

693 PRO: C13/1688/35.

694 PRO: C33/691,f.662.

695 PRO: C13/1678/23.

696 *GM*, Vol.48 (1778), 378-9: see Chapter 11.

697 *GM*, Vol.53 (1783), 421-2.

698 *Critical Review*, Vol.45 (1778), 401-12.

699 *Monthly Review*, Vol.59 (1778), 413-7.

700 *Monthly Review*, Vol.69 (1783), 595.

701 J.M.Kuist, *The Nichols File of the Gentleman's Magazine* (Wisconsin, 1982), General introduction, 4-5.

702 See e.g. C.R.J.Currie and C.P.Lewis, eds., *A Guide to English County Histories* (1994), 99, 145, 159, 401, with regard to William Hutchinson's *Cumberland*, the Revd Philip Morant's *Essex*, the Revd Thomas Fosbrooke's *County of Gloucester*, and the Revd William Thomas's revised edition of Dugdale's *Warwickshire*.

703 *GM*, Vol.60 (1790), 926.

704 *Bibliotheca Topographica Britannica*, No.1 (1780), vi. *Keimelia*: Treasure, store.

705 *British Topography*, Vol.1 (1780), 446-7.

706 Ibid..

707 Francis Grose, *A Classical Dictionary of the Vulgar Tongue* (1768). Described in *DNB* as 'a sort of antiquarian Falstaff', Grose had a varied career, studying art, and becoming at different times Richmond Herald, adjutant and paymaster in the Hampshire Militia,

and captain and adjutant in the Surrey Militia. He and Hasted almost certainly knew each other well, as his wife, Catherine Jordan, came from a Canterbury family, and the vicar of Barming, the Revd Mark Noble, was to describe him as 'an inimitable boon companion' in his *History of the College of Arms* (1804), 434-8.

[708] *GM*, Vol.82 (1812), 189-90 and 672-3.

[709] *GM*, Vol.82 (1812), 104.

[710] For Nichols's 'absorption' of others' work into his own see e.g. C.Phythian-Adams, 'Leicestershire and Rutland', *A Guide to English County Histories*, eds. C.R.J.Currie and C.P.Lewis (1994), 230-232.

[711] See Kuist, *The Nichols File*.

[712] *GM*, Vol.82 (1812), 205.

[713] *GM*, Vol.82 (1812), 419-21. G.M.Arnold, *Robert Pocock, The Gravesend Historian, Naturalist, Antiquarian, Botanist and Printer* (1883).

[714] Hasted, *History*, Vol.I, Preface, i.

[715] Hasted, *History*, Vol.III, 670; 2nd edn., Vol.9, 180-1. Vol.9, 404.

[716] A.M.Everitt, Introduction to the 1972 reprint of Hasted's 2nd edition, xviii.

[717] Hasted, *History*, Vol.III, Preface, i.

[718] Henry H. Drake, ed., *Hasted's History of Kent, corrected, enlarged, and continued to the present time*. Part I. The Hundred of Blackheath (1886). 'To the Reader', n.p., and Introduction, i-xiii.

[719] Ibid..

[720] Ibid..

[721] J.Boyle, *In Quest of Hasted* (Chichester, 1984), 139.

[722] Hasted, *History*, Vol.I, vi; Folkestone Library: Hasted, MS 'History of Folkestone' (942.23 Folk),59-63. Escheat was not finally abolished until 1925.

[723] J.Cantwell, *The Public Record Office, 1838-1958* (1991), 53.

[724] Hasted, *History*, 2nd edn, Vol.1, Preface, xi.

[725] Hasted, *History*, 2nd edn, Vol.2, 342.

[726] Boyle, *In Quest of Hasted*, 99.

[727] Ibid..

[728] Revd S. Ayscough, *A Catalogue of the manuscripts preserved in the British Museum hitherto undescribed* (1782), viii.

[729] C.I.Elton, *The Tenures of Kent* (1867), *passim*.

730 D.Bates, *A Bibliography of Domesday Book* (1986), 84.

731 Alan M. Everitt, *Continuity and Colonization: The Evolution of Kentish Settlement* (Leicester, 1986), xviii.

732 A.M.Everitt, Introduction to 1972 reprint of 2nd edition, v; A.R.Wagner, *English Genealogy* (3rd edn, Chichester 1983), 379.

733 S.E.Brydges, *Autobiography* (1834), 51.

734 LPL: VB 1/11, Act Books of the Archbishop of Canterbury.

735 LPL: VB 1/11 and 1/12, Act Books of the Archbishop of Canterbury. J.Gregory, ed., *The Speculum of Archbishop Thomas Secker* (Church of England Record Society, 2) (1995), 21, notes 'Mr Hasted' as curate of Littlebourne: this is probably a mistake for R.Harvey, who became curate there in 1791.

736 *MJ*, 14 October 1828.

737 See e.g. *MJ*, 28 January 1840.

738 PRO: PROB11/2220/848, and RGM: Hasted family papers (G.208).

739 Ibid..

740 J.Phippen, *Descriptive Sketches of Rochester, Chatham, etc.* (Rochester, 1862), 246-7.

741 RGM: Hasted family papers (G.214).

742 B. Gipps, *Hollingbourne and the Thomas Family* (Hollingbourne, 1991).

743 RGM: Hasted family papers (G.208).

744 Lambeth Archives: Burial Register of St Mary's, Lambeth.

745 MS additions to MS copy of Hasted's 'Anecdotes', now in the possession of Mr Bryan Gipps of Egerton. The date does not agree with that on Hasted's own autograph pedigree of the family, also owned by Mr Gipps, which gives his wife's date of death as December 1804, but this contains several verifiable errors, and the date given in the augmented Anecdotes, with corroborative details concerning Mrs Hasted's burial at Sutton-at-Hone in the same grave as her sister Mrs Mary Dorman, appears to be the more correct. But the MS additions also contain some errors.

746 RGM: Hasted family papers (G.208).

747 PRO: ADM 11/40; Navy List, 1815-1824.

748 MS additions to copy of the Anecdotes; RGM: Hasted family papers (G.214): letters from J.C.Burgoyne to Revd Edward Hasted of December 1853 and January 1854.

749 PRO: PROB11/2184/33, and RGM: Hasted family papers (G.208).

Notes

[750] Ibid..

[751] RGM: Hasted family papers (G.208), letter of 18 November 1853 from Charles James to Joseph Oliver.

[752] RGM: Hasted family papers (G.204), letter from Mr Scobell to Joseph Oliver of 14 December 1853.

[753] CKS: Q/RPL/101, Dartford Land Tax; MALSC: P110/12/11, Overseers' accounts.

[754] RGM: Hasted family papers (G.214), letter of June 1828 from John Pearce to Revd Edward Hasted.

[755] Hasted autograph pedigree, now in the possession of Mr Bryan Gipps. The information relating to Harriet Warington is in another hand.

[756] RGM: Hasted family papers (G.214), letter of 2 July 1828.

[757] Charles's death is given, in another hand, on the Hasted autograph pedigree, in the possession of Mr Bryan Gipps.

[758] CCA: U11/6/2, no.160.

[759] RGM: Hasted family papers (G.214).

[760] Eustace Carey, *Memoir of William Carey, DD* (1836).

[761] Ibid..

[762] RGM: Hasted family papers (G.214).

[763] Ibid..

[764] RGM: Hasted family papers (G.214), letter dated 26 July 1819.

[765] Ibid..

[766] RGM: Hasted family papers (G.214), letter of 1 March 1820.

[767] RGM: Hasted family papers, (G.214) letter of Revd Edward Hasted to Messrs T. and S. Naylor, dated 21 July 1822.

[768] RGM: Hasted family papers (G.214).

[769] RGM: Hasted family papers (G.214), letter of June 1828.

[770] RGM: Hasted family papers (G.214), letter of 2 July 1828.

[771] RGM: Hasted family papers, letter of 12 November 1831.

[772] See e.g. *The New Annual Bengal Directory and General Register for the Year 1824, et seq.*; and *The Bengal and Agra Directory ... for the year 1844*. Francis is erroneously shown here as the surviving brother.

[773] BL, OIOC: N/1/49/f.48.

[774] BL, OIOC: N/1/66/f.264.

[775] Will of George Hasted, dated 17 November 1849: BL, OIOC:L/AG/34/29/82, part 4, 279-280, and PRO: PROB11/2225/38.

[776] Sircar: steward or general factotum; moonshi: interpreter; mooktar: lawyer.

List of Subscribers

John Adams Books, Tonbridge
Jean Adderley, Faversham
Miss Hilary Alpin, Canterbury
J.Douglas Anderson FSA Scot., Pollokshields, Glasgow
L.A.Anderson, Tunbridge Wells
Dr F.W.G.Andrews, Sandwich
Denis Anstey, Snodland
Society of Antiquaries of London
Paul Ashbee, Chedgrave, Norwich
Mrs C.Ashby, Buckingham
John Ashdown, Oxford
Mrs G.M.Atherton, Digges Place, Barham

Mrs Stella Baggaley, Farningham
Derek Barbanell, Washbrook, Ipswich
Mrs E.J.Bassett, Henley Street, Luddesdown
E.F.Bates, Wateringbury
W.Tunstall Bates, Tenterden
Dr Mark Bateson, Canterbury
Mr Peter Batley, Caister-on-Sea, Great Yarmouth
Dennis Beckwith, Otford
Revd Edwin L.W.Bell, Maidstone
Christine Bett, Otford
Dr P.F.J.Betts, Frittenden
Miss E.N.Bickel, Tavistock Place, London
Biddenden Local History Society
Richard N.Bidgood, Witney, Oxon
J.A.Black and P.McFarlane, Sevenoaks
Michael P.Black, Tooting, London
Richard Black, Peckham, London
Tamsin Black, Grenoble, France
John H.Bligh, Rochester
Philip Bowcock, Otford
Dr Jacqueline Bower, Rochester
Dr T.Boyle, Markbeech, Edenbridge
Fred Bromfield, Sevenoaks
Bromley Central Library
Colonel R.P.D.Brook, Chevening
Shiela Broomfield, Hildenborough, Tonbridge
Dr G.P.A.Brown, St John's Jerusalem, Sutton-at-Hone
Mrs J.Buck, Otford
Mike Bundock, Herne Bay

C.F.Burch, Sandwich
Dr Peter John Burville, St Margaret's Bay, Dover
John H.Butcher, Hunton

Canterbury Cathedral Library
F.W.G.Cazalet, Tonbridge
Centre for Kentish Studies, Maidstone
Dr C.W.Chalklin, Guildford, Surrey
Mrs M.Chandler, Otford
Mrs Beryl Coatts, Lydd
Benjamin Cobb, Greenwich, London
Mrs Dorothy Morrow Cobb, Wilmington, Dartford
Robin and Penelope Cook, Bluebell Hill Village, Chatham
Ian Cooling, Wye
Mrs Carol Cooper, Crayford
Cyril Cooper, Brenchley
Mr P.F.Cooper, Rainham
Dr Kevin Brian Cordes, Derby
Mr D.J.Cox, Kingston, Canterbury
Veronica Craig-Mair, Canterbury
Gerald Cramp, Hartley, Dartford
Jean Crane, Adisham
Anthony Cronk FSA, FRSA, Shipton-under-Wychwood, Oxon
Miss G.E.Crowhurst, Gravesend
Dr Paul Cullen, University of Newcastle, Newcastle-upon-Tyne

Gerald Davey, Rolvenden
Lady Donald, Chiddingstone Causeway
Mrs B.Dormer, Maidstone
Dr K.Draper, Chipstead, Sevenoaks
Dr Peter Draper, Stansted, Sevenoaks

Dr Elizabeth Edwards, Rutherford College, University of Kent
Dr Neil Edwards, Grenoble, France
J.Erle-Drax, Bilting House, Bilting
Vaughan Everett, Ulcombe
Professor A.M.Everitt, Kimcote, Lutterworth, Leics.
Peter and Lynne Ewart, Shatterling, Canterbury

Subscribers

John Farrant, Lewes, E.Sussex
Norman L.Farrier, Maidstone
Richard Filmer, Kennington, Ashford
Elizabeth Finn, Ashford
C.E.Stuart Fisher, Sandon, Herts
Colin Flight, Clemson, SC, USA
Dr S.Forsyth, Tonbridge
Mr and Mrs D.J.Fowdrey, Seal
Jean Fox, Seal

Mrs M.C.Gadd, West Malling
J.F.R.Gale, Otford
Mr D.W.Galer, Bexley
Mrs J.Gamon, Black Charles, Underriver
Alan and Mary Gibbins, West Malling
Peter Gibson, South Croydon, Surrey
Mr G.C.B.Gidley-Kitchin, Kemsing
Michael and Nicole Gill, Canterbury
Bryan Gipps, Egerton
John J.T.Glogg, Erith
Malcolm Goldsworthy, Farningham
Janet Grant, Faversham
Steve and Sue Grindlay, Sydenham, London
Guildhall Library, London

Barbara Hale, Chiddingstone Hoath
Hall's Bookshop, Tunbridge Wells
Mr J.B.Hamilton, Snodland
Mr J.G.Harman, Dover
Duncan Harrington, Lyminge
Oliver Harris, London
Frank Harwood, Whitstable
Mrs Sheila Hawes, Bexleyheath
Peter and Elizabeth Hickson, Bexley
Robert H.Hiscock, Gravesend
Historical Manuscripts Commission, London
Mr G.E.Hitchings, Speldhurst
Peter Hobbs, London
John Hori, Rolvenden Layne
Mr and Mrs G. Hornby, Rainham
Mr and Mrs Richard Hoskins, Eythorne
Miss N.M.Huckle, Dartford
Mrs D.J.Hughes, Canterbury
W.D.Hukins, St Michaels, Tenterden
Miss E.P.Humphreys, Godstone, Surrey
J.W.Hurst, West Malling

Institute of Historical Research, London

Miss S.Jellis, Tunbridge Wells
Mrs B.M.Jenkins, Otford
A.R.W. and I.Jones, Crayford
L.B.Jones, Lydd
Sheila M.Judge, Minster, Sheppey

Mrs Joan P.A.Kelly, Dartford
Kemsing Historical and Art Society
Kent Archaeological Society
Kent County Council, Arts and Libraries
Professor D.Killingray, Sevenoaks
John King, Grove Park, London
Lord Kingsdown, Torry Hill, Sittingbourne
The King's School, Rochester
Professor M.A.Knibb, Berkhamsted, Herts
Patricia Knowlden, West Wickham

Edward Lade, Yaldham Manor, Sevenoaks
Lambeth Palace Library, London
Mr R.Langstaff, West Malling
Mrs M.Lawrence, East Peckham
Dr Jean Lawrie, Eynsford
Michael Leach, Ongar, Essex
Peter E.Leach FSA, St Mawes, Cornwall
Lorna J.Lee, Sevenoaks
Mrs C.A.Leighton, Sedbury, Chepstow, Mon.
Mr Michael Lewis, Rochester
Lewisham Local Studies and Archives
John Lindsay, Appledore
R.E.Lloyd-Roberts, Canterbury
John London, Sevenoaks
The London Library, St James's Square
Lyminge Historical Society

Dr Philip MacDougall, Bosham, W.Sussex
Miss K.H.McIntosh, Sturry
Mrs B.Mainprice, Ashurst Wood, W.Sussex
Mrs Pat Manning, Beckenham
G. & D. Marrin & Sons, Folkestone
R.T.Maylam, Yalding
Mrs J.T.Meade, Shoreham
F.G.Meakin, Southfleet
Medway Council
John Mercer, Sidcup
Mrs C.A.Mills, Tunbridge Wells
Paul Minet, Ticehurst, E.Sussex

Subscribers

Major-General The Viscount Monckton of Brenchley, Harrietsham
John F.Moon, Willesborough, Ashford
Pam Morton, Blackheath, London
Peter Mountfield, Seal

The National Trust, Scotney Castle, Lamberhurst
Mr K.G.Newnham, Cranbrook
Mr Brian Nolan, Strood
Mr R.E.Nye, Bearsted

Mr Paul Oldham, Barming
P.R.O'Mahony, Lyminge
John Owen, Throwley

Canon and Mrs J.W.Packer, Bridge
James Packer, Welling
Dr F.H.Panton, Tunstall
Professor E.A.Parker, Canterbury
Dr A.J.Percival, Faversham Society, Faversham
Frances and Eric Percival, Sidcup
Mrs S.M.Petrie, Bells Yew Green, Tunbridge Wells
Dr Antony Pettet, Kingsdown, Deal
Mr Terence Pettet, Eastry
David Pink, Lee, London
Mrs Susan Pittman, Crockenhill, Swanley
Julian Pooley, Surrey History Centre, Woking
Frank Potter, Exeter, Devon
Mr R.W.Potts, Ightham
Miss M.A.Pring, Hollingbourne

The Earl of Radnor, Longford Castle, Salisbury, Wilts
Nigel Ramsay, University College London
S.J.C.Randall, Sevenoaks
Miss J.E.Randles, Sevenoaks
M.M.Raraty, Bridge
Mrs Denise Rason, Orpington
Mr Brian Raynor, Otford
Lynne Rees, Offham
Ian Reid, Hextable
Miss G.Rickard, Canterbury
Philip Riden, University College, Northampton
Keith Ritchie, Longfield
Geoffrey Roberts, Saltwood

Martin Roberts, Bearsted
The Rochester Bridge Trust
W.R.Rogers, Wilmington, Dartford
R.N.Rolinson, Twickenham, Middx
Mr M.J.Rose, Blackheath, London
Mrs K.J.Rowland, Rainham
Arthur Ruderman, Sandgate, Folkestone

Anthony and Jean Samson, Brenchley
The Right Revd Dr R.D.Say, Wye
Dr Rosemary Scott, Stapleford, Cambridge
Sydney Simmons, Tonbridge
P.J.C.Smallwood, Stanford, Ashford
Mrs D.McCall Smith, Chart Sutton
Mrs Evelyn Smith, Otford
Leslie A.Smith, Herne Bay
Paul W.Sowan, South Croydon, Surrey
Dr M.M.N.Stansfield, Merton College, Oxford
Ian and Penny Stewart, Petts Wood, Orpington
Mr.A.G.Stirk, Hythe
Mrs Prue Stokes, Biddenden
Mr S.J.Stringer, Wilmington, Dartford
John B.Sunley, Berkeley Square, London
Mrs M.L.Sutcliffe, Dymchurch
Christine Swift Books, Egerton
Mrs K.Szabo, Beckenham

Peter Tann, Belmont, Faversham
F.H.C.Tatham, Lewes, E.Sussex
Martin I.Taylor, Adisham
Dr Matthew Taylor, St Albans, Herts
Roy and Valerie Taylor, St Albans, Herts
Dr Joan Thirsk, Hadlow
R.G.Thomas, London
S.F.Tully, Maidstone

University of Kent at Canterbury

Muriel Varma, Sidcup
Ms L.P.Veach, Charlton, London
John E.Vigar, Aylesford

Mrs A.J.Wainman, Bicknor
Ian J.B.Walker, Sevenoaks
Charles Wanostrocht, Sandwich
Cliff and Elizabeth Ward, Otford
Wealden Books, Maidstone

Subscribers

Richard and Linda Weeks, Staplehurst
Dorothy and Don Welch, Tunbridge Wells
Mrs M.A.West, West Malling
Frank T.Weston, Edgbaston, Birmingham
Adrian C.Whittaker, Gravesend
Dr John Whyman, Rutherford College, University of Kent
Mr D.E.Wickham, ARHist.S, Belvedere
Miss Olive Wicks, Wallington, Surrey
Mrs M.Wigan, Hurstpierpoint, W.Sussex

J.V.Wilsher, Selling
Alison Wilson, Bromley
Mrs Isabel Wilson, Parkstone, Dorset
Mrs M.D.Windibank, Northfleet
A.W.Wood, Lewisham, London
Janet Wood, Hildenborough, Tonbridge
Miss Mavis Wright, Barming

Mr G.M.U.Young, Tonbridge

Dr Michael Zell, University of Greenwich

Index

Places are – or were previously – in the county of Kent unless otherwise indicated

Abbeville (France), 276-7, 280, 285
Abbott, Charles, (later Lord Tenterden), 216, 395
Abbott, John, 215
Abercrombye, Captain Sir Robert, 50
Abinger (Surrey), 30
Acrise, 260
Adams, Mr, 314
Adisham, 379
Aglionby, Dr William, 152
Aldersbrook (Essex), 94-6
Aldridge, Mrs, see Baptiste, Mrs
Aldridge, Thomas, 41, 56, 59
Alexander, Mr, 101
Alkham, 260
All Souls College, Oxford, 20, 35, 38, 48, 263
Alleengur (India), 405
Allen, Mr, 239
Allhallows, Hoo, 158, 242
America, 65, 168
Amherst, Lord, 257, 400
Andrews, John, 383-4
Antiquaries, Society of, 95-6, 123-4, 126, 135, 138, 140ff, 191, 193, 196, 204, 268, 296, 332
Archer, James, 51, 56-7, 70, 353
Army Lists, 400
Ash, 186
Ashen (Essex), 332
Ashford, 194, 268
Astle, Mrs, 126, 148-9
Astle, Thomas, 5, 24, 95, 113-4, 120-54, 173-4, 178-80, 187-9, 204, 209, 217, 225, 237-9, 243-4, 301, 303, 306, 309, 321-2, 324, 330, 350-1, 376, 382-3
Aubrey, John, 30, 184, 379
Augmentation Office, 125, 128, 188, 204, 376, 381-3
Austen family, 10, 16, 49
Austen, Francis, 194, 249, 372
Austen, Revd Thomas, 16, 242-3
Averie, Samuell, 101, 104, 106
Aylesford, 160

Aylesford, Earl of, 160-1
Aylesford, Lathe of, 237
Ayling, Thomas, 36-7
Ayloffe, Sir Joseph, bt., 114, 124, 139-40, 145-6
Ayres (Ayerst) family, 16, 36, 49
Ayscough, Samuel, 391
Aysted, Rowland de, 4

Bacon, William, 336
Bagnell, John, 7-8
Baker (bookseller), 181
Baker, Henry, 146
Baldwins, 130, 203
Ballie, Bastien, 165
Bankes, Mr, 70
Banks, Joseph (later Sir), 145, 147, 184, 251
Baptist Missionary Society, 401
Baptiste, Mrs (later Mrs Aldridge), 39, 56, 60, 137
Barber-Surgeons, Company of, 82
Barford, Revd Dr William, 211, 213
Bargrave family, 127, 186, 285
Barham Downs, 379
Baring, Alexander (later Baron Ashburton), 349
Barking (Essex), 86, 88-90
Barlow, Francis, 305
Barlow, John, 233, 305, 312-17, 320, 329, 337, 354-5, 361-7, 387-9
Barming, 88, 93, 117, 207-8, 248, 258, 323, 396
Barnardiston, Thomas, 101, 104, 106
Barrell, Revd Edmund, 40, 59-60, 66, 89, 131, 137, 151
Barrington, Hon. Daines, 147-8, 181, 183
Barrow, Isaac, 152
Barry, Hon. John Smith, 216
Barry, Richard, 216
Basire, James, 311
Bassack, William, 165-6, 172
Bastille, 270, 274-5

451

Index

Bates, David, 391
Bath (Somerset), 214, 229, 258, 330, 339, 343, 349-50, 360, 398
Bath Herald, 363, 373
Bathurst family, 260
Bathurst, Edward, 61
Bathurst, Elizabeth, 61
Bathurst, Mary, 61
Bathurst, Revd Richard, 60-1, 200, 249
Bax, Thomas, 220
Bayly, John, 81, 197-8, 233, 235-7, 312, 373, 388
Bean, Stephen, 268
Beanland, John, 76-7
Beauvoir, Revd Dr Osmund, 213-5, 218, 221, 223, 246, 258, 284, 330, 350
Beauvoir, Revd William, 214
Beckenham, 72, 82, 159
Beckwith, Edward, 117-18
Bedell, Mr, 265
Bedford, 57
Bedford family, 40
Bedford, Thomas, 43
Bedfordshire, 101, 105-6
Bekesbourne, 171
Belcher, Edward, 200
Belcher, Martha, 345
Belhouse (Belhus) (Essex), 229, 240
Belmont, 115, 245
Belvidere, 237
Benares (India), 405-6
Bences, Squire, 101
Bengal, 401, 405
Benskin, John, 219
Benson, Revd Dr John, 213
Bentham, Revd James, 184
Berkeley, Revd Dr George, 213, 216
Berkshire, 23-4, 163, 193
Bermondsey (London), 313
Bessborough, Earl of, 169
Best, Caroline, Frances, Isabella and Margaret (das. of T.F.Best), 395
Best, George and Caroline, 395
Best, James, 160, 164, 171-3, 204
Best, Mawdistly, 21
Best, Thomas, 167
Best, Thomas Fairfax, 395
Betenson, Sir Richard, 237
Bethersden, 259
Betteshanger (Betsanger), 262, 266, 289
Bewsborough, Hundred of, 281

Bexley, 31, 79, 147, 159, 198, 213, 215, 234, 247-8, 330, 350
Bexleyheath, 247
Bibliotheca Topographica Britannica, 241, 371-3
Biddenden, 259
Bignel, Mr, 34
Birch, Dr Thomas, 139, 141
Birling, 160
Bishop, Sir Thomas, 243
Blackfriars (London), 329
Blackheath, 43, 159
Blaxland, John, 364
Blenchyndon family, 40, 59, 66
Blomefield, Revd Francis, 184, 193, 363, 374
Blomer, Mrs, 246
Bobbing, 4, 25
Bolland, Mr, 246
Bombay (India), 57
Borlase, Dr, 94, 184
Borrett, John, 39
Borrett, Thomas, 297, 349
Bostock family, 190
Boswell, James, 1, 145
Boteler, Sir Philip, 164, 166
Boteler, Mrs Sarah (née Fuller), 223
Boteler, William, 186, 214, 222-3, 257, 261-2, 266, 278-89, 298-9, 301-4, 307-8, 313, 315-17, 320, 323-6, 330, 358, 384, 389-90
Boudeille, Mr, 269-70
Boughton Aluph, 260
Boughton, Hundred of, 106
Boughton-under-Blean, 256
Boulogne (France), 267-8
Bowes, Andrew Robinson, 299
Boxley, 164, 248-9, 378
Boxley Abbey, 249
Boyle, John, 382, 389-91
Boys family, 108
Boys, Edward, 102
Boys, Mrs Elizabeth (née Wise), 223
Boys, Mrs Jane (née Fuller), 223
Boys, John, 308
Boys, William, 184, 186, 190, 222-3, 237, 255, 257, 261-2, 270, 273-4, 278-85, 289-92, 301-11, 313, 316-17, 330, 389
Boys, William Henry, 223
Boyse, John, 77

Index

Bradborne Place, 237
Bradbourne, 111, 164
Bradley, Thomas, 102
Brander, Gustavus, 140
Brasted, 194-5
Bredhurst, 388
Brett, Dr Nicholas, 187
Brewster, Harriet (later Taylor), 295-6, 337, 342-3, 356-7, 365-6
Bridger, Mrs, 205
Bridges family, 108, 186, 246
Bridges, Sir Brook, bt., 186
Brinkworth, Sarah, 345
Bristow, William, 271, 306-7, 309-10, 316-19, 385-6, 389
British Library, 96, 129, 186, 303, 334
British Museum, 24, 114, 140-1, 145-6, 151, 154, 178, 186, 303, 356, 358, 376, 382
British Topography, 372
Broke, Misses, 197
Bromley, 234, 291, 349
Bromley & Beckenham, Hundred of, 388
Brompton, 201, 240
Brook family, 108
Brooke, George, 299
Brooke, John, 152
Brooke, John Charles, 26, 140
Brookland, 214
Brothertoft (Lincs), 116
Browne, Edmund (Edward), 53-8, 62, 69, 72, 82, 92-4, 244, 328
Browne, Mary, 57, 69-70, 92-3
Bryant family, 16, 49
Brydges, Sir Samuel Egerton, 130, 186, 214, 281, 348, 393
Buckingham, Marquess of, 303, 351
Buckinghamshire, 106
Budgen, William, 365
Bunce family, 108
Bunce, Cyprian Rondeau, 239
Bunce, Sir John, 20
Burges, Thomas, 102
Burgoyne, John Charles, Thomas, and Thomas John, 398
Burnaby, Revd Andrew, 192
Burnley (Lancs), 7-8
Burrell, Mrs, 237
Burrell, Peter, 155
Burton, William, 180, 184
Burville, Revd George, 248

Bury St Edmunds (Suffolk), 332, 334, 336
Buttanshaw (paper-maker), 348
Byng, Hon. John (later Viscount Torrington), 40, 78, 268

Caen (France), 139
Calais (France), 244, 268, 274-6, 285-9
Calcraft, John, 134, 156, 169-70, 174, 203, 275
Calcutta (India), 401, 403
Calne (Wilts), 214
Calvin, Jean, 8
Cambridge, 140, 214, 229
Cambridgeshire, 106
Camden Town (London), 290, 293
Camden, William, 139, 180
Camoens, Luis de, 256
Campbell, Lieutenant John, 50, 75
Canada, 168
Cannon, John, 171-2
Canterbury, *passim,* see esp. 203ff
Canterbury Journal, 227, 229
Cantis, John, 223, 349
Capel, 249
Capel (le-Ferne), 260
Capsell, William, 221
Carey, Revd Dr William, 401-2
Carrington, Clara (later Hasted), 398-9
Carter, George, 216
Carter, William, 222
Caslon, Mr, 228
Cator, John, 159
Catt, John, 268
Cautley, Revd John, 277
Cave, Edward, 369
Cazeneuve, John, 19
Cemp, Mr, 285
Chaddesden (Derbyshire), 261
Chalk, 75, 157-8
Chambers, Samuel, 216
Chancery, 34, 92, 94, 326-8, 346, 359, 363-5, 405
Chapman, Henry, 65
Chapman, James, 156
Chapman, Philip, 211
Chapman, Revd R.H., 360
Chartham Downs, 128

Index

Chatham, 3-4, 10-23, 29, 31-8, 44-54, 114, 160, 164, 171, 173, 191, 201, 239, 247-8, 268, 285, 309, 364-5, 372, 399, 404
Chatham & Gillingham, Hundred of, 388
Chauncy, Sir Henry, 184
Cheam (Surrey), 30-1, 73
Chedham (Sussex), 5
Chelsea (London), 46, 48, 332, 334
Cheltenham (Glos.), 40
Cheriton, 260
Cheshire, 106
Chevening, 194
Chicheley family, 16, 36, 49, 186
Chichester, Mary, 102
Chiddingstone, 194-6
Chiffinch family, 185
Chiffinch, Dorothy, 186
Chiffinch, Thomas, 40, 43
Child, Francis, 160-1
Child, William, 68, 76-7
Chilham Castle, 259
Chilston, 395
Chippenham (Wilts), 330
Chipstead (Surrey), 31, 71, 73
Chislehurst, 309
Chislet, 216, 218-19
Chown, C.H.I., 95
Chrisfield, Richard, 36
Christchurch (Hants), 140
Cirencester (Glos.), 289
Clarendon, Earl of, 102
Clarkson, George, 348, 359, 364-6, 394
Clerkenwell (London), 401, 404
Cliffe, 19, 21-2, 38, 158, 160, 364-5
Clifford, Catherine, 25
Clifford, Sir Coniers, 4, 25-6
Clifford, George, 4, 24-5
Clout, Thomas, 199
Clout, Thomas (junior), 238
Cobham, 29, 197, 200, 235, 376
Cobham Hall, 229, 234-7
Cockran, Colonel, 50
Codsheath, Hundred of, 198
Cogan, John, 102
Cole, Revd William, 214
Colley, Luke, 76
Collings, William and Fanny, 395
Coltman, Mary, 102
Colyer, John, 264

Colyer, Mrs Margaret, see Dorman, Margaret
Comport, George, 365
Compton Bassett (Wilts), 351
Connaught (Ireland), 4, 25
Constant, Joseph, 161
Cooke, Robert, 189
Cooling, 365, 388
Coosens, Richard, 171
Cordwainers, Company of, 99
Cornilo, Hundred of, 281
Cornwall, 63, 106, 146
Corsham (Wilts), 5, 339ff
Corsham Court, 347
Courthope family, 260
Covent Garden (London), 53
Cowden, 194
Cowtan & Colegate, 319
Cox, Thomas, 180
Coxheath, 208
Cranbrook, 259
Crane, Mr, 101
Crane, Terry Pierce, 299
Cray, river, 215, 330, 350
Crayford, 43, 170, 378, 388
Critical Review, 369
Cromp, Revd Pierrepont, 165, 200
Cromwell, Oliver, 99, 102
Croydon (Surrey), 31
Crundale, 260
Currey (solicitor), 364
Curteis, Revd Thomas, 165
Cuxton, 359

D'Aeth, Sir Narborough, bt., 167, 313
Da Costa, Emanuel Mendez, 139, 141
Dacre, Lord, 194, 229, 237, 239-40
Dalison, William, 167
Dalrymple, John, 173
Dalyson, Henry, 38
Darent, river, 66, 69, 74, 82
Darenth, 40, 49, 59, 63, 74
Darnley, Earl of, 44, 194, 197, 229, 234-6, 364
Dartford, 37, 39-40, 43, 45, 56-60, 71, 74, 76, 82, 85-6, 88, 107, 109, 126, 134, 155-9, 163, 167-70, 174, 191, 203, 207, 239, 262, 310-11, 328, 330, 355, 378, 399

454

Index

Dartford and Wilmington, Hundred of, 43
Dashwood, Francis Bateman, 297
Davies, Joseph, 263-4, 327-8, 364
Davies, Joseph Proud, 327-8, 364-5
Davington, 4, 115
Dawney, Mr, 131
Dawson, Thomas, 364
De la Douespe, Revd Ezekiel, 248-9, 394
De Lambert, François Henry, 297
Deal, 194, 225, 253, 257, 292, 379, 397
Debary, Richard, 364-6, 394
Deedes, William, 167, 218, 308, 311
Defoe, Daniel, 146
Delves, Revd William, 216
Denison, Sir Thomas, 172
Denne, Revd Samuel, 192, 271, 273, 291, 302-3, 309-11, 316, 386-7
Denton, 158, 348
Deptford, 155, 171, 378, 385
Derby, Mr, 234
Dering family, 127
Dering, Sir Edward, bt., 44, 59, 125-6, 188, 348, 351, 359
Dering, Revd Dr Heneage, 213
Desbouverie, Laurens, 40
Devonshire, 106
Dine (attorney), 194
Dingley family, 5, 6, 31, 33, 186, 314, 358, 361
Dingley, Elizabeth, 31
Dingley, Sir John, 31
Dingley, Lewis, 5
Dingley, Robert, 31, 78-9, 196, 252
Disney, Revd William, 192, 349
Dix, Revd Joshua, 213-15, 260, 349
Dix, Martha, Edward and Mary, 215
Dixon, Revd Pierce, 165
Dobson, Walter, 102
Doctors' Commons, 139-40, 146, 233-4
Doddington, 200
Dodsley, James, 150-1, 229
Dodsley, Robert, 150
Domesday Book, 131, 187, 303, 373, 389, 392
Dooleypore (India), 405-6
Dorking (Surrey), 30
Dorman family, 59-61, 186, 207, 358
Dorman, Ann, see Hasted, Ann (1732-1803)

Dorman, Mrs Dorothy, 59-60, 78, 118, 208, 331
Dorman, Elizabeth, see Thorne, Mrs Elizabeth
Dorman, John, 59-60, 137, 331
Dorman, John (junior), 60, 87, 89
Dorman, John and Nicholas (twins), 60
Dorman, Margaret (later Pope, then Colyer), 60, 77, 118, 208, 323-4
Dorman, Mary, 60-1, 78, 117-18, 207-8, 249, 258, 323-4, 331, 396-7
Dorman, Thomas, 59-60
Dorset, Duke of, 194, 234, 372
Dover, 122, 167, 188, 194, 201, 225, 244, 256, 280-1, 285, 311-12, 379
Drake, Dr Henry Holman, 381-2
Drew, Mrs, 58
Duane, Matthew, 145-6
Dublin (Ireland), 99, 105, 193, 373
Ducarel, Dr Andrew Coltee, 81, 94, 96, 114, 122, 124, 133-5, 139-41, 144-7, 157, 181, 188-9, 196, 204, 212, 233-4, 236, 240, 257, 277, 306, 330, 376
Duddy, William, 18, 44
Dugdale, Sir William, 122, 178, 180-2, 363, 373-4
Duncombe family, 246
Duncombe, Revd John, 215, 218, 241, 369, 371
Dunkirk (France), 268, 276
Duppa family, 396
Dury, Andrew, 383
Dyke family, 108
Dyke, Sir John Dixon, bt., 156, 203
Dyke, Sir Thomas, bt., 40, 59, 66
Dyke, Thomas (17th c), 102, 106
Dyke, Thomas (18th c), 299

Earle, John and Barbara, 19, 71
East Farleigh, 207, 249
East India Company, 57, 98, 353, 394
East Wickham, 163
Eastchurch, Samuel, 70
Eastling, 4, 19, 37-8, 50, 65, 113, 131, 380
Eastry, 222, 257, 262, 283, 303
Eastry, Hundred of, 281-2
Eaton, Peter, 204
Eden, Master, 404
Eden, Sir Frederick Morton, bt., 308

Index

Edenbridge, 194, 249
Edmondson, Joseph, 130, 135, 189
Edwards, Mary, see Hasted, Mary (née Edwards)
Eldon, Lord, 328
Elers, Paul George, 297
Elham, 260, 348
Ellenborough, Lord, 327
Ellis, George Hasted, 398
Ellis, William, 183
Ellison, Edward, 221
Elmers End, 388
Eltham Palace, 235
Elton, Charles, 391
Elvy, Mr, 76
Elwick, George Geree, 114
Elwick, Nathaniel, 43
Emptage, Mary, 219
Epsom (Surrey), 30
Erith, 40, 59, 87
Esher (Surrey), 53
Essex, 4, 38, 82, 95-6, 101, 106, 114-15, 148, 184, 229, 332
Essex, Robert, Earl of, 102
Eton College, 53, 139, 170
Evans, Samuel, 299
Evelyn, John, 149
Everitt, Professor Alan M., 380, 391-2
Ewell (Surrey), 30
Exeter (Devon), 51, 56
Exning (Suffolk), 348
Eyhorne, Hundred of, 199-201
Eynsford, 349

Fagg, Sir William, bt., 224
Fairfax, Lord, 103
Fairfax, Hon. Robert, 59, 160-1, 164
Fairford (Glos.), 401
Farbrace, Sampson, 194
Farleigh, 248
Farley, Abraham, 187, 303
Farnaby, Sir Thomas, 171-2
Farnborough, 349
Farningham, 40, 77-8, 121, 155
Farrington Gurney (Somerset), 398-9, 406
Faunce family, 29, 59, 66, 127, 156, 158, 192
Faunce, Revd Edmund, 88, 131, 155, 204

Faunce, Thomas, 43, 60, 78, 155-6, 160-2, 171-2
Faussett, Revd Bryan, 64, 122-3, 125-6, 128, 133, 142-3, 185-6, 205, 214, 221, 224
Faussett, Mrs Elizabeth, 204, 224
Faversham, 3, 12, 78-9, 95, 114-15, 117-20, 124-5, 127, 130, 144, 166, 192, 207-8, 230, 248
Faversham, Hundred of, 106
Fawke, Revd Francis, 192
Fell, Mr, 405
Fergusson, Ensign Adam, 50
Ffines, Sir Richard, 188
Finch family, 108
Finchcocks, 61, 200, 249
Fisher, John, 19
Fisher, Thomas, 225, 229
Fitzgerald, Thomas, 253, 397
Flackton, Marrable & Claris, 291
Fleet, Hussey, 399
Fleet Prison, 296-7
Fletcher, John, 171
Fletcher, Thomas, 160-1, 164-5, 173
Folkestone, 194, 226, 229, 233, 259-60, 320, 337
Foote, Mr, 58
Foote, Benjamin Hatley, 164
Foote, Revd Francis Hender, 165, 218
Foots Cray, 163, 197
Fort William College (India), 401
Fortrye family, 29, 186
Fowke, Edward, 59, 66;
Fowle, Revd William Wing, 192, 220, 260
Fox, Charles James, 275
Frampton (Lincs), 116
France, 8, 65, 109, 167-8, 201, 255, 266-92, 313, 316, 326, 347, 358, 377, 397
Francis, Revd Philip, 53
Franklin, Carless, 118
Franklyn (attorney), 194
Franks, 203, 233
Franks, Revd Mr, 46
Frederick, Charles (later Sir), 95, 113-14, 116
French Revolution, 267, 286ff
Friend (tailor), 293
Fright, Richard, 220
Frindsbury, 160

Index

Frinsted, 164, 171
Fruchard, Philip, 36
Fry, Sarah, 345
Fulham (London), 210
Fullagar family, 23
Fullagar, Samuel, 49, 118, 191, 207
Fuller, Jane, see Boys, Mrs Jane
Fuller, Sarah, see Boteler, Mrs Sarah
Fuller, Thomas, 223
Fullerton, John, 40, 43
Fuzzard, John, 254

Gaillard, Captain Richard, 57
Gainsborough, Thomas, 69, 83
Garret, Ann, see Lethieullier, Mrs Ann
Garrett, Thomas and Ann, 82
Gascoyne, Sir Crisp, 86-9, 92, 94
Gavelkind, 47, 57, 62, 183-4
Gentleman's Magazine, 151, 193, 230, 240-1, 250-1, 258, 279, 290, 306, 314-315, 337, 348, 361-2, 369, 371, 373-5
Gibbon family, 186
Gibbon, Edward, 53, 380
Gibbon(s), Thomas, 76-7
Gibbs, Richard, 251-2
Gibson, John and Mary, 163
Gideon, Sir Sampson, 237
Gilbee, Nicholas, 251
Gilbert, Thomas, 165
Gillingham, 19, 38, 160, 388
Gilpin, Mr, 53
Gipps, George, 191, 223
Gipps, Miss, 246
Gloucestershire, 57, 106, 401
Glover, Richard, 164
Godden, George, 264
Godfrey family, 186
Godfrey, Richard, 237
Gofter, Joseph, 205
Golding, Samuel, 268
Goldsmith, Oliver, 180
Goodnestone, 186
Gordon, George, 171
Gordon, William, 174, 204
Gore, Thomas, 219
Goruckpore (India), 405
Goshall, 273
Gosling, John, 6

Gosling, Mary, see Hasted, Mary (née Gosling)
Gostling, Revd William, 184, 205, 211, 213, 225, 237
Goudhurst, 61, 165, 199, 200, 249
Gough, Richard, 140, 192, 271, 291, 302, 309-11, 333, 371-3
Grain, Isle of, 158, 378
Graves, Hasted, 14
Gravesend, 44, 157-9, 172, 221, 375
Grebell, Allan, 349
Greensted Green, 40
Greenstreet, Peter, 106
Greenstreete, Thomas, 20
Greenwich, 43, 115, 139, 156, 165-6, 171, 192, 201, 268
Gregory, Revd Francis, 213, 216
Gregory, William, 216
Grenville, George, 114
Griffin, W., 150-1
Grose, Francis, 372-3
Groves, Ann and William, 163
Guildhall (London), 45-6, 71, 101-6, 111
Guilford, Earl of, 308, 312-13
Gurr, John, 365
Gwynn, William, 54-5

Hacket, Jane, 5
Hackett, Margaret, 5
Hackney (London), 34
Haddock, Nicholas, 164
Hadlow, 249
Hagen, Jacob, 155
Hales, Thomas Pym, 171-2
Halford, Richard, 194
Hall, Mr, 115
Hall, J., 229
Halley, Catherine, 13
Halley, Edmond, 152
Halliday, William and Susan, 344
Halling, 160
Halstead (Essex), 4
Halsted, Henry, 7
Halsted, Joane, 7-8
Halsted, Richard, 7
Halsted, Robert, 7-9, 23
Halsted, Robert (son of William), 8
Halsted, Robert de, 4
Halsted, William, 7-8
Halstow, 20, 22, 38, 76, 158, 251, 364

Index

Hambleton, Betty, 345
Hammond, Denham, 32, 39
Hampshire, 4, 24, 101
Haranc, Mr, 197
Harbledown, 260, 303
Harcourt, James, 359
Harden Huish (Wilts), 330
Hardwicke's Marriage Act, 30
Harris, Mrs, 40, 83
Harris, Dr John, 184, 224-6, 240, 377, 381, 391
Harris, Thomas, 93, 117-19, 207-8
Harrison, Mrs, 205
Hart-Dyke family, 108
Hartlip, 19-20, 76, 364
Harvey, John Springett, 308, 326-7
Harwood, Revd James, 163
Hassell, Revd William, 216
Hassell, William, 216
Hastead, Thomas (father and son), 14
Hasted, Ann (née Dorman, 1732-1803), 31, 60-1, 63-4, 67, 73-4, 78, 97, 117-18, 121-3, 128, 132, 137, 143-4, 169, 174, 196, 204, 207-8, 215, 217, 243, 245, 247-9, 252, 263, 312, 315, 317, 323, 329-31, 356, 361, 393, 397
Hasted, Anne (née Tyler, 1702-1791), 6, 30-4, 40, 45-51, 53-8, 61-2, 70-2, 75, 77-8, 208-12, 217, 223, 245, 252, 257, 263, 290
Hasted, Anne (later Archer, 1729-1762), 33, 35, 37, 46, 49-51, 53, 56-7, 61-2, 353
Hasted, Anne (1765-1839), 135, 212, 217, 245-7, 290, 296, 317, 323-4, 356-7, 359, 393, 396-8, 400
Hasted, Benjamin, 13
Hasted, Charles, 132, 144, 215-16, 245, 252, 257, 290, 296, 309-10, 317, 323-4, 340, 355, 357, 359, 364, 387, 393, 398-400, 404-5
Hasted, Edward (1702-1741), 3, 5, 29-48, 53, 59, 68, 290, 353-4, 361
Hasted, Edward (1732-1812)
  genealogy, 1-6; birth, 3, 33-4; great-grandfather, 6-13; grandparents, 13-24, 34-5; family portraits, 24-7; parents, 29-34, 36-9; death of father, 46-7; Chatham, 48-50; sister's elopement, 51; education, 53; return to Sutton-at-Hone, 56; marriage, 59-62; restoration of St John's Jerusalem, 62-9; purchase of Oakleys, 71; life at St John's, 73-5; death of sister, 76-8; birth of children, 78-9, 132, 148, 169, 175, 217; friendship with John Lethieullier, 81ff; finding of Hill archive, 97-8; work on the History of Sequestrations, 98-107; reception by the county, 108-11; at Throwley: Astle and Wilks, 113-17; the Faversham collectorship, 117-19; work on the *History*, 121-33, 177ff, 248-50; London friends: Ducarel, 133-5, 139; Society of Antiquaries, 138-43, 145; Royal Society, 146-9; *Familiar Letters*, 149-54; work for turnpike trusts, 155-7; on the Commission of Sewers, 158, 221-3; as a warden of Rochester Bridge, 159-62; as a magistrate, 163-7, 218-20; as a Deputy Lieutenant, 167-9; at the assizes, 170-4, 220-1; life in Canterbury, 203ff; removal of mother to Canterbury, 208-12; her London house sold to John Wilkes, 209-10; children: education, apprenticeships, etc, 215-17, 245-7, 252-3, 393ff; publication of Vol.I of the *History*, 226-31, 233-9; reviews, 239-43; liaison with Mary Jane Town, 254-6; death of George, 257-8; financial difficulties, 262-6; flight to France, 267ff; assistance of Boteler, Boys and Revd John Lyon, 280-5; French Revolution, 274ff; return to England, 289; arrest for debt, 293; in the King's Bench prison, 293ff; second edition of the *History*, 305ff; friendship with John Barlow, 305ff; writing of the Anecdotes, 319-20; release from prison, 327-9; work for the Revd Richard Yates, 332-6; master of Hungerford almshouses, 339ff; will, 354-9; death, 360-3.
Hasted, Revd Edward (1760-1855), 3, 7, 9, 24, 27, 78, 121, 138, 215, 217, 223, 245, 247, 249, 252-3, 257, 261, 276-8, 285, 290, 317, 323-5, 331, 337, 340-2, 353-60, 363-6, 393-7, 400, 402-6
Hasted, Edward (1801-1818), 402-3
Hasted, Francis (1795-1844), 402-3, 405-6
Hasted, Francis, 406

458

Index

Hasted, Francis Dingley, 78, 121, 138, 215, 217, 245-7, 252, 257, 324, 328, 355, 357-8, 393, 396-7, 400-2
Hasted, George (1763-1787), 78, 117, 121, 143, 196, 215-16, 245, 247, 252, 254, 257-8, 309, 317, 353, 393, 397
Hasted, George (1798-1850), 402-3, 405-6
Hasted, George Henry, 406
Hasted, John, 402-3
Hasted, John Septimus, 175, 204-5, 207, 215, 245, 252-3, 257, 317, 324, 328, 356-7, 359, 397-400, 406
Hasted, Jonathan, 402
Hasted, Joseph (1662-1733), 3-4, 9-21, 23-5, 29-30, 33, 36-7, 40, 47, 77, 353
Hasted, Joseph (1730-1731), 33
Hasted, Joseph (b. and d. 1769), 207, 393
Hasted, Katherine (née Yardley, 1671-1735), 3, 14-16, 18, 24, 29-30, 34-5, 37, 77, 353
Hasted, Katherine (1766-1842), 126, 148, 217, 245, 290, 323-4, 356-7, 393, 395-7, 400
Hasted, Laurence, 5, 23-4
Hasted, Mary (née Edwards), 3, 12
Hasted, Mary (née Gosling), 3, 6-7, 10-12
Hasted, Mary Anne, 405
Hasted, Mary Barbara Bennet, 215, 217-18, 290, 393
Hasted, Moses (b.?1630), 3-13, 25-7
Hasted, Moses (b.?1659), 11
Hasted, Nathaniel, 3, 9, 13-14, 35, 46
Hasted, Robert, 13
Hasted, Sarah (née Powell), 400-2, 404-5
Hasted, Sarah Anne, 402-3
Hasted, Thomas (b.1665), 10
Hasted, Thomas (b.1680), 12
Hastings, Warren, 1-2
Hatcher, Mr, 206
Hatton family, 190
Hatton, Elizabeth, 221
Hausted, Agnes, 4
Hausted, Revd John, 4-6, 24-6
Hausted, John, 5, 26
Hausted, Richard de, 4
Hausted, William, 4
Hawes family, 16, 49
Hawkinge, 260
Hawkins, Mr, 225

Hawksmoor, Nicholas, 34
Hawley, 4, 37, 39-40, 49, 56, 59, 68, 71, 78, 81-2, 137, 186, 203, 319, 353-4, 356
Hawthorn, Edwarde, 7
Hay (Powys), 403
Hayes, 192
Hayes Place, 291
Hayward, Alderman, 205
Headley (Surrey), 30
Heasted, Moses, 13
Heath, John, 342
Henley, Mrs, 209-10
Henman, Richard and Mathew, 99
Henniker family, 23, 50
Henniker, John (later Sir, later Lord), 23, 50, 309, 311
Henniker, Luce, 23
Henry, David, 369, 371
Heppington, 64, 122-3, 133, 143, 186, 205
Herbelot family, 286-7
Herbert, William, 383
Herefordshire, 73, 106
Herne, 117
Heron, Sir Richard, bt., 259
Heron, Thomas, 259
Hertfordshire, 106
Hever Castle, 237
Hey, Revd Thomas, 192
Hickes, George, 181, 183
Higham, 158
Hill family, 63, 98, 190
Hill, Abraham, 63, 74, 97-100, 148-53
Hill, Mrs Elizabeth, 63
Hill, Frances, 40, 63, 74, 99
Hill, Richard (d.1660), 98-101, 104-6, 151
Hill, Richard (d.1721), 63, 99
Hill, Thomas, 153
Hill, William (17th c), 105
Hill, William (18th c), 63
Hills, Alderman, 11
Hind (attorney), 194
Hobson, William, 101, 104, 106
Hogben, Mr, 200
Hogben, J, 229
Holbrook, Francis, 35
Hollingbourne, 24, 276-7, 317, 324-5, 355, 361, 394-6, 403, 405-6
Hollingworth, Finch, 258

459

Index

Hollis, Thomas, 98
Hone, Nathaniel, 373
Honington Odstock (Wilts), 351
Honywood family, 108
Honywood, Sir John, bt., 297
Hoo, 160, 242
Hoo, Hundred of, 388
Hope, Sir Thomas, 297
Hope, Thomas and Elizabeth, 19, 71
Hopton, Lord, 106
Hopton, Richard, 213
Hornsby family, 29
Hornsby, Richard, 163, 169-71
Horsham manor, 20-1, 38, 76, 263, 364-5
Horsley, John, 179, 181
Horsted, 201
Horton Kirby, 163, 171-2, 233, 324, 329
Horton Priory, 188
Hoskins, Nicholas, 299, 314-15
Hotchkys, Revd Vincent, 172
Hothfield, 165
Hounslow Heath (Middx), 201
Hubbard, James, 76
Hucking, 165, 361, 394
Hughes, Elizabeth, 395
Huguenots, 6-9, 12, 27, 39-40, 191
Hulse family, 129-30
Hulse, Richard, 130, 203
Hume, David, 180
Hungerford Almshouses, 340-7, 352-3, 360-1, 367, 402
Hungerford, Lady Margaret and Sir Edward, 343-4
Hunter, Revd Joseph, 383
Huntingdonshire, 106
Huntingfield Court, 4, 39, 113
Huntingfield manor, 39, 65, 113
Hunton, 255
Hurley (Berks), 163
Husband, Revd Richard, 248
Hutchins, John, 193
Hyde, John, 195
Hyde, Savil(le), 195
Hythe, 194, 379, 386

Ickham, 251
Ightham, 164, 171, 199
India, 1-2, 328, 358-9, 396, 400-1, 405
Indian servants, 406

Ingress, 134, 169, 203
Ives, John, 190, 336

Jacob, Edward, 129-30, 144, 192, 225, 230
James family, 29
James, Charles, 398
James, William (of Ightham), 43, 164, 171-2
James, William (stationer), 71
Jaunpore (India), 405
Jefferys (Jeffreys), William, 365, 395
Jeken, John and Young, 194
Jersey, Earl of, 44, 394
Johnson, Mr, 239-40
Johnson, Fanny, 50
Johnson, Dr Pelham, 50
Johnson, Dr Samuel, 1, 37, 141, 145, 151, 281, 374
Johnson, Thomas, 184
Johnston, W., 151
Jones, Inigo, 236
Jones, Thomas, 170
Jones, William, 293-4
Jordan (attorney), 194
Jumper, William, 205

Kelley, Dr George, (later Sir), 164, 179
Kemsing, 194
Kent Agricultural Society, 349
Kent Archaeological Society, 111, 367
Kentish Chronicle, 319, 363
Kentish Gazette, 50, 162, 206-7, 224-7, 229-31, 256, 258, 267-9, 291, 348-9, 362
Kentish Post, 65, 73, 115, 119, 122-4, 128-9, 131, 169, 211, 218
Kenyon, Lord, 293
Keston, 197, 235
Kettering (Northants), 51
Kidder, Mr and son, 205-6
Kilburne, Richard, 184, 198, 224, 240, 377, 381
Killegrew, Captain, 51, 54
Kilndown, 199
King's Bench Prison, 141, 289ff, 350, 389, 390
King's Lynn (Lynn Regis) (Norfolk), 229
King's School, Canterbury, 131, 214-16, 252, 387, 393, 397

Index

King's School, Rochester, 49, 53
Kinghamford, Hundred of, 388
Kippington, 171
Kirby, John, 165
Kirkby, George, 206, 267, 271, 318, 385
Kirkby, William Comber, 82, 90, 93
Kite, Thomas (father and son), 216
Knight, Richard, 365
Knole (Knoll), 234, 237
Knowler, Mrs Barbara, 217
Knowler, Gilbert, 213, 217-8
Knowlton Court, 313, 379

Lade, Charles, 216
Lade, John, 206, 215, 218
Lade, William, 394
Lambarde, William, 184-5, 224, 240
Lambert, Daniel, 46
Lambeth (London), 313, 396
Lambeth Palace, 95, 132, 139-40, 186, 204, 376
Lamorbey (Lamienby), 31, 78-9, 196
Lampard, John, 45
Lancashire, 7-9, 101, 107
Lane, William, 216
Langley Park, 237
Lansdowne, Marquess of, 382
Larkfield, 164
Larking, John Wingfield, 381
Larking, Revd Lambert Blackwell, 111, 381
Lateward, Richard, 14
Latham, Dr John, 74
Latham, Rice & Co, 282, 285-6
Law, B., 309
Lawson, Revd Johnson, 131
Leaveland (Leveland), 131
Lee, Commissioner, 415
Lee, Mr & Mrs, 40, 59
Leeds, 164, 260
Leeds Castle, 164
Lees Court, 171
Lefroy, Mr, 246
Legeyt, Robert, 349
Legge, Hon. Heneage, 172
Legrand, Mr, 205
Leicestershire, 4, 101, 362
Leigh, 194, 249
Leigh & Sotheby, 302
Leigh family, 40, 59, 66, 186, 190

Leigh, Francis, 43, 78, 156, 203
Leigh, Richard, 78
Leith family, 290
Lenham, 260
Lenham Heath, 200
Letch, J., 145
Lethieullier family, 33, 40, 53, 59, 66, 81-2, 386
Lethieullier, Mrs Ann, 82, 85, 89-92
Lethieullier, Catherine, 40
Lethieullier, Sir John, 39, 82
Lethieullier, John (son of Sir John), 82, 95
Lethieullier, John (1703-1760, son of William), 39, 43, 60, 66, 73, 81ff, 97, 134, 233
Lethieullier, Manning, 93
Lethieullier, Mrs Mary, 82, 91
Lethieullier, Smart, 82, 94-6, 113, 138, 141
Lethieullier, William, 39, 82
Leveux, Jacques, 286
Lewis, Revd Mr, 184, 347
Lewisham, 82, 141, 155, 159, 191, 229
Leybourne Grange, 164
Lidgbird, John, 43
Ligonier, Sir John, 114
Limpsfield (Surrey), 15
Lincoln, Bishop of, 394
Lincoln's Inn, 31, 53-7, 71, 93, 163, 170, 258, 264
Lincolnshire, 38, 116
Linton, 19, 38, 164, 248, 254-5
List, Sarah, 13
Littleton Drew (Wilts), 351
Live, John, 247
Liverpool, Lord, 336
Llandaff (Wales), 268
Loftie, Mrs, 205
Loftie, Revd John, 349
Loftie, William, 349
London, 3-4, 7-10, 13, 15, 21, 23, 26-7, 31-3, 36-7, 39-40, 45, 51, 53-4, 56-8, 71-2, 74-5, 79, 82, 88-9, 93, 99-100, 114, 117, 125, 128, 135, 137ff, 161, 186, 198, 203, 205, 208-9, 212, 224-5, 229, 254, 256, 274, 290-1, 307, 316, 347, 354, 359, 361, 364, 399
London Directory, 399
London Evening Post, 226
London Gazette, 71
Long, William, 221

Index

Longfield, 164
Longford Castle (Wilts), 226, 229
Longley, John, 160
Loose, 248
Love, Nicholas, 161
Low Countries, 8
Lower Halstow, 19, 21-2, 251
Lowth, Charles, 139, 141
Lowth, Revd William, 141, 159, 191, 229
Lucas, Captain Nicholas, 152
Lucas, Sarah, 220
Luddesdown, 29, 196
Ludgater, Mr, 366
Lullingstone, 40, 59, 203
Lushington family, 405
Lushington, Mrs, 205
Lydden, 260
Lydiard (Lidiard) Tregoze (Wilts), 351
Lyminge, 260
Lynch, Revd Dr John, 213, 219
Lynsted (Linstead), 19-22, 35, 38, 47
Lyon, Revd John, 281, 283, 308, 389
Lyttelton, Dr Charles (later Bishop of Carlisle), 95-6, 147

Macaree, Johnson, 224, 349
Macaulay (Macauley), Catherine, 209
Madox, Thomas, 180, 182
Maidstone, 18, 29, 70, 107, 109, 125, 163-6, 169, 171, 178, 184, 201, 203, 208, 229, 243, 248-9, 258, 260, 292, 309, 325, 361, 394-5
Maidstone Journal, 363, 373
Maidstone Museum, 27, 395
Malcher (Melchior), Samuel, 43, 59
Malda (Bengal), 400-2
Man, Miles, 31
Manchester, Earl of, 102
Mann, Galfridus, 69
Mann, Sir Horace, bt., 69, 330
Manning, Richard, 155
Marden, Hundred of, 199
Margate, 225, 359, 378
Market(t) family, 29
Markett, Captain, 43
Marks, Mrs, 329, 331
Marshalsea Prison, 382
Martin, Samuel, 124
Martyn (Martin), Thomas, 190, 333
Marye, Mr, 41, 47-8

Matthew family, 268
Mead, Dr, 95
Medway Navigation Co., 44
Medway, river, 21-2, 44, 159, 179, 379, 388
Meffre, Revd J.C., 347, 360-1, 363
Meggison, Thomas, 196
Meopham, 160
Mercer, Henry, 36, 46, 76-7
Merret, Christopher, 184
Methuen, Paul (later Lord Methuen), 347
Middlesex, 14, 30, 101
Middleton, Hundred of, 200
Middleton, John, 194
Miles, John, 219
Miles, Luke, 76
Miller, Ann, 3, 13
Milles, Dr, 96
Million Bank, 38
Milton, Hundred of, 106
Milton-next-Gravesend, 20, 160, 194, 397
Milton (Regis), 117
Minster (Thanet), 219-20
Mirabeau, Comte de, 276
Mirzapore (India), 406
Monks Horton, 60, 214
Montagu, Lady, 51, 54-5
Monthly Review, 369-70
Moore, Mr, 197
Moore, Archbishop John, 21, 266, 272, 317, 376, 393
Morant, Revd Philip, 96, 114, 126, 133, 148, 184
Mores, Edward Rowe, 96, 190, 193, 241-2, 372
Morgan, George, 220
Morrice, William, 66
Morris, Colonel Staates Long, 400
Mostyn, Revd Roger, 50
Mote, The, 178, 309
Moypaldiggy (India), 401
Mudge, Captain William, 201, 383
Mudnabatty (India), 402
Mumford, John, 88, 207
Musgrave, Joseph, 49-50, 317, 324

Napoleon, 379
Neild, James, 293, 321

462

Index

New Cross Turnpike Trust, 42, 44-5, 75, 155-7, 159
New Romney, 192, 194, 220, 260
Newington (nr Folkestone), 260, 268
Newington (London), 313
Newington (nr Sittingbourne), 4, 19-22, 35-8, 46, 76-7, 258, 353, 364, 395
Newman, John, 151-2
Newport (Isle of Wight), 4-5, 24
Newport (Shropshire), 163
Newton, Sir Isaac, 97
Nichols, John, 141, 193, 241, 271, 301, 306-7, 337, 362, 371-5
Nichols, John Bowyer, 336
Nonington, 201
Norfolk, 229
North, Lord, 313
North, Brownlow (later Bishop of Winchester), 309, 312-13
North Cray, 197
Northall, Robert, 60, 84, 90
Northamptonshire, 51, 57
Northbourne (Norboum), 262, 266, 285, 289
Northfleet, 40, 157, 160, 186, 376
Norton, 251
Nottingham, 3, 13
Nuthall, Thomas, 71

Oakleys (Homefield House), 71-2, 203, 244
Offham, 19, 71
Oglander, Sir John, bt., 5-6
Olantigh, 209
Oliphant, Lord, 54-5
Oliver, Miss, 27
Oliver, Joseph, 27, 395, 398
Oliver, William, 27, 395
Ospringe, 115, 122, 130, 171, 378
Oxenden family, 108
Oxford, 20, 35, 38, 95, 188, 195, 223, 229, 245, 247, 252-3, 293, 393

Paddlesworth, 260
Page family, 16, 36
Page, Revd Charles, 341, 344-7
Page, John, 160-1
Paine, Thomas, 287
Painter-Stainers, Company of, 13-14, 46
Palmer & Co, 403

Papillon, Mrs, 205
Papillon, David, 155
Paramor, John, 223
Paris (France), 124, 152, 214, 274-6, 287
Parkinson, Robert, 12, 14
Parkyns, George, 297
Parry, William, 165
Parsons, James, 146
Partridge (brothers), 305
Pattenson (attorney), 194
Payne (newsagent), 280
Pearce, Bishop, 234
Pearce, John, 404-5
Pedley, George Joseph, 299
Peete, Mr, 310-11
Pegge, Revd Samuel, 240
Peirson, James Bradshaw, 297
Pelham, Thomas, 116
Pembridge (Herefordshire), 73
Penge, 388
Pennant, Thomas, 147, 255, 301
Pennington, William, 263
Pennoyer, William, 99
Penshurst, 44, 158, 194, 221, 336
Penshurst Place, 234
Pepys, Samuel, 97, 153
Percival, Samuel, 39
Perfect, William, 167-8
Perry, George, 145
Petley family, 203
Petley, Charles Carter, 171, 177
Pett, 200
Pett, Katherine, 16
Pett, Peter, 152
Pett, Sir Phineas, 15
Pett, Phineas and John, 16
Pettingall, Dr, 58
Petty Sessions, 107, 109, 173
Peyton, Sir Thomas, 379
Philanthropic Society, 332
Philipott, John, 184-5, 190
Philipott, Thomas, 110, 134, 177-9, 184, 224, 226, 229-30, 240, 377, 381
Picard, Jean Baptiste Francis, 172
Picard, John and Valentine, 129-30
Pitt, William (the younger), 291
Pleydell-Bouverie family, 40
Plot, Dr Robert, 127
Pluckley, 125, 131, 192, 348-9, 351
Pocock, Robert, 375, 399
Pointer family, 290

463

Index

Polhill, Charles, 239
Polhill, Penelope, 239
Pollard, R., 387
Pollexfen, John, 152
Pool Keynes (Wilts), 351
Pope, John, 118, 208
Pope, Matthew, 165
Pope, Mrs Margaret, see Dorman, Margaret
Porion, Nicolas, 275
Postling, 260
Potter, Revd John, 177
Poulton, 260
Poultry Compter, 32, 39-41, 46
Powell, Benjamin (father and son), 401, 403-5
Powell, Samuel, 401, 404
Powell, Sarah, see Hasted, Sarah
Poyntell, Nathaniel, 71
Pratt, Mrs, 78, 121
Pratt, Henry, 251
Pratt, John, 121
Preston (nr Faversham), 115
Price, Mrs, 205
Price, Revd Joseph, 60, 214
Pringle, Sir John, 147
Pritchard (Pritchet), Betty, 345-6
Proby, John, 19
Provenders, 251
Pryce, Dame Elizabeth, 299
Public Record Office, 376, 282-3
Punnett, Thomas Durrant, 249
Purfleet (Essex), 115
Putney (London), 30
Pybus, Charles Small, 308-9, 311-12

Quarter Sessions, 49, 107-9, 163-4, 177, 218, 253
Queenborough, 95, 292, 388
Quelch, William, 170

Radnor, 1st Earl of, 194, 226, 229, 233, 305, 331, 337
Radnor, 2nd Earl of, 259, 320, 331, 337, 339-42, 344-5, 352, 356, 360-1, 363
Rainham, 20, 35, 76, 364
Ransley, John, 165
Ravensbourne, river, 197
Reculver, 379
Redbourne (Lincs), 38

Reeve, William, 102
Reeves, Francis Keate, 297
Reigate (Surrey), 31
Reynolds, Sir Joshua, 83
Richardson (printer), 227, 231, 330
Richardson, Stephen, 76
Richborough Castle, 237
Richmond (Surrey), 30, 55-8, 67
Ricketts, William, 359
Ridley, 239
Rinder, Mrs, 116
Ringslow, Hundred of, 272
Riverhead, 171, 203
Robespierre, Maximilien de, 287
Robinson, Thomas, 183
Roch, Thomas, 205
Rochester, 7-9, 13, 16, 19, 23, 38, 45, 49-50, 53, 76, 88, 132, 135, 140, 151, 157-60, 169, 171, 174, 181, 191, 194-6, 204, 225, 229, 242, 248-9, 251, 360, 364, 388, 400
Rochester, Bishop of, 360
Rochester Bridge, 18, 38, 44, 75, 82, 135, 159-62, 166, 173, 179
Rochester Cathedral, 151
Rock, Mr, 205
Rolfe (attorney), 194, 293, 325-6
Rome House, 48-51, 54
Romney Marsh, 192, 201, 214, 260
Romney, Earl of, 331-2
Romney, Lord, 44, 160-1, 178, 193-4, 309, 331
Romney, Francis, 106
Rooke, Mrs Frances, 177-8, 191
Rookery, The, 39
Roussel, Dr, 205
Row, Sir Henry, 344
Rowe, Revd Henry, 297
Royal English College, St Omer (France), 269, 276
Royal Gunpowder Mills, 115
Royal Navy, 4, 14, 17, 99, 101
Royal Society, 97, 146-9, 151-2, 268, 296
Rugg, John, 293, 325, 327, 364-6
Rugg, Robert, 263-4, 293, 327, 364
Rugg, Robert (junior), 293, 325, 327, 364-6
Russell, William, 171
Rutland, 101
Ruxley, Hundred of, 388
Rye (Sussex), 229, 379

464

Index

Rymer, Thomas, 180, 182, 380
Ryves, Mr, 54

St Alphage's, Canterbury, 6
St Augustine, Lathe of, 218
St Augustine's, Canterbury, 106-7, 312
St Dunstan's, Canterbury, 218, 220, 260
St Dunstan's, Stepney (London), 13
St George's, Canterbury, 3, 12, 205, 207, 213
St George's Fields (London), 293, 329, 337
St James in the Isle of Grain, 19
St John's Jerusalem (Commandery of St John), 40, 65ff, 81-3, 94, 97-9, 130, 133, 137-8, 148-9, 157, 192, 203, 206, 213, 224, 244-5, 331, 343-4, 352
St Margaret's Rochester, 19, 38, 49, 141, 162
St Mary Woolnoth (London), 32-4
St Marylebone (London), 51, 54-5, 366
St Mary's, Lambeth (London), 396
St Nicholas, Rochester, 13
St Omer (France), 268-71, 275-7, 286-7
St Paul, Robert, 203
St Peter's, Canterbury, 3, 6
St Stephen's, Canterbury, 260
Saltwood, 260
Sammes, Aylett, 179
Sandford, Francis, 180, 183
Sandown manor, 282
Sandwich, 186, 194-5, 216, 221-3, 237, 262, 270, 273, 287, 291-2, 308, 379
Sankey, Thomas, 205
Saunders, Revd John, 77
Savary, John, 155
Savin, Mary, 220
Sawbridge, John, 209
Saxby family, 29, 41
Scheldt, river, 287, 292
Scobell, Mr, 399
Scoones, Frances, 258
Scoones, William, 247, 249, 257-8
Scott family, 108
Scrimsour, Mary, 74
Scrimsour, Thomas, 74, 85, 97
Scudamore, William, 325, 327, 364-5
Seal, 194, 239
Seaman, Dutton, 32
Sears, Richard, 76

Seasalter, 260
Secker, Archbishop Thomas, 131-2, 178
Segar, Sir William, 5, 24, 26
Selby family, 29
Senear (?Zennor) (Cornwall), 146
Sevenoaks, 157, 194, 199, 203, 238, 249, 349, 355, 372, 378
Sewers, Commission of, Court of, 44-6, 135, 158-9, 179, 204, 221-3
Seymour, Charles, 230
Shadwell (London), 399
Sheafe, Henry, 38, 44, 48, 53
Sheerness, 44, 158-9, 221, 251
Sheldwich, 256
Shelve, 200
Sheppey, Isle of, 251
Sherlock, Mr, 233
Shooters Hill, 43, 159, 388
Shoreham, 39, 297, 348-9
Shorne, 19, 38
Shorwell (Isle of Wight), 5
Shropshire, 163
Sidney, Sir Philip, 30
Simmons, James, 206, 227, 231, 233, 238, 267, 271, 278-80, 283-4, 301, 306, 312, 315, 318, 349, 379, 385-6
Simmons, John, 325-7, 364-6
Simmons, Samuel, 194
Simmons, Mrs Sarah, 366
Simpkinson, Revd John, 21
Sissinghurst, 166, 169, 172
Sittingbourne, 241, 265, 353
Skilder, Jacob, 76
Slade, John, 361
Slatter (attorney), 293
Smarden, 200, 259
Smith, Benjamin, 205
Smith, John, 19
Smith (Smyth), Mrs, 58, 204
Smith (Smythe) family, 186
Smith, Thomas, 229
Smollett, Tobias, 180
Snodland, 160, 248
Soan, Revd Jonathan, 50
Soan, Martha, 50
Solander, Dr Daniel Carl, 145, 184
Solly family, 186
Solly (attorney), 194
Solly, Joseph, 186
Solly, W. H., 195, 331
Somerden, Hundred of, 198

465

Index

Somerford Keynes (Wilts), 351
Somerset, 398, 406
Somerset Coffee House, 290-2, 295-6, 308
Somner, William, 183, 213, 240
Sonning (Berks), 23-4
Sotheby, Leigh &, see Leigh & Sotheby
South Sea Bubble, 14
Southborough, 249
Southcott, Sir John Thomas, 299
Southfleet, 233, 264
Southwark (London), 85
Spain, 169
Speldhurst, 194
Spelman, Sir Henry, 183
Spitalfields (London), 9, 13
Sprange, Jasper, 198-9
Springett family, 108
Staffordshire, 114
Stalisfield, 113
Stanley (Master in Chancery), 346
Stanley, Josiah, 293
Stanton St Quintin (Wilts), 344
Staplehurst, 199
Stapleton family, 108
Statenborough (Statenborow), 223, 273
Stelling, 260
Stepney (London), 8-9, 13-14, 141
Sterne, Laurence, 379
Stevens, Edmund, 155
Stevens, John, 265
Stewart, William, 32, 41, 46
Stirling, Sir Walter, bt., 349
Stockbury, 200
Stoke, 158
Stonar, 171, 282, 378
Stone, Edward and Hannah, 220
Stones End, 155
Storer, Revd Dr Bennett, 212, 217
Stour, river, 222
Strand (London), 151, 290-2, 330, 334, 364
Streatfeild, Henry, 195-6
Street End, 133
Street, John, 191
Stringer family, 190
Strood, 48, 70, 157, 197, 236
Strype, John, 180, 380
Suffolk, 140, 348
Sun Fire Office, 20, 247
Sundridge, 194-5, 240

Surrenden, Surrenden Dering, 125, 132, 351
Surrey, 15, 30-1, 53, 55, 71, 73, 106, 330, 354-5
Sussex, 21, 30, 378
Sutton (Surrey), 30
Sutton-at-Hone, 39-40, 43, 53ff, 78-9, 81-2, 91, 93, 99, 113, 117, 120, 127-8, 130, 132-3, 137, 139, 144, 146, 148, 151, 155-8, 167, 170-1, 174, 194, 203-4, 207, 218, 244, 249, 255, 328, 331, 348, 386
Sutton Place, 39-40, 59, 66, 73, 81-3, 120, 137, 204, 233
Sutton Valence, 254
Swalecliffe, 260
Swanscombe, 4, 40, 59, 156, 169
Swingfield, 260
Sydney family, 234
Sydney, Viscount, 309

Tancred, Darcy, 264
Tanner, Thomas, 180, 183
Tasker, John, 85, 158, 203-4, 364
Tatton family, 190
Tatton, Revd Dr William, 213, 216
Tatton, William, 216
Taunton (Somerset), 92
Taylo(u)r family, 16, 36, 49
Taylor, Revd Mr, 40, 49, 59
Taylor, Mr J., 199
Taylor, John, 130
Taylor, Robert, 38, 48, 70
Taylor, Samuel, 366
Tempest family, 260
Tenterden, 229
Teston, 164
Teynham, 19-21, 23, 25, 35, 38, 47, 224, 251
Teynham, Hundred of, 106
Teynham, Lord, 25
Thames, river, 56, 379
Thanet, Earl of, 106
Thanet, Isle of, 171, 272, 292, 378-9
Thanington, 260
Thatched House Society, 332
Theobald, Lewis, 20
Thomas, Revd Dr, 401-2
Thomas, Miss, 401
Thomas, Mrs Louisa, 396

466

Thomas, Mark (father and son), 194, 216, 387
Thompson, Captain Ormond, 55
Thoresby, Ralph, 363, 374
Thorley, James, 268
Thorne, Mrs Elizabeth (née Dorman), 60, 78-9, 118, 132, 208
Thorne, Gabriel, 78-9, 117-18, 132, 143, 208
Thorneycroft family, 23
Thornhill, Thomas, 221
Thornhill, Sir Timothy, 380
Thornton, Revd Stephen, 29, 196
Thorpe, Mrs Catherine, 196, 330
Thorpe, Catherine (later Meggison), 196-7, 236, 247
Thorpe, Ethelinda, 196
Thorpe, Dr John, 44, 195-7
Thorpe, John, 79, 140, 147, 159, 162, 181, 195-8, 201, 213, 215, 229, 231, 234-6, 242, 247-8, 252, 257, 306, 330, 350, 400
Thorpe, Revd Robert, 297
Thrale, Ralph, 299
Throwley, 79, 113ff, 143-4, 185, 192
Thurlow, Charles, 216
Thurlow, Edward, 215-16
Thurstone, John, 35
Thurstone, Martha, 35-6
Tilghman, Abraham, 164-5
Times, The, 404
Toft, John, 152
Tomlyn, Thomas, 161, 194, 249
Tomlyn, William, Mary and William, 164
Tonbridge, 131, 247-9, 253-4, 257
Tonbridge, Lowy of, 249
Topham, Mr, 140
Topping, Timothy, 299
Tournay (attorney), 194
Town, Edward, 254-6
Town, Mary Jane, 254-6, 268, 270, 274-6, 283, 286-7, 290-2, 295, 315, 397
Town, Philip and Elizabeth, 255
Townson, John, 173
Travel, Alexander, 151
Trehearne, Mr, 53-4
Tress, William, 76
Tressé, Francis, 240
Tressé, John, 201, 239
Truro (Cornwall), 99

Tryon, Thomas, 43
Tucker, Revd John, 215-16
Tufnail, James, 164
Tufton family, 108, 375
Tunbridge Wells, 164, 199, 253-4, 370
Tunstall, 241, 372
Turner family, 211
Turner, George, 347, 359
Turner, Robert, 99
Tutet, Mark Cephas, 139, 141, 145
Twisden, Judge, 111
Twisden, Sir Roger, bt. (d.1772), 59, 111, 158, 160-1, 164
Twisden, Roger (later Sir, bt.), 204
Twysden, Sir Roger, bt. (d.1672), 107, 111
Tyler, Anne, see Hasted, Anne (1702-1791)
Tyler, George, 30-3
Tyler, George and Louisa (Lovis), 71
Tyler, Henry, 31, 71, 73
Tyler, Hester, 73
Tyler, Richard, 31, 73
Tyler, William, 73
Tyndall, Dr Thomas, 139, 141, 145-6

Udny, George, 401-2
Udny, Robert, 401
Ulcombe, 200, 260
Upchurch, 19-20, 22, 35, 38, 76, 251, 364
Upnor Castle, 114-15

Vacher, Thomas, 20
Vane, Sir Henry, 109
Vane, Viscount, 59
Visitation Returns, 186, 347
Vyse, Mr, 234

Wade, Revd Peter, 248
Wagner, Sir Anthony, 392
Waldershare, 312-13
Waldo, Sir Timothy, 237
Walker family, 14-15, 23, 49
Walker, John, 14
Walker, Katherine, 16
Walker, R., 229
Walker, Richard, 18
Waller, Sir William, 106
Walmer, 308

Index

Walter, Mr, 40
Warburton (Somerset Herald), 127
Ward family, 195
Ward, Anna, 177, 258
Ward, Dr John, 95
Ward, Sarah, 37
Warde, Edward, 163
Waring family, 108, 348
Warington, Harriet (later Hasted), 399
Warwick, Earl of, 51, 54
Watchlingstone, Hundred of, 198
Waterman, Henry, 57, 70
Watson, Colonel, 54
Watson, Lewis Monson (later Lord Sondes), 59, 171-2
Watts, Ralph, 102
Wax Chandlers, Company of, 31-2, 40, 46
Weald, The, 378
Weaver, H., 347
Webb family, 127
Webb, Mrs, 205
Webb, Charles, 218
Webb, Philip Carteret, 181
Webb(e), Nathaniel, 92, 203
Weight, William, 215
Wellard (attorney), 194
West Langdon, 379
West Malling, 167, 248
West Peckham, 348
Westbourne (Sussex), 21
Westcliffe (West Cliffe), 186
Westerham, 194
Westfield (attorney), 194
Westminster (London), 58, 138, 204, 219, 291
Westmorland, Earl of, 44
Weston family, 260
Whatman, James, 248
Wheate, Sir John Thomas, 297
Wheatley family, 40, 59
Wheatley, William, 43
Wheler, Charles Granville, 297
Whiffen, James, 72
White (bookseller), 280, 309
Whiteford, Lt-Colonel, 50
Whitelocke, Anne (later Hill), 99
Whitelocke, Sir Bulstrode, 99
Whitstable, 117, 212, 220-1, 260, 378
Whittingham, William, 229
Whittington (Derbyshire), 240

Whitworth, Charles (later Sir), 108-11, 134, 158, 160, 164-7, 174, 177-9, 372
Wiburn family, 127
Wickham, Humfrey, 188
Wickham, William, 188
Wickhambreux, 192
Wight, Isle of, 4-6, 24, 31, 361
Wildash, Isaac, 160
Wilkes, John, 58, 123-4, 169, 209-10, 274
Wilkes, Polly, 58, 124, 209-10
Wilkins, Robert, 160-2
Wilks, Edward, 78, 95, 113-17, 122, 124, 132, 143, 208, 245
Wilks, Thomas, 116
Willes, Chief Justice, 172
Willett, Ralph, 141
Williams, Dionysius, 146
Williams, John (attorney), 263-4, 325-8, 346, 363-5
Williams, John (prisoner at assizes), 220-1
Williams, John Alexander Vincent, 406
Williams, Manley, 220
Williams, Moses Bellis Taylor, 406
Williams, Rice, 73
Williams, Revd Richard, 324-5, 327, 329, 364
Williams, Sally, 167
Williams, Sir Thomas, 72
Williams, Thomas (attorney), 72-3, 157, 167, 203, 239, 244-5, 262-5, 271, 289, 298, 323-9, 346, 364
Williams, Thomas (stationer), 73
Williamson, Mr, 205
Williamson, Sir Joseph, 152
Willis, Browne, 187
Willoughby de Broke (Willoughby of Brooke), Lord, 195
Willyams family, 246
Willyams, John and Cowper, 216
Wilmington, 40, 68, 82, 87, 91, 137, 192, 271, 291, 302, 386
Wilmot, Sir Robert, bt., 261
Wilsford family, 127, 187
Wilson, Dr, 210
Wiltshire, 330, 342, 348, 351, 353, 361-3, 398
Winchester (Hants), 188, 229, 309
Winchester, Mr, 334
Wingham, Hundred of, 388
Winterborne Bassett (Wilts), 351

Index

Wise, Elizabeth, see Boys, Mrs Elizabeth
Wise, Francis, 95
Witte, Nicholas, 152
Wolverton manor (Isle of Wight), 5, 31, 361
Woodin(g), John, 43
Woolfe, William, 102
Wordsworth, William, 274-5
Worsthorne (Lancs), 7-8
Worth, 282
Wotton, Lady Margaret, 107
Wraight, Henry, 171-2
Wren, Sir Christopher, 34, 149
Wright, Mrs Henry, 27
Wrotham, 164, 177

Wyberton (Lincs), 116
Wye, 187, 260
Wye College, 187, 234, 236

Yardley family, 15-16, 23, 33, 49
Yardley, Katherine, see Hasted, Katherine (1671-1735)
Yardley, Mary, 37
Yardley, Robert, 36-7
Yardley, Susan (later Pett), 16
Yates, Revd Dr Richard, 332-6
Yeoman, Thomas, 222
Yorke, Charles, 118-19
Yorkshire, 9, 101, 107
Young, Arthur, 267, 269, 271